third edition

ACCOUNTING

A SYSTEMS APPROACH

HENRY J. KALUZA
Professor Emeritus
Faculty of Education
University of Western Ontario
London, Ontario

MURRAY B. HOWARD
Northern Collegiate Institute and Vocational School
Sarnia, Ontario

JANET L. KENNEDY AMBACHER, H.B.A., B.Ed., C.A.
Saunders Secondary School
London, Ontario

DARRYL SLYWCHUK
Strathroy District Collegiate Institute
Strathroy, Ontario

McGraw-Hill Ryerson Limited

Toronto Montreal New York Auckland Bogotá Caracas
Hamburg Lisbon London Madrid Mexico Milan New Delhi
Paris San Juan São Paulo Singapore Sydney Tokyo

ACCOUNTING
A Systems Approach

Third Edition

ISBN 0-07-549679-8

1234567890 BP 987654321

Printed and bound in Canada

Canadian Cataloguing in Publication Data
Main entry under title:
Accounting: a systems approach
3rd ed.
ISBN 0-07-549679-8
1. Accounting. I. Kaluza, Henry J.,
HF5635.A33 1991 657 C90-095600-3

Sponsoring Editor: Andrea Crozier
Senior Supervising Editor: Carol Altilia
Copy Editor: Susan Marshall
Designer: Michelle Losier

This book was manufactured in Canada using acid-free paper.

CONTENTS

CHAPTER 4

IDENTIFYING THE BOOKKEEPING BASE OF ACCOUNTING 107

CHAPTER 5

PREPARING FINANCIAL STATEMENTS 163

CHAPTER 6

CLOSING THE LEDGER AND COMPLETING THE ACCOUNTING CYCLE 201

CHAPTER 7

A SECOND RUN THROUGH THE ACCOUNTING CYCLE 257

PART 2
SYSTEMS AND PROCEDURES FOR A SERVICE BUSINESS

CHAPTER 8
INTRODUCING THE ACCOUNTS RECEIVABLE APPLICATION 295

CHAPTER 9
THE ACCOUNTS PAYABLE APPLICATION 345

CHAPTER 10
INTRODUCING PETTY CASH AND BANKING APPLICATIONS 387

CHAPTER 11
EXAMINING THE PAYROLL APPLICATION 427

PART 3
ACCOUNTING CYCLE FOR A MERCHANDISING BUSINESS

CHAPTER 12
INTRODUCING ACCOUNTING CONCEPTS FOR MERCHANDISING BUSINESSES 477

CHAPTER 13
INTRODUCING THE ACCOUNTING CYCLE FOR A MERCHANDISING BUSINESS 507

CHAPTER 14
ACCOUNTING FOR SPECIAL ITEMS 579

CHAPTER 15
REVIEWING AND EXPANDING THE ACCOUNTING OF ADJUSTING ENTRIES 645

CHAPTER 16
COMPLETING THE ACCOUNTING CYCLE 691

PREFACE

This third edition of *Accounting: A Systems Approach* is designed for one-year or a two-year beginning accounting course, primarily at the high school level. It is intended for students who are in accounting courses at the high school level, who wish to register in accounting courses at the university and community college levels, or who desire an introduction to accounting for personal use.

THE PLAN OF THE TEXTBOOK

Organization

The textbook is divided into three parts. Part 1—Chapters 1 to 7—discusses concepts common to all General Ledger systems. In Chapters 1 to 6 the basic financial statements and the simplified accounting cycle are explained in detail via the example of a real estate business. Chapter 7, A Second Run Through the Accounting Cycle is optional, but is included for courses that feature discussion of an eight- or ten-column worksheet with simplified adjustments. Importantly, Chapter 7 should be completed before attempting Chapter 15 in Part 3.

Part 2—Chapters 8 to 11—emphasizes the systems approach with applications for accounts receivable, accounts payable, petty cash and banking, and a salaried payroll. These common accounting applications are illustrated for a small dental practice.

Part 3—Chapters 12 to 16—outlines a complete accounting cycle for merchandising businesses. The topics in these chapters are associated with an introductory accounting course at the advanced level of instruction.

A One-Year Course

The entire textbook is recommended for students requiring an intensive, one-year academic course that serves as the prerequisite for a senior academic accounting course at the high school level. In particular, Chapter 7 is suggested as an early introduction to simplified adjusting entries. A detailed course outline based on the text is recommended so that reasonable coverage of selected problems, mini-cases, and comprehensive case studies is assured. Copies of this detailed course outline should be distributed to students during the first week of the course.

A Two-Year Course

Teachers may wish to use the textbook as part of a two-year clerical or general business program. The first six chapters of Part 1 and all of Part 2 introduce accounting principles and common accounting applications that would be useful, for example, to people who hold clerical positions with service businesses. There is sufficient material in these chapters to form the basis of a one-year course. Chapter 7 is optional for such a one-year course.

In the second year, Chapter 7 of Part 1 and Chapters 8 to 11 of Part 3 may be combined with one semester of accounting applications featuring both manual and microcomputer applications.

NEW FEATURES IN THIS EDITION

Application of the Microcomputer

Microcomputers and software packages, specifically, the electronic spreadsheet and General Ledger system, are unquestionably a trend in the teaching of accounting. Accordingly, *Accounting: A Systems Approach* has three topics that focus on the technological aspect:

- Using Electronic Spreadsheets in Accounting (Topic 4, Chapter 2)
- Applying the Electronic Spreadsheet (Topic 5, Chapter 4)
- Applying the Electronic Spreadsheet and Introducing the General Ledger Accounting Package (Topic 4, Chapter 6)

The student has the option of solving many problems with the electronic spreadsheet and General Ledger applications. However, we recommend that students should solve the problems first manually and then electronically.

Balance Between Procedural and Conceptual Approaches

Much of the current discussion in accounting education has been directed at the choice between procedural and conceptual approaches. At the introductory high school level, we believe in the solution that offers a good balance between the presentation of accounting procedures and accounting theory. Therefore, each topic is structured so that one-half of the problems are procedural. The problems are followed by a selection of mini-cases. For the most part, these mini-cases are short and require the student to apply his or her knowledge of accounting theory and procedures for that topic. The comprehensive case study that appears at the end of each chapter (the case studies for Part 2 are collected together at the end of this part) is an overview of the procedures and the accounting theory for the chapter.

Accounting for the GST

At the time of writing, the federal government is planning to replace the Federal Sales Tax, which is a tax on goods at the manufacturing level, with the Goods and Services Tax (Bill C-62) calculated at a rate of 7% on the sale of goods and or the provision of services. Although Bill C-62 has not been passed, an introduction to the accounting of transactions affected by the GST is important. Consequently, we have revised illustrations of business documents in Part 3 to include the GST. The accounting for the GST follows a spiral development. Initially, all GST transactions are recorded in a current liability account called GST Payable. However, in Chapter 14 where the GST is examined in more detail, alternative methods of tracking the GST are offered to support both manual and computerized applications.

Cash Flow Statement

In support of many teachers' requests, we have recognized the importance of the statement of cash flows by discussing it as a separate topic in Chapter 10, Introducing Petty Cash and Banking Applications.

FEATURES CARRIED FORWARD FROM PRIOR EDITIONS

Key Check Figures

To help students solve assigned problems in the *Study Guide and Working Papers* for Parts 1, 2, and 3, Key Check Figures are given in the working papers section of these books.

Equation Approach

The accounting equation is used to present the introductory accounting cycle. Consequently, a solid foundation of accounting concepts and principles can be laid without the use of accounts, journals, and accounting jargon. In this way, the students learn the **why** before the **how**.

Spiral Development

The topics are arranged to proceed "from the simple to the complex and from the known to the unknown." Thus, the first six chapters of Part 1 give a simplified, that is, without adjustments, version of the accounting cycle by presenting an accounting system for a service business that uses one journal and one ledger. The more complex topics of Part 2 explain special journals and subsidiary ledgers. In Part 3, the special journals, combination journals, subsidiary ledgers, and adjustments are analyzed for a merchandising business.

A Systems Approach

An accounting system may be defined as the method by which a business not only processes its data through the accounting cycle, but also protects its cash and other assets from waste, fraud, and theft. This approach is a fundamental characteristic of the textbook.

Applications of Accounting Theory

Beginning accounting courses at any level of instruction should present an introductory treatment of accounting concepts and Generally Accepted Accounting Principles (GAAPs). Consequently, we offer an introduction to the accounting concepts of entity, going-concern, time-period; to basic GAAPs such as objectivity, cost, revenue, expense, and matching; and to specific disclosure principles required by the *CICA Handbook*.

Current Terminology

Care has been taken to adopt current, precise accounting language throughout the textbook. All accounting terms are highlighted in second colour and are also defined in the margin.

Conversion to SI

In spite of the slow acceptance of the metric system, the style of the textbook conforms to the International System of Units (SI) in accordance with the *Metric Style Guide* published by the Council of Ministers of Education.

Also, by and large, the traditional comma in dollar amounts has been eliminated to conform to the following recommendation of this guide: ". . . the use of the comma to separate sets of three digits to the left of the decimal point is now to be discontinued; a space is left where we used to put a comma." Since the space is optional in a four-digit number, these numbers appear in this way: $4000 or 3263. However, numbers with more than four digits have a space as in, for example, $10 000. In the illustrations, the reader will notice that numbers appear frequently in columns and therefore spaces are retained in four-digit numbers. The style of numbers in spreadsheets conforms to common use.

Marginal Notes, Illustrations, and Icons

Running alongside the text is a wide margin. Key definitions, notes, and accounting concepts and principles are highlighted here.

There are many illustrations in the textbook of accounting records, business forms, and spreadsheets, to name only a few examples. These illustrations elaborate key concepts and reinforce content. We frequently highlight portions of an illustration with a separate illustration to encourage closer examination.

We identify problems that may be solved using electronic spreadsheet software or General Ledger software with icons. For example, this icon indicates that the student may use an electronic spreadsheet. This icon indicates a GL application.

SUPPORTING MATERIALS

An assortment of supporting materials is available to accompany this textbook.

TEACHER'S RESOURCE BOOK AND KEY

This book is divided into nine sections, labelled A to J, which are briefly described below. Many of the sections, namely, B, C, E, F, G, and H, may be reproduced for use in the classroom as aids for encouraging discussion, testing the progress of students, and so on.

A. Instructional Objectives. This section also appears in the student's *Study Guide and Working Papers* for Parts 1, 2, and 3.

B. Solutions. Keys to all problems, mini-cases, and comprehensive case studies are given for each chapter.

C. Chapter Questions. Additional questions and solutions for these questions are offered in this section.

D. Multiple-Choice Questions. The solutions and, where appropriate, detailed explaintions for the multiple-choice questions given in the *Study Guide and Working Papers* are listed here.

E. Supplementary Problems. This sections suggests extra problems for each chapter.

F. Supplementary Case Studies. Additional mini-cases and their solutions are suggested.

G. Progress Tests and Keys. Progress tests, in addition to comprehensive progress tests for Parts 1, 2, and 3 (see Chapters 6, 11, and 16 in the study guide) appear in this section. All solutions are given.

H. Teaching Masters. Teaching masters of the most common forms are presented for each topic area from Chapter 1 to Chapter 16.

I. General Ledger Software and Supporting Manual. One set of disks to suport Summation's® commercial General Ledger module, Version 2.32, and supporting data files are available. In addition, one instruction manual is included to support the General Ledger applications in the textbook. Teachers may duplicate copies of discs and the instruction manuals for their students.

STUDY GUIDE AND WORKING PAPERS FOR PARTS, 1, 2, AND 3

There is a separate study guide and working papers for each of the parts. The study guide lists the instructional objectives for each chapter, in addition to the key terms, chapter questions, a demonstration problem with a suggested solution, and twenty multiple-choice questions.

ACCOUNTING APPLICATIONS

Twelve accounting applications are also published separately from the textbook. In general, these are longer that the topic problems and give the students an opportunity to integrate the material they have learned in preceding chapters. All application problems may be done manually and/or electronically by using school-approved software or the software which accompanies the main text. Some of the applications offer simulated source documents form which students must analyze the transactions before recording their dollar results into accounting records. Other applications offer problems to support the internal control of cash and merchandise inventory and the filing of an individual income tax return for a wage earner and a single proprietorship. There are also problems which are common to accounting for agriculture and fishery businesses. Working papers are included for all applications which require accounting forms.

ACKNOWLEDGEMENTS

We are grateful to the many high school teachers who have made helpful suggestions for topics, problems, mini-cases, comprehensive case studies, and applications for the microcomputer. In particular, the following teachers agreed to review the manuscript and contributed comments: Diana Camerin, Carihi Secondary School, Campbell River, British Columbia; Jim Granville, Cobequid Educational Centre, Truro, Nova Scotia; Paul Ingram, Fundy Regional High School, St. George, New Brunswick; Richard Kelly, Sir Winston Churchill Senior High School, Calgary, Alberta; Anne-Marie Rigaux, St. Johns High School, Winnipeg, Manitoba; Karen Wood, Woburn Collegiate, Scarborough, Ontario.

Several organizations and businesses have contributed to the improvements in this edition. The Canadian Institute of Chartered Accountants allowed us to make reference to several specific financial reporting principles contained the *CICA Handbook*. The Lotus Development Corporation, Microsoft Corporation, the Royal Bank of Canada, and SumWare Corporation kindly granted permission to reproduce some specific spreadsheet illustrations. Michael Murk and Peter Murk of SumWare Corporation permitted us to use the most recent version of Summation in conjunction with selected accounting cycle problems offered in the textbook.

Illustrations Credits

pp. 16, 110, 319, 367, 369, 398, 399, 400, 405, 416, 417, 624, 628, 630, 631, 632, 633, 635, 636, and 637, the Royal Bank of Canada; pp. 59 and 61, Lotus and 1-2-3 are registered trademarks of Lotus Development Corporation. Screen reproduced with permission; pp. 62 and 63, Reprinted with permission. Microsoft is a registered trademark of Microsoft Corporation; p. 111, Courtesy of Bell Canada; p. 128 (for all three items), Photographs taken with permission from Grand & Toy Ltd. from their 1990 catalogue; p. 129 (margin) Courtesy of BASF Canada Inc.; p. 131, Courtesy of IBM Corporation; p. 140, Photograph taken with permission from Grand & Toy Ltd. from their 1990 catalogue; p. 148 (top), Queensway General Hospital, (middle) Reprinted with approval from Nordic Tours Limited, (bottom) Advertisement courtesy of Toshiba of Canada Limited, Consumer Electronics Operations; p. 149, Reprinted with permission from Tetra Pak Inc.; p. 233, (bottom) Courtesy of the Stadium Corporation of Ontario Ltd.; p. 234, Canadian Memorial Chiropractic College; p. 235, With acknowledgement to the H. J. Heinz Company of Canada, Ltd.; p. 236, Courtesy of the Saskatchewan Public Service Commission; p. 237, Kingston Psychiatric Hospital, Ministry of Health, Province of Ontario; pp. 297, 298, 299, 301, 310, 317, 326, 335, 338, and 340, Dental Receipt VS-MR(S) © 1984 Safeguard Business Systems Limited, Mississauga, Ontario; p. 427, Ad illustration courtesy of Sony of Canada Ltd. Sony is a registered trademark of Sony Corporation, Tokyo; p. 428, Published with permission of Employment and Immigration Canada and Supply and Services Canada; pp. 429, 430, 435, 436, 437, 438, 439, 443, 445, 446, 461, 462, 463, Revenue Canada—Taxation. Reproduced with permission of the Minister of Supply and Services Canada; p. 440, Source: Employer Guide, 1990. Published with the permission of Employment and Immigration Canada and Supply and Services Canada, 1990; p. 594, Courtesy of Revenue Canada—Customs and Excise; the Sales Tax Schedule at 8%, page 609, and Form No. (R) 0336P (90-02), page 617, are reprinted with permission from the Ontario Ministry of Revenue, Retail Sales Tax Branch. This latter form is updated regularly. Form No. (R) 0336P (90-02) is also reproduced with the permission of the Queen's Printer for Ontario.

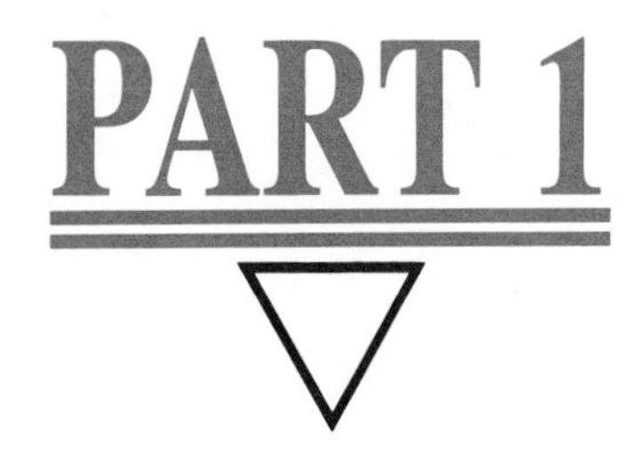

BASIC CONCEPTS IN ACCOUNTING

Part 1 of the text will introduce you to the fundamentals of accounting in two ways:

(1) theoretically, by introducing you to Generally Accepted Accounting Principles (GAAPs) and accounting concepts,

(2) practically, by teaching you how to complete the steps of the accounting cycle for a service business.

Accounting cycle: the procedures of opening a set of accounting records, recording all business events in those records during a specific period, and preparing financial reports and closing those records for that period of time.

In Part 1, you will learn how:

- to maintain a simple set of books and prepare a set of financial statements that are useful for interested persons both within and outside of a service business.
- to complete the steps of a simple accounting cycle first manually, and then electronically by using a microcomputer and spreadsheet software and General Ledger software.

Throughout the seven chapters in Part 1, the simple aspects of accounting theory are presented. This theory explains the importance of the following:

- particular documents
- specific numbers and dates
- basic accounting records such as the system of proofs that is necessary to ensure accuracy of records throughout the entire accounting cycle

CHAPTER 1

ESTABLISHING A BUSINESS

Topic 1
Establishing the Accounting Equation

Topic 2
Introducing the Balance Sheet

Profit-making business: produces goods, sells goods, or sells services.

Accounting is very much a part of every Canadian profit-making business.

Many different kinds of businesses exist in Canada. Farms, steel mills, paper mills, and automobile manufacturers are examples of businesses that produce goods. Other businesses, known as wholesalers, buy goods in large quantities from producers and sell them to retailers, who in turn sell the goods to consumers. Not all businesses, however, produce or sell goods; many — for example, realtors, dentists, lawyers, and dry cleaners — offer services. But all businesses, whether they produce or sell goods or offer services, may be classified according to three forms of ownership:

Forms of ownership: sole proprietorship, partnership, and business corporation.

- sole proprietorship — owned by one person
- partnership — owned by two or more persons
- corporation — owned by one or more persons, and is operated under a government charter

In this chapter, you will be introduced to two accounting concepts related to the creation of any Canadian business.

TOPIC 1 ESTABLISHING THE ACCOUNTING EQUATION

Let's begin with an important question.

What does a person need to start a business?

Your answer will probably include some of the following: money, that is, cash in the bank, a building, equipment and furniture, goods or services to sell, or perhaps a delivery truck.

You and your classmates might have different answers. But let's consider an answer that can apply to all types of businesses. One word—resources—can be used to describe all the items a person needs to start a business.

To start any type of profit-making business, a person needs resources such as land, building, goods for sale, equipment, etc. Since these resources are scarce in the sense that they exist in limited quantities, and since all require effort to produce — through the combination of input, such as machinery, and also labour and management — these resources are called economic resources.

Economic resources: scarce items which require effort to produce and for which a price must be paid.

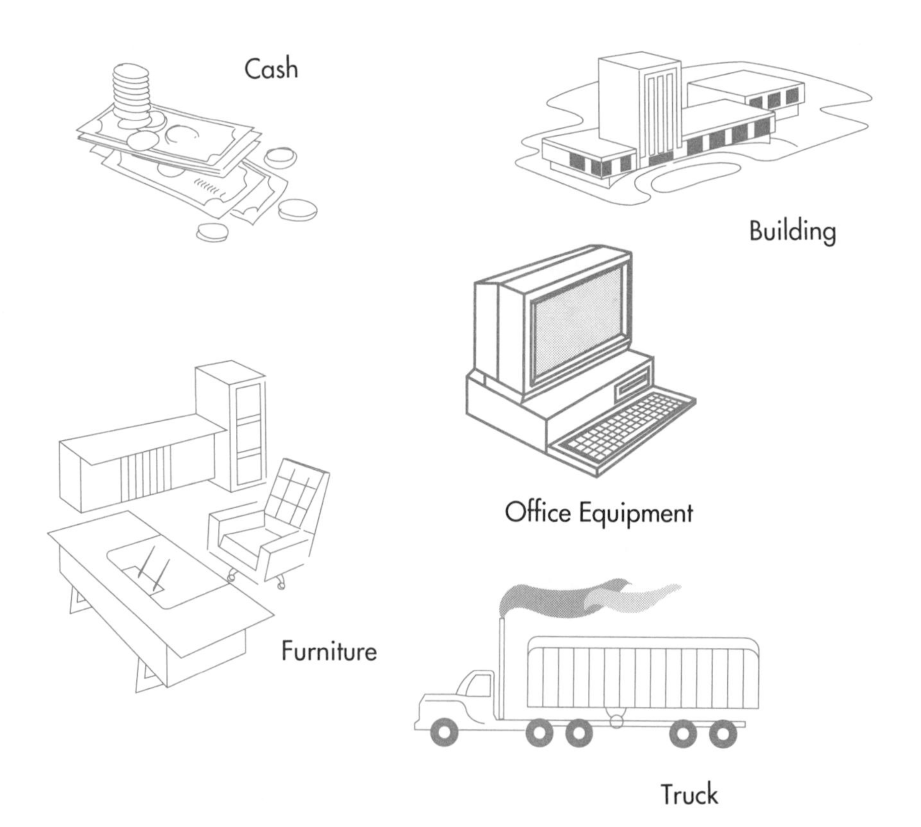

Did your list of resources include people? It is true that people are required to begin any business. But from an accounting standpoint, people are considered a **human resource** or **labour**. Later in the textbook you will learn that a business accounts for this resource with a payroll system. For this reason we exclude this resource from the list of economic resources needed to begin any business. Discussion of this topic is better postponed for an advanced level accounting course. Now consider the following question.

How does a business acquire the economic resources needed to begin operation?

The answer is:

- partly through the investment of the owner or owners
- partly through borrowing

Let's look at each aspect of the answer in detail. For now, we will assume that there is only one owner.

Creditor: a person or business to whom money or goods are owed; one to whom a debt is owed.

Credit: the ability to buy or borrow upon a promise to pay at a later date.

Debt: a sum of money owed by one person (the debtor) to another (the creditor), payable either on demand or at some fixed or determinable future time.

Debtor: a person or business who owes money or goods.

When the owner of a business obtains a loan from a chartered bank, the money is used to purchase economic resources such as equipment, furniture, or delivery trucks. The bank becomes a creditor because it has granted credit — a time period in which to pay back the money borrowed — to the business. Of course, in borrowing from the bank the business has acquired a debt and is a debtor.

Borrowing can also take other forms. For example, a business buys a delivery truck from a truck dealer who allows the business to pay for the truck in 90 days. The dealer, like the bank, is a creditor since credit — 90 days — has been granted to pay for the purchase. Other common terms of credit are 30 and 60 days.

Until a debt that is owed by the business is paid off, a creditor has a **claim** against the economic resources of the business. For example, when money is borrowed from the bank, the bank has a legal claim against the economic resources of the borrower until the debt has been paid. Similarly, if a truck dealer gives a business 60 days to pay for a truck, the dealer has a claim on the borrower's economic resources.

Small claims court: an inexpensive, informal place for settling small disputes, usually of $1000 or less.

Canada's legal system allows creditors to sue debtors for small overdue amounts in an appropriate court. For example, a banker who lent $500 to a business may place a claim before the small claims court of the province in which the business loan was made.

Owner investment: results in claim of owner against economic resources.

Not many new businesses, however, can acquire all the economic resources they need by borrowing. Usually, the owner must invest some of his or her own money in the business. In addition, the owner may invest in furniture or personal belongings in an office. Therefore, another important source of economic resources is owner investment, and if the owner has made an investment to establish the business, he or she, too, has a claim against these resources.

INTRODUCING ACCOUNTING THEORY

Concepts: basic ideas that act as a foundation for all accounting theory.

GAAPs: broad rules or guidelines for preparing financial statements.

Entity concept: one aspect of accounting theory that views the business as being separate, distinct, and apart from its owners.

As you study accounting, you will encounter several concepts and principles of accounting theory. Concepts are the foundation for accounting theory. They provide the theoretical foundation for Generally Accepted Accounting Principles, usually referred to as GAAPs. These principles are broad rules or guidelines that accountants follow in order to produce accounting records that will be alike in structure and comparable to those of businesses of a similar type.

The concept that should be introduced at this time is the entity concept. Accounting theory supports the idea that each business is an economic unit, separate and distinct from its owner and any other business. Therefore, when Mr. Zigone starts a business called Jake's Job—a repair service—his house and the car he drives only for personal use are still owned by him, but the desk and chair he takes to the shop to use at work become economic resources of the new business. The furniture is an example of owner investment. Similarly, the entity concept requires that the new business maintain accounting records that are separate from the family records.

Let's review what we have learned so far.

- To start a business, economic resources are required.
- Some economic resources—for example, cash—come from creditors. The funds are borrowed from creditors who then have legal claim against the economic resources until the debts are paid.
- Some resources are contributed through the investments of the owner, or owners, of the business; therefore, he or she too has a claim against the economic resources of the business.
- Finally, the entity concept states that resources should be separate from the personal belongings of the owner or owners of the business.

Equation: a shorthand way of presenting mathematical or logical relationships.

In the language of accounting, the shorthand way of stating these new ideas is by using an equation. Examine carefully the two equations that follow. Also, study the analysis[1] of each equation given immediately below the equation.

ECONOMIC RESOURCES	=	CLAIMS AGAINST ECONOMIC RESOURCES
$100 000	=	$100 000

[1]In this textbook, analysis means how to learn a topic by breaking it into understandable parts.

Analysis: The first equation says that the economic resources of any business must equal the total claims against the economic resources. In this equation, the total of the economic resources is $100 000. Therefore, the claims against those resources is also equal to $100 000. Notice that the economic resources are placed on the left side of the equation and the claims against the resources appear on the right side.

ECONOMIC RESOURCES	=	CLAIMS OF CREDITORS	+	CLAIM OF OWNER
$100 000	=	$30 000	+	$70 000

Analysis: This second equation is similar to the first; however, it breaks up the claims into two groups. The claims of all the creditors totals $30 000. The amount invested by the owner, or owners, is $70 000. The two sides of the equation must agree; or we also say that the equation is balanced. A quick check shows the total claim against economic resources, $30 000 + $70 000 or $100 000, equals the total economic resources or $100 000.

ANALYZING THE ACCOUNTING EQUATION

Assets: the economic resources of a business.

Liabilities: the claims of creditors against the assets of a business.

Owner's equity: the claim of the owner against the assets of a business.

In the language of accounting, economic resources are known as assets; the claims of creditors are known as liabilities; and the claim of the owner is called owner's equity. (The claim of more than one owner would be known as owners' equity.) We can rewrite the second equation, substituting these accounting terms, to arrive at the equation below, known as the accounting equation.

A	=	L	+	OE
ASSETS	=	LIABILITIES	+	OWNER'S EQUITY
$100 000	=	$30 000	+	$70 000

Analysis: Several important facts about the accounting equation should be remembered, as they will reappear throughout this course in accounting.

- The accounting equation contains three elements: Assets, Liabilities, and Owner's Equity.

- The symbols for the elements are A, L, and OE.
- Assets are shown on the left side of the accounting equation, and Liabilities and Owner's Equity on the right side.
- Assets are the economic resources required to establish any business. They represent what a business **owns**.
- Liabilities are the claims of the creditors against the assets. They represent the **debts** of the business.
- Owner's equity is the claim of the owner against the assets. The term "equity" refers to the claim or right of a person or business to the assets of a business. In this case, the claim or right belongs to the owner. (Thus, one could speak of liabilities as creditors' equity, but this term is not used.)
- On the right side of the accounting equation, you will notice that liabilities appear before owner's equity. This order is very important, for in Canadian courts the claims of creditors are considered before those of an owner or owners. For example, if the business were to be declared bankrupt—that is, incapable of paying its debts—the creditors' claims would have to be satisfied before the owner's in any sale of the assets.
- If you know the value of two of the elements, you can figure out the value of the third element. For example, if:

$$A \text{ (assets)} = \$24\ 000$$
$$L \text{ (liabilities)} = \$4000$$

solve for OE (owner's equity) as follows:

$A = \$24\ 000, L = \$4\ 000, OE = ?$

A	=	L	+	OE
OE	=	A	−	L
OE	=	$24 000	−	$4 000
OE	=	$20 000		

Similarly we can solve for A or L given values for the other elements:

$A = ?, L = \$4\ 000, OE = \$20\ 000$

A =	L	+	OE
A =	$4 000	+	$20 000
A =	$24 000		

$A = \$24\ 000, L = ?, OE = \$20\ 000$

A	=	L	+	OE
L	=	A	−	OE
L	=	$24 000	−	$20 000
L	=	$4 000		

APPLYING THE ACCOUNTING EQUATION

Let's now apply the accounting equation to a specific business. J. Emery Real Estate is a small business that has been established as a sole proprietorship and is owned by Jane Emery. The business consists of buying and selling homes, office buildings, and other types of real estate. Since this business does not produce or sell goods, it is therefore a service business.

J. Emery Real Estate began with the following assets and liabilities: Cash, \$60 000; Automobile, \$15 000; Furniture, \$8000; Office Equipment, \$7000; Bank Loan Payable, \$20 000; Accounts Payable, \$10 000. The business's accounting equation is obtained by classifying these items under the three elements of the equation as follows:

Assets				=	Liabilities		+	Owner's Equity
Cash	Automobile	Furniture	Office Equipment		Bank Loan Payable	Accounts Payable		J. Emery
\$60 000 +	\$15 000 +	\$8 000 +	\$7 000	=	\$20 000 +	\$10 000	+	\$60 000
\$90 000				=	\$30 000		+	\$60 000

Analysis: From studying the business's accounting equation, you will see that the amount of owner's equity is \$60 000. This amount is calculated as follows:

$$A = \$90\,000, L = \$30\,000, OE = ?$$
$$A = L + OE$$
$$OE = A - L$$
$$OE = \$90\,000 - \$30\,000$$
$$OE = \$60\,000$$

Let's examine each element in a little more detail.

Assets Assets, in general, are economic resources owned by a business. Obviously, a business will have many different kinds of assets. Each of these kinds encompasses a number of different items. In accounting practice, related assets are grouped into broad categories rather than dealt with separately. For example, cash in accounting refers not only to money in the form of coins and paper money, but also to cheques, money orders, and credit card receipts received by the business and the amount deposited in the business's bank account.

Cash: currency, cheques, money orders, and bank deposits.

Under **Cash**, J. Emery Real Estate has a large amount, $60 000. The business will need this amount not only to buy more economic resources as needed, but also to pay off debts as they fall due and, in particular, to meet operating expenses. For example, J. Emery Real Estate does not own a building, but rents office space on a regular, monthly basis. Rent and other expenses will be studied later in this textbook. What you should remember now is that cash is an important asset for every business.

Furniture: desk, chairs, tables, etc.

Office equipment: word processors, calculators, photocopiers, cash registers, etc.

The remaining three items under Assets in the accounting equation — Automobile, Furniture, and Office Equipment — require only a brief explanation. Jane Emery needs a car to conduct her business. We assume that she uses it only for business purposes. Furniture refers to such items as desks, chairs, and tables. Office equipment includes calculators, typewriters, word processors, cash registers, photocopiers, and the like.

Liabilities

Most businesses have liabilities or debts to pay. Two very common debts are illustrated in the accounting equation for J. Emery Real Estate — Bank Loan Payable and Accounts Payable.

Bank loan payable: the claim of a bank against the assets of a borrowing business.

First, Bank Loan Payable,[2] or simply Bank Loan, is the accounting term for a loan from a bank. J. Emery Real Estate has borrowed $20 000 from a bank. This amount has been deposited in the name of the business, and it is part of the total cash reported in the assets section.

Accounts payable: amounts owing to creditors (other than banks) for the purchase of goods or services on credit.

The heading Accounts Payable is used to identify amounts due to creditors other than banks for the purchase of goods or services on credit. J. Emery Real Estate has acquired some assets on credit from an auto dealer, a furniture dealer, and an office equipment supplier. In this example, let's assume that these separate amounts are owing: to Bell Furniture Co., $3000; to Ryan Equipment Co., $2000; and to Westown Motors Ltd., $5000. Notice that the sum of these debts is $10 000, the amount reported for accounts payable in the accounting equation.

Mortgage payable: a long-term debt wherein the collateral consists of the property bought.

One other liability is worth mentioning here. In acquiring property —land or a building—some businesses find it necessary to borrow on a long-term basis — for example, for 20 to 30 years. Such a debt is described as a mortgage. A mortgage is a contract or written agreement stating that if a debt is not paid as agreed, the lender may sell the property to obtain the unpaid amount of the debt. This debt is called Mortgage Payable

[2]In accounting language, liabilities are usually identified by the word "payable."

Owner's Equity Owner's equity represents the claim of the owner against the assets of the business—in other words, the financial interest of the proprietor in the business. In the case of J. Emery Real Estate, Jane Emery has equity or a claim against the assets in the amount of $60 000. This claim, like the claims of the creditors, is not against any particular asset but against all assets. Thus, we could say that owner's equity is a **residual** claim—the amount Jane is entitled to **after** the claims of the creditors have been fully satisfied.

TOPIC 1 PROBLEMS

Solving for the unknown element in the accounting equation.

P 1-1 Solve for the unknown in each of the following equations:

	Assets	=	Liabilities	+	Owner's Equity
Example:	$10 000	=	$1200	+	(Answer: $8800)
a.	$500	=	$100	+	?
b.	$4000	=	?	+	$2500
c.	$740	=	$300	+	?
d.	?	=	$800	+	$1000
e.	$9000	=	?	+	$6200
f.	$4800	=	$2100	+	?
g.	$18 000	=	$6900	+	?
h.	?	=	$4500	+	$6900
i.	$1435	=	?	+	$700
j.	$3890	=	0	+	?

Solving for the unknown element.
Itemizing the elements.
Constructing the accounting equation.

P 1-2 On March 10 of this year Jeanne Fung opened an accounting office. The following is a list of her business's assets and liabilities on that date: Accounts Payable, $300; Office Equipment, $4000; Cash, $700; Bank Loan Payable, $3300; Office Furniture, $1900. Determine owner's equity; then write an accounting equation that **itemizes** —gives all the things that make up—the three elements as shown on page 7. *Note:* Keep your answers for use in Problem 1-4.

Solving for the unknown elements.
Itemizing the elements.
Constructing the accounting equation.

P 1-3 Norman Liebenson, owner of the Saskatchewan Garden Maintenance Company, started his business today with the following economic resources and debts: Cash, $1000; Land, $52 000; Building, $124 000; Bank Loan Payable, $8500; Mortgage Payable, $130 000; Maintenance Equipment, $9500; Accounts Payable, $3000; Truck, $8000; and Office Equipment, $900.

a. List assets (beginning with cash) in one column and liabilities in another; then calculate owner's equity.

b. Write the accounting equation for the Saskatchewan Garden Maintenance Company, **itemizing** the three elements. *Note:* Keep your answers for use in Problem 1-4.

MINI-CASES

Identifying the language of accounting.

MC 1-1 Alice Tang has just begun a clothing alteration and repair service called Needles and Pins. She borrowed $15 000 from the bank and opened a bank account in the name of the business, bought a piece of land and a small house which will be her store location for $135 000; took out a mortgage on the land and building, $100 000; bought a used sewing machine on account from Al's Sewing Machines Ltd., $450; bought sewing supplies on credit from Fabrics Unlimited, $250; and bought $700 of other equipment with cash from her personal bank account. *Note:* Divide the cost of purchased property between land ($35 000) and the building ($100 000).

a. Identify each of the items that are involved with Alice's business by using the language of accounting, for example, Cash is an economic resource.

b. Identify each of the people or businesses listed above as a creditor or a debtor and briefly define each of these terms.

c. Prepare an itemized accounting equation for Needles and Pins.

Identifying an accounting concept.

MC 1-2 Igor Sudvanski began a consulting business that he operated out of the basement of his home. He moved some pieces of furniture from his home into the basement office and several other items including: paper, file folders, a stapler, and a filing cabinet.

a. What important accounting concept must Igor keep in mind as he begins the operation of his new business? Briefly explain why this concept is important.

Analyzing the parts of the accounting equation.

MC 1-3 Gerald and Marta were discussing yesterday's lesson on the accounting equation. Gerald said, "I don't understand why we break the three elements into separate items like Cash and Office Furniture. Why don't we just leave those two items under the heading of Assets?"

a. What explanation would you give to Gerald's question?

b. What kind of items are included under Cash and Office Furniture?

INTRODUCING THE BALANCE SHEET

Balance sheet: a financial statement reporting assets, liabilities, and owner's equity as at a certain date.

One important purpose of accounting is to prepare formal reports detailing the assets and the claims against these assets for the benefit of creditors, the owner or owners, or other interested parties. Such a formal report or financial statement is known as a balance sheet.

ANALYZING A BALANCE SHEET

From studying the accounting equation, you have learned that a business's liabilities represent the claims of creditors against its assets, and that owner's equity is the claim of the owner against those assets (Assets = Liabilities + Owner's Equity). The basic structure of a balance sheet is based upon this equation. Compare the equation and balance sheet below. Then study the analysis.

Assets								=	Liabilities			+	Owner's Equity
Cash		Automobile		Furniture		Office Equipment			Bank Loan Payable		Accounts Payable		J. Emery
$60 000	+	$15 000	+	$9 000	+	$7 000		=	$20 000	+	$10 000	+	$60 000
$90 000								=	$30 000			+	$60 000

Heading

Body

J. Emery Real Estate
Balance Sheet
as at September 30, 19 —

ASSETS		LIABILITIES		
Cash	$60 000.00	Bank Loan Payable		$20 000.00
Automobile	15 000.00	Accounts Payable:		
Furniture	8 000.00	Bell Furniture Co.	$3 000.00	
Office Equipment	7 000.00	Ryan Equipment Co.	2 000.00	
		Westown Motors Ltd.	5 000.00	10 000.00
		Total Liabilities		$30 000.00
		OWNER'S EQUITY		
		J. Emery, Capital		60 000.00
Total Assets	$90 000.00	Total Liabilities and Owner's Equity		$90 000.00

Analysis: The balance sheet has two sections, the heading and the body.

- The heading of a balance sheet has three lines and each answers a question: Line 1: **who** (the name of the business); Line 2: **what** (the type of document that follows); Line 3: **when** (the date on which the information is valid).
- The body of the balance sheet has two sides: assets are listed in detail on the left side, and the claims of creditors and the owner on the right side.
- Notice that assets are **itemized**, as in the accounting equation.
- Liabilities are also itemized, and accounts payable are broken down into individual creditors.
- Look at the owner's equity section of the balance sheet. The heading Owner's Equity shows only the total claim of the owner against the assets, but it does not explain the financial interest of the owner. Now notice the heading J. Emery, Capital. The word ''capital'' indicates the amount of the owner's claim against assets that is due to her investment in the business.

Capital: the owner's claim against the assets through personal investment.

Balance sheet equation: the accounting equation represented in the balance sheet.

There are similarities between the accounting equation and the balance sheet. First, since the accounting equation is now represented in the balance sheet, it may be called the balance sheet equation. Second, the balance sheet, like the accounting equation, balances. In other words, total assets equal total liabilities plus owner's equity.

PREPARING THE BALANCE SHEET

Balance sheets are prepared at least once a year. When they are needed more frequently, such as once a month, and where facilities are available, balance sheets are prepared electronically by means of a word processor or a computer.

Don't worry about being asked to prepare a computer program for a balance sheet. The study of how balance sheets and other accounting reports are actually prepared — by typewriter, word processor, printing press, or computer — is part of the study of business data processing. At this stage it is important to acquire only a basic knowledge of the concepts related to the preparation of any balance sheet. The best way to learn how to prepare a balance sheet is by hand.

Business data processing: the study of how business (accounting) information is physically handled and processed.

To help you prepare a handwritten balance sheet, study the illustration on page 15. Let's discuss the various sections.

Heading For a balanced appearance, centre the three lines of the heading over the body. Remember the order of these lines:

- who
- what
- when

Asset Section On the first line, centre the title Assets between the left side of the form and the first money column.

Look carefully at the order of the assets: Cash, Automobile, Furniture, and Office Equipment. This is the order of how quickly each asset can be converted into cash — the liquidity order. Most accountants prefer this order beginning with cash, then followed by all assets which can be converted into cash, and finally, by assets which cannot be converted into cash.

Liquidity order: the order of assets according to how easily the assets may be converted into cash.

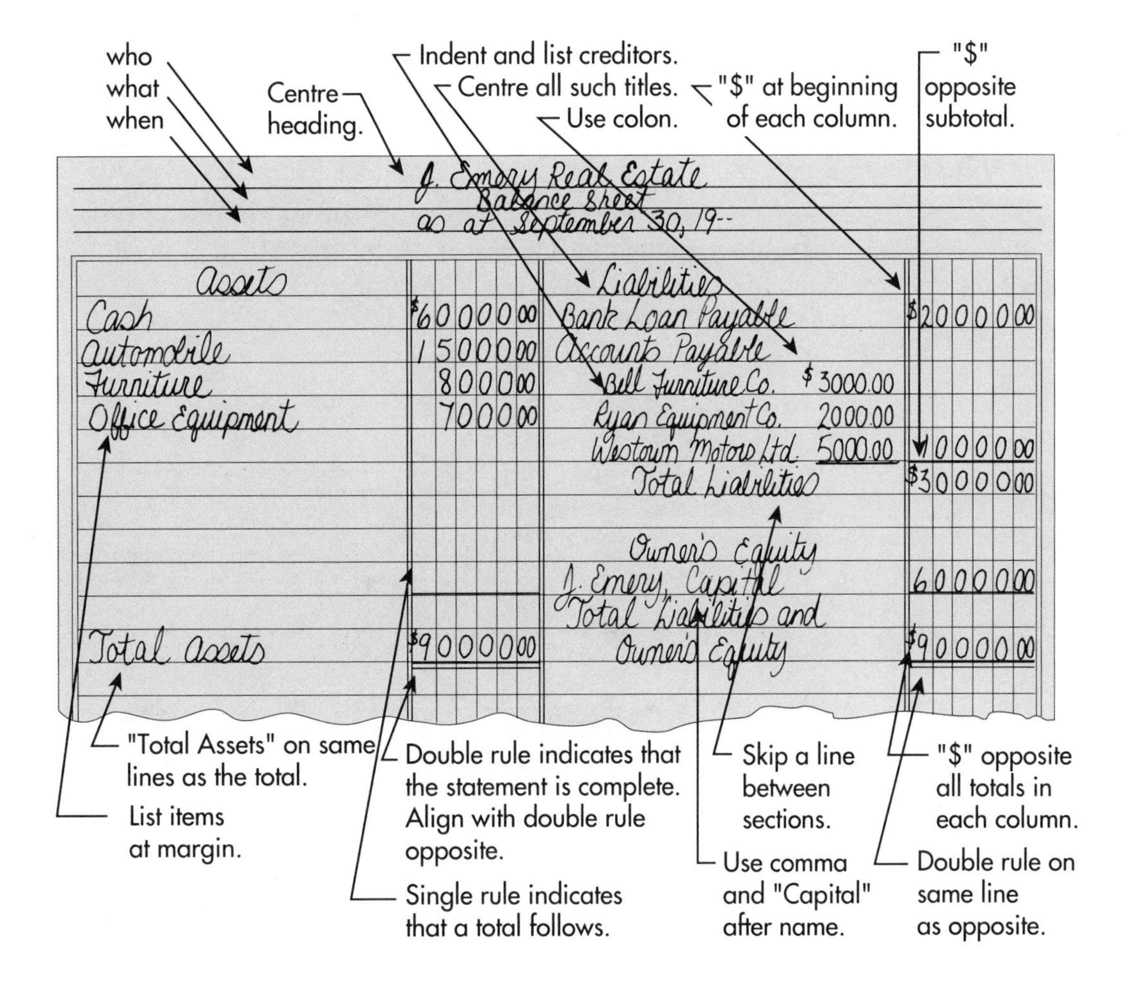

Observe how the assets are entered. With Cash at the beginning, each asset is listed along the left margin. Each word begins with a capital letter. The dollar amount of the asset is recorded on the same line in the money column.

Placement of dollar signs (general rules): (1) with the first amount in a column; (2) with any subtotal or total in a column.

Notice the dollar sign that appears with the first asset in the money column. As a general rule for placement of dollar signs, a dollar sign is shown with the first amount in any column — as illustrated under Liabilities—and with each subtotal and total in a column. In this type of money column decimal points do not appear; also, a column is provided for cents.

Finally, for each even dollar amount, two zeroes in the cents column are added. Do not leave the cents column blank, or use a dash, in a balance sheet form with rules. Above all, a balance sheet is a formal report and should be neat, complete, and legible.

Liability Section

The title Liabilities is centred on the first line of the second side. Liabilities are shown above owner's equity since the claims of the creditors must be satisfied before the claims of the owner in the event of bankruptcy.

Order for listing liabilities: the order of retiring debts; this order is based on the due date.

As with assets, there is a certain order for listing liabilities. Liabilities are debts: those that are to be paid immediately are listed before those that fall due later in, say, 30 days.

Demand loan: repayable when the creditor demands payment.

To understand why a bank loan comes before accounts payable, you must first know something about the types of loans usually granted to businesses. A business loan is generally called a demand loan. To learn the meaning of ''demand,'' study the following illustration.

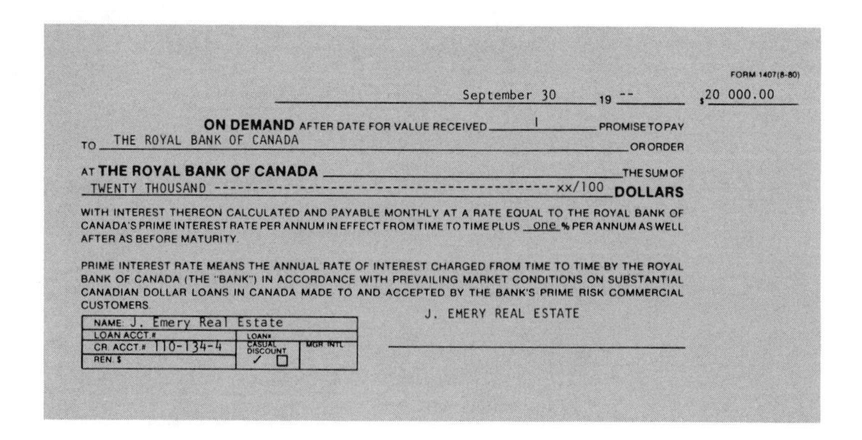
FORM 1407(8-80)

September 30 19 -- $20 000.00

ON DEMAND AFTER DATE FOR VALUE RECEIVED I PROMISE TO PAY

TO THE ROYAL BANK OF CANADA OR ORDER

AT THE ROYAL BANK OF CANADA THE SUM OF

TWENTY THOUSAND --xx/100 DOLLARS

WITH INTEREST THEREON CALCULATED AND PAYABLE MONTHLY AT A RATE EQUAL TO THE ROYAL BANK OF CANADA'S PRIME INTEREST RATE PER ANNUM IN EFFECT FROM TIME TO TIME PLUS one % PER ANNUM AS WELL AFTER AS BEFORE MATURITY.

PRIME INTEREST RATE MEANS THE ANNUAL RATE OF INTEREST CHARGED FROM TIME TO TIME BY THE ROYAL BANK OF CANADA (THE "BANK") IN ACCORDANCE WITH PREVAILING MARKET CONDITIONS ON SUBSTANTIAL CANADIAN DOLLAR LOANS IN CANADA MADE TO AND ACCEPTED BY THE BANK'S PRIME RISK COMMERCIAL CUSTOMERS.

J. EMERY REAL ESTATE

NAME: J. Emery Real Estate
LOAN ACCT #
CR. ACCT # 110-134-4
REN. $
LOAN#
CASUAL DISCOUNT ✓
MGR INTL

Notice that this "I.O.U." is payable to the banker "on demand." This means that the business must repay the bank, with interest, whenever the bank requests payment. By right, the bank can grant the loan today and demand payment tomorrow. Ordinarily, the bank will allow the business to decide when it can pay the debt, as long as the period of time is reasonable. However, the point is that no guaranteed time is stated in the demand note. Since the business can expect that repayment of the loan may be demanded at any time, this liability is usually listed first.

Accounts payable, on the other hand, are shown after the bank loan, since creditors usually give the business a longer time—30, 60 or 90 days—to repay. In the balance sheet for J. Emery Real Estate individual creditors are reported under Accounts Payable.

Those liabilities that must be paid within a year of the date of the balance sheet are placed ahead of those that must be paid over a longer period of time—usually more than one year. For example, a mortgage payable is a long-term debt—for 20 years or more—and, therefore, it is placed at the end of a liability list, as shown below.

One final point should be noted, as also shown below, in the liability section of the balance sheet. To report two or more liabilities, show each liability on a separate line as in the first marginal illustration. Note the use of the dollar sign with the first dollar amount in a money column and opposite Total Liabilities. For one liability, however, only one total is necessary as shown in the second illustration.

Several Accounts Payable

Liabilities		
Bank Loan Payable		$ 2 000 00
Accounts Payable:		
X Company Ltd.	$1 000.00	
Y Company Ltd.	2 000.00	3 000 00
Mortgage Payable		20 000 00
Total Liabilities		$25 000 00

One Liability Only

Liabilities	
Accounts Payable:	
M. Couse Company	$ 1 000 00
Owner's Equity	
J. Kershaw, Capital	39 000 00
Total	$40 000 00

Owner's Equity Section The title Owner's Equity is also centred above its section and one blank line follows this title. As you will recall, owner's equity refers to the claim of the owner against the total assets of the business. Since Jane Emery invested capital of $60 000 in the business, this claim is reported. Remember that the word ''capital'' means investment.

The foregoing notes concern **sole proprietorships**. It is worth mentioning how owner's equity is reported for the two other forms of business ownership. First of all, note that:

- In a **partnership**, the claims of partners against the total assets are usually known as **partners' equity.**
- In a **business corporation**, the owners are called shareholders, and their claims against the assets of the corporation are known as **shareholders' equity**.

Compare the three illustrations below. Notice that, just as the name of a sole proprietor is reported, the names of all the partners are also reported. In the case of shareholders, however, there may be hundreds or even thousands, so that it would be impractical to list the name and equity of each. Instead, **Share Capital** (or **capital stock**) appears, and the total investment by persons holding shares (stock) is given.

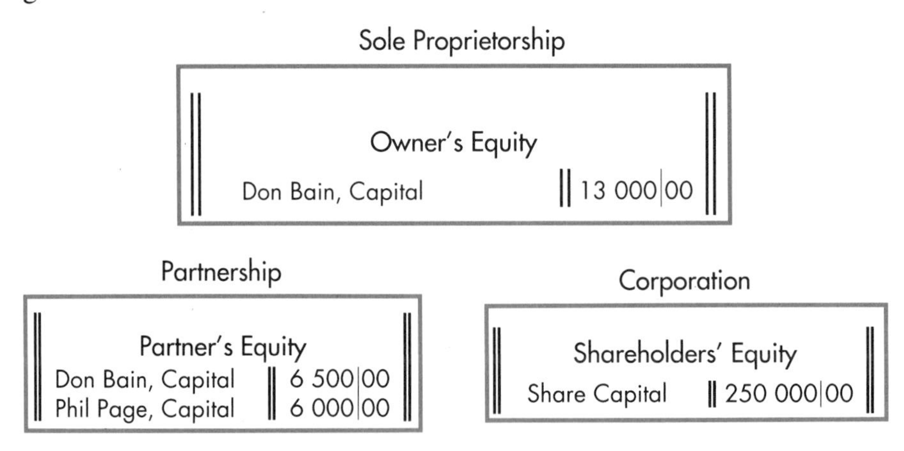

Totals and the Use of Rules After the assets, liabilities, and owner's equity are entered, a line is drawn across each money column (as shown on page 15). Then the columns are added. Both totals — which should be equal — are entered on the first blank line immediately below the ruled line. A dollar sign appears with each total.

Finally, a **double rule** is drawn across each money column to indicate they are complete. A single line indicates addition or subtraction; a double line indicates that the report is complete.

There are two things to note about the style of the document.

No Abbreviations Abbreviations should not be used unless the word or name you are given is already an abbreviation. For example, if the business's name is Fry Co., use the short form given, that is, Co. On the other hand, if the name is Fry Company, write out the full name as given. If a name is too long for one line, use two lines.

This general rule also applies to the date in the heading of a balance sheet. Do not abbreviate the month or the year, and do not use numeric dating, for example, 06 02 91.

12345678901234

too large

too crowded

illegible

just right

Importance of Legibility Make sure your work is legible. One of the most costly problems in business is careless or unreadable writing, especially in the writing of numbers. Ask yourself: *Could someone else read my numbers?*

Here are a few hints to improve your writing of numbers:

- Do not hurry. Take your time to form every number legibly.
- Write the numbers slightly slanted to the right.
- The size of each number should be less than one-half the line space. This leaves enough space above the numbers to make a manual correction, as shown in the margin.

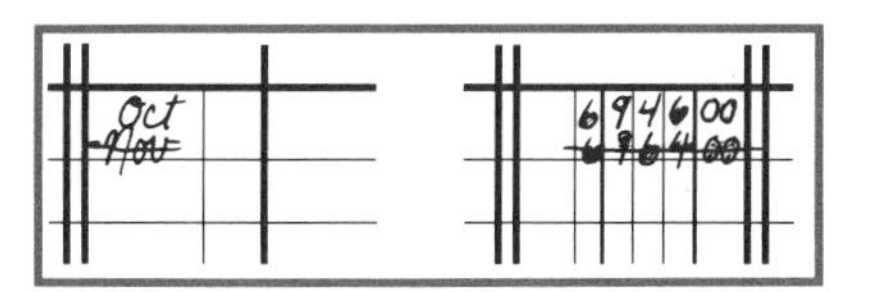

TOPIC 2 PROBLEMS

Preparing a balance sheet from an accounting equation.

P 1-4 Refer to the accounting equations in Problems 1-2 (Jeanne Fung) and 1-3 (Saskatchewan Garden Maintenance Company).

a. Using the accounting equation you solved for Problem 1-2, prepare the opening balance sheet for Jeanne Fung. Assume that there is only one account payable and this is due to Sherlock Office Suppliers, Ltd.

b. Using the accounting equation solved for Problem 1-3, prepare the opening balance sheet for Saskatchewan Garden Maintenance Company. Use today's date. Assume the accounts payable are: Guthrie Home Hardware Ltd., $1000; and P&P Equipment Supplies, Inc., $2000.

Analyzing and classifying accounting equation information.

Preparing a balance sheet from an accounting equation.

P 1-5 The information below reflects Ruth Forrester's Photo Service as at December 31.

a. Classify the financial data by writing an accounting equation. Once you have determined the kind and amount of each asset and liability, use the accounting equation to calculate owner's equity.

(i) The business has $17 000 on deposit in its bank account.
(ii) Office equipment has been acquired at a cost of $3400.
(iii) The business has incurred the following debts to be paid within 60 days: Hay Stationery Ltd., $5400; Lennox Heating Co., $3200; Star Equipment Co., $3700.
(iv) The business owns land that cost $50 000 and a building that cost $100 000.
(v) The business has a 20-year mortgage payable in the amount of $90 000.
(vi) Furniture has been acquired for $8000.

b. When you have completed and balanced the accounting equation, prepare the opening balance sheet of the business.

Preparing a balance sheet from an accounting equation.

P 1-6 Bert Conway began the Pacific Travel Agency on May 1, 19— with these assets and liabilities: Cash, $18 500; Land, $32 000; Building, $85 700; Furniture, $15 600; Office Equipment, $3300; Bank Loan Payable (on demand), $11 000; Mortgage Payable, $100 000; Accounts Payable (Beth Printers Co.), $700.

a. Prepare the balance sheet for Pacific Travel Agency.

MINI-CASES

Presenting items in a specific order in a balance sheet.

Evaluating the accuracy of a financial statement.

MC 1-4 Julienne LeBlanc, a junior accountant, was asked to review the asset section of Highland Landscaping Company's balance sheet. She found the following list of assets:

ASSETS	
Accounts Receivable	$5 000.00
Accounts Payable	1 200.00
Building	89 500.00
Cash	3 500.00
Land	104 000.00
Landscaping Equipment	78 700.00
Office Equipment	21 200.00
Truck	27 500.00
Total Assets	$330 600.00

a. List the errors in accounting concepts and principles that Julienne LeBlanc will most likely find.

b. Name the term that describes how the assets should have been listed in the balance sheet.

c. What is the major error in this portion of the balance sheet?

d. Rewrite this portion of the balance sheet so that its format is correct and it is accurate.

Analyzing the parts of the balance sheet.

MC 1-5 The heading of the balance sheet for J. Douglas's law office reads as follows:

J. Douglas, Barrister and Solicitor
Balance Sheet
as at July 31, 19-

a. What information does each line provide for the reader?

b. Where should the balance sheet heading be positioned in the report?

c. What are the other parts of a balance sheet? What is contained in each of these parts?

Examining format on the balance sheet.

MC 1-6 Alida's accounting teacher has stressed the importance of correct format in preparing a balance sheet.

a. Draw up a list of points to follow for a formal balance sheet presentation.

b. Why is format important? Provide two specific examples in your explanation.

COMPREHENSIVE CASE STUDY 1

Mr. Neville, a teacher of a first-year accounting class, said, ''After having received Wayne Gretzky from the Edmonton Oilers, the owner of the L.A. Kings asked his business's accountant to show Gretzky as one of the valuable assets in a balance sheet. The owner suggested an amount of about $100 000 000.''

He then asked his class to describe any changes that would result on the future balance sheet of the L.A. Kings.

One student, Nicola, said, ''Even though Wayne Gretzky is a valuable player, there would be no change in the balance sheet. Gretzky may be considered a human resource. We learned that accounting accounts for only economic resources.''

Ilan countered with this view, ''Gretzky will make millions of dollars for L.A. for at least seven additional years, so the owner is right. The future balance sheet should report Wayne Gretzky as one of the assets for at least $100 000 000.''

Comparing economic resource accounting to human resource accounting.

a. Whose view do you support? Explain your answer.

CHAPTER 2

ANALYZING CHANGES IN THE ACCOUNTING EQUATION

Topic 1
Analyzing Opening Business Transactions

Topic 2
Analyzing an Expanded Equation

Topic 3
Analyzing the Income Statement and the Related Balance Sheet

Topic 4
Using Electronic Spreadsheets in Accounting

In Chapter 1, you learned that the accounting equation has three elements: assets, liabilities, and owner's equity. In this chapter, you will learn how each of these three elements changes as a result of business transactions.

Business transaction: a financial event that affects assets, liabilities, or owner's equity.

A business transaction is a financial event that affects one or more of the three elements of the accounting equation. When analyzing any financial event, remember the word ''financial'' simply means the event is expressed in terms of dollars or money. In this chapter, you will analyze changes in the accounting equation.

ANALYZING OPENING BUSINESS TRANSACTIONS

To illustrate how business transactions affect the three elements of the accounting equation, we shall look at several business transactions of J. Emery Real Estate. As we know, the accounting equation as at September 30 is as follows:

Assets				=	Liabilities		+	Owner's Equity
Cash	Auto-mobile	Furniture	Office Equipment		Bank Loan Payable	Accounts Payable		J. Emery, Capital
$60 000 +	$15 000 +	$8 000 +	$7 000	=	$20 000 +	$10 000	+	$60 000
$90 000				=	$30 000		+	$60 000

Now study the series of transactions below.

Transaction 1 On October 1, J. Emery Real Estate buys more furniture for $1000 from Enns Furniture Ltd., and pays by cheque.

	Assets				=	Liabilities		+	Owner's Equity
	Cash	Auto-mobile	Furniture	Office Equipment		Bank Loan Payable	Accounts Payable		J. Emery, Capital
Original balance	$60 000 +	$15 000 +	$8 000 +	$7 000	=	$20 000 +	$10 000	+	$60 000
Transaction 1 →	−1 000		+1 000						
New balance →	$59 000	$15 000 +	$9 000 +	$7 000	=	$20 000 +	$10 000	+	$60 000
	$90 000					$30 000		+	$60 000

Analysis: Since the furniture is purchased with cash, only assets are affected by this transaction. The business obtains an additional **asset** — Furniture — by decreasing another **asset** — Cash. Since one asset amount increases while a second decreases by the same dollar amount, the total assets do not change. There is no change on the right side of the accounting equation, and the equation remains **balanced**. The total dollar amount on the left side is equal to the total dollar amount on the right side.

Transaction 2 On October 3, J. Emery Real Estate buys more office equipment — two calculators and one typewriter — for $1200 this time from the Ryan Equipment Co. on 60 days' credit. In other words, the creditor allows 60 days for payment of the debt.

	Assets				=	Liabilities		+ Owner's Equity
	Cash	Auto-mobile	Furniture	Office Equipment		Bank Loan Payable	Accounts Payable	J. Emery, Capital
Original balance	$59 000 +	$15 000 +	$9 000 +	$7 000	=	$20 000 +	$10 000 +	$60 000
Transaction 2 →				+1 200			+1 200	
New balance →	$59 000 +	$15 000 +	$9 000	$8 200	=	$20 000 +	$11 200 +	$60 000
	$91 200				=	$31 200		+ $60 000

Analysis: Two elements of the accounting equation are affected by this transaction. On the left side, the **asset** Office Equipment increases by $1200 because the business now owns more equipment. On the right side of the equation, the **liability** Accounts Payable increases by $1200 because the business now owes more money to its creditors. We can also say that the claims of the creditors against the total assets of the business increase by $1200.

Notice that the owner's equity of $60 000 is not affected by this transaction.

Look closely at the result of this transaction on the accounting equation. With the increase to Office Equipment, the total assets now amount to $90 000 + $1200 or $91 200. The right side also equals $91 200 because the total liabilities increase from $30 000 to $31 200. Since the left side increases by the same amount as the right side, the equation is again balanced.

Transaction 3 On October 4, J. Emery Real Estate returns one calculator costing $200 to Ryan Equipment Co. because it arrived in damaged condition. The creditor accepted the return.

	Assets							=	Liabilities			+	Owner's Equity
	Cash		Automobile		Furniture		Office Equipment		Bank Loan Payable		Accounts Payable		J. Emery, Capital
Original balance	$59 000	+	$15 000	+	$9 000	+	$8 200	=	$20 000	+	$11 200	+	$60 000
Transaction 3 →							− 200				− 200		
New balance →	$59 000	+	$15 000	+	$9 000	+	$8 000	=	$20 000	+	$11 000	+	$60 000
	$91 000								$31 000			+	$60 000

Analysis: Note that, when a business returns an asset purchased on credit but not yet paid for, the asset Cash does not change. The two parts of the equation affected are assets and liabilities, and both decrease. On the left, the **asset** Office Equipment decreases by $200 because the business now owns less equipment. On the right, the **liability** Accounts Payable decreases by $200 because the business owes less money to its creditors. The result is that the equation is still balanced, because the assets on the left side and the liabilities on the right decrease by the same dollar amount.

Transaction 4 On October 5, J. Emery Real Estate writes a cheque for $5000 to Westown Motors Ltd. in payment for the car Jane Emery purchased in September when she established the business. Prior to this payment, Westown Motors Ltd. held claim of $5000 against the total assets of J. Emery Real Estate; the cheque therefore eliminates that claim.

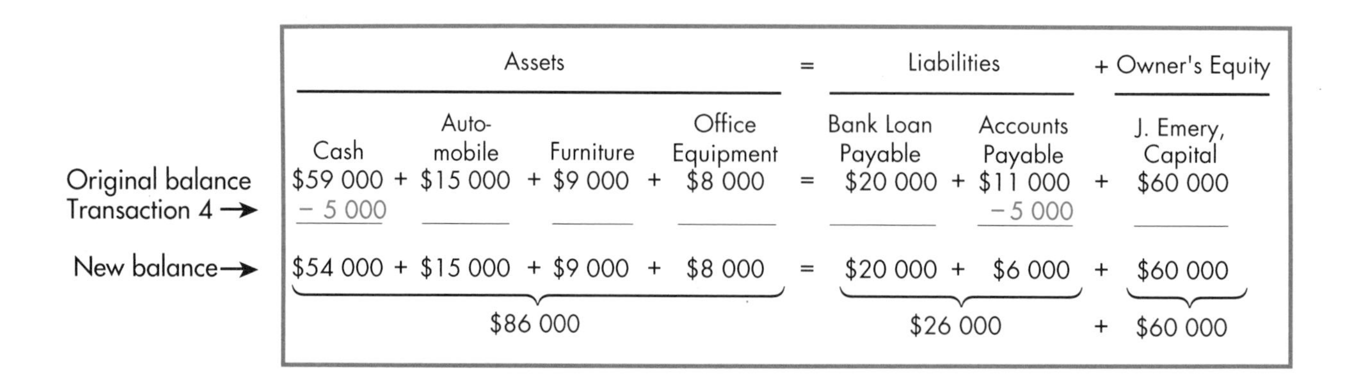

	Assets							=	Liabilities			+	Owner's Equity
	Cash		Automobile		Furniture		Office Equipment		Bank Loan Payable		Accounts Payable		J. Emery, Capital
Original balance	$59 000	+	$15 000	+	$9 000	+	$8 000	=	$20 000	+	$11 000	+	$60 000
Transaction 4 →	− 5 000										− 5 000		
New balance →	$54 000	+	$15 000	+	$9 000	+	$8 000	=	$20 000	+	$6 000	+	$60 000
	$86 000								$26 000			+	$60 000

Analysis: Two elements of the accounting equation are affected by this transaction—Assets and Liabilities. The **asset** Cash decreases by $5000 because the business now has less money. The **liability** Accounts Payable decreases by $5000 because the creditor no longer has a claim against the assets of the business. Since the left and right sides of the equation decrease by the same amount, the equation remains balanced.

Transaction 5 On October 15, J. Emery Real Estate writes a cheque for $4000 to the Royal Bank of Canada in partial payment of the bank loan.

	Assets				=	Liabilities		+ Owner's Equity
	Cash	Auto-mobile	Furniture	Office Equipment		Bank Loan Payable	Accounts Payable	J. Emery, Capital
Original balance	$54 000 +	$15 000 +	$9 000 +	$8 000	=	$20 000 +	$6 000 +	$60 000
Transaction 5 →	−4 000					−4 000		
New balance →	$50 000 +	$15 000 +	$9 000 +	$8 000	=	$16 000 +	$6 000 +	$60 000
	$82 000					$22 000		+ $60 000

Analysis: The analysis of this transaction is much the same as that for Transaction 4: the **asset** Cash and the **liability** Bank Loan Payable each decrease by $4000. Since both sides of the equation decrease by the same amount, the equation remains balanced.

Transaction 6 The previous five transactions have affected only the first two elements of the equation. The transaction at the top of page 28 will affect the third element, Owner's Equity.

	Assets				=	Liabilities		+ Owner's Equity
	Cash	Auto-mobile	Furniture	Office Equipment		Bank Loan Payable	Accounts Payable	J. Emery, Capital
Original balance	$50 000 +	$15 000 +	$9 000 +	$8 000	=	$16 000 +	$6 000 +	$60 000
Transaction 6 →	+3 000							+3 000
New balance →	$53 000 +	$15 000 +	$9 000 +	$8 000	=	$16 000 +	$6 000 +	$63 000
	$85 000					$22 000		+ $63 000

On October 16, Jane Emery decides to increase her investment in the business by taking $3000 from her personal savings account and depositing it into the firm's chequing account.

Analysis: When the owner increases his or her investment in a business, two elements also increase — Assets and Owner's Equity. On the left, the **asset** Cash increases by $3000 because the business now has more money. On the right, the **Owner's Equity** element, J. Emery, Capital increases by $3000 because Jane Emery has now increased her investment in the business. In other words, she has increased her claim against the total assets. Since assets and owner's equity increase by the same amount, while liabilities remain the same, the equation is balanced.

Transaction 7 On October 30, Jane Emery withdraws $2000 from her firm's bank account and deposits it into her personal chequing account.

As sole proprietor of the business, the owner is, of course, entitled to withdraw assets for personal use—in fact, regular cash withdrawals may be required in order to maintain a living. Assets such as office furniture could also be withdrawn for personal use.

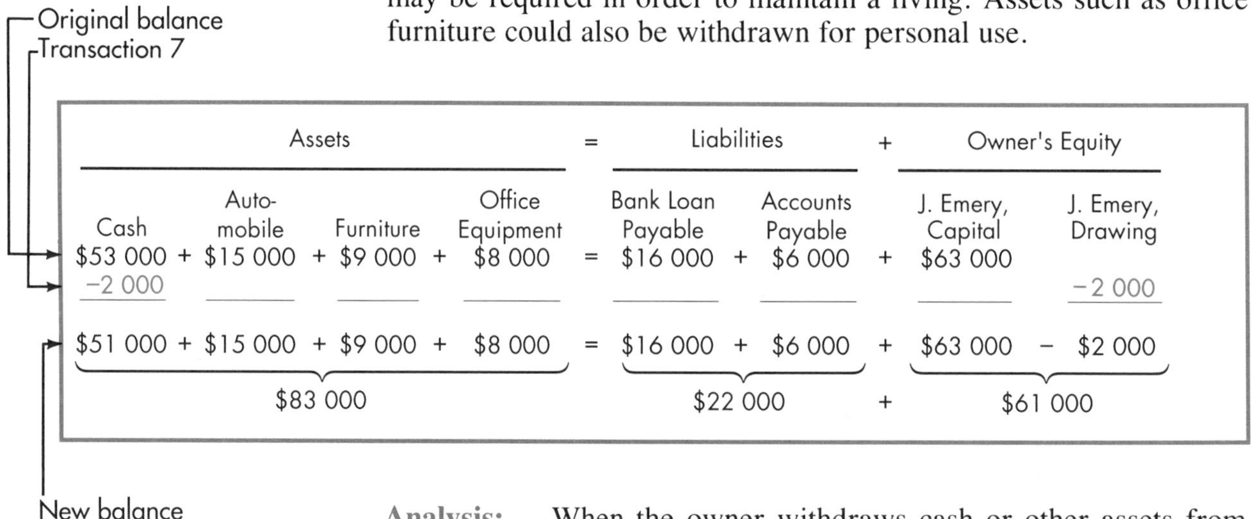

Analysis: When the owner withdraws cash or other assets from the business for personal use, two elements are affected—assets and owner's equity. Both decrease. In this case, the **asset** Cash decreases by $2000 because the business now has less cash.

Of course, the right side of the equation must also decrease by $2000. Since liabilities are not affected by this transaction, it must be owner's equity that is decreased. As you can see from the accounting equation, the decrease is made by subtracting $2000 under a new subheading, **J. Emery, Drawing**.

You might ask: Why not show the decrease to owner's equity under **J. Emery, Capital**? You will remember that capital means investment.

Drawing: a subelement decreasing owner's equity and resulting from the owner's withdrawal of assets for personal use.

Since the original investment has not decreased, we need a new item that will show a decrease in owner's equity, namely, drawing.

Notice that the equation remains balanced since total assets of $83 000 are now equal to total liabilities of $22 000 plus the new owner's equity of $61 000 ($22 000 + $61 000 = $83 000).

PREPARING A SUMMARY TABLE

A useful table for summarizing all of the above transactions is illustrated below. A study of this table will help you solve the problems that follow. Notice at the bottom of the table the reference to the **equality check**, which you can use to confirm whether the sides of the accounting equation are in balance.

SUMMARY TABLE

	ASSETS					= LIABILITIES			+ OWNER'S EQUITY		
Trans-actions	Cash	Auto-mobile	Furni-ture	Office Equip.	Total or Change in Assets	Bk. Loan Payable	Accts. Pay.	Total or Change in Lias.	J. Emery, Capital	J. Emery, Drawing	Total or Change in OE
(Orig. bal)	$60 000	+$15 000	+$8 000	+$7 000	+$90 000	$20 000	$10 000	$30 000	$60 000		$60 000
1	−1 000		+1 000		Ø						
2				+1 200	+1 200		+1 200	+1 200			
3				−200	−200		−200	−200			
4	−5 000				−5 000		−5 000	−5 000			
5	−4 000				−4 000	−4 000		−4 000			
6	+3 000				+3 000				+3 000		+3 000
7	−2 000				−2 000					−2 000	−2 000
Totals	$51 000	+$15 000	+$9 000	+$8 000	$83 000	$16 000	+$6 000	$22 000	$63 000	+$2 000	$61 000

Equality Check: A = L + OE
$83 000 = $22 000 + $61 000
$83 000 = $83 000

TOPIC 1 PROBLEMS

Analyzing business transactions using the accounting equation.

P 2-1 On May 1, the accounting equation for Tuer Service Company is as follows:

Assets					=	Liabilities			+	Owner's Equity
Cash		Truck		Tools		Bank Loan Payable		Accounts Payable		G. Tuer, Capital
$6 000	+	$15 000	+	$4 000	=	$5 000	+	$6 000	+	$14 000

a. Enter the beginning balances of the various items from the accounting equation for Tuer Service Company into a summary table similar to the one illustrated on page 29. In this case there are three assets, two liabilities, and one owner's equity item.

b. Show what happens to the accounting equation as a result of each of Greg Tuer's transactions below.

c. After you have analyzed the final transaction, add up the columns in the table.

d. Do an equality check below the summary table.

Transactions

(i) Bought tools for $3000 on 45 days' credit from Kingston Hardware Ltd.

(ii) Paid $4000 to Belleville Motors Inc. in full payment for the amount owing on the company truck.

(iii) Returned one of the tools costing $400 bought earlier on credit from Kingston Hardware Ltd.

(iv) G. Tuer invested an additional $7000 cash into the business.

(v) Borrowed an additional $8000 cash from the bank and immediately deposited it into the firm's chequing account.

Analyzing business transactions using the accounting equation.

P 2-2 Angela Sousa conducted the following transactions during February for Sousa Stage Sensations.

a. Make a summary table similar to the one on page 29 and enter the following headings: Transactions; Cash; Stage Props; Make-up Supplies; Total Assets; Bank Loan Payable; Accounts Payable; Total Liabilities; A. Sousa, Capital; A. Sousa, Drawing; Total Owner's Equity.

b. Record the effects of the following transactions in the correct columns of the table.

c. After recording the results of the final transaction, add the columns of the table.

d. Do an equality check and list it below the table.

Transactions

(i) Angela transferred $4000 cash from her personal chequing account into a chequing account under the name of Sousa Stage Sensations.

(ii) Angela borrowed $10 000 cash from a local bank and deposited this money into the chequing account of the business.

(iii) Bought stage props from Strathcona Little Theatre costing $4400 on 60 days' credit.

(iv) Bought make-up supplies for $900 cash.

(v) Returned $100 of the make-up supplies because they were damaged.

(vi) Bought additional stage props from Theatre Suppliers Ltd. for $2500 cash.

(vii) Angela withdrew $300 cash for her personal use.

(viii) Issued a cheque in partial payment of the debt to Strathcona Little Theatre, $1000.

(ix) Angela invested personal make-up supplies costing $200.

Analyzing business transactions using the accounting equation.

Preparing an opening balance sheet.

P 2-3 Challenge Problem During November, the following transactions concerning Radio Station CHJK took place.

Nov. 1 A licence was granted to Edna Greenwood for the organization and operation of Radio Station CHJK. Edna Greenwood invested $80 000 cash.

3 Land was purchased for $43 000 from Dwelling Development Company. A cash down payment of $3000 was made, and 90 days' credit extended.

4 A demand loan of $30 000 was obtained from the Royal Bank of Canada.

5 A transmitter was purchased for $55 000 from Radio Specialty, Ltd. A cash down payment of $15 000 was made. The balance is to be paid in monthly instalments of $500, beginning November 18.

6 An office and broadcasting facility was erected at a cost of $68 000, paid in cash.

8 A used compact disc player was purchased for $450 cash from Ferris Music Centre.
11 A tape recorder was purchased for $1250 cash from Ferris Music Centre.
14 A compact disc library was purchased for $5750 from Ferris Music Centre. A cash payment of $1750 was made, with the balance to be paid within 30 days.
16 Part of the compact disc library, originally costing $250, was sold to Civic Recreation Centre for the same price. The Civic Recreation Centre made payment in full by cheque.
18 $500 cash was paid to Radio Specialty, Ltd., as the first instalment due that day.
30 New compact discs were purchased from Ferris Music Centre for $1125, to be paid within 30 days.

a. Analyze and record the impact of each transaction on the accounting equation for this business enterprise by using a summary table with the following column headings: Transaction Date (as opposed to simply transactions); Cash; Land; Building; Transmitter; Broadcasting Equipment; Compact Disc Library; Total Assets; Bank Loan Payable; Accounts Payable; Total Liabilities; Edna Greenwood, Capital.

b. After recording the final transaction, total all columns in the table. Then check if the accounting equation is balanced.

c. Prepare the opening balance sheet for Radio Station CHJK.

MINI-CASES

Examining an accounting concept.

MC 2-1 Roberta and Michelle were discussing a transaction they had encountered while doing their homework. The owner of a business had taken her personal computer into the office at the start of her venture and was using it regularly for business activities. She had paid $900 cash to obtain this computer. Roberta said the computer was a business asset and should be recorded as such, but Michelle thought that because the business had not paid the owner anything for the computer, it must still belong to the owner until the business paid the owner with cash.

a. Whose opinion is correct? Why?

b. Which accounting concept is involved in this case? Explain briefly your reasons.

c. Record the elements of the accounting equation that are affected and explain how they are affected.

Examining an accounting concept.

MC 2-2 George and Kieng were involved with a different homework problem. The owner of XET Co. had employed Willie's Window Washers to clean his home windows the same day that XET Co.'s windows were cleaned. Willie had sent one invoice for both jobs to XET Co. for payment.

a. How would you advise George and Kieng to record this transaction?

b. Which accounting concept is involved in this case? Explain briefly your reasons.

c. Record the elements of the accounting equation that are affected and explain how they are affected.

Discussing proofing steps and techniques.

MC 2-3 Adrian is almost finished his homework. He has just completed the final transaction on an accounting equation summary table.

a. What are the two final steps Adrian has yet to complete?

b. What does Adrian accomplish by completing the final step?

c. Why is this step absolutely essential in accounting? *Hint:* You are working with the accounting equation.

TOPIC 2 ANALYZING AN EXPANDED EQUATION

Revenue and expense transactions: financial events that determine the profit (or loss) of a business.

The primary purpose of a business is to increase the owner's equity by earning a **profit** over a specific period of time. In the language of accounting, the financial events directly related to the calculation of a business profit (or loss) are known as revenue and expense transactions. To record these transactions, we add new items to the right side of the accounting equation. Let's begin by analyzing revenue transactions.

ANALYZING REVENUE TRANSACTIONS

Commissions: the fees a business charges for buying or selling goods, for example, real estate, for clients.

We will analyze two new transactions that affect J. Emery Real Estate, assuming that these transactions follow the last transaction (Transaction 7 of October 30).

Transaction 8 As at October 31, J. Emery Real Estate has received $26 800 in cash, referred to as commissions, for buying and selling homes, land, and other forms of real estate for clients.

Beginning Analysis: Identify what you already know. If the business has received $26 800 cash, then the asset Cash in the equation must be increased by $26 800. Next, the total of the left side of the equation must be changed, since the assets have now increased from $83 000 to $109 800. The accounting equation below illustrates these changes.

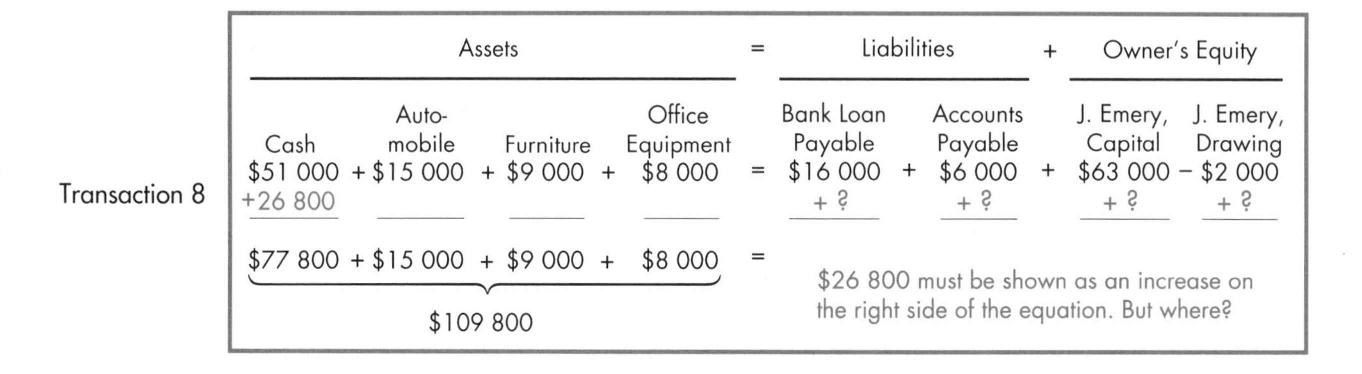

	Assets				=	Liabilities		+	Owner's Equity	
	Cash	Automobile	Furniture	Office Equipment		Bank Loan Payable	Accounts Payable		J. Emery, Capital	J. Emery, Drawing
	$51 000	+ $15 000	+ $9 000	+ $8 000	=	$16 000	+ $6 000	+	$63 000	− $2 000
Transaction 8	+26 800					+ ?	+ ?		+ ?	+ ?
	$77 800	+ $15 000	+ $9 000	+ $8 000	=	$26 800 must be shown as an increase on the right side of the equation. But where?				
	$109 800									

Further Analysis: You now know that when the left side of the equation increases, the right side must also increase by the same amount. But are liabilities affected as a result of the transaction? Obviously not, because liabilities are the debts of the business. Therefore, it must be owner's equity that increases. You have learned that **J. Emery, Capital** represents the claim of the owner through her investment. The commissions earned cannot be described as investment. You have also learned that **J. Emery, Drawing** shows a decrease to owner's equity resulting from an owner's withdrawal of assets for personal use. Again, it would be incorrect to represent commissions under this heading. How then can we represent the increase in owner's equity?

The answer is to add a new item to owner's equity. Study the expanded accounting equation. It includes a new heading **Revenue** to represent such items as commissions.

Final Analysis: J. Emery Real Estate receives $26 800 in cash from commissions. The asset Cash increases by this amount and total assets increase to $109 800. Since the right side of the equation must also increase by the same amount and liabilities are not affected by this transaction, this increase must be reflected in owner's equity. The commissions represent revenue earned for the business and a new heading Revenue is added to the accounting equation. Owner's equity increases by $26 800 and the equation is balanced.

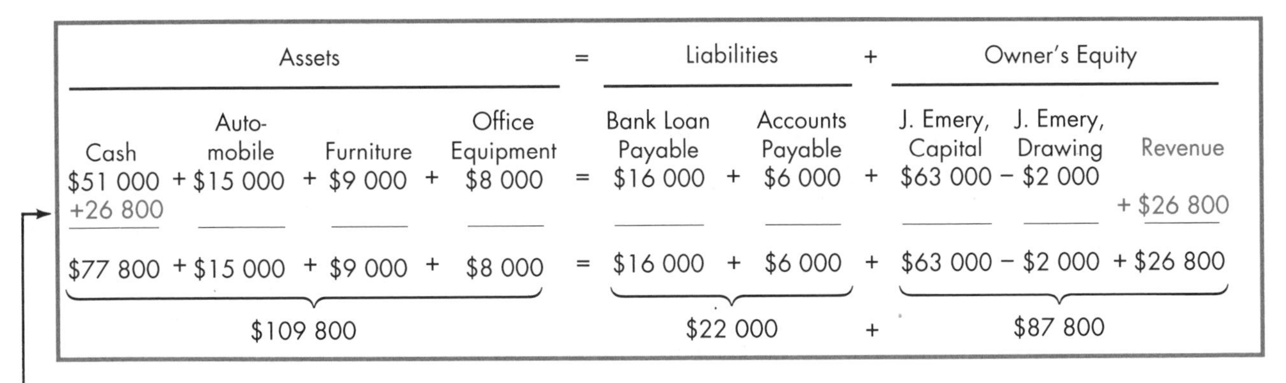

Assets				=	Liabilities		+	Owner's Equity		
Cash	Auto-mobile	Furniture	Office Equipment		Bank Loan Payable	Accounts Payable		J. Emery, Capital	J. Emery, Drawing	Revenue
$51 000	+ $15 000	+ $9 000	+ $8 000	=	$16 000	+ $6 000	+	$63 000	− $2 000	
+26 800										+ $26 800
$77 800	+ $15 000	+ $9 000	+ $8 000	=	$16 000	+ $6 000	+	$63 000	− $2 000	+ $26 800
$109 800					$22 000		+	$87 800		

Transaction 8

Transaction 9 As of October 31, J. Emery Real Estate earned commissions on credit by providing real estate services as follows: $6000 for selling a building for Pat Rogers; $4000 for selling a residence for R. Scobie; and $15 000 for buying properties for Shannon Development Co. All clients, or customers, were given 30 days in which to pay the commissions.

Transaction 9

Assets			=	Liabilities		+	Owner's Equity		
Cash	Accts. Rec.	Auto		Bank Loan Payable	Accounts Payable		J. Emery, Capital	J. Emery, Drawing	Revenue
$77 800 +		+ $15 000 +	=	$16 000	+ $6 000	+	$63 000	− $2 000	+ $26 800
	+$25 000								+ $25 000
$77 800	+ $25 000	+ $15 000 +	=	$16 000	+ $6 000	+	$63 000	− $2 000	+ $51 800
$134 800			=	$22 000		+	$112 800		

Accounts receivable: an asset representing amounts due from customers.

Analysis: The commissions earned on credit increase the assets of the business, as cash received for services rendered also does. However, a credit is treated differently from cash and a new asset Accounts Receivable is added to the equation. We can also say that the business has claims on the property of these customers until their debts are paid. Notice that this new asset is placed after Cash to support the liquidity order. Obviously cash may be drawn upon, deposited, etc., immediately, whereas the customer's debt is repaid some time later.

On the right side of the equation, owner's equity increases by $25 000 because of the additional source of revenue. This increase is shown as a second plus amount (an addition) under **Revenue**. The total revenue for October is now $51 800 ($26 800 in cash commissions plus $25 000 in commissions coming from accounts receivable). Since the two sides of the equation have been increased by the same amount, the equation is in balance.

Revenue: an inflow of assets resulting from the sale of goods or services.

The analysis of Transactions 8 and 9 gives you an excellent definition of revenue: an inflow of cash and accounts receivable resulting from the sale of goods or services.

However, the inflow of cash does not automatically mean revenue has been earned by the business. For example:

- An inflow of cash resulting from a customer's paying a debt means an increase in one asset, Cash, and a decrease in another asset, Accounts Receivable.
- When a business gets cash by borrowing from a bank, this inflow of cash is offset by an increase in liabilities—usually in the form of a demand note payable to the bank.
- Cash can come into a business through additional investment by the owner, in which case assets and owner's equity (under Capital) increase.

Remember that revenue for a given period is equal to the inflow of assets (cash and accounts receivable) during that period from the selling of goods or services. This inflow must be offset by an increase in owner's equity in the accounting equation.

When Is Revenue Recognized? You may be wondering at what point revenue from sales is recognized. For example, should it be recognized at the time the sale is made, or when the cash is received from the customer as in the case of accounts receivable?

As you learned in Chapter 1, Generally Accepted Accounting Principles (GAAPs) are broad accounting rules or guidelines. One of the GAAPs, the revenue principle, may be stated as follows:

Revenue principle: defines revenue, measures revenue, and recognizes revenue.

Revenue must be recognized as at the time of the sale of goods, or as at the time of the rendering of services.

In Transactions 8 and 9, the sales of services were completed when assets such as cash or a promise to pay cash (accounts receivable) were transferred from the buyer to the seller in exchange for the services being completed.

If J. Emery Real Estate had sold goods instead of services, revenue would be recognized when the seller receives cash or the claim to cash (accounts receivable) in exchange for those goods.

Here are two rules to remember when revenue is recognized as being earned:

- In cash sales transactions, sales revenue is earned as at the time when the good or service is received by the buyer and cash is received by the seller.
- In credit sales, revenue is normally recognized as at the time of the sale of goods or as at the time of the rendering of services, and when a sales invoice is available showing credit terms.

ANALYZING EXPENSE TRANSACTIONS

All businesses have expenses, and for one reason only — to support activities that create revenue. For example, when money is spent on employee salaries, advertising, and the use of the telephone to attract customers, revenue may be obtained through the resulting sales.

In accounting terms, expenses are the costs of the goods or services used up by a business to earn revenue.

- Salaries and wages are paid to employees. This cost is offset by the productivity of employees that leads to increased revenue.
- Monthly rent is an expense because the cost of renting office space will be **used up** to provide a place for customers to shop and to house the employees.
- A telephone bill received by a business will be an amount **used up** by the business to support activities which bring in revenue.
- Advertising goods or services of the business attracts customers. This cost is **used up** to help bring in revenue.

Since the amounts paid for salaries, office space, telephone service, advertising, and other expenses are used up in the process of earning revenue, accountants define expenses as the cost of goods or services used up by a business to earn revenue.

Expenses: costs incurred by a business in earning revenue.

The above definition of expenses emphasizes two ideas:

- The cost (dollars) of operating the business must be **used up**.
- Those dollars must be used to earn revenue.

Transaction 10 To create revenue, J. Emery Real Estate incurred several expenses. The business paid a total of $6735 in cash as of October 31 for the following: Rent, $1600; Salaries, $4500; Utilities, $595; and Telephone, $40.

Beginning Analysis: Since the business paid $6735 cash, the left side of the equation decreases because the asset Cash has decreased. Therefore, some element on the right side must decrease by a similar amount. Which element is it?

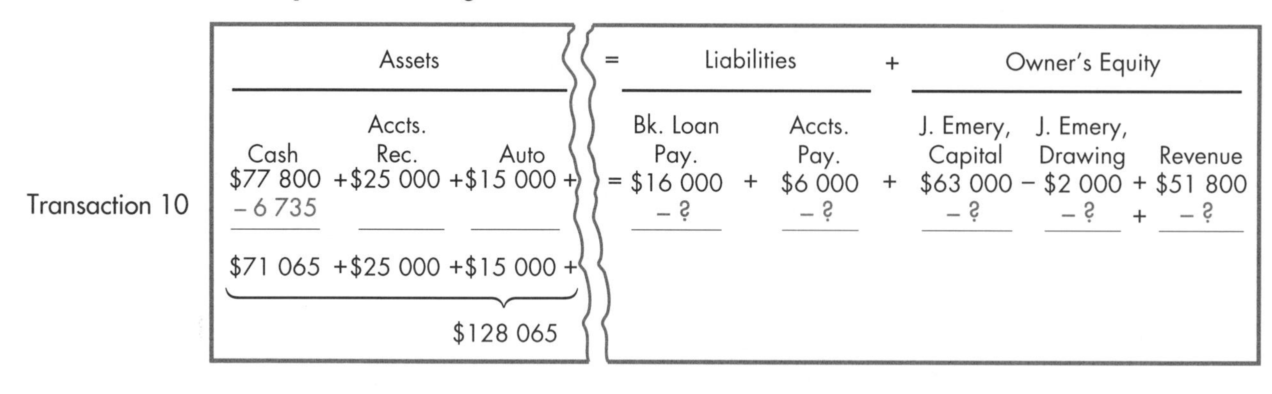

Further Analysis: The element which decreases is not Liabilities because all of the expenses were paid in cash. If your answer is Owner's Equity, you are correct, but which of J. Emery, Capital; J. Emery, Drawing; or Revenue is affected? None of these is the correct account. Remember J. Emery, Capital shows an increase in owner's equity through owner's investment. J. Emery, Drawing shows a decrease to owner's equity through the withdrawal of assets for the owner's personal use. And Revenue illustrates an increase to owner's equity through the inflow of cash and credit received from sales.

How then can we record this decrease in owner's equity? The answer is to introduce a new heading, **Expenses**, illustrated in the accounting equation below.

Transaction 10

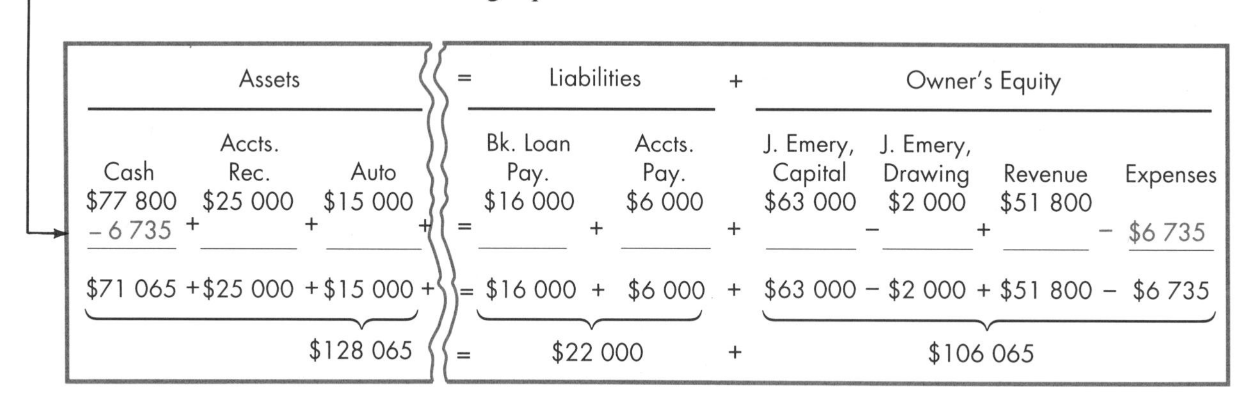

Final Analysis: When a business pays cash for its expenses, the left side of the equation decreases because the **asset** Cash decreases by the amount of the paid expenses. The right side of the equation must also decrease by the same amount. Because liabilities are not affected by the cash transaction, this decrease is recorded under **Expenses** in owner's equity. Note that the minus sign simply shows that this item causes a decrease to owner's equity in the accounting equation. Without subtracting expenses, you could not balance the accounting equation. Check the equation once again to prove this point to yourself.

Transaction 11 On October 31, J. Emery Real Estate receives a bill for $2000 from *The City Record*, a local newspaper, for running three advertisements at different times in October. The bill states that J. Emery Real Estate has a period of 30 days in which to pay.

Analysis: The left side of the accounting equation is not affected because none of the assets are affected. Because J. Emery Real Estate has been given 30 days to pay for the advertising, the **liability** Accounts Payable must be increased to record the new claim of creditors against the total assets of the business. At the same time, the expense **incurred** must be shown as a second minus amount under **Owner's Equity** because expenses cause a decrease to owner's equity.

Transaction 11

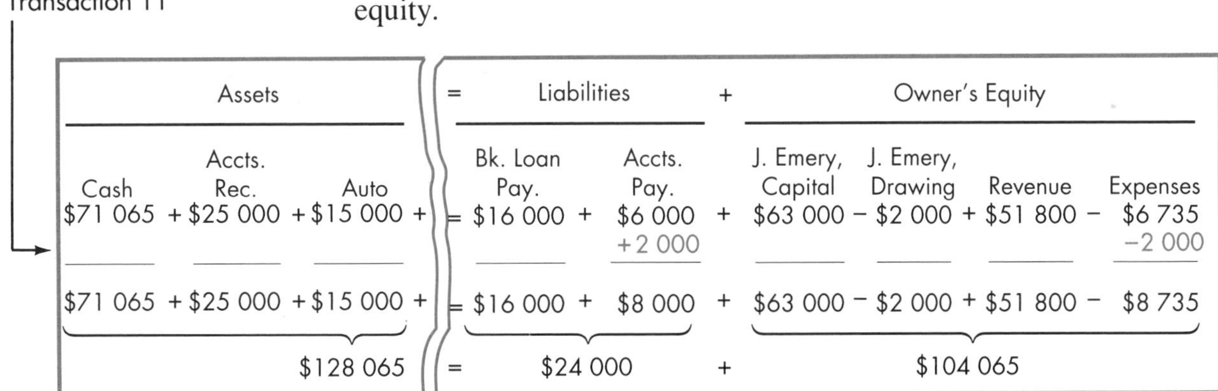

Assets			=	Liabilities		+	Owner's Equity			
Cash	Accts. Rec.	Auto		Bk. Loan Pay.	Accts. Pay.		J. Emery, Capital	J. Emery, Drawing	Revenue	Expenses
$71 065	+ $25 000	+ $15 000 +	=	$16 000 +	$6 000	+	$63 000	− $2 000	+ $51 800	− $6 735
					+2 000					−2 000
$71 065	+ $25 000	+ $15 000 +	=	$16 000 +	$8 000	+	$63 000	− $2 000	+ $51 800	− $8 735
		$128 065	=	$24 000		+	$104 065			

Notice that the increase in liabilities (+$2000) is now offset by the decrease in owner's equity (−$2000). The accounting equation is in balance.

Notice, too, that the total expenses for October, $8735, are shown as a minus amount under **Owner's Equity**. This simply means that owner's equity in the accounting equation has been decreased by this amount.

Expense principle: defines expense, measures expense, and recognizes expense.

The analysis of Transaction 11 introduces a second GAAP — the expense principle for recognizing expenses. Just as revenue was recognized as at a point of sale in an earlier section, the expense principle for recognizing expenses is:

Expenses must be recognized and recorded when they are incurred.

It does not matter whether the business has paid for the expenses; they must always be recognized as soon as they are incurred because they directly offset the earning of revenue within the same time period.

For example, if an advertising expense was incurred during October to increase October sales revenue, it would be incorrect to recognize the expense, for example, in November when the bill is finally paid. Remember these two helpful questions as an aid to recognizing an accounting expense:

- Was the cost incurred (or used up) to earn revenue or to assist in revenue-making activities during a specific time period?
- Does the cost reduce owner's equity in the accounting equation as well as reducing an asset or increasing a liability?

If your answer to both questions is yes, then, under the GAAPs of revenue and expense, you will probably have to recognize a cost of operating the business.

One final point: You now know that revenue is the inflow of cash and accounts receivable. On the other hand, expenses use up economic resources, or result in the **outflow** of assets. As Transactions 10 and 11 showed, this outflow may occur immediately, as a result of paying cash, or later, as a result of paying by credit.

What remains now is to relate the inflow (revenue) to the outflow (expenses) to determine whether the business has made a profit or loss.

MATCHING REVENUES AND EXPENSES

After accounting for revenue and expense transactions for a definite period of time, say one month, you must subtract the total expenses incurred from the total revenue earned to calculate the profit or loss for the period. Before you calculate, you must make sure that revenues and expenses are **matched** for a specific time period. To understand the principle of matching—a GAAP—study the five examples shown on this page and the next page.

Example 1 There is a **mismatch** between revenues and expenses. Why? Revenues and expenses were not calculated for the same time period. A fair report of profit cannot be made. A valid match means **revenues and expenses are related for the same accounting period**.

Revenues (for Oct., Nov., Dec.)	$15 000
Expenses (for Oct., Nov.)	9 000
PROFIT	$ 6 000

Example 2 Obviously, a serious mismatch of revenues and expenses has taken place. It is unfair to report a loss of $10 000 here, because revenues were reported for only six months while expenses for twelve months were deducted from revenues.

Revenues (for 6 months)	$50 000
Expenses (for 12 months)	60 000
LOSS	$10 000

Example 3 This example shows a fair match. Why? Because revenues for one month are matched with expenses for the same month. Since revenues were greater than expenses **for the same period of time**, a profit can be calculated and reported. Notice the use of the term "net profit." "Net" simply means that all revenues and all expenses have been matched.

Revenues (for Sept. 19-5)	$10 000
Expenses (for Sept. 19-5)	4 000
NET PROFIT	$ 6 000

Example 4 This example also shows a fair match. Since total revenues for 19-5 exceeded total expenses for 19-5, a net profit for that year can be calculated and reported.

Revenues (for year 19-5)	$150 000
Expenses (for year 19-5)	115 000
NET PROFIT	$ 35 000

Example 5 Though this example shows a fair match, the result is very different: it shows a net loss for the year. A net loss occurs when total expenses are greater than total revenues for a time period.

Revenues (for year 19-6)	$140 000
Expenses (for year 19-6)	160 000
NET LOSS	$ 20 000

Matching principle: revenues and expenses must be correlated to report the net income (net loss) for an accounting period.

Based on the above examples, the matching principle can be stated as follows:

In reporting the net profit or loss of a business for a financial period, revenues must be matched with those expenses.

That is, revenues of a certain time period (called the **financial** or **accounting period**) must be matched with the related expenses incurred in the same period. Note that the length of the financial period can vary from one month to six months or even a year.

EXAMINING THE NEED FOR A MODERN TERM FOR PROFIT

Net income: the excess of revenue over expenses.

Net loss: the excess of expenses over revenue.

Many years ago, the term ''profit'' was used to report the favourable results of matching revenues with related expenses. However, profit can mean different things to different people. To avoid this confusion, modern accounting practice speaks of income and loss rather than profit and loss. From now on, the student should use net income and net loss. *Remember:* The word ''net'' indicates that all revenues and all expenses have been reported and matched, for the same accounting period.

APPLYING THE MATCHING PRINCIPLE TO THE ACCOUNTING EQUATION

To apply the matching principle, you must rearrange the expanded section—revenue and expenses—of the accounting equation by:

- placing total expenses under total revenue
- calculating the difference between the amounts and listing this as a net income or net loss

Examine the rearranged equation on page 43 for J. Emery Real Estate and study the analysis.

Analysis: We assume the matching principle has been verified for this equation. The excess of revenue over related expenses is net income — which is a plus amount under **Owner's Equity**. In other words, owner's equity increases by the net income for the financial period. Of course, if total expenses had exceeded the total revenue, the final result would have been a **net loss** — a minus amount. This result would naturally mean that the owner's equity for the period decreases by the amount of the loss. Study the two illustrations that follow.

In summary, revenue is the positive or plus part in calculating net income. Expenses are the negative or minus part in calculating net

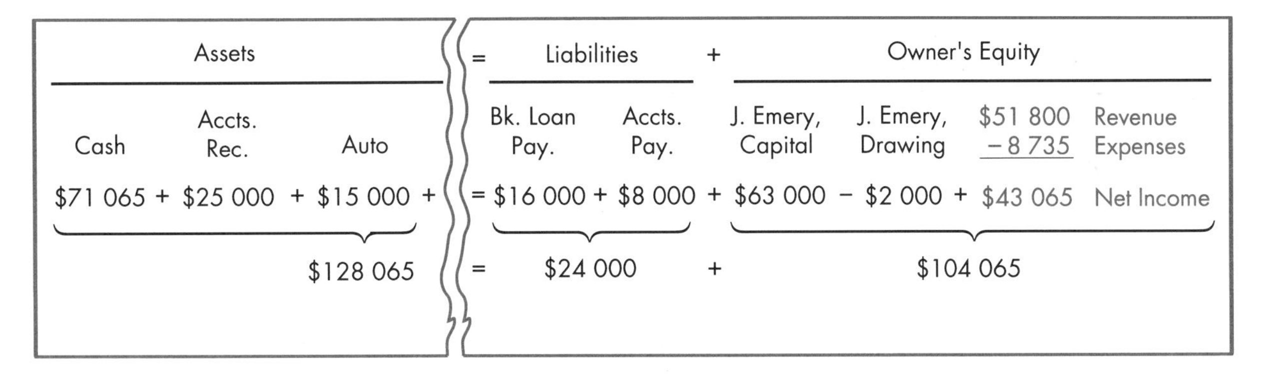

income. The difference between the two will determine whether the owner's equity increases (net income) or decreases (net loss) as a result of the business transactions for a certain period of time.

Owner's Equity			
		Net Income	
		+ $51 800	Revenue
Capital	Drawing	− 8 735	Expenses
$63 000 −	$2 000 +	$43 065	Increase

Owner's Equity			
		Net Loss	
		+ $51 800	Revenue
Capital	Drawing	−80 000	Expenses
$63 000 −	$2 000 −	$28 200	Decrease

PROBLEMS

Analyzing transactions within the expanded accounting equation.

Determining net income or net loss.

P 2-4 The transactions for the month of September are summarized for Chan's Insurance Agency in the accounting equation below.

a. Rearrange the equation to show the matching of revenues and expenses for September.

b. Did this matching produce a net income or a net loss for the period? Explain.

Assets					=	Liabilities	+	Owner's Equity				
Cash		Accts. Rec.		Equip.		Bank Loan Payable		H. Chan, Capital		Revenue		Expenses
$2 510	+	$1 090	+	$6 400	=	$1 000	+	$5 000	+	$8 000	−	$4 000
$10 000					=	$1 000	+	$9 000				

Analyzing transactions within the expanded accounting equation.

Determining net income or net loss.

P 2-5 During the month of June, Bojkovsky Tree Service:

(i)Sold services for cash for $1000.
(ii)Sold services on credit for $3500.
(iii)Bought equipment for $900.
(iv)Received $400 from the sale of services.
(v)Paid $250 to a creditor to pay off an account payable.
(vi)Paid $120 for advertising expense.
(vii)Bought equipment for $300 on credit.
(viii)Paid $130 for utilities.
(ix)Received $250 from a customer to reduce the amount owing to the business.
(x)Paid two employees each $1800 in monthly wages.
(xi)Received $1000 from customers for various credit payments.

a. As at May 31, the business has the assets, liabilities, and owner's equity as shown in the accounting equation that follows. Indicate what happens to the accounting equation as a result of each transaction. The first transaction is done as an example.

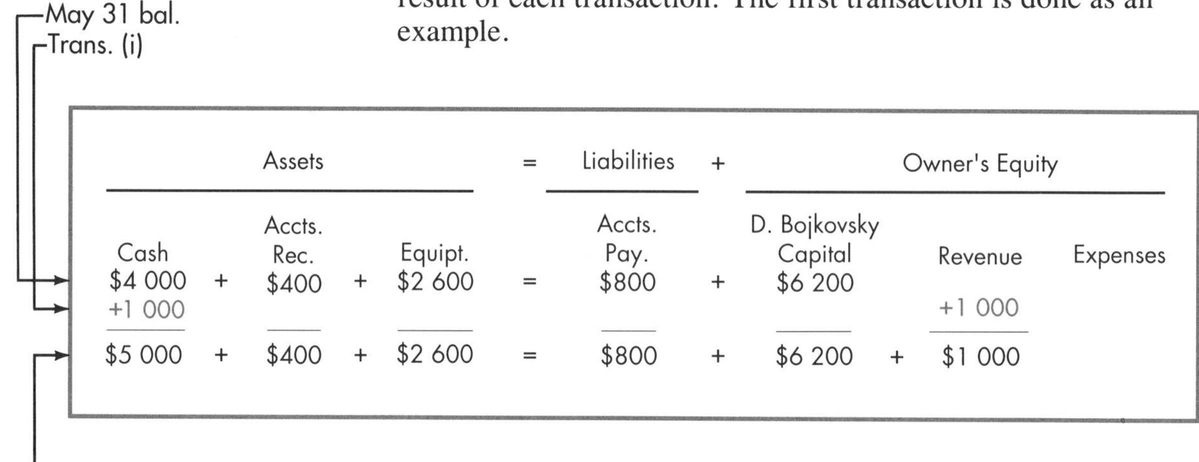

	Assets					=	Liabilities	+	Owner's Equity			
	Cash	+	Accts. Rec.	+	Equipt.	=	Accts. Pay.	+	D. Bojkovsky Capital		Revenue	Expenses
May 31 bal.	$4 000	+	$400	+	$2 600	=	$800	+	$6 200			
Trans. (i)	+1 000										+1 000	
New Balance	$5 000	+	$400	+	$2 600	=	$800	+	$6 200	+	$1 000	

b. Rearrange the resulting equation to illustrate the matching of revenues and expenses for June. Did this matching produce a net income or a net loss for the financial period? Explain.

Analyzing transactions within the expanded accounting equation.

Determining net income or net loss.

P 2-6 Challenge Problem Joan Kara opened a tutoring service in British Columbia under the name J. K. Teaching Services. She employed one person to act as an office secretary and one person to instruct in the marketing and computer areas. The following transactions were recorded during the month of October.

(i)Joan invested $15 000 from her personal saving account in a bank account in the name of J. K. Teaching Services.

(ii) Purchased classroom equipment costing $5000 on 90 days' credit from B. C. Educational Supplies Ltd.

(iii) Purchased two Macintosh® SE® computers and two Imagewriter® printers from Lyons Logic Limited, by issuing a cheque for $9500.

(iv) Returned to B.C. Educational Supplies Ltd. $1500 of the classroom equipment originally purchased on credit.

(v) Invested an additional $10 000 into the business.

(vi) J. K. Teaching Services earned $4200 in fees from the following clients. All clients were allowed 30 days' credit. A. Boushy, $500; V. Prost, $800; F. Rehman, $1300; R. Tuer, $1000; A. White, $600.

(vii) J. K. Teaching Services earned $5400 cash for fees charged for services rendered during the month.

(viii) Joan received a cheque for $800 from V. Prost as payment in full on her account.

(ix) To assist in the earning of revenue during the month of October, J. Kara issued cheques for the following expenses: Rent, $700; Telephone, $55; Office Supplies, $120; Salaries; $1300; Utilities, $90. *Note:* All supplies were used up during the month of October.

(x) J. Kara issued a cheque in the amount of $1000 in partial payment of the account with B. C. Educational Supplies Ltd.

(xi) J. K. Teaching Services received an invoice for October advertising in *The BC Herald*, $210. The newspaper gave the business 30 days from the date of the bill to pay the amount owing.

(xii) Joan withdrew $1100 cash for personal use.

a. Set up an accounting equation with the following accounts under the three elements: Cash; Accts. Rec.; Equipment; Accts. Pay.; J. Kara, Capital; J. Kara, Drawing; Revenue and Expenses. Analyze and record what happens to the accounting equation as a result of each transaction. Use the procedure in Problem 2-5.

b. Rearrange the final equation to illustrate the matching of revenue with related expenses. Did the business produce a net income or a net loss for October? Explain the final effect on owner's equity.

TOPIC 2 MINI-CASES

Identifying correct usage of GAAPs.

MC 2-4 Alain's Bottle Washing Co. performed services for Tonio's Catering Co. on April 3, 19—. Alain's Bottle Washing Co. sent out an invoice for $356 on April 3, indicating that payment was not due until April 30.

a. What GAAP underlies this transaction?

b. What is the key date in this transaction? Why is this date regarded as key?

c. Record the elements that are affected, whether they increase or decrease the accounting equation, and explain why.

Identifying correct usage of GAAPs.

MC 2-5 Tonio's Catering Co. advertised on the local radio station, CKRU. Tonio's Catering Co. received the radio station's monthly invoice on March 29, 19—. The invoice indicated that payment was due by the 15th of the following month.

a. What GAAP underlies this transaction?

b. What is the key date in this transaction? Why is this date regarded as key?

c. Record the elements that are affected, whether they increase or decrease the accounting equation and explain why.

Identifying correct usage of GAAPs.

Calculating net income or net loss.

MC 2-6 Radio station CKRU earned revenues for March totalling $55 000, and has incurred expenses for March totalling $41 000. To date, the station has received only $38 000 of the anticipated revenues, but has paid all but $3000 of the month's expenses.

a. What GAAP underlies this transaction?

b. What is the correct amount for net income (or net loss) in March for CKRU? Explain your calculation.

ANALYZING THE INCOME STATEMENT AND THE RELATED BALANCE SHEET

In Topic 2 you learned how revenue and expense transactions expand the accounting equation under Owner's Equity so that the net income or net loss may be calculated for a certain period of time. The results of this expanded equation may be summarized in two kinds of accounting reports:

- an income statement, which summarizes the revenue and related expenses and reports the net income or net loss for a specific accounting period
- a related balance sheet to report assets, liabilities, and owner's equity as at the end of a specific accounting period

ANALYZING AN INCOME STATEMENT

The basic form of an income statement is based upon the expanded part of the accounting equation. Look closely at the illustration on page 48 (top), and then identify the following features.

- An income statement has two sections, heading and body.
- The heading has three lines: line 1 shows the name of the business; line 2, the name of the financial statement; line 3, the specific accounting period for which revenues and expenses are matched.
- At the beginning of the body is a summary of the reported revenue for the accounting period.
- Revenue is followed by expenses for the same accounting period. Notice that total expenses are shown in order to match this amount against the reported revenue.
- The result of operating the business—the net income or net loss for the accounting period—concludes the income statement.

PREPARING AN INCOME STATEMENT

In Chapter 1 you learned that a balance sheet is prepared at least once a year for interested parties such as creditors, and that the people who manage a business may prepare them as often as once a month. You were also told that this financial statement is usually printed — by typewriter, printing press, computer, or word processor. These facts apply as well to the preparation of an income statement. However, as with the balance sheet, you can learn the important guidelines for preparing an income statement by doing some by hand as on page 48 (bottom). By the time you have finished this chapter you will also have had the opportunity to complete some of the exercise problems using an electronic spreadsheet.

Heading Notice that the heading of an income statement answers the questions **who**, **what**, and **when**.

The **when** is very important; it explains the accounting period covered by the statement. In the income statement illustrated for J. Emery Real Estate, the accounting period is one particular month,

Assets			=	Liabilities		+	Owner's Equity		
Cash	Accts Rec.			Bk. Loan Pay.	Accts Pay.		J. Emery, Capital	J. Emery, Drawing	+$51 800 Revenue – 8 735 Expenses
$71 065 +	$25 000 +	···	=	$16 000 +	$8 000	+	$63 000 −	$2 000 +	$43 065 Net Income
$128 065			=	$24 000		+	$104 065		

J. Emery Real Estate
Income Statement
For the Month Ended October 31,19—

Revenue		
Commissions Earned		$51 800. 00
Expenses:		
Salaries Expense	$4 500.00	
Rent Expense	1 600.00	
Utilities Expense	595.00	
Telephone Expense	40.00	
Advertising Expense	2 000.00	
Total Expenses		8 735.00
Net Income		$43 065.00

October. Note that this period **has ended**, and the transactions matching revenue and related expenses are recorded. Thus, it would be incorrect to use the expression "ending" in the date line.

J. Emery Real Estate
Income Statement
For the Month Ended October 31, 19--

Revenue:		
Commissions Earned		$51 800 00
Expenses:		
Salaries Expense	$4 500 00	
Rent Expense	1 600 00	
Utilities Expense	595 00	
Telephone Expense	40 00	
Advertising Expense	2 000 00	
Total Expenses		8 735 00
Net Income		43 065 00

Once the accounting period has been established, it must be stated on the date line on the statement. For example, if the accounting period covers three months—say January, February, and March—the date line would read "For the Quarter Ended March 31, 19— " or "For the Three Months Ended March 31, 19—." If the accounting period covers a calendar year, the date line would read "For the Year Ended December 31, 19—."

Revenue Section On the first line at the margin, enter the title Revenue followed by a colon. Underneath, indent and list the sources of revenue, beginning each word with a capital letter. When there is only one source, as in the example for J. Emery Real Estate, show the amount directly in the second money column. If there are several sources, as in the example below, the individual amounts would be listed in the first money column and the total amount in the second money column with an appropriate descriptive line such as "Total Revenue."

Revenue:				
Admissions Revenue	$8 000	00		
Concessions Revenue	4 500	00		
Parking Fees Earned	2 500	00		
Total Revenue			$15 000	00

The source of revenue depends on the nature of a business's operations. Retailing, wholesaling, and manufacturing businesses earn revenue mainly by selling goods, so they describe their source as sales revenue or simply Sales. Service businesses report their main source of revenue by describing the nature of their business operations. Businesses that charge a commission for their services may report their revenue as **Commissions Earned**.

Sales: the main source of revenue for firms that sell goods.

Many service businesses are professional — law, medicine, dentistry, accountancy, etc. These businesses charge a fee for their services. Therefore, their income statements usually describe their main source of revenue as Professional Fees Earned or Fees Earned

Fees earned: the main source of revenue for professionals such as doctors and lawyers.

Expense Section On the line below the last entry in the revenue section, enter the title Expenses followed by a colon. Indent and list the expenses beneath this title. Begin every word with a capital letter. If there is only one expense, list the amount in the second money column. If there is more than one expense, as there usually is, the amount for each expense is listed in the first money column, and the figure for total expenses is recorded in the second money column (that is, the main money column for reporting the match-up of revenue with related expenses). *Note:* In order to be consistent with the revenue section, a descriptive statement should be included. By showing the total expenses in the same column as the total revenue, you have indicated the principle of matching all revenues against all expenses for the same accounting period.

Reporting a Net Loss

Total Revenue	$18 000	00
Total Expenses	20 000	00
Net Loss	$ 2 000	00

Net Income or Net Loss Section

The income statement concludes with net income or net loss — the final result of operating a business for an accounting period. First draw a single line across the money column under the amount of the total expenses. Next, subtract the total expenses from the total revenue and record the difference in the second money column on the next line. (In the example illustrated for J. Emery Real Estate, the result is a net income; if the total expenses were greater than the total revenue for the accounting period, you would show the final result under Net Loss.) Finally, draw a double line under the amount for net income, or loss, to indicate the match of revenue and related expenses, and thus the statement is complete.

Dollar Signs

Since an income statement is a **formal** financial statement, dollar signs should appear with the first amount in each money column and the final result in the second money column. Refer to the income statements illustrated so far in this chapter for the correct placement of dollar signs.

At this point, you should have no difficulty in defining the term Income Statement. One good definition is a financial report of revenues, expenses, and the net income or net loss for a definite accounting period. Another is a financial report of the match of revenues and expenses for a stated accounting period. Remember that any definition must include the idea of a definite accounting period that has **ended**.

Income statement: a financial report of the results of matching revenues with related expenses for a definite accounting period.

PREPARING A RELATED BALANCE SHEET

In the income statement for J. Emery Real Estate, the net income reported ($43 065) agrees with the amount shown in the accounting equation. It is important to remember, however, that this income is the amount remaining after revenues and related expenses have been matched for an accounting period. If revenue means an inflow of assets (cash and/or accounts receivable) through sales, and if expenses mean an outflow of assets (cash) or an increase in liabilities (incurring an expense through a liability), then certain balances must also be updated to reflect these changes. To report the new balances in assets, liabilities, and owner's equity as at the end of the accounting period, a new balance sheet must be prepared immediately after the income statement.

Analysis: Look at the illustration on page 52 and study the following points.

- The heading of the new balance sheet reports a different date from that of the opening balance sheet. Here, the balance sheet reports the assets and the claims against those assets as at October 31. In other words, the new balances for assets, liabilities, and owner's equity are reported as at October 31.

- There is only one new point concerning the asset side of the balance sheet. Accounts Receivable (an asset) is reported immediately after Cash, because the business expects to collect amounts due from customers within 30 days. The customers' names and the amounts of their debts are listed in a separate column. The total is then placed in the main column.

- Amounts owing to creditors are reported in Liabilities as at October 31. These amounts will differ from those reported in the opening balance sheet of September 30 because of transactions during October. The firm now owes the bank only $16 000, not $20 000. Under Accounts Payable, the business no longer owes money to Westown Motors Ltd.; therefore, no debt is reported.

  However, because of Transaction 11, a new creditor, *The City Record*, is listed. Also, a new balance is reported for Ryan Equipment Co., because $3000 is the new amount owing as at October 31. No change has been reported for Bell Furniture Co., because no transaction involving this creditor took place in October.

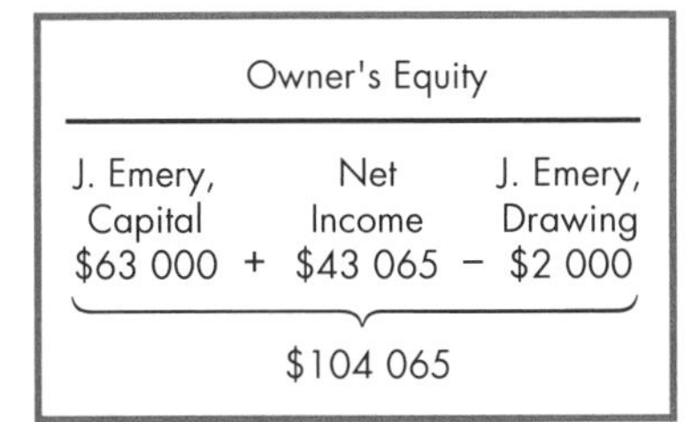

A = $128 065, L = $24 000, OE = ?

A	=	L	+	OE
OE	=	A	+	L
OE	=	$128 065	+	$24 000
OE	=	$104 065		

- From the owner's standpoint, the most important information is reported in the Owner's Equity section of the new balance sheet. To understand this section, remember the meaning of owner's equity: **the claim the owner has against the total assets of the business.** In the opening balance sheet, the owner had only one claim: $60 000 through an investment (capital). One month later, however, the owner's equity section reports two claims: the investment of $63 000 ($60 000 plus an additional investment) and the net income of $43 065 earned through business operations.

Assets					=	Liabilities		+	Owner's Equity		
Cash	Accts. Rec.	Auto	Furn.	Office Equip.		Bk. Loan Pay.	Accts. Pay.		J. Emery, Capital	Net Income	J. Emery, Drawing
$71 065	+ $25 000	+ $15 000	+ $9 000	+ $8 000	=	$16 000	+ $8 000	+	$63 000	+ $43 065	− $2 000
$128 065					=	$24 000		+	$104 065		

J. Emery Real Estate
Balance Sheet
as at October 30, 19—

ASSETS			LIABILITIES		
Cash		$71 065.00	Bank Loan Payable		$ 16 000.00
Accounts Receivable:			Accounts Payable:		
Pat Rogers	$ 6 000.00		Bell Furniture Co.	$ 3 000.00	
R. Scobie	4 000.00		The City Record	2 000.00	
Shannon Development Co.	15 000.00	25 000.00	Ryan Equipment Co.	3 000.00	8 000.00
			Total Liabilities		$ 24 000.00
Automobile		15 000.00			
Furniture		9 000.00			
Office Equipment		8 000.00			
			OWNER'S EQUITY		
			J. Emery, Capital	$ 63 000.00	
			Add: Net Income	43 065.00	
				106 065.00	
			Deduct: Drawing	2 000.00	
			Total Owner's Equity		104 065.00
Total Assets		$128 065.00	Total Liabilities and Owner's Equity		$128 065.00

- Note that net income is added to the capital part of owner's equity. The total is a claim against the total assets of the business. The final equation has been rearranged to show this new total.
- The last part of the Owner's Equity section shows the deduction for withdrawals under **Drawing**. (As you will recall, the owner has the right to withdraw assets for personal use.) Here, the owner's withdrawal of $2000 of assets decreases owner's equity to $104 065. Notice that the total of owner's equity agrees with the results when you solve the accounting equation for owner's equity. You should always make this calculation when you solve problems on the balance sheet.

- Observe that the deduction for Drawing comes **after** net income is added to capital. This order is also shown in the rearranged accounting equation. To understand why, remember that a person who invests money hopes to make profits (net income). A sole owner does not expect to be paid a salary for working in his or her business. The owner's main goal is to increase his or her equity, which results from the business earning **net** income. Of course, before those net incomes can be calculated, the owner will have to withdraw cash in order to live. In accounting, these drawings are considered to be distributions of profit—payments made before the net income has been computed and reported. That is why it is very important to report withdrawals only **after** net income has been added to capital in the owner's equity section.

Drawings: payments made in anticipation of profits (net income).

Since the owner's withdrawals represent payments made in advance out of net income, owner's withdrawals are **not** business expenses. No transaction involving the withdrawal of assets for the owner's personal use should ever be reported in the income statement. Remember the accounting definition of expenses: costs of goods and services used up by the business to **earn revenue.** When an owner withdraws assets for **personal** use, the asset is used up but no revenue is earned from that withdrawal.

For the above reasons, always report Drawings in the balance sheet after Net Income is added to Capital.

- The illustration of the components of owner's equity on page 52 showed Net Income being added to Capital. Suppose, however, there was a net loss during the accounting period. This would be reported on the balance sheet as a **deduction** from Capital. Again, show any drawings after reporting the net loss. The illustration below is an example.

Total Liabilities		$24 000
OWNER'S EQUITY		
J. Emery, Capital ..	$63 000	
Less: Net Loss	3 000	
	60 000	
Less: Drawing	2 000	
Total Owner's Equity		58 000
Total *L* + *OE*		$82 000

PROBLEMS

Preparing an income statement.

P 2-7 Cindy Vandenberk operates the Diamond Theatre, which derives revenue from admissions, parking fees, and operating concessions. Between January 1 and December 31 of this year, the Diamond Theatre reported revenues and expenses as shown below.

a. Prepare an income statement for the accounting period.

Admissions Revenue	$202 000
Telephone Expense	112
Salaries Expense	96 300
Advertising Expense	6 000
Insurance Expense	1 500
Parking Fees Earned	23 570
Concessions Revenue	37 500
Miscellaneous Expense	56
Building Rental Expense	18 000
Utilities Expense	3 000
Film Rental Expense	52 175
Projection Rental Expense	4 800

Preparing an income statement and a related balance sheet.

P 2-8 Refer to the solution for Problem 2-6 (J. K. Teaching Services).

a. Prepare an income statement for J. K. Teaching Services, for the accounting period given.

b. Prepare a related balance sheet reporting the assets and claims against assets as at the end of the accounting period.

Analyzing transactions using the accounting equation.

Preparing an income statement and a related balance sheet.

P 2-9 Challenge Problem D. Egyed organized a book-binding company on May 1 of this year. The business earns revenue by binding books by several methods. These include: hard-back bindings, soft-back bindings, and plastic and metal spiral bindings. The business conducted the following business transactions during May.

May 1 Egyed invested $250 000 cash by opening a bank account in the name of the business, Egyed Book Binders.

3 Purchased book-binding equipment from Thorne Industries Ltd. at a cost of $8500. A cash down payment of $3500 was made and balance is owing in 60 days.

5 Purchased a truck from Watertown Motors for $15 000. A cash down payment of $1000 was required when the contract was signed. The first payment will be due June 3.

6 Bought insurance for the truck for $970 cash.
6 D. Egyed purchased a piece of land and a building suitable for use as an office at a cost of $185 000. The land was valued at $45 000. A cheque was issued for the full amount of the purchase.
7 Bought office equipment at a cost of $8000 from Taylor Suppliers. Payment was due in ten days.
7 Issued a cheque for $6500 for binding supplies to be used in May.
8 The business completed delivery of an order from the Lambton County Board of Education to rebind 5000 textbooks at $2.00 per book (hard cover). The agreement called for payment within 30 days after delivery.
11 The business completed the binding of 10 000 copies of a new soft-cover book being published by McGraw-Hill Ryerson Limited. The business received payment of $22 000 in full.
12 Issued a cheque for $350 to pay the PUC for utilities.
13 Issued a cheque for $99 to pay the telephone bill received on May 9.
15 Paid the employees $7900 in salaries for the first half of May.
17 Paid $8000 to Taylor Suppliers. This is payment in full for the office equipment.
18 Received $300 from Dow Chemical of Canada for the binding of 200 spiral-bound training manuals.
21 Issued a bill totalling $15 000 to the Chamber of Commerce to soft-cover bind 25 000 tourist booklets. The Chamber was given 30 days to pay the bill.
23 Issued a cheque for $650 to Union Gas Limited to pay for heating costs.
23 Borrowed $3200 from the Royal Bank of Canada. This is a demand loan and was deposited into the business's bank account.
26 Completed the binding of 1000 soft-cover orientation books for Lambton College. Payment of $700 was due by month end.
31 Issued a cheque for $85 for gas and oil expense for the truck.
31 Received payment in full of $700 from Lambton College.
31 D. Egyed withdrew $2500 cash for personal use.
31 Paid the employees $7900 in salaries for the second half of May.

31 Paid $1500 to the Royal Bank of Canada on the demand loan.

31 Shell Canada Limited required the binding of 300 reference manuals in a metal spiral. Total payment of $450 is due in 10 days.

a. Set up a summary table on two pages as follows. On a left-hand page, make columns for (1) Transaction Date; (2) Cash; (3) Accts. Rec.; (4) Land; (5) Building; (6) Truck; (7) Office Equipment; (8) Binding Equipment; (9) Total Assets. On the right-hand page, make columns for (10) Bank Loan Payable; (11) Accts. Pay.; (12) Total Liabilities; (13) D. Egyed, Capital; (14) Revenues; (15) Expenses; (16) D. Egyed, Drawing; (17) Total Owner's Equity.

b. Analyze each business transaction by recording the effects on the elements of the accounting equation in the appropriate columns of the table.

c. After recording the final transaction, total the columns. Then do an equality check on the main elements of the accounting equation.

d. Prepare an income statement for the first month's operations. *Hint:* There are three sources of revenue and seven expenses to report in the statement.

e. Prepare the related balance sheet reporting the details of individual assets, liabilities, and the owner's equity as at May 31.

MINI-CASES

Examining financial statements and GAAPs.

MC 2-7 An income statement has many of the same parts as a balance sheet. There are also significant differences in the form and functions of the two statements.

a. What GAAP underlies every income statement?

b. What is the significant difference between the heading of the income statement and that of the balance sheet? Explain.

c. Which statement is dependent upon the other? Explain.

Identifying the kinds of information gained from financial statements.

MC 2-8 The ABC Company just prepared an income statement for the six months ended June 30, and a related balance sheet as at June 30. These financial statements provide the reader with specific information about that business.

a. What are the key pieces of information provided to the reader by the income statement?

b. What are the key pieces of information provided to the reader by the balance sheet?

Examining how GAAPs affect the preparation of financial statements.

MC 2-9 Triple Star Real Estate Company has just completed and published its year-end financial statements. The owner, Ralph Farnworth, was asked by a business associate if Triple Star Real Estate Company's statements comply with GAAPs. Ralph Farnworth asks you the following question to assist him in determining an answer to his associate's question.

a. What GAAPs that you have studied to date are directly involved in the preparation and presentation of the income statement and balance sheet of a business?

USING ELECTRONIC SPREADSHEETS IN ACCOUNTING

In Chapter 1 and this chapter you were introduced to the accounting equation and applied it to the preparation of income statements and related balance sheets. So far you have prepared financial statements manually, using pen and paper. In this topic, you will discover the capabilities of electronic spreadsheets and learn how to prepare income statements and balance sheets using an electronic spreadsheet.

Electronic spreadsheet: an applications program in which the computer's memory serves as a large worksheet.

With the introduction and wide use of microcomputers in the mid-1970s, software companies developed a powerful worksheet called the electronic spreadsheet. This new applications software combines the convenience and familiarity of a pocket calculator with the powerful memory and electronic screen capabilities of the microcomputer.

The first successful electronic spreadsheet software, called VisiCalc™ as illustrated on page 58, was introduced in 1978. Many new spreadsheets have since been developed; several of the most popular are listed in the side margin. Today's spreadsheets are very sophisticated and are usually integrated with a word processing package, a data-base package, a graphics package, or a communication package.

Enable®
Excel®
Jazz®
Lotus 1-2-3®
Multiplan®
Q Spread®
Quattro®
SuperCalc IV®
Symphony®
Twin/1•2•3®

The electronic spreadsheet is similar to a columnar worksheet, allowing you to record and organize information, but also acting as a very powerful calculator. In addition, by utilizing the **built-in functions** of the spreadsheet and formulas prepared by the user, the user

G15 (V) +F15/F6*100

	A	B	C	D	E	F	G
1	The Baird Real Estate Company						
2	Income Statement						
3	For the Month Ended October 31, 19-1						
4							
5	REVENUE:						%
6	Commissions Earned					2180.00	100.00
7							
8	EXPENSES:						
9							
10	Advertising Expense				210.00		9.63
11	Salaries Expense				900.00		41.28
12	Telephone Expense				48.00		2.20
13	Utilities Expense				19.00		0.87
14					-------		
15	Total Expenses					1177.00	53.99
16						-------	
17	Net Income - Net Loss					1003.00	46.01
18						=======	

Built-in functions: preprogrammed instructions that enable the user to perform specific operations, without actually having to develop the instructions.

"What if" situation: a valuable analytical tool which enables the user to examine the effects of a proposed change to an existing spreadsheet.

can introduce changes to the exercise as **"what if"** situations. For example, what if you had a list of expenses that you wished to total? By using the sum function, you could have the computer add the column of numbers and place the total automatically in a cell. Then, if you wanted to know what would happen to the total if the third number in the list was twice as much, you would type in the new amount and the computer would automatically recalculate the new total. The spreadsheet is an excellent tool for calculating sales projections, income taxes, financial ratios, cost estimates, accounts receivable, accounts payable, and payrolls.

EXPLAINING THE CHARACTERISTICS OF THE ELECTRONIC SPREADSHEET

As shown on page 59, the electronic spreadsheet is simply a series of columns and rows that make up what are commonly referred to as

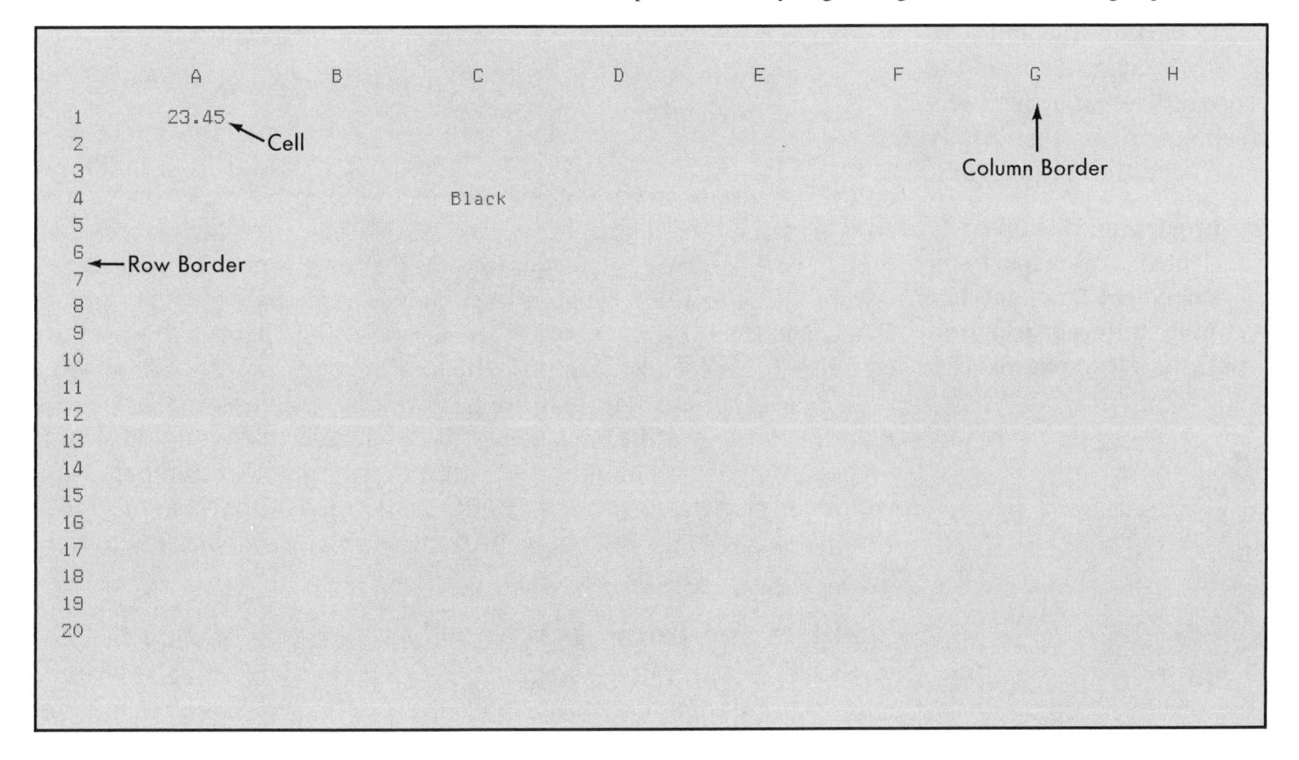

Cell: the working location on the spreadsheet defined by column and row co-ordinates, for example, A1 or D10.

Label: information that is descriptive in nature and not intended for the purpose of making calculations.

Formula: a mathematical expression designed to complete a specific function.

Copy (replicate): duplication of information in another cell location thus enabling the information to automatically be used in that new cell.

"cells." Columns are usually labelled by letters (A, B, C, . . . AA, . . . BC), while rows are labelled by numbers (1, 2, 3, . . . 56, . . . 256). By referring to a column and then a row, you can identify the co-ordinates of any cell on the spreadsheet. In the illustration above find the number 23.45 at "A1" or the word "BLACK" at "C4." All electronic spreadsheets use labels to record alphanumeric information such as headings and descriptions, **numbers** to record numeric information that will be used to make calculations, and formulas. Using the electronic spreadsheet the user can:

- scroll to various locations
- insert and delete columns and rows
- use a GOTO command to move to a specific location
- call up built-in commands that will carry out specific mathematical operations; for example, sum a column or find an average
- copy information and place it in different selected locations
- introduce various number formats, for example, dollar signs, or decimal places
- export and import information between the electronic spreadsheet and other types of programs, such as word-processing or data-base

Exporting: the ability to transfer from the spreadsheet all or part of a document to another totally different program.

Importing: the ability to transfer all or part of a document from another totally different program back into the spreadsheet.

- cut and paste information from one location to another
- transfer automatically information between two or more electronic spreadsheets.

Literally, anything that can be done with pencil and paper on columnar paper can be done on the electronic spreadsheet. The major advantage of the electronic spreadsheet is that calculations are completed very quickly and accurately. Furthermore, one can create "what if" situations, change one or more numbers in the spreadsheet, and then instantaneously see the resulting changes to the entire electronic spreadsheet. Suppose the total revenue figure on an income statement doubled because the advertising expense for a specific month tripled. What effect would those changes have on net income or net loss for the month? By simply changing two numbers, you would immediately see the result. As spreadsheets become more complex, "what if" situations provide an instant view of any projection you might choose to make.

Features for Lotus 1-2-3® Lotus 1-2-3® is a software program that is, like most programs, continually undergoing revisions. Each time the manufacturer updates the software, new features are included in the package. Therefore, it will be important that you determine the version of the software before you begin working with any spreadsheet. Lotus 1-2-3® will operate on IBM equipment and on most IBM compatibles.

Integrated package: a software package that enables the user to exchange information between the programs within the package.

Refer to the initial Lotus screen on the opposite page as you study the following paragraph. Lotus 1-2-3® is an **integrated package** incorporating a spreadsheet, a data base and graphics.

Lotus 1-2-3® has two menus, a main menu and a submenu. The main menu is displayed at the top of the screen and the submenu lies immediately beneath the main menu. Both menus are called up by the slash (/) key. The various commands can then be engaged by either highlighting the appropriate command and pressing enter or by striking the first letter of the desired command. The program's built-in commands and functions enable the user to carry out specific operations very quickly and easily. For example, the COPY command transfers a piece or pieces of information from a particular location to another location on the spreadsheet.

Note that Lotus 1-2-3® does not restrict the length of information placed in a given cell, but will permit the text to extend into adjacent cells. If a company name is too long to fit in one cell, say A1, it will extend into cell B1 without any problem unless something has been previously entered into B1. This is particularly valuable when recording headings or descriptive statements that are wider than any given column.

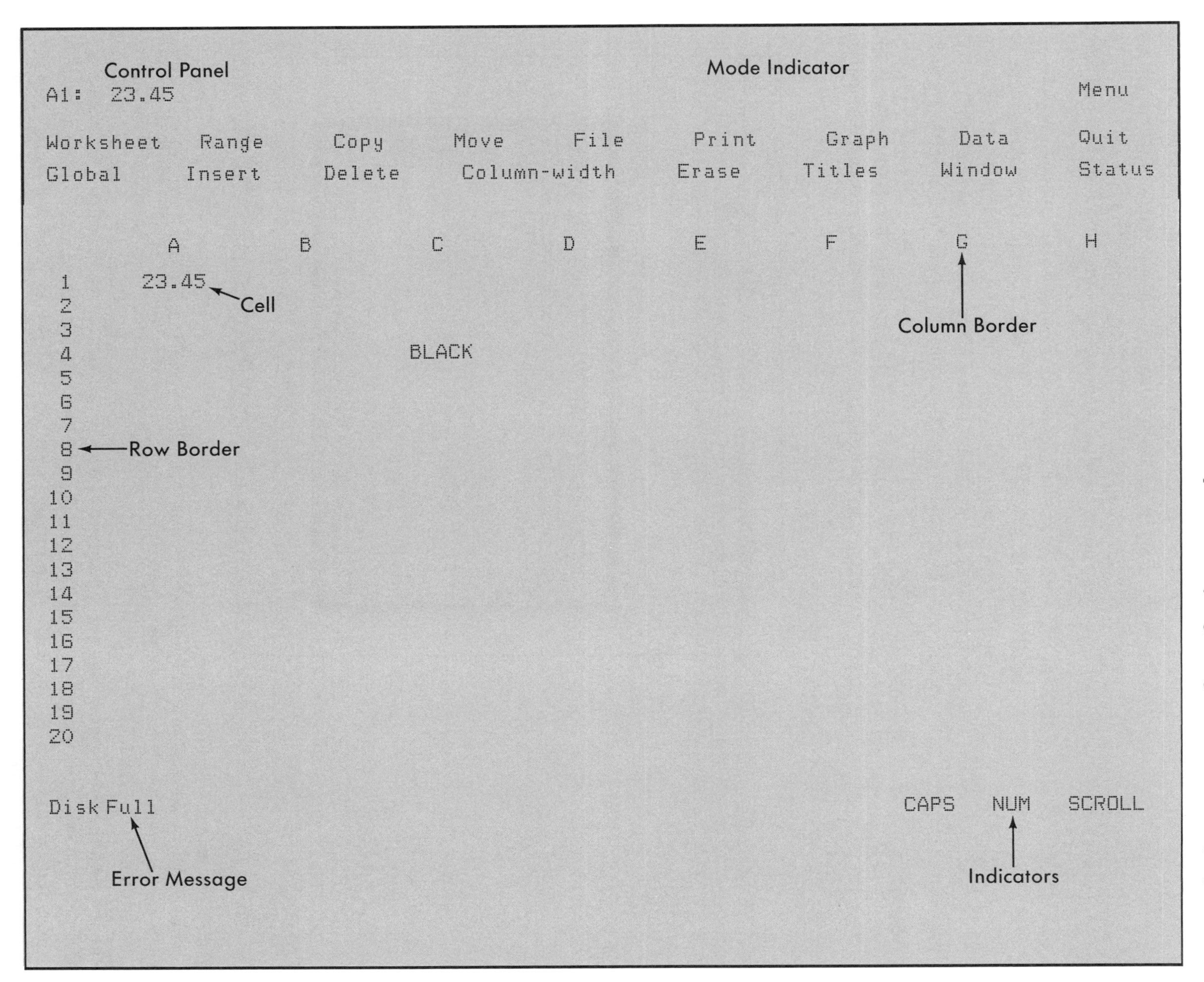
Control Panel
Mode Indicator
A1: 23.45
Menu
Worksheet Range Copy Move File Print Graph Data Quit
Global Insert Delete Column-width Erase Titles Window Status
A B C D E F G H
1 2 3 4 5 6 7 8 9 10 11 12 13 14 15 16 17 18 19 20
23.45
Cell
Column Border
BLACK
Row Border
Disk Full
Error Message
CAPS NUM SCROLL
Indicators

Several of the features which you will become involved with later in this topic include: formatting individual and multiple cells in a variety of ways, copying, centring, right and left justification, adjusting column widths, saving, printing, erasing, and inserting and deleting columns and rows.

Features of Excel® Excel® will run on IBM® equipment and on most IBM® compatibles, as well as the Apple® Macintosh®. This textbook will discuss how to use Excel® on the Macintosh® specifically. However, the concepts would be similar on an IBM. Excel® is an integrated package that incorporates a spreadsheet, a data base, and graphics like Lotus 1-2-3®. Commands are found on a single menu bar that is displayed across the top of the screen, as illustrated below.

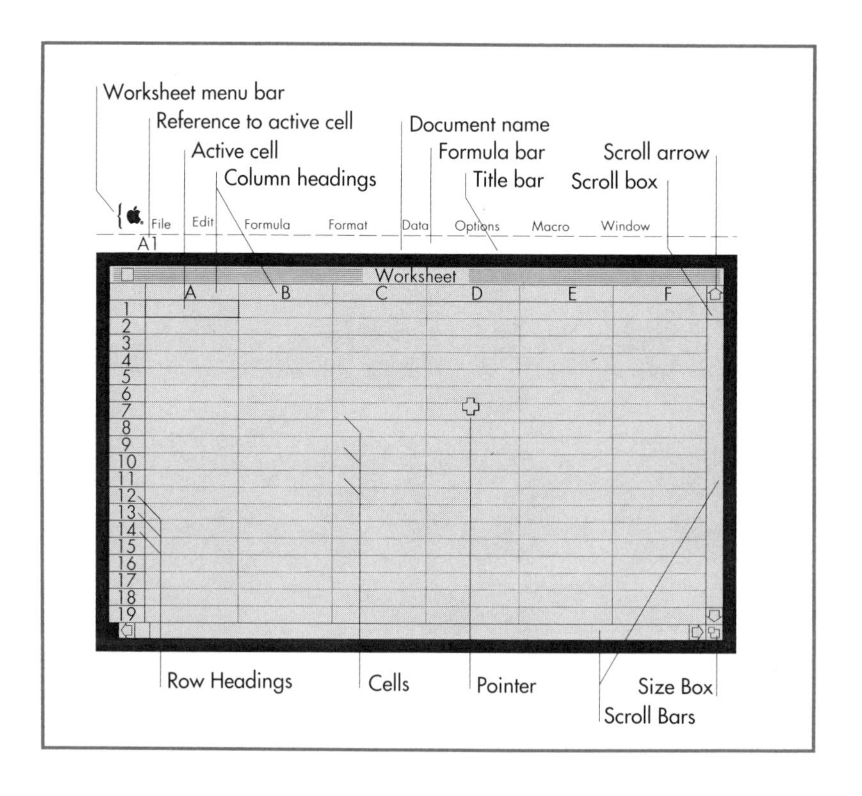

Pull-down menu: a feature which permits the user to access the main menus. The user highlights the principal item and then the sub-menu items drop down into view much like pulling down a blind in a window.

One of the major differences of Excel® is the **"pull-down" menu**. The Macintosh® version of Excel® allows the user to call up commands by keystrokes, but its design promotes the use of a mouse that requires considerably fewer instructions to operate. The mouse is an input device that permits the user to move the cursor around the screen and highlight specific portions easily, so that some action can be carried out. The user can locate a command by using the mouse to pull down a menu. The desired command is then selected simply by highlighting it. Often, a selected command will display a window on the screen asking you to select additional features, once again by using the mouse. Excel®, like Lotus 1-2-3®, does not restrict the

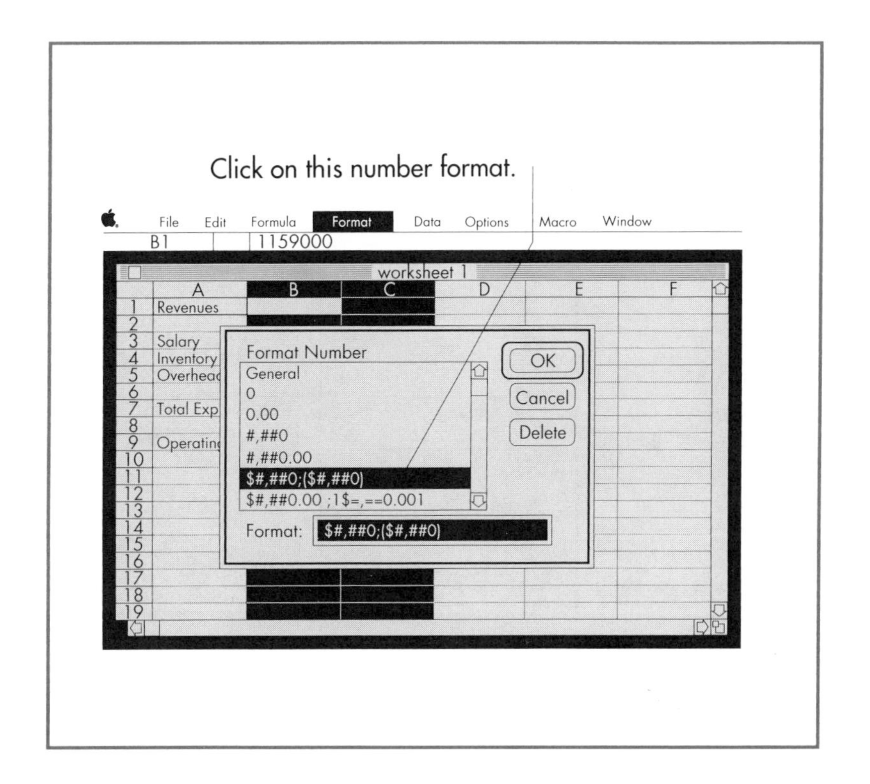

length of information that can be placed into a given cell and contains all the other features identified in the Lotus 1-2-3® description. Both of these packages are very sophisticated and contain many additional features that are beyond our present needs. The chart on the following page compares the features for each of the electronic spreadsheets described earlier.

SOLVING ACCOUNTING PROBLEMS WITH ELECTRONIC SPREADSHEETS

You can now examine how an income statement and a related balance sheet are prepared using an electronic spreadsheet. Refer to the illustrations on the following pages (65 to 68) for the J. Emery Real Estate income statement and related balance sheet. Compare these statements to those prepared manually and illustrated on pages 15 and 48.

Now let's illustrate a simple "what if" situation and observe the effects on both the income statement and the related balance sheet. Suppose Jane Emery earns commissions of $50 000 instead of $51 800. Observe that not only the Commissions Earned line is affected, but also the Net Income line in the income statement and the owner's equity section of the balance sheet. Because there was a change in the revenue account Commissions Earned, there must also be an equivalent change in the cash and/or accounts receivable account(s). In this case, the change is reflected in the Cash account

FEATURE	LOTUS 1-2-3	EXCEL
Version	2.01	1.5
Size	256 columns by 8192 rows	256 columns by 16 384 rows
Standard Set Columns	9 characters	10 characters
Menu(s)	Called up by the SLASH (/) key	Menu Bar with pull-down menus accessed with a mouse or by command key and selected coded keys
Windows	limited availability	used extensively
Macros	available	available
Function Keys	selected uses	not used
Mouse or Equivalent	may be available	used extensively

on the balance sheet. Note as well the change in the assets, the liabilities, and the owner's equity totals. By using formulas to make all calculations and transfer of numbers from the income statement to the balance sheet, all the above changes to the statements can be accomplished by changing only two numbers.

It is important to notice the power that the "what if" situation provides Jane Emery. She now possesses the ability to examine a variety of potential changes in her business and an easy way to observe the effects of those changes. Thus, she has a very fast and powerful analysis tool at her fingertips. Examine the "what if" situations illustrated in the spreadsheets on pages 67 and 68.

```
EG: (F2) [W9] 10000                                                    READY

          A         B         C         D         E         F         G         H

1    J. Emery Real Estate
2    Income Statement
3    For the Month Ended October 31, 19-
4
5    REVENUE:
6    Commissions Earned                             51800.00
7
8    EXPENSES:
9    Salaries Expense                     4500.00
10   Rent Expense                         1600.00
11   Utilities Expense                     595.00
12   Telephone Expense                      40.00
13   Advertising Expense                  2000.00
14                                        -------
15   Total Expenses                                  8735.00
16                                                  --------
17   Net Income - (Loss)                            43065.00
18                                                  ========
19
20
09   Oct. 91   10:07   PM                                      NUM
```

	E	F	G	H	I	J	K	L	M
1				J. Emery Real Estate					
2				Balance Sheet					
3				as at October 31, 19--					
4									
5		ASSETS					LIABILITIES		
6	Cash			71065.00		Bank Loan Payable			16000.00
7	Accounts Receivable:					Accounts Payable:			
8	Pat Rogers		6000.00			Bell Furniture Co.		3000.00	
9	R. Scobie		4000.00			The City Record		2000.00	
10	Shannon Development		15000.00	25000.00		Ryan Equipment Co.		3000.00	8000.00
11	Co.					Total Liabilities			24000.00
12	Automobile			15000.00					
13	Furniture			9000.00			OWNER'S EQUITY		
14	Office Equipment			8000.00		J. Emery, Capital		63000.00	
15						Net Income (-Loss)		43065.00	
16								106065.00	
17						J. Emery, Drawing		2000.00	
18						Total Owner's Equity			104065.00
19									
20						Total Liabilities and			
21	Total Assets			128065.00		Owner's Equity			128065.00
22									
23									
24									
25									

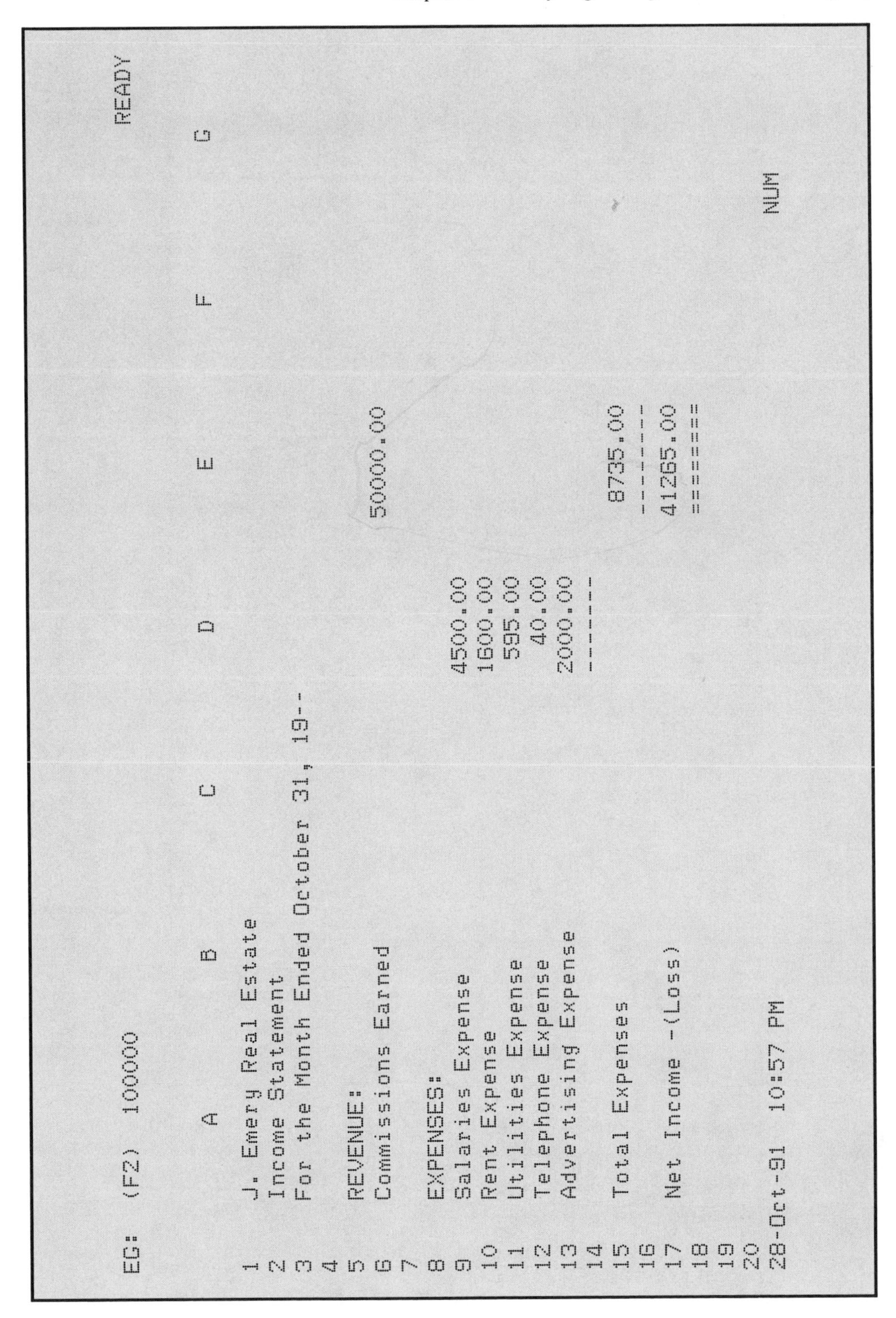

```
EG: (F2) 100000                                                            READY

        A            B            C            D            E        F        G
1   J. Emery Real Estate
2   Income Statement
3   For the Month Ended October 31, 19--
4
5   REVENUE:
6   Commissions Earned                                       50000.00
7
8   EXPENSES:
9   Salaries Expense                            4500.00
10  Rent Expense                                1600.00
11  Utilities Expense                            595.00
12  Telephone Expense                             40.00
13  Advertising Expense                         2000.00
14                                              --------
15  Total Expenses                                           8735.00
16                                                           --------
17  Net Income -(Loss)                                       41265.00
18                                                           ========
19
20
28-Oct-91  10:57 PM                                         NUM
```

	E	F	G	H	I	J	K	L	M
1				J. Emery Real Estate					
2				Balance Sheet					
3				as at October 31, 19--					
4									
5		ASSETS					LIABILITIES		
6	Cash			69265.00		Bank Loan Payable			16000.00
7	Accounts Receivable:					Accounts Payable:			
8	Pat Rogers		6000.00			Bell Furniture Co.		3000.00	
9	R. Scobie		4000.00			The City Record		2000.00	
10	Shannon Development		15000.00	25000.00		Ryan Equipment Co.		3000.00	8000.00
11	Co.					Total Liabilities			24000.00
12	Automobile			15000.00					
13	Furniture			9000.00			OWNER'S EQUITY		
14	Office Equipment			8000.00		J. Emery, Capital		63000.00	
15						Net Income (-Loss)		41265.00	
16								104265.00	
17						J. Emery, Drawings		2000.00	
18						Total Owner's Equity			102265.00
19									
20						Total Liabilities and			
21	Total Assets			126265.00		Owner's Equity			126265.00
22									
23									
24									
25									

TOPIC 4 PROBLEMS

Exploring the use of an electronic spreadsheet.

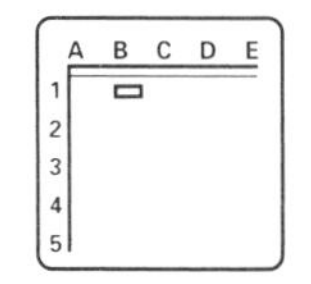

P 2-10 Refer to your solution for Problem 2-7 (Diamond Theatre). Cindy Vandenberk operates the Diamond Theatre, which derives revenue from admissions, parking fees, and concessions. Between January 1 and December 31 of this year, the Diamond Theatre reported revenues and expenses as shown below. Prepare an income statement for the accounting period.

Admissions Revenue	$202 000
Telephone Expense	112
Salaries Expense	96 300
Advertising Expense	6 000
Insurance Expense	1 500
Parking Fees Earned	23 570
Concessions Revenue	37 500
Miscellaneous Expense	56
Building Rental Expense	18 000
Utilities Expense	3 000
Film Rental Expense	52 175
Projection Rental Expense	4 800

a. Using the hand-out material supplied by your instructor, complete the income statement for the Diamond Theatre using an electronic spreadsheet. Print a copy of the income statement for your notes. Compare the printout to the handwritten income statement in your notes.

b. Complete the ''what if'' situations below. Print a copy of each situation, and then compare the original statement to the statement produced after each ''what if'' situation. What if the Admissions Revenue was cut in half? What if the Film Rental Expense tripled?

c. What advantages are there for a business to use ''what if'' situations?

Preparing an income statement and a balance sheet using an electronic spreadsheet.

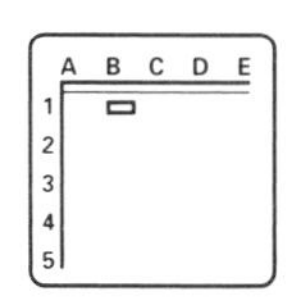

P 2-11 Refer to your solution for Problem 2-8 (J.K. Teaching Services).

a. Using your manually completed income statement for J.K. Teaching Services, and the handout material provided by your instructor, prepare the income statement using an electronic spreadsheet.

b. Using the completed balance sheet for J.K. Teaching Services, and the handout material provided by your instructor, prepare the balance sheet using an electronic spreadsheet. Notice how the net income (loss) figure of the income statement is automatically tied into the owner's equity section of the balance sheet. Print a copy of the income statement and balance sheet for your notes.

c. What if total expenses increased by 12%? What if the additional investment was only $2000 instead of $10 000? Take particular note of the changes that occur in the owner's equity section of the balance sheet when changes are made in the income statement. Print a copy after each "what if" situation, and then compare the original statements to the statements produced after each "what if" situation.

Preparing financial statements on a spreadsheet without step-by-step instructions.

Examining the information required with a loan application.

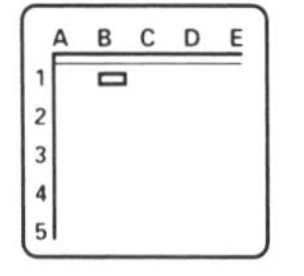

P 2-12 Refer to your solution for Problem 2-9 (Egyed Book Binders).

a. Using the knowledge you have acquired by completing Problems 2-10 and 2-11, and your completed handwritten statements, prepare the income statement and related balance sheet for Egyed Book Binders using an electronic spreadsheet. Print a copy of the income statement and balance sheet for your notes.

b. Assume the following "what if" situations: (1) All the revenue figures in the business were cut in half. (Change the original figures by building a formula that will divide each revenue number in half.) (2) All but $100 in the Accounts Receivable had been converted into cash. (3) The business borrowed an additional $5000 from the bank. Produce a hard copy printout after each "what if" situation, and then compare the original statements to the statements produced after each "what if" situation.

MINI-CASES

Examining features of electronic spreadsheets.

MC 2-10 Martine just finished the financial statements for World Wide Widgets using an electronic spreadsheet package. One of her colleagues, Tuan, who was not familiar with the use of a spreadsheet, observed the final product and commented on the neatness of the presentation. However, Tuan replied, "It must be difficult to learn to use the computer and very time consuming to prepare the statements this way. Besides, if you have to make changes, it would take forever to retype all that work."

a. How would you expect Martine to respond to Tuan's comments regarding the difficulty of using the computer?

b. What major advantages could Martine point out to Tuan regarding the time it takes to prepare financial statements on a spreadsheet?

c. What is it that Tuan does not understand about the use of a spreadsheet when changes are required? What is the other important feature available to the spreadsheet user regarding changes to the presentation?

Examining features of electronic spreadsheets.

MC 2-11 Ricardo Consiglio recently took over the management of Consolidated Storage Company. He has observed that financial statements are prepared using an electronic spreadsheet, and expressed the following concerns to you. ''What happens if the employee is interrupted and must leave the machine for a short period of time? What happens if the employee is not finished at the end of the day? Does the machine have to be left on all night? What happens if the power goes off in the office?''

a. Answer Mr. Consiglio's questions to the best of your knowledge.

Examining how GAAPs affect the use of spreadsheets.

MC 2-12 Jorge and Bill have been discussing the use of the electronic spreadsheet for the preparation of financial statements. Bill believes that the spreadsheet will prepare statements that comply better with GAAPs than handwritten statements.

a. What comments would you make to Jorge and Bill regarding their concerns?

COMPREHENSIVE CASE STUDY 2

Fred Katch owns the Economy Car Rental Company near a newly built international air terminal. Since the opening of the airport, Fred's business has increased beyond his original expectations of five years ago. In fact, business has been so good that he cannot meet the requests of customers on weekends. Fred decides to borrow $75 000 from his bank in order to buy an additional fleet of five cars. With his application for a loan, he includes a statement saying that his car rental business is estimated to be worth $150 000. In analyzing the application, the bank manager states that he is impressed with the possible bright future of the business, but before he can make a final decision he will require additional information about the earning power of the business and about the current financial position of the business.

Examining how financial statements are used to determine if a business should be granted a loan for the purpose of expansion.

a. Why would the bank manager request more finanical information on the business before making a decision to grant the loan?

b. What financial statements should Fred have submitted with his loan application?

c. Why would the bank manager be interested in learning about the earning power of the business?

d. If you were the bank manager, would you consider any factors other than those shown on the financial statements in determining whether or not to approve the loan?

e. Do you believe Fred should have applied for the loan in the first place? Explain your answer.

CHAPTER 3

USING ACCOUNTS

Topic 1
Establishing Accounts

Topic 2
Recording Asset and Liability Changes in T-Accounts

Topic 3
Recording Owner's Equity Changes in T-Accounts

In Chapters 1 and 2 you analyzed business transactions that affected the key elements of the accounting equation. For example, you will recall that when a customer paid cash to repay a debt to a business, the asset Cash increased and the asset Accounts Receivable decreased — both on the left side of the equation. On the other hand, when a business paid cash for a debt, eliminating the claim of a creditor, the asset Cash decreased on the left side and the liability Accounts Payable decreased on the right side.

Now suppose that during a normal business day the asset Cash was involved in 300 transactions. To find out the balance of Cash at the end of the day: (1) Would you record the increases and decreases to Cash directly in one equation as illustrated? (2) Would you prepare 300 separate accounting equations? (3) Or would you prepare a new balance sheet after each change in Cash?

Recording changes directly on the accounting equation is inefficient.

A			=	L	+	OE
Cash	Accounts Receivable	Office Equipment		Accounts Payable		Owner's Capital
~~$8 000~~ +	~~$500~~ +	~~$3 500~~	=	~~$2 000~~	+	~~$10 000~~
~~$8 500~~	Ø	$4 500		~~$1 200~~		$14 000
~~$7 500~~				$ 500		
~~$6 700~~						
~~$6 000~~						
$10 000						

Account: a device for recording the effects of transactions under one title.

Obviously, all of these are inefficient ways to record the daily changes to an asset like Cash. (Choice 3 would involve 300 separate balance sheets!) A new device is needed to record changes to the items in the accounting equation—namely, the account.

ESTABLISHING ACCOUNTS

Several different forms of accounts are in actual use; only a very simple one is presented here—other forms will be introduced in later chapters. This simple account resembles the accounting equation. Just as the equation has two sides, so this device has two sides also, as shown here.

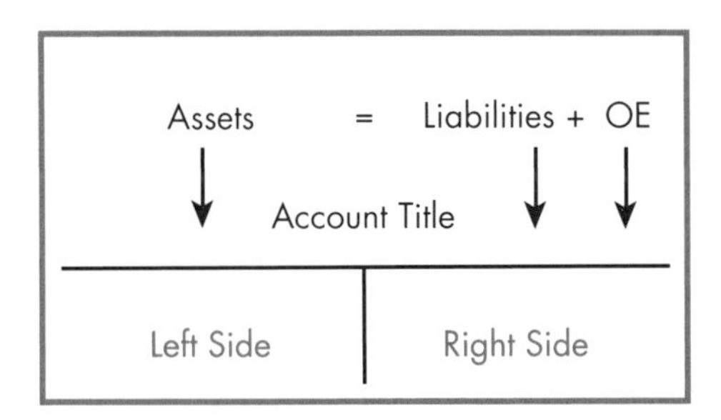

The various account forms illustrated at the top of the next page, each of which is in the shape of a large T, may be called **T-accounts**. The name of the account above the horizontal line matches the item in the accounting equation. A separate account can be used for each asset and liability, and for each part of owner's equity.

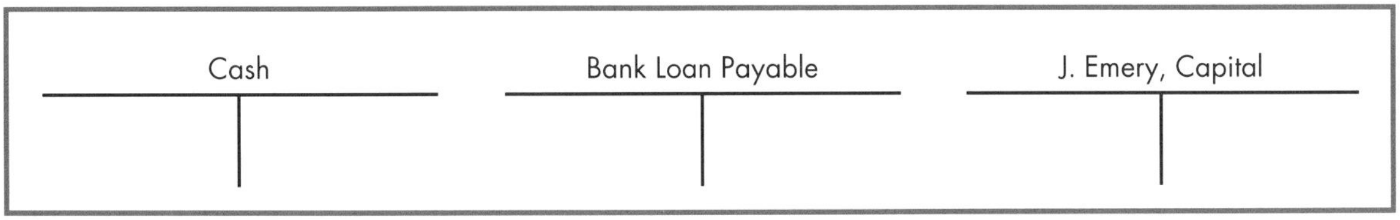

Cash		Bank Loan Payable		J. Emery, Capital	

DEFINING DEBITS AND CREDITS

Debit: the left side of an account.

Credit: the right side of an account.

In the language of accounting, the left side of every account is known as the debit (DR.) side and the right side is known as the credit (CR.) side. When you see a reference to the debit side of an account, you should always think only of the left side of that account. When you see a reference to the credit side, think only of the right side. Do not attach any further meaning to debit and credit. The term "debit" refers to the **left** side, and the term "credit" to the **right** side, of an account.

Account Title	
DEBIT (DR.) SIDE (left side)	CREDIT (CR.) SIDE (right side)

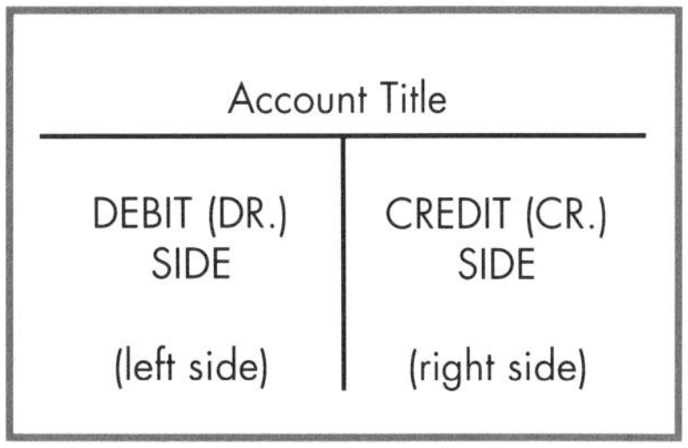

OPENING ACCOUNTS

Look again at the first accounting equation for J. Emery Real Estate, illustrated below with a number of T-accounts. Do you see any relationship between the position of each element in the accounting equation and the position of the dollar amount in each T-account?

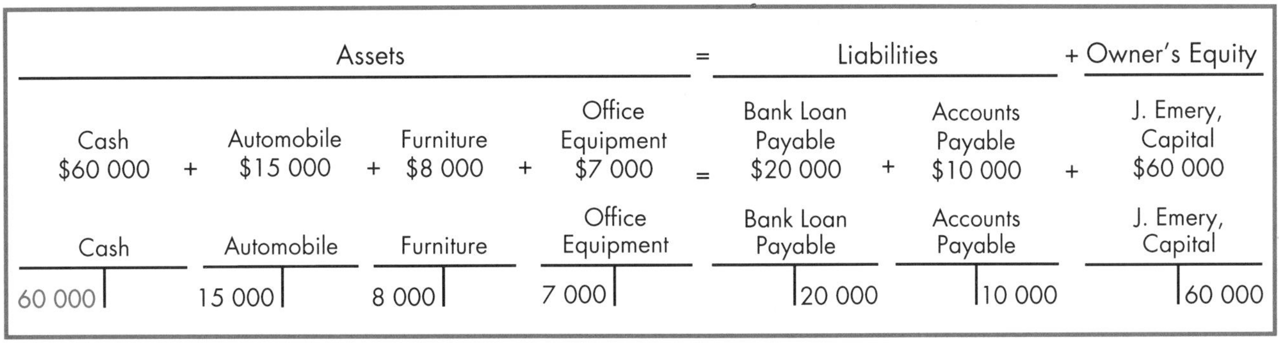

Assets								=	Liabilities				+ Owner's Equity
Cash $60 000	+	Automobile $15 000	+	Furniture $8 000	+	Office Equipment $7 000		=	Bank Loan Payable $20 000	+	Accounts Payable $10 000	+	J. Emery, Capital $60 000

Cash		Automobile		Furniture		Office Equipment		Bank Loan Payable		Accounts Payable		J. Emery, Capital	
60 000		15 000		8 000		7 000			20 000		10 000		60 000

Positions of Opening Balances

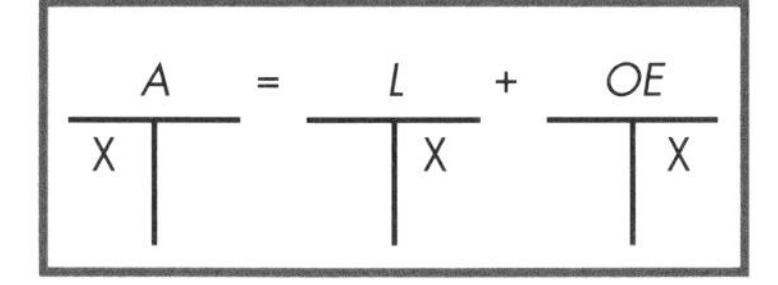

As you can see, each entry—which we describe as the first—in the T-accounts appears on the same side that the account appears in the equation. These entries are called **opening balances**. Because assets are located on the left side of the accounting equation, all assets will show their beginning balances on the left side, that is, the debit side.

Where would you locate the opening balance amounts for the liabilities and the owner's equity subelement Capital? On the credit side, of course, because liabilities and owner's equity are placed on the credit (right) side of the accounting equation. You should now have little difficulty in understanding this important rule.

Rule for Opening Accounts

An account is opened by placing its beginning amount, called an opening balance, on the same side that the account appears in the accounting equation.

OPENING ACCOUNTS FOR A BUSINESS

To illustrate how accounts are actually established for a business, consider the example of J. Emery Real Estate in Chapter 1. Jane Emery began her business on September 30 by buying and investing in assets. Against these assets, two claims were made: (1) the total claims of creditors, called liabilities, and (2) the claim of the owner, called owner's equity. Thus, an accounting equation was formed for Jane Emery's new business.

For the beginning accounting equation, a beginning balance sheet was prepared so that the elements of the equation could be summarized in a more detailed financial report. Since this opening balance sheet contains the same information as the accounting equation, it is possible to also use this information to open a set of accounts for the business. Compare how the opening balance sheet relates to the T-accounts in the illustration on the opposite page.

From the illustration, you can easily see the similarities. There are, however, important differences:

- Each asset account has the date of the opening balance sheet on the debit (left) side of the account. The opening balances for these accounts must also be placed on the left (debit) side.
- For all liabilities and the owner's equity accounts, the date of the opening balance sheet is identified on the credit side. The opening balance for each account must also be placed on the credit (right) side.
- A separate account is opened for each creditor so that the amount owed to each can be quickly calculated. The abbreviation "Accts. Pay." is placed before the creditor's name to identify it as an account payable. (When the business has customer

J. Emery Real Estate
Balance Sheet
as at September 30, 19 —

ASSETS		LIABILITIES		
Cash	$60 000.00	Bank Loan Payable		$20 000.00
Automobile	15 000.00	Accounts Payable:		
Furniture	8 000.00	Bell Furniture Co.	$3 000.00	
Office Equipment	7 000.00	Ryan Equipment Co.	2 000.00	
		Westown Motors Ltd.	5 000.00	10 000.00
		Total Liabilities		$30 000.00
		OWNER'S EQUITY		
		J. Emery, Capital		60 000.00
Total Assets	$90 000.00	Total Liabilities and Owner's Equity		$90 000.00

Cash

Debit	Credit
19— Sept. 30 60 000	

Automobile

Debit	Credit
19— Sept. 30 15 000	

Furniture

Debit	Credit
19— Sept. 30 8 000	

Office Equipment

Debit	Credit
19— Sept. 30 7 000	

Bank Loan Payable

Debit	Credit
	19— Sept. 30 20 000

Accts. Pay./Bell Furniture Co.

Debit	Credit
	19— Sept. 30 3 000

Accts. Pay./Ryan Equipment Co.

Debit	Credit
	19— Sept. 30 2 000

Accts. Pay./Westown Motors Ltd.

Debit	Credit
	19— Sept. 30 5 000

J. Emery, Capital

Debit	Credit
	19— Sept. 30 60 000

ASSETS $90 000 = LIABILITIES $30 000 + OWNER'S EQUITY $60 000

accounts, the short form "Accts. Rec." is placed before the customer's name to identify it as an account receivable.)

- Dollar signs are not required when recording dollar amounts in T-accounts because they are not formal financial reports like the income statement and the balance sheet.
- There is no **account** called "Owner's Equity." Since this term means **all** the claims of the owner against the total assets of the business, a T-account must be opened for each claim of the owner. In this case, Jane Emery made an investment, and an account called "Capital" is opened to show this claim.

OPENING THE LEDGER

Ledger: a file or group of accounts.

When accounts have been opened for all assets, liabilities, and the owner's equity, the entire group of accounts forms the ledger. Strictly speaking, a ledger is a file containing all the accounts of a particular type or nature; in actual practice, there are many different types and forms of ledgers. Some of these will be examined in future chapters. At this point, think of "the ledger" as simply the group of T-accounts.

Note that the ledger on page 77 for J. Emery Real Estate contains all of the accounts as they are found in the beginning accounting equation. Each opening balance relates directly to the location in which that account is found in the accounting equation, namely, $A = L + OE$. Therefore, asset accounts which are found on the left side of the equation have opening balances on the debit or left side of the account; liability and owner's equity accounts have opening balances on the credit or right side of the account.

J. Emery Real Estate
Summary of Ledger Account Balances
as at September 30, 19 —

TOTAL DEBIT (LEFT) BALANCES			TOTAL CREDIT (RIGHT) BALANCES	
Cash	$60 000.00		Bank Loan Payable	$20 000.00
Automobile	15 000.00		Accts. Pay./Bell Furniture Co.	3 000.00
Furniture	8 000.00		Accts. Pay./Ryan Equipment Co.	2 000.00
Office Equipment	7 000.00		Accts. Pay./Westown Motors Ltd.	5 000.00
			J. Emery, Capital	60 000.00
Total Debits	$90 000.00		Total Credits	$90 000.00
Total Assets	$90 000.00	=	Total Liabilities + Owner's Equity	$90 000.00

To prove this point, check the T-account ledger. The debit or left-side balances represent assets in the equation, while the total credit right-side balances represent total liabilities plus owner's equity. The equation in the ledger will always show that the total debits are equal to the total credits.

PROBLEMS

Preparing opening balances.

Preparing total proofs.

P 3-1 Refer to the opening balance sheet solved for Problem 1-4 **b** (Saskatchewan Garden Maintenance Company).

a. Open a T-account ledger, including every asset and liability, and the owner's equity. For each account enter the date and the opening balance.

b. Prepare a summary of ledger account balances similar to that illustrated on page 78. What do the totals prove?

Preparing opening balances.

Preparing total proofs.

P 3-2 Refer to the opening balance sheet solved for Problem 2-3 (Radio Station CHJK).

a. Open a T-account ledger including every asset and liability, and the owner's equity. For each account enter the date and the opening balance.

b. Prepare a summary of ledger account balances similar to that illustrated on page 78. What do the totals prove?

Analyzing and recording transactions on the equation.

Preparing a balance sheet.

Preparing total proofs.

P 3-3 Challenge Problem The following financial events or transactions took place over several days in April in order to establish Peter's Programming Service. The service is owned by Peter Ramlagen.

(i) Peter Ramlagen invested $15 000 cash by placing it into the bank account of Peter's Programming Service.

(ii) Peter purchased computer equipment costing $8000 from Larry's Computer Store on 60 days' credit.

(iii) He purchased with cash several pieces of computer software from Software Unlimited Inc., costing $4300.

(iv) Peter returned computer equipment originally purchased on credit for $500 from Larry's Computer Store.

(v) He borrowed $6000 from the bank, signing a demand note. The money was immediately deposited to the business's bank account.

(vi) Computer Office Furniture was purchased from Manley's Ltd. costing $7300. The terms of the purchase were: 20% in cash; the balance on 90 days' credit. Peter issued a cheque for the correct amount. *Note:* Use the Computer Equipment account.

a. Analyze and record the effects of each transaction on the accounting equation for Peter's Programming Service by using a summary table with the following columns: Transaction No.; Cash; Computer Equipment; Computer Software; Total Assets; Bank Loan Payable; Accts. Pay./Larry's Computer Store; Accts. Pay./Manley's Ltd.; P. Ramlagen, Capital.

b. Total all items in the table. Then do an equality check.

c. Prepare the opening balance sheet for Peter's Programming Service as at April 12, current year.

d. Open a T-account ledger for each asset, liability, and owner's equity account listed in the opening balance sheet.

e. Prepare a summary of ledger balances similar to that illustrated on page 78. What do the totals prove?

MINI-CASES

Discussing debit-credit theory.

MC 3-1 Manny and Julian are discussing the new terms debit and credit that they were taught today. Julian says, "Debits are put on the left side because assets are found on the left side of the accounting equation, and credits are put on the right side of the equation."

a. Will Julian be successful in correctly recording business transactions with his present understanding of debits and credits?

b. What is the correct meaning of the terms "debit" and "credit" as they relate to accounting?

c. Give an example of a transaction that will work if Julian applies his rule for debits and credits.

d. Give an example of a transaction that will NOT work if Julian applies his rule for debiting and crediting.

Preparing opening entries.

MC 3-2 Wolf Moritz began a repair shop by investing $500 of his own money and his personal tools for which he paid $1500 cash. He also borrowed $300 from the bank. To keep track of what he had done, Wolf prepared the following list: "Things the business owns: Cash, $800; Tools, $1500. Things the business owes: To the bank, $300."

a. Is this a satisfactory method for recording the opening information for Wolf's business?

b. What key information did Wolf not include in his list?

c. Using T-accounts and the accounting equation as a heading, prepare the necessary accounts and record the opening balances for Wolf Moritz's new business. Briefly, write a note explaining to Wolf what you did and why.

Determining what constitutes a ledger.

MC 3-3 B. M. Y. Co. begins business operations with five asset accounts, two liability accounts, and the owner's capital account. Margaret says to Willard, "This company cannot have a ledger. Eight accounts are not enough to be described as a ledger."

a. Is Margaret's statement correct?

b. If her statement is correct, how many accounts must a business have in order to have a ledger? If not, briefly explain what is meant in accounting by the term "ledger."

RECORDING ASSET AND LIABILITY CHANGES IN T-ACCOUNTS

In this topic, you will learn how to use debits and credits to record changes in asset and liability accounts. However, the rules for using debits and credits to record changes in the owner's equity section of the equation will be studied in Topic 3.

It is very important to learn not only how the increases and decreases are recorded in asset and liability accounts, but also why each increase or decrease is recorded on a particular side of an account. Here is the rule for recording an increase to any account:

Rule for Increasing All Accounts

An increase in an account is recorded on the same side that the account appears in the accounting equation.

Let's apply this rule to the recording of increases in asset accounts.

Rule for Recording Increases in Asset Accounts

An increase in an asset account is recorded on the debit side, because assets appear on the left side of the accounting equation.

This rule explains why increases in asset accounts are recorded on only one side of the account. Since asset accounts are located on the left side of the equation, an increase to any asset account must be recorded on the same side, that is, on the debit side. For example,

Cash	
DR. (Increase side)	CR.
5 000	

suppose a transaction causes an increase of $5000 to the cash account. To record this increase, you would simply show the $5000 on the left or debit side of the cash account as shown in the margin.

Debiting: recording an amount on the left side.

Accountants sometimes use short expressions such as "Debit Cash for $5000." All this means is to record the $5000 on the left side of the cash account. And instead of saying "recording Cash with an amount on the left side," accountants simply say "debiting Cash." Thus, the **noun** "debit" means the left side of the account, and the **verb** "debit" means **to record** an amount on the left side of the account.

Let's now apply the rule for recording increases to *liability* accounts.

Rule for Recording Increases in Liability Accounts

An increase in a liability account is recorded on the credit side, because liabilities appear on the right side of the beginning accounting equation.

The above rule is easy to understand because it is logical. Since liabilities are located on the right side of the accounting equation, all liabilities must be increased on that side, that is, on the credit side. For example, to record an increase of $100 to Accounts Payable, you would credit this account as shown at the top in the left-hand illustration on page 83.

Crediting: recording an amount on the right side.

In recording the credit, one is of course crediting the account.

If accounts are increased on the side on which they appear in the accounting equation, the following rule makes sense.

Rule for Decreasing All Accounts

A decrease in an account is recorded on the side opposite to that on which the account appears in the accounting equation.

Let's apply this to the recording of decreases in asset accounts.

Rule for Recording Decreases in Asset Accounts

A decrease in an asset account is recorded on the side opposite to the one on which the element *A* appears in the accounting equation —in other words, the credit side.

The above explains why decreases are recorded on only one side of asset accounts. Decreases must be recorded on the credit side because that is the side opposite to the one on which the account appears in the accounting equation. For example, to decrease the Cash account by $400, you would credit it as shown at the bottom in the marginal illustration.

The rule for recording decreases can now be applied to all liability accounts as follows.

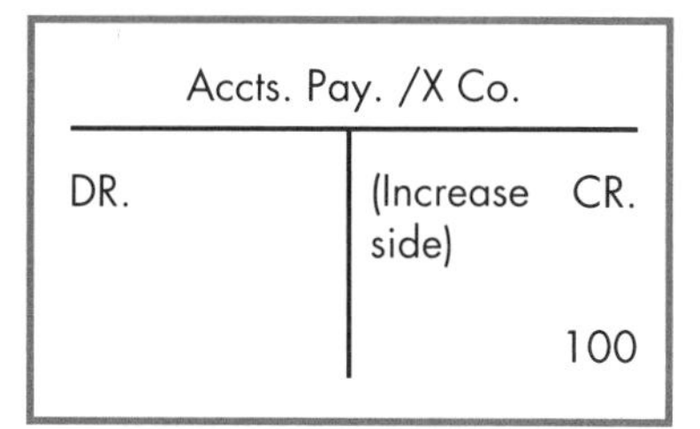

Cash	
DR. (Increase side)	(Decrease side) CR.
	400

Rule for Recording Decreases to Liability Accounts

A decrease in a liability account is recorded on the side opposite to the one on which the element *L* appears in the accounting equation — in other words, the debit side.

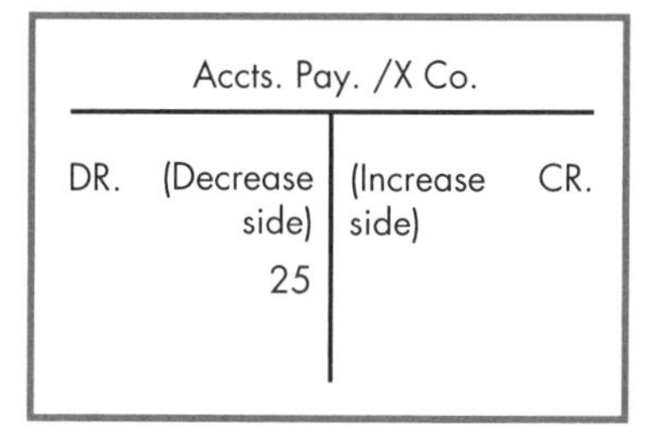

For example, to record a decrease of $25 to Accts. Pay./X Co., debit the account as shown in the margin. Why? The rule says that all decreases must be recorded on the side opposite to the one on which the account appears in the accounting equation. Since liabilities are found on the right side, the opposite is the left (debit) side.

Here's a good question. *On what side would you show the balance in any account after recording any increases or decreases?* The following rule makes accounting sense.

Rule for Showing a Normal Balance in an Account

The balance of an account will normally appear on the same side that the account appears in the accounting equation.

This final rule is an important one. It explains how you would place the difference between the total debits and the total credits recorded in any account. Suppose the Cash and the Accounts Payable accounts contained entries as illustrated in the margin.

Account balance: the difference between the total debits and the total credits.

The Cash account shows a record of two debits and two credits. The difference between the total debits and total credits is $5000 and is called the account balance. Since the Cash account, an asset, appears on the left side of the equation, it normally has a **debit** (DR.) balance. In other words, total debits are usually greater than total credits in accounts on the left side of the equation.

Cash	
DR.	CR.
5 000	400
2 000	1 600
7 000	2 000

$5 000 debit balance

Accts. Pay./X Co.	
DR.	CR.
25	400

$375 credit balance

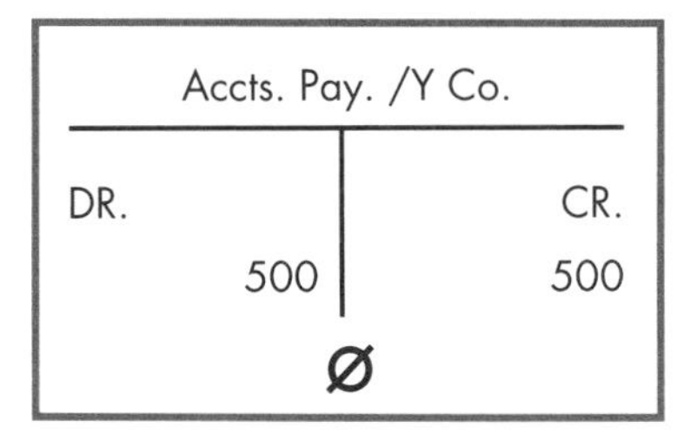

In the case of a liability account, total credits are normally greater than total debits. A liability account, therefore, is expected to have a **credit** (CR.) balance. This follows from the general rule because all liabilities are found on the right or credit side of the equation.

Suppose the debit side and the credit side of an account are equal. How would you identify the balance? Of course, it would be a zero balance. One way to show an account with such a balance is to write a large zero with a slash as illustrated in the margin.

Here's a useful summary of the basic rules for recording increases and decreases to asset and liability accounts:

A		=	*L* + *OE*	
Asset Accounts			Liability Accounts	
DR. (Left)	(Right) CR.		DR. (Left)	(Right) CR.
Record increases here.	Record decreases here.		Record decreases here.	Record increases here.

- **All** accounts are **increased** on the **same** side as the one on which the account appears in the accounting equation.
- **All** accounts are **decreased** on the **opposite** side to the one on which the account appears in the accounting equation.
- **Asset** accounts (which appear on the left side of the accounting equation) are **increased on the debit side** and **decreased on the credit side**.
- **Liability** accounts (which appear on the right side of the accounting equation) are **increased on the credit side** and **decreased on the debit side**.
- The balance of **any** account will normally be placed on the **same** side as the one on which the account appears in the accounting equation.
- The balance of an **asset** account will normally be on the **debit** side.
- The balance of any **liability** account will normally be on the **credit** side.

ILLUSTRATING ASSET AND LIABILITY CHANGES IN T-ACCOUNTS

For the October transactions for J. Emery Real Estate, the opening balances are recorded in T-accounts.

October 1 J. Emery Real Estate buys more furniture for $1000 from Enns Furniture Ltd., and pays by cheque.

ANALYSIS CHART

What Happens	Accounting Rule	Accounting Entry
The asset Furniture increases by $1000.	To increase an asset, debit the account. *Reason:* Assets increase on the side on which they appear in the accounting equation—the debit side.	Debit: Furniture $1000
The asset Cash decreases by $1000.	To decrease an asset, credit the account. *Reason:* Assets decrease on the side opposite to that on which they appear in the accounting equation—the credit side.	Credit: Cash $1000

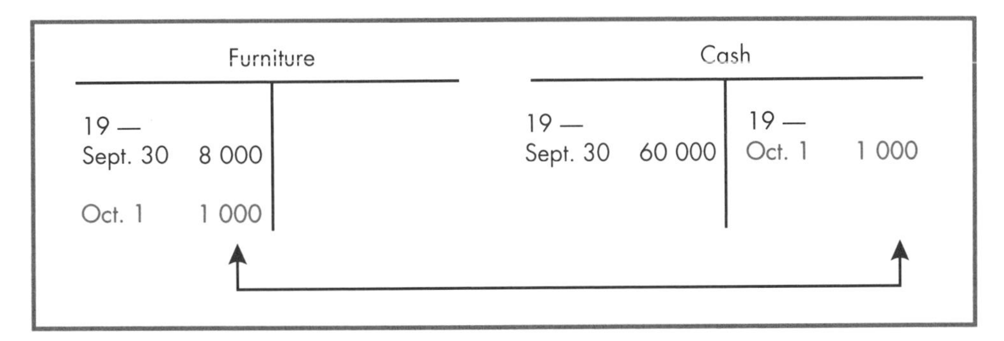

Analysis: In recording this first transaction, notice that only two asset accounts are affected.

(1) Since the Furniture account must be increased, the amount must be recorded on the debit side. This follows the rule that increases in an account always occur on the same side that the account appears in the accounting equation.

(2) Since the business has given a cheque in payment, the asset Cash must be decreased. In accordance with the rule for decreasing an account, the amount of the cheque must be recorded on the credit side of the Cash account.

Here is another important point. The transaction results in an increase to one asset account and a decrease to another, by the same dollar amount. In fact, this is the same transaction you studied in Topic 1 of Chapter 2. But in this chapter, the analysis has to be done in terms of debits and credits. Thus, you say that one asset account is debited and another is credited for the same amount. In other words, the debit entry is the same as the credit entry. This idea is emphasized by the arrows in the two T-accounts on page 85. When you analyze a recorded transaction, always check that debits and credits are equal.

October 3 J. Emery Real Estate buys more office equipment for $1200 from the Ryan Equipment Co. on 60 days' credit.

ANALYSIS CHART

What Happens	Accounting Rule	Accounting Entry
The asset Office Equipment increases by $1200.	To increase an asset, debit the account. *Reason:* Assets increase on the side on which they appear in the accounting equation — the debit side.	Debit: Office Equipment $1200
The liability Accts. Pay./Ryan Equipment Co. increases by $1200.	To increase a liability, credit the account. *Reason:* Liabilities increase on the side on which they appear in the accounting equation — the credit side.	Credit: Accts. Pay./Ryan Equipment Co. $1200

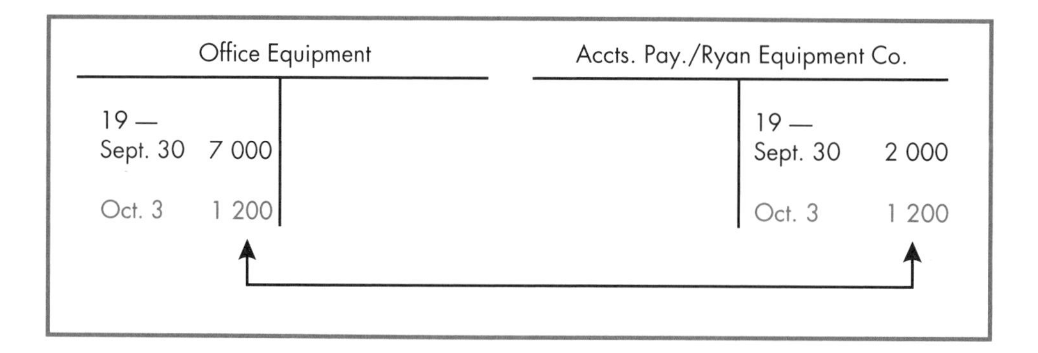

Analysis: Two different accounts are affected by this second transaction. Both the asset Office Equipment and the liability Accts. Pay./Ryan Equipment Co. increase. The Office Equipment account is debited for $1200 and the Accts. Pay./Ryan Equipment Co.

account is credited for the same amount. Again the debit dollar amount is equal to the credit dollar amount.

October 4 J. Emery Real Estate returns one calculator costing $200 to Ryan Equipment Co. because it arrived damaged. The creditor has accepted the return.

Analysis: The two accounts affected by this transaction decrease by the same amount. Since a piece of office equipment has been returned, the asset Office Equipment must be decreased by the amount of the return. And since J. Emery Real Estate no longer owes the $200 to Ryan Equipment, the liability Accts. Pay./Ryan Equipment Co. decreases by $200, as the analysis chart shows. The rule says that, to record a decrease to any liability account, the amount must be recorded on the side opposite to the one on which the element *L* appears in the accounting equation. Office Equipment is credited because all assets decrease only on the side opposite to the one on which the element *A* appears in the accounting equation.

ANALYSIS CHART

What Happens	Accounting Rule	Accounting Entry
The liability Accts. Pay./Ryan Equipment Co. decreases by $200.	To decrease a liability, debit the account. *Reason:* Liabilities decrease on the side opposite to that on which they appear in the accounting equation.	Debit: Accts. Pay./Ryan Equipment Co. $200
The asset Office Equipment decreases by $200.	To decrease an asset, credit the account. *Reason:* Assets decrease on the side opposite to that on which they appear in the accounting equation.	Credit: Office Equipment $200

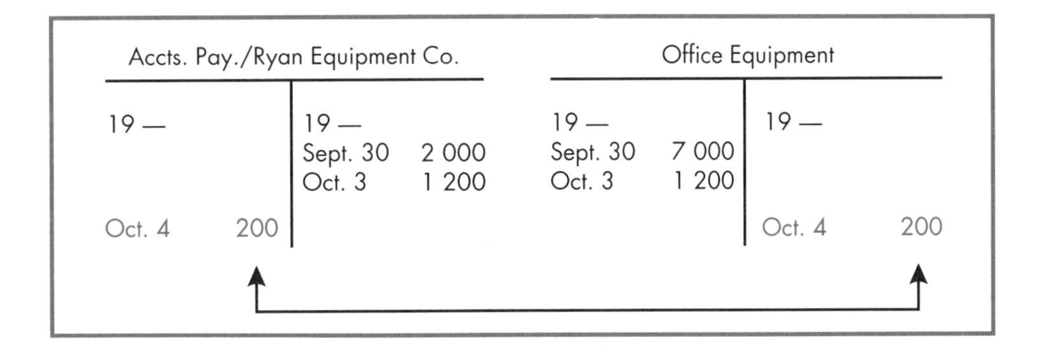

Double-entry system: the system of recording transactions now in general use in modern accounting practice: For every transaction, the debit entry or entries must equal the credit entry or entries.

Note that for the third time in a row, a business transaction has resulted in an accounting entry that debits one account and credits another with the same dollar amount. In fact, as a rule, equal debits and credits must be recorded for every business transaction. This is the double-entry system.

October 5 J. Emery Real Estate makes out a cheque for $5000 to Westown Motors Ltd.

ANALYSIS CHART

What Happens	Accounting Rule	Accounting Entry
The liability Accts. Pay./Westown Motors Ltd. decreases by $5000.	To decrease a liability, debit the account. *Reason:* Liabilities decrease on the side opposite to that on which they appear in the accounting equation.	Debit: Accts. Pay./Westown Motors Ltd. $5000
The asset Cash decreases by $5000.	To decrease an asset, credit the account. *Reason:* Assets decrease on the side opposite to that on which they appear in the accounting equation.	Credit: Cash $5000

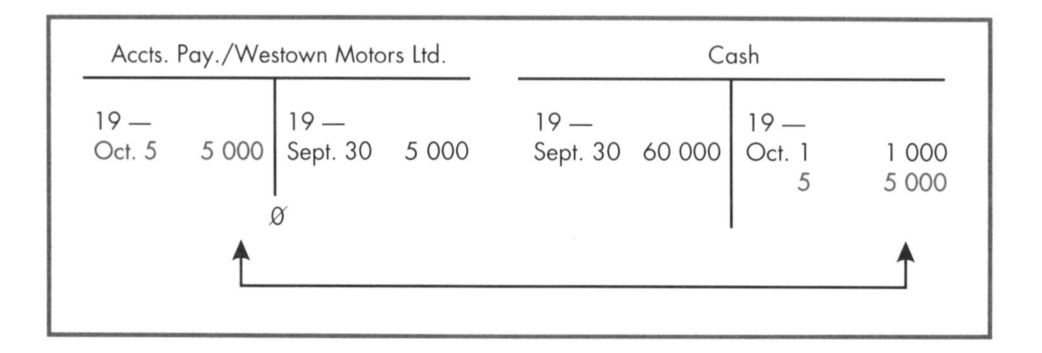

Analysis: Notice the use of the double-entry system in the record of this transaction. The total of the debit entry is equal to the total of the credit entry — $5000. Notice also the large zero with the slash, centred at the bottom under the debit to Accts. Pay./Westown Motors Ltd. It is customary to show this large "no-balance" sign in the account when the recording of an entry results in a zero balance.

October 15 J. Emery Real Estate makes out a cheque for $4000 to the Royal Bank of Canada in partial payment of the bank loan.

Analysis: You should now be able to interpret on your own the double-entry system of recording transactions in T-accounts.

ANALYSIS CHART

What Happens	Accounting Rule	Accounting Entry
The liability Bank Loan Payable decreases by $4000.	To decrease a liability, debit the account. *Reason:* Liabilities decrease on the side opposite to that on which they appear in the accounting equation.	Debit: Bank Loan Payable $4000
The asset Cash decreases by $4000.	To decrease an asset, credit the account. *Reason:* Assets decrease on the side opposite to that on which they appear in the accounting equation.	Credit: Cash $4000

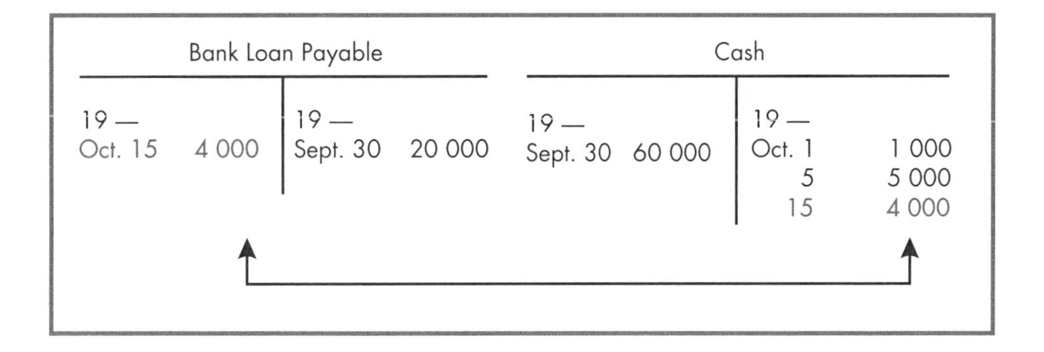

Here are three guidelines that will help you analyze business transactions in the problems that follow:

- Every transaction affects **at least** two accounts.
- If **only** two accounts are affected, the debit entry in the one account must be equal to the credit entry in the other.
- If **more than** two accounts are affected, the total debits must be equal to the total credits.

Once you have determined the accounts involved in the transaction, you can apply the basic rule for increasing and decreasing amounts.

One final point: Notice that in all transactions analyzed and recorded so far, the debit side of the entry is given first, before the credit side. It is good procedure to always think of the debit entry as coming before the credit entry.

PROBLEMS

Calculating account balances.

P 3-4 Study the following T-accounts.

Cash	
5 000	700
200	1 800
300	500
	600
	100

Accts. Rec./J. Forrester	
200	200

Supplies	
700	200

Equipment	
1 200	
1 800	

Accts. Pay./Chayka Corp.	
500	1 200
600	

Dale Green, Capital	
100	5 000
	300

a. Determine the balance for each and indicate whether it is a debit or credit by entering DR. or CR. in the appropriate space.

b. Below the T-account ledger, prove that the accounting equation is in balance, and within the ledger, by completing the totals for $A = L + OE$.

Analyzing transactions using debits and credits.

P 3-5 On a form similar to the one below, show what happens to the fundamental elements—assets or liabilities—in each transaction, and name the accounts that are involved.

Example: Purchased land for cash in the amount of $60 000.

DEBIT ENTRY		CREDIT ENTRY	
What Happens	Account Debited	What Happens	Account Credited
Assets increase	Land	Assets decrease	Cash

(i) Bought supplies for $250 cash.
(ii) Bought equipment for $1200 from XYZ Co. on account.
(iii) Bought a building costing $145 000 on a 30-year mortgage payable.
(iv) Returned $300 of the equipment bought from XYZ Co. on account.
(v) Received $450 from a customer in partial payment on an account owing.
(vi) Borrowed $10 000 from the bank by signing a demand note.
(vii) Paid $500 to XYZ Co. in partial payment of the amount owing.
(viii) The owner invested in a truck valued at $6500.

Analyzing transactions using T-accounts.

Preparing a balance sheet.

P 3-6 Challenge Problem Jennifer Pong established a sole proprietorship accounting office under her name, J. Pong, C.A. The following transactions took place.

May 1 Jennifer deposited $10 000 in personal funds into a bank account in the name of the new business.
2 She bought two used IBM XT® personal computers for the office at a total cost of $2400 from IBM Co. The terms were 30 days' credit.
3 She bought one desktop electronic calculator from Monroe Co. for $600. Issued a cheque in payment.
4 She decided that only one of the personal computers was needed for the office. Instead of returning one, she agreed to sell it at cost to a friend. The friend, R. Stevens, agreed to pay J. Pong, C.A., $1200 within 30 days. *Hint:* This transaction does not involve a sale of services. It simply eliminates the cost of one piece of office equipment.
5 She purchased one IBM Model 30® personal computer for $4000. The terms were one-half cash, the balance owing to IBM Co. on 30 days' credit.
8 She bought three more calculators for the office from Monroe Co. at a total cost of $1800. The terms allowed for 30 days' credit.
9 She returned one of the calculators bought on credit on May 8 from Monroe Co., because it was the wrong model. It had cost $600.
10 She borrowed $12 000 cash from the bank signing a demand note. This amount was deposited immediately into the business's bank account.

11 She bought a car from Westown Motors for business use. The cost was $14 000. The terms were 20% in cash and the rest on 30 days' credit.

15 She purchased desks, chairs, and tables from Office Specialty Ltd. The total cost was $6500. The terms given were 30 days' credit.

17 One of the desks purchased on May 15 proved to be defective. Jennifer returned it to Office Specialty Ltd. for a full credit of $500—the price shown on the bill made out to J. Pong, C.A.

30 She issued a cheque to IBM Co. for $2400 in full payment for the PCs bought on May 2.

30 She issued a cheque to Monroe Co. for $1200 in full settlement of the balance owing to this creditor.

31 R. Stevens paid $600 cash in part payment of the debt owing to J. Pong, C.A.

31 Jennifer purchased accounting and tax books to be used as a professional library in the business. She issued a cheque for $4000 to C.C.H. Canadian Limited for the total cost of the books.

a. Set up a T-account ledger for J. Pong, C.A., with the following accounts: Cash; Accts. Rec./R. Stevens; Office Equipment; Furniture; Automobile, Accounting Library; Bank Loan Payable; Accts. Pay./IBM Co.; Accts. Pay./Monroe Co.; Accts. Pay./Office Specialty Ltd.; Accts. Pay./Westown Motors; J. Pong, Capital.

b. Record each of the transactions by date in the T-account ledger. Use only the accounts set up for the business.

c. After you record the final transaction, calculate the balance for each account. Draw a single line across the entire account and show the balance below this line on the correct side as shown below.

Cash	
4 000	200
100	800
1 900	1 000
Balance 4 000	

d. Prepare a Summary of Account Balances as at May 31. It should prove that the accounting equation agrees with the balances of the ledger accounts.

e. The banker has asked the owner to provide a copy of the business's latest balance sheet, in support of the existing demand loan. Prepare the balance sheet in good form. Report the assets and claims against the assets as at May 31.

MINI-CASES

Analyzing an incorrect double entry.

MC 3-4 Tellerant Company's junior bookkeeper recorded the purchase of office supplies for cash in the following manner:

Cash		Accts. Rec.	
1 000		1 000	

a. Provide the correct solution for the junior bookkeeper.

b. Briefly explain how you arrived at this solution.

Studying debiting and crediting in liability accounts.

MC 3-5 A liability is an amount owing to an outside business.

a. Write three separate and complete transactions, each one for a different liability account. You may use cash in only one of the transactions. At least one of the transactions must cause the liability account to be debited and at least one of the transactions must cause the liability account to be credited.

b. Briefly explain how one determines if a liability account is to be debited or credited.

Examining debiting and crediting of asset and liability accounts.

MC 3-6 Examine the two separate transactions A and B in the T-accounts below.

Cash		Accts. Rec.		Accts. Pay.	
A 1 500	B 2 000		A 1 500	B 2 000	

a. Determine and state what kind of transaction supports each of these entries.

b. Briefly explain how the above debits and credits were determined.

TOPIC 3 RECORDING OWNER'S EQUITY CHANGES IN T-ACCOUNTS

Owner's equity is the claim of the owner against the total assets as shown in the accounting equation and as reported by the balance sheet at the end of the financial period. In Chapter 2, you learned that owner's equity may change as a result of these types of business transactions:

- additional investment by the owner of the business
- revenue
- expense
- a withdrawal of assets for the owner's personal use

An account called ''Owner's Equity'' as such does not exist in accounting. You must remember this before you use debits and credits to record changes to owner's equity. Let's review the complete accounting equation:

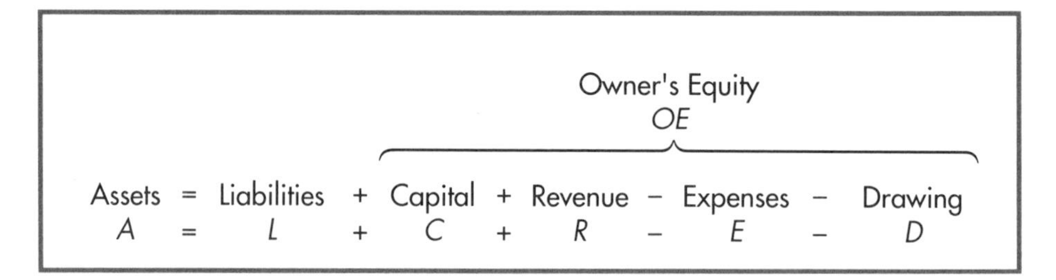

It shows four separate sections under owner's equity:

- **Capital**: the owner's investment
- **Revenue**: the inflow of cash and accounts receivable resulting from sales
- **Expenses**: the operating costs incurred in bringing revenue into the business
- **Drawing**: the withdrawal of assets for the owner's personal use

This accounting equation also shows these important facts about owner's equity:

- Capital transactions cause an increase to owner's equity (*OE*) in the accounting equation, so there is a plus sign in front of *C*.
- Revenue transactions cause an increase to *OE*, so there is a plus sign in front of *R*.

- Expense transactions cause a decrease to *OE*, so there is a minus sign in front of *E*.
- Drawing transactions cause a decrease to *OE*, so there is a minus sign in front of *D* in the equation.

It follows, therefore, that four separate accounts are needed to record those transactions that cause increases and decreases to Owner's Equity—capital, revenue, expenses, and drawing.

APPLYING DEBIT AND CREDIT RULES TO RECORD CHANGES TO OWNER'S EQUITY

The rules in Topic 2 for increasing and decreasing asset and liability accounts can also be used for recording changes to the owner's equity. But there is one more point. Since owner's equity, by itself, is not an account, you must use a separate account for each transaction that causes an increase, and a separate account for each transaction that causes a decrease, to owner's equity in the accounting equation. Study the two rules that follow.

Rule for Recording an Increase to Owner's Equity

An increase to owner's equity is recorded in the account that causes an increase to *OE* in the accounting equation, and on the side on which owner's equity is placed in the accounting equation—the credit side.

This rule says that you must first identify what item causes the increase to owner's equity. For example, an additional investment of cash by the owner causes an increase to assets on the left side of the equation. A similar increase results on the right side to owner's equity. Since the increase to owner's equity was caused by owner investment, the Capital account is used to record this increase. Because owner's equity appears on the credit (right) side of the accounting equation, the increase will be recorded on the credit side of the Capital account.

Rule for Recording a Decrease to Owner's Equity

A decrease to owner's equity is recorded in the account that decreases *OE*, and on the side opposite to the one on which owner's equity appears in the accounting equation—the debit side.

This rule follows the rule given for all accounts. To decrease any element of the accounting equation (*A, L,* or *OE*), you have to use the opposite side. In the case of owner's equity, the debit (left) side must be used.

RECORDING CAPITAL TRANSACTIONS

Perhaps the most fundamental business transaction is the initial investment of the owner in his or her business. For example, when the owner invests cash to establish a business, the Cash account is opened with a debit balance. Likewise, the owner's Capital account is opened with a credit balance. If an additional investment is made later on, an accounting entry must be made to record the increase to Owner's Equity and an increase to Cash or another asset.

October 16 Jane Emery decides to increase her investment in the business by taking $3000 from her personal savings account and depositing the cash into the business's chequing account.

ANALYSIS CHART

What Happens	Accounting Rule	Accounting Entry
The asset Cash increases by $3000.	To increase an asset, debit the account. *Reason:* Assets increase on the side on which they appear in the accounting equation.	Debit: Cash $3000
Owner's Equity in the accounting equation increases by $3000.	To increase Owner's Equity, credit the account which caused the increase. *Reason:* Owner's Equity can increase only on the side on which it appears in the accounting equation—the credit side.	Credit: J. Emery, Capital $3000

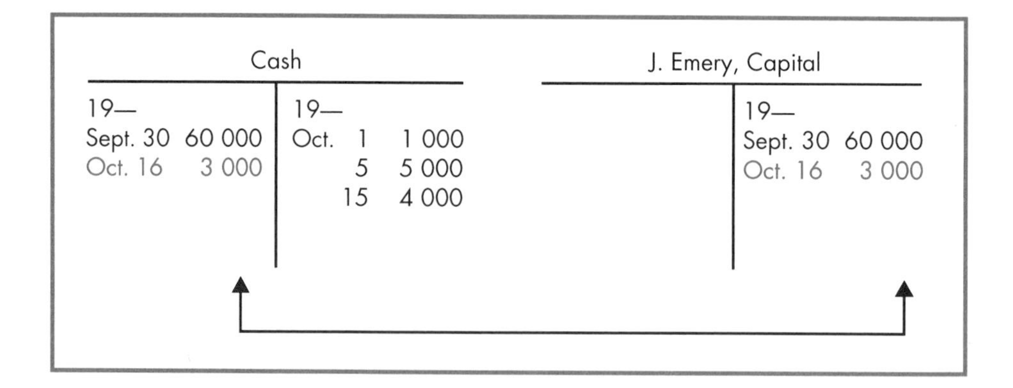

Analysis: In the double entry shown below, the asset Cash is debited for an increase of $3000. You already know that all increases to assets, shown on the left side, must be balanced by similar increases on the right side of other accounts. Since the owner has invested additional cash, that is, owner's equity, on the right side of the equation, must also increase. Under owner's equity, investment is recorded under Capital. Therefore, the increase must be recorded in the Capital account, on the credit side.

RECORDING DRAWING TRANSACTIONS

When an owner withdraws cash from the business for personal use, a subelement called Drawing is used to record the transaction.

October 30 Jane Emery withdraws $2000 from her business's bank account and deposits it into her personal chequing account.

ANALYSIS CHART

What Happens	Accounting Rule	Accounting Entry
Owner's Equity in the accounting equation decreases by $2000.	To decrease Owner's Equity, debit the account which caused the decrease. *Reason:* Owner's Equity can decrease only on the side opposite to that on which it appears in the accounting equation—the debit side.	Debit: J. Emery, Drawing $2000
The asset Cash decreases by $2000.	To decrease an asset, credit the account. *Reason:* Assets decrease on the side opposite to that on which they appear in the accounting equation—the credit side.	Credit: Cash $2000

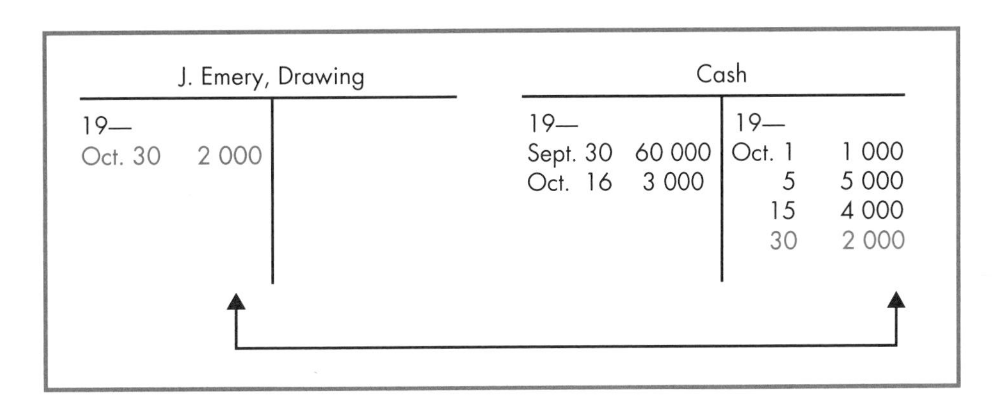

Analysis: From the chart, you can see Owner's Equity is decreased by $2000. The rule to decrease elements of the equation says to record a decrease in the account that decreases. Here, the Drawing account is used to record the decrease to owner's equity. This decrease must be recorded on the side opposite to the one on which the element is located in the equation—the debit side.

The credit entry is easy to follow because you have now analyzed many entries that decrease the Cash account.

Do not confuse the owner's withdrawals of cash for personal use with expense transactions. For example, it would be a serious accounting error to consider a monthly cash withdrawal by the owner of a business as his or her salary. True, an owner uses all or part of his or her time to carry on the business. But the owner invests money and time in the business for one reason only: to make as much income as possible. The owner's incentive is the healthy increase in his or her equity in the business that will result if the business earns a large net income. All of the owner's ''salaries'' must be accounted for as a debit to his or her Drawing account.

Watch out for other kinds of transactions dealing with personal withdrawals by the owner. For example, an owner of a business may issue a cheque to pay a **home** telephone bill. In this case, again, the owner's Drawing account must be used to show a decrease to owner's equity. Of course, a credit to Cash would be made to record the decrease to the Asset account. It would be a serious error to debit an expense account — for example, Telephone Expense — since this account only records **business** expenses.

RECORDING REVENUE TRANSACTIONS

As you will recall, revenue is the inflow of cash and accounts receivable that result from the sale of goods or services. It causes an increase in owner's equity in the accounting equation. To record this increase in a ledger, a revenue account must be credited.

October 31 J. Emery Real Estate has received $26 800 cash for buying and selling homes, land, and other forms of real estate for a variety of clients.

ANALYSIS CHART

What Happens	Accounting Rule	Accounting Entry
The asset Cash increases by $26 800.	To increase an asset, debit the account. *Reason:* Assets increase on the side on which they appear in the accounting equation.	Debit: Cash $26 800
Owner's Equity in the accounting equation increases by $26 800.	To increase Owner's Equity, credit the account which caused the increase. *Reason:* Owner's Equity can increase only on the side on which it appears in the accounting equation — the credit side.	Credit: Commissions Earned $26 800

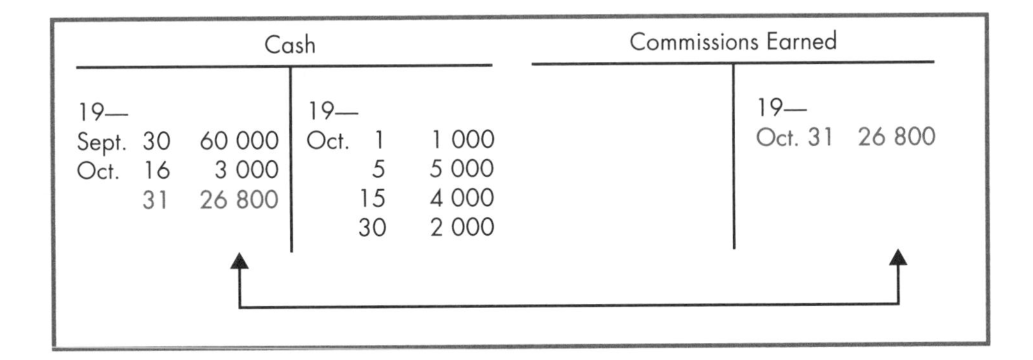

Analysis: As explained in Chapter 2, the name of the revenue account depends on the nature of the business's operations. Since a real estate broker earns revenue by charging a commission, the revenue account would usually be called "Commissions Earned," as it is here. Dentists, lawyers, doctors, accountants, and other professionals charge a fee for their services, so it is common to see a revenue account called "Professional Fees Earned," or Fees Earned. Retail stores sell goods, and the revenue account is usually called "Sales Revenue" or Sales.

October 31 J. Emery Real Estate earned commissions on credit by providing real estate services as follows: $6000 for selling a building for Pat Rogers; $4000 for selling a residence for R. Scobie; $15 000 for buying properties for Shannon Development Co. All clients were given 30 days in which to pay.

Analysis: The credit to the revenue account Commissions Earned should be easy to follow. Observe carefully the debits to each of the three customer accounts. Obviously, the total of the three debits must be equal to the one credit to the revenue account.

ANALYSIS CHART

What Happens	Accounting Rule	Accounting Entry
Three assets increase as follows: Accts. Rec./Pat Rogers by $6000; Accts. Rec./R. Scobie by $4000; Accts. Rec./Shannon Development Co. by $15 000	To increase assets, debit the separate accounts involved.	Debit: Accts. Rec./Pat Rogers $6000 Accts. Rec./R. Scobie $4000 Accts. Rec./Shannon Development Co. $15 000
There is a second inflow of revenue causing an increase of $25 000 to *OE* in the accounting equation.	To increase *OE*, credit the account which caused the increase. (Here, it is revenue that caused it.)	Credit: Commissions Earned $25 000

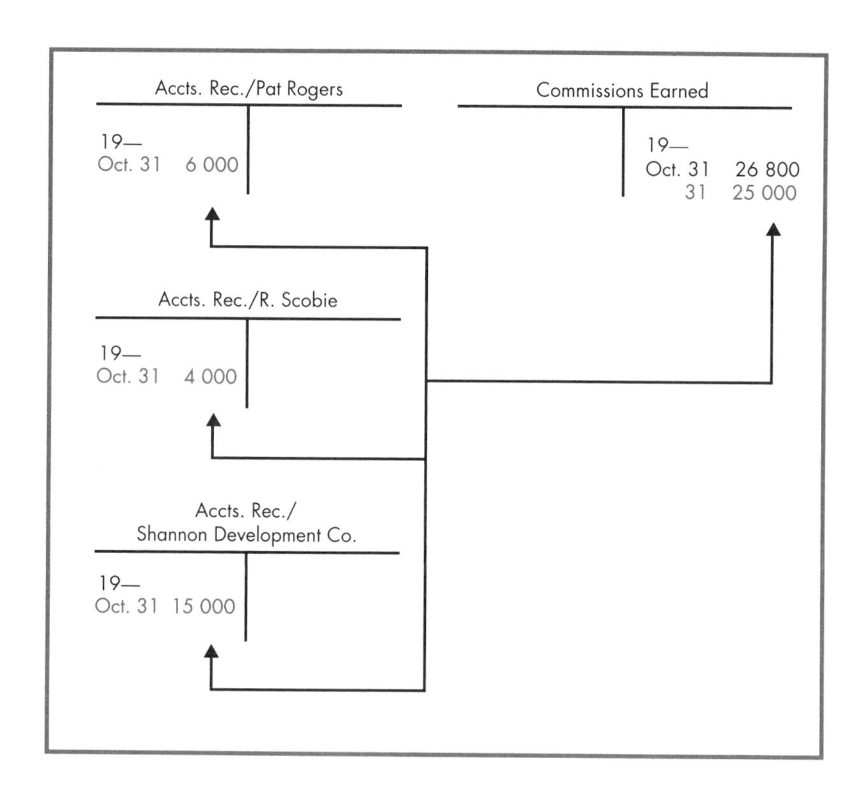

RECORDING EXPENSE TRANSACTIONS

Chapter 2 explained the nature of a business expense and how it results in a decrease to Owner's Equity in the accounting equation. This is an important point because it explains why the **debit** side of an expense account must be used to record any expense transaction. Also, expenses may be incurred because of an immediate cash payment or because of owing a sum through a liability. Study the analysis of how the next two expense transactions are recorded.

October 31 J. Emery Real Estate pays $6735 cash for the following expenses: Rent, $1600; Salaries, $4500; Utilities, $595; Telephone, $40.

ANALYSIS CHART

What Happens	Accounting Rule	Accounting Entry
Four expenses are incurred. These cause *OE* in the accounting equation to decrease by their sum.	To decrease Owner's Equity, record the amount in the account that caused the decrease, on the side opposite to that on which *OE* is placed in the accounting equation.	Debit: Rent Expense $1600 Salaries Expense $4500 Utilities Expense $595 Telephone Expense $40
The asset Cash decreases by the sum of the expenses, $6735.	To decrease an asset, credit the account.	Credit: Cash $6735

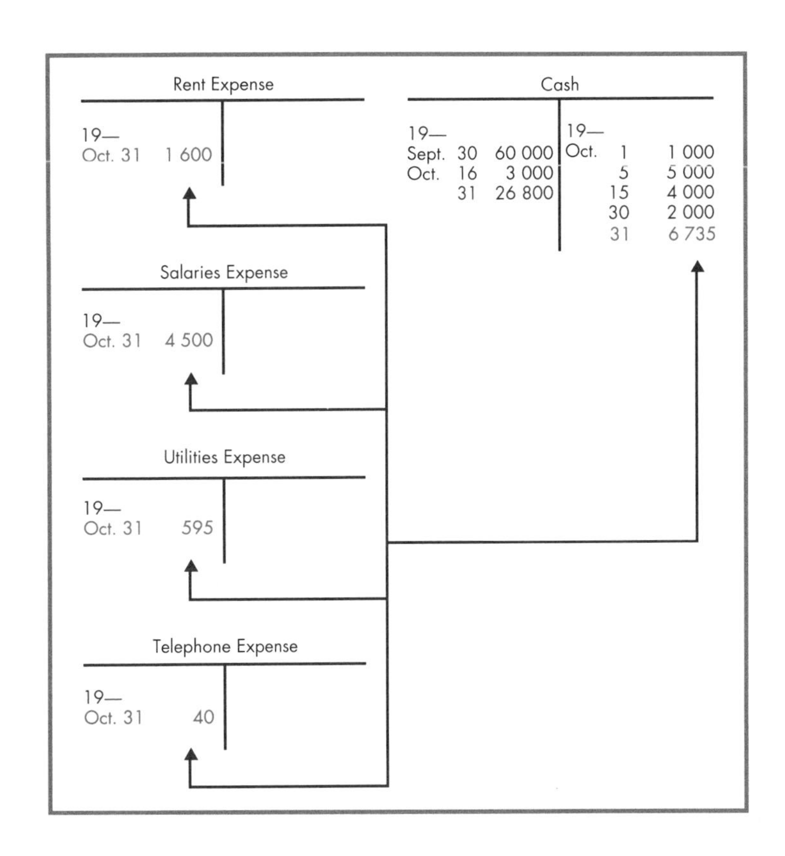

Analysis: Notice that a separate expense account describing the cost used up is shown. A separate expense account gives better information to the owner, who must make sure that those costs do not get too high. Notice also that the total of the debits equals the one credit.

October 31 J. Emery Real Estate receives a bill for $2000 from *The City Record,* a local newspaper, for the running of three advertisements at different times during October. The bill allows the business a period of 30 days in which to pay.

ANALYSIS CHART

What Happens	Accounting Rule	Accounting Entry
An expense for advertising is incurred. This expense decreases Owner's Equity by $2000 in the accounting equation.	To decrease Owner's Equity, debit the account which caused the decrease. *Reason:* Owner's Equity can decrease only on the side opposite to that on which *OE* appears in the accounting equation—the debit side.	Debit: Advertising Expense $2000
The liability Accts. Pay./The City Record increases by $2000 in the accounting equation.	To increase a liability, credit the account. *Reason:* Liabilities appear on the right side of the equation. Thus, the increase side is the credit side.	Credit: Accts. Pay./The City Record $2000

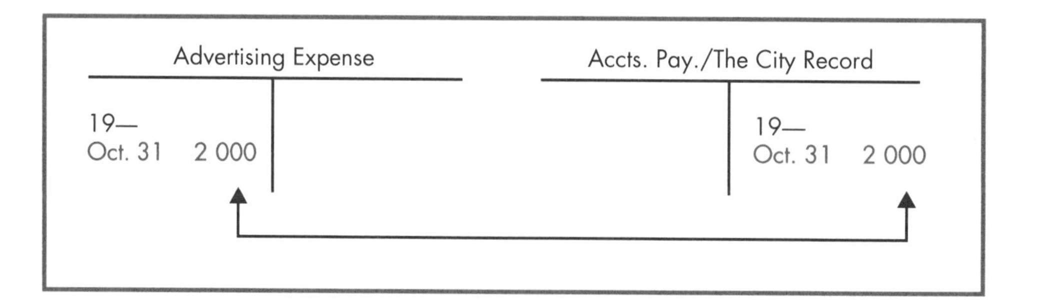

Analysis: Once again a separate expense account is required to describe the cost used up. This time, however, the business has been given 30 days in which to pay, requiring an increase in a liability account, Accts. Pay./The City Record. Notice the importance of recording this expense in October, even though no cash is paid out as yet, in order that the business complies with the matching principle mentioned in Chapter 2.

PROBLEMS

Analyzing transactions using debits and credits.

P 3-7 Refer to Problem 2-5. Set up a separate T-account for each of the eleven transactions shown for Bojkovsky Tree Service. Use an account called "Tree Service Revenue" for all transactions involving the sale of services. Always show the debit entry on the left side.

Analyzing transactions using debits and credits.

Proving the balance.

P 3-8 Refer to Problem 2-9 (Egyed Book Binders).

a. Set up the following T-account ledger for Egyed Book Binders: Cash; Accts. Rec./Chamber of Commerce; Accts. Rec./Lambton College; Accts. Rec./Lambton County Board of Education; Accts. Rec./Shell Canada Limited; Land; Building; Binding Equipment; Office Equipment; Bank Loan Payable (Truck); Accts. Pay./Taylor Supplies; Accts. Pay./Thorne Industries; Accts. Pay./Watertown Motors; D. Egyed, Capital; D. Egyed, Drawing; Hard-Cover Binding Revenue; Soft-Cover Binding Revenue; Spiral Binding Revenue; Binding Supplies Expense; Insurance Expense; Utilities Expense; Telephone Expense; Salaries Expense; Heat Expense; Gas and Oil Expense.

b. Record the transactions for May in the T-accounts established for Egyed Book Binders. Use only the accounts set up in **a** above. Show the date of each transaction in the appropriate accounts.

c. Calculate and show the balance on the correct side of the account at the close of business on May 31.

Preparing opening balances.

Analyzing transactions using debits and credits.

Calculating account balances.

Preparing an income statement and related balance sheet.

P 3-9 Challenge Problem On September 1, Elina Li began the Triple M Real Estate Co. with the following assets and liabilities: Cash, $10 000; Office Supplies, $800; Furniture, $6000; Office Equipment, $2500; Bank Loan Payable (on demand), $7000; Accts. Pay./Global Office Supplies, $1500.

a. Set up the T-account ledger for Triple M Real Estate.

b. Record the opening balances in the appropriate accounts. Check the total debits and credits of these accounts to prove that the equation is in balance as at September 1. *Hint:* One element must be calculated.

c. Record the following transactions in September in the T-accounts established for Triple M Real Estate. Identify each transaction by date.

Sept. 2 Elina Li made an additional investment of $8000 in the business.
2 She bought a car from Willard Motors Ltd. She paid $500 down, and balance of $9500 is to be paid in 90 days.
3 She bought a new computer for the office from C. & C. Computers for $2400 on 60 days' credit.
4 E. Li sold a home for Shelley MacIntosh. She paid a selling commission to E. Li of $1350 cash.
5 She paid $2800 cash for rent.
6 She sold a piece of land for G. Da Silva. The commission amounted to $435. The invoice allowed credit terms of 30 days.
8 She paid $60 for newspaper advertising in the local paper.
10 She bought a new home for R. Carlisle. The client paid the commission of $2125 in full.
11 She sold a home for E. Liberi. The commission of $3390 was paid in full.
12 E. Li made a partial payment of $1000 on the bank loan.
14 The business paid $1500 to Global Office Supplies in full.
15 She received $50 on account from G. Da Silva.
17 She paid the heat expense for the business in cash, $210.
19 She bought office space for V. J. Plumbers Ltd. The commission totalled $1550. V. J. Plumbers Ltd. was allowed 30 days to pay.
23 She paid the utilities bill for $380 with cash.
24 She bought a home for Gordon Wilson. Mr. Wilson paid the commission in full, $3330.
25 She paid $45 cash for additional office supplies.
30 She paid the monthly salaries of the business's three employees. Each employee received $1200. The employees were paid by cheque.
30 She bought warehouse space for Samson Hardware Ltd. Payment of the commission of $1670 was made in full.
30 E. Li paid herself a salary of $1700.
30 She bought a condominium for Mrs. Richards, who paid the business immediately with a cheque for $6900.
30 She received $1000 rental revenue from Fernando Leone. Fernando sublets the top floor of the building that Triple M Real Estate Co. rents.

d. Calculate the balance of each account at the close of business on September 30. Show each balance on the correct side of the account.

e. Prepare a Summary of the Ledger Account Balances as at September 30 to prove that the accounting equation is in balance with the ledger.

f. From the Summary, prepare an income statement for the month of September.

g. From the Summary and the result of the income statement, prepare a balance sheet in good form as at September 30.

MINI-CASES

Analyzing the debiting and crediting of owner's equity.

MC 3-7 Jordan and Martin were discussing the following transaction: J. Grassi, the owner of T. & J. Comp., received the monthly business telephone bill, $45. J. Grassi decided to write one cheque on the bank account of the business to pay the business and his personal telephone bill, $18. Jordan thinks the entry should use the Cash account and the Telephone Expense account. Martin thinks that the owner should not make any entry because the owner is paying his personal telephone bill.

a Is either student's opinion correct?

b. What factors determine which accounts should be used in this transaction?

c. What rules determine the debits and credits in this transaction?

d. Record in T-account format the correct entry.

Analyzing the debiting and crediting of owner's equity.

MC 3-8 Refer to Mini-Case 3-7, but assume that J. Grassi paid the business and personal telephone bills with a single cheque written against his personal account.

a Is either student's opinion correct?

b. What factors determine which accounts should be used in this transaction?

c. What rules determine the debits and credits in this transaction?

d. Record in T-account format the correct entry.

Explaining the debiting and crediting of revenue accounts.

MC 3-9 Marilyn Hutnik operates a consulting business and uses one revenue account called Consulting Fees Earned. The new bookkeeper is uncertain as to how to record revenue transactions.

a. Explain the rules for debiting and crediting revenue accounts.

b. Prepare two typical narrative transactions that would involve this revenue account. *Note:* Prepare one for cash, and one on account.

COMPREHENSIVE CASE STUDY 3

The owner of Brown Consulting Services—a single proprietorship—seeks your help to prepare a year-end income statement which will be included in the owner's personal income tax return. You learn the following facts through an examination of the business's ledger.

(i) The total sales for the year amount to $125 000.

(ii) The total expenses charged against the business amount to $100 000.

(iii) Among the expenses, the Owner's Salary Expense account showed a debit balance of $24 000. You find that the owner paid himself a monthly salary of $2000.

(iv) An analysis of the Telephone Expense account revealed a debit balance of $360. Of this amount, only $200 represented the actual business expense; the remainder represented the payment of all telephone bills for the owner's home.

(v) One expense account, called Golf and Country Club Expense, showed a debit balance of $2000. This amount represented the owner's yearly dues to a private golf club in the community.

Preparing a condensed income statement.

a. Prepare a condensed income statement showing total revenue, total expenses, and the net income that should be reported for income tax purposes.

Making suggestions for improved accounting practices.

b. What suggestions would you offer in the proper accounting of the owner's personal expenses? How would you explain your recommendations to the owner?

CHAPTER 4

IDENTIFYING THE BOOKKEEPING BASE OF ACCOUNTING

At this point you are ready to learn how to perform accounting in a more organized way so that you can prepare financial statements easily and accurately at the end of each accounting period. This organized way of accounting is a series of steps known as the accounting cycle

Accounting cycle: the complete sequence of accounting activities repeated in every accounting period.

In this chapter, you will be shown the first four steps of the accounting cycle.

TOPIC 1 ORIGINATING TRANSACTION DATA

Accountants cannot make a record of any financial event unless there is tangible and objective proof that a business transaction has taken place. To understand the meaning of "objectivity," think of the word "object." An object is something you can see. When you can see something, you know it is real. Accountants then record business transactions given information in objects called "source documents," on the basis of the objectivity principle:

Objectivity principle: accounting data should be verifiable.

All accounting transactions must be supported by business papers called source documents.

Source documents: business forms (papers) that give evidence of business transactions on a certain date.

Four common source documents are the opening balance sheet, invoice, cheque record, and remittance slip.

The First Balance Sheet When a business is established, the details of assets, liabilities, and owner's equity are presented in the **first balance sheet**. This becomes the source document as at the date when the owner begins his or her business. Of course, this date is the one reported in the heading of the balance sheet. Then a T-account is opened for each asset and liability, and also for the owner's Capital account as at the opening balance sheet date.

Handwritten Sales Slip

The Invoice When a business buys an asset either with cash or on credit, the seller completes a bill of sale often called the sales invoice or simply the **invoice**.

The name of the document varies according to the type of each business. The bill of sale may be called an invoice, a sales slip, a sales ticket, or a cash register tape. Regardless of its name, the buyer will receive the original, which becomes the source document for the transaction.

For example, when J. Emery Real Estate bought additional office equipment costing $1200 from the Ryan Equipment Co. on 60 days' credit, the company issued a document known as an invoice, as illustrated.

HYDE PARK HARDWARE
482-3310

00 00.50 HD

00 00.04 TX

00 00.54

THANK YOU

4654 13 JUN 90

Cash Register Tape

RYAN EQUIPMENT CO.
379 KING STREET
KITCHENER, ONTARIO N2G 1G6

INVOICE
No. 04879

SOLD TO:
J. Emery Real Estate
Any Street
Any Town, Canada

INVOICE DATE: 19– 10 03
TERMS: Net, 60 days
SHIPPED VIA: Truck

SHIP TO:
Same

QUANTITY	DESCRIPTION	UNIT PRICE	AMOUNT
2	Electronic Printing Calculators, Model 15X, Serial Numbers 487876 and 787877	$200.00	$400.00
1	Electronic Typewriter, Model AC5, Serial Number 878994	800.00	800.00
	Total Amount Payable		$1 200.00

Purchase invoice: a copy of an invoice, received by the buyer, to give evidence of the purchase made.

Sales invoice: a source document that gives evidence of a sale.

This invoice is called the purchase invoice by the buyer, because he or she receives the original for buying the asset. An accounting copy of the invoice is kept by the seller and becomes the source document for the sale—that is, it proves in the seller's books that a sale occurred. The seller's name for it is the sales invoice. A good way to remember the difference between the terms "sales invoice" and "purchase invoice" is to follow the arrows in the diagram below. *Remember*: The two are the same document—the invoice—looked at from two different points of view—the seller's and the buyer's.

The invoice can also be used to originate a sale of services. A telephone bill is a good example. For the user of telephone services, the telephone bill is the source document for proving the telephone expense transaction. For the telephone company—the seller of these services—a copy of the source document becomes the sales invoice, allowing the revenue earned to be recorded for the period.

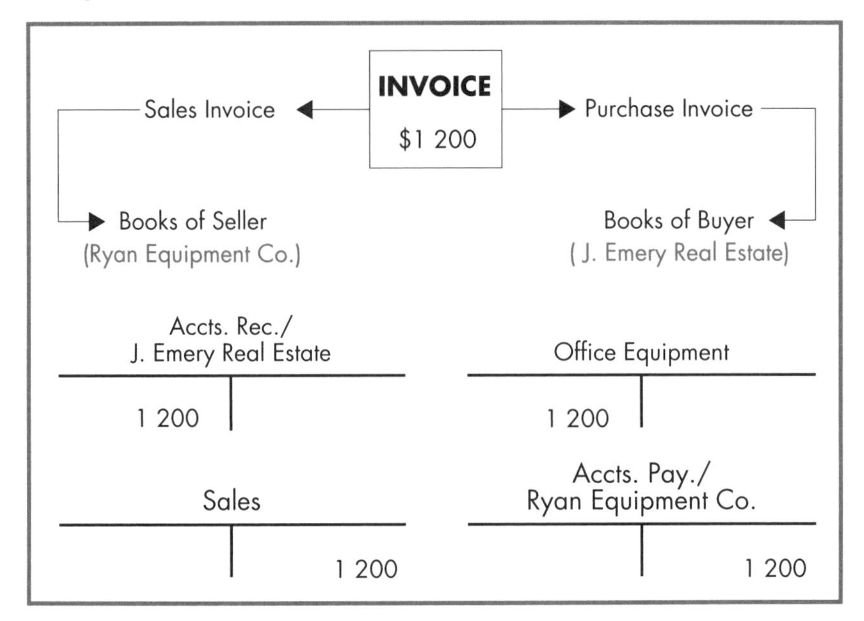

The Cheque Record Many businesses use a **cheque record** as evidence of each cash payment. It may take many forms: one is the cheque stub. Study the stub and the attached cheque shown below, along with the telephone bill illustrated on the opposite page. The cheque is in payment of the telephone bill for October.

In this example, J. Emery Real Estate has two documents proving that a cash payment occurred. The cheque stub is the main source document, and the bill marked ''Paid'' becomes a supporting source document. With this objective evidence, the accountant can record the result of the transaction by debiting the Telephone Expense account, and crediting the Cash account, for the amount shown on the cheque record.

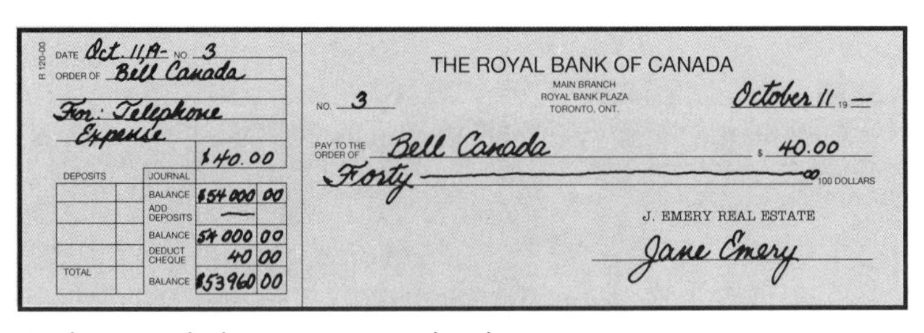

Cheque stub: kept by buyer as a record of the cash payment.

Completed cheque: sent to the seller of services (Bell Canada).

Bell Member of Telecom Canada

TELEPHONE NUMBER	DATE	AMOUNT DUE	AMOUNT PAID
709 555 1212	1989 11 10	40.00	40.00

6555 1212 12301 006

0 123 xxxx 1 90 90

PLEASE DETACH AND
RETURN – DO NOT STAPLE

J. EMERY REAL ESTATE
123 ANY STREET
ANYTOWN, CDN M4B 1E4

065353512125320001233911100000410000000000051964

* * * DETACH HERE * * *

INQUIRIES DIAL '0'

PAGE	TELEPHONE NUMBER	DATE
1	709 555 1212	19-- 10 10

* * * ACCOUNT SUMMARY * * *

	SERVICES		30.00
	EQUIPMENT RENTALS		6.45
	TAX – FED.	1.54	
	TAX – PROV.	3.37	4.91
	OTHER CHARGES OR CREDITS		
	TAX – FED.		
	TAX – PROV.		
	CHARGEABLE MESSAGES		
PREVIOUS BALANCE	TAX – FED.		
	TAX – PROV.		
PAYMENTS	LATE PAYMENT CHARGE		
ADJUSTMENTS	DIRECTORY ADVERTISING		
BALANCE FORWARD	+ TOTAL CURRENT CHARGES		40.00
	= AMOUNT DUE		40.00

PLEASE PAY THIS AMOUNT UPON RECEIPT

PAYMENTS AND ADJUSTMENTS PROCESSED AFTER
19-- 10 10 WILL BE REFLECTED ON YOUR NEXT ACCOUNT

Paid
Oct. 11
Cheque
No. 3

THE LATE PAYMENT CHARGE RATE OF INTEREST IS 1.75% MONTHLY
(23.14% PER ANNUM)

Bell See reverse for more information

Bill: marked "Paid" with cheque number and date.

Remittance slip: a source document proving the receipt of a customer's cheque.

The Remittance Slip When a customer pays a debt by cheque, many businesses prepare a business form called the remittance slip. The slip becomes the source document for the record of the dollar amount received. The document may also be called a receipt.

J. EMERY REAL ESTATE
Any Street
Any Town, Canada

Account Copy
Payment Receipt No. 001

Name Pat Rogers
100 Main Street
Yourtown, Canada

Date Nov. 1 19–

CASH ☐
CHEQUE ☑
MONEY ORDER ☐

Received Payment on Account.

Clerk A.B.

Amount Received: $500.00

The remittance slip above would be prepared **before** the customer's cheque is deposited into J. Emery Real Estate's bank account. This is important, because accounting requires evidence that a cheque has been received. Once prepared, the remittance slip becomes the source document for analyzing and recording a debit to Cash and a credit to Accts. Rec./Pat Rogers for the amount of the cheque ($500 in this case).

The chart below summarizes the source documents identified for the transactions of J. Emery Real Estate during October.

Transaction	Source Document
Oct. 1 J. Emery Real Estate buys additional furniture for $1000 from Enns Furniture Ltd., and pays by cheque.	1. Cheque stub 2. Invoice from Enns Furniture Ltd. (marked *Paid* with cheque number and date)
Oct. 3 J. Emery Real Estate buys additional office equipment costing $1200 from the Ryan Equipment Co. on 60 days' credit.	Invoice from Office Equipment Co. (which becomes the purchase invoice)
Oct. 4 J. Emery Real Estate returns one piece of office equipment, a calculator, costing $200 to Ryan Equipment Co. because the equipment arrived in damaged condition. The creditor accepts the return.	1. Copy of letter (a note to the creditor) stating the details of the return of the equipment 2. The creditor usually mails a note after receiving the returned goods. The note is attached to the source document above.
Oct. 5 J. Emery Real Estate writes out a cheque for $5000 to Westown Motors Ltd.	Cheque stub
Oct. 15 J. Emery Real Estate writes out a cheque for $4000 to the Royal Bank of Canada in part payment of the bank loan payable.	Cheque stub

(Continued.)

Oct. 16 Jane Emery decides to increase her investment in the business by taking $3000 from her personal savings account and depositing the cash into the firm's chequing account.	1. Note called a *memorandum* (or *memo*), which is usually prepared to identify the additional investment 2. Copy of the deposit slip, which shows the amount invested in the firm's bank account
Oct. 30 Jane Emery withdraws $2000 from her firm's bank account and deposits it into her personal chequing account.	Cheque stub
Oct. 31 J. Emery Real Estate has received $26 800 cash for buying and selling homes, land, and other forms of real estate for a variety of clients.	1. Copies of the individual sales invoices (sales slips) totalling $26 800 for commissions earned 2. Copy of a deposit slip showing the total cash received, $26 800, deposited into the firm's bank account
Oct. 31 J. Emery Real Estate earned commissions on credit by providing real estate services as follows: $6000 for selling a building for Pat Rogers; $4000 for selling a residence for R. Scobie; $15 000 for buying properties for Shannon Development Co. All clients were given 30 days to pay the commissions.	Copies of the invoices (totalling $25 000) made out to these customers.

PROBLEMS

Examining and analyzing an invoice.

P 4-1 Study the invoice on the next page. Then answer the questions.

a. Who is the seller?

b. Who is the buyer?

c. Who prepared the source document?

d. How do you know whether the invoice gives evidence of a credit sale?

e. What was sold to the buyer?

f. Why is an invoice number an important feature of every invoice?

g. How was the amount owing calculated?

h. By what date must the buyer pay the amount owing?

i. What amount will be charged if the buyer does not pay according to the terms given in the invoice?

j. In one sentence, describe the transaction from the viewpoint of the seller.

J. EMERY REAL ESTATE
MEMBER BROKER
Any Street
Any Town, Canada
Telephone: 471-8622

INVOICE NO. 00007
INVOICE DATE: October 31, 19 –
TERMS: Net 30 days

Pat Rogers
68 Central Avenue
Yourtown, Canada

For the following services rendered:		Amount
Oct. 30/ --	Sold building located at 40 Main Street West, under your name, for $120 000	
Commission:	5% of the amount equal to the sales price	$6 000.00
	Please Pay This Amount	$6 000.00

When Remitting: Please indicate Invoice No. on reverse of your cheque.
Interest will be charged at 2% per month on overdue accounts (after 30 days from Invoice Date).

k. Show the double entry by using T-accounts that would be made in the seller's books.

l. In one sentence, describe the transaction from the viewpoint of the buyer.

m. Show the double entry by using T-accounts that would be made in the buyer's books. *Hint:* An expense account must be debited.

Identifying source documents.

P 4-2 Refer to Problem 3-6 (J. Pong, C.A.). For each of the business transactions outlined for J. Pong, C.A., name a source document, and a supporting document, if necessary. Use a form similar to the one below.

Date	Transaction	Source Document

Identifying source documents.

P 4-3 Refer to Problem 3-9 (Triple M Real Estate Co.). For each of the business transactions outlined for Triple M Real Estate Co., name a source document. Also suggest any supporting document where needed. Use a form similar to the one used for Problem 4-2.

MINI-CASES

Examining a GAAP and how it relates to transaction data.

MC 4-1 Walter Koenig recently obtained a part-time job with a small local business. One of Walter's new functions is to do simple bookkeeping entries. Walter has never taken any accounting courses and he has asked you to assist him in understanding the documents that he has been given in order to prepare the bookkeeping entries. He has been given ten invoices and a remittance slip.

a. In general, what is the one term that would be given to these documents?

b. What GAAP supports the use of these documents? Briefly explain the meaning of this term.

c. List three other documents that would be commonly used in business.

Listing the information found in a sales invoice.

Developing the format for an invoice.

MC 4-2 You have been asked by your employer to design a sales invoice for the company. The company specializes in decorating fancy cookies and cake products. The terms offered to clients are net 30 days.

a. Make a list of the points that should be included on the invoice.

b. Prepare a rough layout of what the actual invoice might look like.

c. What GAAP supports the use of this document? Briefly explain the meaning of this term.

Analyzing the paper flow involved in a business transaction.

MC 4-3 The owner of Holiday Sports Suppliers would like to know what source documents are involved in a complete transaction from the time an item is ordered, paid for, sold, and the funds collected and banked.

a. List the source documents involved in the situation described above.

b. Briefly describe the function of each of these documents.

c. What GAAP supports the use of these documents? Briefly explain the meaning of this term.

JOURNALIZING TRANSACTION DATA

In Chapter 3, you learned how to record the debits and credits for each business transaction directly in a T-account ledger. All business transactions could be recorded in accounts, but there are several disadvantages to recording debits and credits only in the ledger.

- Each transaction has a debit and a credit entry. These entries would appear separately in at least two different accounts, but which ones? You would have to search the entire ledger in order to match the debit entry to a credit entry for one complete business transaction.
- The accounts do not display, in any kind of order, a listing of all the business transactions that occurred on any given day. Again, you would have to search through all the accounts to discover how many business transactions occurred on a given day.
- If an error were made in the debit or credit entry, the error would be difficult to locate quickly because the double entry has been recorded into two or more accounts.

Journal: a daily record of business transactions in debit and credit form; a book of original entry.

To overcome these disadvantages, many accounting systems make an accounting record known as the **journal** before the debits and credits are entered into the ledger accounts. The journal is like a diary: it shows, for each day, the debits and credits analyzed from the source documents. The debits and credits can later be transferred to individual ledger accounts. Under this system, the debit and credit entries appear for the first time, in date order, in the journal. The journal is also known as the **book of original entry**.

Before we examine how transactions are recorded in a journal, the following points should be considered.

General Journal: a two-column journal.

Journalizing: the process of analyzing transactions into debits and credits, and recording the results in a journal.

- There are many different kinds of journals. One is the two-column form called the General Journal. This is a simple way of journalizing—analyzing a transaction and recording the debits and credits in the journal.
- Journalizing does not require any additional (new) knowledge of how to debit and credit accounts.

You will learn how to record journal entries manually, then in an electronic spreadsheet, and finally by using a General Ledger accounting package in Chapter 6. Generally, journalizing is done either manually or on a computer using a General Ledger accounting package. We will begin by journalizing manually because it is easier to learn. In fact, the practice of recording transactions manually in some journals persists even in some large businesses that use computers.

For most business transactions to be recorded in the journal, one or more source documents provide the accounting data. Journalizing, therefore, follows taking information from source documents and is the second step in the accounting cycle.

JOURNALIZING: AN ILLUSTRATION

Suppose that, on November 3, a business bought two desks costing $300 each from Wood Company on 30 days' credit. In journalizing this transaction, follow these steps:

Step 1 Analyze the effects of the transaction in the usual way, but this time try to think of the debit entry before the credit entry. (To review the rules for debiting and crediting accounts, go back to Chapter 3.) The T-account analysis follows:

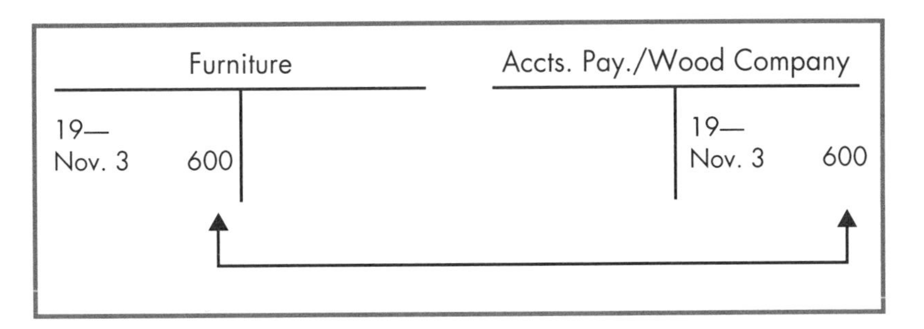

Step 2 Study the General Journal page illustrated below.

All journal sheets are numbered consecutively. In this illustration, "page 10" appears on the top line of the journal, because earlier transactions were recorded on previous pages.

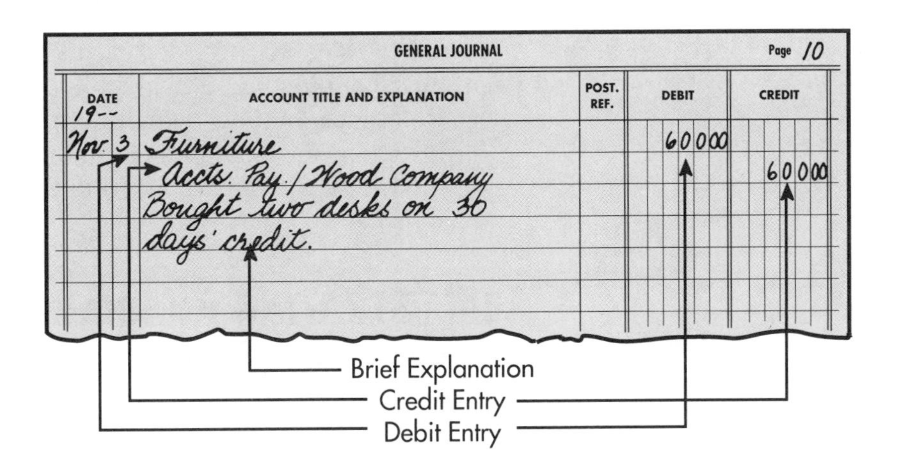

The year and month are written at the top of every journal page.

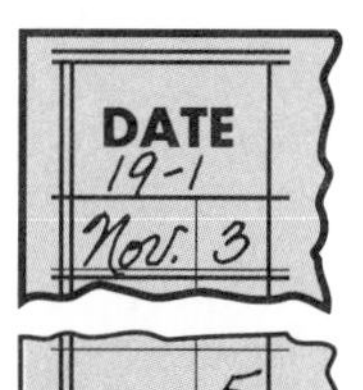

Only the day of the month is recorded for the next transaction on the same journal page.

When the month changes on the same journal page, the new month is written.

When the year changes on the same journal page, the new year and month are written.

Next, record the date of the transaction in the Date column. When you begin a page of the journal, indicate the year in the date column, below the heading. You will probably want to abbreviate the date because space is limited. Enter it into the left side of the date column and write the day of the month of the transaction on the right side.

For subsequent transactions, only the day of the month is recorded. The month and year are repeated only at the top of a new page, or when either the month or the year changes, as illustrated in the margin.

Step 3 Write the title of the account to be debited in the Account Title and Explanation column. Then carefully enter the debit amount in the debit column (the left-hand money column). Notice that the dollar sign has been omitted. It is only in the income statement, the balance sheet, and other formal financial reports that dollar signs appear. The journal is not a **formal** financial statement.

Step 4 On the line below the debit entry, indent about 1.5 cm from the date column and write the title of the account to be credited. The reason for indenting is simply to make it easier to distinguish the credit entry from the debit entry. It may remind you to indent if you remember that credit means ''to the right.'' Then enter the amount in the credit column (the right-hand money column).

Step 5 Finally, on the line below the credit entry in the Account Title and Explanation column, record an explanation of the transaction. In the example, the account title for the debit entry does not explain what type of furniture was acquired; however, a short, clear explanation is shown. In addition, many accountants like to see an identification of the source documents involved.

The Posting Reference Column A narrow column to the left of the debit column is identified with Post. Ref. This is the Posting Reference column, which is **not** used in the journalizing procedure. Rather, this column is used in **posting** (transferring) data to the ledger, which will be explained in the next topic.

ILLUSTRATING JOURNAL ENTRIES

To illustrate how a set of journal entries is recorded in a two-column General Journal, the earlier transactions for J. Emery Real Estate are first presented by date, transaction, and source document as follows:

Date		Transaction	Source Document
19—			
Sept.	30	Jane Emery began the firm J. Emery Real Estate with the following assets and liabilities: Cash, $60 000; Automobile, $15 000; Furniture, $8000; Office Equipment, $7000; Bank Loan Payable, $20 000; Accts. Pay./Bell Furniture Co., $3000; Accts. Pay./Ryan Equipment Co., $2000; Accts. Pay./Westown Motors Ltd., $5000. The opening balance sheet was prepared.	Opening balance sheet as at Sept. 30.
Oct.	1	J. Emery Real Estate buys more furniture for $1000 from Enns Furniture Ltd., and issues Cheque No. 1 in payment.	Cheque record; purchase invoice marked *Paid*
	3	J. Emery Real Estate buys more office equipment—two calculators and one typewriter—costing $1200 from the Ryan Equipment Co. on 60 days' credit.	Purchase invoice
	4	J. Emery Real Estate returns one calculator costing $200 to Ryan Equipment Co. because the equipment arrived in damaged condition. The creditor has accepted the return.	Copy of letter, note, or return slip
	5	J. Emery Real Estate makes out Cheque No. 2 for $5000 to Westown Motors Ltd.	Cheque record
	11	Cheque No. 3 is issued in payment of a business telephone bill for $40.	Cheque record
	12	Cheque No. 4 is issued in payment of the monthly rent, $1600.	Cheque record; landlord's bill marked *Paid*
	15	Cheque No. 5 is issued for $4000 to the Royal Bank of Canada in part payment of the bank loan payable.	Cheque record
	16	Jane Emery decides to increase her investment by taking $3000 from her personal savings account and depositing the cash into the firm's chequing account.	Memo; copy of bank deposit slip
	18	Cheque No. 6 is issued to Public Utilities Commission, in payment of $595 utilities bill.	Cheque record; utilities bill marked *Paid*
	20	$13 400 cash is received for commissions earned buying and selling real estate. (The invoice slips are numbered 00001, 00002, 00003, and 00004.)	Individual sales invoices; copy of bank deposit slip.
	30	Cheque No. 7 in the amount of $2000 is issued to Jane Emery for personal use.	Cheque record
	31	$13 400 cash is received for commissions earned from real estate transactions. (Invoice slips 00005 and 00006.)	Individual sales invoices; copy of bank deposit slip
	31	Cheque No. 8 in the amount of $2250 is issued to clerk Wendy Thomas for monthly salary; also cheque No. 9 in the amount of $2250 to clerk Jim Trafford for monthly salary.	Individual cheque records

(Continued.)

Oct.	31	The following sales invoices are issued: No. 00007 to Pat Rogers for $6000 in commissions earned selling a building for the client; No. 00008 to R. Scobie for $4000 in commissions earned selling a residence for the client; No. 00009 to Shannon Development Co. for $15 000 in commissions earned buying properties for the client. Terms for all customers: net 30 days.	Copies of the invoices
	31	A bill for $2000 is received from *The City Record* for advertisements during the month. Terms: net 30 days.	Purchase invoice

The following points will help you to understand the entries in the General Journal for J. Emery Real Estate:

- The journal pages are numbered consecutively.
- The first column is for the date of the transaction. This date is usually taken from a source document, the date in the journal is also the date of the transaction document. If there were no source document, the date in the journal would become the date of the transaction.[1]
- A line is skipped after each entry. In a two-column journal, this spacing causes each entry to stand out clearly.

Opening entry: the first entry to establish an account.

- The first entry is known as the opening entry because it identifies the accounts that open a set of accounting records for a beginning balance sheet of the new business.

Compound entry: an entry that involves more than two accounts.

- An entry which includes more than one debit and more than one credit, such as the opening entry in the illustration, is called a compound entry. In every compound journal entry, the debits are listed before the credits, and the total of all the debits must be equal to the total of all the credits. This total is not shown in a two-column journal but should be checked mentally before the next journal entry is done.
- Only **complete** journal entries are shown on a journal page. In other words, a transaction is not recorded unless there are enough lines to journalize all of it, including the brief explanation. This is for the reader's convenience. It is better to leave a

[1]For example, an entry to correct an error in journalizing would be recorded in the General Journal without a supporting source document. The date of record is the date entered in the journal. Hence, the journal becomes the objective evidence for the correcting entry. Similarly, many adjusting entries are made without supporting source documents. Therefore, the General Journal becomes important evidence to verify the entries posted to ledger accounts.

GENERAL JOURNAL — Page

DATE 19-1		ACCOUNT TITLE AND EXPLANATION	POST. REF.	DEBIT	CREDIT
Sept.	30	Cash		60000 00	
		Automobile		15000 00	
		Furniture		8000 00	
		Office Equipment		7000 00	
		Bank Loan Payable			20000 00
		Accts. Pay./Bell Furniture Co.			3000 00
		Accts. Pay./Ryan Equipment Co.			2000 00
		Accts. Pay./Westown Motors Ltd.			5000 00
		J. Emery, Capital			60000 00
		To record the opening			
		balance sheet into accounts.			
Oct.	1	Furniture		1000 00	
		Cash			1000 00
		Cheque No. 1 to Enns Furniture			
		Ltd. for additional furniture.			
	3	Office Equipment		1200 00	
		Accts. Pay./Ryan Equipment Co.			1200 00
		2 calculators and 1 typewriter			
		on 60 day's credit.			
	4	Accts. Pay./Ryan Equipment Co.		200 00	
		Office Equipment			200 00
		Returned 1 calculator received			
		in damaged condition.			
	5	Accts. Pay./Westown Motors Ltd.		5000 00	
		Cash			5000 00
		Cheque No. 2 on account.			
	11	Telephone Expense		40 00	
		Cash			40 00
		Cheque No. 3 to Bell Canada.			

few blank lines at the bottom of a page than to use two pages to record an entry.

- Page 3 of the General Journal shows how a correction is made (page 123). The clerk simply ruled out the mistake with a single neat line and neatly inserted the correct amount in full above, with his or her initials. Thus, the reader can see the error, the correction, and who made the correction. An error is never erased.

GENERAL JOURNAL — Page 2

DATE		ACCOUNT TITLE AND EXPLANATION	POST. REF.	DEBIT	CREDIT
19-					
Oct.	12	Rent Expense		1 600 00	
		Cash			1 600 00
		Cheque No. 4 for monthly rent.			
	15	Bank Loan Payable		4 000 00	
		Cash			4 000 00
		Cheque No. 5 to The Royal Bank of Canada in part payment of demand loan.			
	16	Cash		3 000 00	
		J. Emery, Capital			3 000 00
		Additional investment.			
	18	Utilities Expense		595 00	
		Cash			595 00
		Cheque No. 6 to Public Utilities Commission.			
	20	Cash		13 400 00	
		Commissions Earned			13 400 00
		Invoices 00001, 00002, 00003, and 00004.			
	30	J. Emery, Drawing		2 000 00	
		Cash			2 000 00
		Issued Cheque No. 7 to owner for personal use.			
	31	Cash		13 400 00	
		Commissions Earned			13 400 00
		Invoices 00005 and 00006.			

EXAMINING ADVANTAGES OF THE JOURNAL

From a study of the journal entries illustrated on the pages 121 to 123, you may see the following advantages of a journal:

- The journal lists all the financial events by date. Thus, if you needed information about a transaction months or even years ago, all you would need is the date of the transaction to find it in the journal.

GENERAL JOURNAL — Page 3

DATE 19-1		ACCOUNT TITLE AND EXPLANATION	POST. REF.	DEBIT	CREDIT
Oct.	31	Salaries Expense		4 500 00	
		Cash			4 500 00
		Cheque No. 8 for $2 250 to			
		Wendy Thomas; Cheque No. 9			
		for $2 250 to Jim Trafford.			
	31	Accts. Rec./Pat Rogers		6 000 00	
		Accts. Rec./R. Scobie		4 000 00	
		Accts. Rec./Shannon Development Co.		15 000 00	25 000 00 HJK ~~24 000 00~~
		Commissions Earned			
		Sales Invoices issued as			
		follows: No. 00007 to Pat			
		Rogers; No. 00008 to			
		R. Scobie; No. 00009 to			
		Shannon Development			
		Co. Terms on all			
		invoices: 30 days.			
	31	Advertising Expense		2 000 00	
		Accts. Pay./The City Record			2 000 00
		Advertising bill, terms given: net 30 days			

- Since the journal provides a record of all transactions in date order, you can compare the volume of transactions from day to day.
- Because the equality of debits and credits can be checked at a glance, errors can be discovered before the transactions are transferred to the ledger.
- The journal not only shows all numerical information about a transaction in one place, but also explains the transaction.
- The journal is a factual proof of financial events in case such proof should be required in a court of law, or if any source document should be lost or destroyed.

PROBLEMS

Preparing General Journal entries.

P 4-4 On a sheet of two-column General Journal paper, record the following transactions. Explain each entry, and use a second sheet of journal paper if necessary. Because the owner is starting the business, start with page 1.

Nov. 1 Jim Edgar began his business, J. Edgar Consulting Services, with the following assets and liabilities: Cash, $2500; Office Supplies, $1450; Accts. Pay./G. Health Suppliers, $800. (Remember that the debits must equal the credits in the journal entry.)

2 Issued Cheque No. 001 to pay for additional office supplies. $150.

4 Performed consulting services for A. Lee. Issued Sales Invoice No. 01 for $450 and extended 30 days' credit. (Use Consulting Fees Earned as your revenue account.)

6 Issued Sales Invoice No. 02 to Tankers Ltd. for $950. The firm paid immediately in full.

7 Issued Cheque No. 002 to Bell Telephone in full payment of the invoice received today, $67.

10 Issued Cheque No. 003 for $700 in full payment of the monthly rent.

12 Issued Cheque No. 004 for $200 in partial payment of the account with Accts. Pay./G. Health Suppliers.

15 Received $500 cash from T. Byers, payment in full for consulting services performed. Sales Invoice No. 03.

16 Bought a Macintosh® SE computer® for the office from D. Moyer Computers Ltd. on account, $3000. The firm gave us 30 days to pay. (Open a new account.)

17 Borrowed $5000 from the Royal Bank of Canada. The funds were deposited into the bank.

20 Performed consulting services for Lambton Industries Inc. on account. Issued Sales Invoice No. 04 for $1200. Jim Edgar extended 30 days' credit.

23 Jim Edgar took out an advertisement in the local newspaper for one week. He issued Cheque No. 005 as payment in full, $350.

25 Paid the Public Utilities Commission for the monthly utilities with Cheque No. 006 for $440.

30 Issued Sales Invoice No. 05 to Oriole Industries Ltd. for services performed. Oriole Industries Ltd. paid in full with Cheque No. 3456, $3200.

30 J. Edgar withdrew $250 for personal use. Cheque No. 007 was issued to complete this withdrawal.

Preparing an opening General Journal entry.

Preparing General Journal entries.

P 4-5 Refer to Problem 3-9 (Triple M Real Estate Journal). Use two-column General Journal paper to record the opening entry for Triple M Real Estate Co. *Hint:* Remember the Capital account. Then journalize the remainder of the business transactions for the month of September. An explanation is required for each journal entry. Identify all issued source documents in your journal explanations. Begin with No. 310 for the first sales invoice and No. 605 for the first issued cheque.

Preparing General Journal entries.

P 4-6 Challenge Problem Journalize the transactions below. Select the account titles from the following list: Cash; Accts. Rec./A. Couse; Accts. Rec./B. Doan; Accts. Rec./C. Fairs; Accts. Rec./D. Good; Accts. Rec./E. Hey; Accts. Rec./J. Pool; Land; Building; Automobiles; Office Equipment; Bank Loan Payable; Accts. Pay./Ace Motors; Accts. Pay./The Daily News; Accts. Pay./Esso Oil Co.; Accts. Pay./Public Utilities Commission; Mortgage Payable; Jawed Iqbal, Capital; Jawed Iqbal, Drawing; Rental Revenue; Advertising Expense; Utilities Expense; Repairs Expense; Telephone Expense; Salaries Expense; Gasoline Expense. Provide a brief explanation for each entry. It may be necessary to begin a new journal page.

Oct. 1 Jawed Iqbal deposited $400 000 cash into Car Rental System's bank account.

2 Land was purchased on the company's behalf for $35 000; a building on the land was also purchased for $65 000. A cash payment of $30 000 was made using Cheque No. 001, and a 20-year mortgage note was signed for the balance.

3 Twenty new automobiles were purchased at $8700 each from Ace Motors. A cash down payment of $50 000 was made using Cheque No. 002, the balance to be paid in 60 days.

4 An automobile was sold to J. Pool, one of the company's employees, at cost. Pool paid $1000 in cash and agreed to pay the balance within 30 days.

5 An automobile proved to be defective and was returned to Ace Motors. Ace Motors reduced the amount owing by Car Rental System by $8700.

9 $5000 cash was borrowed from the bank on a demand note.

10 A cash register and office desk were purchased for $3200, payment being made on Cheque No. 003.

27 The hydro bill from the Public Utilities Commission amounted to $75, to be paid before November 10.

28 Repair bills for servicing automobiles totalled $2400, and were paid by issuing Cheque No. 004.

29 Gasoline charges totalled $4000, payable in 30 days to Esso Oil Co.

30 Salaries amounting to $6800 were paid to employees; cheques numbered 005, 006, and 007 were issued.

31 An accounting of $17 000 cash was obtained by renting cars to cash customers for the month. Invoices numbered 01, 02, 03, 04, and 05 were issued.

31 Revenue totalling $11 700 was earned in October through car rentals on a credit of 30 days to the following customers: Invoice No. 06, A. Couse, $2400; Invoice No. 07, B. Doan, $3000; Invoice No. 08, C. Fairs, $900; Invoice No. 09, D. Good, $2700; Invoice No. 10, E. Hey, $2700.

31 Jawed Iqbal withdrew $1200 cash for personal use using Cheque No. 008.

31 Cheque No. 009 for $56 was issued to Bell Canada to pay the monthly telephone bill.

TOPIC 2 MINI-CASES

Analyzing General Journal entries.

Correcting General Journal entries.

MC 4-4 Alana Grigas is the employee responsible for the General Journal of Takei Legal Associates. After having examined the past week's journal transactions, she has extracted the following General Journal entry prepared by A. Freer, a new accounting clerk. Takei Legal Associates made a partial payment of $110.00 on Invoice No. 2858 dated July 3, 19–1 from Stark's Stationery Ltd. The journal information came from the cheque stub No. 878 and was dated July 6, 19–1.

GENERAL JOURNAL Page

DATE		ACCOUNT TITLE AND EXPLANATION	POST. REF.	DEBIT	CREDIT
19-1					
July	7	Cash			878 00
		Accts. Rec./Stark's Stationery		878 00	
		Payment in full on Invoice No. 2885			
		with Cheque No. 110.			

a. Why do you think Alana may be concerned? List each concern.

b. Briefly describe why each of these areas is a concern to Alana.

c. Prepare what you believe is the correct General Journal entry.

Examining the importance of the General Journal.

MC 4-5 Reid and Natale were overheard discussing the importance of the General Journal in the accounting cycle. Reid said, "I don't need to waste my time writing all of the transaction information in the General Journal. I record it all in the ledger accounts. There are no advantages to writing it again in the General Journal."

a. What points could Natale make to convince Reid that the General Journal has real worth and that it should be kept in the accounting cycle?

Analyzing the General Journal explanation.

MC 4-6 Ivan was extremely disappointed with the results of his last assignment. The transactions that he journalized were generally well done, but he had not included a single explanation even though the instructions had specifically stated that explanations were to be included. Ivan said, "Anyone who knows what they are doing can tell everything about a transaction just by looking at the accounts and the amounts!"

a. Briefly, give Ivan three reasons why an explanation should be included with any journal entry. Try to be as specific as possible.

b. Support each of your reasons above with a specific General Journal entry.

POSTING TRANSACTION DATA

A chronological record of business transactions in a journal has many uses; however, accounts that classify accounting information under one title are also needed, so that a set of financial statements can be prepared at the end of any accounting period. Also, during the accounting period, the owner will want information such as:

- How much cash is available in the bank account?
- How much is owing from customers on account?
- How much is owing to the bank?
- How much is owing to creditors on accounts payable?
- How much revenue has been earned?
- How many expenses have been incurred?

Posting: transferring debits and credits from the journal to the ledger.

While the journal will have a record of all transactions, it would be inefficient to search the journal for all entries affecting one account. Therefore, once the debits and credits have been recorded in the journal, accounting information must be transferred from the journal to the individual accounts in the ledger. The process is called posting.

INTRODUCING THE MODERN LEDGER

Ledger (1): the book of secondary or final entry.

You learned in Topic 2 that business transactions are analyzed and recorded in debit and credit form for the **first** time in the journal; hence, the journal was called the ''book of original entry.'' Since these debits and credits are then transferred to the ledger, you could say the ledger is the ''book of secondary entry''; but no further transfer of debits and credits is required and, therefore, the ledger is better called the ''book of final entry.''

Historically, the collection of individual accounts, called a ledger, was a bound book. This was the basis for the original definition of the ledger as the ''book of accounts.'' Today, the term ''book'' is still used, even though many other different forms of the ledger exist. Some of these include:

- a loose-leaf binder which holds individual ledger sheets
- a ledger tray which holds individual ledger cards
- a filing tub or cabinet which holds individual ledger folders and files

These methods offer a great deal of flexibility in adding, deleting, and rearranging individual accounts or groups of accounts.

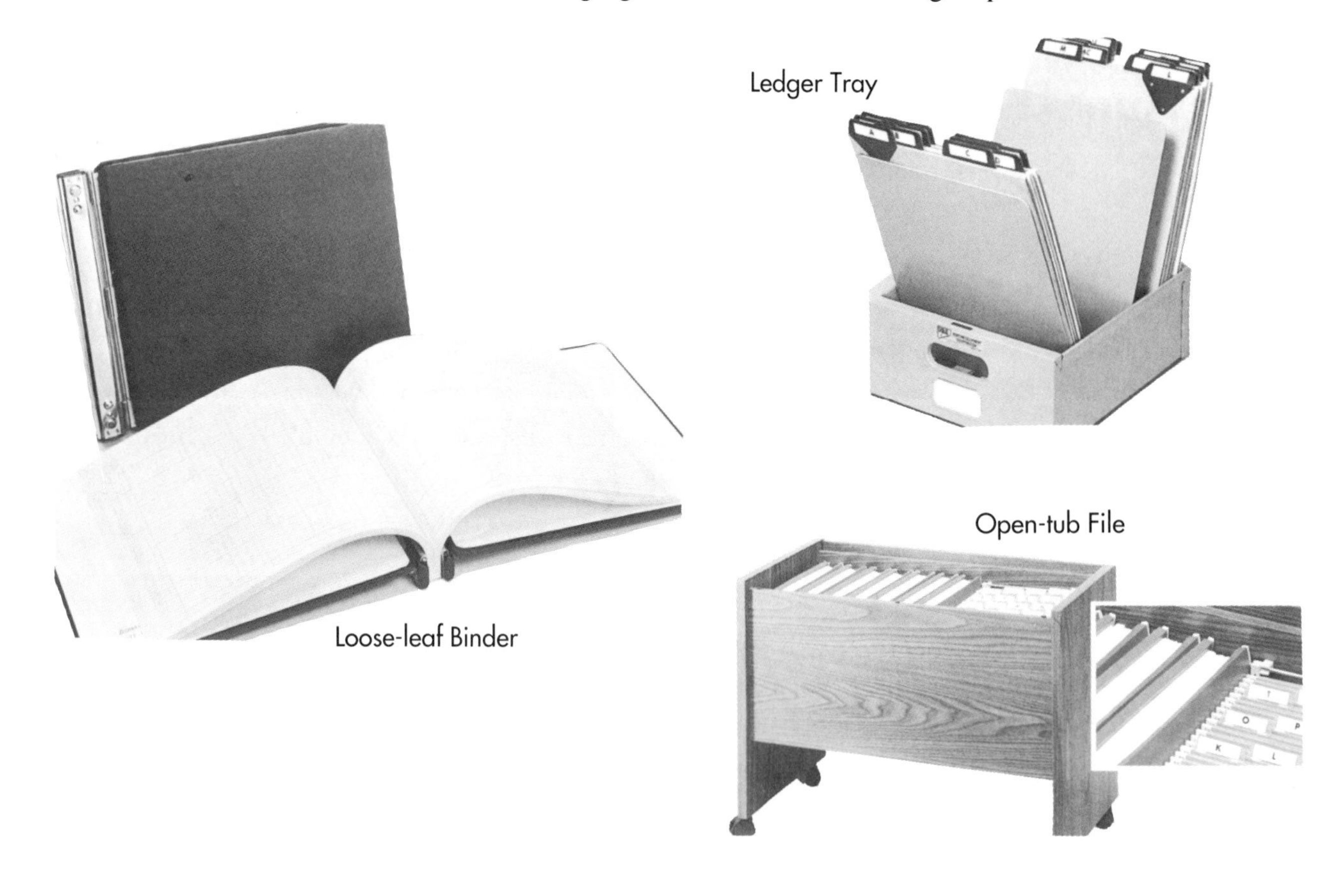

The most modern method of processing a ledger is by computer. The ledger files are stored on magnetic tape or disk allowing great flexibility including very rapid access and addition and deletion of information and files. A modern ledger, then, is a group of accounts filed according to the method of data processing used by the business.

Ledger (2): a group or file of accounts; the book of final entry.

EXPLORING THE NEED FOR A FORMAL LEDGER ACCOUNT

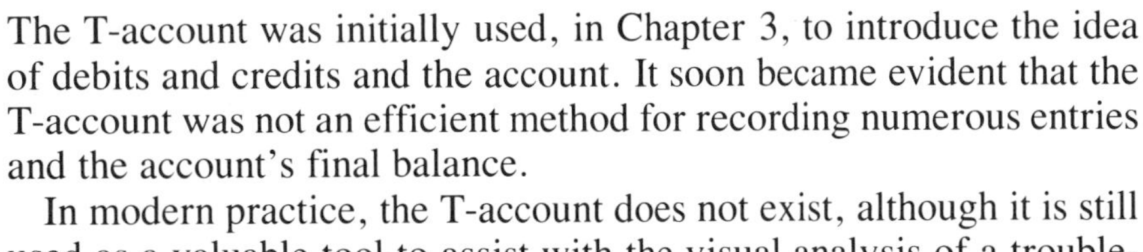

The T-account was initially used, in Chapter 3, to introduce the idea of debits and credits and the account. It soon became evident that the T-account was not an efficient method for recording numerous entries and the account's final balance.

In modern practice, the T-account does not exist, although it is still used as a valuable tool to assist with the visual analysis of a troublesome transaction. Instead, forms are designed according to the type of information required from the account and the method of processing data used in the business's accounting system. For example, an account form posted by hand will be quite different from one posted by computer. One type of account form that is widely used is the three-column form as shown below.

Analysis: The three money columns are:

- the **debit** column, where the debits from the journal are recorded
- the **credit** column, where the credits are recorded in the credit column of the journal
- the **balance** column, where the balance remaining in the account is recorded immediately after the debit or credit has been posted from the journal to the ledger

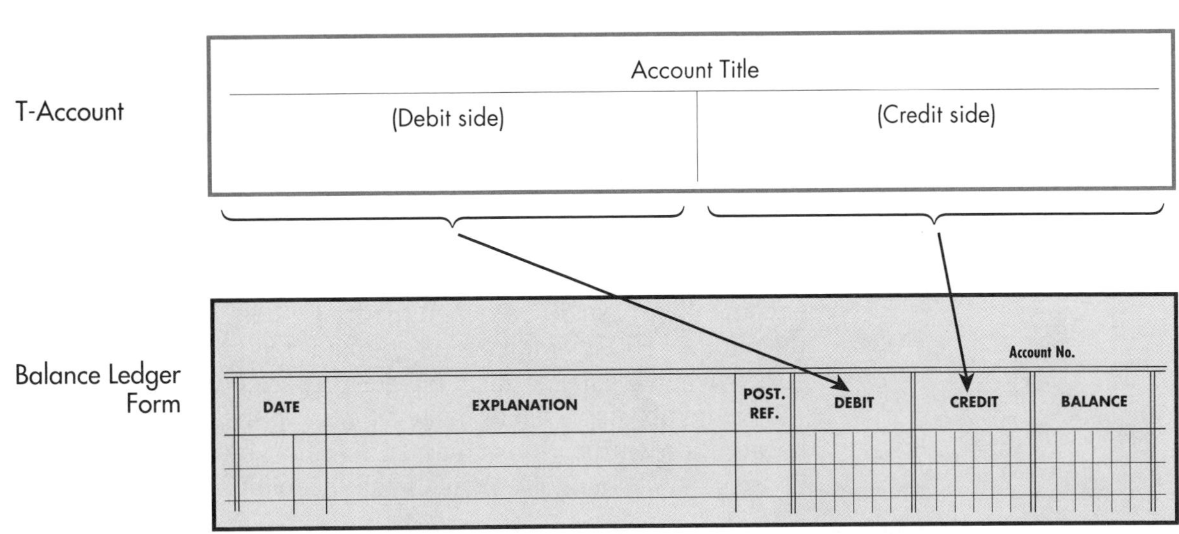

Since the current balance is shown after each posting, the three-column form is more commonly called the balance ledger form.

Balance ledger form: a three-column account with a "running balance" column.

The other columns in the balance ledger form are:

- **Date** This column shows the date of the business transaction as recorded in the journal.
- **Explanation** This shows a brief explanation. Often, the source document is identified or an unusual entry is explained. A description is not necessary, however, for every entry in the ledger account because the source of—or reference for—posting is usually given in the next column.
- **Post. Ref. (Posting Reference)** This column shows the name of the journal and the page from which the information has been transferred.

When the name of the account is shown, it appears at the left, above the date column. However, accounts are usually identified by a number code at the top right-hand side of the balance ledger form. These accounts are filed in the General Ledger.

General Ledger: the ledger filing those accounts which supply information for the preparation of financial statements.

ORGANIZING THE CHART OF ACCOUNTS

The number code given to each account identifies the account and indicates the order in which this account is listed in the General Ledger. Such a number plan is important because it enables financial statements to be prepared later from the numeric sequence of accounts in the General Ledger. The complete list of account titles and the number codes assigned to them is called the Chart of Accounts.

Chart of Accounts: a numbering plan, listing all account titles in the order in which they appear in the accounting equation, and the numbers assigned to them.

Many number plans are in use today. The three-digit plan is common. A three-digit plan for J. Emery Real Estate is shown at the top of the opposite page.

Notice that the first digit of the code identifies the major class of accounts, while the second and third digits provide a further breakdown. For example, account numbers beginning with 1 indicate asset accounts; those beginning with 2 indicate liability accounts; and so on. The next two digits indicate the position of the account within its group. Most charts of accounts leave gaps in the sequence of numbers so that new accounts can be added later on. Notice also that an account is not usually assigned the first whole number. For example, the number 100 is omitted here so that it may be used for the heading Assets when a balance sheet is later prepared on a computer listing.

This numbering system makes it easy to locate an account quickly because it identifies it as an asset, liability, owner's equity, revenue, or expense account. Remember that accounts related to the balance

J. Emery Real Estate
Chart of Accounts

ASSETS
101 Cash
103 Accts. Rec./Pat Rogers
104 Accts. Rec./R. Scobie
105 Accts. Rec./Shannon Development Co.
110 Automobile
112 Furniture
114 Office Equipment

LIABILITIES
201 Bank Loan Payable
202 Accts. Pay./Bell Furniture Co.
203 Accts. Pay./The City Record
204 Accts. Pay./Ryan Equipment Co.
205 Accts. Pay./Westown Motors Ltd.

OWNER'S EQUITY
301 J. Emery, Capital
302 J. Emery, Drawing

REVENUE
401 Commissions Earned

EXPENSES
501 Rent Expense
502 Telephone Expense
503 Utilities Expense
504 Salaries Expense
505 Advertising Expense

Chart of Accounts

Asset accounts:	101 through 199
Liability accounts:	201 through 299
Owner's Equity accounts:	301 through 399
Revenue accounts:	401 through 499
Expense accounts:	501 through 599

sheet are given lower code numbers while accounts related to the income statement are given higher ones.

POSTING TO THE LEDGER

The mechanics of posting to the ledger will vary from business to business. It will naturally depend on the method of processing used: by hand or by computer. The manual method has been chosen for this chapter to simplify matters. You will be introduced to the posting function using a computer General Ledger accounting package in the last topic of Chapter 6.

The illustration at the top of the next page outlines the steps for posting the opening entry for J. Emery Real Estate. The top portion of the General Journal shows how the first account, Cash, is posted to the Cash account in the General Ledger.

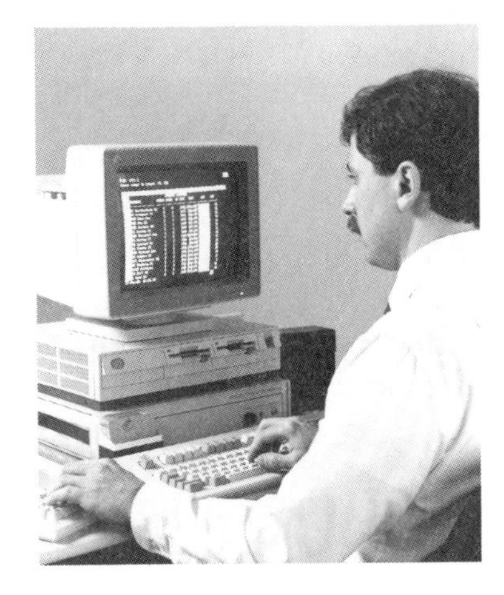

Step 1: Locate the ledger account. For the first account recorded in the General Journal, locate the ledger account.

Step 2: Record the date. Record the date in the date column of the ledger account. It should be exactly the same as the date recorded on each source document and the journal record.

Record the year, month, and day for the first entry only. Do not continue to write the month or the year for the rest of the entries

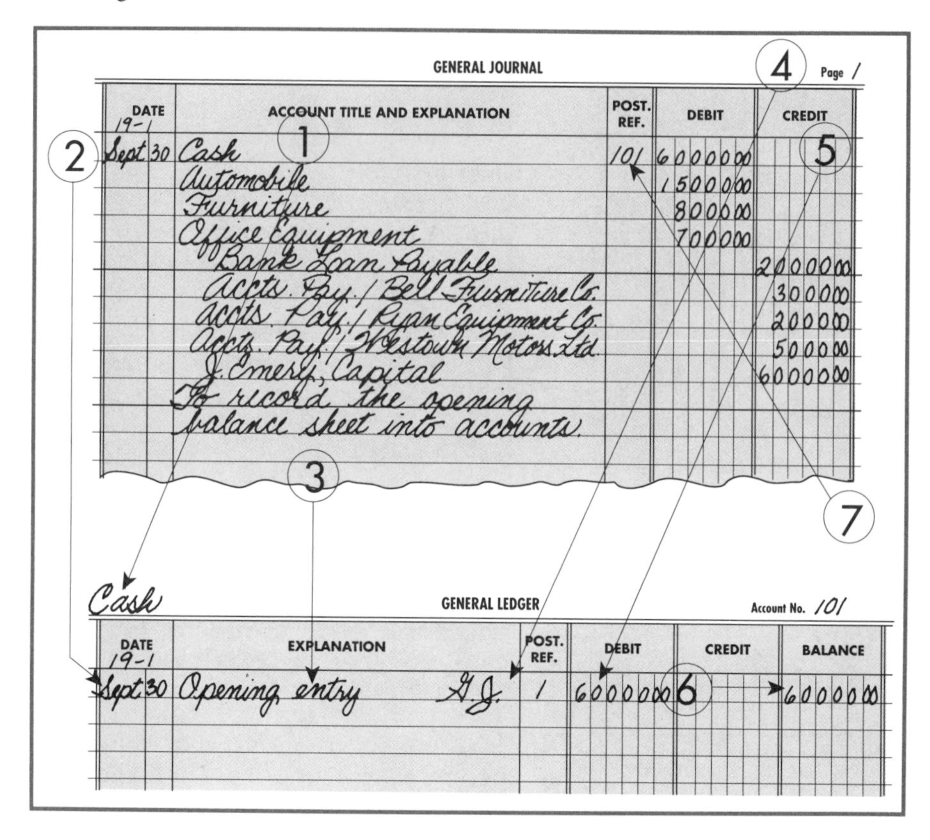

unless a change is involved or the account must be continued on another page.

Step 3: Show an explanation, if needed. Enter an explanation of the entry, if one is needed to make the entry clear. In the Cash account shown, the words "Opening entry" are written to distinguish this as the opening balance. In practice, however, the Explanation column in the General Ledger is seldom used. The posting reference to the corresponding journal page allows a clerk or accountant to quickly locate a complete explanation of the transaction.

Step 4: Fill out the Post. Ref. column of the account. Just before the Post. Ref. column of the account, enter the letters G.J. (for General Journal). Then, enter the number of the journal page from which the entry is being posted. In the example, the source of posting reference is G.J. 1, referring to page 1 of the General Journal.

Step 5: Record the amount in the correct money column. Since Cash has been debited in the journal, this debit amount is transferred to the debit column of the ledger. (Make sure you have copied the figure correctly. Most errors in ledger work in a manual system are due to careless copying of numbers.)

Step 6: Record the correct balance in the balance column. Since there is only a debit amount in the Cash account and no previous debits or credits, no calculation is necessary here. The debit amount is the balance.

Return to the General Journal, and in the Post. Ref. column, enter the number of the ledger account to which the journal entry has been posted. In the example, the number 101 appears in the Post. Ref. column of the General Journal to show that the Cash account has been posted.

Important: Recording the accounting number of the account posted in the Post. Ref. column of the General Journal must be the last step in posting. Why? If you place the account number in the Post. Ref. column of the journal before posting the entry, and then were interrupted, you could easily forget to post the entry. Always remember to record the account number in the journal only after having posted and recorded the balance in the Balance column of the ledger account.

When you have finished posting the first account, locate the next one. If the transaction involves a debit, repeat the foregoing procedure. If it involves a credit, apply the same procedure but with one change: record the amount in the credit column.

LOOKING AT GENERAL LEDGER ACCOUNTS AFTER POSTING

The illustrations that follow on the next few pages show how the accounts should look after the opening entries, and a selection of the other transactions of J. Emery Real Estate have been posted from the General Journal to the General Ledger. (See pages 134 to 137.) *Remember:* Account numbers are entered in the Post. Ref. column in the General Journal only **after** each entry is posted.

CALCULATING A NEW BALANCE

From the foregoing it would seem simple to calculate the current balance of an account in a balance ledger form. Let us check this by calculating the new balances in three accounts.

In the Cash account shown on page 135, Account No. 101, the opening entry on September 30 shows a debit balance of $60 000. This balance does not need to be identified as a debit balance because

GENERAL JOURNAL Page 1

DATE 19-1		ACCOUNT TITLE AND EXPLANATION	POST. REF.	DEBIT	CREDIT
Sept.	30	Cash	101	60 000 00	
		Automobile	110	15 000 00	
		Furniture	112	8 000 00	
		Office Equipment	114	7 000 00	
		Bank Loan Payable	201		20 000 00
		Accts. Pay./Bell Furniture Co.	202		3 000 00
		Accts. Pay./Ryan Equipment Co.	204		2 000 00
		Accts. Pay./Westown Motors Ltd.	205		5 000 00
		J. Emery, Capital	301		60 000 00
		To record the opening			
		balance sheet into accounts.			
Oct.	1	Furniture		1 000 00	
		Cash			1 000 00
		Cheque No. 1 to Enns Furniture			
		Ltd. for additional furniture.			
	31	Advertising Expense	505	200 00	
		Accts. Pay./The City Record	203		200 00
		Advertising bill; terms			
		given: net 30 days.			

(as you learned from the accounting equation) assets normally have debit balances.

The second posting, on October 1, shows a credit of $1000 from issuing a cheque to buy additional furniture. Since this cheque decreases Cash, the account is credited, and the new balance is $59 000. This balance is understood to be a debit, because all assets are found on the debit (left) side of the accounting equation.

On October 5, J. Emery Real Estate issued Cheque No. 2 in payment of the account payable to Westown Motors Ltd. Since this payment decreases the amount of cash, the account is credited, and the balance is now calculated at $54 000 ($59 000 − $5000).

Similar decreases in the Cash account appear as of October 11, 12, and 15. For each of these postings, the Cash account is **credited**. The balance after posting the decrease on October 15 is $48 360 ($53 360 − $5000).

On October 16, however, the Cash account shows a **debit** posting of $3000. This results in an increase to the Cash account. The new balance is $51 360 ($48 360 + $3000). Further debits will be added

General Ledger

Cash — Account No. 101

DATE		EXPLANATION	POST. REF.	DEBIT	CREDIT	BALANCE
19-1						
Sept.	30	Opening entry	G.J. 1	60000.00		60000.00
Oct.	1		G.J. 1		1000.00	59000.00
	5		G.J. 1		5000.00	54000.00
	11		G.J. 1		40.00	53960.00
	12		G.J. 2		1600.00	52360.00
	15		G.J. 2		4000.00	48360.00
	16		G.J. 2	3000.00		51360.00
	18		G.J. 2		595.00	50765.00
	20		G.J. 2	13400.00		64165.00
	30		G.J. 2		2000.00	62165.00
	31		G.J. 2	13400.00		75565.00
	31		G.J. 3		4500.00	71065.00

Accts. Rec./Pat Rogers — Account No. 103

DATE		EXPLANATION	POST. REF.	DEBIT	CREDIT	BALANCE
19-1						
Oct.	31	Invoice 00007	G.J. 3	6000.00		6000.00

Accts. Rec./L. Scobie — Account No. 104

DATE		EXPLANATION	POST. REF.	DEBIT	CREDIT	BALANCE
19-1						
Oct.	31	Invoice 00008	G.J. 3	4000.00		4000.00

Bank Loan Payable — Account No. 201

DATE		EXPLANATION	POST. REF.	DEBIT	CREDIT	BALANCE
19-1						
Sept.	30	Opening entry	G.J. 1		20000.00	20000.00
Oct.	15		G.J. 2	4000.00		16000.00

Accts. Pay./Ryan Equipment Co. — Account No. 204

DATE 19-1		EXPLANATION	POST. REF.	DEBIT	CREDIT	BALANCE
Sept.	30	Opening entry G.J.	1		2 000 00	2 000 00
Oct.	3	G.J.	1		1 200 00	3 200 00
	4	G.J.	1	200 00		3 000 00

Accts. Pay./Westown Motors Ltd. — Account No. 205

DATE 19-1		EXPLANATION	POST. REF.	DEBIT	CREDIT	BALANCE
Sept.	30	Opening entry G.J.	1		5 000 00	5 000 00
Oct.	5	G.J.	1	5 000 00		—0—

J. Emery, Capital — Account No. 301

DATE 19-1		EXPLANATION	POST. REF.	DEBIT	CREDIT	BALANCE
Sept.	30	Opening entry G.J.	1		60 000 00	60 000 00
Oct.	16	G.J.	2		3 000 00	63 000 00

J. Emery, Drawing — Account No. 302

DATE 19-1		EXPLANATION	POST. REF.	DEBIT	CREDIT	BALANCE
Oct.	30	G.J.	2	2 000 00		2 000 00

Commissions Earned — Account No. 401

DATE 19-1		EXPLANATION	POST. REF.	DEBIT	CREDIT	BALANCE
Oct.	20	G.J.	2		1 340 00	1 340 00
	31	G.J.	2		1 340 00	2 680 00
	31	G.J.	3		2 500 00	5 180 00

Rent Expense — Account No. 501

DATE 19-1		EXPLANATION	POST. REF.	DEBIT	CREDIT	BALANCE
Oct.	12		G.J. 2	1600 00		1600 00

Important: Although the accounts illustrated on the previous pages show several accounts on one page, in actual practice under a manual system each account would be shown on a separate sheet or card, as illustrated below.

GENERAL LEDGER

Account Name J. Emery, Capital — Account No. 301

Date 19-1		Explanation	Post. Ref.	Debit	Credit	Balance
Sept	30	Opening entry	G.J. 1		60000 00	60000 00
Oct.	16		G.J. 2		3000 00	63000 00

to the previous balance and further credits will be subtracted, so that the current balance is always shown in the account.

Look at Account No. 205 on page 136, the Accts. Pay./Westown Motors Ltd. liability account. The opening entry shows a credit balance. This balance need not be identified as a credit balance because liabilities normally have credit balances in the accounting equation, as do the Capital and Revenue accounts found under the Owner's Equity element.

The second entry shows a debit of $5000, which is a result of a cheque issued to this creditor. Since this is a liability account and the debit must show a decrease, the new balance is calculated by subtracting the debit from the current (credit) balance. This calculation gives a "zero balance" or "no balance." The "no-balance" sign is written in the balance column.

Now look at Account No. 401, Commissions Earned, on the same page. This is a revenue account and will normally have a credit balance, because revenue causes an increase to owner's equity in the accounting equation. Of course, each new credit entry will be added to the balance because commissions earned result in increases to owner's equity. For the Commissions Earned account, and for all revenue accounts, every balance is understood to be a CR. balance.

REVIEWING THE ACCOUNTING CYCLE

You have now been introduced to the first three steps in the accounting cycle:

- Step 1: originating
- Step 2: journalizing
- Step 3: posting

PROBLEMS

Opening ledger accounts.

Posting to the General Ledger.

P 4-7 Refer to Problem 4-4 (J. Edgar Consulting Services). Assume that the following General Ledger accounts have been identified from the Chart of Accounts for J. Edgar Consulting Services: Cash, 101; Accts. Rec./Lambton Industries Inc., 105; Accts. Rec./A. Lee, 108; Office Supplies, 115; Office Equipment, 120; Bank Loan Payable, 201; Accts. Pay./G. Health Suppliers, 205; Accts. Pay./D. Moyer Computers Ltd., 210; J. Edgar, Capital, 301; J. Edgar, Drawing, 302; Consulting Fees Earned, 401; Telephone Expense, 505; Rent Expense, 510; Advertising Expense, 515; Utilities Expense, 520.

a. Post the journal entries made in Problem 4-4 to the General Ledger. *Note:* Save the journal and ledger for use in the next topic of this chapter.

Opening ledger accounts.

Posting to the General Ledger.

P 4-8 Refer to Problem 4-5 (Triple M Real Estate Co.). Assume that the following general ledger accounts have been identified from the chart of accounts for Elina Li's Triple M Real Estate Co.: Cash, 101; Accts. Rec./G. Da Silva, 105; Accts. Rec./V.J. Plumbers, 108; Office Supplies, 115; Furniture, 120; Office Equipment, 125; Automobile, 130; Bank Loan Payable, 201; Accts. Pay./C. & C. Computers, 205; Accts. Pay./Global Office Supplies, 210; Accts. Pay./Willard Motors Ltd., 215; E. Li, Capital, 301; E. Li, Drawing, 302; Commissions Earned, 401; Rental Revenue, 403; Rent Expense, 505; Advertising Expense, 510; Heat Expense, 515; Utilities Expense, 520; Salaries Expense, 525.

a. Post the journal entries made in Problem 4-5 to the General Ledger. *Note:* Save the journal and ledger for use in the next topic of this chapter.

Organizing a Chart of Accounts.

Opening ledger accounts.

Posting to the ledger.

P 4-9 Challege Problem Refer to the General Journal you made for the Car Rental System in Problem 4-6.

a. Go through all entries made in the journal and set up a chart of accounts for Jawed Iqbal's business. Follow the plan in the chart illustrated on page 131.

b. Using your chart, set up a General Ledger for the Car Rental System.

c. Post the journal entries made in Problem 4-6 to the General Ledger. *Note:* Save the journal and the ledger for use in the next topic of this chapter.

MINI-CASES

Designing a Chart of Accounts for a larger business.

Discussing the importance of account numbers.

MC 4-7 Single X Company is a very small business and uses a very simple chart of accounts to number its ledger accounts. Triple X Company, however, is very large and has several hundred asset accounts and over one hundred liability accounts.

a. Suggest a numbering system that would suit each company.

b. Why are ledger accounts assigned a number?

Analyzing and discussing the posting procedure.

MC 4-8 Hans often takes shortcuts when posting in order to save time. He will often ignore posting references or fill them all in at once. In addition, he often posts one account, for example, Cash, out of several journal entries at the same time.

a. Explain to Hans why these are very weak accounting procedures. Make certain you include the reasons why posting is done in a repetitive manner.

Discovering, describing, and correcting errors in a ledger account.

MC 4-9 D. Jeong has asked you to examine the following ledger account that was prepared by an inexperienced part-time bookkeeper.

a. List and describe each of the errors that you detect in the bookkeeper's work.

b. Prepare a correct version of the ledger Cash account.

GENERAL LEDGER

Cash — Account No. 101

DATE 19-1		EXPLANATION	POST. REF.	DEBIT	CREDIT	BALANCE
May	10	Rec'd on acct.	GJ2	200 00		$ 200 00
May		Payment on acct.	GJ1		150 00	350 00
	14	Loan from the bank	GJ2	5000 00		5355 00
	15	Payment on acct.			500 00	3855 00
	16	Additional Invest.	GJ3	1000 00		4585 00
		Final Total				$1 4345 00

TOPIC 4 PREPARING ACCOUNTING PROOFS

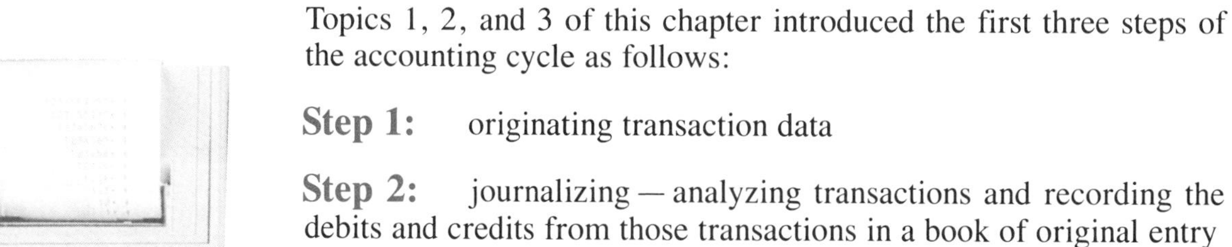

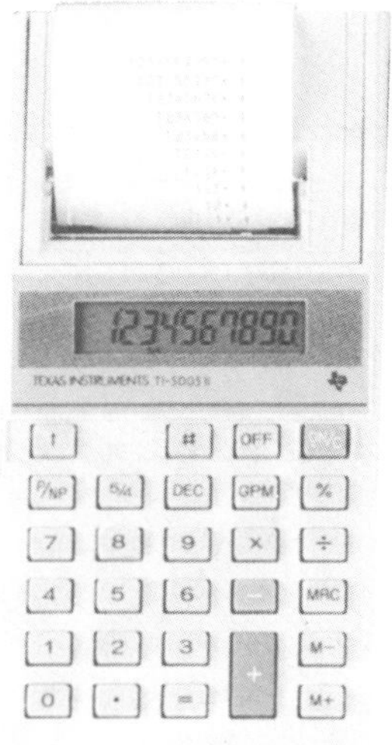

Topics 1, 2, and 3 of this chapter introduced the first three steps of the accounting cycle as follows:

Step 1: originating transaction data

Step 2: journalizing — analyzing transactions and recording the debits and credits from those transactions in a book of original entry

Step 3: posting — transferring debits and credits from the journal to the ledger

After the third step, financial statements can be prepared from the accounts filed in the General Ledger. Before such statements are prepared, however, accountants recommend making a number of accounting **proofs** — procedures to ensure (1) that the data recorded in the journal and the ledger are accurate and (2) that all transactions have been accounted for.

PREPARING THE JOURNAL PROOF

The double entry in the journal is a sound checking system in itself. For each transaction, a debit and credit is recorded and these amounts are equal. This important rule of "debits equal credits" makes it possible to prove the journal page in two ways:

- by routinely totalling each column on a journal page **before** any posting is done
- by totalling the money columns **before** turning to a new page

A journal proof is prepared either manually or by using a computer program. A simplified computer method is presented using an electronic spreadsheet in Topic 5 of this chapter and a sophisticated method using a general ledger accounting package is presented in Chapter 6. A short description of the manual preparation of a journal proof is given below.

In the manual method, an adding machine or a calculator with a tape printer is often used to perform the addition. In fact, any type of adding machine that will give you a printout is preferred so that you can check your calculations directly against the original data. The illustration on page 142 shows the addition of the debit and credit columns on page 1 of the General Journal for J. Emery Real Estate.

Journal proof: the total of the debit column is equal to the total of the credit column on a journal page.

If the two totals agree, then this is reasonable mathematical proof that the figures in the journal are accurate. This proof is commonly known as the journal proof. Posting can now be done to the ledger, and page 2 of the journal can be set up without fear that an error may exist in the previous page.

As you can see from the illustration, when these machine tapes are saved and kept with accounting records, a reference notation is made at the top of the tape. Sometimes, the tapes are attached to the documents being proved.

Important warning: It is considered good accounting practice to double-check the figures against the source document and make sure the debits equal the credits **before** recording the next transaction.

PROVING INDIVIDUAL ACCOUNT BALANCES

Instead of rechecking each horizontal calculation in an account, you can easily check the account's final balance on rough paper or with the aid of an electronic calculator.

When using the "rough-paper" approach for an account which usually has a debit balance, first add the debit column and record the total. Next add the credit column and record the total beneath the debit total. Subtract the credit total from the debit total. Your answer should be the same as the final balance in the account. For example,

GENERAL JOURNAL Page

DATE 19-1		ACCOUNT TITLE AND EXPLANATION	POST. REF.	DEBIT	CREDIT
Sept.	30	Cash		60 000 00	
		Automobile		15 000 00	
		Furniture		8 000 00	
		Office Equipment		7 000 00	
		Bank Loan Payable			20 000 00
		Accts. Pay./Bell Furniture Co.			3 000 00
		Accts. Pay./Ryan Equipment Co.			2 000 00
		Accts. Pay./Westown Motors Ltd			5 000 00
		J. Emery, Capital			60 000 00
		To record the opening			
		balance sheet into accounts.			
Oct.	1	Furniture		1 000 00	
		Cash			1 000 00
		Cheque No. 1 to Enns Furniture			
		Ltd. for additional furniture.			
	3	Office Equipment		1 200 00	
		Accts. Pay./Ryan Equipment Co.			1 200 00
		2 calculators and 1 typewriter			
		on 60 days' credit.			
	4	Accts. Pay./Ryan Equipment Co.		200 00	
		Office Equipment			200 00
		Returned 1 calculator received			
		in damaged condition.			
	5	Accts. Pay./Westown Motors Ltd.		5 000 00	
		Cash			5 000 00
		Cheque No. 2 on account.			
	11	Telephone Expense		40 00	
		Cash			40 00
		Cheque No. 3 to Bell Canada.			

Journal Proof
Page 1
Oct. 11, 19-1

```
        0.00 T

60 000.00 +
15 000.00 +
 8 000.00 +
 7 000.00 +
 1 000.00 +
 1 200.00 +
   200.00 +
 5 000.00 +
    40.00 +
97 440.00 T

20 000.00 +
 3 000.00 +
 2 000.00 +
 5 000.00 +
60 000.00 +
 1 000.00 +
 1 200.00 +
   200.00 +
 5 000.00 +
    40.00 +
97 440.00 T
```

the final balance of the Cash account in J. Emery Real Estate's General Ledger is a debit of $71 065—debits are greater than credits—as illustrated opposite. If the account usually has a credit balance, begin with the credit column first and proceed in the same manner.

Once you have checked and proved the final balance in the account, it is useful to indicate it as a DR. or CR. balance. Of course, the final balance in a Cash account will be a DR. balance, as illustrated.

Here are the steps for checking the same Cash account if you use an adding machine or an electronic calculator tape.

- Clear the machine of any previous figures. Then enter each **debit** figure with the **plus** (+) bar.

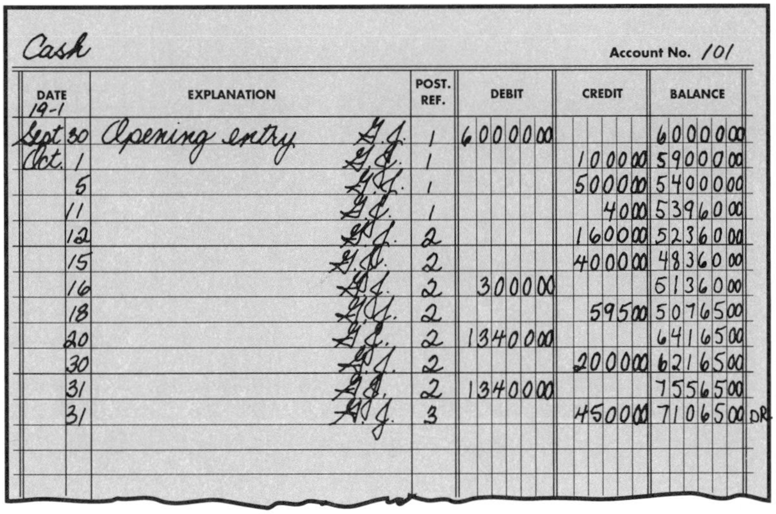

Cash Account No. 101

DATE 19-1		EXPLANATION	POST. REF.	DEBIT	CREDIT	BALANCE
Sept.	30	Opening entry	G.J. 1	60 000.00		60 000.00
Oct.	1		G.J. 1		1 000.00	59 000.00
	5		G.J. 1		5 000.00	54 000.00
	11		G.J. 1		40.00	53 960.00
	12		G.J. 2		1 600.00	52 360.00
	15		G.J. 2		4 000.00	48 360.00
	16		G.J. 2	3 000.00		51 360.00
	18		G.J. 2		595.00	50 765.00
	20		G.J. 2	13 400.00		64 165.00
	30		G.J. 2		2 000.00	62 165.00
	31		G.J. 2	13 400.00		75 565.00
	31		G.J. 3		4 500.00	71 065.00 DR.

Total debits	$89 800
Total credits	−18 735
Cash balance	$71 065 DR.

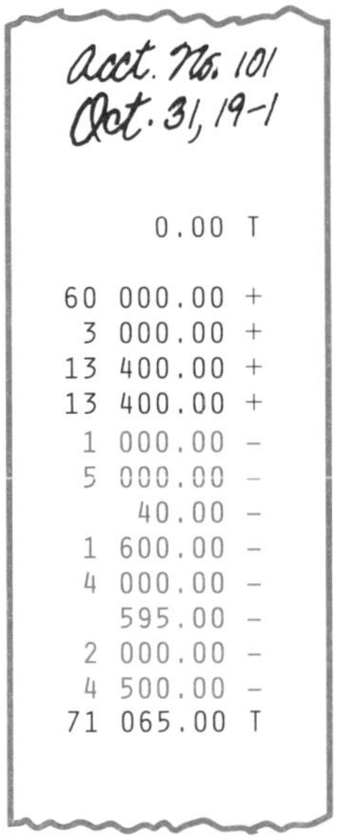

Acct. No. 101
Oct. 31, 19-1

```
      0.00 T

60 000.00 +
 3 000.00 +
13 400.00 +
13 400.00 +
 1 000.00 -
 5 000.00 -
    40.00 -
 1 600.00 -
 4 000.00 -
   595.00 -
 2 000.00 -
 4 500.00 -
71 065.00 T
```

- Next, enter each **credit** figure with the **minus** (−) bar.
- Press the total key.

If the figures have been entered correctly, the total should verify the final balance in the account. In the case of this Cash account, the margin illustration gives the final result in the line "71 065 T."

Here are the steps for checking an account which must have a final CR. balance. In J. Emery Real Estate's General Ledger, Account No. 204 is a liability account. The final balance is checked on an electronic calculator as illustrated below.

- Clear the machine of any previous figures. Then enter each **debit** figure with the **plus** (+) bar.
- Next, enter each **credit** figure with the **minus** (−) bar.

After the last credit figure is entered, press total. For a liability account, the final total should be interpreted as a CR. balance. Depending on the machine, the balance will print either in red with a star or the letters CR. beside it, or in black with a minus sign.

It is useful to show the final balance as a DR. or CR., but this should be done only after you have proved its accuracy. In the case of Account No. 204 (at the top of page 144), the final balance on the proof will be shown as $3000 CR.

You should now have little difficulty in determining whether an account has a final debit or credit balance. Chapter 3 gave you three rules for increasing and decreasing accounts. The third is well worth repeating.

The balance of an account is recorded on the same side as that on which the account appears in the accounting equation.

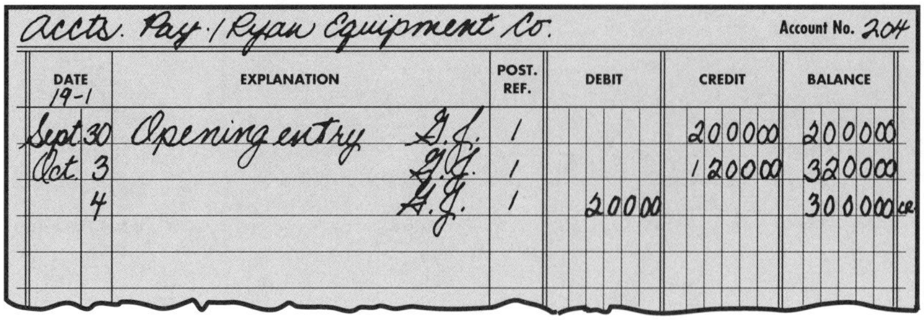

Accts. Pay./Ryan Equipment Co. Account No. 204

DATE 19-1		EXPLANATION	POST. REF.	DEBIT	CREDIT	BALANCE
Sept.	30	Opening entry	G.J. 1		2 000 00	2 000 00
Oct.	3		G.J. 1		1 200 00	3 200 00
	4		G.J. 1	200 00		3 000 00 CR.

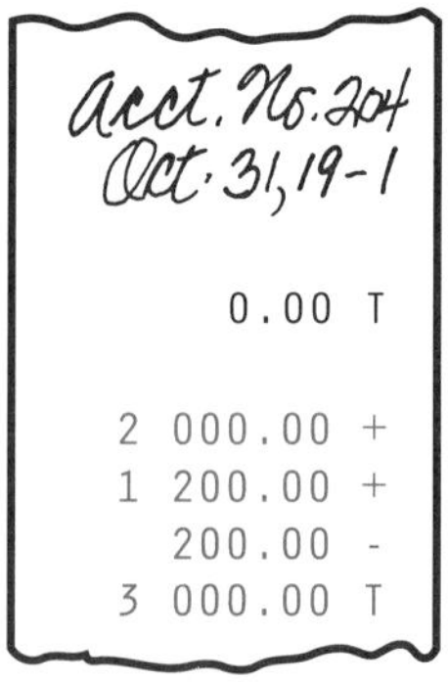

Acct. No. 204
Oct. 31, 19-1

0.00 T

2 000.00 +
1 200.00 +
200.00 -
3 000.00 T

Applying this rule to the classes of accounts introduced in the chart of accounts, you can now show this summary:

Asset	Type of Final Balance Normally Shown
Asset	DR., because assets are found on the left side of the accounting equation
Liability	CR., because liabilities are found on the right side of the accounting equation
Owner's Equity elements:	
Capital	CR., because the owner's investment increases *OE* in the accounting equation
Drawing	DR., because owner's drawings decrease *OE* in the accounting equation
Revenue	CR., because revenue accounts increase *OE* in the accounting equation
Expense	DR., because expense accounts decrease *OE* in the accounting equation

PROVING THE LEDGER

If the debits and credits are posted correctly to the accounts, the ledger must balance, not only in the individual ledger accounts but overall.

Actually, you have already learned how to "prove the ledger." In Chapter 3, after completing the T-account ledger, you were asked to do a summary to prove that the accounting equation is in balance within the T-account ledger. This summary showed that the total of the debit balances agreed with the total of the credit balances in the ledger. Such a summary is known as a **trial balance**

Examine the following illustration.

J. Emery Real Estate
Trial Balance
October 31, 19–1

ACCOUNT TITLE	ACCT. NO.	DEBIT	CREDIT
Cash	101	71 065.00	
Accts. Rec./Pat Rogers	103	6 000.00	
Accts. Rec./R. Scobie	104	4 000.00	
Accts. Rec./Shannon Development Co.	105	15 000.00	
Automobile	110	15 000.00	
Furniture	112	9 000.00	
Office Equipment	114	8 000.00	
Bank Loan Payable	201		16 000.00
Accts. Pay./Bell Furniture Co.	202		3 000.00
Accts. Pay./The City Press	203		2 000.00
Accts. Pay./Ryan Equipment Co.	204		3 000.00
J. Emery, Capital	301		63 000.00
J. Emery, Drawing	302	2 000.00	
Commissions Earned	401		51 800.00
Rent Expense	501	1 600.00	
Telephone Expense	502	40.00	
Utilities Expense	503	595.00	
Salaries Expense	504	4 500.00	
Advertising Expense	505	2 000.00	
		138 800.00	138 800.00

Formal trial balance: a list or summary of the balances of accounts in a ledger as at a certain date.

PREPARING THE FORMAL TRIAL BALANCE

Study these points as you refer to the illustration above:

- Check the accuracy of the final balance reported in each account in the ledger, and show whether it is a debit or a credit balance by placing DR. or CR. after it.
- To begin the trial balance, centre a three-line heading as shown. The heading answers three questions: **who** (the name of the business); **what** (the name of the accounting proof); and **when** (the date as of which the summary is prepared).
- Deal with the accounts in the order in which they are filed in the General Ledger. List only accounts that have a non-zero balance. Balanced accounts are not listed in the trial balance. Write the account title and the account number in their respective columns, and the account balance in the appropriate money column.

- After all the account balances have been entered, draw a single line across both money columns and total the columns. If you have journalized and posted correctly, the total debit balances will equal the total credit balances. If this happens, the trial balance is then completed by drawing a double line across both money columns and the account number column.

You may wonder what "trial" means. In simple terms, you are putting the General Ledger "on trial" for accuracy. If $A = L + OE$, then this equation as it is represented in the ledger must balance.

You may also be wondering: If all expense account balances and owner's drawing account balances are shown on the right side of the accounting equation, why are they listed as debit balances? The answer is that since all accounts have only two sides, debit and credit, any account causing a decrease to owner's equity must be shown on the side opposite to that on which owner's equity is found in the accounting equation. So when you list a debit balance for any expense account or for the owner's drawing account, you are recognizing that these accounts **decrease** owner's equity.

On the other hand, the owner's capital account and all revenue account balances **increase** owner's equity. Since all increases to owner's equity are shown on the side on which owner's equity is found in the equation, these account balances are always listed in the credit column of the trial balance.

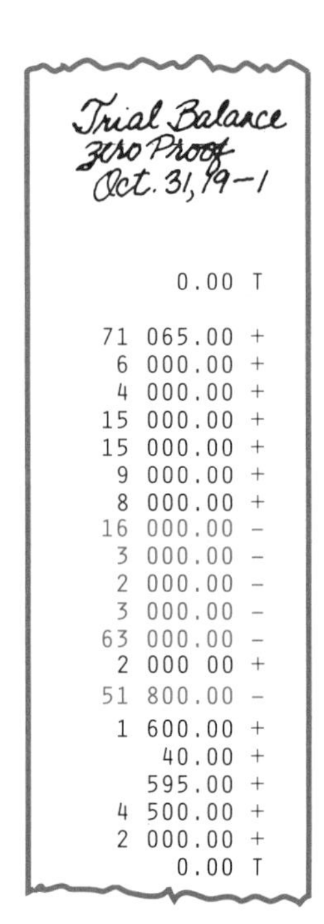

Informal Trial Balance

PREPARING AN INFORMAL TRIAL BALANCE

When a formal trial balance is not required, an adding machine that will print out a tape may be used. To save time, the accounts with a balance can be entered directly onto the machine tape from the ledger. Here are the main procedures for a quick trial balance:

- Check the accuracy of the balance in each account and indicate whether it is a debit or a credit. (Place a large "DR." or "CR." to the right of the final balance.)
- Clear the machine with the TOTAL key.
- Listing all accounts in the account number order, enter all debit balances on the machine with the plus (+) key and all credit balances with the minus (–) key.
- When the last balance has been listed, press the TOTAL key to print the result.

If the result is a zero, you have a zero proof and the ledger is in balance — total debits equal total credits.

Zero proof: deducting all of the credit balances from all of the debit balances to give a zero balance.

If the result is not zero, an error exists in the ledger and the tape can be used to find it. (Of course, it may happen that an error has been made in producing the zero proof.)

A	=	L	+	C	+	R	−	E	−	D
$128 065	=	$24 000	+	$63 000	+	$51 800	−	$8 735	−	$2 000
$128 065	=	$128 065								

USING THE TRIAL BALANCE

A trial balance is useful because:

- It proves the equality of the total debits and credits in the General Ledger.
- It lists all the account balances, giving a brief picture of every account that has a balance in the ledger.
- It is a basis for the preparation of financial statements.

REVIEWING THE ACCOUNTING CYCLE

Although each of the accounting proofs presented in this topic is important, the taking of the trial balance is the key checkpoint before any financial statements are prepared.

Here are the steps in the accounting cycle we have covered so far:

Step 1: originating transactions from source documents

Step 2: journalizing—analyzing and recording transactions from source documents to a book of original entry

Step 3: posting—transferring debit and credit information from the journal to the ledger

Step 4: preparing a trial balance

DEFINING BOOKKEEPING

Bookkeeping: the process of journalizing business transactions, posting transactions to ledger accounts, and proving the ledger to be in balance.

With the completion of the trial balance stage of the accounting cycle, you can now learn the meaning of bookkeeping

In simple terms, bookkeeping is journalizing, posting, and preparing the trial balance. It thus consists of steps 2, 3, and 4 of the accounting cycle.

Accounts Payable Clerk

The Queensway General Hospital has an immediate full-time opening for an individual with previous Accounts Payable experience. The successful candidate must have experience on a cumputerized system, good typing and communication skills.

Please apply to:

Human Resources Dept.
Queensway General
Hospital

Formerly, nearly everyone who worked with financial records was called a bookkeeper. (Records were actually kept in book form for many years.) As financial record-keeping grew in importance, the term ''accountant'' came into popular usage.

Today, the accountant is usually responsible for establishing and maintaining an entire accounting system, interpreting the results of recorded data to management, and assisting in management decisions. The bookkeeper — who works for an accountant — records transactions, posts to the ledger, and provides mathematical checks of documents, journals, account balances, and the ledger.

SENIOR BOOKKEEPER

Nordic Tours, a mid-size travel wholesale company, has a position open for a full-charge Bookkeeper.

Candidate must have 5-10 years of diversified experience. Responsibilities include some budget control, supervising and handling of several sets of books up to and including monthly financial statements as well as some administrative responsibilities. Experience on computerized systems a definite asset. Salary will be commensurate with experience and will be complimented by a comprehensive range of employee benefits.

Reply in confidence to:

NORDIC

In large organizations, especially where computers are now used to process accounting data, the term ''bookkeeper'' is gradually disappearing and ''accounting clerk'' is taking its place. In small businesses the person in charge of financial records is still called a bookkeeper, even though he or she may be performing the duties of an accounting

Accounts Receivable Clerk

Toshiba of Canada Limited, Consumer Electronics Operations, is seeking a person to work in their Accounts Receivable Department. Experience in account reconciliation, preparation of bank deposits and data entry is required.

Please mail your resume to:

Toshiba of Canada Limited

Tetra Pak Inc. is a world leader in the supply of form-fill-seal packaging systems for liquid foods. Because of a steadfast commitment to high quality product, superior service and innovative development, Tetra Pak is experiencing unparalleled growth. Currently we have the following opportunity available at our Aurora facility.

Cost Accountant

Responding to the Plant Accountant, initial responsibilities will include various reconciliations, analysis of operating results and variances, and ensuring departmental responsibilities are completed.

Duties will also include the preparation of numerous monthly management information reports for both the financial and production management teams on inventory/production and capital acquisitions and control activities.

Tetra Pak's accounting and production reporting is fully computerized requiring previous experience with numerous software packages. The successful applicant will also have a minimum of 2 years' experience in a costing environment and be presently pursuing a CMA designation.

In addition to the above qualifications, the ability to think clearly and function well as a member of a team is essential. Tetra Pak offers a competitive salary commensurate with experience and comprehensive benefits package. Qualified candidates are invited to submit a resume in strict confidence to:

Personnel Department, Tetra Pak Inc.

Tetra Pak Inc.

clerk. It is important to realize that even small businesses have access to microcomputers. Powerful electronic spreadsheets and General Ledger accounting packages enable even a small business to complete some or all of the accounting cycle electronically. Details on how this can be accomplished will be presented in Topic 5 of this chapter (more uses of the spreadsheet) and in Chapter 6 (an introduction to a GL accounting package).

In general, the following distinction can be made. The accountant holds a professional position, and the bookkeeper or accounting clerk performs clerical duties under the supervision of an accountant.

PROBLEMS

Preparing accounting proofs.

P 4-10 Refer to the journal you prepared for Problem 4-4 and the ledger for Problem 4-7 (J. Edgar Consulting Services).

a. Make a journal proof for each page of the General Journal used to solve Problem 4-4 (J. Edgar Consulting Services). Use separate paper or use a tape if you have access to an adding machine or a calculator.

b. Check the accuracy of the final balance for each account in the General Ledger in Problem 4-7. Then print DR. or CR. in the General Ledger after each final balance.

c. Prepare a formal trial balance of the General Ledger done for Problem 4-7. Use November 30 as the date.

d. If you have access to an adding machine or calculator with a printer, prepare a zero proof or a quick trial balance of the General Ledger you prepared in Problem 4-7.

Preparing accounting proofs.

P 4-11 Refer to the journal you made up for Problem 4-6 (Car Rental System) and the ledger for Problem 4-9 (Car Rental System).

a. Make up a journal proof for each page of the General Journal used to solve Problem 4-6. Use separate working paper or use a tape if you have access to an adding machine or a calculator.

b. Check the accuracy of the final balance for each account in the General Ledger in Problem 4-9. Then print DR. or CR. in the General Ledger after each final balance.

c. Prepare a formal trial balance of the General Ledger done for Problem 4-9. Use October 31 as the date.

d. If you have access to an adding machine or a calculator with a printer, prepare a zero proof or a quick trial balance of the General Ledger you prepared in Problem 4-9.

Creating a Chart of Accounts.

P 4-12 Challenge Problem Babyland Diaper Service began operations on March 1 with the following accounts.

a. Create a Chart of Accounts and assign appropriate account numbers.

Opening the ledger accounts.

b. Open each of the ledger accounts with its appropriate account name and number from the Chart of Accounts.

Journalizing and posting transactions.

c. Journalize the transactions that follow. Include a brief explanation.

Preparing accounting proofs.

d. Post the journal entries to the ledger accounts.

e. Prepare the accounting proofs that you believe are necessary to this point in the accounting cycle. Explain briefly why you

Explaining the importance of the accounting proofs.

would want each of these proofs. Are there any of these proofs that could have been prepared by some other method? Explain.

Mar.	1	Christina Rade, the owner, borrowed $5000 from the bank and invested $1000 of her personal funds into the business. She made a deposit of $6000 cash into a bank account in the name of Babyland Diaper Services.
	1	Bought supplies for the business from ABC Wholesale Supplies on account, $480. Terms were 30 days. C. Rade decided to expense the entire amount of the supplies.
	2	Bought a new washer from Sears Canada Ltd., $600. Issued Cheque No. 001.
	2	C. Rade brought a old clothes dryer from home to use in the business. The dryer was appraised at $200.
	3	C. Rade issued Cheque No. 002 to A. B. Rental Services for $450 to pay the monthly rent for the business office space.
	4	A delivery truck was purchased from Wellington Motors for $15 000. A cash down payment of $1000 was made using Cheque No. 003, with the balance to be paid in 90 days.
	7	Performed services for Mrs. B. McNally over the past week on account, $43. The payment terms of the business are net 30 days.
	7	Performed services for Mrs. T. Oshiro over the past week. The business received payment in full, $57.
	11	Bought gas for the truck with personal funds, $20.
	14	Received cash from several customers for services performed, $280.
	30	Paid PUC for monthly services with Cheque No. 004, $95.
	31	Received payment in full from B. McNally.
	31	C. Rade used $10 of supplies for personal use.

TOPIC 4 MINI-CASES

Identifying errors in the journal.

MC 4-10 A portion of a General Journal including the journal proof is illustrated on the next page.

a. Identify the errors and their causes.

Determining reasons for preparing accounting proofs.

b. What is another method for calculating a journal proof?

c. Why is this accounting proof an important procedure to complete before other accounting steps take place?

GENERAL JOURNAL — Page 31

DATE 19–9		ACCOUNT TITLE AND EXPLANATION	POST. REF.	DEBIT	CREDIT
July	10	Cash		500	
		Fees Earned			500
		For services performed			
	10	Telephone Expense		53	
		Cash			35
		Monthly telephone bill Cheque No. 583			
	11	Cash		100	
		Accts. Rec./Tools & Trade Comp.		789	
		Fees Earned			789
		Performed services for Cash & on acct.			
				1 432	1 324

Preparing accounting proofs.

Identifying possible errors.

Identifying possible weaknesses in the accounting proofs.

MC 4-11 The Accts. Rec./Tri-State Comp. account is illustrated below.

Accts. Rec./Tri-State Comp. — Account No. 115

DATE 19–9		EXPLANATION	POST. REF.	DEBIT	CREDIT	BALANCE
Jan.	18	Invoice No. 6387	GJ 11	1 230 00		1 320 00
	19	Rec'd. on account	GJ 11		800 00	520 00
	19	Invoice No. 6388	GJ 12	1 580 00		2 000 00
	20	Invoice No. 6389	GJ 13		1 800 00	3 800 00
	21	Rec'd. on account	GJ 13		600 00	3 200 00

a. Complete the individual account balance proof.

b. Does the proof indicate any problems? What are they?

c. Does the proof identify all types of errors that can occur in the ledger account? If not, what are they? Does this account contain any such problem? How would you correct this error?

Recalling definitions.

Decribing methods for preparing accounting proofs.

Identifying the importance of accounting proofs.

MC 4-12 "A list or summary of the balances of accounts in the ledger as at a certain date."

a. What does this statement define?

b. Describe two methods for preparing this summary.

c. Why is it important to prepare this summary?

d. List the steps required in the accounting cycle to get you to this step. Would an accountant work on each of these jobs? Explain why or why not.

APPLYING THE ELECTRONIC SPREADSHEET

Until now, you have used the electronic spreadsheet only to prepare income statements and related balance sheets. In this chapter, you will learn how:

- to journalize in the General Journal
- to post to the General Ledger
- to prepare a variety of accounting proofs, including a journal proof and a trial balance

First let's review the strengths and weaknesses of the electronic spreadsheet. Then we will discuss various applications.

REVIEWING THE STRENGTHS OF THE ELECTRONIC SPREADSHEET

Each of the following are strengths of the electronic spreadsheet in accounting.

- You can choose from a large number of electronic spreadsheets.
- You can use an electronic spreadsheet on most computer systems.
- You can pick from a wide variety of computer system price ranges and features.

The electronic spreadsheet is perfectly suited to the mathematical calculations required in accounting. These include such operations as adding, subtracting, and averaging.

Its formula capability enables the user to make calculations on specific cells and then update calculations instantaneously if a change or changes are made to any of the specified cells. This is the ''what if'' power of the electronic spreadsheet.

- The electronic spreadsheet has the ability to apply a specific formula throughout the spreadsheet. You will remember that this was called **copying** or **replication**. This enables the user to repeat a specific calculation at different places with a different set of numbers in the spreadsheet. This can be particularly useful when there is a repetitive operation to carry out such as totalling one or more additional columns by using a formula previously created.
- The user can easily adapt the electronic spreadsheet to individualized and very specific jobs.

LOOKING AT THE WEAKNESSES OF THE ELECTRONIC SPREADSHEET

The following are a few weaknesses of the electronic spreadsheet in accounting.

- Less expensive electronic spreadsheets may not have the features or physical size that are needed by the user to solve complex accounting problems.
- Some packages require considerable computer memory in order to operate.
- The electronic spreadsheet is not designed to easily integrate a variety of accounting activities such as journalizing, posting from the journal to the ledger, preparing a trial balance, and then preparing financial statements. These activities are programmed into the General Ledger accounting packages that will be discussed in Chapter 6.
- The user must learn how to develop the formula and use the power of the electronic spreadsheet for specific accounting uses.

SPECIFICALLY APPLYING THE ELECTRONIC SPREADSHEET

Now let's examine each accounting cycle step that you have studied and determine if the electronic spreadsheet could be adapted to that accounting operation. The steps of the accounting cycle studied to date include:

- originating transaction data
- journalizing
- posting
- preparing a trial balance
- preparing the income statement and related balance sheet

There are additional steps yet to be learned in the accounting cycle, but these will be addressed later in Chapter 6.

The electronic spreadsheet will not be a useful tool for you in the origination of transaction data. It is, however, perfectly suited for demonstrating the power of the computer in journalizing.

Examine the structure of the General Journal.

- The General Journal requires five columns of varying widths: Date, Account/Explanation, Posting Reference, Debit and Credit. The electronic spreadsheet is made up of columns and rows and the columns can easily be changed to almost any width desired. Therefore, the formatting of the spreadsheet for use as a journal is very simple.

- The recording of actual journal entries is as easy as the manual recording of journal entries. The date is recorded, the name of the account, the appropriate debit or credit entry, and finally an explanation is input.
- The next step in journalizing would be to perform a journal proof. You will remember that this was accomplished by totalling, either manually or with the aid of a calculator, both the debit and credit columns. These two totals should add to the same number if the journal is correct. When you use the electronic spreadsheet, you can program the computer to calculate these two totals by means of the **sum command**. This command adds all the cells in the debit column, produces a total, and then repeats that same operation for the credit column. There are several advantages in using the computer. These include:
- The computer is much faster in producing the totals.
- The computer's calculation will be completely accurate. No error is possible.
- There is no possibility of an input error. No numbers need to be re-entered into a calculator. Instead, the appropriate information is simply highlighted on the computer screen and the computer completes the calculation.

The illustration on page 156 demonstrates a sample General Journal page.

It is important to realize that there are some limitations to the electronic spreadsheet. These include:

- Headings and a new page number are not automatically created at the top of each new journal page. A user can easily copy the headings using the **copy command**, but it would still be necessary for the user to complete this task at the beginning of each new page.
- Posting is **not** done automatically. In fact, maintaining a ledger on an electronic spreadsheet is not an efficient process. Posting references in the General Journal would have to be entered at a later date either using the computer or manually on a printout of the General Journal.

The next step in the accounting cycle is posting. Because the electronic spreadsheet is not an **integrated accounting package**, it is not designed to, nor was it intended to, act as a General Ledger package. As a result, the electronic spreadsheet is not easily used as a General Ledger for the following reasons:

	A	B	C	D	E	F
1	General Journal				Page 1	
2						
3	Date	Account Title and Explanation	PR	Debit	Credit	
4						
5	19--					
6	Sept.30	Cash		60000		
7		Automobile		15000		
8		Furniture		8000		
9		Office Equipment		7000		
10		Bank Loan Payable			20000	
11		Accts. Pay./Bell Furniture Co.			3000	
12		Accts. Pay./Ryan Equipment Co.			2000	
13		Accts. Pay./Westown Motors Ltd.			5000	
14		J. Emery, Capital			60000	
15		To record the opening balance				
16		sheet into accounts.				
17						
18	Oct. 1	Furniture		1000		
19		Cash			1000	
20		Cheque # 1 to Enns Furniture				
21		Ltd. for additional furniture.				
22				91000	91000	
23						
24						
25						
26						

A26

- Ledger accounts will vary in size depending upon the number of transactions affecting that account. Therefore, it is very difficult to know how much space to assign to each ledger account.
- Because of the first problem with the headings and also that a business can have many ledger accounts to maintain, the ledger requires large amounts of space and computer memory. This is not efficient use of the electronic spreadsheet.
- Finally, and most importantly, there is no efficient way to transfer the information from the journal to the appropriate ledger account.

The following step in the accounting cycle—the preparation of the trial balance — is once again, perfectly suited to the electronic spreadsheet. The following steps would enable the user to prepare a trial balance, illustrated on page 158. Read each step carefully and then refer to the illustration that follows.

- The trial balance requires four columns: the account name, the account number, the debits, and the credits. As before, these columns require different widths, and these columns can be altered quickly.
- The heading occupies the first three lines. This can be placed against the left margin or centred over the body of the trial balance.
- The individual accounts, account numbers, and debit or credit balances are then transferred from the General Ledger into the appropriate columns.
- Instead of manually adding or totalling with a calculator, you total the debit and credit columns using the **sum command**. To save additional time and avoid any opportunity for error, use the **copy command** to complete the preparation of the formula for the credit column after you have prepared the formula for the debit column.
- Finally, you can complete a **zero proof** of the trial balance by adding one more column to the electronic spreadsheet. In the column immediately to the right of the credit column, build a formula that enters the debit column cell as a positive number and the credit column cell as a negative number. Then use the **copy command** to fill all of the remaining cells in the column with that same formula. The result will be a listing of all the account balances in the proofing column as either a positive or negative number. Total the column by using the **sum command** and you have a zero proof.

These steps should sound very familiar, because the procedure you used to produce a zero proof on a calculator is very similar. The only

	A	B	C	D	E	F
1	J. Emery Real Estate					
2	Trial Balance					
3	October 31, 19--					
4						
5						
6	Account Title	Acct	Debit	Credit		
7		No.				
8						
9	Cash	101	71065		71065	
10	Accts. Rec./Pat Rogers	103	6000		6000	
11	Accts. Rec./R. Scobie	104	4000		4000	
12	Accts. Rec./Shannon Development Co.	105	15000		15000	
13	Automobile	110	15000		15000	
14	Furniture	112	9000		9000	
15	Office Equipment	114	8000		8000	
16	Bank Loan Payable	201		16000	-16000	
17	Accts. Pay./Bell Furniture Co.	202		3000	-3000	
18	Accts. Pay./The City Press	203		2000	-2000	
19	Accts. Pay./Ryan Equipment Co.	204		3000	-3000	
20	J. Emery, Capital	301		63000	-63000	
21	J. Emery, Drawing	302	2000		2000	
22	Commissions Earned	401		51800	-51800	
23	Rent Expense	501	1600		1600	
24	Telephone Expense	502	40		40	
25	Utilities Expense	503	595		595	
26	Salaries Expense	504	4500		4500	
27	Advertising Expense	505	2000		2000	
28			-------	-------		
29			138800	138800	0	
30			=====	=====		
31						
32						

A32

difference is that you had to input all that information into the calculator. The work was completed by using the spreadsheet in three short and easy steps.

PROBLEMS

Developing a trial balance on the electronic spreadsheet.

Examining "what if" situations.

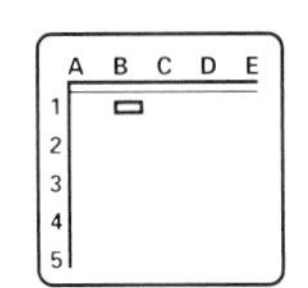

P 4-13 Refer to Problem 4-4 (J. Edgar Consulting Services).

a. Use the step-by-step instructions provided by your instructor for preparing the General Journal. Complete a journal proof. Print a copy of the General Journal for your notes and compare it to the manual copy you prepared earlier in your workbook.

b. Complete the following "what if" situations, print a copy of the new General Journal and compare it to the original printout.

i) "What if" J. Edgar borrowed $17 000 from the Royal Bank instead of $5000 on November 17?

ii) "What if" the Macintosh® SE® computer bought on the 16th cost $2798 instead of $3000?

iii) What changes automatically and ensures that you completed the changes correctly?

Developing a trial balance on the electronic spreadsheet.

Examining "what if" situations.

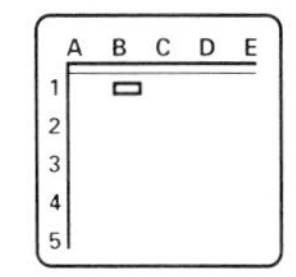

P 4-14 Refer to Problem 4-10 (J. Edgar Consulting Services).

a. Use the step-by-step procedures supplied by your instructor to complete the trial balance for J. Edgar Consulting Services. Prepare the "zero-proof" column, and then print a copy of the trial balance for your notes. Compare the printout to the work you completed earlier in the chapter.

b. Complete two "what if" situations as follows:

i) What if the Cash account and the Capital account increased by $3500 each?

ii) What if the Drawing account increased by $750 because we failed to record a cash withdrawal? (*Remember:* At least two accounts will be affected.)

Take particular notice of the effect that the changes have on the totalling and the zero-proof procedures.

MINI-CASES

Discussing the advantages and disadvantages of using an electronic spreadsheet vs. a simple manual system.

MC 4-13 A. Fonzerelli operates an automobile storage and finish-restoring service. His business has been operating for three years and all accounting records have been maintained manually. Richard, a friend of the owner and a classmate of yours in accounting class wants to introduce Mr. Fonzerelli to the possible uses of an electronic spreadsheet in his business.

a. List the manual accounting activities that could be completed on an electronic spreadsheet.

b. What are the advantages to be gained by converting these accounting activities over to the computer?

c. Are there potential disadvantages that should be considered before such a step is taken?

Discussing the pros and cons of the posting procedure in an electronic spreadsheet.

MC 4-14 Kwong is a computer fanatic and believes that ledger accounts can be included in an electronic spreadsheet along with a General Journal and that posting can be completed electronically.

a. Is Kwong correct? Is it possible to complete both journalizing and posting using an electronic spreadsheet?

b. Discuss the pros and cons, and then draw a conclusion as to possibility of success of such an endeavour.

COMPREHENSIVE CASE STUDY 4

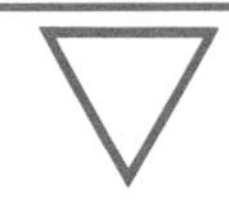

Robert Gauthier is the owner of RG Computer Consulting Services. The business has been in operation since August 1 and it has been growing steadily. Robert has kept very good journal records, but he thinks of his ledger accounts as being second in importance. Robert wants to prepare a set of financial statements for the end of September. You have been asked to assist in the preparation of these statements. Robert has given you all the journals, and presented below is a list of the accounts of the business. Robert has also provided you with a piece of paper that indicates the dates and amounts of cash he has withdrawn from the business since August 1. The total of the withdrawals is $525.

SUMMARY OF ACCOUNT BALANCES

Accts. Pay./Telmark Co.	$ 650
Accts. Rec./W. Wrongton	125
Office Equipment	12 600
Bank Loan Payable	8 000
Consulting Fees Earned	4 400
Advertising Expense	600
Accts. Rec./P. Langton	450
Accts. Pay./ABC Furniture	1 200
Rent Expense	800
Office Furniture	4 300
Utilities Expense	345
Supplies Expense	475
R. Gauthier, Drawing	?
R. Gauthier, Capital	?
Automobile	7 650
Cash	1 950

Analyzing accounting records.

Calculating missing data.

Preparing financial statements.

a. Calculate the missing balances.

b. Prepare a formal trial balance for RG Computer Consulting Services at September 30. If possible, use an electronic spreadsheet for this task and print a copy of the trial balance.

c. If the ledger accounts had not been usable, what would you have had to do in order to make them usable? Where would you obtain that information?

Constructively criticizing methods of recording and the accounting system.

d. Prepare a formal income statement and a formal related balance sheet for Robert Gauthier's business.

e. What comments would you make and what advice would you give to Robert regarding his present accounting system and maintenance of accounting records?

PREPARING FINANCIAL STATEMENTS

Topic 1

Introducing the Six-Column Worksheet

Topic 2

Preparing the Financial Statements

Topic 3

Interpreting an Income Statement and Balance Sheet

Chapter 4 introduced the first four steps of the accounting cycle:

(1) originating transaction data from source documents

(2) journalizing source documents

(3) posting data to the ledger

(4) preparing a trial balance

These steps lead to one goal—to prepare a set of financial statements.

When a trial balance is correct and contains only a short list of General Ledger accounts, a set of financial statements can be easily prepared. However, many accountants first prepare a working paper called the **worksheet**.

TOPIC 1 INTRODUCING THE SIX-COLUMN WORKSHEET

The worksheet is a working paper that summarizes all information needed to prepare an accurate set of financial statements. The worksheet is not regarded as part of the permanent accounting records of a business. It is only temporary, and you may prepare the worksheet neatly in pencil, so that you can easily correct errors.

The worksheet illustrated below has six columns.

J. Emery Real Estate
Worksheet
For the month ended October 31, 19-1

	ACCOUNT TITLE	ACCT. NO.	TRIAL BALANCE		INCOME STATEMENT		BALANCE SHEET		
			DEBIT	CREDIT	DEBIT	CREDIT	DEBIT	CREDIT	
1	Cash	101	71 065.00						1
2	Accts. Rec./Pat Rogers	103	6 000.00						2
3	Accts. Rec./R. Scobie	104	4 000.00						3
4	Accts. Rec./Shannon Dev. Co.	105	15 000.00						4
5	Automobile	110	15 000.00						5
6	Furniture	112	9 000.00						6
7	Office Equipment	114	8 000.00						7
8	Bank Loan Payable	201		16 000.00					8
9	Accts. Pay./Bell Furn. Co.	202		3 000.00					9
10	Accts. Pay./The City Press	203		2 000.00					10
11	Accts. Pay./Ryan Equip. Co.	204		3 000.00					11
12	J. Emery, Capital	301		63 000.00					12
13	J. Emery, Drawing	302	2 000.00						13
14	Commissions Earned	401		51 800.00					14
15	Rent Expense	501	1 600.00						15
16	Telephone Expense	502	40.00						16
17	Utilities Expense	503	595.00						17
18	Salaries Expense	504	4 500.00						18
19	Advertising Expense	505	2 000.00						19
20			138 800.00	138 800.00					20
21									21
22									22
23									23
24									24
25									25
26									26

Analysis: Examine the following about the worksheet for J. Emery Real Estate:

- The three-line heading answers the same three questions as in the income statement: **who** (the name of the business); **what** (the name of the working paper); and **when** (the date of the accounting period). Notice that the date line reads "For the Month Ended" because the worksheet includes the income statement, which is based on a specific period that has ended on October 31.

- The body consists of these columns: **Account Title**, for all General Ledger accounts having a balance at the end of the accounting period; **Account Number**, for the account number of each account listed. For the **Trial Balance**, **Income Statement**, and **Balance Sheet** columns, two money columns—debit and credit—are given.

Worksheet: an expanded trial balance, in which account balances are classified and sorted. The worksheet provides information to prepare formal financial statements.

Because it begins with a trial balance and is expanded to include other statement columns, the worksheet may be defined as an expanded trial balance.

The Income Statement and Balance Sheet columns at the right are referred to as the "financial statement columns."

COMPLETING THE SIX-COLUMN WORKSHEET

To complete a six-column worksheet, follow the steps. After reading the instructions for each step, look at the completed worksheet illustrated on page 166.

Step 1: Complete the Heading. Remember: The date line always reports the length of the accounting period that has ended. It is important to recognize that the link which connects the financial statement columns is the accounting period. As you now know from the matching principle, the net income (or net loss) is the result of matching revenues with related expenses for a definite period.

Step 2: Copy the Trial Balance to the Worksheet. Enter the account titles, account numbers, and the debit and credit balances exactly as listed for the trial balance. Include the totals to prove that the General Ledger is in balance. It should also be noted that some businesses do not prepare a formal trial balance. Instead, they copy the trial balance information directly from the General Ledger accounts to the worksheet.

Step 3: Transfer and Separate the Balances. The next step is to divide the information in the trial balance between the income statement and the balance sheet. Remember these two rules when copying balances from the trial balance to the related financial statement column.

- Copy a debit balance to the debit side of the related financial statement.

J. Emery Real Estate
Worksheet
For the Month Ended October 31, 19–1

	ACCOUNT TITLE	ACCT. NO.	TRIAL BALANCE		INCOME STATEMENT		BALANCE SHEET		
			DEBIT	CREDIT	DEBIT	CREDIT	DEBIT	CREDIT	
1	Cash	101	71065 00				71065 00		1
2	Accts. Rec./Pat Rogers	103	6000 00				6000 00		2
3	Accts. Rec./R. Scobie	104	4000 00				4000 00		3
4	Accts. Rec./Shannon Dev. Co.	105	15000 00				15000 00		4
5	Automobile	110	15000 00				15000 00		5
6	Furniture	112	9000 00				9000 00		6
7	Office Equipment	114	8000 00				8000 00		7
8	Bank Loan Payable	201		16000 00				16000 00	8
9	Accts. Pay./Bell Furn. Co.	202		3000 00				3000 00	9
10	Accts. Pay./The City Press	203		2000 00				2000 00	10
11	Accts. Pay./Ryan Equip. Co.	204		3000 00				3000 00	11
12	J. Emery, Capital	301		63000 00				63000 00	12
13	J. Emery, Drawing	302	2000 00				2000 00		13
14	Commissions Earned	401		51800 00		51800 00			14
15	Rent Expense	501	1600 00		1600 00				15
16	Telephone Expense	502	40 00		40 00				16
17	Utilities Expense	503	595 00		595 00				17
18	Salaries Expense	504	4500 00		4500 00				18
19	Advertising Expense	505	2000 00		2000 00				19
20			138800 00	138800 00	8735 00	51800 00	130065 00	87000 00	20
21						8735 00			21
22	Net Income					43065 00	→	43065 00	22
23							130065 00	130065 00	23
24									24
25									25
26									26

- Copy a credit balance to the credit side of the related financial statement column.

The accounting equation is represented in the balance sheet. Therefore, asset, liability, and owner's equity accounts are transferred to the balance sheet. Since the income statement reports revenues and expenses, these accounts are transferred to the income statement.

Analysis: The first account balance, Cash, shows a debit balance of $71 065. Cash is an asset account and all assets are recorded in the balance sheet. Therefore, copy this amount, $71 065, to the **debit** column under the **Balance Sheet** heading.

Since the next six accounts are all assets, with debit balances, they are copied to the **debit** column of the **balance sheet**.

The Bank Loan Payable, on Line 8, has a credit balance of $16 000. This is a liability account and all liabilities are recorded in the balance sheet. Therefore, copy this **credit** balance to the **credit** column of the **balance sheet**. Follow the same procedure for the three accounts payable that follow.

The owner's Capital account is listed on Line 12. Copy the **credit** balance of this account to the **credit** column of the **balance sheet.**

Next is the owner's drawing account. Copy the **debit** balance of this account to the **debit** column of the **balance sheet.** Why? Because all drawings are eventually reported in the balance sheet as a deduction from owner's equity.

Commissions Earned is the next account. Since this is a revenue account with a **credit** balance, copy the balance to the **credit** column of the **income statement**.

Five expense accounts are listed next. Since each shows a **debit** balance, copy each balance to the **debit** column of the **income statement**.

Step 4: Add the Financial Statement Columns. Draw a single line across all statement columns as shown. Then add the figures in the debit and credit columns for both the Income Statement and the Balance Sheet. The totals are written below the single line.

Step 5: Complete the Income Statement Section. Since the income statement is shown as debit and credit columns, the procedure to prepare an income statement is slightly different.

Completing the Income Statement Section: Calculating a Net Income

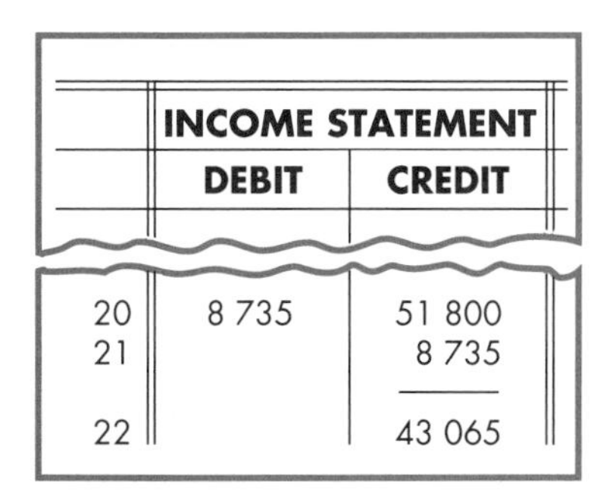

	INCOME STATEMENT	
	DEBIT	CREDIT
20	8 735	51 800
21		8 735
22		43 065

- Below the totals, place the **smaller amount** under the larger one. In the example, $8735 is placed under $51 800 in the credit column.
- Draw a single line under the smaller amount to indicate a calculation.
- Subtract the two figures and enter the answer on the next line. Since the smaller figure normally represents total expenses, and since this figure is subtracted from the larger total revenue, the answer must be the net income for the month. Thus, in the example, the net income is $43 065, shown on line 22 of the worksheet. See also the marginal illustration.
- Finally, at the far left of the worksheet, in the Account Title column, enter the words "Net Income."

Step 6: Complete the Balance Sheet Section. This is the last step, which is highlighted at the top of page 168.

- Copy the net income along the same line to the **credit** column of the balance sheet. Why? Since the net income in the income statement shows a credit balance, owner's equity in the balance sheet must also show a credit balance. In the illustration, this

Completing the Balance Sheet Section:
Reporting a Net Income

INCOME STATEMENT		BALANCE SHEET		
DEBIT	CREDIT	DEBIT	CREDIT	
8 735	51 800	130 065	87 000	20
	8 735			21
	43 065 →		→ 43 065	22
		130 065	130 065	23

increase to the credit side is emphasized with an arrow, which you may wish to use at this stage.

- Draw a single line across both the debit and the credit columns of the Balance Sheet section to indicate a calculation.
- Total the Balance Sheet columns. The sums must agree, and in this example, the sums are both $130 065.
- Finally, draw a double line across both financial statement columns as shown.

The worksheet is now complete.

CALCULATING AND REPORTING A NET LOSS

In J. Emery Real Estate's worksheet, the **match-up** between the total revenue and the total expenses in the income statement resulted in a net income. Suppose, however, that the total expense (the total of the debit column) is greater than the total revenue (the total of the credit column). Then matching revenue with related expenses would show a net loss.

The procedure for reporting a net loss on the worksheet is shown on the opposite page. Note that the total of the debit column of the income statement is greater than the total of the credit column. This means that the total expense is greater than the total revenue. The match-up is done by placing the $14 000 under the $15 000 in the greater column. The net debit balance is copied to the debit column of the Balance Sheet column, because a net loss decreases owner's

Calculating and Reporting a Net Loss

INCOME STATEMENT		BALANCE SHEET		
DEBIT	CREDIT	DEBIT	CREDIT	
15 000	14 000	74 600	75 600	20
14 000				21
1 000 →		→ 1 000		22
		75 600	75 600	23

equity in any balance sheet. The Balance Sheet columns will balance now that the net loss has been transferred to the debit side.

Finally, the words ''Net Loss'' are entered on the far left side of the worksheet in the Account Title column and a double line is drawn across the financial statement columns to complete the worksheet.

TOPIC 1 PROBLEMS

Preparing a six-column worksheet.

P 5-1 A trial balance of the General Ledger for the St. John's Rental Company was taken after the first month's business as at May 31, and revealed the following balances: Cash (101), $5600; Accts. Rec./R. Dowber (105), $85; Accts. Rec./Talbot Construction Co. (107), $2400; Accts. Rec./Weima Contractors (109), $4850; Office Equipment (130), $6500; Delivery Truck (150), $9400; Bank Loan Payable (201), $3000; Accts. Pay./Gautreau Equipment (205), $1200; Accts. Pay./Southend Suppliers (208), $900; R. McTavish, Capital (301), $16 213; R. McTavish, Drawing (302), $500; Rental Fees Earned (401), $12 800; Rent Expense (501), $4000; Telephone Expense (505), $55; Utilities Expense (510), $325; Office Supplies Expense (515), $103; Advertising Expense (520), $210; Truck Expense (525), $85.

Prepare a six-column worksheet for the St. John's Rental Company for the month ended May 31.

Preparing a six-column worksheet.

P 5-2 After the first year of business for Louis's Fix-It Shop, the following balances were listed in the business as at October 31, 19—. Cash (101), $10 600; Accts. Rec./P. Doran (105), $250; Accts. Rec./Kapplan Co. (107), $147; Repair Supplies (109),

$2300; Land (125), $12 000; Building (128), $35 000; Repair Equipment (130), $4750; Delivery Truck (150), $11 300; Bank Loan Payable (201), $4500; Accts. Pay./Albert & Son Suppliers (205), $986; Accts. Pay./Packer Parts Ltd. (208), $900; Mortgage Payable (240), $29 000; L. Sanchez, Capital (301), $26 216; L. Sanchez, Drawing (302), $7500; Fees Earned (401), $32 800; Property Taxes Expense (501), $3000; Telephone Expense (505), $559; Utilities Expense (510), $1375; Office Supplies Expense (515), $587; Advertising Expense (520), $989; Truck Expense (525), $1045; Interest Expense (530), $3000.

Prepare a six-column worksheet for Louis's Fix-it Shop for the year ended October 31, 19—.

Preparing a six-column worksheet.

P 5-3 After the first year of business, the Maritime Survey Co. showed the following year-end General Ledger account balances as at December 31: Cash (101), $9250; Government of Canada Bonds (102), $10 000; Accts. Rec./Dartmouth Construction (103), $2400; Accts. Rec./Halifax Properties (104), $1600; Accts. Rec./Saint John Construction (105), $3500; Land (110), $25 000; Building (112), $75 000; Survey Equipment (114), $30 000; Office Equipment (116), $5000; Trucks (118), $36 000; Bank Loan Payable (201), $4500; Accts. Pay./Fredericton Supply (202), $3000; Accts. Pay./Newcastle Motors (203), $2500; Salaries Payable (204), $1200; Mortgage Payable (220), $48 000; Don Kelly, Capital (301), $50 930; Don Kelly, Drawing (302), $32 000; Fees Earned (401), $188 870; Interest Revenue (402), $1000; Salaries Expense (501), $41 970; Survey Supplies Expense (502), $1800; Office Supplies Expense (503), $2400; Telephone Expense (504), $890; Utilities Expense (505), $1950; Insurance Expense (506), $390; Maintenance Expense (507), $11 250; Gasoline Expense (508), $3800; Truck Repairs Expense (509), $1200; Property Taxes Expense (510), $1200; Bank Interest Expense (520), $400; Mortgage Interest Expense (521), $3000.

Prepare a six-column worksheet for the Maritime Survey Co. *Special Instructions*: This worksheet will require the use of two pages. Draw a single line across all money columns after the second-last line (line 23) of the first worksheet form. On the last line (line 24), in the Account Title column, write "Totals Carried Forward." Show the total in each money column.

On the second page, show in the heading the title "Worksheet, Page 2" and the date of the accounting period. Then, on the line below the heading Account Title, write "Totals Brought Forward." Copy all the totals from the first page to this line in the proper money columns.

You can then complete the worksheet in the usual way.

Preparing a six-column worksheet. Save the solution to Problem 5-4 for use in Chapter 6.

P 5-4 Refer to Problem 4-10 (J. Edgar Consulting Services) on page 150 and prepare a six-column worksheet for this business for the month ended November 30, 19-1.

MINI-CASES

Analyzing the procedure in order to prepare financial statements in a business.

MC 5-1 Grease and Oil Services just completed six months of operations in the fiscal year that will end December 31, 19—. All postings to the General Ledger are complete, but the owner, Miki Milina, is uncertain what to do before producing a new balance sheet.

a. Assist Miki by suggesting what accounting records she needs to prepare before the balance sheet can be completed. Explain why she needs each of these accounting records.

b. What date should be used on any accounting records produced at this time? Explain.

Identifying the GAAP related to the income statement.

MC 5-2 A completed six-column worksheet reflects at least one GAAP that you have studied in this textbook relating to the income statement.

a. Identify the GAAP involved.

b. Explain how this GAAP is demonstrated in the preparation of a worksheet.

Identifying the GAAP related to the worksheet.

MC 5-3 Examine the worksheet on page 172 and identify the errors located in the worksheet.

a. Briefly describe each error you have located and how it could be corrected.

b. Prepare a correct version of the worksheet.

c. Identify the GAAP involved in the preparation of a worksheet.

Scarborough Cleaning Service
Worksheet
For the Year Ended December 31, 19-1

	ACCOUNT TITLE	ACCT. NO.	TRIAL BALANCE DEBIT	TRIAL BALANCE CREDIT	INCOME STATEMENT DEBIT	INCOME STATEMENT CREDIT	BALANCE SHEET DEBIT	BALANCE SHEET CREDIT	
1	Cash	101	2 500 00				2 500 00		1
2	Accts. Rec./Aladin Lamps	104	850 00				850 00		2
3	Accts. Rec./Miloom Manor	106	235 00				235 00		3
4	Accts. Rec./Peterson Co.	108	480 00				480 00		4
5	Cleaning Equipment	120	10 200 00				10 200 00		5
6	Truck	125	8 700 00				8 700 00		6
7	Bank Loan Payable	201		3 500 00			3 500 00		7
8	Accts. Pay./ABC Co.	206		280 00				280 00	8
9	Accts. Pay./Talbot Equip.	208		1 200 00				1 200 00	9
10	R. Podgorski, Capital	301		13 705 00				13 705 00	10
11	R. Podgorski, Drawing	302	8 000 00		8 000 00				11
12	Cleaning Service Revenue	401		31 650 00		31 650 00			12
13	Cleaning Supplies Exp.	501	1 360 00		1 360 00				13
14	Gas & Oil Expense	505	300 00		300 00				14
15	Wages Expense	510	16 000 00		16 000 00				15
16	Equipment Repairs Expense	515	150 00						16
17	Utilities Expense	520	1 200 00						17
18	Telephone Expense	525	360 00						18
19			50 335 00	50 335 00	25 660 00	31 650 00	28 175 00	15 185 00	19
20						25 660 00			20
21						5 990 00		5 990 00	21
22							28 175 00	21 175 00	22
23									23
24									24
25									25
26									26

PREPARING THE FINANCIAL STATEMENTS

This section deals with preparing financial statements from a completed worksheet. Also, it presents some new Generally Accepted Accounting Principles (GAAPs) for reporting the balance sheet.

PREPARING THE INCOME STATEMENT

The first financial statement to be prepared is the income statement. The data for preparing the income statement are found under the Income Statement heading. Portions of the worksheet and the income statement for J. Emery Real Estate are shown on the next page.

J. Emery Real Estate
Worksheet
For the Month Ended October 31, 19–1

ACCOUNT TITLE	INCOME STATEMENT	
	DEBIT	CREDIT
Commissions Earned		51 800
Rent Expense	1 600	
Telephone Expense	40	
Utilities Expense	595	
Salaries Expense	4 500	
Advertising Expense	2 000	
	8 735	51 800
		8 735
Net Income		43 065

J. Emery Real Estate
Income Statement
For the Month Ended October 31, 19–1

Revenue:		
Commissions Earned		$51 800 00
Expenses:		
Rent Expense	$ 1 600 00	
Telephone Expense	40 00	
Utilities Expense	595 00	
Salaries Expense	4 500 00	
Advertising Expense	2 000 00	
Total Expenses		8 735 00
Net Income		$43 065 00

PREPARING THE RELATED BALANCE SHEET

As you have learned, the related balance sheet is prepared **after** the income statement. Of course, the data for the balance sheet are found in the columns headed Balance Sheet on the worksheet.

Account form: a balance sheet with assets on the left side, and the claims against them on the right.

Report form: a balance sheet with assets, liabilities, and owner's equity arranged vertically.

In Chapter 2, the balance sheet was prepared with the assets on the left side and the claims against those assets on the right, as in the accounting equation, $A = L + OE$. This form is also known as the account form type of balance sheet, because it has two sides. But the account form is only one way to report a balance sheet. Another method is shown in the illustration on page 175. It is called the report form. Examine it first, and then study the following points.

- In the heading, Line 1 reports the name of the firm, Line 2 the name of the document, and Line 3 the **as at** date on which the assets, liabilities, and owner's equity are reported.
- The body reports the details of $A = L + OE$. Note that the three elements of the accounting equation are placed **vertically**.
- It is easier to prepare a balance sheet in the report form because you do not need to balance the totals of $A = L + OE$ on the same line.
- No matter which form is used, all balance sheets should report useful information about the assets, the liabilities, and the owner's equity. In earlier chapters, you learned a simple form of balance sheet. In the illustration on page 175, notice that the

Classified balance sheet: one in which assets and liabilities are reported under meaningful groups or classes.

liabilities have been divided into groups or classes. Such a balance sheet is called a classified balance sheet**.** Since the elements of the accounting equation are also reported vertically here, it may be referred to as a **classified balance sheet prepared in report form**.

Assets may be put into as many as six classes, but only two are shown in the illustration: current assets and fixed assets. Liabilities may be put into as many as four classes, but only one class, current liabilities, is shown. (A second class will be presented later.)

REPORTING CURRENT ASSETS

Current assets: assets which can be converted into cash within one year of the balance sheet date (introductory definition).

The meaning of current assets reflects the liquidity order of reporting assets—that assets are reported in the order of how easily they can be converted into cash.

In the case of J. Emery Real Estate, Accounts Receivable are reported directly after Cash because the business expects to collect from the customers within a short time—perhaps 30 days.

Current Assets:	
Cash	$ 6 400
Canada Savings Bonds	20 000
Accounts Receivable	1 200

Canada Savings Bonds are reported before Accounts Receivable, as shown in the margin. This is because these bonds can be converted into cash by ''cashing them in'' at the bank or through a broker.

This definition of current assets is introductory because other current assets are included in this class which are **not** converted into cash. You will learn about these assets, as well as other aspects of current asset accounting, later in this chapter and in Chapter 15.

Finally, note that the total of current assets is reported. This total always appears on a balance sheet.

REPORTING FIXED ASSETS

Fixed assets: tangible, long-lived assets held for use within the firm to support revenue-making activities for several years beyond the balance sheet date.

Fixed assets are also known as **long-lived assets**, **operational assets**, **plant assets**, or **property**, **plant**, and **equipment**. Being more or less permanent in nature, they are not normally converted into cash. Instead, they are kept in the business to assist in revenue-making activities for several years beyond the balance sheet date. Fixed assets are always reported under a separate heading in the balance sheet.

Look at the Fixed Assets section in the handwritten balance sheet for J. Emery Real Estate (opposite page). Notice the words ''at cost'' after ''Fixed Assets.'' They are put there because of a very important GAAP called the **cost principle**. It may be introduced as follows:

GAAP for Cost (introductory definition).

All assets purchased by a business must be recorded as follows: (1) The cost of all assets is the original purchase price. This price is known as the cost price or cost value. (2) The original cost values of assets must be retained throughout the accounting cycle.

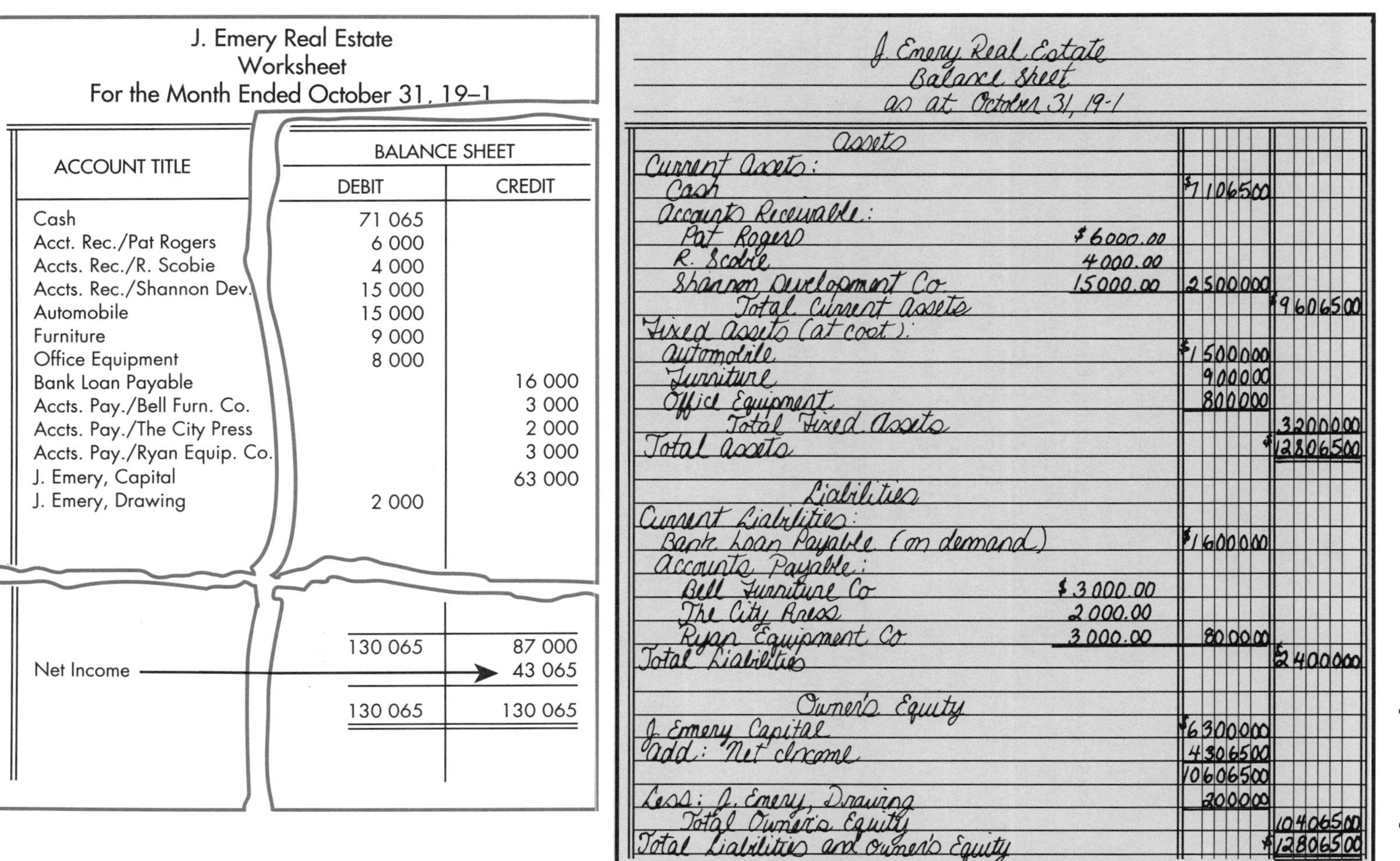

J. Emery Real Estate
Worksheet
For the Month Ended October 31, 19–1

ACCOUNT TITLE	BALANCE SHEET	
	DEBIT	CREDIT
Cash	71 065	
Acct. Rec./Pat Rogers	6 000	
Accts. Rec./R. Scobie	4 000	
Accts. Rec./Shannon Dev.	15 000	
Automobile	15 000	
Furniture	9 000	
Office Equipment	8 000	
Bank Loan Payable		16 000
Accts. Pay./Bell Furn. Co.		3 000
Accts. Pay./The City Press		2 000
Accts. Pay./Ryan Equip. Co.		3 000
J. Emery, Capital		63 000
J. Emery, Drawing	2 000	
	130 065	87 000
Net Income →		43 065
	130 065	130 065

J. Emery Real Estate
Balance Sheet
as at October 31, 19-1

Assets			
Current Assets:			
Cash		$71 065.00	
Accounts Receivable:			
Pat Rogers	$6000.00		
R. Scobie	4000.00		
Shannon Development Co.	15000.00	25 000.00	
Total Current Assets			$96 065.00
Fixed Assets (at cost):			
Automobile		$15 000.00	
Furniture		9 000.00	
Office Equipment		8 000.00	
Total Fixed Assets			32 000.00
Total Assets			$128 065.00
Liabilities			
Current Liabilities:			
Bank Loan Payable (on demand)		$16 000.00	
Accounts Payable:			
Bell Furniture Co	$3000.00		
The City Press	2000.00		
Ryan Equipment Co	3000.00	8 000.00	
Total Liabilities			$24 000.00
Owner's Equity			
J. Emery Capital		$63 000.00	
Add: Net Income		43 065.00	
		106 065.00	
Less: J. Emery, Drawing		2 000.00	
Total Owner's Equity			104 065.00
Total Liabilities and Owner's Equity			$128 065.00

Cost price (sometimes known as historical cost price): the price originally agreed upon by buyer and seller.

When applied to fixed assets, the cost principle assures readers of financial statements that these assets are reported in the balance sheet on the basis of what it cost the business to obtain them. For example, if a parcel of land cost $20 000 ten years ago, the cost principle requires accountants to report it at its original cost, $20 000 — even if it can now be bought or sold for $50 000. To avoid any misunderstanding, the words "at cost" are used, either after the particular asset or after the class name Fixed Assets.

Fixed Assets (at cost):	
Automobile	$15 000
Furniture	9 000
Office Equipment ...	8 000

Though we have been talking about assets, the cost principle sets guidelines for recording every element and subelement in the accounting equation. It also sets guidelines for transactions when a cash price is not involved. Since these areas of applying the cost principle can become very complex, they are best studied in more advanced courses. In this chapter, and later ones, always show the words "at cost" after **Fixed Assets** on a balance sheet.

In the illustration, notice that **total fixed assets** is reported. And finally when the report form of balance sheet is used, a double line is drawn below total assets. This closes the asset section so that this figure is separate from the figures for liabilities and owner's equity.

REPORTING CURRENT LIABILITIES

Current liabilities: debts owing which will fall due within one year of the balance sheet date.

Liabilities, like assets, are reported on a balance sheet under groups or classes of accounts. A common group is current liabilities

Current liabilities are debts the business expects to pay within one year of the balance sheet date. For J. Emery Real Estate, note that the bank loan is payable "on demand." This means that the bank can ask the realtor to pay back the loan at any time. Therefore, it is reported as the first current liability on the balance sheet.

Amounts owing to creditors, too, would normally have to be paid within one year of the balance sheet date. Thus, the illustrated balance sheet also reports Accounts Payable as a current liability.

Although the balance sheet shows only two current liabilities, it is useful to remember that **any debt which will be paid out of current funds (funds available under current assets) should be included in current liabilities**. Keep this in mind when you study other balance sheets in this book.

In this balance sheet, the total of current liabilities is also the total liabilities. When only one class of liabilities is reported, the total is commonly shown as "Total Liabilities." When more than one class of liabilities is reported, the total of each class should be shown.

The owner's equity section was explained in Chapter 2.

PRESENTING THE CLASSIFIED BALANCE SHEET IN ACCOUNT FORM

When the balance sheet is to be included in a published annual report, most Canadian businesses prefer to use the report form described earlier. However, some businesses still prefer the account form with two pages, the left page listing the assets and the right page listing the liabilities and the owner's equity elements.

Study the illustrated balance sheet for Southview Cleaning Shop.

- You will notice that for each page, there is a main column in addition to subcolumns. The subcolumns list groups of individual accounts; the main columns list totals.

Southview Cleaning Shop
Balance Sheet
as at December 31, 19—

ASSETS

Current Assets		
Cash		$ 2 250.00
Government of Canada Bonds		10 000.00
Accounts Receivable		
Alma Services	$2 000.00	
Vancouver Auto	2 800.00	4 800.00
Total Current Assets		17 050.00
Fixed Assets (at cost)		
Land (security for mortgage payable)		10 000.00
Building (security for mortgage payable)		50 000.00
Dry Cleaning Equipment		20 000.00
Delivery Equipment		12 000.00
Office Equipment		5 000.00
Total Fixed Assets		97 000.00
Total Assets		$114 050.00

LIABILITIES

Current Liabilities		
Bank Loan Payable (on demand)		$ 2 000.00
Accounts Payable:		
Bute Supply Co.	$1 500.00	
Kingsway Ltd.	3 500.00	5 000.00
Property Taxes Payable		200.00
Current portion of mortgage payable		1 000.00
Total Current Liabilities		8 200.00
Long-Term Liabilities		
10% Mortgage Payable, due 1999 (secured by land and building)	$20 000.00	
Less current portion	1 000.00	
Total Long-Term Liabilities		19 000.00
Total Liabilities		$ 27 200.00

OWNER'S EQUITY

L.A. Fortier, Capital	$71 850.00	
Add: Net Income for Year	40 000.00	
	111 850.00	
Less: Withdrawals	25 000.00	
Total Owner's Equity		86 850.00
Total Liabilities and Owner's Equity		$114 050.00

- In the Current Asset section, two accounts receivable are listed in the subcolumn. Below this list is a single line which indicates a calculation. All of the assets are listed in the main column. The single rule below "4 800.00" indicates that the figures above it will be added. The rule below "17 050" indicates a total.

- The five fixed assets are also presented in the same way. You can identify the subtotal of each group of assets quickly, as they appear to be enclosed between two single rules. The final total is underlined by a double rule.

- In the liability section on the right page, observe the two classes of debts: **current liabilities** and **long-term liabilities**.
  As we have said, current liabilities consist of all the debts of the business payable within one year of the balance sheet date. Long-term liabilities, on the other hand, represent the debts of a business that are **not** due within one year. The illustration highlights one common long-term debt, mortgage payable.

Long-term liabilities: debts which, in the ordinary course of business, are not liquidated within one year of the balance sheet date.

- A mortgage is a pledge of property to a creditor as security against a debt (the loan of money). Since a pledge of property is involved, accountants report as much information as possible about a mortgage. For example, if a fixed rate of interest is used, the interest rate payable on the mortgage should be reported, as well as the due date.

- The mortgage is "secured by land and building." This means that the lender of the money (the mortgagee) will have a claim on the firm's land and building if the borrower (the mortgagor) fails to make the payments.

- On the asset side of the balance sheet under Fixed Assets, notice that the land and building are pledged as securities against the mortgage. After each asset the words "security for mortgage payable" appear in parentheses. Thus, the reader of the balance sheet knows which liabilities are secured and which assets are pledged as securities.

- The current portion of the long-term debt is reported under Current Liabilities. This is important, because any portion of long-term debt payable within a year—out of current funds or assets—should be included in current liabilities.

- You will notice that the current portion of the mortgage payable is reported twice: under Current Liabilities as a current liability and also under Long-Term Liabilities as a deduction from the original long-term debt. This reports the amount to be paid beyond a year from the balance sheet date.

- Finally, on the left page total assets must be reported on the same line as the total liabilities and owner's equity on the right page.

REVIEWING THE ACCOUNTING CYCLE

We have now covered these steps in the accounting cycle:

- Step 1: originating the transaction data
- Step 2: journalizing
- Step 3: posting
- Step 4: preparing the trial balance
- Step 5: preparing the worksheet
- Step 6: preparing financial statements

PROBLEMS

Preparing an income statement and related balance sheet in report form.

P 5-5 Using the completed worksheet for Problem 5-1, prepare an income statement and a classified balance sheet in report form for the St. John's Rental Company.

Preparing an income statement and related balance sheet in account form.

P 5-6 Using the completed worksheet for Problem 5-2, prepare an income statement and a classified balance sheet in account form for Louis's Fix-It Shop. *Important*: Of the $29 000 balance reported for Mortgage Payable, $2500 is due within one year of the balance sheet date. The mortgage is secured by the pledging of land and a building. Finally, the final amount payable on the mortgage is due in 15 years.

Preparing an income statement and related balance sheet in report form.

P 5-7 Using the completed worksheet for Problem 5-3, prepare an income statement and a classified balance sheet in report form for the Maritime Survey Co. *Important*: Assume that the mortgage payable carries a fixed rate of interest at 7 1/2%. Of the $48 000 balance reported on the mortgage payable, assume that $5000 is payable within one year of the balance sheet date. The mortgage is secured by the pledging of the company's land and buildings. Assume that the mortgage payable is due 20 years from now.

Preparing an income statement and related balance sheet in report form. Save the solution to P5-8 for use in Chapter 6.

P 5-8 Using the completed worksheet for Problem 5-4, prepare an income statement and a classified balance sheet in report form for J. Edgar Consulting Services.

MINI-CASES

Examining GAAPs as they relate to the financial statements.

Determining the effects of an unrecorded transaction on the financial statements.

MC 5-4 W. Geer has been examining the financial statements for her firm, Geer Services Company, for the quarter ended July 31, 199-. She has noted the following key figures and has asked you for your assistance in resolving the following problem.
Total Revenue, $56 780; Total Expenses, $43 566; Net Income, $13 214; Total Current Assets, $15 900; Total Fixed Assets, $89 740; Total Assets, $105 640; Current Liabilities, $28 500; Total Owner's Equity, $77 140.

She has discovered an unrecorded sales invoice describing a cash transaction for services performed for $250 dated July 27, 199-.

a. What GAAP does this unrecorded sales invoice relate to?

b. What GAAP does the unrecorded transaction relate to?

c. What two accounts are affected by this unrecorded transaction?

d. What would be the effects on the Income Statement and Balance Sheet? **(i)** Describe the effects in words and then **(ii)** show the changes based on the key figures provided above.

Reconstructing lost and/or partially destroyed documents.

MC 5-5 You have just been hired to take over the duties of Mr. Deverell, who has been called out of town on an emergency. He had been completing the financial statements for the business, and had completed the job before the emergency. Unfortunately, in his excitement and haste to depart, he destroyed the worksheet, and the statements were badly soiled when the contents of a coffee cup were spilled on them. The illustration on the opposite page is what you have to work with.

a. What accounting records are needed for you to reproduce the worksheet? the financial statements?

b. Assuming that you have access to only the soiled financial statements, reproduce as much of the missing information as possible.

c. Prepare the statements in good form for the owner of the business.

	A	B	C	D	E	F
1			ABC Company			
2			Income Statement			
3			For the Three Months Ended		July 31, 199-	
4	[illegible]					
5	[illegible]					
6	[illegible] Earned				4[illegible]	
7	[illegible]					
8	EXPENSES					
9	Heat Expense			4500.00		
10	Telephone Expense			200.00		
11	Wages Expense			3750.00		
12	Utilities Expense			690.00		
13	Supplies Expense			1315.00		
14	Rent Expense			12000.00		
15	Total Expenses				[illegible]	
16					[illegible]	
17	Net Income (-Loss)				[illegible]	
18					[illegible]	
19			[illegible]			
20			[illegible]			
21			[illegible]			
22			[illegible]			
23			[illegible]			
24	[illegible]		[illegible]			
25	[illegible] ASSETS		[illegible]			
26	Cash				3580.00	
27	Accounts Receivable/P. Bowen			350.00		
28	Accounts Receivable/R. McCarty			895.00	[illegible]	
29	Supplies on Hand				[illegible]	
30	Total Current Assets				[illegible]	5595.00
31						
32	FIXED ASSETS (at cost)					
33	Office Equipment				6500.00	
34	Mac[illegible]				25900.00	
35	Tru[illegible]				11600.00	
36	To[illegible]					44000.00
37	To[illegible]					49595.00
38		[illegible]				
39		[illegible]	OWNER'S EQUITY			
40	CURRENT [illegible]					
41	Bank Lo[illegible]				13000.00	
42	Accoun[illegible]rs				2250.00	
43	Total [illegible]					15250.00
44						
45	OWNER'S EQUITY					
46	Roy Hassen, Capital				16000.00	
47	Net Income				23145.00	
48					39145.00	
49	Roy Hassen, Drawing				4800.00	
50	Owner's Equity					34345.00
51	Total Liabilities and Owner's Equity					49595.00

Identifying financial statement errors; preparing statements in correct form.

MC 5-6 A junior clerk was asked to prepare the financial statements for the business in order to determine if he was ready for a promotion. Examine the statements below.

a. Identify any errors in the statements.

b. Prepare the statements correctly.

c. What would be your recommendation regarding the promotion of the clerk?

Communications Services
Income Statement
As at May 30, 199–

Revenue			
Fees earned		$67 800 00	
Less: Rent Expense		12 000 00	$55 800 00
Total Revenues			
Expenses			
Wages Expense		$18 000 00	
Telephone Expense		566 00	
Office Supplies Expense		525 00	
Utilities Expense		1 546 00	
Heat Expense		896 00	
		21 533 00	
		34 267 00	

Communications Services
Balance Sheet
As at May 30, 199–

Assets			
Current Assets			
Cash	$6800 00		
Supplies on Hand	460 00	$	
Accounts Receivable / ABLE Co.		1500 00	
Accounts Receivable / BAKER Co.		1800 00	
Total Current Assets			$10560 00
Fixed Assets			
Automobile		15000 00	
Office Equipment		12000 00	
Canada Savings Bonds		7500 00	
Land		16000 00	
Building		87500 00	
Total Fixed Assets		138000 00	138000 00
Total Assets			$148560 00
Liabilities & Owner's Equity			
Current Liabilities			
Accounts Payable / Yerger Ltd.			$2400 00
Long-Term Liabilities			
Bank Loan Payable	$12000 00		
Mortgage Pay	65000 00		
			77000 00
			79400 00
Owner's Equity			
L. Pearson Capital		$64893 00	
Net Income		34267 00	
		99160 00	
L. Pearson, Drawings	$30000 00		
Owner's Equity			69160 00
Total Liabilities & Owner's Equity			$148560 00

INTERPRETING AN INCOME STATEMENT AND BALANCE SHEET

You have learned how to prepare two of the most important financial statements — the income statement and the balance sheet. No matter how you prepare these statements, by hand or by computer, it is important to understand and interpret both statements. What does an income statement say, and what does a balance sheet say, to readers?

REVIEWING GENERALLY ACCEPTED ACCOUNTING PRINCIPLES

Basic accounting principles: broad accounting guidelines followed by professional accountants in all countries.

When you hear the phrase ''basic accounting principles,'' you may think of those broad principles which are accepted in all countries in which accounting is carried on as a profession.

So far, you have learned the following GAAPs: the revenue principle, the expense principle, the matching principle, the objectivity principle, and the cost principle.

- **Revenue principle**: This GAAP assumes you can define revenue, and it says that revenue must be recognized at the time when the sale of services (or goods) is made, and not when the cash is received from the customer.
- **Expense principle**: This GAAP assumes you can define expense, and it says that an expense must be accounted for when it is incurred, and not when the cash payment is made.
- **Matching principle**: Revenues recognized during one accounting period must be matched with expenses incurred during the same accounting period. On the basis of this recognition, the net income or net loss can be calculated. The accounting period may be any designated length of time up to one year.
- **Objectivity principle**: Before a transaction can be recorded, it must have occurred. Physical proof or evidence is required to prove that a transaction took place, and such evidence is called a source document.
- **Cost principle**: First, all assets must be accounted for on the basis of how much was paid to get those assets. Second, these same cost figures must be kept in the asset accounts even if the so-called market or current value has gone up.

These are only five of at least ten basic accounting principles. Others will be discussed in later chapters in the text.

EXPLAINING SPECIFIC ACCOUNTING PRINCIPLES

Specific accounting principles: more specific guidelines followed by accountants in a particular country.

***CICA Handbook*: published by the Canadian Institute of Chartered Accountants, containing specific accounting guidelines for use in Canada.**

Every country also follows its own specific accounting principles which serve as guidelines for accountants practising in that country. Canada's three accounting bodies are the Canadian Institute of Chartered Accountants (CICA), which grants the C.A. designation, the Society of Management Accountants of Canada, which grants the C.M.A. designation, and Certified General Accountants' Assocation of Canada, which grants the C.G.A. designation. Each of these professional accounting bodies follows the *CICA Handbook* published by the Canadian Institute of Chartered Accountants, which contains more specialized guidelines. Since they concern financial reporting requirements, these guidelines are often collectively called the **financial reporting principle**.

Here are the guidelines you have learned so far:

- Financial statements should be prepared in such form and use such words and classifications that readers can easily understand the information being reported.
- Assets reported on the balance sheet should be classified under at least two classes: current and fixed.
- The main items making up current assets should be reported separately, for example, cash, marketable securities, and accounts receivable.
- Fixed assets should be recorded by major category; for example, land, building, and machinery.
- The cost value of fixed assets should be disclosed on every balance sheet.
- If assets of the business are promised as security against liabilities, the nature of such assets should be disclosed. In other words, readers of the balance sheet should know which assets have been pledged as security against which debts.
- Liabilities reported on the balance sheet should be classified under at least two headings: current and long-term.
- The current liability section reports all debts payable within one year from the date of the balance sheet, for example, bank loans, accounts payable, other loans payable, taxes payable, and current payments of long-term debt.
- If any of the liabilities are secured, they should be stated separately and the fact that they are secured should be indicated.
- Any portion of a long-term debt obligation payable within a year out of current funds should be included in the current liabilities.

- The income statement should report at least the following items: the main sources of revenue earned by the business for a specific accounting period, the major expenses incurred for the same period, and the net income or net loss for the period.
- The financial statements of an unincorporated business (sole proprietorship) should clearly indicate the name of the business and, when necessary, the name of the owner.
- Any "salary" paid to the owner of a single proprietorship should be considered part of the payment of the net income to the owner. Such "salaries" should be accounted for in a separate, drawing account.

It should be kept in mind that other countries may follow different principles from the ones above.

WHAT AN INCOME STATEMENT SAYS

Let us summarize what you have learned so far about the income statement.

- Every income statement follows the matching principle: revenues earned for an accounting period are matched with the expenses incurred for the same period. Remember that, regardless of how complex the income statement appears to be, only two key elements are reported: revenue and expenses.
- The heading of any income statement tells the reader the name of the business, the name of the statement, and the length of the accounting period for which revenues and expenses have been matched. It is important to understand that this accounting period has **ended**. The date line should contain the word "ended" (not "ending").
- The income statement reports the main and secondary source(s) of revenue earned by the business during the accounting period. For example, the main source of revenue for a dental practice is fees for services rendered. Thus, professional fees earned would be the main or primary source of revenue. The firm may also have invested money in Canada Savings Bonds. The interest earned from the bond investment would be the firm's secondary source of revenue. Other common sources of secondary revenue are the dividends earned from investing in stocks, and rental revenue earned from renting part of the firm's land or building.

Main or primary source of revenue: regular operations of the business that bring in revenue.

Secondary source of revenue: a source of revenue which is not part of the regular operations of the business, usually an investment.

- Various terms are used by business to describe their main source of revenue. The nature of the main business operation will give you a hint. Service firms sell services so their main source of revenue depends on what their services are. A realtor charges a commission for buying and selling properties so his or her main source of revenue would be given as **Commissions Earned**. Most professional practices, such as those of lawyers, doctors, dentists, and accountants, charge fees for their services and would report their main source of revenue as **Fees Earned**. If a business buys and sells a good, as do retailers or wholesalers, that firm would report their main source of revenue as **Sales Revenue** or Sales.

- What meaning has been given to the term "revenue"? The revenue principle defines the main source of business revenue as an inflow of assets (cash and/or accounts receivable) from the sale of goods and services. For a service firm this means that revenue must be recognized when the services are rendered. For example, when a dentist performs dental services such as giving an X-ray or cleaning and examining a patient's teeth, the total of the bill must be recognized as revenue earned. The dentist does not wait until the cash is received to recognize revenue.
- Every source of revenue should be traced back to a source document. Of course, this important idea comes from the objectivity principle. The reader of an income statement must have confidence that all revenues reported are accurate. To give this confidence, special accountants called auditors are hired to ensure that all business transactions are supported by source documents.

Auditors: specialized accountants who conduct an examination of the accounting records and other supporting evidence of a business.

- The expense principle gives the meaning of expenses and guides accountants in deciding when to record expenses in accounting records.
- Business expenses, of course, are the costs of operating a business. For example, when a telephone is used in a dentist's practice, the cost of using the telephone helps bring in revenue. In accounting language, that cost is "used up" and so becomes **expired**. That expired cost is accounted for as a business expense and reported under Telephone Expense. All expired costs, therefore, are business expenses.

Expired costs: expenses to be matched against revenue in the income statement.

- The expense principle not only defines an expense but tells readers when those expenses are to be accounted for. Expenses are recorded when they are **incurred** and not when they are eventually paid. For example, a telephone bill received today shows the cost of business telephone use during a period of time. The expense should be recognized and recorded at that time. If a cheque is issued immediately, then the expense is recognized along with the cash payment. However, if management decides to wait until next month to pay, the expense must be recorded through an account payable.

- All expense transactions must be recorded in accordance with the objectivity principle. The income statement is based on this principle, since all reported expenses can be traced to source documents.
- The result of matching revenues with related expenses—the net income or net loss—may be considered the most important piece of information reported by the income statement.

  When the statement is called the "income statement," the net result would be reported as **net income.** Some businesses, however, prefer to name their statement the Earnings Statement (or Statement of Earnings). In this case, the net result would be reported as **net earnings**.

  Earnings Statement: another name for the income statement.

  Many years ago, firms called their statement the Profit and Loss Statement; the net result in the statement was therefore called **net profit**.

  Profit and Loss Statement: an old name for the income statement.

  The terms "net income," "net earnings," and "net profit" all have the same meaning. However, net profit is rare in today's accounting practice.
- It is important to remember that net income is related to the matching principle. To put it simply, net income is made up of more revenue than matched expenses. If revenue refers to an inflow of assets, and expenses refer to expired costs, net income must mean that the business has increased the dollar amount of assets during the accounting period. On the other hand, if a net loss is the result, this means that the total dollar amount of assets must have decreased during the accounting period.

WHAT AN INCOME STATEMENT DOES NOT SAY

An income statement is a historical statement reporting the matching of revenues with related expenses for a period that has ended.

In interpreting an income statement for a given accounting period, many persons try to read too much into the document. Here are a few of the things an income statement does **not** say:

- An income statement does not predict the net income for any **future** accounting period. It is merely a matching of revenues and related expenses for a period which has ended—a historical report of revenues and expenses for a past accounting period. Since the future is filled with uncertainty, the reader of a historical income statement cannot rely on the reported results of any single year for an indication of future results. However, by comparing income statements of past accounting periods, for example, ten-year periods or five-year periods, one may be able to predict with greater confidence the future of a business. Management may try to predict the future by examining a budgeted income statement, which would be described as such.

Budgeted income statement: a statement estimating future revenues matched with future expenses in order to predict net income or net loss for some future accounting period

An income statement reports only a fair approximation of net income for an accounting period.

- An income statement, even if it is well prepared, does not provide an exact measurement of net income for the accounting period. Here is why. Ideally, all expenses should be identified with certain revenues during a specified accounting period. However, it is often impossible to get a precise matching. For example, it is difficult to assign the costs of such items as an advertising expense. Consider the management decision to incur an advertising cost of $1000 in order to produce revenue for the month of December. If revenues from sales totalled $5000 for December, there is no guarantee that the benefits of using up the $1000 of advertising cost did bring in exactly $5000 of revenue. Furthermore, some of January's revenue was probably a result of the advertising expense of December. So, whenever it is difficult to measure the benefits of any cost used up to bring in revenue, one simply accounts for the entire cost as an expense in the time period when the expense was incurred.

True profit: the difference between total funds invested over the life of the business and funds realized from sale of the business.

- An income statement does not report the so-called ''true profit'' of any business. Rather, it reports the profit for the accounting period. To get the true profit, you would have to calculate the difference between the assets invested during the lifetime of the business and the amount finally received from remaining assets after winding up the business. You would also have to deduct any withdrawals of funds made by the owner during the lifetime of the business, because personal withdrawals are actually payments made out of profits in advance of accounting for them. Suppose, for example, that your total investment in a business over 20 years amounted to $100 000, and that during this period your withdrawals for personal use totalled $240 000. Suppose also that after 20 years you sold the business for $160 000 cash. Your true profit, therefore, would be $160 000 + $240 000 − $100 000 or $300 000 for the 20 years.

  Owners and other interested persons need, not this ''true profit,'' but periodic information on the progress of the business. To get this information, accountants prepare income statements at least annually, and in a great many cases quarterly, or even more often.

Net income does not mean cash.

- Some readers of net income statements, unfortunately, interpret net income as cash. Always keep in mind that net income is the **excess of revenue over the related expenses** for a specific accounting period. Cash has very little to do with the determination of net income. Some are misled into thinking that, since revenue is the inflow of cash and expense is the outflow, the difference must be a cash balance. True, revenue refers to an inflow of cash (or claims to cash) and expense to an outflow for some of the operating expenses. But cash is often reused as soon as it becomes available. For example, sales revenue is often used to buy other assets for the purpose of bringing in more revenue. Or the cash may be invested in bonds and stocks so that revenue from secondary sources may flow in. Another point to consider is that not all expenses result in an outflow of cash. For example, the business may have incurred an advertising expense on 30 or 60 days' credit. Later on in this book, you will also learn that for some expenses, such as depreciation, there is **no** cash outflow.

In accounting, expenses must be treated as **expired costs**. And net income must always be regarded as the net increase to owner's equity as a result of having revenues greater than their related expenses for a given accounting period.

Summary An income statement reports mainly the following information:

- the sources of revenue earned for a given accounting period
- those expenses which are related to the revenue for the same accounting period
- the result of matching the two—the net income or net loss

WHAT A BALANCE SHEET SAYS

Here is a summary of what you have learned so far about the balance sheet.

Accounting entity: the business as a unit distinct from its owner(s), for accounting purposes.

- A balance sheet gives the reader the name of the business in the first line of the heading. This name also identifies the accounting entity. This means that accounting separates the idea of the business from that of the owner or owners. For example, when J. Emery invested some of her own money in her real estate business, only the amount of that investment is included in the assets of J. Emery Real Estate. The accountant is not concerned with Emery's **personal assets** such as her home, car, or boat. Nor is accounting concerned with the owner's personal debts. It is concerned with the accounting entity—J. Emery Real Estate.
- A balance sheet gives readers a detailed summary of the assets, and claims against those assets, as at a particular date. The details about the assets come from the accounts in the General Ledger. As well, the details of the claims of creditors come from the balances of the liability accounts filed in the General Ledger. And the claims of the owner come from the balance of the

owner's Capital account in the General Ledger, plus the net income (or less the net loss) reported by the income statement, less the balance of the owner's Drawing account in the General Ledger.

- A balance sheet provides the reader with information about the financial position of the firm with regard to its ability to pay current debts. If all debts payable out of current funds are reported correctly under current liabilities, the reader can turn to the list of current assets to see if there are enough funds. For example, by comparing the available current assets against the current debts of J. Emery Real Estate, you learn that the firm has $71 065 of potential cash available to clear the total current debts of $24 000. This would suggest that the business is in a favourable financial position not only to meet its obligations to creditors, but also to pay expenses in operating the business.
- A balance sheet gives the reader a view of the firm's financial position to carry on its business operations. Such an interpretation may be made by analyzing the fixed assets section. For example, in the case of J. Emery Real Estate, the reader can see that the business has $32 000 of fixed assets to assist in revenue-making activities.
- Finally, a balance sheet reveals the strength of the owner's claim against the assets. In the case of J. Emery Real Estate, the claim appears to be a strong one. The balance sheet as at October 31, 19— shows total assets of $128 065. Of this total, creditors claim $24 000 or approximately 19%. J. Emery's claim of $104 065 is approximately 81%. You must remember, however, that this is a residual or remaining claim because the claims of creditors must always be satisfied before the owner's claim.
- In accordance with specific guidelines published in the *CICA Handbook*, a balance sheet tells the reader which debts are secured.
- In accounting, any liability that is reported as secured has one or more assets pledged as the security. Again in accordance with the *CICA Handbook*, a balance sheet will report which assets have been pledged.

A balance sheet can say other things to readers, but further analysis cannot be done until you learn more about additional assets, liabilities, and owner's equity elements, and, especially, how they are applied to different types of businesses.

WHAT THE BALANCE SHEET DOES NOT SAY

One of the most important problems facing many readers of a balance sheet is the possibility of misinterpretation. Here is a summary of some of the things that a balance sheet does **not** say.

- A balance sheet does not report the details of how profits were made by the business. These details are reported in the income statement.
- A balance sheet does not show the claims of creditors and the owner against specific assets. For example, the total claim of the creditors reported in J. Emery Real Estate, $24 000, is not against the cash of the business or against any other specific asset. Nor is the claim of J. Emery, the owner, against any specific asset. The claims are **against the assets in general** — the total assets only.
- The word ''Capital'' under the owner's equity must not be interpreted as cash. Although it is true that the owner has invested money, it is also true that the new business has used some of this money to acquire additional assets. No balance sheet, therefore, reveals how money invested by the owner has been used by the business. Because balance sheets do not disclose actual transactions, it is important that the meaning of **capital** be restricted only to **investment**. A correct interpretation of J. Emery, Capital, therefore, is J. Emery's claim against total assets through her investment.
- This final limitation is very important to remember. A balance sheet does not report the so-called market value, current value, or worth of any business. Unfortunately, many readers believe that the total assets represent a bundle of future cash resources. While there is little difficulty in assigning a dollar value to **current** assets such as cash and accounts receivable, there are **fixed** assets to consider as well. Such assets are kept by the business to produce revenue and not to be converted into cash.

In Topic 2, you learned that accountants follow the basic guideline called the cost principle. This principle means that accountants are required to record assets on the basis of the dollars that have been used to buy these economic resources. Therefore, the dollar amounts listed on the balance sheet do not indicate the prices at which assets could be sold. In the language of business, the value of an asset simply means ''the cost of the asset'' and not its present value or worth.

Value: in accounting, the cost of assets.

You have also learned that to avoid any reader misunderstanding, accountants are directed in the *CICA Handbook* to disclose the cost of reporting assets. For this reason, all fixed assets are reported "at cost."

Unexpired costs: assets carried forward in the balance sheet to be expired in some future accounting period.

You can now learn a second way to define assets in general. If assets are reported at cost and are still usable to produce revenue, then at least part of these costs must not have been used up—in other words, they are unexpired costs. All assets, therefore, represent unexpired costs reported on the balance sheet to be used up in the future. As you have learned from analyzing the income statement, all costs used up become expired costs and are reported as expenses matched against revenue in the period in which they expired. In Part 3 of this textbook, you will learn how assets which start as unexpired become expired, and how these expired costs are transferred to expense accounts.

The illustration following should clarify the differences between unexpired and expired costs.

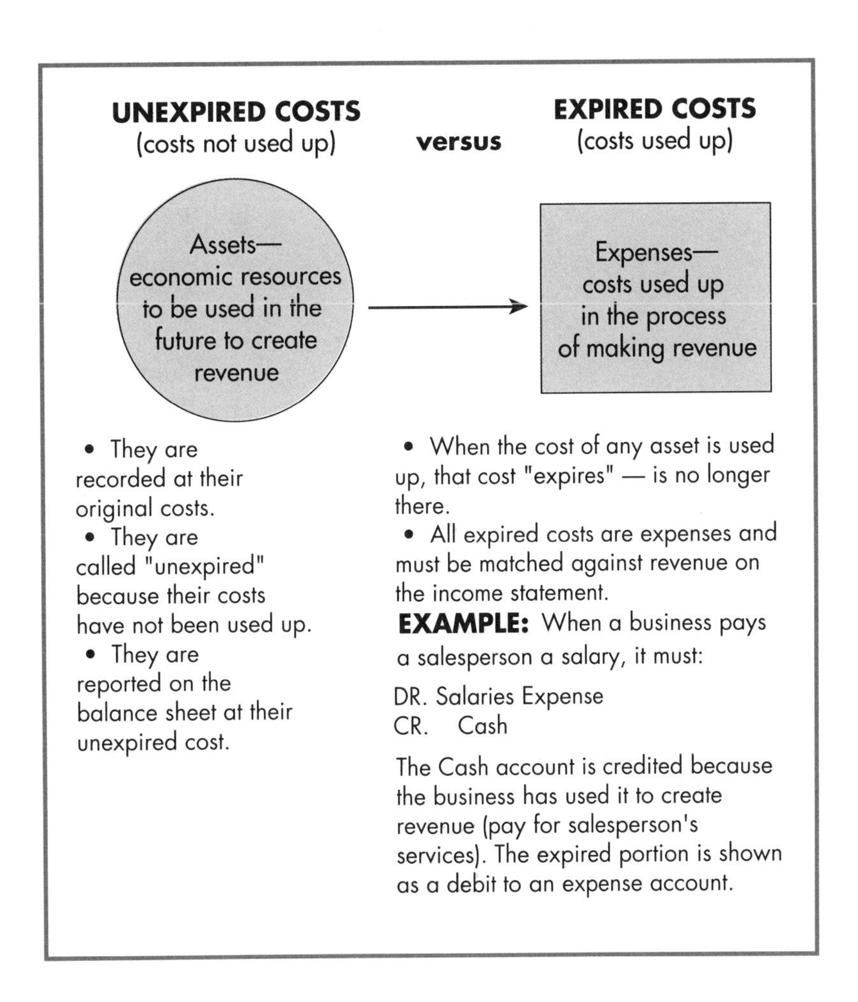

Summary: A balance sheet is a statement of a business's financial position that gives three main pieces of information:

- It summarizes assets, liabilities, and owner's equity as at a specific date.
- It allows the reader to analyze the financial position of the business—its ability to meet its debts.
- It allows the reader to analyze those economic resources to be used that will bring in revenue for the firm.

Balance sheet: a statement of financial position.

A balance sheet, therefore, may properly be interpreted as a **statement of financial position**.

TOPIC 3 PROBLEMS

Identifying and correcting statement heading errors.

P 5-9 In each of the income statement headings shown below, determine if there are any errors that make it difficult to interpret the statement correctly. Then, if errors exist, rewrite any heading that does not conform to current accounting practices.

a.
Stratford Drama Services
For the month ended July 31, 19—
Income Statement

b.
Leafy Tree Services
As at November 31, 19—

c.
Glass Cleaners EXTRAORDINARY
Earnings Statement
For the Three Months Ending March 31, 19—

d.
Statement of Profit and Loss
Hapworth Legal Systems
February 28, 19—

Identifying and correcting statement heading errors.

P 5-10 In each of the balance sheet headings shown below, determine if there are any errors that make it difficult to interpret the statement correctly. Then, if errors exist, rewrite any heading that does not conform to current accounting practices.

a.
Computer Programming Services
Statement of Financial Position
As at June 30, 19—

b.
Green Thumb Garden and Lawn Comp.
Balance Sheet
For the month ended January 31, 19—

c.

Beau's Banquet Business
Statement of Asset Worth
September 30, 19—

Listing business operations and types of revenue.

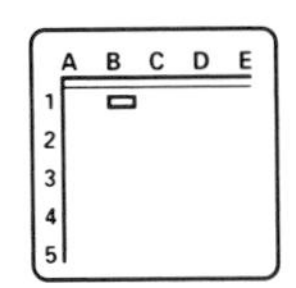

P 5-11 On a form similar to the one below, enter the following types of businesses in column (1): bank, manufacturer of steel products, wholesale merchandiser, doctor, retail clothier, lawyer, newspaper company, dentist, accountant, mortgage and savings corporation, telephone company, airline company, movie theatre, real estate agency, insurance agency.

Then complete columns (2) and (3) for each type of business listed.

Type of Business (1)	Main Business Operations (2)	Description of Revenues (3)
EXAMPLE: Bank	Lending of money	Interest revenue

Preparing an income statement and related balance sheet in accordance with accounting guidelines.

Interpreting the completed financial statements.

P 5-12 Given the trial balance for Bird's View Touring Co. and the following additional information you are to prepare:

a. An income statement for the four months ended May 31, 19—.

b. A balance sheet on May 31, 19—.

Additional Information:

(i) The current portion of the mortgage payable is $1200.

(ii) The mortgage is for 25 years at an annual interest rate of 11.5%. It is secured by the land and office building.

Bird's View Touring Co.
Trial Balance
May 31, 19—

		Debits	Credits
Cash	101	$ 10 000	
Canada Savings Bonds	105	3 000	
Accounts Receivable	110	600	
Office Supplies on Hand	115	750	
Land	150	11 000	
Office Buiding	160	35 700	
Airplanes	170	97 800	

(Continued on next page.)

(Continued.)

Tour Equipment	175	1 400	
Bank Loan Payable	201		$ 8 000
Accounts Payable	210		3 600
Mortgage Payable	250		29 000
F. Schwartz, Capital	301		89 665
F. Schwartz, Drawing	302	4 500	
Touring Fees Earned	401		34 600
Chartering Fees Earned	403		6 500
Telephone Expense	501	125	
Fuel Expense	505	2 900	
Plane Maintenance Expense	510	1 300	
Insurance Expense	515	800	
Hangar Rental Expense	520	400	
Utilities Expense	525	120	
Wages Expense	530	750	
Office Supplies Expense	535	220	
		$171 365	$171 365

c. Answer each of the following questions as they relate to the financial statements of Bird's View Touring Co.: **(i)** What is the total of the Current Assets? **(ii)** What is the total of the Current Liabilities? **(iii)** What percentage claim have the creditors on the total assets? **(iv)** What is the residual claim of owner (in dollars) on the total assets?

TOPIC 3 MINI-CASES

Examining the balance sheet for errors in presentation.

Preparing a formal balance sheet.

Interpreting the financial statements.

MC 5-7 The balance sheet for Fantastic Fishing is illustrated on the opposite page.

The bank loan is payable on demand. The current portion of the Mortgage Payable is $2200. The mortgage is secured by the fishing boat. The net income for the month of August is $12 600. The amount of drawings by the owner for the month of August is $2300.

a. List and explain your criticisms of the Balance Sheet for Fantastic Fishing.

b. Using the above data, prepare a balance sheet in report form that meets the requirements of the Generally Accepted Accounting Principles and the specific guidelines from the *CICA Handbook* studied so far.

Fantastic Fishing
Balance Sheet
as at August 31, 19—

ASSETS		LIABILITIES	
Cash	$ 3 500	Accounts Payable	$ 2 700
Accounts Receivable	1 400	Bank Loan Payable	8 500
Office Supplies	250	Mortgage Payable (15 years)	82 000
Fishing Tackle and Equipment	16 200	Total Liabilities	$ 93 200
Fishing Boat	98 000		
		OWNER'S EQUITY	
		M . Suzuki, Capital	26 150
Total	$119 350	Total	$119 350

c. Answer the following questions on interpreting this balance sheet. **(i)** Who is the owner of the business? **(ii)** Does the owner represent the accounting entity? Explain why or why not. **(iii)** What is the claim of creditors against the economic resources? **(iv)** What is the single largest asset by dollar amount? **(v)** How was that asset in **(iv)** financed? **(vi)** Can the business successfully meet its debts? Easily or with difficulty? Explain. **(vii)** Does the owner have a weak or strong claim against the the economic resources of the business? Explain your answer. **(viii)** Does the balance sheet report the profit of the business? **(ix)** What is meant by the word ''demand'' in demand loan payable? **(x)** Does the balance sheet report the true worth of the business? Explain your answer.

Examining dollar changes in fixed assets.

MC 5-8 Amelia Schumacher owns a quilting and craft business which operates in three locations in Vancouver. The land and building accounts are listed on her balance sheet at a total cost of $110 000. Recently, a group of doctors offered Amelia $150 000 for the land and building, which are near a major hospital. Amelia was quite surprised at this offer since it represented three times what she originally paid for the property. However, with this offer, Amelia now believes that she should increase her land and building accounts to reflect the increased value of her property. Furthermore, based on this information, Amelia believes she should increase the amount expressed on the balance sheet for the other two pieces of land and property. If you were her accountant, what advice would you give her regarding the recording of the first asset in question and the other two assets that she is concerned about? How would you justify your position?

Analyzing a business's balance sheet.

MC 5-9 The balance sheet for Central Rent-A-Car is illustrated below:

Balance Sheet
Central Rent-A-Car
For the Year Ended December 31, 19—

ASSETS		**LIABILITIES**	
Cash	$ 100	Accounts Payable	$ 9 000
Automobiles	25 500	Bank Loan Payable (on demand)	1 000
Furniture	5 000	3-year Note Payable due December 31, 19-4	18 000
Office Equipment	6 000	J. Taylor, Capital	9 000
Accounts Receivable	400	Net Income for Year	18 000
J. Taylor, Drawing	18 000		
Total Assets	$55 000	Total Liabilities	$55 000

The three-year note payable was made out to City Chev-Olds Ltd. This note was secured by pledging the entire amount reported for Automobiles. The current portion of the long-term note payable is $6000.

a. List and explain your criticisms of the above balance sheet.

b. Using the above data, prepare a balance sheet in report form that meets the requirements of the basic accounting principles and the specific guidelines studied so far.

c. Answer the following questions on interpreting the balance sheet. **(i)** Does Rent-A-Car own premises from which it can conduct business operations? Explain why or why not. **(ii)** What is the claim of creditors against the assets of the business? **(iii)** Analyze the financial position of this business as to its ability to meet debts. **(iv)** Does the owner have a strong or weak claim against the assets of the business? Explain your answer. **(v)** Is the business in a strong financial position to create revenue through the service of renting cars? Explain your answer. **(vi)** Summarize the main weaknesses of this business as you have concluded from our analysis of the business's balance sheet.

COMPREHENSIVE CASE STUDY 5

After the second year of business, Miller's TV Repair Service reported the following year-end trial balance.

Miller's TV Repair Service
Trial Balance
December 31, 19-2

Cash	101	$ 10 000	
Canada Savings Bonds	102	15 000	
Accts. Rec./F. Allen	103	1 000	
Accts. Rec./S. Foster	104	800	
Accts. Rec./A. Leung	105	210	
Repair Service Equipment	120	18 000	
Truck	122	15 000	
Office Equipment	124	2 400	
Bank Loan Payable (on demand)	201		$ 3 000
Accts. Pay./Aurora Ltd.	202		210
Accts. Pay. Markham Supply	203		1 100
Wages Payable	204		400
Business Licence Fee Payable	205		200
3-Year Note Payable	220		12 000
J. Miller, Capital	301		53 542
J. Miller, Drawing	302	24 000	
Repair Services Revenue	401	68 940	
Bond Interest Earned	402		1 800
Property Rent Expense	501	9 600	
Wages Expense	502	36 920	
Business Licence Fee Expense	503	200	
Advertising Expense	504	1 400	
Telephone Expense	505	360	
Utilities Expense	506	1 300	
Supplies Expense	507	870	
Truck Repairs Expense	508	1 200	
Gas and Oil Expense	509	1 120	
Interest Expense	520	1 812	
		$210 132	$72 252

Here is some additional information:

(i) The 3-year note payable is a written promise to pay Canada Trust by no later than December 31, 19-5. According to the agreement, $4000 is due to be paid within one year of the balance sheet date. Also, the note payable is secured by pledging of the firm's repair service equipment.

(ii) Due to an obvious error in reporting an account balance, the trial balance does not balance.

Preparing a six-column worksheet, an income statement, and a classified balance sheet in report form.

a. Find the error. Show a correct trial balance on a six-column worksheet.

b. Complete the six-column worksheet.

c. Prepare an income statement in good form.

d. Prepare a classified balance sheet in report form.

Analyzing an income statement and a balance sheet.

e. Now using the completed income statement and balance sheet answer the following questions: **(i)** What is the name of the primary source of revenue? If there is more than one primary revenue, name them. **(ii)** Is there any secondary sources of revenue in this business? If so, name them. **(iii)** Does the business own property? Explain how you know this and indicate the source(s) of your information. **(iv)** What GAAP is responsible for the third line of the income statement heading? What do you learn from this line of the heading? **(v)** What GAAP influences the preparation of the Fixed Asset section of the balance sheet of a business? What is one feature of the balance sheet presentation that is influenced by the GAAP you just named?

CHAPTER 6

CLOSING THE LEDGER AND COMPLETING THE ACCOUNTING CYCLE

Topic 1
Closing the Ledger

Topic 2
Completing the Accounting Cycle

Topic 3
Learning About Careers and the Process of Accounting

Topic 4
Applying the Electronic Spreadsheet and Introducing the General Ledger Accounting Package

You will study the remaining steps of the accounting cycle in this chapter. The first six steps are: (1) originating transaction data, (2) journalizing, (3) posting, (4) preparing the trial balance, (5) preparing the six-column worksheet, and (6) preparing financial statements. Topics 1 and 2 deal with steps 7 and 8, respectively.

CLOSING THE LEDGER

THE NEED FOR CLOSING

At the end of an accounting cycle, you will hear the expression "closing the ledger" or "closing the books." The word "closing" has special meaning. To understand the reasons for closing, study the illustration below for J. Emery Real Estate.

At the top is the accounting equation. This represents the transactions that have ended as at October 31, 19—, the end of the accounting cycle. Notice that net income is added to owner's equity before the drawing is deducted. The total for owner's equity is $104 065. This figure is also reported in the partial balance sheet. Capital is also reported consistently in all items as $63 000.

So far, this information presents nothing new to you; however, you will recall from Chapter 2 that capital is the claim of the owner against the assets of the business. As at October 31, this claim has increased to $104 065, yet the balance of the Capital account in the General Ledger and partial trial balance does not show this increase. In effect, the balance in the Capital account is $104 065 at the end of the account-

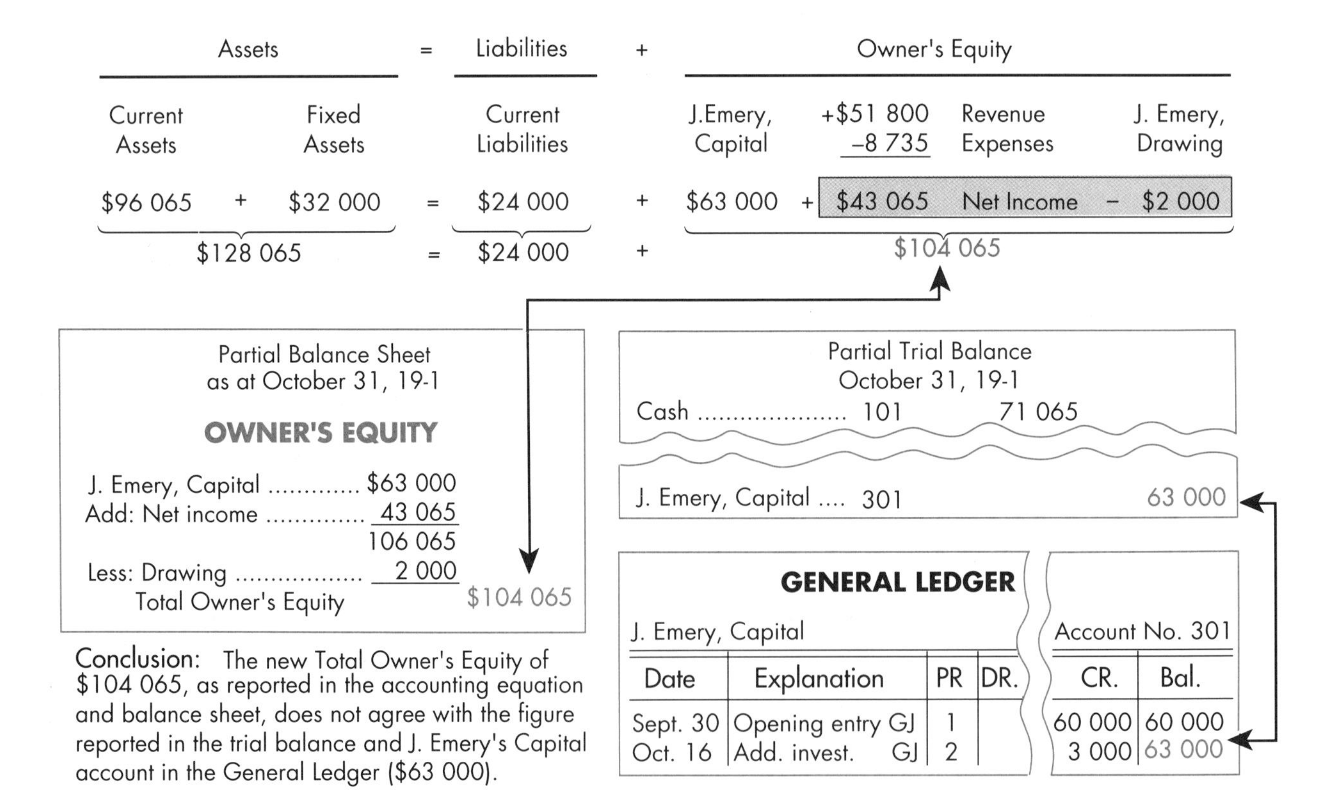

Conclusion: The new Total Owner's Equity of $104 065, as reported in the accounting equation and balance sheet, does not agree with the figure reported in the trial balance and J. Emery's Capital account in the General Ledger ($63 000).

ing cycle and the ledger and trial balance must show this increase.

Now we can begin to see the need for closing the ledger. Simply, closing the ledger is a method of adding the net income to the owner's Capital account so that the balance of this account will agree with the total owner's equity of the balance sheet and the accounting equation at the end of an accounting cycle. As you will learn shortly, the balances of the expense and revenue accounts — in other words, net income or net loss — are transferred to the Capital account. For now, keep in mind that the ledger must agree with the balance sheet and the accounting equation.

There is another reason for closing the ledger. As you know, the calculation of net income is the result of matching revenues for a certain accounting period with related expenses for that accounting period. Also, it is important for a year-end matching to occur so that the net income for the year can be reported to interested persons outside the business. (One of these interested parties is the federal department of taxation—Revenue Canada. The department requires all businesses to report their net income (or net loss) at least once a year.)

Now, if the revenue and expense accounts contain balances for a specific year, these figures cannot appear in the next accounting period. If they did, the next year's figures would contain not only the current year's amounts, but also last year's. That is why the balances of all revenue and all expense accounts at the end of the accounting year must be ''closed''—equal to zero. By closing all revenue and all expense accounts, these accounts are cleared to receive the figures of revenue and expense for the next accounting period.

We can summarize the two reasons for closing. First, there is the need for updating the Capital account balance so that it agrees with the total owner's equity in the balance sheet. This account is balanced by transferring the net income through ledger accounts to the Capital account. Second, it is necessary to clear all revenue and expense accounts at the end of the accounting period so that they can receive only the figures of the next period. To do this, all revenue and expense accounts must be closed (equal to zero). Keep these two reasons in mind when you go through the actual mechanics of closing the ledger.

UNDERSTANDING THE MECHANICS OF CLOSING

To understand the actual mechanics of closing, it is helpful to first visualize the process with T-accounts. In the illustration (page 204 top), the separate stages of the closing process are numbered in chronological order. You will observe that one new account, **Revenue and Expense Summary**, appears. (Another name is Income Summary.) Can you guess its nature and purpose? Follow the sequence closely; then study the number-keyed explanation that follows.

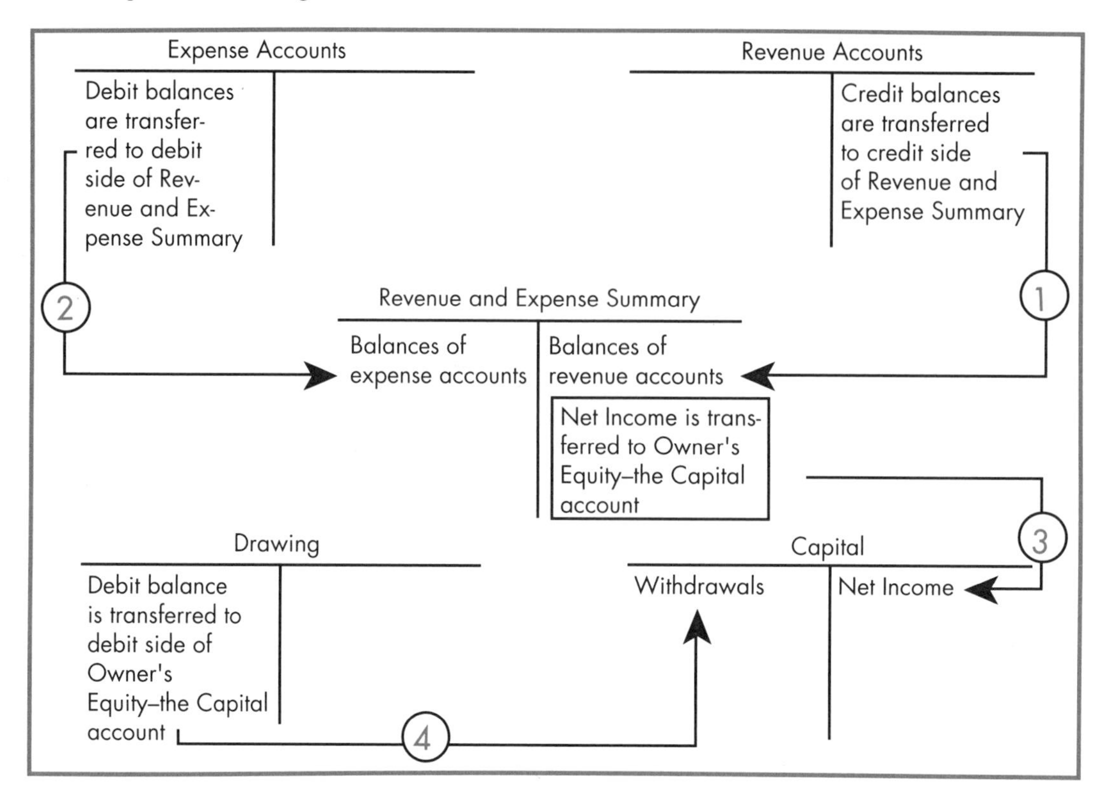

1. Transfer Revenue Account Balances. The first step in closing the ledger is to transfer the revenue for the accounting period to a special summary account called Revenue and Expense Summary (often abbreviated as R & E Summary). To make this transfer, the Revenue account or accounts must be debited and the Summary account must be credited. Once this double entry is posted, the Revenue account will be closed. Thus, the balance of the account will be zero, and the Summary account will have a credit balance.

For J. Emery Real Estate, this entry is shown in T-accounts as follows:

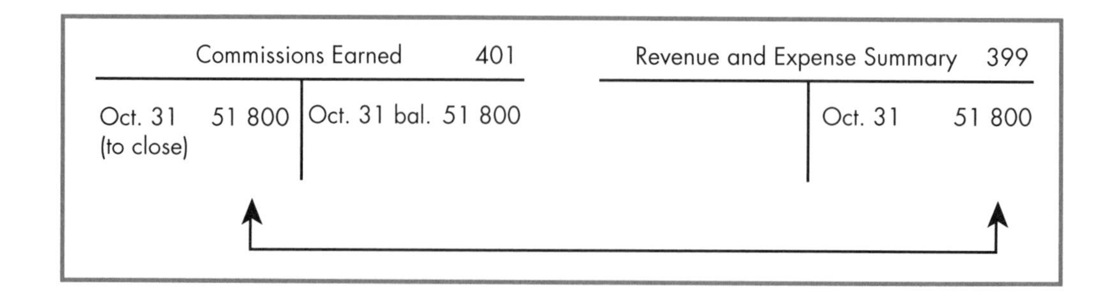

2. Transfer Expense Account Balances. The second step is to transfer the total expenses of the accounting period to the R & E Summary account. This transfer is made by debiting the Summary account with the total expenses and crediting each individual expense account. Once this compound entry is posted, the individual expense accounts will be closed, while the Summary account lists the total expenses for the accounting period. This compound entry is shown below.

Revenue and Expense Summary 399	
Oct. 31 8 735 (total expenses)	Oct. 31 51 800 (total revenue)

3. Transfer the R & E Summary Balance to the Capital Account. Look at the R & E Summary account illustrated below. What does the credit figure represent? Obviously, the revenue for the accounting period. What does the debit figure represent? The total related expenses for the accounting period. By now, you should realize the purpose and the function of the R & E Summary account. As the name suggests, it summarizes the revenue and related expenses in the General Ledger. Actually, you can think of this account as the income statement in the ledger.

Revenue and Expense Summary 399	
Oct. 31 8 735 (total expenses)	Oct. 31 51 800 (total revenue)
	Oct. 31 balance 43 065
	This account has a credit balance. It must be the net income.

If the credit side is greater than the debit side, what will the balance be called? The answer is "net income" since there is an excess of revenue over related expenses. This net income, or credit balance, is then transferred (cleared) to the owner's capital account by debiting the R & E Summary account and crediting the Capital account. This entry may be shown in T-account form as follows:

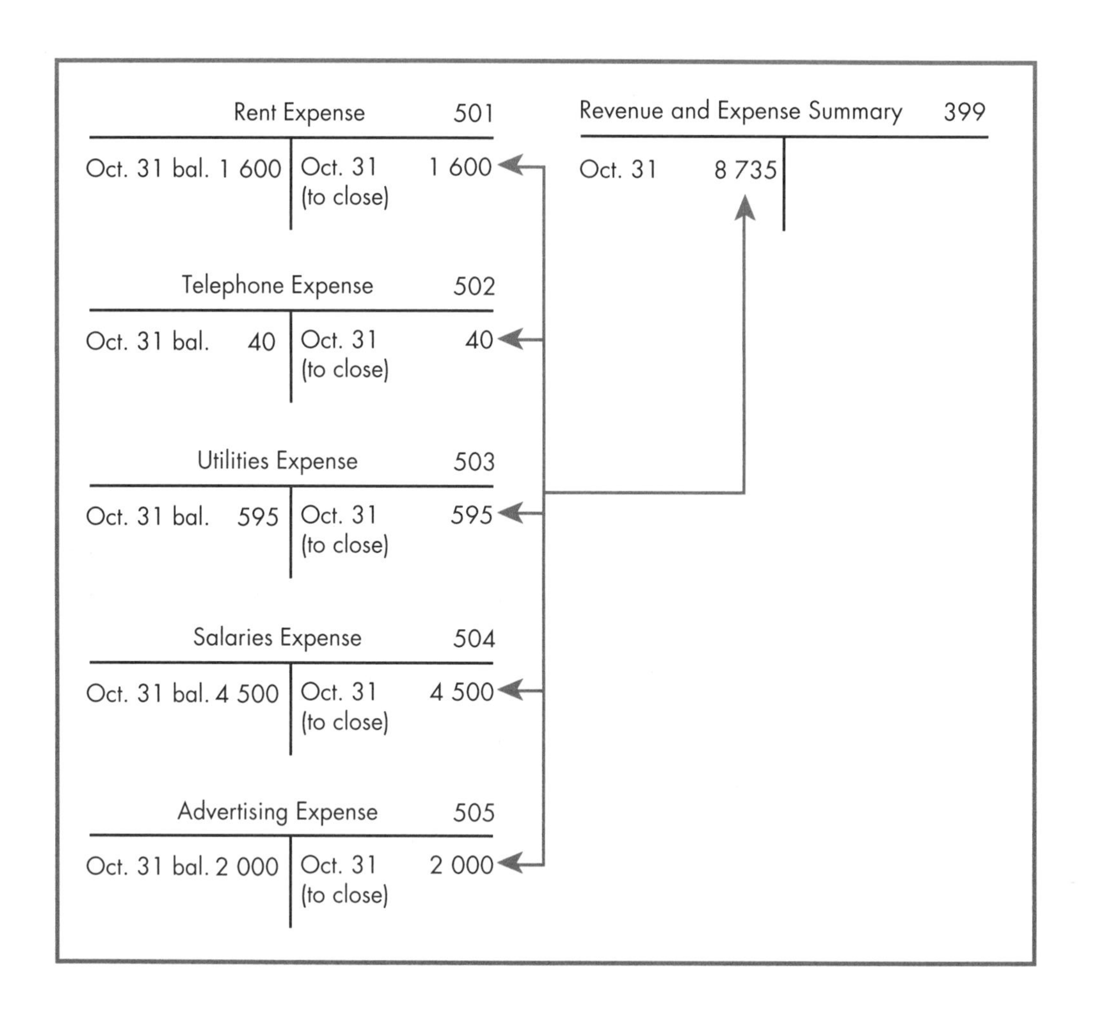

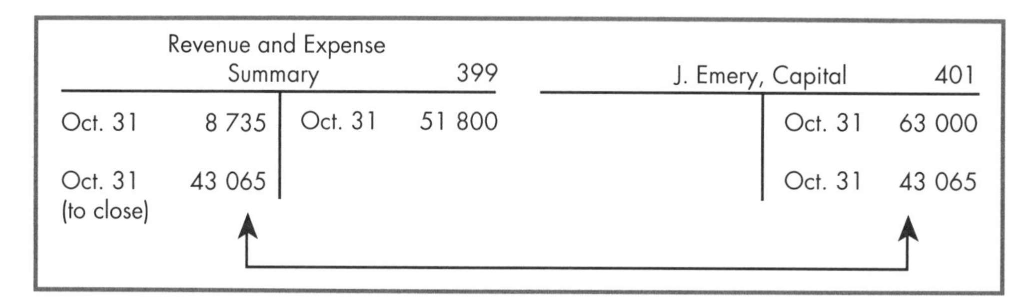

The R & E Summary account is now zero because the credit balance of $43 065 (the net income) has been transferred to the owner's

Capital account. This transfer shows that the net income has been added to the owner's Capital account.

If there was a debit balance in the Summary account, this debit balance would mean a net loss, since there would be an excess of expenses over related revenue. Of course, this net loss would be transferred to the owner's Capital account by debiting the Capital account and crediting the Summary account. Study the analysis of the following T-account:

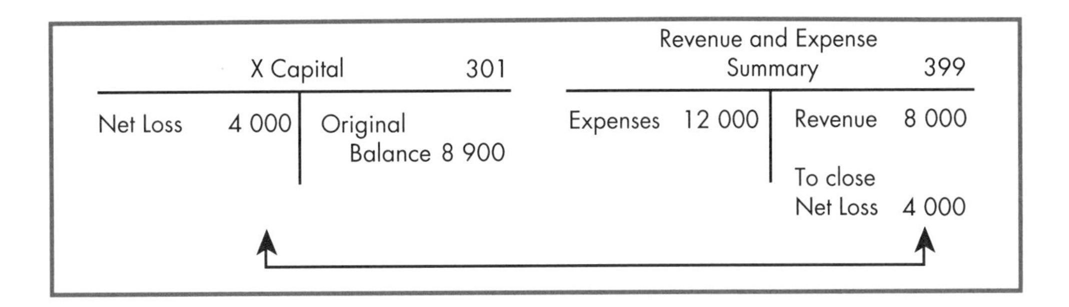

In this closing entry above, the net loss of $4000 (the debit balance in the Summary account) is transferred to the debit side of the owner's Capital account. Since the owner's Capital account is part of owner's equity in the accounting equation, this debit has the effect of decreasing owner's equity in the equation. The same idea was shown on the worksheet: Net loss was transferred from the debit column of the income statement section to the debit column of the balance sheet.

Note the account number given to this R & E Summary account: Account No. 399. Since the idea of the Summary account is to allow the transfer of net income (or net loss) to the owner's Capital account, you can say that the Summary account is related to owner's equity in the General Ledger. For this reason, many charts of accounts will show the Summary account under Owner's Equity.

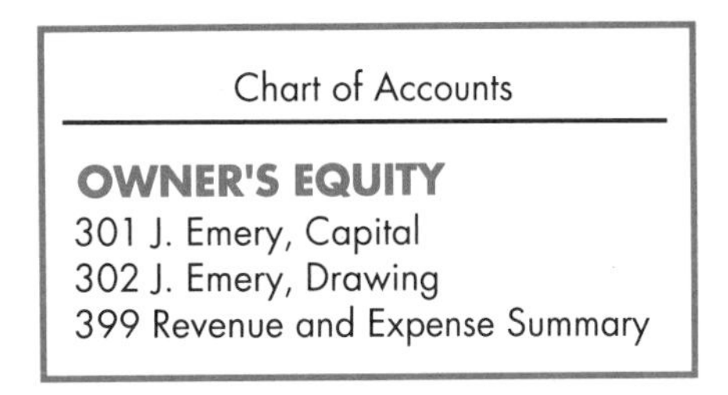

4. Transfer Drawings to the Capital Account. The final step in closing is to transfer the owner's Drawing to the owner's

Capital account by debiting the Capital account and crediting the Drawing account. This last step is identical to the sequence used in the accounting equation and the balance sheet.

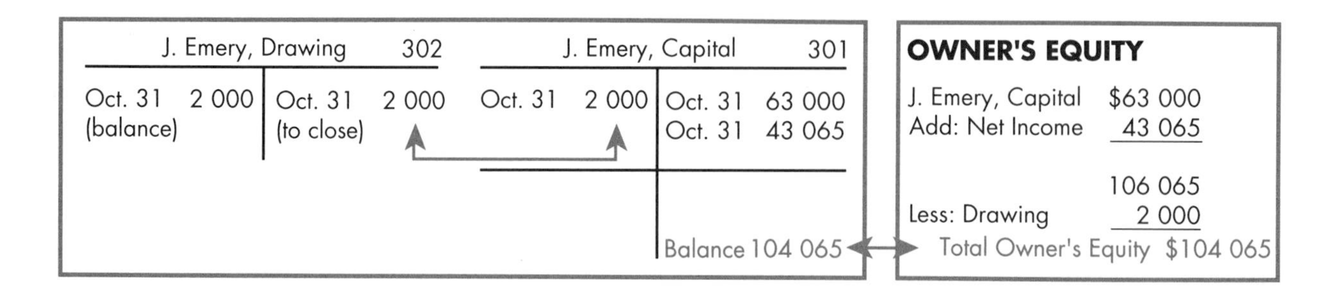

Once this entry is posted, the Drawing account is closed and the Capital account agrees with the new total for owner's equity as shown by the balance sheet and accounting equation.

ILLUSTRATING HOW TO CLOSE THE LEDGER

The General Ledger for J. Emery Real Estate will be used to illustrate the actual closing process. Although closing would normally occur at the end of a complete fiscal (accounting) year, we will close the ledger at the end of one month for J. Emery Real Estate for the sake of simplicity. It is essential to remember one other point: Journal entries must come before all ledger postings. Follow the illustrations on the next pages. Then study the summary.

Summary Closing the ledger, or "closing the books," is done at the end of the accounting year for two reasons:

- to update the Capital account so that its balance agrees with the total owner's equity figure (as in the balance sheet and accounting equation) at the end of an accounting period.
- to prepare the ledger so that the revenue and expense amounts for the next accounting period can be recorded without mixing them with amounts from the previous accounting period

Temporary accounts: revenue and expense, R & E Summary, and drawing accounts.

To close the ledger, all revenue and expense accounts are cleared. Because these accounts are closed at the end of the accounting period, they are known as the temporary accounts of the General Ledger. On the other hand, the balance sheet accounts (except for the owner's Drawing) are not closed. Therefore, all balance sheet accounts, except Drawing, are permanent accounts.

The owner's Drawing account must be considered a temporary account because its balance is closed and transferred to the owner's

Permanent accounts: asset, liability, and capital accounts.

Capital account. This means that the only permanent owner's equity account in the General Ledger is the owner's Capital account.

Revenue and Expense Summary: a temporary account used to transfer (clear) the net income (net loss) to the owner's capital account.

Remember, too, that the Revenue and Expense Summary account is itself a temporary owner's equity account because it is used only at the end of the accounting period when the books are being closed. Nevertheless, it serves two very useful functions in the accounting cycle: (1) it simplifies the closing of the temporary revenue and expense accounts, and (2) it provides a convenient record of the net income (or net loss) for the accounting period in the ledger.

Closing the ledger is the seventh and the next to last step of the accounting cycle. Try naming all seven in order.

Finally, let's review the GAAPs and concepts studied so far and introduce two new accounting concepts. You will recall the discussion concerning the matching principle, the revenue and expense principles, the cost principle, and the objectivity principle.

Going-concern concept: assumes that a business will continue to operate in order to meet planned objectives.

The going-concern concept states that a business will continue to exist and operate indefinitely unless an unforeseen event forces the business operation to cease. This assumption of long life supports the reporting of the business assets at a dollar figure that can be identified and verified.

Financial statements and the closing of the General Ledger must be done at regular intervals to measure and determine particular accounting information for decision-making purposes and to meet government regulations, that is, income tax filing. The time-period concept supports this need. The most common time period is one year, which is the basis for filing income tax.

Time-period concept: assumes the need to divide the life of a business entity into convenient time periods.

All of the GAAPs and concepts build a framework for the practical application of accounting.

GENERAL JOURNAL Page 4

DATE		ACCOUNT TITLE AND EXPLANATION	POST. REF.	DEBIT	CREDIT
19-1					
Oct.	31	Commissions Earned	401	51 800 00	
		Revenue and Expense Summary	399		51 800 00
		To close the revenue account.			
	31	Revenue and Expense Summary	399	8 735 00	
		Rent Expense	501		1 600 00
		Telephone Expense	502		40 00
		Utilities Expense	503		595 00
		Salaries Expense	504		4 500 00
		Advertising Expense	505		2 000 00
		To close the expense accounts.			
	31	Revenue and Expense Summary	399	43 065 00	
		J. Emery, Capital	301		43 065 00
		To transfer the net income.			
	31	J. Emery, Capital	301	2 000 00	
		J. Emery, Drawing	302		2 000 00
		To transfer the drawings.			

Important: The presence of account numbers in the Post. Ref. column suggests that all accounts on this page have been posted to the General Ledger.

General Ledger
(after closing entries have been posted)

Cash Account No. 101

DATE		EXPLANATION		POST. REF.	DEBIT	CREDIT	BALANCE
19-1							
Sept.	30	Opening entry	G.J.	1	60 000 00		60 000 00
Oct.	1		G.J.	1		1 000 00	59 000 00
	5		G.J.	1		5 000 00	54 000 00
	11		G.J.	1		40 00	53 960 00
	12		G.J.	2		1 600 00	52 360 00
	15		G.J.	2		4 000 00	48 360 00
	16		G.J.	2	3 000 00		51 360 00
	18		G.J.	2		595 00	50 765 00
	20		G.J.	2	13 400 00		64 165 00
	30		G.J.	2		2 000 00	62 165 00
	31		G.J.	2	13 400 00		75 565 00
	31		G.J.	3		4 500 00	71 065 00

Accts. Rec./Pat Rogers — Account No. 103

DATE 19-1		EXPLANATION	POST. REF.	DEBIT	CREDIT	BALANCE
Oct.	31	Invoice 00007	G.J. 3	6000 00		6000 00 DR.

Accts. Rec./R. Scobie — Account No. 104

DATE 19-1		EXPLANATION	POST. REF.	DEBIT	CREDIT	BALANCE
Oct.	31	Invoice 00008	G.J. 3	4000 00		4000 00

Accts. Rec./Shannon Development Co. — Account No. 105

DATE 19-1		EXPLANATION	POST. REF.	DEBIT	CREDIT	BALANCE
Oct.	31	Invoice 00009	G.J. 3	15000 00		15000 00 DR.

Automobile — Account No. 110

DATE 19-1		EXPLANATION	POST. REF.	DEBIT	CREDIT	BALANCE
Sept.	30	Opening entry	G.J. 1	15000 00		15000 00 DR.

Furniture — Account No. 112

DATE 19-1		EXPLANATION	POST. REF.	DEBIT	CREDIT	BALANCE
Sept.	30	Opening entry	G.J. 1	8000 00		8000 00
Oct.	1		G.J. 1	1000 00		9000 00 DR.

Office Equipment — Account No. 114

DATE 19-1		EXPLANATION	POST. REF.	DEBIT	CREDIT	BALANCE
Sept.	30	Opening entry	G.J. 1	7000 00		7000 00
Oct.	3		G.J. 1	1200 00		8200 00
	4		G.J. 1		200 00	8000 00 DR.

Bank Loan Payable — Account No. 201

DATE 19-1		EXPLANATION	POST. REF.	DEBIT	CREDIT	BALANCE
Sept.	30	Opening entry	G.J. 1		20 000 00	20 000 00
Oct.	15		G.J. 2	4 000 00		16 000 00

Accts. Pay./Bell Furniture Co. — Account No. 202

DATE 19-1		EXPLANATION	POST. REF.	DEBIT	CREDIT	BALANCE
Sept.	30	Opening entry	G.J. 1		3 000 00	3 000 00

Accts. Pay./The City Record — Account No. 203

DATE 19-1		EXPLANATION	POST. REF.	DEBIT	CREDIT	BALANCE CR.
Oct.	31		G.J. 3		2 000 00	2 000 00

Accts. Pay./Ryan Equipment Co. — Account No. 204

DATE 19-1		EXPLANATION	POST. REF.	DEBIT	CREDIT	BALANCE
Sept.	30	Opening entry	G.J. 1		2 000 00	2 000 00
Oct.	3		G.J. 1		1 200 00	3 200 00
	4		G.J. 1	200 00		3 000 00 CR.

Accts. Pay./Westown Motors Ltd. — Account No. 205

DATE 19-1		EXPLANATION	POST. REF.	DEBIT	CREDIT	BALANCE
Sept.	30	Opening entry	G.J. 1		5 000 00	5 000 00
Oct.	5		G.J. 1	5 000 00		—0—

J. Emery, Capital — Account No. 301

DATE 19-1		EXPLANATION	POST. REF.	DEBIT	CREDIT	BALANCE
Sept.	30	Opening entry	G.J. 1		60 000 00	60 000 00
Oct.	16		G.J. 2		3 000 00	63 000 00
	31	Net income	G.J. 4		43 065 00	106 065 00
	31	Drawings	G.J. 4	2 000 00		104 065 00

J. Emery, Drawing — Account No. 302

Date 19-1	Explanation	Post. Ref.	Debit	Credit	Balance DR.
Oct. 30		G.J. 2	2,000.00		2,000.00
31	To J. Emery, Capital	G.J. 4		2,000.00	0

Revenue and Expense Summary — Account No. 399

Date 19-1	Explanation	Post. Ref.	Debit	Credit	Balance
Oct. 31	Total revenue	G.J. 4		51,800.00	51,800.00
31	Total expense	G.J. 4	8,735.00		43,065.00
31	To close net income	G.J. 4	43,065.00		0

Commissions Earned — Account No. 401

Date 19-1	Explanation	Post. Ref.	Debit	Credit	Balance
Oct. 20		G.J. 2		13,400.00	13,400.00
31		G.J. 2		13,400.00	26,800.00
31		G.J. 3		25,000.00	51,800.00 CR.
31	To R+E Summary	G.J. 4	51,800.00		0

Rent Expense — Account No. 501

Date 19-1	Explanation	Post. Ref.	Debit	Credit	Balance DR.
Oct. 12		G.J. 2	1,600.00		1,600.00
31	To R+E Summary	G.J. 4		1,600.00	0

Telephone Expense — Account No. 502

Date 19-1	Explanation	Post. Ref.	Debit	Credit	Balance DR.
Oct. 11		G.J. 1	40.00		40.00
31	To R+E Summary	G.J. 4		40.00	0

Utilities Expense — Account No. 503

DATE 19-1		EXPLANATION	POST. REF.	DEBIT	CREDIT	BALANCE DR.
Oct.	18		G.J. 2	595 00		595 00
	21	To R+E Summary	G.J. 4		595 00	-0-

Salaries Expense — Account No. 504

DATE 19-1		EXPLANATION	POST. REF.	DEBIT	CREDIT	BALANCE DR.
Oct.	31		G.J. 3	4500 00		4500 00
	31	To R+E Summary	G.J. 4		4500 00	-0-

Advertising Expense — Account No. 605

DATE 19-1		EXPLANATION	POST. REF.	DEBIT	CREDIT	BALANCE DR.
Oct.	31		G.J. 3	2000 00		2000 00
	31	To R+E Summary	G.J. 4		2000 00	-0-

TOPIC 1 PROBLEMS

Preparing a six-column worksheet.

P 6-1 After one year's operations, the trial balance for VanderHoeven's Camera Repair Shop is illustrated on the opposite page.

a. From the trial balance, prepare a six-column worksheet.

Preparing a set of financial statements.

b. From the completed worksheet, prepare a set of financial statements. Use the report form of the balance sheet.

Opening the General Ledger.

c. From the trial balance, set up a General Ledger for VanderHoeven's Camera Repair Shop. Include an account for Revenue and Expense Summary (No. 399). Show all account balances carried forward as of December 31, 19–1. For example, the Cash account would be opened as illustrated also on the opposite page.

Journalizing the closing entries.

d. Journalize the required closing entries in the General Journal, beginning with page 12.

Posting the closing entries to the General Ledger.

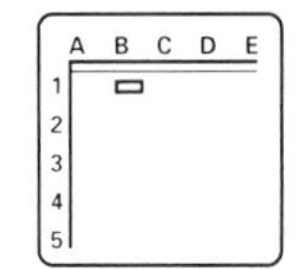

e. Post the closing entries to the appropriate ledger accounts. *Note:* The new balance in L. VanderHoeven, Capital, after all postings are complete, should be $21 870. Does your balance agree?

VanderHoeven Camera Repair Shop
Trial Balance
as at December 31, 19–1

Account	No.	Debit	Credit
Cash	101	$ 2 100	
Accts. Rec./S. Abbott	105	800	
Accts. Rec./K. Martindale	107	350	
Accts. Rec./B. Maxwell	109	150	
Repair Equipment	130	15 650	
Office Equipment	140	6 850	
Bank Loan Payable (on demand)	201		$ 3 000
Accts. Pay./Camera Parts Ltd.	205		400
Accts. Pay./Precision Tools Inc.	207		630
L. VanderHoeven, Capital	301		13 800
L. VanderHoeven, Drawing	302	8 500	
Repairs Revenue	401		35 000
Telephone Expense	501	600	
Advertising Expense	503	1 200	
Utilities Expense	505	4 300	
Rent Expense	507	5 200	
Wages Expense	510	6 000	
Supplies Expense	512	1 130	
		$52 830	$52 830

Cash — Account No. 101

DATE		EXPLANATION	POST. REF.	DEBIT	CREDIT	BALANCE DR.
19–1						
Dec.	31	Balance forward	✓			2 100 00

Preparing a six-column worksheet.

Preparing financial statements from the worksheet.

Opening the General Ledger.

P 6-2 Linda To is the owner and operator of Sparkle Car Wash. Her business's year-end trial balance is shown on the following page.

Additional information:

(i) The long-term note is due in the year 19-8.

(ii) The long-term note is secured by the pledging of the Car Wash Equipment.

(iii) The current portion of the long-term note is $8000.

a. From the trial balance, prepare a six-column worksheet.

Sparkle Car Wash
Trial Balance
as at September 30, 19–3

Cash	101	$ 5 300	
Marketable Securities	105	18 000	
Accts. Rec./ABC Car Rentals	110	480	
Accts. Rec./Tony's Taxi Service	112	220	
Land	130	12 000	
Car Wash Equipment	140	95 000	
Car Vacuuming Equipment	145	8 500	
Office Equipment	150	3 000	
Bank Loan Payable (on demand)	201		$ 15 000
Accts. Pay./Auto Cleaning Supplies Ltd.	205		440
Accts. Pay./Pasquin's Plumbing Co.	210		850
Long-Term Note Payable	240		53 000
L. To, Capital	301		68 110
L. To, Drawing	302	22 000	
Car Washing Revenue	401		71 000
Vacuuming Equipment Revenue	403		5 500
Advertising Expense	501	600	
Telephone Expense	503	500	
Utilities Expense	505	15 000	
Wages Expense	507	23 500	
Cleaning Supplies Expense	509	4 500	
Vacuuming Supplies Expense	511	300	
Interest Expense	520	5 000	
		$213 900	$213 900

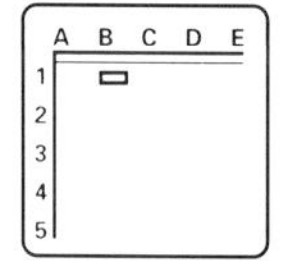

b. From the completed worksheet and additional information given in the question, prepare a set of financial statements. Use the report form of the balance sheet.

c. From the trial balance, set up a General Ledger for Sparkle Car Wash. Include an account for Revenue and Expense Summary (Acct. No. 399). Show all account balances carried forward as of September 30, 19-3.

Journalizing the closing entries for the year-end.

d. Journalize the required closing entries in the General Journal, beginning with page 27.

Posting the closing entries to the General Ledger.

e. Post the closing entries to the appropriate ledger accounts. *Note:* The new balance in the account L.To, Capital—after all postings—should be $73 210. Does your balance agree?

P 6-3 The year-end trial balance for Paul's Armoured Car Service is illustrated below:

Paul's Armoured Car Service
Trial Balance
as at November 30, 19–2

Account	No.	Debit	Credit
Cash	101	$ 200	
Accts. Rec./C. Price Co.	102	5 000	
Accts. Rec./B. Walker & Sons	103	3 000	
Land	110	4 000	
Garage Buildings	112	16 000	
Armoured Cars	114	18 000	
Office Equipment	116	4 000	
Bank Loan Payable	201		$ 4 000
Accts. Pay./Daily News	202		1 500
Accts. Pay./Exeter Supply Co.	203		4 500
Accts. Pay./Farr Motors Ltd.	204		6 000
Mortgage Payable	220		30 000
Paul Williams, Capital	301		22 500
Paul Williams, Drawing	302	12 000	
Fees Earned	401		60 000
Wages Expense	501	54 000	
Advertising Expense	502	1 200	
Repairs Expense	503	1 800	
Gasoline and Oil Expense	504	3 100	
Insurance Expense	505	1 500	
Utilities Expense	506	1 800	
Telephone Expense	507	200	
Miscellaneous Expense	508	300	
Bank Interest Expense	520	400	
Mortgage Interest Expense	521	2 000	
		$128 500	$128 500

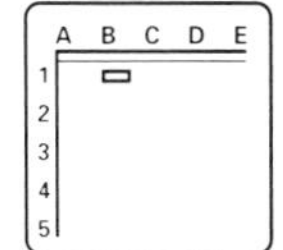

Additional information:

(i) The bank loan is payable on demand.

(ii) The mortgage payable is due on November 30, 20-2.

(iii) It is secured by the pledging of the cost of both the land and the garage buildings.

(iv) The current portion of the mortgage payable, due within the next accounting year, is $3000.

Preparing a six-column worksheet.

a. From the trial balance, prepare a six-column worksheet.

Preparing financial statements from the worksheet.

b. From the completed worksheet and additional information, prepare a set of financial statements in good form. Use the report form of the balance sheet.

Opening the General Ledger.

c. From the trial balance, set up a General Ledger for Paul's Armoured Car Service. Include an account for the Revenue and Expense Summary (No. 399). Show all account balances carried forward as at November 30, 19-2.

Journalizing the closing entries for the year-end.

d. Journalize the required closing entries in the General Journal, starting with page 15.

Posting the closing entries to the General Ledger.

e. Post the closing entries to the appropriate ledger accounts. *Note:* The new balance in the owner's Capital account, after all postings are complete, should be $4200. Does your balance agree?

Opening the General Ledger.

P 6-4 The completed worksheet for J. Edgar Consulting Services is found in Problem 5-4 on page 171.

Journalizing the closing entries for the year-end.

a. From the trial balance, set up a General Ledger for J. Edgar Consulting Services. Include an account for Revenue and Expense Summary (No. 399). Show all account balances carried forward as of November 30, 19-1.

Posting the closing entries to the General Ledger.

b. Journalize the required closing entries in the General Journal, starting with page 15.

Save the solution to Problem 6-4 for Topic 2.

c. Post the closing entries to the appropriate ledger accounts.

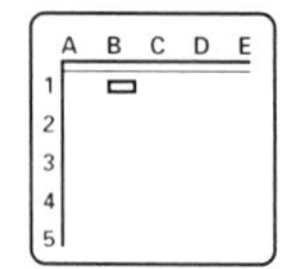

TOPIC 1 MINI-CASES

Listing all the temporary accounts in a business.

Identifying a student error and explaining why the answer is incorrect.

Explaining temporary and permanent accounts.

MC 6-1 During a class discussion following the topic of "closing the ledger," Mrs. Mauro, the teacher, asked the class to list all the "temporary" accounts of a business. Nelson gave the following answer. "The accounts receivable and accounts payable accounts are temporary accounts because they are often closed to a 'zero balance' whenever the customer pays their account in full or whenever the business pays any outstanding debt in full."

a. State why Nelson's answer is incorrect. Where is his understanding at fault?

b. Give a brief explanation of a temporary and a permanent account.

Listing all the permanent accounts of a business.

c. List the types of accounts that are considered temporary and those that are considered permanent.

Closing the Drawing account.

Explaining the effect(s) on the financial statements if a revenue, expense, or drawing account is omitted.

MC 6-2 Jeannette, while working with three fellow students, made the following observations: (1) Anton had closed the revenue and expense accounts. However, he had not closed the Drawing account as he prepared the closing entries. (2) Martha, on the other hand, had closed the Drawing account into the owner's Capital account. (3) Tyler closed the Drawing account as part of the closing entry to transfer all expenses to the Revenue & Expense Summary. Jeannette is not sure which classmate's work is accurate and has asked you the following questions.

a. Whose work is correct and whose is incorrect? Briefly, explain why you made that particular choice.

b. Suppose one or more revenue and expense accounts were omitted in the closing procedure. Would these omissions have any effect on the preparation of year-end financial statements? Explain.

c. What would be the effect on a set of books if the Drawing account was not closed at year-end?

Examining the checking procedures to ensure accuracy in the closing procedure.

Identifying key numbers in the R & E Summary account.

MC 6-3 Assume that you have just completed the closing entries for a business. Accounting offers several methods of checking the accuracy of your work at several key locations throughout the accounting cycle as identified in the separate cases that follow.

a. The total of the expenses is a debit figure in the Revenue and Expense Summary account. Name the two places in the business's books and/or statements where this figure can be found and confirmed.

b. The total of the revenues is a credit figure in the R & E Summary account. Name the two places in the business's books and/or statements where this figure can be found and confirmed.

c. What does the balance in the R & E Summary account represent? Name the three places in the business's books and/or statements where this figure can be found and confirmed.

d. After all the revenue, expense, and drawing accounts and the R & E Summary account has been closed, the Capital account has a new balance. In what statement can this new balance be found? Specifically, in what section of that statement can this figure be found?

TOPIC 2 COMPLETING THE ACCOUNTING CYCLE

After closing entries have been posted, the General Ledger should reveal these facts:

- All revenue and expense accounts, the Revenue and Expense Summary account, and the owner's Drawing account should have zero balances.
- Only the accounts that supply data for the year-end balance sheet should contain balances. Remember, however, the Drawing account has been closed.
- The balance in the owner's Capital account should agree with the total of Owner's Equity in the year-end balance sheet.

Postclosing trial balance: a trial balance taken after closing the ledger.

Once the ledger is closed, an after-closing trial balance called the postclosing trial balance is prepared. This procedure represents the final step in any accounting cycle. The postclosing trial balance for J. Emery Real Estate is illustrated below:

J. Emery Real Estate
Postclosing Trial Balance
October 31, 19–1

ACCOUNT TITLE	ACCT. NO.	DEBIT	CREDIT
Cash	101	71 065 00	
Accts. Rec./Pat Rogers	103	6 000 00	
Accts. Rec./R. Scobie	104	4 000 00	
Accts. Rec./Shannon Development Co.	105	15 000 00	
Automobile	110	15 000 00	
Furniture	112	9 000 00	
Office Equipment	114	8 000 00	
Bank Loan Payable	201		16 000 00
Accts. Pay./Bell Furniture Co.	202		3 000 00
Accts. Pay./The City Press	203		2 000 00
Accts. Pay./Ryan Equipment Co.	204		3 000 00
J. Emery, Capital	301		104 065 00
		128 065 00	128 065 00

From the postclosing trial balance, you can see that the balance sheet accounts are the only ones listed. As explained in Topic 1, these accounts are **permanent** because their balances are carried forward into the next accounting period. On the other hand, all revenue and expense accounts, the Revenue and Expense Summary account, and the owner's Drawing account do not appear in the postclosing trial balance because their account balances are closed (equal to zero). For this reason, these accounts are only **temporary** — their balances are reduced to zero at the end of each accounting cycle.

If the columns in the postclosing trial balance agree, then the revised accounting equation, after closing the ledger, must also balance. You can easily check the accounting equation as follows:

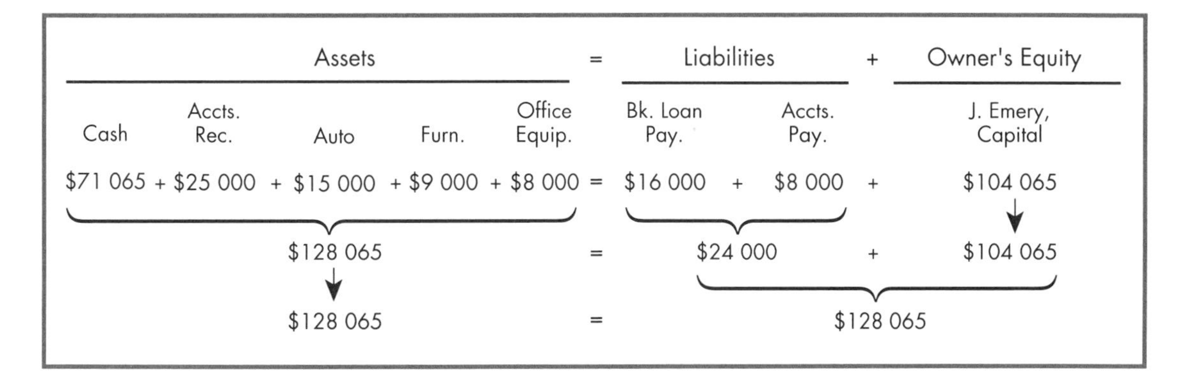

SUMMARIZING THE ENTIRE ACCOUNTING CYCLE

The preparation of the postclosing trial balance completes the accounting cycle. The cycle begins with originating data from source documents and ends with preparing a postclosing trial balance. The cycle is repeated for the next accounting period. To review, follow the eight steps in the accounting cycle that are illustrated below.

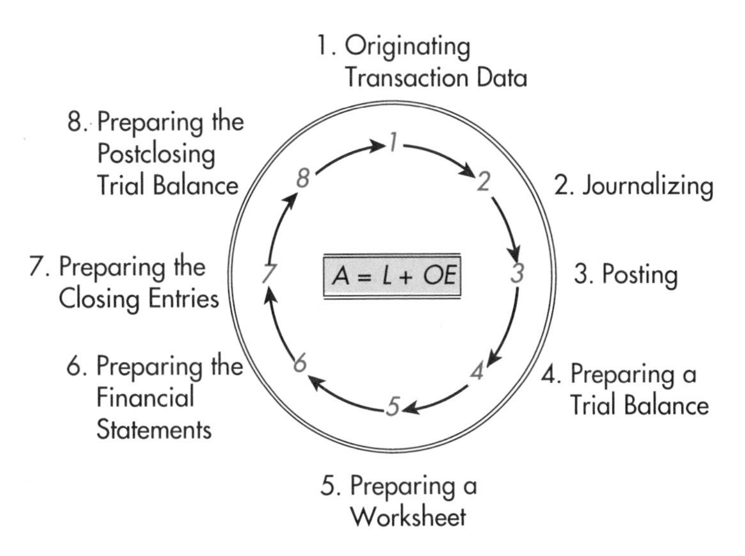

PROBLEMS

Preparing a postclosing trial balance and an accounting equation from a postclosing trial balance.

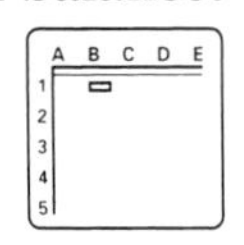

P 6-5 Refer to your solution from Problem 6-1 (VanderHoeven's Camera Repair Shop).

a. From the General Ledger, prepare a postclosing trial balance for VanderHoeven Camera Repair Shop.

b. Prepare a final accounting equation from the postclosing trial balance to prove that the equation balances. For Accounts Receivable and Accounts Payable, show totals only.

Preparing a postclosing trial balance and an accounting equation from a postclosing trial balance.

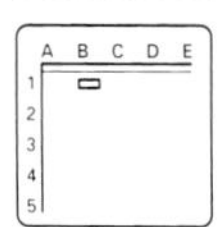

P 6-6 Refer to your solution from Problem 6-2 (Sparkle Car Wash).

a. From the General Ledger, prepare a postclosing trial balance for Sparkle Car Wash.

b. Prepare a final accounting equation from the postclosing trial balance to prove that the equation balances. For Accounts Receivable and Accounts Payable, show totals only.

Preparing a postclosing trial balance and an accounting equation from a postclosing trial balance.

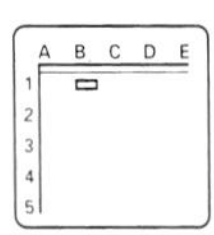

P 6-7 Refer to your solution from Problem 6-3 (Paul's Armoured Car Service).

a. From the General Ledger, prepare a postclosing trial balance for Paul's Armoured Car Service.

b. Prepare a final accounting equation from the postclosing trial balance to prove that the equation balances.

Preparing a postclosing trial balance and save the solution to Problem 6-8 for use in Chapter 6.

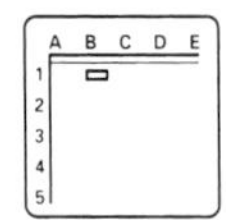

P 6-8 Refer to your solution for Problem 6-4 (J. Edgar Consulting Service).

a. From the General Ledger, prepare a postclosing trial balance for J. Edgar Consulting Services.

MINI-CASES

Listing the accounts not found in the the postclosing trial balance.

MC 6-4 Bella just finished the postclosing trial balance in the first problem that she was assigned for homework. Andrea, a student from the other accounting class which has not yet discussed closing

Listing the steps to do from the worksheet to the postclosing trial balance.

Analyzing the importance of the postclosing trial balance.

the books, asks Bella why her trial balance has no expenses listed in it.

a. What accounts other than expenses are missing from a postclosing trial balance?

b. List the steps to prepare a postclosing trial balance from a completed worksheet that Bella should outline for Andrea. (Prepare this list in point form.)

c. What should Bella tell Andrea about the importance of completing a postclosing trial balance?

Listing the steps for detecting errors in a postclosing trial balance.

Identifying accounting records that assist in correcting errors.

MC 6-5 James just completed his postclosing trial balance, but unfortunately it does not balance.

a. List the steps that James should follow to locate his error.

b. Name three accounting records that contain the information that James needs to locate and correct errors in the postclosing trial balance.

Identifying errors in a postclosing trial balance.

MC 6-6 Study the postclosing trial balance for Tsui's Travel Service that follows:

Postclosing Trial Balance
Tsui's Travel Service
For the Year Ended December 31, 19–1

Cash	$ 2 800	
Accounts Receivable/P. Faling	240	
Accounts Receivable/B. Hartford	160	
Office Supplies	300	
Land	14 700	
Building	48 000	
Automobile	21 000	
Office Equipment	6 000	
Bank Loan Payable	10 000	
Accounts Payable/Delta Suppliers		$ 500
Mortgage Payable		30 000
T. Tsui, Capital		37 700
T. Tsui, Drawing	6 000	
Service Fees Earned		21 000
	$109 200	$89 200

Analyzing methods for detecting common errors.

a. List the five errors in this postclosing trial balance.

b. Two of these errors were made at closing. Identify each of these errors.

Examining limitations of the postclosing trial balance in locating errors.

c. What check should have been made that would have caught the errors in **b** assuming that financial statements are correct?

d. Would the postclosing trial balance reveal the errors in **b** if everything else was done correctly? Explain why.

Preparing a corrected postclosing trial balance.

e. Prepare a correct postclosing trial balance. What accounts in the postclosing trial balance must change, in what way, or by how much?

LEARNING ABOUT CAREERS AND THE PROCESS OF ACCOUNTING

System flowchart: a chart showing the flow of procedures, and the flow of data and documents, in an accounting system.

To learn about some of the possible careers in accounting, it is necessary to know first what makes up the entire accounting process within any business. An accounting system flowchart will show you the process. Study the flowchart on the opposite page.

ANALYZING THE SYSTEMS FLOWCHART

Think of a large rectangle as a business of any size or kind. Steps of the accounting process which take place within the business are shown inside the rectangle; those which take place outside the business are shown outside the rectangle.

Within any business organization, all accounting begins with the **origination of data**. In a systems flowchart, the **input symbol** has been used to show this data coming into the business.

Not all data or information, however, results in business transactions. Therefore, the flowchart **decision symbol** asks an important question: *Is an accounting entry required?* For example, a person may offer the owner a sum of money to buy the business. This offer will not become a business transaction because the ''transaction'' is not complete unless the offer is accepted by the owner. Instead, the

Input Symbol

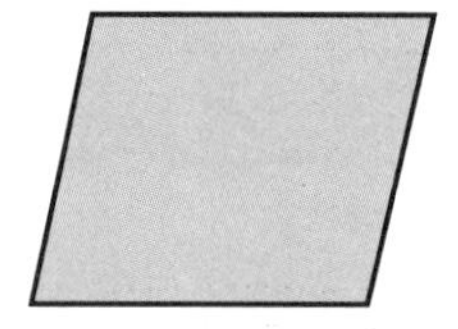

Indicates data put into the system

Decision Symbol

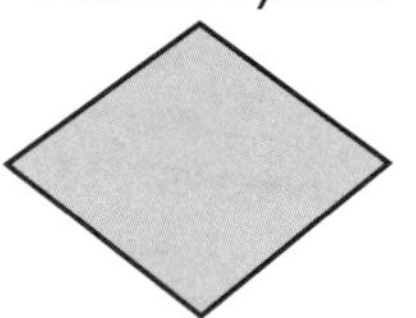

Indicates that a decision must be made

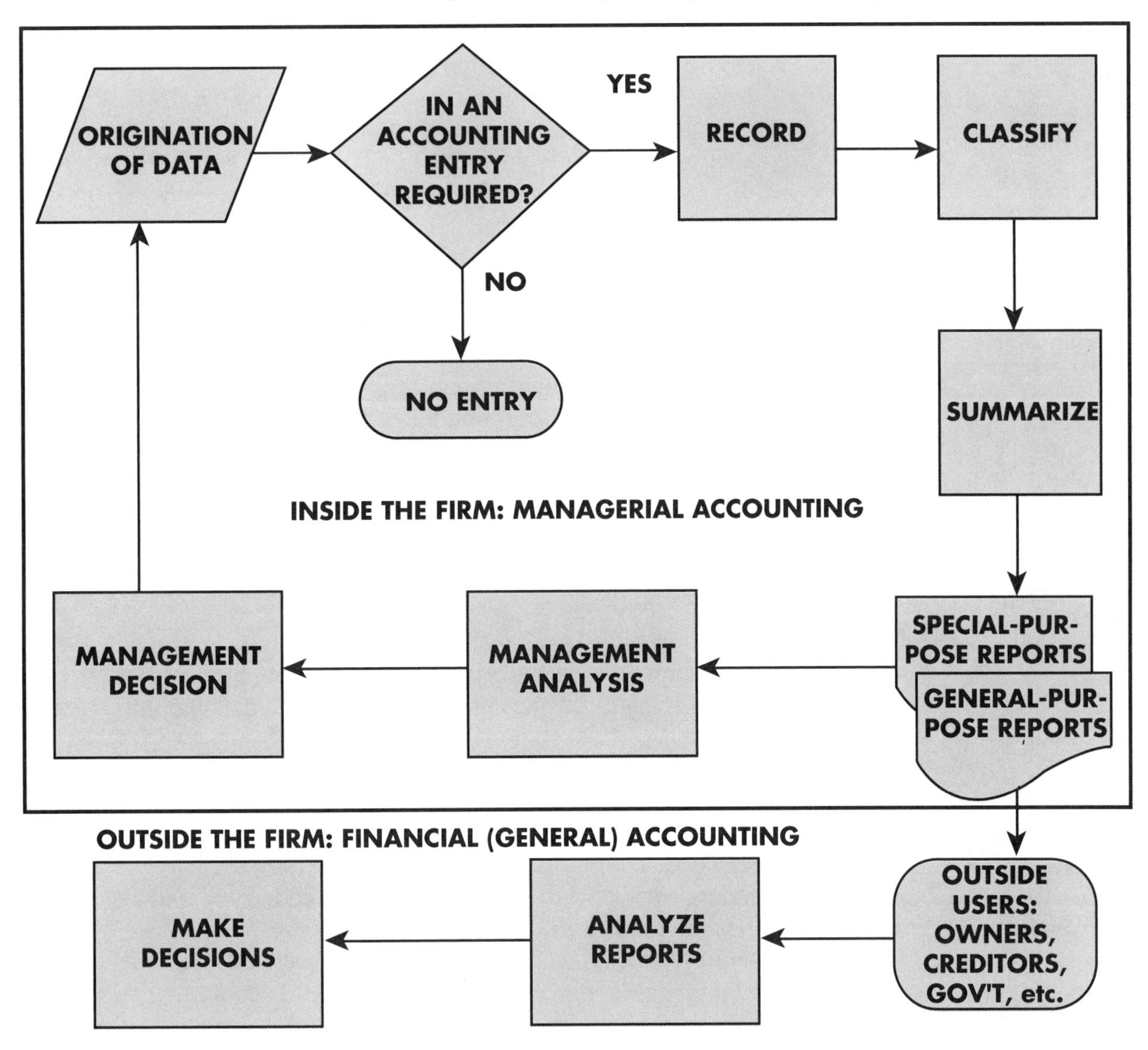

owner rejects the offer and the systems flowchart shows a "no" answer to the question by means of the arrow pointing to the **terminal point.** The **terminal symbol** ends any further consideration of this data.

Terminal Symbol

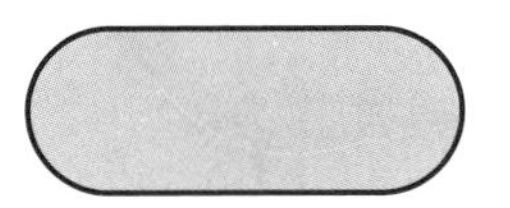

Indicates the ending in a flowchart

On the other hand, much of the data originating within the business will form completed business transactions—for example, when a sale of goods or services is made to a customer. This is shown on a source document called an invoice, which records the results of the transaction.

All completed business transactions will enter the accounting process. The systems flowchart now shows a "YES" answer with an

Process Symbol

Indicates that an activity of some kind must be performed

Document (Report) Symbol

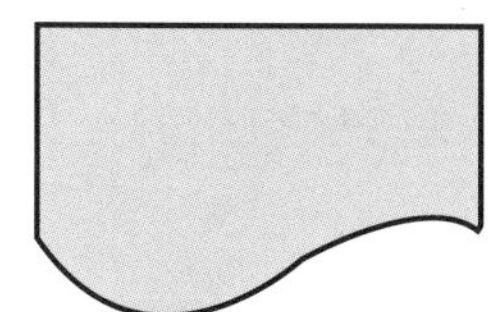

Indicates any source document: journals, ledgers, trial balances, financial statements, and other accounting statements and reports

Special-purpose reports: detailed sales reports, expense reports, budgets, and other financial reports aimed at the managers ("insiders") of a business.

Managerial accounting: that part of the accounting process which prepares special-purpose reports to meet the needs of managers.

General-purpose reports: financial statements prepared in accordance with GAAPs and for "outsiders."

arrow leading to the symbol labelled RECORD, which refers to the recording of the results of that transaction.

The action of recording is shown in the chart by the **process symbol**. You already know that a record of any business transaction is made by analyzing the information shown by the source document and recording that information in a journal — that is, journalizing those business transactions.

The arrow now leads from RECORD to another process symbol labelled CLASSIFY. Classifying accounting information means simply to post accounting data to appropriate accounts in a ledger file.

The next arrow leads to SUMMARIZE. Many different summaries are made before accounting reports are prepared—the trial balance is one example of a valuable summary of General Ledger accounts before financial statements are prepared.

The chart now shows the output of reports. The reports are indicated in the chart by the **document** or **report symbol**. Two distinct types of reports are produced by the accounting process, one aimed at persons within the business, the other at persons outside of the business.

Reports which stay **in** the business are called special-purpose reports. These are produced for management. Examples are reports for periodic sales, expense reports, budgets, and monthly financial statements.

The chart shows that these special-purpose reports may serve as the basis for a management decision that sets off a new series of economic events. Such a decision may result in the recording of more business transactions, ending in another series of reports.

Because special-purpose reports are intended for managerial decision making only, the system flowchart shows this "flow" of the accounting process as one main branch of accounting. This branch is called managerial accounting or management accounting. As you will learn shortly, many careers are possible in this branch of accounting.

The other type of report shown in the flowchart is a general-purpose report for interested parties **outside** the business. These outsiders include owners who do not manage their own businesses, such as shareholders of corporations. Other interested outsiders could be potential investors, banks and other lending institutions, government agencies, and labour unions. *Note:* Since a symbol for "outsiders" does not exist, a symbol has been selected for our purposes. It is not basic to accounting systems flowcharting.

For outside groups, the reports must be general in nature, so that all outsiders can use them. The traditional year-end financial statements — year-end income statements and balance sheets — make up these reports. With these, the would-be lender will want to analyze and interpret the business's financial position to decide whether the business is secure and offers a good return on investment.

For obvious reasons, general-purpose financial statements must be prepared according to pre-established guidelines — GAAPs. In Chapter 5 you learned that every country follows basic accounting principles, and also specific ones as published by that country's leading accounting authority (the *CICA Handbook* in Canada). Since general-purpose financial statements are prepared only for outside parties, in accordance with GAAPs, this branch of accounting is referred to as financial accounting or general accounting.

Financial (general) accounting: that part of the accounting process which prepares general-purpose statements for outside users.

The following table summarizes the main features between financial accounting and managerial accounting. See also the illustrated employment ads.

THE TWO BRANCHES OF ACCOUNTING COMPARED

Financial (General)	Managerial
1. Deals with the preparation of useful general-purpose reports aimed at interested parties outside the firm.	1. Deals with the preparation of useful specific purpose reports aimed at managers inside the firm.
2. The reports must be general in nature, in order to be of interest to many different outsiders such as business owners who do not manage (shareholders), potential investors, bankers and other creditors, labour unions, and Revenue Canada Taxation.	2. The reports must be specific in nature, to be of interest to specific managers such as sales managers, production managers, and purchasing managers.
3. Common examples of general reports are the year-end financial statements such as the income statement and the balance sheet.	3. Common examples of specific reports are a variety of sales reports for different marketing managers, cost and expense reports for purchasing and production managers, specific budgets for specific managers, and monthly financial statements.
4. To be useful to outsiders, all general-purpose reports (year-end financial statements) must be prepared in accordance with GAAPs.	4. For specific-purpose reports to be useful, GAAPs do not have to be followed. For example, a budgeted income statement is only an estimated forecast of future net income which matches estimated revenues and estimated expenses for a future period.

Your study of the system flowchart should enable you to understand the following definition:

A Modern Definition of Accounting

Accounting may be described as the process of recording, classifying, and summarizing business transactions so that useful specific-purpose reports can be prepared for management decision-making, and useful general-purpose reports in accordance with GAAPs can be prepared for interested parties outside the business.

ACCOUNTING CAREERS

Large businesses often hire clerks to work in a particular area of the business's accounting. For example, an accounts receivable clerk will work in the accounts receivable department, a payroll clerk will work in the payroll department, and so on. Such an area of accounting may be called an accounting application.

Accounting application: the several accounting activities related to one area of the firm's accounting. For example, all accounting related to customer accounts forms the accounts receivable application.

Smaller businesses, however, do not divide their accounting duties into departments. Instead, they may hire only one clerk — the bookkeeper — to do the work of several.

Most large businesses employ one or more professional accountants, who supervise the clerks. In small businesses, the owner-manager may hire a professional accounting business to set up the business's accounting system and to look after the preparation of financial statements on a regular basis. Of course, the bookkeeper in this small business would follow the accounting system designed by the professional accountant.

To become an accounting clerk or bookkeeper normally requires a high-school education. One or more high-school courses in accounting would help you get started in a clerical position. To become a professional accountant, however, you will need more education.

BECOMING A PROFESSIONAL ACCOUNTANT

In Canada, three accounting bodies have been created by law to educate and train professional accountants:

- the Canadian Institute of Chartered Accountants, whose members are entitled to the designation Chartered Accountant, or C.A.
- the Society of Management Accountants, whose members are entitled to the designation Certified Management Accountant, or C.M.A.
- the Canadian Certified General Accountants' Association, whose members are entitled to the designation Certified General Accountant, or C.G.A.

In all three cases, the letters C.A., C.M.A., and C.G.A. do not indicate university degrees — universities do not award these letters. They are, rather, **professional designations**.

C.A.: the designation for Chartered Accountant.

The Chartered Accountant (C.A.) To be able to write the letters "C.A." after your name, you must complete the requirements of your provincial Institute of Chartered Accountants. For example, the Institute of Chartered Accountants of Ontario controls the program for education and training of students to become C.A.s in Ontario. Briefly, here are the requirements to become a C.A. in Ontario. Although there are minor differences in other provinces, the majority have the same requirements.

- A university degree such as a B.A. (Bachelor of Arts), B.Sc. (Bachelor of Science), B. Comm. (Bachelor of Commerce), or M.B.A. (Master of Business Administration) is necessary. However, you must take 51 credit hours of university courses, in courses recognized as acceptable. The courses may be divided into two classes: ''pure'' and ''related.''
- In pure accounting courses, a minimum grade of 60% is normally required. The recognized pure accounting courses are:

Financial Accounting: When you complete this text, you will have covered only a few of the topics in an introductory course on financial accounting. If you continue your education, there are many other topics which have to be covered in depth at the university level.

Management Accounting: This is sometimes called Cost and Management Accounting.

Auditing: This prepares a person to examine the records and financial reports of a variety of businesses and business corporations.

Taxation: This covers the details of individual and corporate income tax.

- The recognized ''related'' accounting courses for which university passing grades are required are:

Computer Science: No professional accountant can practise without some exposure to the computer.

Quantitative Methods: This is a specialized course in business statistics.

Business Finance: This is sometimes called Financial Management.

Economics: This is an introduction to the two main fields of economics, called Macroeconomics and Microeconomics.

Business Law: This is sometimes called Commercial Law.

Introduction to Business: This is an introduction to how businesses are formed and managed.

- You must be hired by a C.A. business to obtain on-the-job training. (In general, C.A. businesses require a university degree with at least 28 credit hours of approved accounting and related courses before students are hired.)
- After completing the 51 semester-hour credits, C.A. students are required to complete three admission examinations in the areas of accounting, auditing, and taxation before they are permitted to enter the C.A. School of Accountancy program. The School of Accountancy program is designed to prepare the applicant for

the C.A.'s Uniform Final Examination (UFE). Upon the successful completion of the Uniform Final Examination and the experience requirement, the student is awarded the C.A. designation.

New C.A.s may open their own public accounting office, or they may be employed in private or government positions. The majority of C.A.s specialize in fields like external auditing, taxation, and information systems. These careers and others are summarized at the end of this topic.

C.M.A.: the designation for Certified Management Accountant.

The Certified Management Accountant (C.M.A.) Like the C.A., the C.M.A. is a professional. A C.M.A. can specialize in either of two separate branches of accounting—public accounting and management accounting. Public accounting primarily deals with the areas of audit and tax. The management accountant primarily deals with the use of financial and strategic information to improve decision making and profitability within an organization. Although there is a certain overlap in duties, there are several clear distinctions between these two branches of accounting.

The governing body for C.M.A.s is the Society of Management Accountants of Canada. Each province is also organized into a branch or chapter. For example, the Society of Management Accountants of Ontario supervises the education and training of C.M.A.s for Ontario. Like C.A.s, the C.M.A.s must complete an educational program. The academic requirements for accreditation as a C.M.A. include the following:

- the completion of the Society's pre-professional program requirement;
- the successful completion of the Professional Accreditation Examination, Part I; and
- the successful completion of the Professional Accreditation Examination, Part II.

For details concerning any of the above, consult the latest C.M.A. education calendar. When accreditation is received by the student, he or she is entitled to use the designation of C.M.A.

Unlike the C.A. program, a candidate for a C.M.A. designation may be considered without a business university degree. However, the student without this post-secondary education will be required to complete the necessary courses to meet the pre-professional program.

C.G.A.: the designation for Certified General Accountant.

The Certified General Accountant (C.G.A.) The C.G.A., too, is a professional accountant who qualifies for a variety of career positions.

C.G.A.s are organized under a national body, the Certified General Accountants' Association of Canada. This association also has a chapter in each province and territory. For example, the Certified General Accountants Association of Ontario governs the education and training of students in Ontario.

Like C.A.s and C.M.A.s, C.G.A.s need to pass an approved list of "pure" and "related" accounting courses. The courses for "Program 90" include:

Financial Accounting 1
Financial Accounting 2
Financial Accounting 3
Financial Accounting 4
Financial Accounting 5 (an option at level five)
Managerial Mathematics and Economics 1
Economics 2
Quantitative Methods 2
Managerial Accounting 1
Managerial Accounting 2
Managerial Accounting 3 (an option at level 5)
Managerial Information Systems 1
Managerial Information Systems 2 (an option at level 5)
Taxation 1
Taxation 2 (an option at level 5)
Finance 1
Finance 2
Auditing 1
Auditing 2
Management Auditing 1 (an option at level 5)
Microcomputer Tutorial

As part of the student's level five requirements, the C.G.A. program permits the student to specialize in one of three areas: Financial Management, Management Accounting, or Public Practice. Each area of expertise directs the student to a set of more specific course choices, thus the optional courses in level five.

- Examinations are required for each of the courses with a passing grade of 65%. Assignment work throughout the course must be submitted and at a passing level in order to qualify to write the exam.
- There is a strict ten-year time limit for completion of the C.G.A. program.

- The C.G.A.s also require a minimum of two years' practical work experience. They also outline three levels of responsibility and experience that are required. These levels must be compatible with the level of study with which the student is involved.
- When accreditation is received by the student, he or she is entitled to use the designation of C.G.A.

In a manner similar to the C.M.A. program, the C.G.A. program will accept students with a minimum of a secondary school education, but will also offer course exemptions for approved university and/or community college courses.

OBTAINING MORE THAN ONE DESIGNATION

The three Canadian accounting bodies have a working relationship enabling them to confer each other's designations. For example, a C.M.A. graduate with a university degree may become a C.A. in Ontario by completing twelve semester-hour subject requirements, the practical experience requirements, the School of Accountancy, and the Uniform Final Examination. Similarly, a C.A. can become a C.M.A. or a C.G.A. by completing the requirements of the provincial chapter of the accounting body.

SUMMARIZING ACCOUNTING CAREERS

Accountants tend to specialize just as lawyers and doctors do. The large field of accounting is composed of three sectors:

- public accounting
- private accounting
- governmental accounting

CHARTERED ACCOUNTANT

QUALIFIED C.A. with at least 3 years' experience required by medium-sized accounting firm with rapidly growing practice. Ideal candidate will be an independent self-starter and able to supervise staff. Respond in confidence to—

Public Accounting A public accountant is one who offers professional services to the public for a fee. Many small businesses will hire a public accountant rather than employ an accountant themselves.

An accountant in public practice may work alone or in partnership, or may be a member of a large business with many partners and offices throughout the country. Some of the larger businesses have branches in several countries. The chief areas in which the public accountant will serve are:

General accounting: In this area, the public accountant may check the accounting records once a month, prepare monthly statements, and eventually the year-end statements.

External auditing: To perform an audit, the public accountant makes a careful review of the accounting system and the financial

CHARTERED ACCOUNTANTS

Progressive, expanding CA firm in North Toronto requires graduates with 1-2 years' post qualification experience to handle an account group.

The successful candidates must be capable of supervising staff and dealing directly with clients in tax planning and consulting to medium-sized businesses. Professional development program provided "in house" to assist in career growth.

Please reply in confidence to—

statements of the business.

This independent service is especially important to corporations because the owners — the shareholders — rely on the audit to present the financial statements fairly and consistently.

Tax services: The public accountant is often called upon to prepare the annual tax returns of individuals, small businesses, and large businesses. Another important service is to offer tax plans so that the client can pay as little income tax as possible within the framework of Canada's complex tax laws.

Management advisory services: The public accountant may advise the management of the business on matters such as classifying job positions and the hiring of qualified people. In recent years, very large public accounting businesses have organized special departments that give advisory services to management about company mergers and employee pension plans.

Systems design and installation: The public accountant may be hired to study a business's system of processing accounting information and suggest changes in the overall accounting system.

In Canada, the majority of accountants in public practice are C.A.s.

ACCOUNTING OPPORTUNITY

We are looking for a first-rate individual to join our first-rate facility!

You have at least one year of experience in a computerized accounting environment, have experience in A/P, A/R, and general ledger and preferably have completed the first year of a recognized accounting program.

This position requires a bright individual with a high-energy level possessing excellent interpersonal, communication and organizational skills who enjoys working in a fast-paced team environment.

We offer excellent benefits, competitive salary and an exciting environment. If you can meet this challenge, send resume to:

Stadium Corporation of Ontario Limited
300 The Esplanade W
Suite 3000
Toronto, Ontario
M5V 3B2

Courtesy of the Corporation of Ontario Ltd.[A]

Private Accounting Accountants hired as employees of a business that is not a public accounting business — such as Stelco — are said to be in private accounting.

There are far more private accountants than public accountants. Their chief employers are business corporations that may have several hundred employees working in a number of special accounting departments. In these businesses, accountants are hired to perform functions ranging all the way from general (financial) accounting duties to such management functions as cost accounting, budgeting, internal auditing, and other special phases of management accounting.

Controller or comptroller: the chief accounting officer in a large business.

The chief accounting officer in a large business is generally called the controller or comptroller because he or she not only manages the accounting staff, but also is part of the management team responsible for controlling the financial operation of the business. One attraction of the accounting or finance department in a large corporation is the fact that the accounting division has often been the springboard for promotion to key jobs in sales, purchasing, production planning, manufacturing, and personnel. Indeed, it is quite common for vice-presidents and presidents to hold accounting titles such as C.A., C.M.A., and C.G.A.

Financial Analyst

H.J. Heinz, an ideal place to apply your skills and enjoy career growth, has this opportunity in the Profit Planning Department which will allow you to realize your goals at our Canadian Head Office.

Reporting to the Administrator, Profit Planning, you will be responsible for assisting in the development, analysis and consolidation of information necessary to support the forecasting cycle. This includes monthly financial forecasts, monthly actual analysis, budgets, and five-year business plans.

As a university or college graduate in the 3rd or 4th level of the CMA/CGA program, you have one to two years experience in forecasting and budgeting within a consumer products environment. In addition to being ambitious and well organized, you are an excellent communicator and have experience with Lotus 1-2-3.

We offer a competitive salary, generous benefits and, importantly, excellent opportunities for advancement and professional development. Please send your resume, in confidence, to: **Human Resources Department, H.J. Heinz Company of Canada Ltd.**

No agency solicitation considered.

Government Accounting Governments at all levels — federal, provincial, and municipal — hire accountants to perform specialized services. Of course, the federal government is the largest employer of accountants who may perform such services as preparing budgets, auditing the accounting records of departments, or examining the millions of income tax returns filed by individuals and corporations.

Provincial governments, too, hire accountants but on a smaller scale. These accountants would perform services such as preparing budgets, auditing the accounting records of various provincial departments, and examining income tax returns and sales tax returns for that province.

Financial Officer

$40,300 - $47,900

Join the senior management team of the MINISTRY OF HEALTH'S Kingston Psychiatric Hospital, a regional facility with a 23-million dollar budget, employing more than 700 staff. Reporting to the hospital administrator, you will: plan, develop and implement financial services; direct a staff of 15 providing financial services responsive to changing needs and priorities while making the best use of available resources; help develop/implement overall hospital administrative programs. The ministry has a smoke-free workplace policy.

Qualifications: Excellent knowledge of government financial and administrative control systems; excellent analytical and conceptual skills; good problem-solving and interpersonal skills; familiarity with computer and software applications; sound knowledge of accounting and financial-management principles and techniques acquired through study and membership in a recognized accounting association.

Municipalities may hire an accountant to act as the city or town treasurer and to perform services such as audits and the preparation of budgets.

Fund accounting: the accounting of government funds which are used for a variety of purposes.

Another important field of governmental accounting is made up of accountants who are hired to assist appointed and elected representatives in administering the many separate funds that have been set up for specific purposes. Because each fund is kept separate, and because there are income or loss concepts in the same sense as in private accounting (though governments are not designed to make profits), governmental accounting is often known as fund accounting.

PROBLEMS

Identifying the action words of the accounting cycle.

P 6-9 Three key action words within the accounting process are shown in column (1) below.

Key Concepts from the Accounting Process (1)	Matching Words from the Accounting Cycle (2)
Recording	
Classifying	
Summarizing	

a. Complete column (2) by giving the one word or words from the steps of the accounting cycle which match(es) the meaning of the word in column (1).

b. Give one word which defines all the words in both columns. *Hint:* The correct word has been used in an earlier chapter.

Identifying career opportunities in accounting.

P 6-10 Search newspapers and magazines for classified ads announcing positions in bookkeeping, management accounting, and financial (general) accounting. From the advertisements, list the following information: title of the position, starting salary, education or knowledge required, experience (if any), and type of work performed.

MINI-CASES

Researching the accounting bodies in Canada.

MC 6-7 Helen and her brother Miguel are interested in becoming professional accountants. They discover that their school library lacks information on professional careers as accountants. Obtain information from each of the three accounting bodies, C.A.s, C.M.A.s, and C.G.A.s, and prepare a summary of the major areas of stress and expertise that each body focuses on. Include information on student entrance requirements, course requirements, methods of course presentation, and examinations and testing requirements.

Interviewing a professional accountant.

MC 6-8 A visitor to an introductory accounting class was introduced as M. S. Taylor, B.A., M.B.A., with experience as a financial executive with a local auto dealer. Following the visitor's presentation and departure, several students questioned whether the guest possessed an accounting designation. Seek out and interview at least one person from the community who has an accounting designation. Prepare a summary of their accounting experience, their educational background, a description of their present job, the level of responsibility of their job, and the possibility of promotion.

Analyzing the events of a business.

MC 6-9 Several significant happenings in the life of a business are listed below. For each of these events, explain whether or not it will enter into the accounting process.

Identifying events affecting the accounting process.

a. Vaughan Minor invested $50 000 cash under the firm name Vaughan Minor, Chartered Accountant, and deposited it into the bank account.

b. The owner looked at three different office buildings in order to decide where to establish his public accounting practice.

c. A cheque for $700 was made out to City Properties Ltd. for the payment of one month's office space in City Towers.

d. Vaughan Minor interviewed three candidates for the position of office receptionist.

e. The owner was permitted to try out three different microcomputer systems without charge.

f. The owner signed a contract to purchase one of the tested microcomputer systems. Payment was to be made in 60 days.

g. Lawrence Philp, C.A., opened a competing accounting practice in an office building across the street.

h. Lawrence Philp, C.A., offered Vaughan Minor $20 000 cash to join him as an equal partner in a firm to be called Philp and Minor, Chartered Accountants.

APPLYING THE ELECTRONIC SPREADSHEET AND INTRODUCING THE GENERAL LEDGER ACCOUNTING PACKAGE

Chapters 2 and 4 introduced the applications of an electronic spreadsheet in accounting. You have learned how to prepare income statements, balance sheets, the general journal, and accounting proofs using an electronic spreadsheet.

In Chapter 5, you became familiar with a six-column worksheet. In this topic in particular you will learn that the electronic spreadsheet is perfectly suited for preparing a worksheet. In fact, with the special features you have already learned, such as copying, summing, and preparing and using formulas, the electronic spreadsheet becomes a powerful tool for examining worksheets.

The second computer application you will be introduced to in this topic is the General Ledger accounting package. Like the electronic spreadsheet, this package, commonly referred to as a GL package, uses the speed and accuracy of the computer to great advantage.

Just as the electronic spreadsheet is very general in nature and can have many non-specific uses, the GL package is far more powerful and sophisticated than the electronic spreadsheet, and much more specific in its accounting applications. Each of these computer applications are invaluable tools when used wisely and correctly.

PREPARING A SIX-COLUMN WORKSHEET USING AN ELECTRONIC SPREADSHEET

The worksheet can be prepared using an electronic spreadsheet in much the same way as it was manually prepared in Chapter 5, Topic 1. Refer to the six-column worksheet for J. Emery Real Estate on page 166 and recall its parts:

(1) the three-part heading

(2) the account titles, or names

(3) the account numbers

(4) the Trial Balance columns

(5) the Income Statement columns

(6) the Balance Sheet columns

Examine each of the illustrations that follow as you read the description of how the worksheet is constructed using the electronic spreadsheet.

Headings and Account Titles The heading traditionally has three lines at the top of the worksheet and is centred over it. Because the width of the columns has not yet been established, we will delay placing the heading. Instead, beginning at cell A5, record and centre each column heading.
the title ''ACCOUNT NAME'';
in B5 ''ACCT.'' and in B6 ''NO.'';
in C5 ''TRIAL'' and C6 ''DR.'';
in D5 ''BALANCE'' and D6 ''CR.'';
in E5 ''INCOME'' and E6 ''DR.'';
in F5 ''STATEMENT'' and F6 ''CR.'',
in G5 ''BALANCE'' and G6 ''DR.'';
and in H5 ''SHEET'' and H6 ''CR.''.

GOTO A7 and record each of the account names in the trial balance. Several of the accounts will not fit into the nine or ten spaces usually assigned by the program. In fact, the longest item is 28 characters long, so the account name column must be expanded to hold at least this number. The column width is reset by using the command line.

Next, a glance tells you that the column heading ''ACCT.'' is the longest item in this column and is five characters long. Notice how each column is adjusted in width to accommodate the longest item, either in the heading or the body. Adjust the column width accordingly and then record each of the account numbers in the corresponding cell in column B. Finally, the correct debit or credit balance of each account is recorded in columns C or D. Add a single line under the trial balance columns. The next step is total the columns. Remember that the trial balance proves that the total debits equal the total credits. By using the sum function the debit and credit columns can be totalled. This is an important step because nothing further should be done in the worksheet until the debit and credit totals equal. Refer to the illustration below.

Sum function: a special function of an electronic spreadsheet that automatically totals a selected group of numbers.

ACCOUNT NAME	ACCT.	TRIAL	BALANCE	INCOME	STATEMENT	BALANCE	SHEET
	NO.	DR.	CR.	DR.	CR.	DR.	CR.
Cash	101	71065					
Accts. Rec./Pat Rogers	103	6000					
Accts. Rec./R. Scobie	104	4000					
Accts. Rec./Shannon Dev. Co.	105	15000					
Automobile	110	15000					
Furniture	112	9000					
Office Equipment	114	8000					
Bank Loan Payable	201		16000				
Accts. Pay./Bell Furn. Co.	202		3000				
Accts. Pay./The City Press	203		2000				
Accts. Pay./Ryan Equip. Co.	204		3000				
J. Emery, Capital	301		63000				
J. Emery, Drawing	302	2000					
Commissions Earned	401		51800				
Rent Expense	501	1600					
Telephone Expense	502	40					
Utilities Expense	503	595					
Salaries Expense	504	4500					
Advertising Expense	505	2000					
		138800	138800				

Now you can use another powerful feature of the electronic spreadsheet. With the copy command, you can copy or transfer the cells containing expense account amounts to the corresponding cells of the income statement. Next, you can copy the revenue account cell to the corresponding income statement cell, then the debit account cells to the balance sheet, and finally the credit account cells to the balance sheet. Refer to the illustration on page 242.

Copy command: another special function of an electronic spreadsheet that enables the user to copy designated number(s) and transfer them to another location within the spreadsheet.

ACCOUNT NAME	ACCT.	TRIAL	BALANCE	INCOME	STATEMENT	BALANCE	SHEET
	NO.	DR.	CR.	DR.	CR.	DR.	CR.
Cash	101	71065				71065	
Accts. Rec./Pat Rogers	103	6000				6000	
Accts. Rec./R. Scobie	104	4000				4000	
Accts. Rec./Shannon Dev. Co.	105	15000				15000	
Automobile	110	15000				15000	
Furniture	112	9000				9000	
Office Equipment	114	8000				8000	
Bank Loan Payable	201		16000				16000
Accts. Pay./Bell Furn. Co.	202		3000				3000
Accts. Pay./The City Press	203		2000				2000
Accts. Pay./Ryan Equip. Co.	204		3000				3000
J. Emery, Capital	301		63000				63000
J. Emery, Drawing	302	2000				2000	
Commissions Earned	401		51800		51800		
Rent Expense	501	1600		1600			
Telephone Expense	502	40		40			
Utilities Expense	503	595		595			
Salaries Expense	504	4500		4500			
Advertising Expense	505	2000		2000			
		138800	138800				

Then, you must total the statement columns. Before totalling, underline each column. This is best accomplished by using the copy command to copy the line or rule from one of the trial balance columns. If you use the sum function to total the entire debit column of the income statement, then use the copy command to reproduce the formula automatically for each of the three remaining columns.

Next, place the total expense figure under the total revenue figure so that the net income can be calculated. By assigning the cell beneath the revenue figure equal to the total expense cell, you will have the opportunity to use the spreadsheet for ''what if'' situations. This use will be demonstrated later in the topic. Notice, even when you type in the cell location of the total expense, the actual number is still displayed. Next, place a single line under the total expenses. On the line below, create a formula in the cell where the net income or net loss will be displayed. Remember to identify the net income (loss) in the account name column as soon as the calculation is complete. Now because you know the net income will cause the capital account to increase, place the net income figure in the credit column of the balance sheet. Be sure to type in a cell location, not a number, to make the best use of the spreadsheet capability. Place a single line beneath both balance sheet columns and enter a formula to calculate the totals for each balance sheet column. Finally, place a double line beneath the Income Statement and Balance Sheet columns. Refer to the illustration below.

ACCOUNT NAME	ACCT. NO.	TRIAL BALANCE DR.	TRIAL BALANCE CR.	INCOME STATEMENT DR.	INCOME STATEMENT CR.	BALANCE SHEET DR.	BALANCE SHEET CR.
Cash	101	71065				71065	
Accts. Rec./Pat Rogers	103	6000				6000	
Accts. Rec./R. Scobie	104	4000				4000	
Accts. Rec./Shannon Dev. Co.	105	15000				15000	
Automobile	110	15000				15000	
Furniture	112	9000				9000	
Office Equipment	114	8000				8000	
Bank Loan Payable	201		16000				16000
Accts. Pay./Bell Furn. Co.	202		3000				3000
Accts. Pay./The City Press	203		2000				2000
Accts. Pay./Ryan Equip. Co.	204		3000				3000
J. Emery, Capital	301		63000				63000
J. Emery, Drawing	302	2000				2000	
Commissions Earned	401		51800		51800		
Rent Expense	501	1600		1600			
Telephone Expense	502	40		40			
Utilities Expense	503	595		595			
Salaries Expense	504	4500		4500			
Advertising Expense	505	2000		2000			
		138800	138800	8735	51800	130065	87000
					8735		
Net Income					43065		43065
						130065	130065

Examine next the following "what if" situation. Suppose that Jane Emery earned an additional $3000 in commissions from, for example, Pat Rogers. This would cause an increase to the account Accts. Rec./Pat Rogers and also to the revenue account Commissions Earned. Assume that you change the trial balance by adding $3000 to each of the accounts affected. Accts. Rec./Pat Rogers should now read $9000 and Commissions Earned, $54 800. The new total of the trial balance would be $141 800. Because a formula was used to produce the trial balance total, the new totals are automatically updated when the corrections are made. The figures in the statements, however, remain unchanged because numbers, not formulas, were copied. In order to use the power of the spreadsheet, the cell formula must be copied into the two accounts affected. Notice that as soon as these changes are made, all other totals are immediately and accurately updated. Finally, at B1, B2, and B3, enter the three-line heading as shown on page 166. Refer to the illustration below.

J. EMERY REAL ESTATE
WORKSHEET
FOR THE MONTH ENDED OCTOBER 31, 19-1

ACCOUNT NAME	ACCT. NO.	TRIAL BALANCE DR.	TRIAL BALANCE CR.	INCOME STATEMENT DR.	INCOME STATEMENT CR.	BALANCE SHEET DR.	BALANCE SHEET CR.
Cash	101	71065				71065	
Accts. Rec./Pat Rogers	103	9000				9000	
Accts. Rec./R. Scobie	104	4000				4000	
Accts. Rec./Shannon Dev. Co.	105	15000				15000	
Automobile	110	15000				15000	
Furniture	112	9000				9000	
Office Equipment	114	8000				8000	
Bank Loan Payable	201		16000				16000
Accts. Pay./Bell Furn. Co.	202		3000				3000
Accts. Pay./The City Press	203		2000				2000
Accts. Pay./Ryan Equip. Co.	204		3000				3000
J. Emery, Capital	301		63000				63000
J. Emery, Drawing	302	2000				2000	
Commissions Earned	401		54800		54800		
Rent Expense	501	1600		1600			
Telephone Expense	502	40		40			
Utilities Expense	503	595		595			
Salaries Expense	504	4500		4500			
Advertising Expense	505	2000		2000			
		141800	141800	8735	54800	133065	87000
					8735		
Net Income					46065		46065
						133065	133065

INTRODUCING THE GENERAL LEDGER ACCOUNTING PACKAGE

GL package: an accounting software package that enables the user to perform all or most steps of the accounting cycle on the computer.

As powerful and flexible as the electronic spreadsheet is, it is not designed for, nor useful for, all accounting applications. As you have discovered working through the accounting cycle, virtually all parts of the accounting cycle are integrated. The electronic spreadsheet does not readily provide the needed integration features to make it a useful tool throughout all steps of the accounting cycle. Another type of software package provides this advanced level of integration: the General Ledger Accounting Package or GL package.

What requires integration in accounting? First, let's examine the first three steps in the accounting cycle and focus on how information is transferred.

- Originating information from source documents: the source documents provide the necessary information to prepare journal entries. No integration is required.

  Journalizing: As you have experienced manually, journalizing involves recording the date, the debit accounts, and the credit accounts, the amounts, and usually an explanation. The transfer of information between the journal and the ledger requires integration.
- Posting: Posting means to copy the amounts in the journal to the appropriate ledger accounts. Each time a posting takes place, a new balance must be calculated either manually or with a calculator.

A General Ledger package requires the same input of accounts and amounts as the manual system when journalizing. However, the clerk must use a GJ grid as defined under the GL package. With experience, you can become very efficient with this type of journalizing. However, the one major difference from the manual system is that all accounts are identified by an account number. Therefore, when the journal entry is recorded, the user inputs the account numbers, not the account names. The computer then identifies the account in the Chart of Accounts — which has previously been input — and records the account name in the journal grid automatically. Furthermore, the computer assumes the dollar amount to be recorded will be that account's usual balance, for example, Cash would be automatically assumed to be a debit. Before the entry is input, the program requires confirmation of the balance or that it be changed appropriately.

Good practice in the manual system requires that each journal entry be verified for debit-credit equality before posting takes place. GL packages check for this equality automatically and will not permit you to proceed further until the journal's debits and credits balance.

Now the GL package demonstrates one of its major advantages. The user now directs the computer to post the journal entry. Electronically, and with great speed and complete accuracy, the appropriate accounts are posted automatically. The manual repetitive work of making individual entries is eliminated.

PREPARING THE TRIAL BALANCE

When the trial balance is prepared manually, all the accounts with a balance are listed and then totalled to check for debit-credit equality.

The GL package completes this task automatically. Therefore, any copying or totalling errors are eliminated and calculating is faster.

PREPARING WORKSHEETS AND FINANCIAL STATEMENTS

Next the GL package has the capability of producing complete financial statements, given that considerable set-up has been completed in the Chart of Accounts. Each account must be coded with an account number. (Recall the reference to account numbers in the journal discussion.) This account number coding includes every account, as well as headings, subtotals, and totals. Each of the codes assigns rank determining the location of that item on the statements. Therefore considerable preliminary work is necessary if the statements are to be produced correctly at some later date. Note, however, that once the set-up is complete, financial statements can be prepared as frequently as required.

CLOSING THE GENERAL LEDGER

Manual closing is the posting of journal entries to the ledger. Closing is carried out automatically by the GL package with each revenue or expense account brought to zero and closed to the Capital account.

In both the manual and computer applications, reference is made to month-end and year-end closings. If you examine a company using a manual system in practice, month-end closings virtually never occur. Why? There are two main reasons: (1) In a manual system it is too much work. A business cannot afford the labour hours it takes to complete the accounting entries required in closing the books. (2) If a business closed its books each month, it would be nearly impossible to calculate the year-to-date total figures. Imagine how much work would be required to determine totals for each expense account at the end of a quarter, six months, or a full year. Therefore, in a manual system, the books are rarely closed except for once a year. It is important to note that in textbook applications, students often are asked to close at the end of a month to simulate, with simple numbers, the steps that normally only take place once a year.

Why then does the GL package offer a month-end closing option and what actually takes place? The computer only pretends to close each revenue and expense account, but it does not make the account equal to zero as it does during the year-end closing sequence. Instead, the computer determines the closing amount and transfers the duplicate amounts to a "dummy" account that calculates the net income or net loss and supplies the necessary information for the production of month-end statements without actually affecting the working accounts of the business. In addition, the computer also maintains what is called a year-to-date set of totals so that the user can request current year-to-date statements and account totals.

Finally, at the actual year-end the GL package will make each revenue account equal to zero, calculate the net income or net loss, and place the calculated amount in the owner's Capital account. One journal entry is necessary, the closing entry for the owner's Drawing account. Remember, the computer will post that entry automatically. Simply, the computer stores the account balances in what are called "buckets." Each account can store fourteen balances — the current balance which is set equal to zero at the start of each month, twelve past period balances, and an accumulator. When a transaction takes place, the amount is added to the accumulator and then stored as a current balance. Remember when month-end closing took place, the accumulator was not cleared, only duplicated for use in the dummy account. At year-end closing, however, the temporary accounts were cleared and made equal to zero, with the exception of the Drawing account.

PRE-CLOSING GENERAL LEDGER — JANUARY 31, 1991

1991 (current) 1990

	Jan 1991	Dec.	Nov.	Oct.	Sept.	Aug.	July	June	May	Apr.	Mar.	Feb.	Jan.	
Period / Account	Current	–1	–2	–3	–4	–5	–6	–7	–8	–9	–10	–11	–12	–13
Cash in Bank	$10	7	14	35	–5	7	–15	–20	10	25	16	12	6	420
Accounts Receivable	$112	76	84	92	71	63	43	32	46	76	87	98	116	809

Year-End Indicator

Current Period Balance

12 Past Period Balances

Accumulator Balance

POST-CLOSING GENERAL LEDGER — FEBRUARY 1, 1991

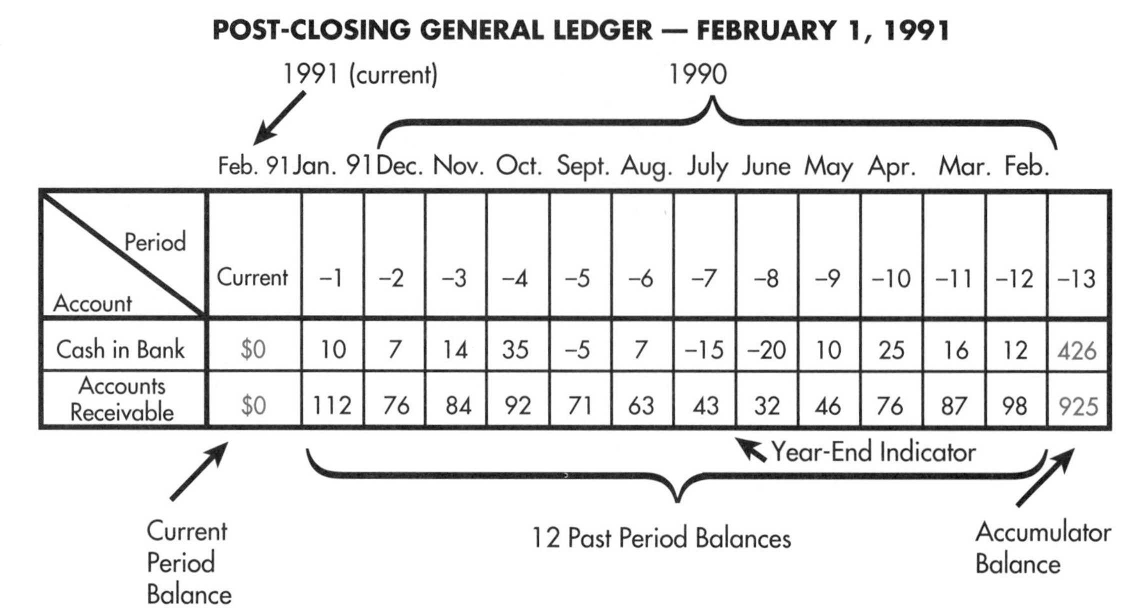

Account \ Period	Current	−1	−2	−3	−4	−5	−6	−7	−8	−9	−10	−11	−12	−13
Cash in Bank	$0	10	7	14	35	−5	7	−15	−20	10	25	16	12	426
Accounts Receivable	$0	112	76	84	92	71	63	43	32	46	76	87	98	925

EXAMINING THE INTEGRATION FEATURES OF A GL PACKAGES

Most GL packages are purchased as part of an overall general accounting package that includes programs not only to process the General Ledger, but also subsidiary ledgers like accounts receivable and accounts payable. General accounting packages are ''general'' because their programs can be applied to several different types of businesses. However, customized packages are required for businesses like medical and dental practices. A sophisticated general accounting package will include such accounting fuctions as:

- a **General Ledger module** includes many of the items described above.
- an **Accounts Receivable module** provides subsidiary accounts receivable capability
- an **Accounts Payable module** provides subsidiary accounts payable capability
- an **Inventory module** provides perpetual inventory capability
- an **Invoicing module** provides the ability to produce industry standard invoices
- a **Payroll module** provides the capability of preparing payroll on the computer.

The user of the general accounting package should be able to operate each of these modules independently from the General Ledger or with full integration.

Batch processing: the collection of accounting data over a period of time after which the data are processed as a group against a particular accounting file.

Real-time accounting: the accounting of source documents and related accounts without a time delay.

Mainframe computer: a large-scale, expensive computer capable of processing billions of characters of information at great speed.

Minicomputer: a scaled-down, less expensive mainframe.

Microcomputer: a desktop or personal computer, based on a microprocessor, that is typically used by one person.

RAM (Random Access Memory): temporary, internal memory that is lost as soon as the power is shut off.

Floppy disk drive: a secondary storage device that usually comes in 5-1/4 or 3-1/2 inch sizes.

Printer: an output device used to produce printed material (hard copy) for the use of its reader(s).

Typically, general accounting packages are designed to input information by batch processing or real-time accounting. Batch processing, as the name suggests, involves inputting a large number or batch of entries. For example, three days' business transactions might be entered into the computer at one time. This system is commonly used for very large computers and mainframes, although some packages are designed to run this way on microcomputers. The major advantage is the speed with which the input takes place. The disadvantages include the lengthy time needed to prepare the input and the delay between the actual transaction and entry of that information into the computer. Real-time accounting involves direct interaction between the user and the computer at the time the transaction takes place. The major advantage is the immediate updating of accounting information. For example, when an invoice is prepared using real-time accounting, the invoice is immediately produced for the customer and inventory records and accounts receivable records can immediately be updated. The major disadvantage is that the user must have access to the computer at all times. This can be costly.

A variety of computer configurations are required for the various general accounting packages found on the market today. These configurations fall into two categories: The first is the type of computer used to run the system; and the second is the specific need for a microcomputer system.

- Originally only very expensive mainframe computers had the power and memory size to handle the complexity of a general accounting package.
- The minicomputer was the next type of computer capable of handling the general accounting package. This computer was less expensive, but still had the necessary power and memory size.
- Finally, general accounting software was developed and improved as the power and memory size of the microcomputer grew.

  Accounting packages are still being run on mainframe and minicomputers in many businesses, but the most dramatic growth in the use of these packages has been in smaller businesses as the microcomputer has become more powerful and more affordable. General accounting software packages vary in their microcomputer requirements. These requirements can vary as follows.

- The most basic computer configuration needed to run a general accounting package requires 640 K of internal RAM (random access memory) and two floppy disk drives and a printer. (It may be possible to operate the system with one floppy disk drive, but it would prove most inconvenient and very impractical.)

- As the software package increases in overall size and complexity, the internal memory (RAM) of the computer system must increase. It is becoming commonplace for microcomputers to come equipped with a minimum of one megabyte (1000 K) of internal memory and many can be expanded to two, five, or more megabytes of internal memory.

Megabyte: 1024 kilobytes of memory in the computer.

- A great number of microcomputer systems also come equipped with built-in and/or external hard-disk capability. Hard-disk capacities run from 20 to 60 megabytes of storage with 20- or 40-megabyte systems being most popular. It is impractical to run many general accounting packages if your computer does not have hard-disk capability. A hard-disk system provides the user with greatly increased storage capability and speed.

Hard disk: a storage mechanism placed either internally or externally in a computer system.

Menu: a list of choices offered to the user that guides the user to a specific option offered by the program.

Most accounting software packages operate via a series of menus. The menus guide the user through the package by offering a series of choices. The first menu is very general in nature, but with each choice that is made, the menus that follow become more specific in nature. For example, the first menu (often called the Master System Menu) of a general accounting package appears as follows:

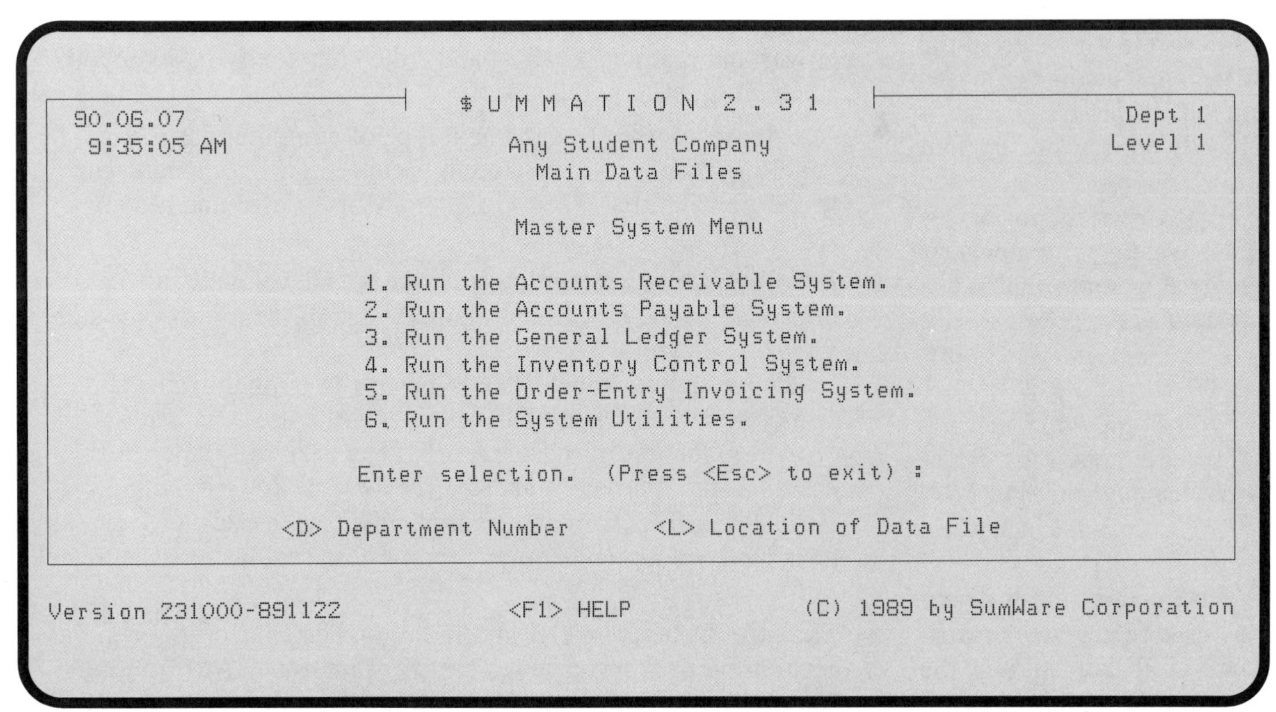

General Accounting Package Master System Menu

As you can see, the user has six choices:

1. Run the Accounts Receivable System
2. Run the Accounts Payable System
3. Run the General Ledger System
4. Run the Inventory System
5. Run the Order-entry/Invoicing System
6. Run the Systems Utilities

Notice that each menu must provide the user with a method of escaping from that menu.

If the user chooses choice 3, the General Ledger System, the following menu would appear:

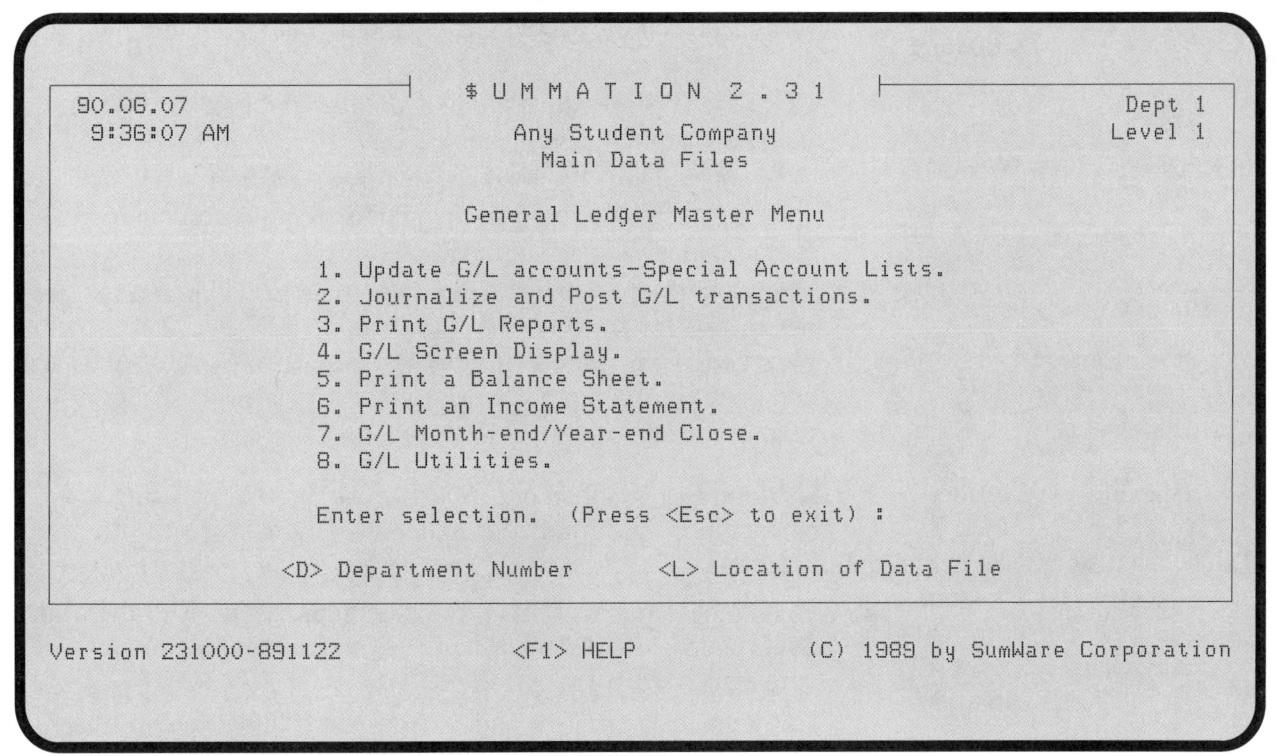

General Ledger Master System Menu

This menu provides the user with eight different options. Each of these options relates specifically to a General Ledger operation. If the user chooses one of these items, there are two possibilities: a more specific menu or a specific accounting operation.

All general accounting packages require the user to be familiar with basic accounting knowledge and double-entry bookkeeping. You should now be able to appreciate and have an understanding of what the system is doing for you.

PROBLEMS

Opening a new spreadsheet.

Preparing a worksheet from a given trial balance.

Answering a "what if" situation.

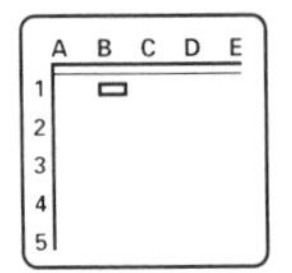

P 6-11 Return to Problem 6-1 (VanderHoeven Camera Repairs Shop). By using the trial balance provided, your manual solution, and detailed instructions concerning the use of a spreadsheet provided by your instructor, complete the following tasks.

a. Open a new spreadsheet on the computer and transfer the trial balance accounts, account numbers, and amounts into the spreadsheet.

b. Copy the appropriate amounts from the trial balance into the income statement and balance sheet.

c. Total and rule off the worksheet. Print a copy of your spreadsheet if possible and then compare your computer work to the manual work completed in Topic 1.

d. Complete the following "what if" situation. What if a service performed for B. Maxwell amounting to $263 was not recorded? Print a copy of your spreadsheet if possible and then compare your computer work to the original worksheet prepared in **c**.

Opening a spreadsheet.

Preparing a worksheet from a given trial balance.

Answering a "what if" situation.

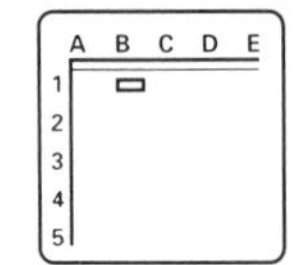

P 6-12 Return to Problem 6-2 (Sparkle Car Wash). By using the trial balance provided, and your manual solution, complete the following tasks.

a. Open a new spreadsheet on the computer and transfer the trial balance accounts, account numbers and amounts into the spreadsheet.

b. Copy the appropriate amounts from the trial balance into the income statement and balance sheet.

c. Total and rule off the worksheet. Print a copy of your spreadsheet if possible and then compare your computer work to the manual work completed in Topic 1.

d. What if an invoice for cleaning supplies received from Auto Cleaning Supplies Ltd. amounting to $861 was not recorded? The firm is given 30 days to pay. Print a copy of your spreadsheet if possible and then compare your computer work to the original worksheet prepared in **c**.

Opening a GL package.

Journalizing, posting, and preparing a trial balance and financial statements from a set of transactions.

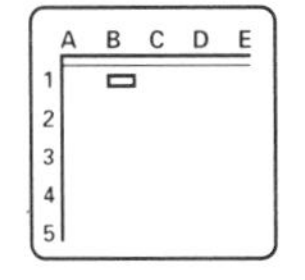

P 6-13 Return to the problems for J. Edgar Consulting Services (Problems 4-4, 4-7, and 4-10). By using the transactions provided, your manual solution, and detailed instructions concerning the use of a GL package provided by your instructor, complete the following tasks.

a. By following the detailed instructions provided to you, load the GL package and move through the menus until you reach the journalizing function. Complete the journal entries for the problem and run the appropriate program to obtain a printout of all General Journal entries.

b. Review three of the accounts affected by the journalizing in **a**, print a detailed report of these accounts; time permitting, print a detailed report of the entire General Ledger; and, finally, have the computer print out a trial balance from the ledger accounts.

c. Have the computer prepare an income statement and balance sheet for the month-end.

MINI-CASES

Examining procedures to ensure safety of data files.

MC 6-10 An inexperienced data entry clerk used a popular microcomputer GL package to process 1000 transactions over four days. After completing 680 transactions, a power surge occurred that completely eliminated these data files. The frustrated accounting clerk was required to begin again, but instead resigned and left for home.

a. What precautions should have been taken to ensure the safety of all accounting data files?

Comparing manual accounting to computerized accounting.

MC 6-11 Two students were overheard discussing the merits and limitations of computerized general accounting versus the traditional manual method.

Sarah strongly supported the move to microcomputer GL packages for all businesses. In support, Sarah believes that, in time, microcomputers will eliminate the need for the traditional manual method. On the other hand, Chuan supported the use of microcomputers for only mid-sized and large businesses. Chuan believes that the traditional manual method will always be needed by small businesses.

a. Use your experience and knowledge gained from Problem 6-13 to write a short report giving the advantages and limitations of a microcomputer GL package for small business accounting systems. End your report with your opinion regarding the debate between Sarah and Chuan.

Comparing batch processing to real-time accounting.

MC 6-12 Mauro, after using a real-time and a batch system to process a GL problem, supported only the batch system. On the other hand, Margarette argued in support of only real-time accounting.

a. Which system do you prefer? Write a short report giving your reasons.

COMPREHENSIVE CASE STUDY 6

Bright Brass Refinishing Company is owned and operated by A. Laddin. After one year of operation, Alice wanted to know what dollar amount she now had invested in the business. Her initial investment had been $10 000 and she had withdrawn for personal living expenses $1000 per month during the year.

Assume for the year total revenue of $53 000 and total expenses of $41 000.

Demonstrating the closing sequence.

a. Use T-accounts and general account headings, for example, Total Revenue, to demonstrate the closing entries for the business.

Calculating the new investment amount.

b. Was the business profitable during this past year? Provide a dollar figure. How did you arrive at that figure? (Show your work.)

c. What is the dollar figure in Alice's capital account after one full year of operation? Support your answer with numbers from **a**.

Analyzing and discussing potential accounting errors.

d. Explain to Alice how it is possible for the business to have made a profit while her capital account is the same as when the business began.

e. Why could Alice not claim her living expenses as an operating expense? Explain. If it was possible, would that have changed the final outcome in **c** and **d**?

f. If **e** was possible, what would the advantage have been to Alice?

CHAPTER 7

A SECOND RUN THROUGH THE ACCOUNTING CYCLE

Topic 1
Adjusting for Prepaid Expenses

Topic 2
Adjusting for Depreciation Expense

Topic 3
Expanding the Six-Column Worksheet to Ten Columns

In preceding chapters, you learned the eight steps of the accounting cycle: (1) originating information through source documents, (2) journalizing, (3) posting, (4) preparing the trial balance, (5) preparing the worksheet, (6) preparing financial statements (the income statement and the balance sheet), (7) closing the books, and (8) preparing the postclosing trial balance. Furthermore, you have learned that each of these steps had a very specific purpose. Once one cycle is complete, another can be started by using the information in the postclosing trial balance.

In earlier topics, we have assumed that **all** revenues and **all** expenses are recorded during an accounting period. And, it was very important that revenues were matched with related expenses to report a fair net income or loss for the accounting period.

In practice, however, not all revenues and expenses are recorded during the accounting period. For example, the business may have acquired office supplies costing $1000 at the beginning of the accounting period. Assume that the cost is recorded in a current asset account. During the period some of these supplies, say $800, are used to support revenue-making activities. Therefore, at the end of the accounting period, only $200 of the original supplies are on hand.

How would this situation be recorded in the accounts? At the end of the accounting period, there is on record an Office Supplies on Hand account (a current asset) showing $1000. However, only $200 supplies are actually on hand at this time. In addition, there is no recorded expense of using $800 of supplies during the accounting period. Because this expense of using supplies is not recorded, net income would be overstated. Similarly, the current asset Office Supplies on Hand would also be overstated.

The theory of accounting requires the correct application of the matching principle. To resolve the obvious mismatch in this example —an unrecorded expense used to assist in revenue-making activities —an adjustment must be made to record the expense and decrease the current asset. In the language of accounting, the mismatches are corrected through **adjusting entries**.

In practice, adjustments may be required for recorded and unrecorded revenues, and also for recorded and unrecorded expenses. To keep matters simple, only the adjustments for unrecorded expenses will be presented here. Additional adjustments will be examined in Part 3.

ADJUSTING FOR PREPAID EXPENSES

To understand the concept of a prepaid expense and how it is adjusted at the end of an accounting period, study these transactions of Delta Real Estate.

June 1 Delta Real Estate issues a cheque for $200 to purchase enough office supplies to last several months. The cost is recorded in an asset account Office Supplies on Hand.

This transaction would result in the following T-account analysis:

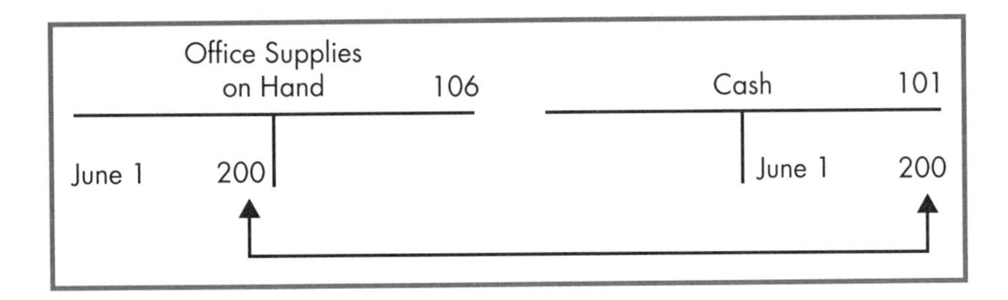

Analysis: Since the company issues a cheque, Cash is credited. The cash is used to acquire an asset—office supplies. Supplies is an asset acquired under the cost principle; therefore, it must be debited.

These supplies are expected to last for more than one accounting period. Because more than one accounting period will benefit from the expenditure, this asset is known as a prepaid expense. To be more exact, the prepaid expense is a **current** asset because its cost will be used up or will expire usually within one year of the date of the balance sheet. At the end of each period, the portion of the cost that has expired must be determined, and an adjustment is made to transfer the expired portion from the asset account to the appropriate expense account.

Prepaid expense: an expense payment made in advance to benefit more than one accounting period; hence, a current asset whose cost will be used up in the very near future.

Examine the following transaction.

June 30 In preparation for month-end financial statements, Delta Real Estate takes a physical count of office supplies and discovers $125 of unused supplies.

Office Supplies Count	
June 1	$200
Less: Office Supplies count, June 30	125
Supplies Used	$ 75

The margin shows the calculation that is now required. The result is that $75 of office supplies were used during the month of June. The asset account Office Supplies on Hand should be adjusted to reflect this remaining cost. The necessary General Journal entry is illustrated below.

June 30	Office Supplies Expense	75	
	Office Supplies on Hand		75
	To adjust the Office Supplies on Hand account for the month ended June 30.		

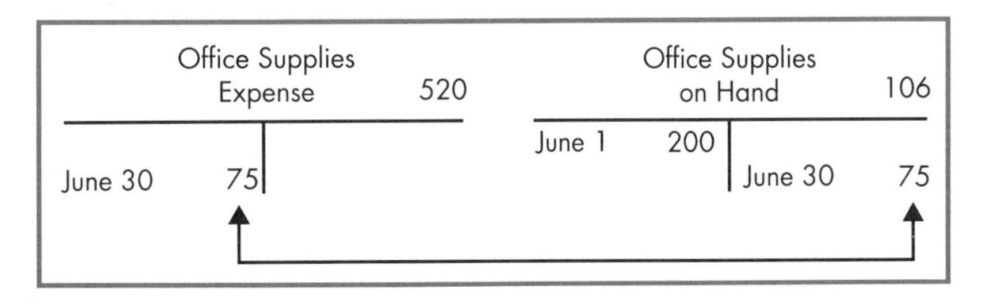

Analysis:

- Credit the asset account Office Supplies on Hand for $75 (supplies used).
- Debit the expense account Office Supplies Expense. This records the dollar amount of office supplies used during the month.

The adjustment corrects the cost value of the asset so that it will reflect the unused or unexpired cost of office supplies in the current asset section of the balance sheet. The amount used—the expired cost — will also be reported, but in the expense section of the income statement. The adjustment updates both accounts, and the expense of the period is matched with the revenues of that period.

If the adjustment is not made, what would happen?

- Revenue and expenses would be mismatched.
- Expenses would be understated by $75, because the used portion of office supplies is not recorded.
- Net income would be overstated by $75.
- Owner's equity, specifically capital, would be overstated by $75.
- The asset section of the balance sheet would be overstated by $75, because the unused portion of the asset account would not have been reduced by the amount used during June.

Prepaid insurance: a prepaid expense account identifying the unused amount of insurance coverage still owned by the business.

Prepaid Insurance Another prepaid expense in business is insurance. Insurance is purchased on assets (such as equipment, automobiles, buildings, and inventory) to ensure against loss due to theft, fire, flood, etc. Insurance premiums are paid in advance, usually on a yearly basis and in a lump sum. When insurance is purchased, the asset Prepaid Insurance is debited. The lump sum applies to the entire year, and if the accounting period is only one month, then only one-twelfth is used up. Therefore, this account should be adjusted periodically.

June 1 Delta Real Estate issues a cheque for $600 for insurance on the automobile of the business.

The following General Journal entry is recorded:

June 1	Prepaid Insurance	600	
	Cash		600
	To pay for a one-year insurance policy.		

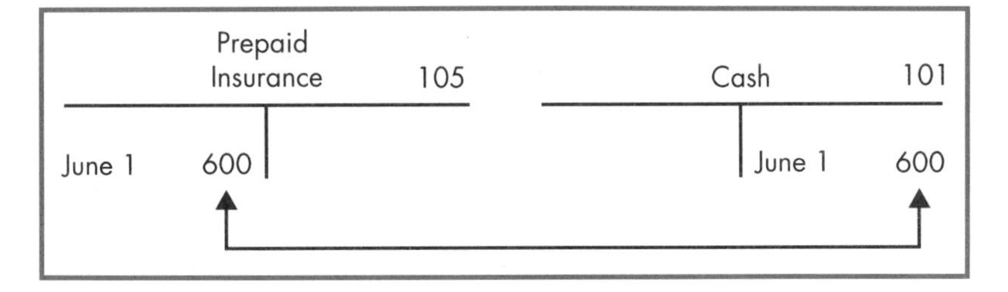

Analysis:

- The company bought 12 months of insurance coverage for $600 ($50/month). The business now owns insurance coverage for one year with an unexpired cost on June 1 of $600.
- Since a cheque was issued, Cash is credited.

June 30 At the end of June, one month of the insurance coverage or cost has expired. In other words, one-twelfth of the insurance coverage has been used. The Prepaid Insurance account must be adjusted, and the expired portion (1/12 of $600 or $50) of the premium is debited to the expense account Insurance Expense.

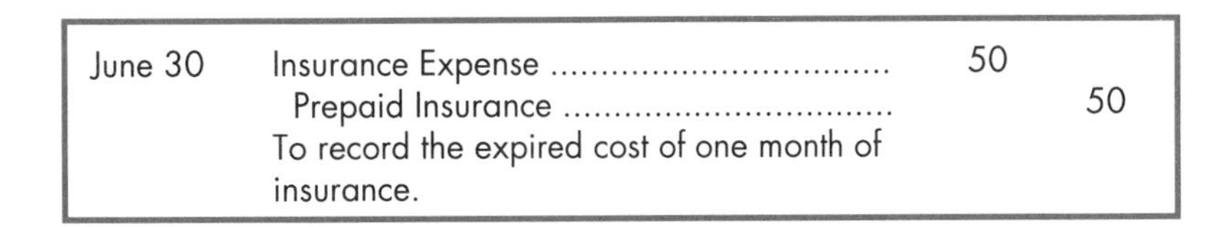

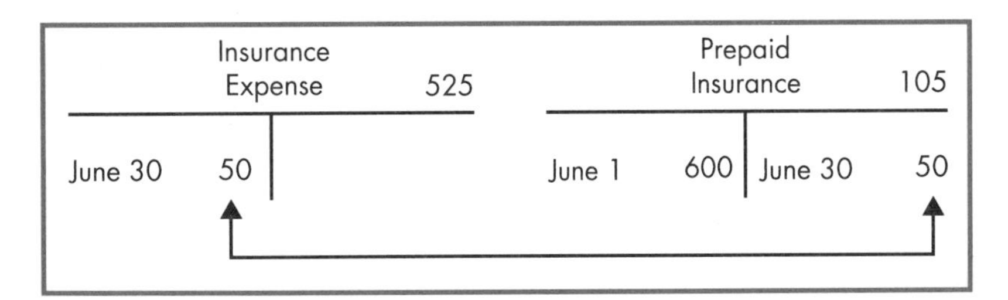

The company now owns 11 months of insurance coverage. The unexpired portion is $550. The current asset account Prepaid Insurance reflects this amount, due to the adjustment.

Other Prepaid Expenses Other prepaid expenses are rent and advertising. Any time an expense is paid in advance and can be applied to more than one accounting period, it may be recorded as a prepaid expense. *Note:* If a firm pays for its rent only one month in advance, it is very unlikely that the company will call that amount prepaid rent. Instead, because it will last less than one accounting period, it will be expensed immediately and listed as rent expense in the journal entry.

REDEFINING CURRENT ASSETS

As you learned in Chapter 6, current assets can be converted into cash within one year of the date of the balance sheet. With the introduction of prepaid expenses, however, this definition is expanded as follows:

Current assets consist of cash and other economic resources that are reasonably expected to be realized in cash, sold, or consumed during the normal operating cycle of the business.

Note that two distinct types of assets are included in this definition:

Operating cycle: the time it takes to complete the following: (1) performance of a service; (2) collection of cash from the accounts receivable.

- assets, such as accounts receivable, that are intended to be converted into cash during the normal operating cycle of the business. The operating cycle is the average time period between the performance of a service on account and the collection of cash from the accounts receivable. Most often this period is one year (or less) from the date of the balance sheet.
- assets to be consumed during the operating cycle of the business. These are identified as prepaid expenses—expenses which are unexpired costs (current assets) when they are acquired. Generally, they are expected to be consumed—or their costs to expire—within one year of the date of the balance sheet. Remember, the expired cost of such prepaid expenses must be transferred to expense accounts through adjusting entries.

In presenting the current asset section on any balance sheet, place those assets that are to be realized in cash before assets that will expire their costs while being used to support revenue-making activities. Prepaid expenses may be listed separately or grouped under a subheading as shown in the following illustration.

Delta Real Estate
Partial Balance Sheet
as at June 30, 19 -1

Current Assets:		
Cash		$ 8 796.00
Accounts Receivable		5 400.00
Supplies on Hand	$125.00	
Prepaid Insurance	550.00	675.00
Total Current Assets		$14 871.00

TOPIC 1 PROBLEMS

Preparing adjusting journal entries.

P 7-1 Prepare the appropriate adjustment entries in the General Journal, page 25, for each of the following, unrelated situations. Date all entries as at December 31, the year-end. (Include an explanation.)

a. Supplies on Hand, January 2: $600; Supplies on Hand, December 31: $25.

b. Supplies on Hand, December 1: $55; Supplies on Hand, December 31: $15.

c. Supplies on Hand, January 2: $800; Supplies on Hand, December 31: nil.

d. Prepaid Insurance, May 1: $600; Prepaid Insurance, December 31: $200.

e. A one-year insurance policy was prepaid on August 1. The annual premium was $1200.

f. A cheque for $450 was issued to City Realty for three months' advance office rent on December 1.

g. Insurance policy 10A was acquired on April 1 at a cost of $1200 for one year. A second policy, 10B, was acquired on November 30 at a cost of $1800, also for a twelve-month period.

Preparing adjusting journal entries.

P 7-2 The XYZ Company had shop supplies costing $425 at the beginning of the year. During the year the company acquired additional supplies totalling $575. At the year-end the physical count of supplies revealed a balance of $260. Prepare the necessary adjusting entry as of December 31. (Use the title Shop Supplies.) *Hint:* T-accounts might prove useful.

Preparing adjusting journal entries.

Posting adjustments to T-accounts.

P 7-3 Given the following T-accounts and information, prepare adjusting entries on July 31 to update both accounts and post your journal entries to the T-accounts.

Office Supplies on Hand 105		Prepaid Insurance 108	
July 1 120		July 1 300	

(i) A physical count of supplies indicates 200 units at $0.50 per unit.

(ii) The July 1 entry represents a one-year policy bought on that date.

MINI-CASES

Preparing adjusting journal entries.

Identifying GAAPs involved with adjustments.

Discussing the effects of adjustment errors on financial statements.

MC 7-1 Delta Comp. issued Cheque No. 456 for $700 on October 1, 19-1 to *The Daily News* for four months of newspaper advertisements.

a. Record the year-end adjusting entry in the General Journal on December 31, 19-1.

b. What GAAP would have been violated if this adjusting entry had not been completed?

c. What financial statement(s) would be affected if this adjustment had not been completed? Use actual numbers in your explanation.

d. Show by means of T-accounts what the balances would be before and after the required adjustment.

Explaining the need for adjustments.

MC 7-2 XYZ Company just completed its second year of operations. The owner wants to know why she must count the office supplies when this is such a busy time of the year for her business.

a. Explain the need for a physical count of office supplies at the end of the accounting year. Emphasize the GAAP affected in your discussion.

b. Discuss a possible remedy that XYZ Company might explore for closing at this very busy time of the year.

Drafting a memo to analyze the correct method of preparing adjusting entries.

MC 7-3 J. & M. Real Estate orders supplies from a local stationery store every three months. The business pays for its office space at the beginning of each month. Additional information at month-end is given as follows:

June	1	Office supplies costing $800 were purchased on account from ABC Suppliers.
	1	The monthly rent of $1000 was paid by issuing Cheque No. 873.
	30	Office supplies still on hand totalled $560.

If this business prepares adjustments at the end of every month, prepare a short memo directed "To: F. Milsom, Owner, J. & M. Real

Estate,'' recommending how the business should record the additional information given at month-end. Also include in your memo a short paragraph explaining why you would record the two situations given on June 1 differently. Finally, end your memo by identifying and explain the GAAP which influences the way you would record these situations. Begin your memo with the following subheadings: (1) TO:, (2) FROM: (show your name), (3) DATE: (show current date), and (4) SUBJECT: Preparing and Explaining Adjusting Entries.

TOPIC 2 ADJUSTING FOR DEPRECIATION EXPENSE

The ordinary meaning of depreciation as commonly defined does not apply to the study of accounting. Depreciation has a different meaning in accounting.

One way to understand depreciation is through the analysis of why any business acquires fixed assets such as a building, equipment of various sorts, machinery, delivery truck, etc. Examine the questions and answers that follow.

- *Why does a business acquire fixed assets like a building?*
  A business acquires fixed assets to carry on business.
- *What is meant by the phrase ''to carry on business''?*
  The chief purpose of any business operation is to make money. This is accomplished by producing revenue in excess of the expenses incurred in a particular accounting period.

This last answer is most important, for it leads to the acknowledgement of a very important principle in the study of accounting.

Fixed assets, such as buildings, machinery, and delivery trucks, are acquired to produce revenue or to support revenue-making activities.

You can think of fixed assets as providing services to the business over a period of years. For example:

(1) Acquiring a building may be regarded as payment in advance for several years' supply of housing services. The building ''houses'' the sales personnel who sell the services; it ''houses'' the equip-

ment and office personnel required to support the operations of the business; it "houses" the customers who come to the business location. The building is acquired to **support revenue-making activities** for a number of years to come. It was not acquired for the purpose of **resale**. If it were, it would cease to operate the moment the building was sold.

(2) A delivery truck which has been purchased offers transportation services to the business for a period of years or so many thousands of kilometres. The purpose of acquiring the truck is to **support revenue-making activities** of the business. It has not been acquired for resale.

Remember, fixed assets have been acquired to **produce revenue or support revenue-making activities** for years to come.

There are a number of points that you should now become familiar with. Study each of these factors as they relate to depreciation.

- The GAAP applied to the reporting of fixed assets on the balance sheet is the **cost principle**. All fixed assets are reported in accounts and in the balance sheet on the basis of their original cost.
- Accountants can only estimate how long a particular asset will assist in the production of revenue for the business. In the case of a building, it may be 10, 15, or 20 years or more. A truck may last for 200 000 km. It is important to realize that under any circumstances this determination of useful life is only an estimate.
- One thing is for certain: The asset will not last forever. Two important factors must be considered. Physical wear and tear and exposure to the outside elements limit the useful life of any fixed asset. A delivery truck is exposed to sun, snow, rain, and wind. It is driven thousands of kilometres and subjected to a variety of road conditions in all types of weather. All these circumstances cause what is called physical deterioration. Similarly, an older building is not nearly as attractive to shop in as a new and modern building. The faster, more powerful computer system that will be available six months from the date you purchased your computer is a perfect example of the second factor called obsolescence

Physical deterioration: wear and tear resulting from use and climatic factors.

Obsolescence: the process of becoming out of date that occurs through technical innovation.

You have learned two important accounting concepts: (1) that fixed assets are acquired by business to produce revenue or support revenue-making activities; and (2) that physical deterioration and obsolescence limit the length of time that fixed assets can generate revenue. The next set of questions will introduce a third important concept.

- Let's assume (1) management has decided that the estimated useful life of the building is 20 years and (2) the building will be worthless at the end of that time. What would management expect from the use of the building in that 20 years? Management would expect the building to assist in revenue-making operations for the next 20 years.
- If the building was acquired at the beginning of this year for $48 000 to create revenue for 20 years, should the business charge this year's net income, $15 000, with the entire cost of the building? In other words, should the accountant show an expense of $48 000 in this year's income statement? In a word, no.
- Why would it be incorrect to match the entire cost of the building with this year's income statement? This cost would be expensed for only one year, while the building will produce revenue for another 19 years. The fairest method is to spread the cost as evenly as possible over the useful life of the asset, that is, to spread the cost of $48 000 over 20 years.

The last answer brings us to the GAAP of matching revenues and expenses within the same accounting period. Since the building is to produce revenue for 20 years, a fair portion of the cost of the building must be matched in each of those 20 years. This important concept of matching costs is illustrated through the following series of diagrams.

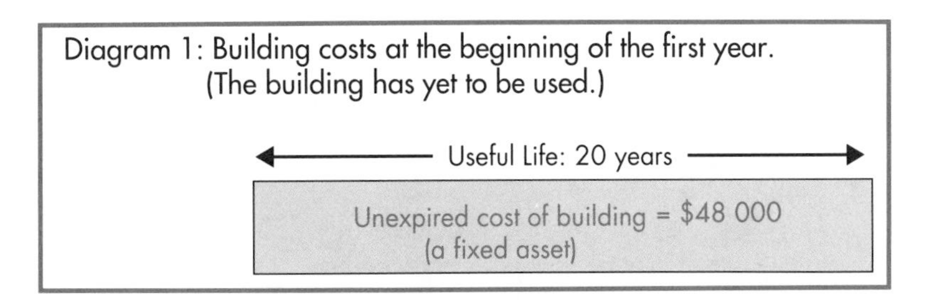

Observe from the diagram that the cost of the building is analyzed at the beginning of the first year. None of the cost of the building is charged against the revenue until the building is used. Since the building has yet to be used, the cost is said to be **unexpired**. Any unexpired cost that will produce revenue or support revenue-making activities for a period longer than one accounting period (a year) will be reported on the balance sheet under the heading **Fixed Assets** (or Plant and Equipment or Long-Lived Assets). As you will recall, unexpired costs such as prepaid assets are reported under **Current**

Assets, because their costs are expected to expire within one year of the date of the balance sheet. Now let's examine what happens at the end of the first year of using the building to produce revenue.

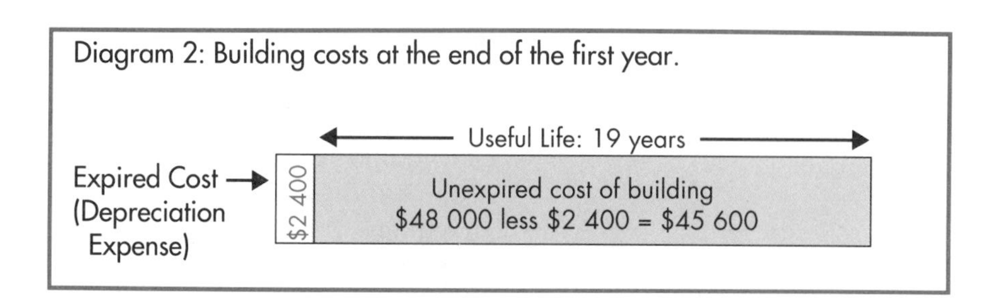

This second diagram reveals an expired cost portion of $2400; that is, $2400 of the cost of the building has been used up at the end of the first year. The expired cost is 1/20 of $48 000, since the building is estimated to have a useful life of 20 years. As you will recall from the study of prepaid expenses, the expired cost must be separated from the unexpired cost and recognized as an expense. In accounting, the expired cost of a fixed asset is known as depreciation expense. It is important to emphasize that depreciation expense is the used (expired) cost portion of a fixed asset for a particular accounting period. Examine the next diagram.

Depreciation expense: the expired cost of using a fixed asset.

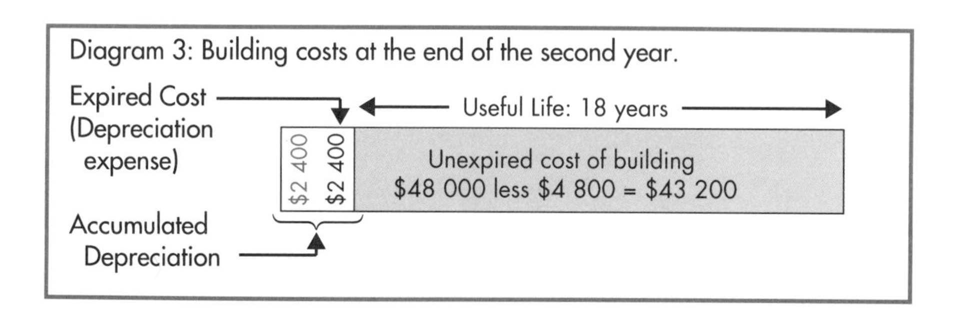

When the building costs are analyzed at the end of the second year, two important concepts are evident. From the diagram, notice that the expired cost for the second year is the depreciation expense for that year. Notice, too, that the first and second years' depreciation expense (expired costs) are added together or accumulated as accumulated depreciation. This second concept is very important, for it is used to report the unexpired cost of the building at the end of the second year. The partial balance sheet illustrated in the margin shows

Accumulated depreciation: the total of the expired costs of any one asset.

Partial Balance Sheet (as at the end of the second year)	
Fixed Assets (at cost):	
Building	$48 000
Less: Accumulated Depreciation	4 800
	$43 200

the original cost of the building less its accumulated depreciation. In other words, the reader of the balance sheet should interpret this calculation as the original cost of the fixed asset less the accumulation of expired costs. You will find that this report is required for all fixed assets whose costs expire over their useful life. The next diagram shows the concepts of depreciation expense and accumulated depreciation.

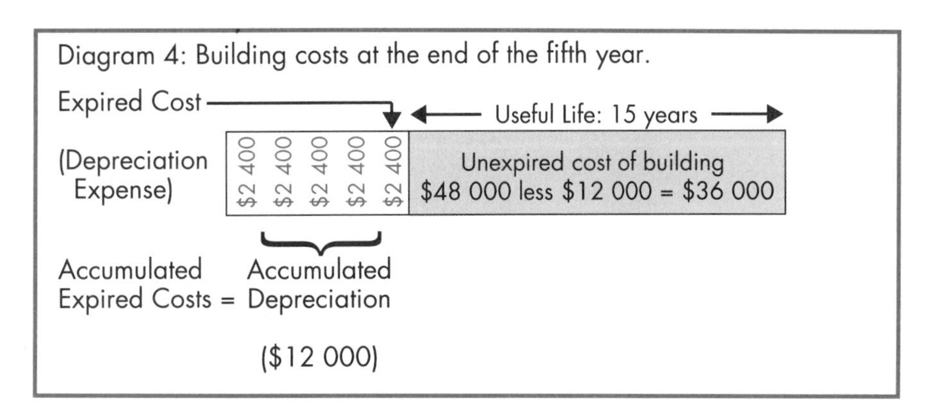

Partial Income Statement For the Year Ended December 31, 19-5	
Operating Expenses:	
Depreciation Expense on Buildings	$2 400

Partial Balance Sheet as at December 31, 19-5	
Fixed Assets (at cost):	
Building	$48 000
Less: Accumulated Depreciation	12 000
	$36 000

Notice that the expired cost (depreciation expense) is pointed out for the fifth year. This calculation is no different from the previous ones, since 1/20 of the original cost has been identified. The concept of accumulating the depreciation expense over five years is clearly shown. At the end of the fifth year the accumulated expired cost of the building is $12 000. This amount would be reported as the fixed asset amount on the fifth year's balance sheet. Of course, the depreciation expense of $2400 would be matched against the revenue of the fifth year to calculate fairly the net income (or loss) for that accounting period.

The concept of spreading the cost of the building over its useful life may be illustrated in diagrams to the end of the twentieth year. Obviously, the last diagram would show a depreciation expense of $2400 for the twentieth year and an accumulated depreciation of $48 000. Thus, no unexpired cost of the building would remain. The process of depreciating the asset is complete and we can define depreciation:

Depreciation is a process of allocating the cost of a fixed asset over its estimated useful life. It is not a process of evaluation.

This definition emphasizes the process of allocation—spreading the cost of the assets over its useful life. In accounting, depreciation must refer to the process of converting the original cost of fixed assets into expenses, that is, into expired costs. In other words, the expired cost calculated for a specific period must be matched against the revenue earned for the same period. Failing to provide for depreciation expense would result in understating the net income.

There is, however, one fixed asset that does not depreciate—land. The cost of land must not be matched against the revenue of any accounting period. There are two reasons why land does not depreciate: (1) Land is acquired solely with the idea of serving as a site on which the depreciable building will be constructed. (2) Land is regarded as having unlimited life because its cost can be recovered once the building is, for example, torn down. On any balance sheet, therefore, land is placed under **Fixed Assets** at its original cost, but there will be no accumulated depreciation. For this reason, land must be separated from Buildings on a balance sheet.

RECORDING DEPRECIATION EXPENSE

On the basis of your experience with other adjusting entries, you should have a good idea of how the depreciation entry will be recorded. Check your thoughts against the illustration on the opposite page.

Analysis:

- The debit entry describes a specific depreciation account.
- In the chart of accounts the company assigns a separate depreciation expense account for each asset being depreciated. Depreciation expense, like any other expense, is matched against the revenues of the period. For this reason the company must calculate the depreciation expense at year-end for that accounting period, in order to match the correct amount of depreciation expense against the corresponding revenues.
- The depreciation expense is closed at period-end to the Revenue and Expense Summary account as part of the routine of closing. This routine was discussed in detail in Chapter 6.
- The credit entry is an accumulated depreciation account.
- In the chart of accounts the company assigns each accumulated depreciation account to its related fixed asset account. Accumulated Depreciation/Building is the contra account of Building. A contra account is an account in direct opposition to its related account, which in this case is the Building account. This contra asset account is used in conjunction with the asset Building to reflect a true net cost figure of the building. Several different contra accounts will be identified later.

Contra account: an account that offsets another account.

GENERAL JOURNAL Page 20

DATE 19-2	ACCOUNT TITLE AND EXPLANATION	POST. REF.	DEBIT	CREDIT
Dec. 31	Depreciation Expense/Building	510	2 400 00	
	Accumulated Depreciation/Building	112		2 400 00
	To record one year's depreciation on the building.			

Delta Real Estate
Chart of Accounts

EXPENSES

510 Depreciation Expense/Building
511 Depreciation Expense/Warehouse Equipment
512 Depreciation Expense/Office Equipment
513 Depreciation Expense/Delivery Trucks

Delta Real Estate
Chart of Accounts

FIXED ASSETS

110 Land
111 Building
112 Accumulated Depreciation/Building
113 Warehouse Equipment
114 Accumulated Depreciation/Warehouse Equipment
115 Office Equipment
116 Accumulated Depreciation/Office Equipment
117 Delivery Trucks
118 Accumulated Depreciation/Delivery Trucks

- The cost principle requires that a business always reports fixed assets at their original cost price. Only when the accumulated depreciation is deducted from the original price can the unexpired cost of that fixed asset be accurately presented. This accumulated depreciation account will not be closed at the end of the accounting period, because it represents the accumulation of depreciation expense. Look for a related accumulated depreciation account with every fixed asset account—except, of course, Land.

CALCULATING STRAIGHT-LINE DEPRECIATION

Straight-line method: one of the most common methods to determine an amount of depreciation expense per year.

The spreading out of depreciation in equal amounts over several periods is known as the straight-line method. It is very popular and the calculation is as follows:

$$\text{Straight-line Depreciation} = \frac{\text{Asset Cost} - \text{Disposal Value}}{\text{Estimated Life}}$$

Disposal value: estimated value of the fixed asset when it is sold, scrapped, or traded (also referred to as a scrap value or salvage value).

The asset cost is the original cost figure of the asset. The disposal value, also referred to as salvage value, is the estimated value of the fixed asset when it is sold, scrapped, or traded. The **estimated useful life** is management's best determination of the useful life of the asset and is the key part of the calculation. Since the estimated useful life and the disposal value are estimates, the final calculation of depreciation is also an estimate.

There are several other methods of estimating depreciation, and we will examine some of those methods later.

ILLUSTRATING DEPRECIATION ENTRIES

January 1, 19-1 A cheque is issued for $5200 to purchase furniture for an office.

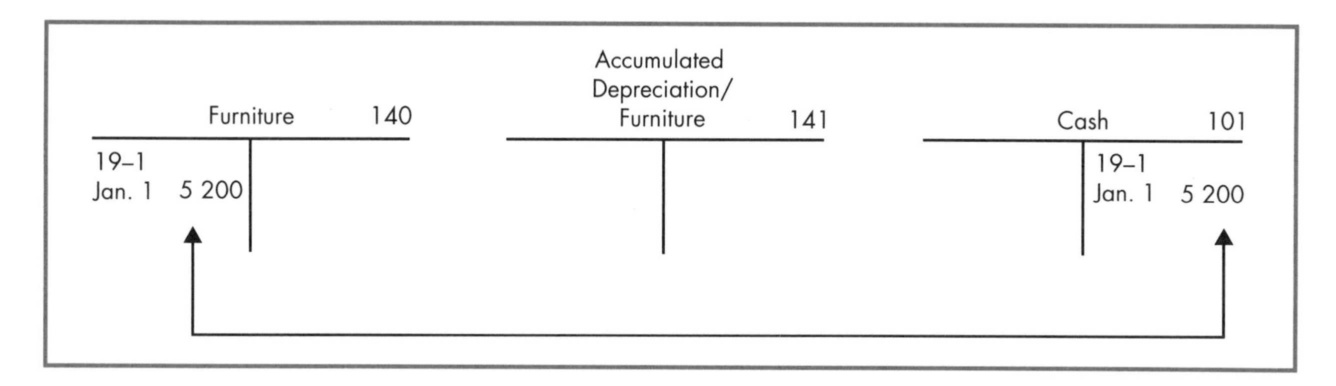

Analysis:

- The entry of the cash purchase of the office furniture is recorded with a debit to Office Furniture and a credit to Cash.
- Notice the contra asset account, Accumulated Depreciation/ Office Furniture, listed beside the asset account Office Furniture. Since the asset has just been purchased, there is no amount recorded in this account yet.

December 31, 19-1 An adjustment entry is made to record the dollar amount of using the furniture for one year. Management has estimated a useful life of ten years and a disposal value of $200 for this office furniture.

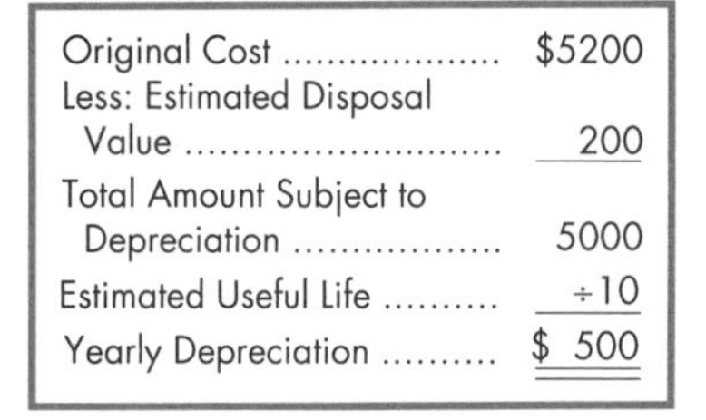

Original Cost	$5200
Less: Estimated Disposal Value	200
Total Amount Subject to Depreciation	5000
Estimated Useful Life	÷10
Yearly Depreciation	$ 500

Analysis:

- The straight-line method is used to calculate the depreciation expense. The numbers given are substituted into the equation shown earlier. The margin shows another method of arriving at the same figure.

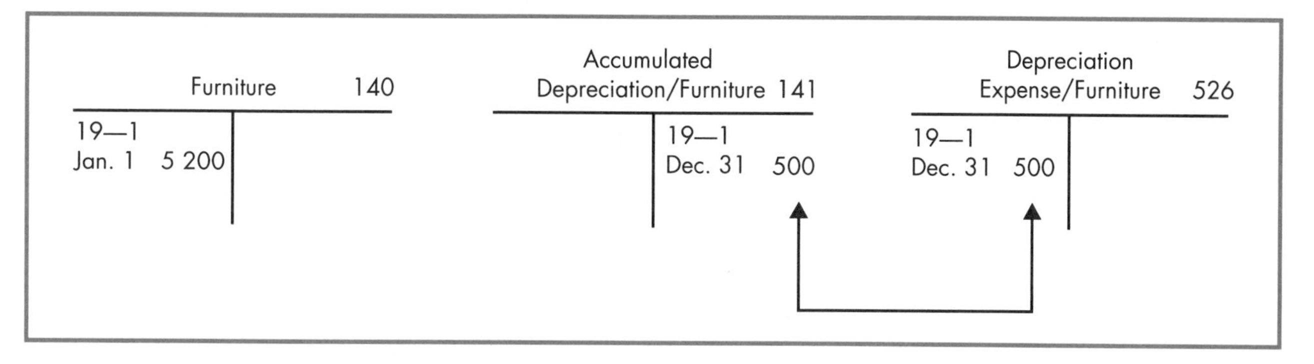

- From the original cost price, subtract the disposal value. This represents the unexpired cost to be allocated over the next ten years.
- Since all years are considered identical under the straight-line method, simply divide by 10 and your answer is one full year of depreciation for the next five years. If you wished to know the depreciation by month, you would divide one year's depreciation by 12.
- Notice that there is no change to the fixed asset Furniture; instead the amount is recorded, as a credit, to the contra account, Accumulated Depreciation/Furniture.

Book value: original asset cost less accumulated depreciation.

- The current unexpired value of the furniture or the book value is the difference between the two accounts.
- In each subsequent year, the Accumulated Depreciation/Furniture account will increase by $500 until at the end of the tenth year the business will dispose of the asset. *Note:* The entries for the disposal of the asset will be handled in a later chapter in the text.

PROBLEMS

Calculating the dollar amounts for several adjustments.

Preparing General Journal entries to record the adjustments.

P 7-4 B. T. Latimore Services has asked you to make the dollar calculations and prepare the General Journal entries for each of the following unrelated adjustment situations. Assume that the firm's year-end is December 31, 19-4 and that adjustments have previously been completed once a year. Prepare charts, similar to the one shown at the top of page 274, illustrating the year-by-year depreciation amounts and the accumulated depreciation for each separate fixed asset.

Preparing depreciation charts for the fixed assets.

Year	Asset Cost	Annual Depreciation	Accumulated Depreciation
19-2	$18 000*	$3 600	$3 600
19-3	$14 400**	$3 600	$7 200

*$19 800 – $1 800 **$18 000 – $3 600

(i) The firm bought a warehouse for $83 000. Its useful life is estimated at 25 years with a disposal value of $3000.

(ii) A computer system cost the firm $10 800 and its useful life is estimated to be 7 years. The firm believes the disposal value will be approximately $3800.

(iii) The business vehicle was bought on January 1, 19-2 at a cost of $19 800. It is expected to have a useful life of 5 years and disposal value of $1800.

(iv) The business equipment was recently upgraded at a total cost of $23 450 on July 1, 19-4. It is expected to have a useful life of 3 years with no disposal value at the end of its useful life.

Calculating the depreciation expense of an asset.

Preparing the ledger accounts for the accumulated depreciation.

P 7-5 Timberwolf Trapping Services recently purchased a new all-terrain vehicle with four-wheel drive for $25 700. The firm estimated its useful life at 4 years with no salvage value at all.

a. Calculate the depreciation expense for each year of the vehicle's useful life.

b. Complete the three-column ledger card for the vehicle and the accumulated depreciation account for each year of the vehicle's life.

Calculating the depreciation expense of an asset.

Journalizing adjustment entries.

P 7-6 Screen Repairs Services bought a piece of land for $12 000 and a small building on the land for $38 000. The owner believes the building will be useful for 7 years and that at the end of this time it will have a disposal value of $1600.

a. Make all necessary depreciation calculations on the land and building for the first year.

b. Prepare all necessary General Journal entries for the calculations made in **a**.

MINI-CASES

MC 7-4 When preparing several adjustments for the month ended May 31, 19—, a junior accountant made several errors.

Determining errors in the General Journal entries.

Preparing correct journal entries.

Identifying the GAAPs affected in the case.

(i) The Supplies on Hand account was adjusted from $120 to $80.

19—			
May 23	Supplies on Hand	80	
	Supplies Expense		80
	To adjust the supplies on hand account.		

(ii) A building was purchased May 1, 19—at a cost of $25 000. Useful life is estimated to be 4 years and the disposal value is estimated to be $1000.

19—			
May 31	Depreciation Expense/Building	500	
	Accum. Deprec./Building		500
	To record one month of depreciation expense.		

(iii) The firm bought a piece of equipment for $1320 cash on May 1, 19—. It had an estimated useful life of twelve months and disposal value of $120.

19—			
May 31	Depreciation Expense/Equip	110	
	Accum. Depreciation/Equip		110
	To record one month of depreciation expense.		

a. Describe briefly in writing the errors in each of the adjusting entries.

b. Show the correct journal entry for each error.

c. Indicate in each case if a GAAP is affected. If yes, identify the GAAP and indicate how it was violated.

Determining the correct definition of accounting.

Examining accounting terminology.

MC 7-5 Examine each of the following definitions for depreciation.

(i) A procedure in which the cost or other recorded value of a fixed asset less estimated residual value (if any) is distributed over the asset's estimated useful life in a systematic and rational manner.

(ii) A decrease in the value of property through wear and tear, deterioration, or obsolescence.

Discussing the GAAPs that affect depreciation.

a. Which of these two is a correct accounting definition? Why?

b. What is the key word in a description of depreciation process?

c. What are the two key GAAPs applied to depreciation?

d. What are three synonyms for the term "disposal value"?

Analyzing an adjustment situation and preparing the appropriate journal entry.

MC 7-6 Adjustments play a very important role in ensuring correct and up-to-date figures in the income statement and the balance sheet. Assume that a Prepaid Insurance account with a balance of $600 is adjusted to show only two-thirds of that balance.

Dealing with adjustment entries.

a. What is the General Journal entry to record this adjustment?

b. Where are adjustments usually computed and listed before they are journalized? What is the advantage of using this document?

Analyzing accounting errors as a result of adjustment errors.

c. Assume that this adjustment was forgotten and therefore not recorded. What statement(s) would be affected? What areas would be affected and what would be the dollar effect on each of the statements?

Naming the GAAPs affected by the faulty analysis of adjustment transactions.

d. What GAAP is being affected in this case and specifically how is it misinterpreted?

EXPANDING THE SIX-COLUMN WORKSHEET TO TEN COLUMNS

In Topic 1 of Chapter 5 you prepared six-column worksheets. You will recall the column headings were Trial Balance, Income Statement, and Balance Sheet. Now that you can prepare adjustments for prepaid assets and depreciation on fixed assets, you must expand the worksheet to include these adjustment calculations. Remember that the worksheet is an accountant's tool for expanding the trial balance for computing, classifying, and sorting account balances to prepare the period-end financial statements. It is not a permanent document of the firm, and is usually prepared in pencil. This is the only document where erasing is permissible. Follow this step-by-step procedure in order to expand and complete the ten-column worksheet.

Step 1: Completing the Trial Balance Section

(1) Place the heading at the top of the worksheet. Remember that it must answer the questions who, what, and when. The date identifies the accounting period (in this case "For the Year Ended December 31, 19–2").

(2) Transfer the period-end account balances of the General Ledger to the Account Title column and the first two money columns of

the Trial Balance section. Check to ensure that the debits equal the credits before proceeding. It is important that you realize that no adjusting entries have been completed at this point. Refer to the illustration of a worksheet on page 278. Note that the account numbers have been included in a separate column.

(3) Next you must expand the worksheet from six columns to ten columns. Immediately after the Trial Balance money columns, insert two new headings: Adjustments and the Adjusted Trial Balance. Each has two money columns. You now have a ten-column worksheet. In practice, worksheets may contain six, eight, ten, or more columns. In this textbook, you will deal only with the six- and ten-column worksheets.

(4) Finally, you should be able to identify a number of accounts within the trial balance that may require adjusting entries (prepaid assets and accumulated depreciation). The lack of related expired cost (expense) accounts for any of these accounts indicates that the trial balance values are unadjusted figures.

Step 2: Completing the Adjustment Section Examine the illustration on page 278 and determine which of the accounts require adjusting entries. These include: (106) Supplies on Hand, (108) Prepaid Insurance, (109) Prepaid Advertising, (111) Accumulated Depreciation/Automobile, and (113) Accumulated Depreciation/Furniture. In practice, adjusting entries are examined and recorded in the worksheet before they are journalized and posted. Because the trial balance information has not been updated, additional information must be provided in order for you to complete the adjustment section of the worksheet. Such information might include:

- a month-end count of the supplies
- the unused portion of the prepaid insurance and prepaid advertising
- the depreciation calculations for the automobile and furniture, and office equipment. Each of these various adjustments will now be examined. *Remember:* You will be looking at **changes**. The letters A through E in the following headings refer to the letter codes discussed.

A. Adjusting for Supplies Used Refer to the illustration of the worksheet and locate the Supplies on Hand account. You should find a debit balance for $900. This represents the amount of supplies on January 1, 19–2. Assume that the unused supplies have been counted on December 31, 19–2 and that the total is $300. The change is $600 ($900 – $300). Supplies costing $600 have been used up (expired)

Note: The cents columns have been omitted in order to show the entire worksheet.

Rapid Clairet Delivery Service
Worksheet
For the Year Ended December 31, 19-2

Account Title	Acct. No.	Trial Balance Debit	Trial Balance Credit	Adjustments Debit	Adjustments Credit	Adjusted Trial Balance Debit	Adjusted Trial Balance Credit	Income Statement Debit	Income Statement Credit	Balance Sheet Debit	Balance Sheet Credit
Cash	101	52550									
Accts. Rec./Cary Lee	103	2000									
Accts. Rec./Martin Mantha	104	1200									
Accts. Rec./Donald Wheeler	105	4000									
Supplies on Hand	106	900									
Prepaid Insurance	108	600									
Prepaid Advertising	109	750									
Automobile	110	19000									
Accumulated Depreciation/Auto.	111		900								
Furniture	112	6300									
Bank Loan Payable	201		16000								
Accts. Pay./Bell Furniture Co.	202		3000								
Accts. Pay./CKEE Radio	203		600								
Accts. Pay./Ryan Equip. Co.	204		3000								
R. Clairet, Capital	301		36500								
R. Clairet, Drawing	302	24000									
Delivery Fees Earned	401		120000								
Rent Expense	501	7200									
Telephone Expense	502	500									
Utilities Expense	503	1000									
Salaries Expense	504	60000									
		180000	180000								

resulting in an expense, Supplies Expense. To record this change, debit $600 to Supplies Expense and credit the Supplies on Hand by $600. Now study the illustration on page 280 to see how these two accounts are illustrated. The credit column of the adjustments section lists the Supplies on Hand entry. Since there is no Supplies Expense account listed, the entry is recorded in the Account Title column, beneath the trial balance items. The debit entry for Supplies Expense is then recorded in the debit column of the adjustment section. Each adjustment, as it is recorded, should be identified with a letter. This will permit easy identification of the related entries and assist in the preparation of General Journal entries in the future.

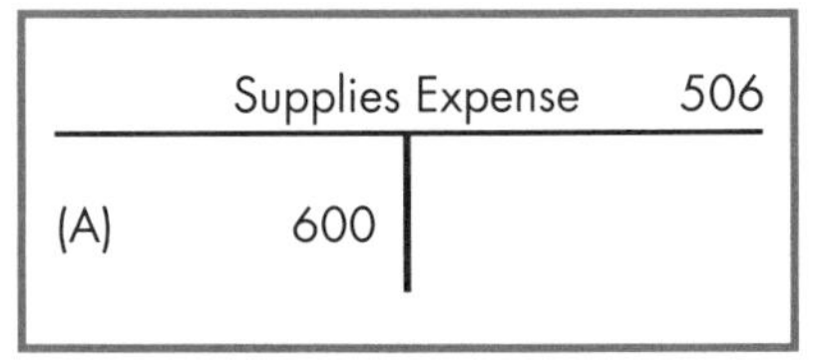

Summary: (1) Analyze the complete double entry. T-accounts are often useful (see margin). (2) Record the entries opposite the accounts in the appropriate debit or credit column or open any account not previously listed in the trial balance. (3) Letter-code all adjustments for reference and ease of journalizing in the future.

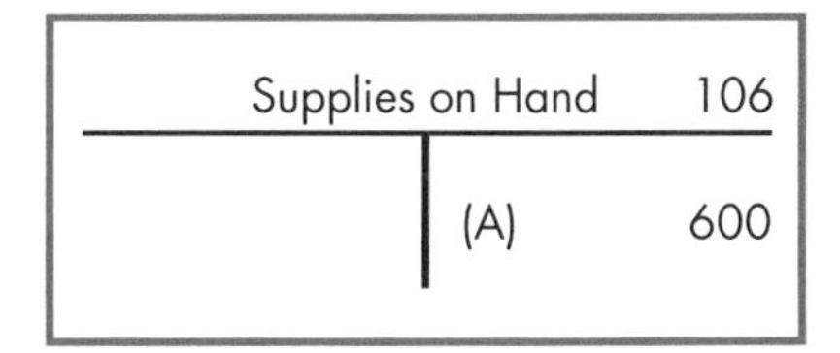

B. Adjusting for Expired Insurance Assume that your insurance policy was bought on September 1, 19-2 for $600. The cost per month is $50 ($600 ÷ 12). Four months of the insurance premium have been used up at December 31, 19-2. Therefore, adjustment B is entered to debit Insurance Expense and credit Prepaid Insurance for $200.

C. Adjusting for Prepaid Advertising Assume that a three-month block of radio advertising time was bought on October 1, 19–2 for $750. The cost per month is $250 ($750 ÷ 3). The adjusting entry required is to debit Advertising Expense and then to credit Prepaid Advertising. The letter reference is C.

Automobile Cost	$19 000
Disposal Value	1 000
Depreciation Base	$18 000

Useful life is 5 years

Annual Depreciation

$$= \frac{\$19\ 000 - 1\ 000}{5}$$

= $3 600 per year

Depreciation per month
= $3 600 ÷ 12 = $300
... for 3 months
$300 x 3 = $900

D. Adjusting for the Automobile Assume that the automobile cost the firm $19 000 on October 1, 19–1. The firm estimates that there will be disposal value of $1000 and that the useful life will be five years. Therefore, three months (October, November and December of 19–1) have been recorded in the Accumulated Depreciation/ Auto. account ($900). Examine the marginal calculation.

Refer to the illustration and locate the Accumulated Depreciation/ Auto. account which indicates a credit balance of $900. Remember that this is the contra account of the asset Automobile and by deducting the amount of the Accumulated Depreciation/Auto. account from the Automobile account you can determine the book value of the

Rapid Clairet Delivery Service
Worksheet
For the Year Ended December 31, 19-2

Account Title	Acct.	Trial Balance		Adjustments		Adjusted Trial Balance		Income Statement		Balance Sheet	
	No.	Debit	Credit	Debit	Credit	Debit	Credit	Debit	Credit	Debit	Credit
Cash	101	52550									
Accts. Rec./Cary Lee	103	2000									
Accts. Rec./Martin Mantha	104	1200									
Accts. Rec./Donald Wheeler	105	4000									
Supplies on Hand	106	900			(A) 600						
Prepaid Insurance	108	600			(B) 200						
Prepaid Advertising	109	750			(C) 750						
Automobile	110	19000									
Accumulated Depreciation/Auto.	111		900		(D) 3600						
Furniture	112	6300									
Bank Loan Payable	201		16000								
Accts. Pay./Bell Furniture Co.	202		3000								
Accts. Pay./CKEE Radio	203		600								
Accts. Pay./Ryan Equip. Co.	204		3000								
R. Clairet, Capital	301		36500								
R. Clairet, Drawing	302	24000									
Delivery Fees Earned	401		120000								
Rent Expense	501	7200									
Telephone Expense	502	500									
Utilities Expense	503	1000									
Salaries Expense	504	60000									
		180000	180000								
Supplies Expense	506			(A) 600							
Insurance Expense	505			(B) 200							
Advertising Expense	507			(C) 750							
Depreciation Expense/Auto	510			(D) 3600							
Depreciation Expense/Furniture	511			(E) 500							
Accumulated Depreciation/Furn.	113				(E) 500						
				5650	5150						

asset. Therefore, the book value of the automobile after three months must be $18 100 ($19 000 – $900). When you examine the trial balance, however, you will realize that the adjustment for the full year of 19–2 has not yet been completed. You have already calculated the yearly amount, $3600. The entry required is to debit Depreciation Expense/Auto. and to credit Accumulated Depreciation/Auto. Once again, notice the letter D. Also each asset account has its own accumulation account and expense account.

Useful life is 10 Years

Furniture Cost	$6 300
Disposal Value	300
Depreciation Base	$6 000

Annual Depreciation

$$= \frac{\$6\,300 - 300}{10}$$

= $600 per year

Depreciation per month
= $600 ÷ 12
= $50

... per ten months
= $50 x 10
= $500

E. Adjusting for Furniture Assume that the furniture cost the firm $6300 on March 1, 19–2. The business estimates that there will be a disposal value of $300 and that the useful life will be ten years. Therefore, ten months of depreciation, $500, must be recorded for 19–2. See the calculation in the margin. Since no previous depreciation has been recorded on furniture, observe that both the depreciation expense and accumulated depreciation accounts are shown below the trial balance as the letter E.

Step 3 Completing the Adjusted Trial Balance Section

After all adjustments are recorded and the balance totals are completed, the next step is to correct or to update the trial balance figures by transferring them to the Adjusted Trial Balance section. For example, the Cash account amount of $52 550 is transferred directly to the adjusted trial balance section as a debit for $52 550 because there was no adjustment. (See the illustration on page 282.) The same procedure works for the accounts receivable accounts. Note, however, the next account Supplies on Hand. This account has a balance of $900 in the trial balance section. There is a credit adjustment equal to $600. Subtract the credit adjustment from the debit figure in the trial balance section ($900 – $600). The difference of $300 is transferred to the appropriate column in the adjusted trial balance.

Next, examine the Prepaid Insurance account. Once again the credit adjustment is subtracted from the debit trial balance figure. The figure transferred to the adjusted trial balance debit column is $400 ($600 – $200).

Then examine the Prepaid Advertising account. The credit adjustment is subtracted from the debit trial balance figure and the balance is transferred to the debit column of the Adjusted Trial Balance. Check the figure in the illustration after you attempt this calculation yourself. Finally, if the adjustments created an additional account

Rapid Clairet Delivery Service
Worksheet
For the Year Ended December 31, 19-2

Account Title	Acct. No.	Trial Balance Debit	Trial Balance Credit	Adjustments Debit	Adjustments Credit	Adjusted Trial Balance Debit	Adjusted Trial Balance Credit	Income Statement Debit	Income Statement Credit	Balance Sheet Debit	Balance Sheet Credit
Cash	101	52550				52550					
Accts. Rec./Cary Lee	103	2000				2000					
Accts. Rec./Martin Mantha	104	1200				1200					
Accts. Rec./Donald Wheeler	105	4000				4000					
Supplies on Hand	106	900			(A) 600	300					
Prepaid Insurance	108	600			(B) 200	400					
Prepaid Advertising	109	750			(C) 750	0					
Automobile	110	19000				19000					
Accumulated Depreciation/Auto.	111		900		(D) 3600		4500				
Furniture	112	6300				6300					
Bank Loan Payable	201		16000				16000				
Accts. Pay./Bell Furniture Co.	202		3000				3000				
Accts. Pay./CKEE Radio	203		600				600				
Accts. Pay./Ryan Equip. Co.	204		3000				3000				
R. Clairet, Capital	301		36500				36500				
R. Clairet, Drawing	302	24000				24000					
Delivery Fees Earned	401		120000				120000				
Rent Expense	501	7200				7200					
Telephone Expense	502	500				500					
Utilities Expense	503	1000				1000					
Salaries Expense	504	60000				60000					
		180000	180000								
Supplies Expense	506			(A) 600		600					
Insurance Expense	505			(B) 200		200					
Advertising Expense	507			(C) 750		750					
Depreciation Expense/Auto	510			(D) 3600		3600					
Depreciation Expense/Furniture	511			(E) 500		500					
Accumulated Depreciation/Furn.	113				(E) 500						
				5650	5150	184050	184050				

after the original trial balance, transfer those amounts directly to the adjusted trial balance section. Now draw a single line across both columns of the adjusted trial balance and total the debit and credit columns. Again, these two columns must agree. If they do not, locate the error before you proceed. After agreement is obtained, double-underline the two columns.

Step 4: Moving the Adjusted Trial Balance Amounts into the Statement Columns After the Adjusted Trial Balance columns have been proved correct, the individual amounts are copied to one column of either the Income Statement section or the Balance Sheet section. Here are two rules that will help you to move an amount to the correct location.

(1) Move a debit amount from the Adjusted Trial Balance to the debit column of the appropriate financial statement section. For example, a Cash debit will be transferred to the debit side of the Balance Sheet section. Similarly, the debit for Rent Expense would be entered in or copied to the debit column of the Income Statement section.

(2) Move a credit amount from the Adjusted Trial Balance to the credit column of the appropriate financial statement section. For example, the Accumulated Depreciation/Auto. account shows a credit balance in the Adjusted Trial Balance. Transfer this credit balance to the credit column of the Balance Sheet. Similarly, the credit balance for Delivery Fees Earned represents a revenue account. Copy this balance to the credit column of the Income Statement.

Analysis: Each account balance in the Adjusted Trial Balance section must be transferred to either the debit or the credit column of the related statement section. Assets, liabilities, and the owner's equity capital and drawing accounts must be moved to the **Balance Sheet** columns. Similarly, revenue and expense accounts must be transferred to the correct **Income Statement** columns. (See page 284.)

Step 5: Calculating the Net Income (or Net Loss) and Completing the Worksheet After all amounts have been transferred, the totals of the statement must be calculated and entered. If you are uncertain of the procedure, return to Topic 1, Chapter 5 on pages 166 and 169 for assistance.

COMPLETING THE ACCOUNTING CYCLE

In Chapter 6, you completed the accounting cycle by closing the books and preparing a postclosing trial balance. By expanding the

Rapid Clairet Delivery Service
Worksheet
For the Year Ended December 31, 19-2

Account Title	Acct. No.	Trial Balance Debit	Trial Balance Credit	Adjustments Debit	Adjustments Credit	Adjusted Trial Balance Debit	Adjusted Trial Balance Credit	Income Statement Debit	Income Statement Credit	Balance Sheet Debit	Balance Sheet Credit
Cash	101	52550				52550				52550	
Accts. Rec./Cary Lee	103	2000				2000				2000	
Accts. Rec./Martin Mantha	104	1200				1200				1200	
Accts. Rec./Donald Wheeler	105	4000				4000				4000	
Supplies on Hand	106	900			(A) 600	300				300	
Prepaid Insurance	108	600			(B) 200	400				400	
Prepaid Advertising	109	750			(C) 750	0				0	
Automobile	110	19000				19000				19000	
Accumulated Depreciation/Auto.	111		900		(D) 3600		4500				4500
Furniture	112	6300				6300				6300	
Bank Loan Payable	201		16000				16000				16000
Accts. Pay./Bell Furniture Co.	202		3000				3000				3000
Accts. Pay./CKEE Radio	203		600				600				600
Accts. Pay./Ryan Equip. Co.	204		3000				3000				3000
R. Clairet, Capital	301		36500				36500				36500
R. Clairet, Drawing	302	24000				24000				24000	
Delivery Fees Earned	401		120000				120000		120000		
Rent Expense	501	7200				7200		7200			
Telephone Expense	502	500				500		500			
Utilities Expense	503	1000				1000		1000			
Salaries Expense	504	60000				60000		60000			
		180000	180000								
Supplies Expense	506			(A) 600		600		600			
Insurance Expense	505			(B) 200		200		200			
Advertising Expense	507			(C) 750		750		750			
Depreciation Expense/Auto	510			(D) 3600		3600		3600			
Depreciation Expense/Furniture	511			(E) 500		500		500			
Accumulated Depreciation/Furn.	113				(E) 500						500
				5650	5150	184050	184050	74350	120000	109750	64100
									74350		
Net Income									45650		45650
										109750	109750

worksheet and adding adjustments to your knowledge, you have not changed any of the procedures of closing. If you encounter any difficulty in the closing of the books refer back to Topics 1 and 2 of Chapter 6.

PROBLEMS

Transferring the figures to the worksheet trial balance.

Preparing the adjustments on the worksheet

Completing the worksheet.

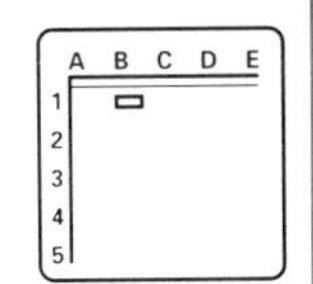

P 7-7 Illustrated below is the month-end trial balance for L. Hill Computer Programming Services.

L. Hill Computer Programming Services
Trial Balance
January 31, 19–1

Account Title	Acct. No.	Debit	Credit
Cash	101	$ 8 900	
Accounts Receivable	105	5 600	
Prepaid Insurance	110	1 200	
Supplies on Hand	112	4 500	
Prepaid Rent	114	4 800	
Computer Equipment	150	21 000	
Office Furniture	160	4 000	
Accum. Deprec./Off. Furniture	161		$ 210
Office Equipment	170	1 300	
Bank Loan Payable	201		5000
Accounts Payable	205		800
L. Hill, Capital	301		23 260
L. Hill, Drawing	302	3 500	
Programming Revenue	401		34 300
Telephone Expense	501	360	
Heat Expense	503	1 200	
Utilities Expense	508	700	
Wages Expense	512	6 300	
		$63 360	$63 360

Additional Information:

(i) The firm's year-end is December 31. However, adjustments and worksheets are prepared at the end of each month to report monthly financial statements.

(ii) The firm bought computer equipment on January 31, 19-1 at a total cost of $21 000. The firm estimated the equipment would have a useful life of three years and the disposal value would be $3000.

(iii) The firm paid rent on a month-by-month basis until January 1. At this time the firm prepaid one full year of rent, $4800.

(iv) The firm bought one year of insurance coverage on January 1, 19-1, $1200.

(v) The supplies on hand at the end of January totalled $3900.

(vi) The office furniture was purchased for $4000 on June 1, 19-0 (previous year). The useful life is estimated to be ten years with a disposal value of $400.

(vii) The office equipment cost $1300 and has a disposal value of $100. The estimated useful life is expected to be five years. This equipment was purchased on January 1, 19-1.

a. Transfer the trial balance to the ten-column worksheet.

b. Complete the adjustments in the worksheet. Remember to assign a letter code to each adjustment.

c. Complete the adjusted trial balance to ensure that the totals are equal.

d. Complete the income statement and balance sheet columns of the worksheet.

Opening the worksheet with the trial balance information.

P 7-8 Challenge Problem The Markowski Bookkeeping Services prepared their year-end trial balance on September 30, 19-3, as illustrated on the opposite page.

Completing adjustments.

Completing a worksheet.

Journalizing adjustments.

Preparing a formal income statement and balance sheet.

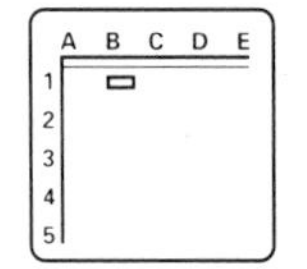

Additional Information:

(i)The firm makes adjusting entries only once at the end of the year. The year-end is September 30.

(ii)Supplies costing $235 are unused at year-end.

(iii)A one-year insurance policy was bought on January 2, 19-3.

(iv)The building was acquired seven years ago on October 1. The estimated useful life is expected to be 30 years with a disposal value of $10 000.

(v)The office equipment was bought on January 2, 19-3. Its estimated useful life is 4 years with no disposal value.

(vi)The office furniture was bought on October 2, 19-2. Its estimated useful life is three years with disposal value of $300.

(vii)The bank loan is a demand loan with an interest rate of 10.5%. (Interest on this loan has been ignored in this question.)

(viii)The mortgage payable is a 25-year term at 8%, and is secured by the land and building. The current portion of the mortgage

Markowski Bookkeeping Services
Trial Balance
September 30, 19–3

Account Title	Acct. No.	Debit	Credit
Cash	101	$ 3 800	
Accounts Receivable	105	4 300	
Supplies on Hand	110	1 000	
Prepaid Insurance	112	1 800	
Land	140	42 500	
Building	145	145 000	
Accum. Deprec./Building	146		$ 27 000
Office Equipment	150	2 400	
Office Furniture	154	3 000	
Accum. Deprec./Off. Furn.	155		900
Bank Loan Payable	201		11 000
Accounts Payable	205		4 300
Property Taxes Payable	210		2 400
Mortgage Payable	250		80 000
Barb Markowski, Capital	301		72 640
Barb Markowski, Drawing	302	26 100	
Bookkeeping Fees Earned	401		95 000
Consulting Fees Earned	403		23 500
Telephone Expense	508	1 100	
Utilities Expense	510	1 800	
Property Taxes Expense	512	8 300	
Advertising Expense	515	5 200	
Heat Expense	525	17 000	
Wages Expense	530	49 000	
Postage Expense	535	240	
Maintenance Expense	540	2 900	
Miscellaneous Expense	550	1 300	
		$316 740	$316 740

payable is $4000. Interest expense has been ignored in this problem.

(ix) All depreciation is calculated using the straight-line method.

a. Transfer the trial balance to the ten-column worksheet.

b. Complete the adjustments in the worksheet. Remember to assign a letter code to each adjustment.

c. Complete the adjusted trial balance to ensure that the totals are equal.

d. Complete the Income Statement and Balance Sheet columns of the worksheet.

e. Record the adjustments in the General Journal from the worksheet.

f. Prepare a formal income statement and a classified balance sheet in report form from the worksheet.

Creating a Chart of Accounts.

Journalizing the trial balances.

P 7-9 Use your school's microcomputer's General Ledger software or Summation's General Ledger System to simulate the accounting of Markowski Bookkeeping Services, Problem 7-8, in this chapter. Suggested step-by-step procedures are as follows:

a. Create a General Ledger of accounts to support accounts illustrated in the trial balance on page 287. Add accounts to cover all adjusting entries shown by your manual solution to Problem 7-8. Also add heading and subheading accounts to support the future printout of financial statements. (The data files in support of the Summation package already contain the Chart of Accounts for Markowski Bookkeeping Services.)

b. Use the System Utilities to change the company name to your name as for example, ''Singh Bookkeeping Services.'' Also make changes in accounts 302 and 303 to reflect your name, Capital and your name, Drawing. (Check the detailed supplement or your software's technical reference manual on the procedures to make these changes.)

c. Print a hard copy of the chart of accounts.

d. Print a ''dummy'' set of financial statements to check the placement of heading and subheadings, and subtotal and total levels. Make appropriate changes in the Chart of Accounts to obtain an acceptable set of financial statement printouts.

e. Use the appropriate General Journal grid programmed for your General Ledger software to journalize the trial balance illustrated on page 287. For the Description, type ''Balance forward.''

f. Print a hard copy of the General Journal showing the correct journalizing of **e** above.

g. Prepare a printout of the trial balance before adjustments on September 30, 19-3 for your firm's bookkeeping services.

h. If your printout of the trial balance contains worksheet columns for adjustments and the adjusted trial balance, enter the adjustment solved for Problem 7-8 and one more to support the transfer of the current portion of mortgage payable, $4000, from the Mortgage Payable account to a current liability account you should create called "Cur. Portion/Long-Term Debt." *Note:* Use appropriate working forms if your software package does not support the printout of a worksheet. Complete the worksheet to the end of the adjusted trial balance. Check all totals.

i. Enter all adjustments through your software's journal entry grid. Post all adjustments.

j. Print a hard copy of the general journal showing all adjustments. Double-check to see that all adjustments have been accounted for. If errors have been made, return to the journal entry grid, enter an entry to reverse the entire error entry, and then enter the correct adjustment.

k. Print the income statement, balance sheet and, if possible, any supporting schedule such as one that supports the details of the Owner's Equity section of the balance sheet.

l. Use the appropriate program within your GL software to do a year-end closing.

m. Journalize and post the closing of the Drawing account.

n. Print a postclosing trial balance.

o. Compare your statements and postclosing trial balance with those done in the manual solution of Problem 7-8. The key figures should match.

MINI-CASES

Discussing the usefulness of a ten-column worksheet.

MC 7-7 The ten-column worksheet is never presented to the general public as are the income statement and the balance sheet. However, the worksheet can be an extremely useful tool for an accountant.

a. Write a report discussing the useful features of the ten-column worksheet and how each of these features assists the accountant with his or her work.

Calculating depreciation expense.

MC 7-8 Alred and Elina were discussing the calculations of depreciation expense of a $100 000 building, which has an estimated useful life of 30 years and a disposal value of $10 000. Alred thinks that the depreciation expense calculation is an accurate figure, but Elina states that it is only a wild guess and that the figure has no real accuracy at all.

Discussing the usefulness of the estimated figures used in depreciation calculations.

a. Prepare the calculation for the first year of depreciation expense. Show your work.

b. Discuss the merits of each person's opinion.

c. State your opinion regarding the discussion and support it with accounting theory (that is, GAAPs).

Discussing the advantages and disadvantages of using a Revenue and Expense Summary account in closing the books.

MC 7-9 Closing the books at year-end results in all revenue, expense, and drawing accounts being brought equal to zero. These amounts ultimately are closed to the owner's Capital account. Students initially learning the closing procedure are encouraged to use a Revenue and Expense Summary or Income Summary account, but in actual practice, both manually and on the computer, the closing results go directly to the Capital account(s) of the business.

a. Discuss the advantages and disadvantages of both methods from the perspective of: **(i)** a beginning student; **(ii)** a practising accountant.

COMPREHENSIVE CASE STUDY 7

Assume that you are the manager of a bank branch in your community and that your signature is required before any bank loan is granted. Suppose now that two applications for a business loan (on a demand basis) have been placed before you: one application from Ali's Radio & TV Service for a loan of $5000; and a second application from Farrell's Stenographic Service for a similar amount of $5000. As part of each application, you require that a balance sheet reporting the financial position of the business is filed. The loan applications attached to each statement are illustrated below and on the next page.

Ali's Radio & TV Service
Balance Sheet
as at October 31, 19-2

ASSETS		LIABILITIES	
Current Assets:		Current Liabilities:	
Cash	$ 2 000	Wages Payable	$ 4 000
Accounts Receivable	8 000	Accounts Payable	36 000
Total Current Assets	10 000	Current Portion of Long-term Debt	5 000
		Total Current Liabilities	45 000
Fixed Assets (at cost):		Long-term Liabilities:	
Land (security for mortgage payable)	30 000	Mortgage Payable (20 years) (secured by land and building)	50 000
Building (security for mortgage payable)	40 000	Less: Current Portion	5 000
		Total Long-term Liabilities	55 000
Tools	5 000	Total Liabilities	100 000
Office Equipment	4 000		
Delivery Truck	21 000	**OWNER'S EQUITY**	
Total Fixed Assets	100 000	Ali Best, Capital	40 000
		Less: Net Loss	30 000
		Total Owner's Equity	10 000
Total Assets	$110 000	Total Liabilities and Owner's Equity	$110 000

Farrell's Stenographic Service
Balance Sheet
as at October 31, 19-2

ASSETS			LIABILITIES		
Current Assets:			Current Liabilities:		
Cash	$40 000		Accounts Payable	$ 7 000	
Accounts Receivable	5 000		Salaries Payable	3 000	
Total Current Assets	45 000		Total Liabilities	10 000	
Fixed Assets (at cost):			**OWNER'S EQUITY**		
Office Equipment	25 000				
Furniture	5 000		B. Farrell, Capital	50 000	
Delivery Equipment	15 000		Add Net Income for Year	30 000	
Total Fixed Assets	45 000		Total Owner's Equity	80 000	
Total Assets	$90 000		Total Liabilities and Owner's Equity	$90 000	

Analyzing financial statements in order to determine a company potential for obtaining a loan.

a. Would you grant a bank loan to both businesses? Give reasons for your decision.

SYSTEMS AND PROCEDURES FOR A SERVICE BUSINESS

General Ledger (GL) application: updating the GL to prepare financial statements.

In Part 1, you were introduced to a simple accounting cycle and the basic concepts of accounting systems. Also, Part 1 emphasized the use of the General Ledger to prepare useful financial statements at the end of each accounting period. This use of the General Ledger is known as the General Ledger (GL) application.

Although the General Ledger application is very important, it is not the only one used in accounting today. In this part, you will learn about these common applications for:

- individual accounts receivable (the accounts receivable application)
- individual accounts payable (the accounts payable application)
- the details of a business's payroll (the payroll application)
- petty cash and banking procedures (petty cash and banking application)

Such accounting is known as the **accounts receivable application**, the **accounts payable application**, the **payroll application**, and the **petty cash and banking application**.

BOOKKEEPER/Clerk to work in law firm. Experience in computer systems necessary. Duties include journal entries, A/R, A/P. Salary negotiable.

BOOKKEEPER/Secretary, experienced to trial balance, Bedford, ACCPAC & WP50, A/R, A/P, inventory, filing, bank reconciliation. Salary $25 000.

INTRODUCING THE ACCOUNTS RECEIVABLE APPLICATION

Topic 1
Originating and Analyzing Dental Charges

Topic 2
Journalizing and Posting Dental Charges

Topic 3
Controlling Cash Receipts

Topic 4
Journalizing and Posting Cash Receipts

Topic 5
Explaining Month-End Procedures and Introducing the One-Write System

Assume that a small dental practice has been operating for the first year under the name John H. Johnson, D.D.S. To assist with his practice, Dr. Johnson has hired a dental assistant/hygienist and a front-office person who is both receptionist and secretary, and also bookkeeper. As the bookkeeper, this person is responsible for completing all steps of the accounting cycle discussed in Part 1.

In this first year, the dental practice's accounting system uses the General Ledger application. Illustrated below is the Chart of Accounts for the General Ledger at the end of the first year of operation. Notice that not all accounts have been included in this chart. Some will be added as they are presented, while others are complex and will be discussed in Part 3.

John H. Johnson, D.D.S.
Dental Surgeon
Chart of Accounts

CURRENT ASSETS
101 Cash
102 Bank Deposit Receipts
103 Accts. Rec./Ms. Mary Brown
104 Accts. Rec./B. Campbell
105 Accts. Rec./T. Douglas
106 Accts. Rec./Ms. B. Farr

FIXED ASSETS
110 Dental Equipment
112 Office Equipment

CURRENT LIABILITIES
201 Bank Loan Payable
202 Accts. Pay./Denco Supply
203 Accts. Pay./Mardan Business Systems Ltd.

LONG-TERM LIABILITIES
210 5-Year Note Payable

OWNER'S EQUITY
301 John H. Johnson, Capital
302 John H. Johnson, Drawing
399 Revenue and Expense Summary

REVENUE
401 Professional Fees Earned
402 Interest Revenue

EXPENSES
501 Rent Expense
502 Salaries Expense
503 Dental Supplies Expense
504 Office Supplies Expense
505 Telephone Expense
506 Utilities Expense
507 Lab Fees Expense
508 Professional Fees Expense
530 Interest Expense

You can see that the Chart of Accounts is getting quite large due to the individual listing of accounts receivable and accounts payable. The Chart of Accounts will continue to grow as Dr. Johnson's business prospers. To solve this problem you will learn how to keep track of all the customer accounts in a separate book. This is known as the accounts receivable application. The supplier accounts (the accounts payable application) will be dealt with in Chapter 9.

Accounts receivable application: all accounting dealing with customer accounts.

ORIGINATING AND ANALYZING DENTAL CHARGES

PREPARING A PATIENT LEDGER CARD

Assume that a new family—the Garcias: Domaso, his spouse, Lucia, and their children, Anita, and Don—visit Dr. Johnson's dental practice to receive dental services. Before any such services can be rendered, the dental clerk will prepare, under a manual system, a new patient ledger card as illustrated below.

STATEMENT

JOHN H. JOHNSON, D.D.S.
Dental Surgeon
ANY STREET – ANY TOWN, CANADA
TELEPHONE 576-5950

MR.
MRS.
ANITA
DON

Mr. D. Garcia
Any Street
Any Town, Canada

NUMERO NUMBER	DATE	DESCRIPTION	HONORAIRES CHARGE	PAIEMENT PAYMENT	SOLDE COURANTE CUR. BAL.

SAFEGUARD BUSINESS SYSTEMS
FORM ARL-MS-4 BIL.
COPYRIGHT REGISTERED © 1984

S.V.P. PAYEZ LE DERNIER MONTANT DANS CETTE COLONNE
PLEASE PAY THE LAST AMOUNT IN THIS COLUMN

A–One Surface Amalgam
AA–Two Surface Amalgam
AAA–Three Surface Amalgam
BR–Bridge
CB–Cosmetic Bonding
CL–Cleaning
CR–Crown
DR–Denture Repair
E–Exam
EN–Endodontic Treatment
FD–Full Denture
FL–Fluoride Treatment
LAB–Laboratory Fee
MA–Missed Appointment
NC–No Charge
OR–Orthodontics
OS–Oral Surgery
PCC–Previously Charged on Account
PD–Partial Denture
PT–Periodontal Treatment
REC–Recall Exam
REL–Reline
TF–Temporary Filling
TT–Tissue Treatment
WF–White Filling
X–Extraction
XR–X-Ray

THIS IS A COPY OF YOUR ACCOUNT AS IT APPEARS ON YOUR LEDGER CARD

This card is a record of the dental fees charged to the family and the cash payments received from this family. After each charge or payment is recorded, the balance is calculated. This balance is the amount owing to Dr. Johnson from this family of patients.

PREPARING A DENTAL FEE BILL

Dental fee bill: a source document showing charges to and payments from dental patients.

The source document used by the majority of dental practices to record services performed by the dentist is called the dental fee bill.

Transaction 1 Let's assume that Lucia came for an examination, X-ray, and cleaning. The dental fee bill is completed as follows.

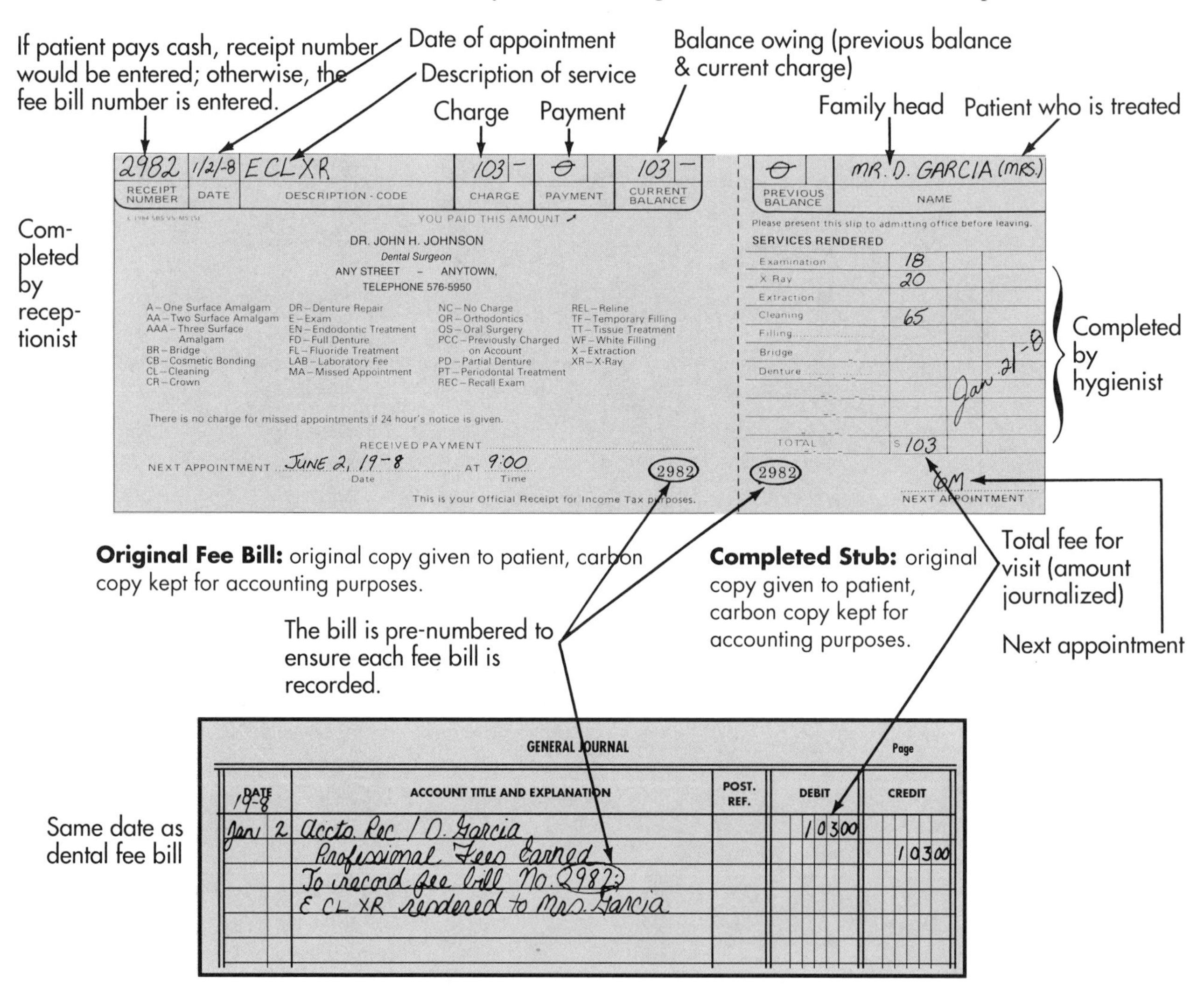

The accounting entry to record the charges shown in the fee bill is illustrated in the General Journal above. It shows a debit to the asset account Accts. Rec./D. Garcia and a credit to the revenue account Professional Fees Earned. The posting of this entry to the individual patient ledger card is illustrated on page 310.

Transaction 2 Domaso Garcia and his daughter, Anita, receive dental services on the same day. Anita has an X-ray, examination, and cleaning for a total fee of $78. Mr. Garcia then has two white fillings inserted for a fee of $73. In some dental practices, the above transactions would be completed on the stub and fee bill as follows. *Note:* Some dental practices might prefer to issue separate fee bills, one for services to Anita, the other to Mr. Garcia. Both fees, however, would be charged to the Garcia family patient ledger card.

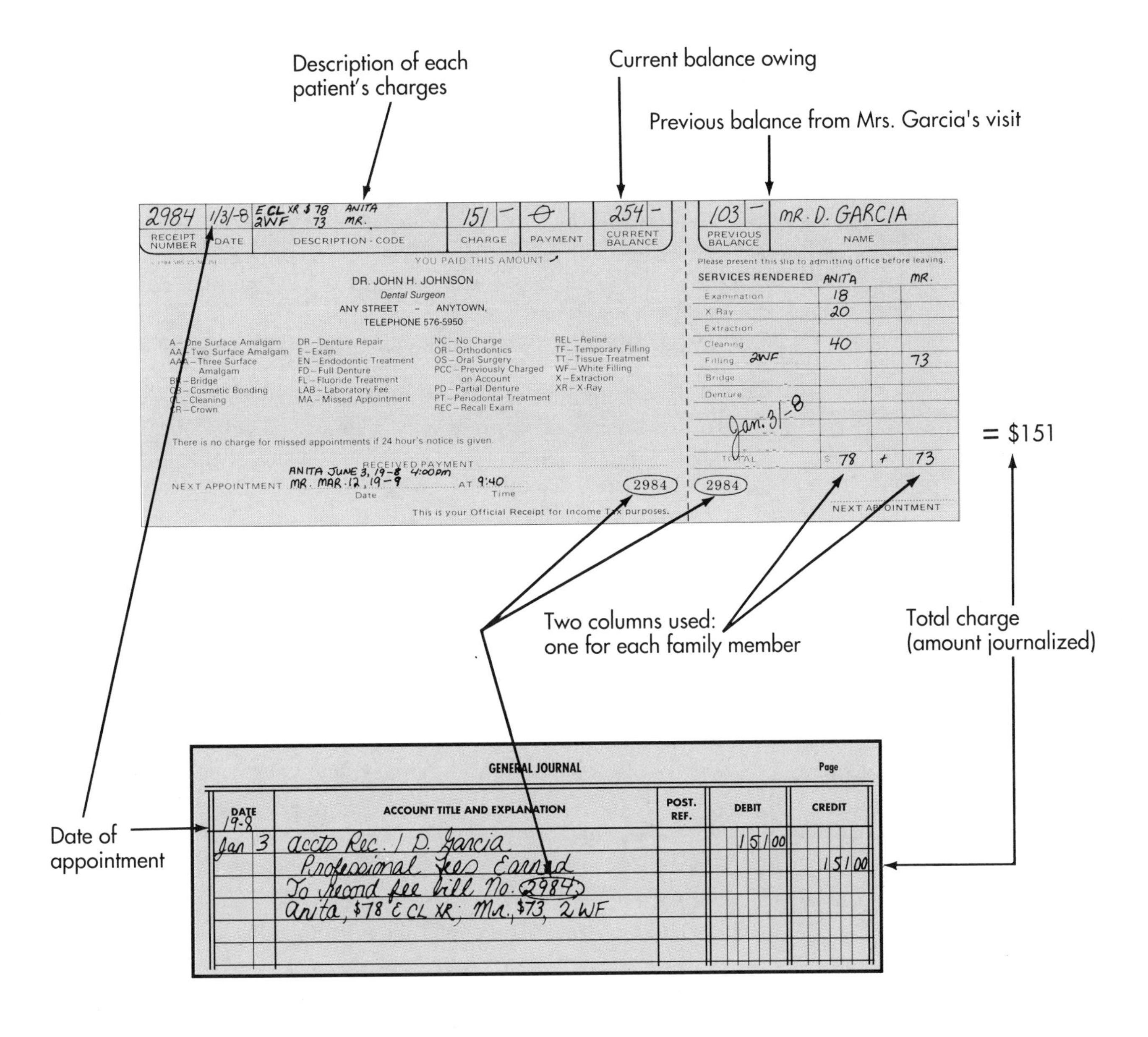

ANSWERING IMPORTANT QUESTIONS ON GAAPs

You have learned how a dental charge originates on a two-part source document called a dental fee bill. It is also important to know how to apply the GAAPs related to this source document.

- *What* basic *GAAP is recognized with the creation of a dental fee bill?*
  The objectivity principle.
- *What is the essential meaning of the objectivity principle?*
  Think of the word "object." An object can be seen. It is real. In accounting, every transaction must be real. That is, you should be able to prove that the transaction actually took place. The objectivity principle says that there must be evidence to prove the existence of every accounting transaction. That proof or evidence is known as the source document.
- *What other* basic *GAAP is recognized with the creation of the dental fee bill?*
  The revenue principle.
- *What two things does the revenue principle say when applied to the dental fee bill?*
  First, it defines revenue as the inflow of assets (accounts receivable in this case) resulting from the sale of dental services. Second, it is the guideline for recognizing revenue. In a service firm, revenue is recognized only after services have been completed. This recognition is easy because a source document—here, the dental fee bill—shows the details of the services rendered.

PROBLEMS

Setting up the records for new patients.

Preparing dental fee bills and journalizing.

P 8-1 The first patient of Dr. Lien Chang's practice is Helga Vandenberk. Her husband, Howard Vandenberk, pays the family bills. The Vandenberks have two children, Roberta and Tom. Helga Vandenberk has received the following dental services: examination, $18; X-ray, $20; cleaning, $65. No payment was made on the day of the services, December 2, 19–7. The next appointment is in 6 months.

a. Prepare the new patient's ledger card. Make up a suitable address for the family.

b. Prepare the stub of the dental fee bill. Show how it would be completed with the breakdown of services rendered and total as of December 2. The stub is numbered 0001.

c. Prepare the fee bill portion of the bill. The next appointment is booked for June 2, 19-8, 09:00.

d. In General Journal form, analyze the accounting of the dental fee bill.

Analyzing the parts of a dental fee bill.

P 8-2 Illustrated below is a completed dental fee bill and stub for Dr. Lien Chang's practice.

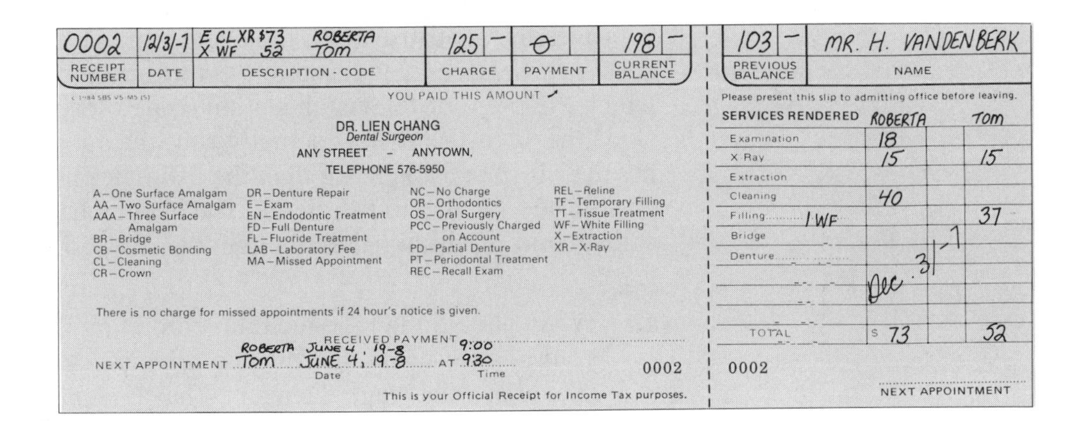

RECEIPT NUMBER	DATE	DESCRIPTION - CODE	CHARGE	PAYMENT	CURRENT BALANCE
0002	12/3/-1	E CL XR $73 ROBERTA X WF 52 Tom	125 —	⊖	198 —

PREVIOUS BALANCE	NAME
103 —	MR. H. VANDENBERK

YOU PAID THIS AMOUNT ↗

DR. LIEN CHANG
Dental Surgeon
ANY STREET - ANYTOWN,
TELEPHONE 576-5950

A–One Surface Amalgam
AA–Two Surface Amalgam
AAA–Three Surface Amalgam
BR–Bridge
CB–Cosmetic Bonding
CL–Cleaning
CR–Crown
DR–Denture Repair
E–Exam
EN–Endodontic Treatment
FD–Full Denture
FL–Fluoride Treatment
LAB–Laboratory Fee
MA–Missed Appointment
NC–No Charge
OR–Orthodontics
OS–Oral Surgery
PCC–Previously Charged on Account
PD–Partial Denture
PT–Periodontal Treatment
REC–Recall Exam
REL–Reline
TF–Temporary Filling
TT–Tissue Treatment
WF–White Filling
X–Extraction
XR–X-Ray

There is no charge for missed appointments if 24 hour's notice is given.

RECEIVED PAYMENT
NEXT APPOINTMENT ROBERTA JUNE 4, 19-8 9:00
Tom JUNE 4, 19-8 AT 9:30
Date Time

0002

This is your Official Receipt for Income Tax purposes.

Please present this slip to admitting office before leaving.

SERVICES RENDERED	ROBERTA	Tom
Examination	18	
X Ray	15	15
Extraction		
Cleaning	40	
Filling 1 WF		37
Bridge		
Denture		
	Dec. 3/-1	
TOTAL	$ 73	52

0002

NEXT APPOINTMENT

a. How many parts are there to this source document? Name them.

b. What is common to these parts? Why is this item important?

c. When is the top line of the stub portion completed?

d. Where did the previous balance come from?

e. How many important columns appear at the top edge of the left or fee bill portion?

f. Name the three money columns from left to right on the dental fee bill. What are these called in accounting terms?

g. How is the explanation of dental services recorded on the dental fee bill?

h. What is the total fee charged on the bill? How is the amount calculated?

i. What amount is currently owed by the patient? How is this amount calculated?

j. Analyze the results of the source document by showing the accounting entry in General Journal form.

k. Name two basic GAAPs which can be related to this completed source document. Explain them.

MINI-CASES

Applying the revenue principle.

MC 8-1 A small advertising agency has just started up and its management is making decisions regarding its system for recording sales and accounts receivable. The agency designs advertisements for various clients. Once the client has approved the design and chosen the type of media, the agency arranges for the advertisements to appear on radio, television, or in the newspaper. When the client approves the advertisement, the agency prepares an invoice for the cost of its service in addition to the **estimated** cost of the service which the radio or television station or newspaper will provide. Once the advertisement is actually run, the agency is sent an invoice. If the cost is more than the estimate, then the agency sends an adjusted invoice to the client. The agency has found that these adjustments are minimal and amount to about 5% of the total service fee.

a. When should the revenue be recorded by the agency? Support your answer using the revenue principle. *Hint:* You need to decide at what stage the agency has completed their service for a client.

Applying the objectivity principle.

MC 8-2 Rosemary Pouliot, an accountant, provides services for a charitable organization. She spends 25 hours providing the services and her normal rate is $50 per hour. Ms. Pouliot will not bill the organization for her services. Instead, she asks for a tax receipt showing a charitable donation to the organization in the amount of $1500.

a. In how many ways could the organization journalize this transaction? Explain whether any accounting fees should be recorded and, if so, the dollar amount that should be recorded. *Hint:* The accountant wants to claim a donation in excess of the fair value of the work she has performed. This would mean that the charity would have to record revenues in excess of the fair value of the work performed. You must decide whether this is reasonable given what you know about the objectivity principle.

JOURNALIZING AND POSTING DENTAL CHARGES

In this topic, you will learn how to record all dental fees and why they are recorded in a special journal. You will also be introduced to a special ledger that contains all of the individual patient accounts. Since the General Ledger is maintained, posting is done twice.

EXAMINING THE NEED FOR A FEES EARNED JOURNAL

Suppose all the dental fee bills are summarized for the month of January. The summary is presented below. Assume that all Dr. Johnson's patients do not pay at the time of their appointment.

Summary of Dental Fee Bill Charges

19-8			
Jan.	2	2982	To Lucia Garcia (new patient). E CL XR, charge of $103.
	2	2983	To Ms. Mary Brown, EXT, charge of $35.
	3	2984	To Mr. Garcia and daughter Anita: Mr. Garcia, two WF, charge of $73; Anita, E CL XR, charge of $78. Total charge of $151.
	3	2985	To Mary, daughter of Mr. B. Campbell, for temporary filling. Total fee of $56.
	5	2987	To David, son of Mr. R. Diloreto (new patient), for examination, X-ray, and cleaning. Total fee, $132.
	8	2990	To Helena and Dimitri, children of Mr. J. Kantzos (new patient). Helena's treatment: exam, X-ray, cleaning, and fluoride, $144. Dimitri's treatment: exam, X-ray, and cleaning, $92. Total charge of $236.
	9	2991	To Mr. T. Jacques (new patient). Exam, X-ray, and cleaning; total fee of $103.
	10	2994	To Ms. Clemence Lee (new patient). EXT, charge of $50.
	11	2995	To David, son of Mr. W. Maksymiuk (new patient). Exam, X-ray, and root canal treatment. Total fee of $285.
	13	2997	To Mr. R. Diloreto, for examination, X-ray, and cleaning. Total fee of $103.
	14	2998	To Mr. J. Kantzos, for exam, X-ray, and cleaning. Total fee, $103.

17 2999 To Vina Aveiro (new patient). Total charge of $1000 for a bridge.
18 3000 To Mr. T. Jacques. Total fee of $600 for a crown.
20 3002 To Ms. Christine Zander (new patient). Exam, X-rays, root canal treatment, $692.
22 3003 To Mr. H. Chan (new patient). Exam, X-ray, cleaning, $103.
24 3005 To Ms. Clemence Lee, cleaning, $65.
25 3006 To Mr. D. Cook (new patient). Exam, X-ray, cleaning, $103.
26 3007 To Andrew, son of Mr. D. Cook. Exam, X-ray, cleaning, $103. Also to Brenda, daughter of Mr. Cook. Exam, X-rays, cleaning, $103. Total bill, $206.
29 3009 To Mr. S. Lesniak (new patient). Exam, X-ray, cleaning, $103.
30 3010 To Mr. H. Chan. Root canal treatment plus crown, $992.
31 3011 To Ms. Gwenda Tuck (new patient). Exam, X-ray, and partial denture, $567.
31 3012 To Mr. H. Chan. Lab fee of $156.
31 3014 To Ms. Anne Gomes (new patient). Total fee of $750 for bridge.

Now suppose that the above 23 transactions were recorded in a General Journal as shown below.

GENERAL JOURNAL Page 53

DATE 19-8		ACCOUNT TITLE AND EXPLANATION	POST. REF.	DEBIT	CREDIT
Jan.	2	Accts. Rec./D. Garcia		103 00	
		Professional Fees Earned			103 00
		To record fee bill No. 2982;			
		E C/ XR rendered to Mrs. Garcia.			
	2	Accts. Rec./Mary Brown		35 00	
		Professional Fees Earned			35 00
		To record fee bill No. 2983;			
		tooth extraction.			
Jan.	31	Accts. Rec./Ms. A. Gomes		750 00	
		Professional Fees Earned			750 00
		To record fee bill No. 3014;			
		services rendered, bridge.			

Until now, you have analyzed each fee charged by debiting Accounts Receivable/(Name of Patient) and crediting the revenue account Professional Fees Earned. If all 23 transactions were recorded in the General Journal, this would mean that Accounts Receivable would be debited, and Professional Fees Earned credited, 23 times. Furthermore, if each entry required at least three or four lines (one for the debit entry, one for the credit entry, and one or two for the brief explanation), the entire 23 transactions would use at least 69 or 92 writing lines. Moreover, a typical dental practice would probably have 15 to 20 similar transactions **per day**. Add to this other business transactions which may also be recorded in the General Journal, and you would probably have to search through many pages of the journal to find the total fees earned for a given day or month. To overcome these difficulties, many firms use a special journal to record revenue earned called the Fees Earned Journal.

ILLUSTRATING THE FEES EARNED JOURNAL

Fees Earned Journal: a special journal recording all fees earned in chronological order.

The next illustration shows how the 23 transactions discussed above may be recorded in the special revenue journal called the Fees Earned Journal. In actual practice, this journal is custom-designed to meet the needs of individual firms. For example, some firms may prefer to use only one money column to record dental fees earned. Such is the case when a firm uses a one-write system to record all charges. Other businesses may prefer to use a Fees Earned Journal with several money columns.

Study the one-column Fees Earned Journal presented on the opposite page.

Analysis:

- Since the Fees Earned Journal records all revenue earned, this journal is in effect the revenue journal.
- As in all journals, page numbers are given on the top line.
- The main column headings are: Receipt Number, to record the number on the fee bill; Date, to record the transaction date appearing on the source document; Account Debit, to record each account debited in each transaction; Description Code, to record the description code of the dental services provided; Post. Ref. (Posting Reference), to be used later to transfer each amount debited to appropriate accounts; and Amount, to record the dollar result of each fees earned transaction.

After studying the headings, you may ask yourself: *Where is the column to record the credit to Professional Fees Earned?* For each

FEES EARNED JOURNAL Page 1

RECEIPT NUMBER	DATE		ACCOUNT DEBIT	DESCRIPTION CODE	POST. REF.	AMOUNT	
2982	Jan	2	D. Garcia	E CL XR (Mrs.)		103	–
2983		2	Ms. Mary Brown	EXT		35	–
2984		3	D. Garcia	E CL XR (anita) 2 WF (Mr.)		151	–
2985		3	B. Campbell	TF (Mary)		56	–
2987		5	R. Diloreto	E CL XR (David)		132	–
2990		8	J. Kentzoo	E XR CL FL (Helena) E XR CL (Dimitri)		236	–
2991		9	T. Jacques	E CL XR		103	–
2994		10	Ms. C. Lee	EXT		50	–
2995		11	W. Makoymuik	E XR RCT (David)		285	–
2997		13	R. Diloreto	E CL XR		103	–
2998		14	J. Kantzoo	E CL XR		103	–
2999		17	Ms. V. Aveiro	BR		1000	–
3000		18	T. Jacques	CR		600	–
3002		20	Ms. C. Zander	E XR RCT		692	–
3003		22	H. Chan	E CL XR		103	–
3005		24	Ms. C. Lee	CL		65	–
3006		25	D. Cook	E CL XR		103	–
3007		26	D. Cook	E CL XR (Brenda + andrew)		206	–
3009		29	S. Lesniak	E CL XR		103	–
3010		30	H. Chan	RCT CR		992	–
3011		31	Ms. G. Tuck	EXR PD		567	–
3012		31	H. Chan	Lab fee		156	–
3014		31	Ms. A. Gomes	BR		750	–

line entry, the credit is understood as having been recorded each time the debit entry is made. The total of credits for each month is posted at the end of a month.

You can now see one of the main advantages of any special journal: recording the complete entry on one line. However, think of each transaction in General Journal form so you can record correctly the debit entry. For example, in the first transaction, the entry in General Journal form shows four lines as shown on page 307. That same entry, with all information, is recorded on one line in the special journal. Remember, however, that the credit to Professional Fees Earned is understood and will be seen as part of the total credits at the end of the month.

Here are three more points to keep in mind:

- All receipt numbers will be accounted for in the Fees Earned Journal. For example, receipt number 2986 is missing in the illustration above. This would suggest that 2986 was used to record no fee charged but only the receipt of cash on account. As you will learn in Topic 4, payments of cash received will be recorded in another special journal.

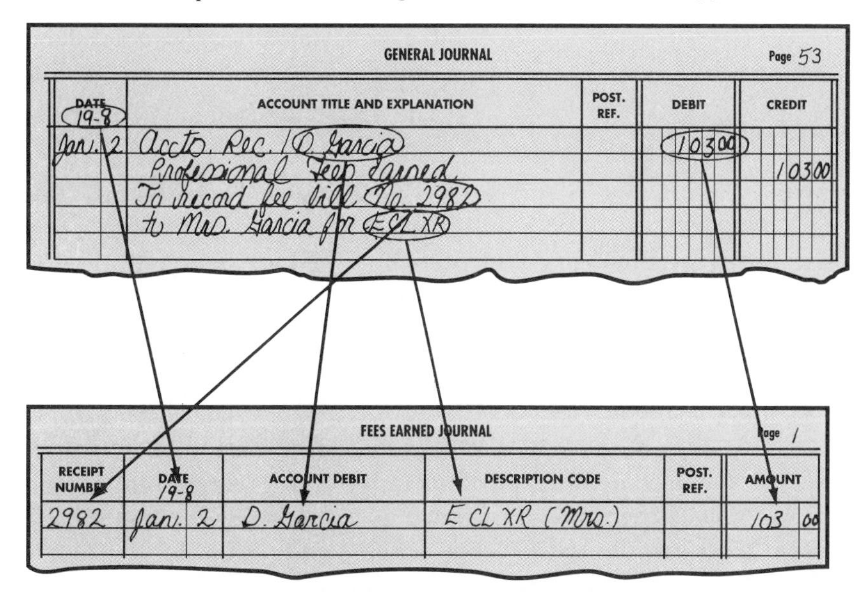

- There are no "cents" amounts recorded for dental fees charged. This practice is common in dental and other practices using the manual method. It reduces errors in adding long columns of figures.
- When only dollars are used in journals and ledger accounts, it is permissible to show a dash instead of ciphers (zeros). The dash should not be used when reporting dollars in financial statements. Such statements are treated as **formal** accounting reports. Journals and ledgers, on the other hand, are internal records.

LOOKING AT THE NEED FOR AN ACCOUNTS RECEIVABLE LEDGER

In Part 1 of this book, all transactions involving accounts receivable were posted to a few individual customer accounts that were filed together with other asset accounts in the same general ledger. In practice, however, nearly all professional practices (dental, law, accounting, etc.) have a large number of individual accounts receivable. So do nearly all other businesses which sell services (or goods) on credit. Consider the following problems of using only one ledger:

- It would become quite crowded.
- It would be heavy and awkward to work with.
- Only one person could post at any one time.
- The trial balance would take several pages.

- If the trial balance did not balance, it would be very difficult to find the error within a reasonable time.
- The Current Asset section of the balance sheet would be very long.

Accounts Receivable Ledger: the file of all individual customer or patient accounts.

To overcome these problems, the majority of firms will file individual customer accounts in a separate ledger called the Accounts Receivable Ledger (or **customers' ledger**, or, in a dental practice, **patients' ledger**).

ORGANIZING A SEPARATE ACCOUNTS RECEIVABLE LEDGER

Accounts Receivable: a current asset account in the General Ledger.

When individual customer accounts are pulled from the original or main ledger, it is important to remember that a general account known as Accounts Receivable must be kept in the General Ledger. The process of pulling out the four individual patient accounts at the start of January, 19-8 to replace them with one account for Dr. Johnson's dental practice is shown next.

Analysis: Study the illustration on page 309 and note the following facts:

- There are two ledgers: the Accounts Receivable Ledger containing the individual patient (customer) accounts, and the main ledger, the General Ledger, which now contains the general account called Accounts Receivable.
- The Accounts Receivable account in the General Ledger will show the total amount owed by all the customers. For example, the opposite illustration shows Accounts Receivable with a total balance of $320. This total is seen clearly on the debit side of the Accounts Receivable account in the General Ledger.
- This Accounts Receivable account is said to ''control'' the individual patient accounts recorded on the patient ledger cards because the sum of the balances on the cards must be equal to the balance in the Accounts Receivable account. Therefore, this account may be called Accounts Receivable Control. In practice, the word ''control'' is usually dropped from the account name because it is understood.
- The General Ledger is the **main ledger**—that is, it contains all of the information necessary to prepare financial statements. The Accounts Receivable Ledger is a secondary or a subsidiary ledger. The subsidiary ledger does not contain all of the accounts of the business; it contains only *one class* of account. In a large accounting system, there will always be one General Ledger and one or more subsidiary ledgers.

Accounts Receivable Control: the General Ledger account which contains the total of all individual customer account balances. (In practice, the word control is not used, since it is understood.)

Subsidiary ledger: a secondary ledger which stores the details of all the accounts of only one type.

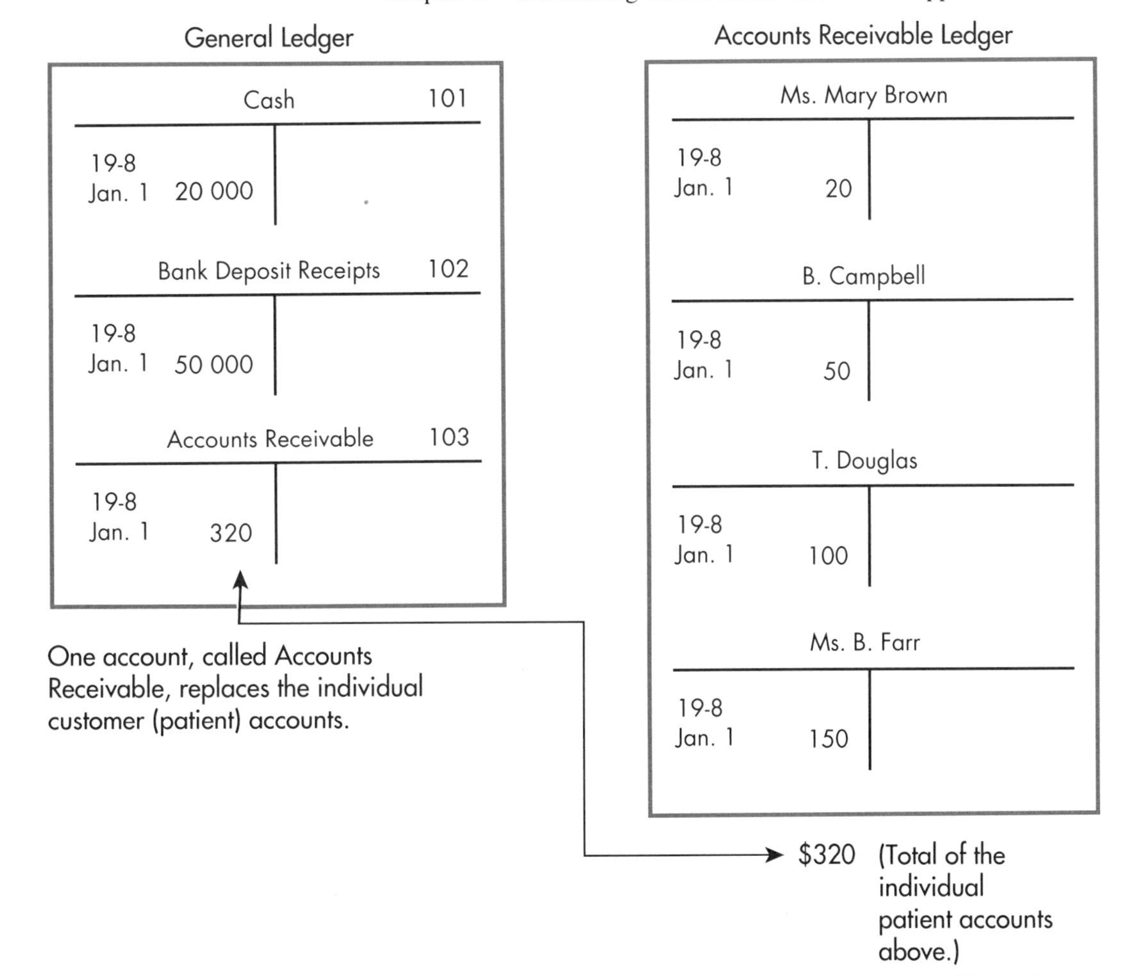

- Accounts stored in the subsidiary ledger are coded differently from the accounts filed in the General Ledger. In the T-account illustration above, the accounts in the Accounts Receivable Ledger are kept in alphabetical order. On the other hand, the accounts in the General Ledger are filed in numerical order as listed by a chart of accounts.
- In the case of an actual dental practice, the subsidiary Accounts Receivable Ledger is the box or drawer that contains all the individual patient cards filed alphabetically.

POSTING INDIVIDUAL CUSTOMER ACCOUNTS

When a General Ledger and an Accounts Receivable Ledger are both used, the posting of credit sales—cash is not paid at the time sale is made or service is performed—is done twice: once to the customer's account in the Accounts Receivable Ledger; and once to the Accounts Receivable Control account in the General Ledger. The posting to the subsidiary ledger is daily so that the balance owing can be known at any time. Usually this posting is done immediately after entering the transaction in the Fees Earned Journal. The entry may be made from the source document or from the Revenue Journal. We will illustrate the method of posting from the Revenue Journal.

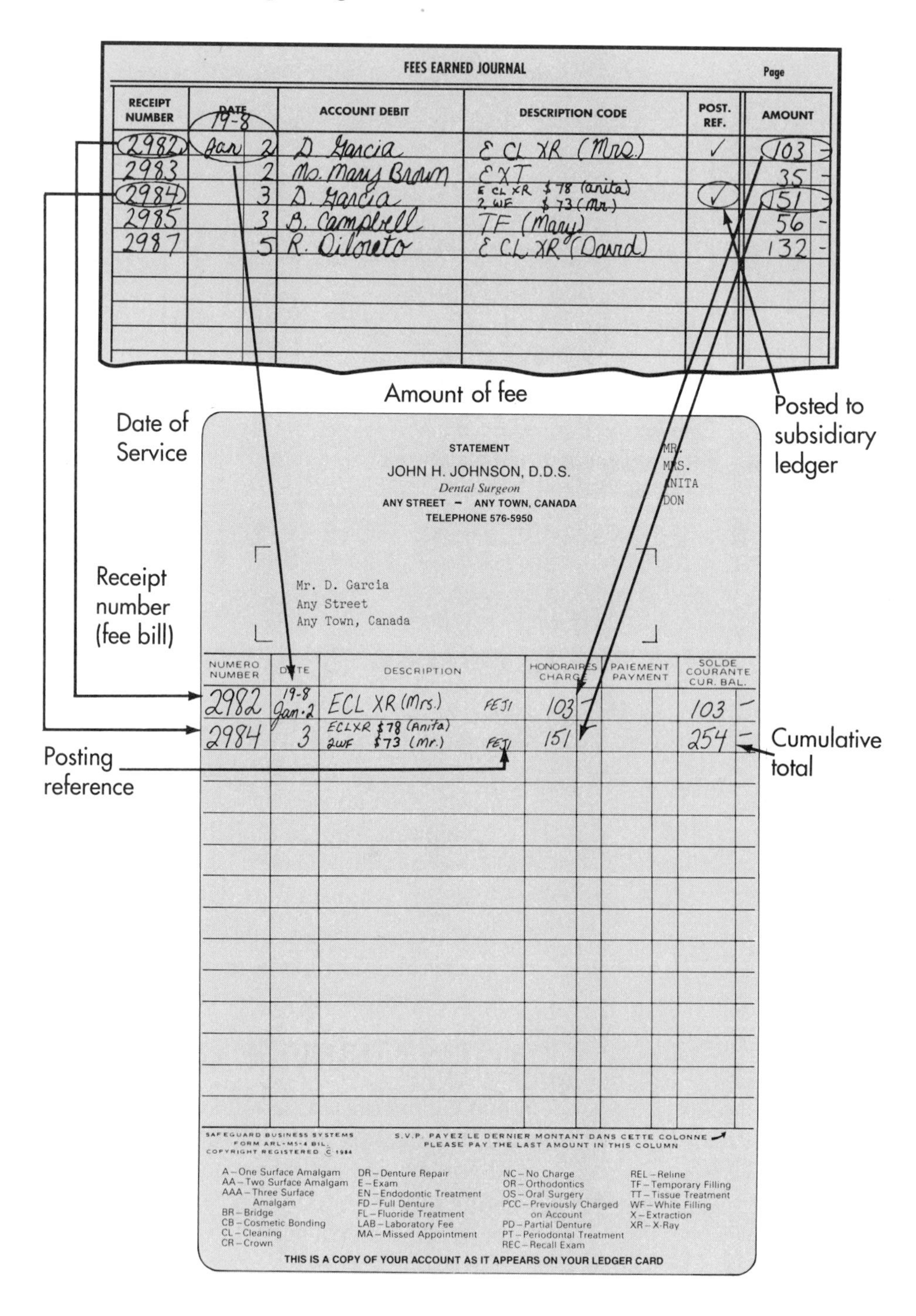

POSTING TO THE GENERAL LEDGER

As discussed earlier, the main advantage of the special journal is that you save time posting monthly totals to the General Journal instead of posting each individual transaction. However, it is important to check the accuracy of the journal before it is posted. In this way errors can be caught at various stages in the accounting cycle. Some checking procedures are as follows:

(1) Use an adding machine to obtain the correct total amount in the journal. Check the tape against the Amount column.

(2) Add the amount column and place a total in pencil just below the last amount entered. This is known as a pencil footing or pinhead total. Read the column and, if the pencil total agrees with the tape total, record the total in pen on the next available line.

Pencil footing: small, pencilled figures entered at the foot (bottom) of a money column.

The steps used for posting to the General Ledger are illustrated below.

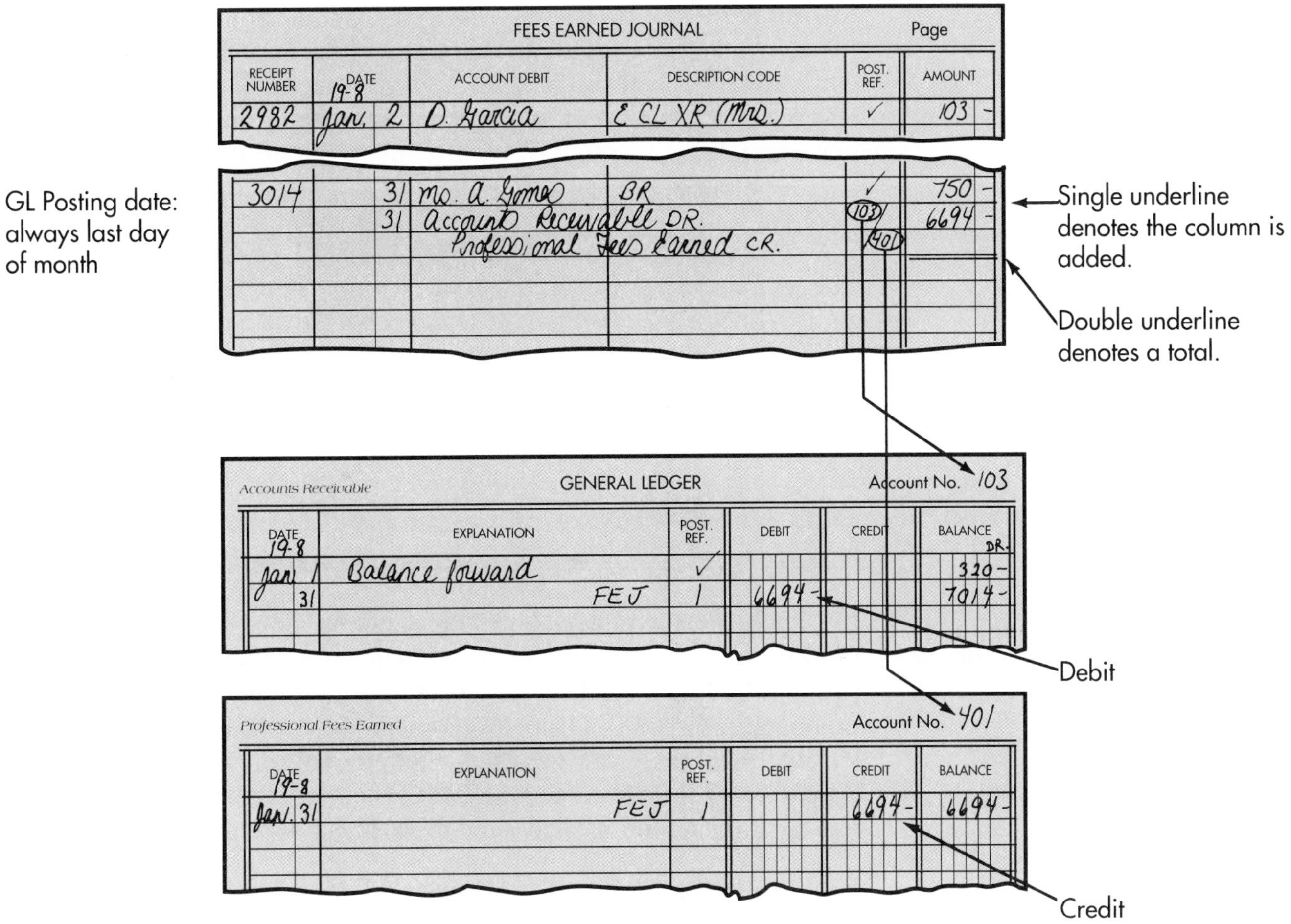

FEES EARNED JOURNAL — Page

RECEIPT NUMBER	DATE 19-8		ACCOUNT DEBIT	DESCRIPTION CODE	POST. REF.	AMOUNT
2982	Jan.	2	D. Garcia	E CL XR (Mrs.)	✓	103 -
3014		31	Ms. A. Gomes	BR	✓	750 -
		31	Accounts Receivable DR.		103	6694 -
			Professional Fees Earned CR.		401	

GL Posting date: always last day of month

Single underline denotes the column is added.

Double underline denotes a total.

Accounts Receivable — GENERAL LEDGER — Account No. 103

DATE 19-8		EXPLANATION	POST. REF.	DEBIT	CREDIT	BALANCE DR.
Jan.	1	Balance forward	✓			320 -
	31	FEJ	1	6694 -		7014 -

Debit

Professional Fees Earned — Account No. 401

DATE 19-8		EXPLANATION	POST. REF.	DEBIT	CREDIT	BALANCE
Jan.	31	FEJ	1		6694 -	6694 -

Credit

LOOKING AT THE ADVANTAGES OF THE SPECIAL JOURNAL

Here are the main advantages to using a special journal to record the professional fees earned:

- Only one line is needed to record an entry in a special journal. Thus, valuable time and space are saved.
- The dollar amount is written only once for each double entry because the credit to Professional Fees Earned is understood.
- Time is saved because only the total is posted to the General Ledger at the end of the month—as a debit to Accounts Receivable and as a credit to Professional Fees Earned.
- Division of responsibility among accounting clerks is possible. In a large business, only one clerk instead of several can be responsible for recording and posting accounts receivable.

Other Special Journals As you can see from the Fees Earned Journal, a special journal is used to record transactions that are similar and very repetitive in nature. Other special journals exist in the efficient organization of any accounting system for most businesses. For example, the inflow of cash is highly repetitive and, therefore, justifies the use of a special journal to record cash receipts. The Cash Receipts Journal will be dealt with in Topic 4.

A special journal such as the Fees Earned Journal does **not** eliminate the need for a General Journal. Think of the General Journal as the non-specialized journal. It is the record that contains the entries that cannot be recorded in a special journal. The General Journal is used to record the opening balance sheet of a new firm. Remember, special journals are used to record transactions that are similar and repetitive.

PROBLEMS

Setting up the books for a dental practice and journalizing dental fee bills.

P 8-3 Dr. L.M. Munro opened his dental practice during the final week of January, 19-7 with the following assets and liabilities: Cash, $5000; Government of Canada Bonds, $30 000; Dental Equipment, $40 000; Office Equipment, $10 000; Bank Loan Payable, $5000; Accts. Pay./Bell Equipment Ltd., $10 000; Accts. Pay./Riverside Systems Ltd., $2000. The transactions below represent the dental fees charged to various patients in that week.

Jan. 26	0001	To Ms. M. Micsinski, E CL. Total fee, $103.
27	0002	To Susan, daughter of Mr. L. McGraw. E 2BW CL, $93.

28	0003	To Mr. L. McGraw, CR. Total fee of $370.
28	0004	To Mr. S. Katz, Lab fee of $175.
29	0005	To Richard and Ronald, sons of Mr. S. Ketcheson. Richard, E CL, $65. Ronald, E XR 2WF, $59.
30	0006	To Ms. J. Laing, E BW CL, $106.
31	0007	To Mr. I. Ryder, E CL, $103.

a. Record the opening entry for Dr. Munro's dental practice in the General Journal.

b. Analyze each of the above dental charges in General Journal form in the same journal as used in **a** above. Show a complete explanation for each entry.

c. Record the transactions analyzed in **b** on page 1 of a Fees Earned Journal.

Using a Fees Earned Journal.

P 8-4 The summary of transactions below represents the dental fees charged to various patients of Dr. Lien Chang's dental practice for the month of December, 19-7.

Dec.	2	0001	To Mr. H. Vandenberk for dental services rendered to Mrs. Vandenberk. Total fee for E CL XR, $103.
	3	0002	To Mr. H. Vandenberk for dental services rendered to the two children: Roberta, E CL XR, $73; Tom, XR 1WF, $52.
	4	0003	To Mr. Geoff Dean, XR WF, $43.
	4	0004	To Mr. H. Vandenberk, E CL, $103.
	5	0005	To Mrs. B. Liepner, spouse of Mr. M. Liepner, XR WF, $78.
	8	0006	To Mrs. E. Revell, for E XR and EN (endodontics), $252.
	9	0007	To Mr. T. Taller, for E CL, $103.
	10	0008	To Mr. T. Murphy, for 2WF, $44.
	11	0009	To Ms. L. Kretchman, for E CL, $103.
	14	0010	To Mr. B. Gibson, $143, for dental services performed on two children: Don, for CL, $40; David, for E CL, $63.
	15	0011	To Mrs. Vandenberk, spouse of H. Vandenberk, for 2WF, $63.
	16	0012	To Ms. M. Kingsbury, for CR, $600.
	17	0013	To Ms. C. Pratt, for BR, $280.
	18	0014	To Mr. R. Kendall, for E CL, $103.
	21	0015	To Mr. M. Robineau, for lab fee, $335.
	22	0016	To Mr. Jack Wilson, for E CL, $103.

23	0017	To Ms. M. McKim, for E BW CL, $108.
24	0018	To Ms. B. Johnson, for lab fee, $195.
27	0019	To Mr. D. Schearer, for PFM (type of crown), $289.
30	0020	To Mr. D. Milks, for 1WF, $52.
30	0021	To Mrs. J. Borron, spouse of Mr. Wm. Borron, for E CL, $103.
31	0022	To Mr. Wm. Borron, for E CL, $103.
31	0023	To Ms. Mary Ryan, for E 2BW CL, $122.
31	0024	To Ms. V. Hume, for E 2BW 1PA CL, $179.

a. Record the same transactions on page 1 of a Fees Earned Journal.

Creating and posting from an Accounts Receivable Ledger.

P 8-5 Refer to Problem 8-3 (Dr. L.M. Munro's dental practice) and the solution for that problem.

a. Open separate patient accounts receivable cards for Mr. S. Katz, Mr. S. Ketcheson, Ms. J. Laing, Mr. L. McGraw, Ms. M. Micsinski, and Mr. I. Ryder. Invent appropriate mailing addresses.

b. Post the transactions from the Fees Earned Journal (from Problem 8-3) to the individual patient accounts in the Accounts Receivable Ledger.

c. Total the Fees Earned Journal. Record the appropriate double entry for this total; post the total to appropriate General Ledger accounts; and rule off the special journal for the month.

Creating and posting from an Accounts Receivable Ledger.

P 8-6 Refer to Problem 8-4 (Dr. Lien Chang's dental practice) and the solution for that problem.

a. List all the patients identified in the December transactions. Then arrange the names in alphabetical order.

b. From that list, set up an Accounts Receivable Ledger in T-account form.

c. Post the transactions from the Fees Earned Journal to the T-accounts set up for the Accounts Receivable Ledger.

d. Set up a patient's ledger card for Mr. H. Vandenberk. Post the transactions from the Fees Earned Journal to this account.

e. Total the Fees Earned Journal and show this total **journalized** for the month of December. Then rule off the journal for the month.

f. Set up the two appropriate General Ledger accounts and post the total from the Fees Earned Journal to these accounts.

MINI-CASES

Debating the uses of an Accounts Receivable Ledger.

MC 8-3 Two students are discussing the newly learned procedures for the accounts receivable application. The first student says that she feels the Accounts Receivable Ledger (that is, the patient ledger cards) are a waste of time and that the total in the Fees Earned Journal should just be posted to the Accounts Receivable account in the General Ledger to eliminate all the double-posting required. The second student replies that there are many advantages to setting up a separate ledger for patient accounts.

a. Defend both sides of the discussion adding your own observations about the additional procedures and advantages or disadvantages encountered when using an Accounts Receivable Ledger.

Designing a system to ensure all revenues are collected.

MC 8-4 Kristian Teleki owns a pet-sitting business. When pet owners are away, Kristian feeds, walks, and cares for the pets. If the pet has other special needs, the pet owner makes special arrangements with Kristian. Kristian charges by the day and adds any fees for special care to the daily fee. When the pet owner returns, he or she pays him. One day Kristian is talking to you about his business. He says, ''I record all of my duties on my calendar at home but when I compare the number of days I have worked with the revenues I have collected I always seem to be short.''

a. Suggest a system that will help Kristian with this problem.

Analyzing the effect of posting errors.

MC 8-5 The accounts receivable clerk has posted the Accounts Receivable Ledger and the General Ledger, but the balances are not equal. When she reviews her work, the clerk finds that she has missed posting a month's transactions to one patient's account.

a. What effect does this omission have on the two ledgers? Are any other records affected by this error? How can the omission be corrected?

CONTROLLING CASH RECEIPTS

The owners of a business rely on an accounting system to ensure that:

- All cash receipts are recorded efficiently and accurately.
- The cash is protected from fraud (dishonesty) and outright theft.

To ensure that the receipt of cash is controlled, a business takes these basic measures:

- pre-numbering source documents
- preparing a daily cash proof
- setting up a business chequing account
- depositing cash receipts intact
- making daily deposits
- dividing responsibilities among employees
- using a special journal to record cash receipts

Since these measures are taken within the business, they are called—as a whole—an internal control system. As a business grows, the need to control cash becomes more complex and additional measures are required.

Internal control system: activities organized within a business for the purpose of (1) protecting its assets against waste, fraud, and theft and (2) ensuring the accuracy and reliability of the data in accounting reports.

PRE-NUMBERING SOURCE DOCUMENTS (RECEIPTS)

Whenever cash is received, a pre-numbered receipt should be completed. The term "pre-numbered" means that each separate document is printed with a number. The receipt will indicate:

- the amount received
- the date the cash is received
- who made the payment
- why the payment was made

Some examples of these receipts are:

- cash register tape
- sales slip
- cash receipts, illustrated at the top of page 317
- receipted fee bills (for example, in our dental practice), illustrated below the first illustration on page 317

With pre-numbered receipts, you can check the sequence of receipts to ensure that all of them are recorded in the business's accounts. It does not restrict someone from simply not preparing a receipt and then taking the cash. However, if this happens often, the customers will complain that they are being asked to make unfair and excessive payments and the owner(s) will investigate the situation.

Note: In the illustrations that follow ROA means "Received on Account."

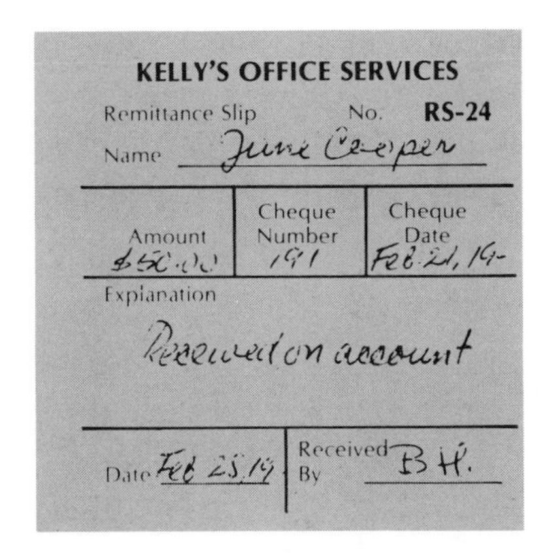

KELLY'S OFFICE SERVICES

Remittance Slip No. **RS-24**

Name June Cooper

Amount	Cheque Number	Cheque Date
$50.00	191	Feb. 21, 19-

Explanation

Received on account

Date Feb 25, 19 Received By B.H.

2401 CAMBIE ST. ACCT. COPY—PAYMENT RECEIPT

BUXTON'S VANCOUVER, B.C.

069868

ACCOUNT NO. 13071 CLERK #104 25.92/100

NAME Dunster, S. F.

ADDRESS 89-904 Clarke Rd.

Port Moody, B.C.

CASH ☐

CHEQUE ☒

MONEY ORDER ☐

DATE: -- 10 15

YEAR MONTH DAY

PAYMENT ON ACCOUNT ☒ DEPOSIT ON LAY-A-WAY ☐

DEPOSIT ON C.O.D. ☐ DEPOSIT ON SPECIAL ORDER ☐

RECEIPT NUMBER	DATE	DESCRIPTION - CODE	CHARGE	PAYMENT	CURRENT BALANCE
2986	1/8/-8	ROA	-0-	50 —	-0-

PREVIOUS BALANCE	NAME
50 —	MS. MARY BROWN

YOU PAID THIS AMOUNT

DR. JOHN H. JOHNSON

Dental Surgeon

ANY STREET - ANYTOWN,

TELEPHONE 576-5950

A – One Surface Amalgam
AA – Two Surface Amalgam
AAA – Three Surface Amalgam
BR – Bridge
CB – Cosmetic Bonding
CL – Cleaning
CR – Crown
DR – Denture Repair
E – Exam
EN – Endodontic Treatment
FD – Full Denture
FL – Fluoride Treatment
LAB – Laboratory Fee
MA – Missed Appointment
NC – No Charge
OR – Orthodontics
OS – Oral Surgery
PCC – Previously Charged on Account
PD – Partial Denture
PT – Periodontal Treatment
REC – Recall Exam
REL – Reline
TF – Temporary Filling
TT – Tissue Treatment
WF – White Filling
X – Extraction
XR – X-Ray

There is no charge for missed appointments if 24 hour's notice is given.

RECEIVED PAYMENT L.F.

NEXT APPOINTMENT .... AT 2986

Date Time

This is your Official Receipt for Income Tax purposes.

Please present this slip to admitting office before leaving.

SERVICES RENDERED

Examination
X Ray
Extraction
Cleaning
Filling
Bridge
Denture

ROA $50 Jan 8/-8

TOTAL $

2986

NEXT APPOINTMENT

PREPARING A DAILY CASH PROOF

The daily cash proof will verify that the total cash on hand is equal to the total cash as recorded in the receipts. In this way, the cash deposit and the accounting entry can be verified before they are completed.

Ideally, the person who receives the cash should not also prepare the proof; instead, the proof should be prepared by a supervisor or the owner. In practice the proof used will vary according to the needs of the business, and we will show you an example of one proof.

Cash Register Tapes When a cash register system is used, the clerk is generally instructed to prepare a daily cash summary form from the actual count. In other words, the clerk counts the total amount of cash in the till at the end of the shift. To provide for maximum control, the clerk would prepare this daily cash summary without knowing the totals on the cash register tape.

A supervisor should then check that the count is equal to

- the total of the cash sales on the cash register tape, **plus**

- the total of the cash received on account, **plus**

Change fund: a small amount of currency used to make change.

- the amount of the change fund, that is, the money that was in the till when the cashiers started their shift, **less**
- any money removed from the drawer to refund a customer's return of merchandise.

Look closely at the illustration below.

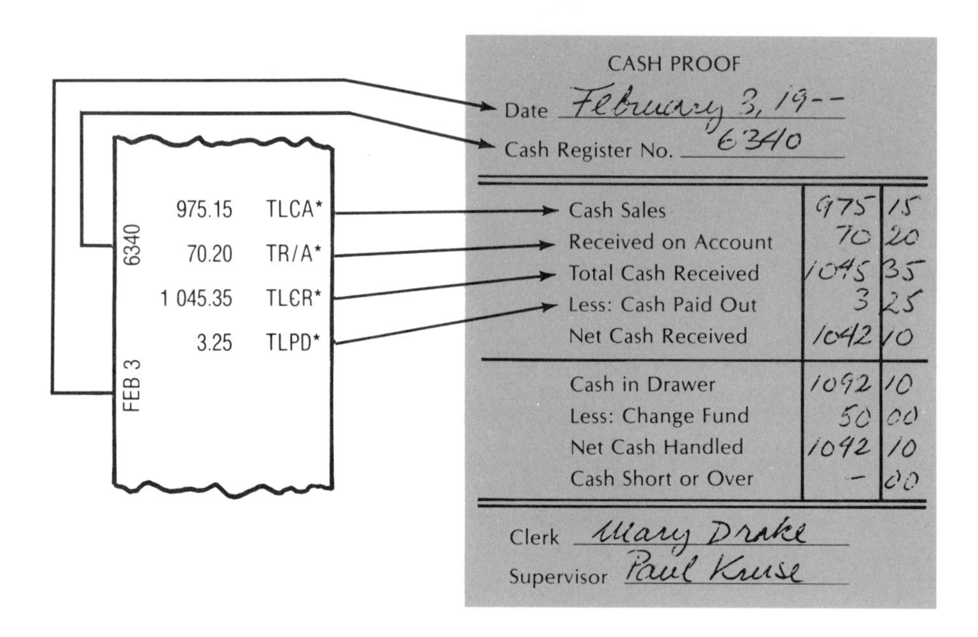

CASH PROOF

Date February 3, 19--

Cash Register No. 6340

Cash Sales	975	15
Received on Account	70	20
Total Cash Received	1045	35
Less: Cash Paid Out	3	25
Net Cash Received	1042	10
Cash in Drawer	1092	10
Less: Change Fund	50	00
Net Cash Handled	1042	10
Cash Short or Over	–	00

Clerk Mary Drake

Supervisor Paul Kruse

SETTING UP A BUSINESS CHEQUING ACCOUNT

Current account: a business bank account used to account for a business's cash receipts and cash payments.

A business chequing account, called a current account, ensures a measure of control over a business's most valuable asset — cash. A current account provides the business with the following advantages:

- The bank acts as custodian of the business's cash to safeguard the asset while it remains on deposit. The business can then keep large sums of money away from its place of business.
- All payments for business expenses can be controlled by the owner who signs the cheques, ensuring that payment is for an actual business expense. The cheques then become valuable source documents providing proof that transactions took place.
- The business receives monthly statements showing all the transactions that affect the bank account. These statements can be compared to the accounting records of the business to ensure all cash transactions have been recorded. This procedure will be expanded in Chapter 10.

DEPOSITING CASH RECEIPTS INTACT

This control measure places great emphasis on the word "intact." "Intact" means that **all** cash received must be deposited into the firm's current account. Never should even one dollar of cash receipts be used to make any payment. This ensures that total cash recorded can be verified against total cash received. For this purpose all cheques received should be stamped "For Deposit Only" which will ensure that the entire cheque amount is deposited into the business's current account.

DEPOSITING CASH DAILY

All cash should be deposited daily. Any delay increases the danger of theft. Many banks provide access during non-business hours by way of a night deposit box.

Deposit slips should always be prepared in duplicate. Most banks provide businesses with deposit books that allow a carbon copy of the deposit slip to be made. The original slip is stamped (with the date and the name and branch of the bank) and kept by the bank and the carbon copy or duplicate is stamped and kept by the business. This copy provides the business with a permanent record of the deposit which may be used to clear up any discrepancy between the business's records and the monthly bank statement and may be used to audit the accounting records. An example of a cash proof is provided below.

CURRENT ACCOUNT
DEPOSIT SLIP

ROYAL BANK

Oct. 25, 19--
DATE

DEPOSITOR'S INITIALS: P.M. | TELLER'S INITIALS:

CREDIT ACCOUNT OF

Sportsman Specialty Shop
843 Driftwood Rd.
Any Town, Canada

PLEASE LIST FOREIGN CHEQUES ON A SEPARATE DEPOSIT SLIP

VISA AND CHEQUES		DETAILS	CASH (INCL. COUPONS)
250.00	VISA VOUCHER TOTAL	18 X 1	18.00
359.10		12 X 2	24.00
(see cheque list attached)		5 X 5	25.00
		7 X 10	70.00
		2 X 20	40.00
		1 X	50.00
		X	
		COIN	38.67
		CANADIAN CASH TOTAL	265.67
TOTAL	609.10	VISA & CHQS FORWARDED	609.10
U.S. CASH		RATE	
U.S. CHQS		RATE	
NET DEPOSIT			874.77

⑆0000 2⑈003⑆ 51

Cheque List
Deposit
Oct. 25, 19--

0.00 T

18.00
20.90
19.40
10.00
28.70
35.80
30.00
17.45
46.30
40.00
55.65
20.00
16.90

359.10 T

DIVIDING RESPONSIBILITIES AMONG EMPLOYEES

If the owner cannot be involved in the daily activities of the business, the responsibility of handling cash should be separated from the responsibility of recording cash. In other words, those employees who handle an asset should not also record transactions relating to that asset.

This measure provides control over cash in two ways:

- Cash received by one person can be checked against the cash receipts recorded by a separate person. For example, refer to the daily cash proof on the opposite page.
- Cash must be deposited the day it is received, or the bank statement will not agree with the accounting records. This ensures that the money is not used, for whatever reason, by an employee for a few days before it is actually deposited.

USING A SPECIAL JOURNAL TO RECORD CASH RECEIPTS

Cash Receipts Journal: a special journal in which only cash receipts are recorded.

Since transactions involving cash receipts are routine and occur on a daily basis, many firms will use a special journal known as the Cash Receipts Journal. This special journal will be discussed in the next topic.

The system of cash control is illustrated on page 321. Try to identify the basic measures for controlling cash.

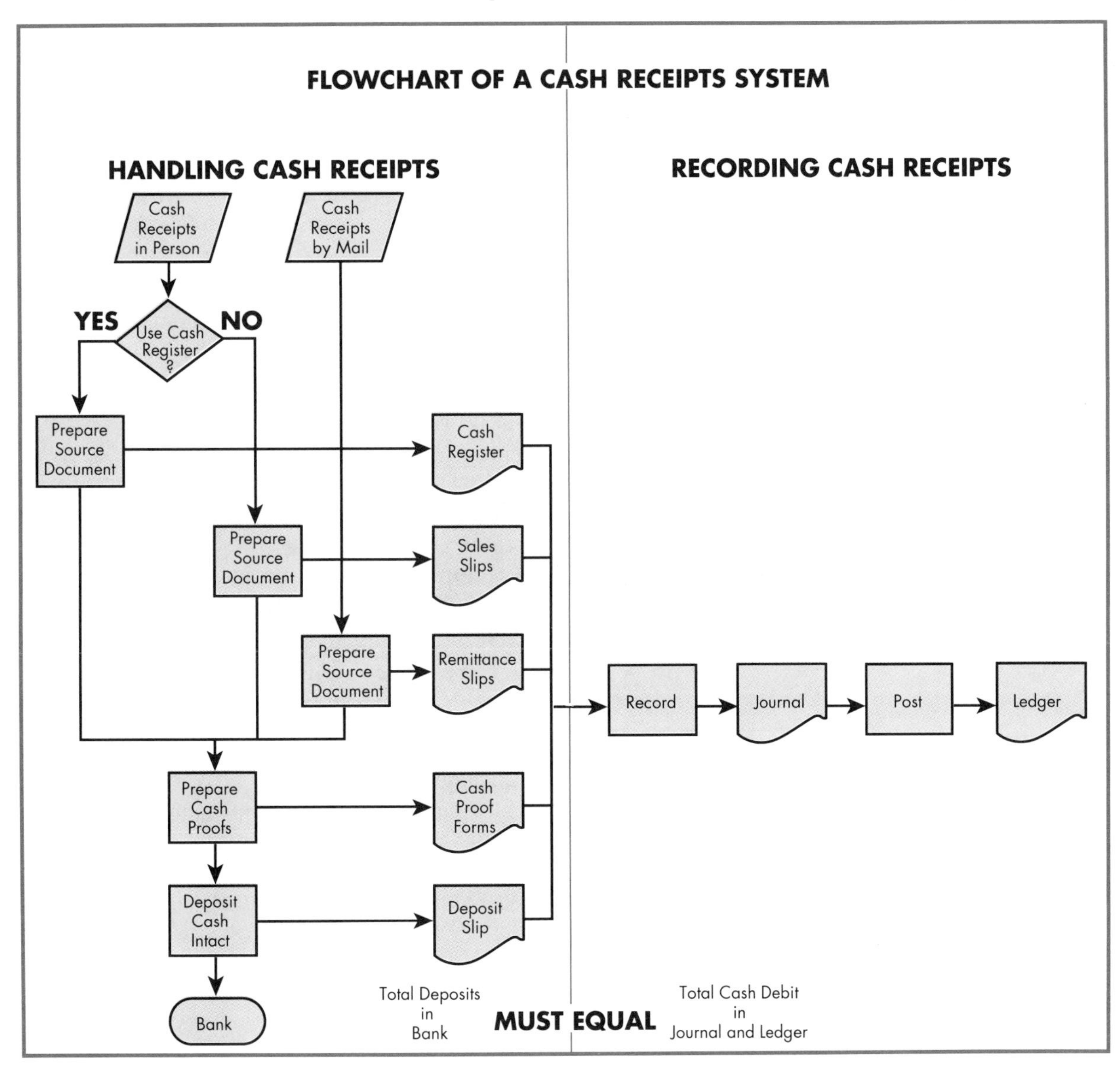

TOPIC 3 PROBLEMS

Preparing a fee bill when cash is received.

P 8-7 The four transactions below represent only a portion of the cash receipts transactions of Dr. Lien Chang's dental practice.

Dec. 4 0003 To Mr. Geoff Dean, XR WF, $43 (X-ray = $15, WF = $28). Mr. Dean promptly paid $43 in cash.

17	0013	To Ms. C. Pratt, $280, for BR. Ms. Pratt issued a cheque for $80 in part payment.
31	0025	Received a cheque for $100 from Mr. H. Vandenberk in part payment of his account.
31	0026	Received a cheque for $103 from Mr. Jack Wilson in full settlement of account.

a. For each dental transaction, prepare the stub and the main dental fee bill portion. Use your initials to indicate the receipt of the bill where necessary.

b. Analyze each dental transaction in General Journal form. As part of the explanation, indicate in which special journal the transaction would be recorded.

Preparing a deposit slip.

P 8-8 Using today's date, prepare a deposit slip for The Janzen Shop, located at 5 Bolton Avenue in your town or city. The firm has a current account numbered 110-734-2 at a nearby bank. A summary of the cash receipts shows the breakdown illustrated below. *Note:* If you have access to an adding machine, itemize the cheques on it and attach the adding machine tape to the deposit slip. If you do not, itemize the cheques on a separate sheet. Record the total of the cheques in the Cheque section of the slip and write the short note ''See separate tape attached.''

Bank of Canada Notes	Coins
2 fifty-dollar bills	148 dollar coins
97 twenty-dollar bills	185 quarters
35 ten-dollar bills	210 dimes
138 five-dollar bills	321 nickels
270 two-dollar bills	380 pennies

Cheques from

D. Shearer, $78.50	D. Stevenson, $110.00	K. Gloster, $24.80
J. MacLean, $62.30	K. Hartsell, $89.00	M. Elliot, $129.75
E. Carleton, $37.90	S. Lindeblom, $23.10	G. McSweeney, $98.40
M. Farewell, $56.00	R. Lewis, $198.75	G. Leal, $225.80
D. Merizzi, $68.90	D. Walduck, $32.80	J. Harrington, $98.56

Preparing a daily cash proof.

P 8-9 You are a cashier supervisor at a retail outlet. At the end of your shift one of the cash drawers contains the following cash:

Bank of Canada Notes	Coins	Cheques
5 fifty-dollar bills	120 dollar coins	$125
30 twenty-dollar bills	84 quarters	$95
46 ten-dollar bills	40 dimes	$178
59 five-dollar bills	38 nickels	
33 two-dollar bills	205 pennies	

The cash register tape provides you with the following information:

Total cash sales	$1 318.30
Cash received on account	845.00
Expenses paid out of drawer	4.65
Daily change fund	50.00

a. Prepare a daily cash proof.

b. What steps would you take if there is a discrepancy in **daily cash proof** between the money in the drawer and the information on the cash register tape?

MINI-CASES

For each case below, identify why cash control is inadequate and suggest an internal control measure that would solve the problem.

Suggesting cash controls for a parking garage.

MC 8-6 Tim George, the owner of a city parking lot, charges a flat fee of $5. He hires two attendants: one to collect cash and supervise parking during the day, and the other to do the same during the evening. To simplify his records system, Tim instructs each attendant to turn over all cash collected at the end of the shift with a simple summary showing the number of parked cars under his or her supervision.

Suggesting cash controls relating to banking procedures.

MC 8-7 Lucy Trocchi, the manager of a large clothing store, has a current account with a nearby bank but, for personal reasons, prefers to deposit cash receipts at the end of the week only. For safekeeping prior to the weekly bank deposit, she puts the cash into a vault in her office. Lucy's weekly cash receipts are in the range of $25 000 to $40 000.

Suggesting cash controls for revenue collections.

MC 8-8 The Students' Council is having a dance, and members are selling tickets for the dance. The tickets are printed with the date and time of the dance. The ticket sellers are also organizing the dance. The treasurer has told them that it would be easier if they paid for any decorations, etc., with the ticket proceeds and then submit to the treasurer the remaining cash after school on the day of the dance.

JOURNALIZING AND POSTING CASH RECEIPTS

With a copy of the source document to prove the existence of a cash receipts transaction, you can now proceed to the second and third steps of the accounting cycle: to record the debits and credits of the cash receipts in a journal and to post the transactions to appropriate accounts.

In this topic, you will learn how to record cash receipts transactions in a special Cash Receipts Journal and to post those transactions from this journal to appropriate accounts in the Accounts Receivable Ledger and the General Ledger.

EXPLORING THE NEED FOR A CASH RECEIPTS JOURNAL

When cash receipt transactions are recorded in a two-column General Journal, the Cash account is debited. The account which is credited depends upon the source of the cash. The two most common sources are cash sales and payments from debtors. A dental practice records a cash sale when a patient pays for services before leaving the office. In the first case, Fees Earned would be increased or credited and in the second case the account receivable would be reduced or credited. Since these entries occur many times in an accounting period, it is easier to summarize them in one journal and then post only monthly to the General Ledger. We discussed the Fees Earned Journal in Topic 2. In this topic, we will examine the special journal for recording cash receipts.

ILLUSTRATING THE CASH RECEIPTS JOURNAL

The illustrations will assume all cash receipts are for payments on account. A Cash Receipts Journal is illustrated on the next page.

POSTING THE CASH RECEIPTS JOURNAL

As you know, posting means transferring information from a journal to an appropriate account in a ledger. When a special journal like the Cash Receipts Journal is used together with the General Ledger and Accounts Receivable Ledger, it is helpful to think of posting in not one but two stages:

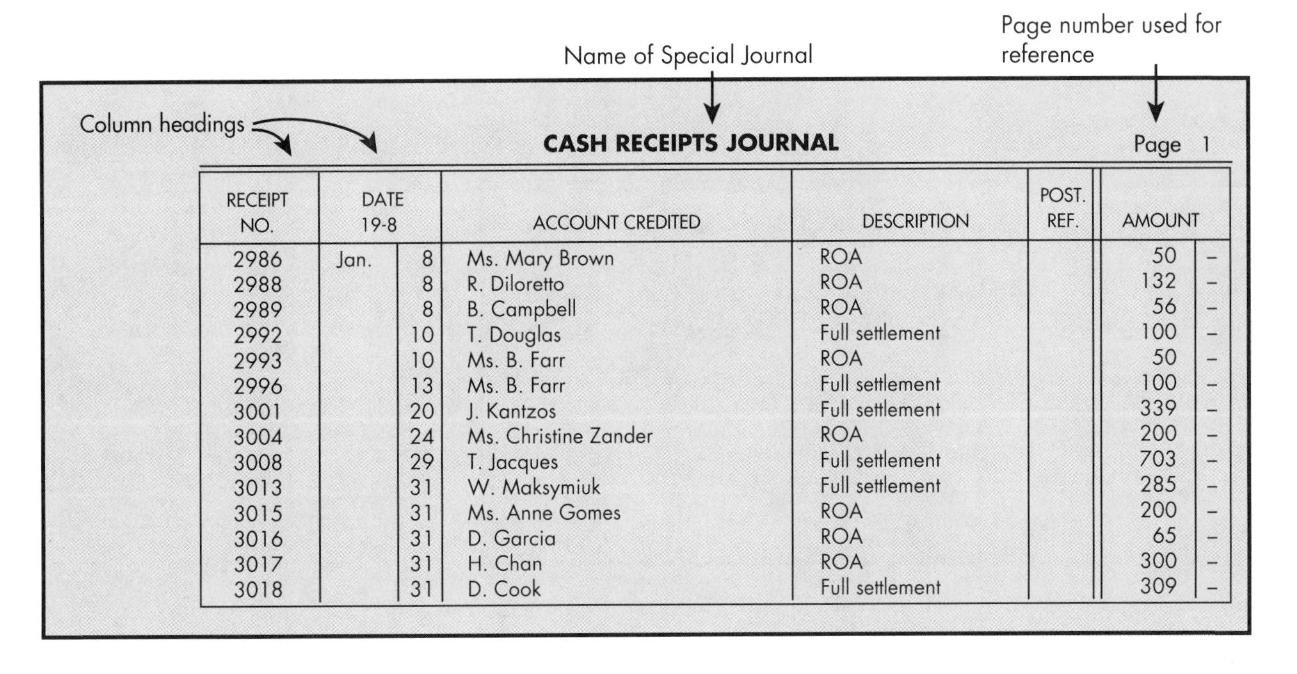

CASH RECEIPTS JOURNAL Page 1

RECEIPT NO.	DATE 19-8		ACCOUNT CREDITED	DESCRIPTION	POST. REF.	AMOUNT	
2986	Jan.	8	Ms. Mary Brown	ROA		50	–
2988		8	R. Diloretto	ROA		132	–
2989		8	B. Campbell	ROA		56	–
2992		10	T. Douglas	Full settlement		100	–
2993		10	Ms. B. Farr	ROA		50	–
2996		13	Ms. B. Farr	Full settlement		100	–
3001		20	J. Kantzos	Full settlement		339	–
3004		24	Ms. Christine Zander	ROA		200	–
3008		29	T. Jacques	Full settlement		703	–
3013		31	W. Maksymiuk	Full settlement		285	–
3015		31	Ms. Anne Gomes	ROA		200	–
3016		31	D. Garcia	ROA		65	–
3017		31	H. Chan	ROA		300	–
3018		31	D. Cook	Full settlement		309	–

- a daily posting (illustrated on page 326) to the Accounts Receivable Ledger (for example, a patient ledger card)
- a month-end posting (illustrated on page 327) of the Amount column total to the Cash account (debit) and Accounts Receivable Control account (credit) and also the Revenue account (Fees Earned) (credit) in the General Ledger

LISTING THE ADVANTAGES OF THE CASH RECEIPTS JOURNAL

Let's summarize the main advantages of using a special journal to record all cash receipts:

- Only one line is required to record an entry in the Cash Receipts Journal; this saves time and space.
- The dollar amount is written only once for each double entry because a Cash debit is understood.
- Valuable time is saved because only the total is posted to the General Ledger at the end of the month. The total is posted to Cash debit, and to the controlling account, Accounts Receivable credit.

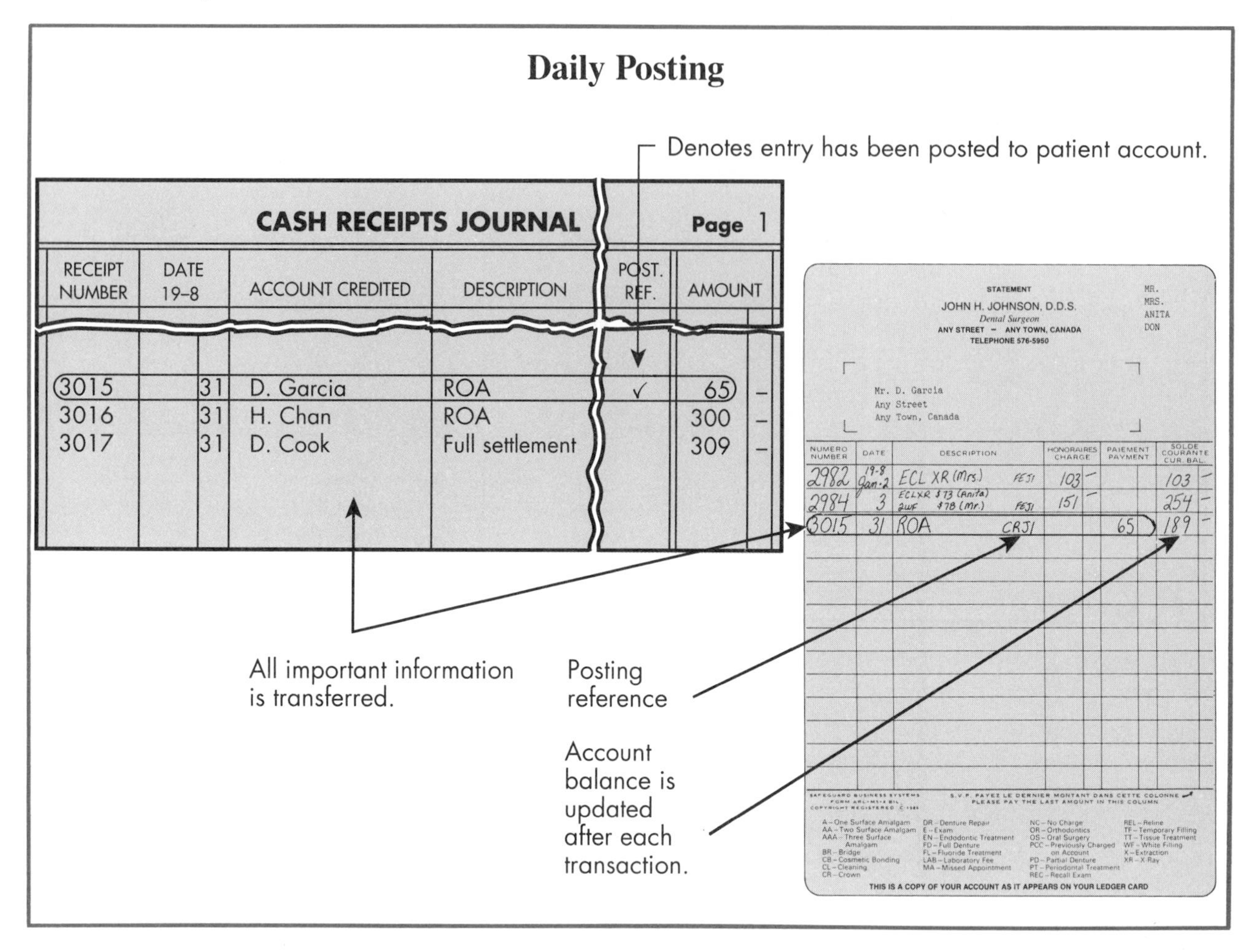

CASH RECEIPTS JOURNAL — Page 1

RECEIPT NUMBER	DATE 19-8	ACCOUNT CREDITED	DESCRIPTION	POST. REF.	AMOUNT
3015	31	D. Garcia	ROA	✓	65 —
3016	31	H. Chan	ROA		300 —
3017	31	D. Cook	Full settlement		309 —

STATEMENT
JOHN H. JOHNSON, D.D.S.
Dental Surgeon
ANY STREET – ANY TOWN, CANADA
TELEPHONE 576-5950

MR.
MRS.
ANITA
DON

Mr. D. Garcia
Any Street
Any Town, Canada

NUMERO NUMBER	DATE	DESCRIPTION		HONORAIRES CHARGE	PAIEMENT PAYMENT	SOLDE COURANTE CUR. BAL.
2982	19-8 Jan. 2	ECL XR (Mrs.)	FEJ1	103 —		103 —
2984	3	ECLXR $73 (Anita) 2WF $78 (Mr.)	FEJ1	151 —		254 —
3015	31	ROA	CRJ1		65	189 —

SAFEGUARD BUSINESS SYSTEMS

S.V.P. PAYEZ LE DERNIER MONTANT DANS CETTE COLONNE
PLEASE PAY THE LAST AMOUNT IN THIS COLUMN

A – One Surface Amalgam
AA – Two Surface Amalgam
AAA – Three Surface Amalgam
BR – Bridge
CB – Cosmetic Bonding
CL – Cleaning
CR – Crown
DR – Denture Repair
E – Exam
EN – Endodontic Treatment
FD – Full Denture
FL – Fluoride Treatment
LAB – Laboratory Fee
MA – Missed Appointment
NC – No Charge
OR – Orthodontics
OS – Oral Surgery
PCC – Previously Charged on Account
PD – Partial Denture
PT – Periodontal Treatment
REC – Recall Exam
REL – Reline
TF – Temporary Filling
TT – Tissue Treatment
WF – White Filling
X – Extraction
XR – X-Ray

THIS IS A COPY OF YOUR ACCOUNT AS IT APPEARS ON YOUR LEDGER CARD

- A division of responsibility among accounting clerks is made possible. In a large firm, one clerk can be responsible for recording and posting credits to Accounts Receivable.

LOOKING BRIEFLY AT THE FEDERAL SALES TAX

The federal government has proposed a 7% Goods and Services Tax (GST). This tax will be levied on services. Therefore, the Fees Earned amount plus the tax amount will total the debit made to Accounts Receivable. Since at the time of writing, physicians' and dentists' fees are to be exempt from the tax, we will not include the tax in our illustrations. The accounting of the GST is treated in Part 3 of the text.

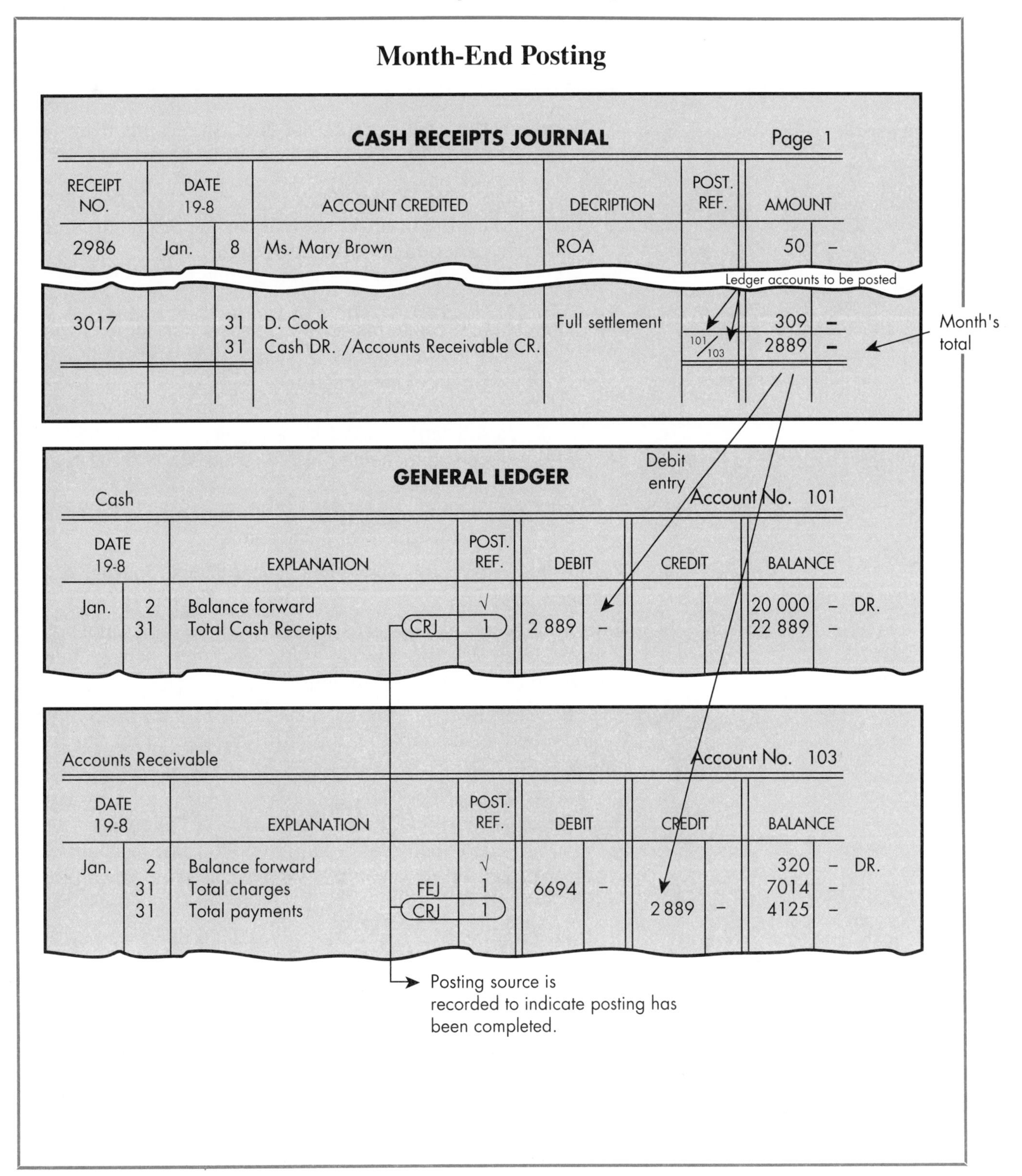
Month-End Posting
CASH RECEIPTS JOURNAL
Page 1
RECEIPT NO.
DATE 19-8
ACCOUNT CREDITED
DECRIPTION
POST. REF.
AMOUNT
2986
Jan.
8
Ms. Mary Brown
ROA
50 –
Ledger accounts to be posted
3017
31
D. Cook
Full settlement
309 –
31
Cash DR. /Accounts Receivable CR.
101/103
2889 –
Month's total
GENERAL LEDGER
Debit entry
Cash
Account No. 101
DATE 19-8
EXPLANATION
POST. REF.
DEBIT
CREDIT
BALANCE
Jan.
2
Balance forward
√
20 000 – DR.
31
Total Cash Receipts
CRJ 1
2 889 –
22 889 –
Accounts Receivable
Account No. 103
DATE 19-8
EXPLANATION
POST. REF.
DEBIT
CREDIT
BALANCE
Jan.
2
Balance forward
√
320 – DR.
31
Total charges
FEJ 1
6694 –
7014 –
31
Total payments
CRJ 1
2 889 –
4125 –
Posting source is recorded to indicate posting has been completed.

PROBLEMS

Journalizing cash receipts.

P 8-10 The transactions below represent the cash receipts from various patients of Dr. L.M. Munro's dental practice for the final week of January, 19-8.

Jan. 26	0001	Ms. M. Micsinski today issued a cheque for $103 in full payment of the dental fee.
28	0003	Mr. L. McGraw issued a cheque for $93 in part payment of his account.
30	0008	Ms. J. Laing paid $106 cash to clear her account.
31	0009	Mr. I. Ryder issued a cheque for $103 in full payment of his dental fee.
31	0010	Received a cheque for $363 from Mr. L. McGraw in full settlement of his account.
31	0011	Received a cheque for $50 from Mr. S. Katz in part payment of his account.
31	0012	Received a cheque for $100 from Mr. S. Ketcheson in part payment of his account.

a. Record the transactions above in a Cash Receipts Journal. Begin on page 1.

b. Refer to Problem 8-5 and its solution. Post the transactions from the Cash Receipts Journal to the separate patient accounts receivable cards used for Problem 8-5.

c. Total the Cash Receipts Journal and show this total **journalized** for the month of January. Then rule off the journal for the month.

d. Set up two General Ledger accounts and post the total from the Cash Receipts Journal to these accounts. *Note:* The Cash account has a debit balance forward of $5000; the Accounts Receivable controlling account has a debit balance forward of $1593.

Journalizing and posting cash receipts to only the General Ledger.

P 8-11 Brian Prong, C.A., owns and operates a tax service bureau in a medium-sized community. All clients are given 30 days in which to pay their bills. Brian uses pre-numbered fee bills which serve also as official receipts when cash is received on account.

a. Open General Ledger accounts and enter account balances forwarded as of March 1, 19-8 as follows: Cash (101), $29 000; Accounts Receivable (103), $4500; Office Equipment (110), $6500; Automobile (112), $20 000; Bank Loan Payable (201), $1200; B. Prong, Capital (301), $58 800.

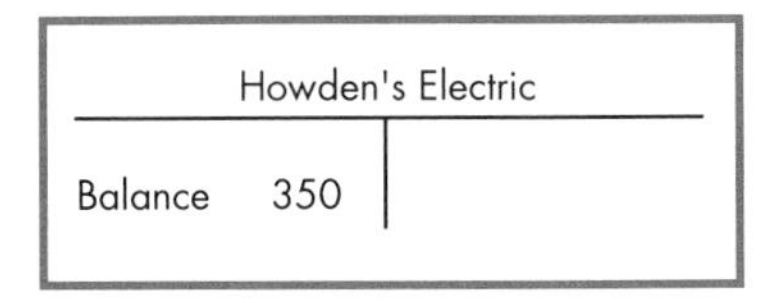

b. Set up a T-account Accounts Receivable Ledger for the following clients: Howden's Electric (balance, $350 DR.), Munro Boats (balance, $650 DR.), J. North (balance, $2000 DR.), Orr Cleaners (balance, $1000 DR.), Wm. A. Smith (balance, $500 DR.). *Note:* In setting up each T-account, show the balance on the proper side. This balance represents the balance carried forward from the previous accounting period.

c. Record the following cash receipts transactions in a Cash Receipts Journal. Number the page with 12.

Mar. 4 Receipt No. 6040. Issued to Howden's Electric for cheque received in full payment of account.
6 Receipt No. 6041. Received a cheque for $650 from Munro Boats in full settlement of account.
10 Receipt No. 6042. J. North appeared at the office to issue his cheque for $1000 in part settlement of his account.
22 Receipt No. 6043. Received a cheque for $500 from Orr Cleaners on account.
28 Receipt No. 6044. Received a cheque for $500 from Wm. A. Smith in full settlement of account.

d. Post the daily entries from the Cash Receipts Journal to the appropriate accounts.

e. Check the addition (using an adding machine tape or the footing procedure), total, and then rule off the Cash Receipts Journal for the month.

f. Post the month-end total from the Cash Receipts Journal to the General Ledger.

Journalizing and posting cash receipts to Accounts Receivable Ledger and General Ledger.

P 8-12 The transactions below represent the cash received from various patients of Dr. Lien Chang's dental practice for the month of December, 19-7.

Dec. 4 0003 Received $43 in cash from Mr. Geoff Dean in full settlement for the dental services rendered today.
17 0013 Received a cheque for $80 from Ms. C. Pratt in part payment of the dental fee charged today.
31 0025 Received a cheque for $100 from Mr. H. Vandenberk in part payment of his account.
31 0026 Received a cheque for $103 from Mr. Jack Wilson in full settlement of account.
31 0027 Received a cheque for $78 from Mr. M. Liepner in full settlement of account.
31 0028 Received a cheque for $252 from Ms. E. Revell in full settlement of account.

31	0029	Received a cheque for $103 from Mr. T. Taller in full settlement of account.
31	0030	Received a cheque for $44 from Mr. T. Murphy in full settlement of account.
31	0031	Received a cheque for $103 from Ms. L. Kretchman in full settlement of account.
31	0032	Mr. B. Gibson appeared at the office to pay $50 cash in part payment of his account.
31	0033	Received a cheque for $100 from Ms. M. Kingsbury in part payment of her account.
31	0034	Received a cheque for $103 from Mr. R. Kendall in full settlement of account.

a. Record the transactions above in a Cash Receipts Journal, page 1.

b. Use the T-accounts in the Accounts Receivable Ledger solved for Problem 8-6 to post the transactions from the Cash Receipts Journal to the individual patient accounts.

c. Use the patient's ledger card set up for Mr. H. Vandenberk in Problem 8-6 to show how this family card would receive the appropriate posting from the Cash Receipts Journal.

d. Check the addition of the Cash Receipts Journal using an adding machine tape or the footing procedure. Total and record the appropriate double entry for this total, then rule off the Cash Receipts Journal for the month.

e. Post the month-end total from the Cash Receipts Journal to the General Ledger. *Note:* The Cash account shows a balance of $10 000. Check the solution to Problem 8-6 for the correct balance forward for Accounts Receivable DR.

MINI-CASES

Designing a Cash Receipts Journal.

MC 8-9 You have been asked by a friend for advice about how to record revenue. Your friend is a student who earns extra money by providing various services to homeowners who wish to have their homes looked after while they are away. These services include: house-sitting; lawn care; pet-sitting; and snow removal. Your friend charges each homeowner on a weekly basis for the house- and pet-sitting, and charges a flat rate each time he mows the lawn or shovels the driveway. He collects the cash upon the return of the homeowner or at the time a lawn is mowed or a driveway shovelled.

a. Design a Cash Receipts Journal for your friend. Make sure to describe why each piece of information recorded in your journal is necessary.

Comparing the special journal to the General Journal.

MC 8-10 Two students were overheard exchanging different views on recording the following transaction: Kim Hall opened a dental practice by investing $100 000 cash in a bank chequing account under the business name, Kim Hall, D.D.S.

Student A insisted that a debit to Cash and a credit to Kim Hall, Capital for $100 000 should be recorded in the Cash Receipts Journal.

Student B countered by insisting that the double entry be recorded in the General Journal.

a. Which student is correct? Give reason(s) to support your answer.

EXPLAINING MONTH-END PROCEDURES AND INTRODUCING THE ONE-WRITE SYSTEM

So far in this chapter you have gone through the first three steps of the accounting cycle for transactions affecting customer (patient) accounts:

Step 1: Originating transaction data through the analysis of the charge on the dental fee bill, and of the payment on the receipted dental fee bill.

Step 2: Journalizing the dental fee in the Fees Earned Journal and journalizing the cash received in the Cash Receipts Journal.

Step 3: Posting transactions daily from the Fees Earned Journal and the Cash Receipts Journal to the patient accounts in the Accounts Receivable Ledger, and posting the monthly total from those special journals to appropriate accounts in the General Ledger.

This topic involves the fourth step of the accounting cycle: preparing monthly trial balances.

PREPARING MONTHLY TRIAL BALANCES

When a General Ledger and one or more subsidiary (secondary) ledgers are used in an accounting system, it is important that a trial balance be taken at the end of each month for each ledger. Also, when many customer account balances appear in the Accounts Receivable Ledger, it is most important to prepare what is known as an **aged trial balance** at month-end.

PREPARING THE GENERAL LEDGER TRIAL BALANCE

In the General Ledger trial balance, all accounts with balances are listed in the order in which they appear in the ledger. The only difference from the trial balances studied earlier is that the controlling account for accounts receivable appears instead of the listing of the individual customer (patient) account balances. Similarly, the controlling account for accounts payable appears instead of the individual creditor accounts. In the case of Dr. Johnson's dental practice (assuming that the fees charged and cash receipts represent the only transactions for the first month of the new accounting period), the monthly General Ledger trial balance would appear as follows:

John H. Johnson, D.D.S.
Trial Balance
January 31, 19–8

ACCOUNT TITLE	POST. REF.	DEBIT		CREDIT	
Cash	101	22 889	00		
Bank Deposit Receipts	102	15 680	00		
Accounts Receivable	103	4 125	00		
Dental Equipment	110	70 000	00		
Office Equipment	112	4 000	00		
Accounts Payable	202			10 000	00
5-Year Note Payable	210			30 000	00
John H. Johnson, Capital	301			70 000	00
Professional Fees Earned	401			6 694	00
		116 694	00	116 694	00

Trial balance: a summary of General Ledger account balances.

The above illustration merely shows the heading Trial Balance. It is understood that the words "General Ledger" go along with this heading; a quick glance at the accounts listed will support this idea. So when you merely see the title "Trial Balance," think of the report as the **General Ledger Trial Balance**.

PREPARING THE ACCOUNTS RECEIVABLE TRIAL BALANCE

Schedule of Accounts Receivable: a list of individual customer account balances.

Posting to the various customer accounts in the Accounts Receivable Ledger is done on a daily basis. To check on the accuracy of this posting for the whole month, the balances of all the accounts in the Accounts Receivable Ledger at the end of the month are listed in a form called the Schedule of Accounts Receivable, as shown below.

John H. Johnson, D.D.S.
Schedule of Accounts Receivable
January 31, 19-8

V. Aviero	1000	00
M. Brown	5	00
B. Campbell	50	00
H. Chan	951	00
R. Diloreto	103	00
A. Gomes	550	00
D. Garcia	189	00
C. Lee	115	00
S. Lesniak	103	00
G. Tuck	567	00
C. Zander	492	00
Total Accounts Receivable	4 125	00

Accounts Receivable — Account No. 103

DATE 19-8		EXPLANATION	POST. REF.	DEBIT		CREDIT		BALANCE		
Jan.	2	Balance forward	✓					320	–	DR.
	31	Total charges FEJ	1	6 694	–			7 014	–	
	31	Total payments CRJ	1			2 889	–	4 125	–	

The total of the Schedule of Accounts Receivable at the end of the month must agree with the balance of the Accounts Receivable controlling account in the GL (General Ledger). In effect, a type of **trial balance** has been made to prove that the subsidiary ledger agrees with the related controlling account in the GL. Notice also the title of the report. The term "Accounts Receivable Trial Balance" might have been used, but to avoid confusion with the trial balance of the

GL, Schedule of Accounts Receivable will be used throughout this textbook.

If the total of the Schedule of Accounts Receivable agrees with the balance in the Accounts Receivable controlling account, the posting to the subsidiary ledger is proved to be accurate. If they are not identical and the General Ledger trial balance has been proved, there must be errors or omissions in the subsidiary ledger. For example, a clerk may have posted a charge directly to a patient's account without including this charge in the Fees Earned Journal. Of course, the mistakes must be identified and corrected before any financial statements are prepared. In general, as a useful internal control measure, **it is essential that the Accounts Receivable account in the General Ledger agree with the Accounts Receivable subsidiary ledger before any financial statements are prepared**.

PREPARING THE AGED TRIAL BALANCE

When a firm has many customer accounts with month-end balances as shown by the Schedule of Accounts Receivable, it is common to prepare an aged trial balance of those receivables.

Aged trial balance: a list of customer account balances according to their "age" (current, 31–60 days, 61–90 days, or over 90 days).

What is meant by "aged"? "Aged" refers to how each customer's month-end balance is listed and indicates whether that balance is currently due or overdue. In giving credit terms, most firms usually award their reliable customers with 30 days from the date of the bill to pay their account in full. Any such balance in a customer's account is then regarded as current—not past due.

On the other hand, if a customer's account balance shows an amount not paid for, say, 40 days from the date of the bill, accountants say that this amount is past due or is **aged** beyond 30 days. To control these past-due or older account balances, accountants recommend the classification of aged amounts under at least the following headings: **31–60 days**, **61–90 days**, and **over 90 days**.

Suppose a patient's account shows the information on page 334.

To age this account, one would say that the $81 shown on Jan. 14, 19-2 is past due between 31–60 days. Therefore, the $81 would be entered in the 31–60 days aged column. The remaining $622 (balance owing of $703 less the $81) is not past due because the date of the charge, February 10, 19-2 is within the current 30-day credit period. This amount would be reported in the current column of the aged trial balance as illustrated.

Analysis: As you can see, amounts past due are clearly indicated. Now the owner/manager must collect the amounts. The longer the amounts remain past due, the less likely the firm will collect these amounts. Remember these important points:

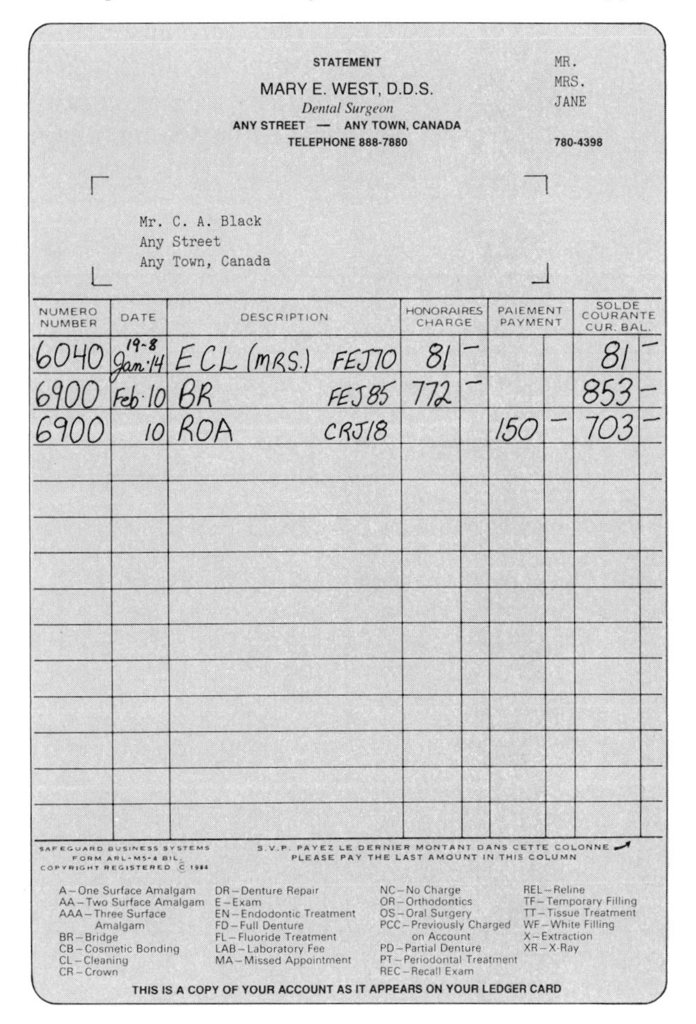

STATEMENT

MARY E. WEST, D.D.S.
Dental Surgeon
ANY STREET — ANY TOWN, CANADA
TELEPHONE 888-7880

MR.
MRS.
JANE

780-4398

Mr. C. A. Black
Any Street
Any Town, Canada

NUMERO NUMBER	DATE	DESCRIPTION		HONORAIRES CHARGE	PAIEMENT PAYMENT	SOLDE COURANTE CUR. BAL.
6040	19-8 Jan. 14	E CL (MRS.)	FEJ70	81 —		81 —
6900	Feb. 10	BR	FEJ85	772 —		853 —
6900	10	ROA	CRJ18		150 —	703 —

SAFEGUARD BUSINESS SYSTEMS
FORM ARL-MS-4 BIL.
COPYRIGHT REGISTERED © 1984

S.V.P. PAYEZ LE DERNIER MONTANT DANS CETTE COLONNE
PLEASE PAY THE LAST AMOUNT IN THIS COLUMN

A–One Surface Amalgam
AA–Two Surface Amalgam
AAA–Three Surface Amalgam
BR–Bridge
CB–Cosmetic Bonding
CL–Cleaning
CR–Crown
DR–Denture Repair
E–Exam
EN–Endodontic Treatment
FD–Full Denture
FL–Fluoride Treatment
LAB–Laboratory Fee
MA–Missed Appointment
NC–No Charge
OR–Orthodontics
OS–Oral Surgery
PCC–Previously Charged on Account
PD–Partial Denture
PT–Periodontal Treatment
REC–Recall Exam
REL–Reline
TF–Temporary Filling
TT–Tissue Treatment
WF–White Filling
X–Extraction
XR–X-Ray

THIS IS A COPY OF YOUR ACCOUNT AS IT APPEARS ON YOUR LEDGER CARD

- Overdue accounts receivable may never be collected. This means having to account for what are known as bad debts. Of course, bad debts result in extra expenses which decrease the firm's net income and even may result in a net loss. (The accounting of bad debts is explained in Chapter 15.)
- Overdue accounts receivable mean that the owner has no money coming in within an expected time (within 30 days). This means a poor **cash flow**. If money is not coming in on time from receivables, the owner may have to borrow money to pay the firm's accounts payable. And borrowing money means extra accounting for an extra cost called interest expense, which can also lead to future net losses.

- Overdue accounts receivable also mean that the business cannot invest the amounts which should be flowing in. If the business thus loses the opportunity to invest, it is actually losing the chance to make more money through interest earned or dividends earned on investments. We call such losses "opportunity costs."

Mary E. West, D.D.S
Aged Trial Balance as of February 28, 19-8

Family Name	Phone No.	Total Owing	Current	Days Past Due			Current Month	
				31-60	61-90	Over 90	Debits	Credits
J. Acker	487-7890	42.00				42.00		
C.A. Black	780-4398	703.00	622.00	81.00			772.00	150.00
S. Byrd	459-6070	204.00			204.00			
J. Cruse	236-8902	59.00		52.00		7.00	52.00	100.00
E. Doney	679-4598	100.00				100.00		
E. Flynn	579-8945	19.00	153.00			19.00		
B. Goetz	887-4532	153.00	100.00				153.00	
E. Harris	334-2378	100.00	100.00				100.00	
J. Jacobs	456-0990	981.00	2.00	100.00	100.00	681.00	100.00	
L. Larsen	324-0345	109.00		107.00			302.00	300.00
M. Matz	567-9823	20.00			20.00			
H. Novak	456-4588	15.00	375.00			15.00		
W. Petty	234-6789	523.00		148.00			875.00	500.00
J. Robey	788-8000	306.00	2.00	274.00		32.00	274.00	400.00
T. Schmidt	471-8666	109.00		107.00			302.00	300.00

Controlling a firm's accounts receivable, therefore, is just as important as controlling the asset Cash. One way of controlling accounts receivable is to take time to (1) prepare an aged trial balance each month, (2) study the results, and (3) take steps to get the debtors to pay.

For Dr. Johnson's practice, an aged trial balance as of February 28, 19-8, from the data presented in this chapter, is illustrated on page 337.

PREPARING THE STATEMENT OF ACCOUNT

Statement of account: a statement mailed monthly to a customer showing the balance the customer owes.

One step taken by many firms to control their accounts receivable is to prepare a statement of account. In some businesses, a statement of account is mailed to each customer (or patient) showing a month-end balance on the Schedule of Accounts Receivable. Since preparing and mailing many monthly statements is costly, dental practices (and

John H. Johnson, D.D.s
Aged Trial Balance

Family Name	Phone No.	Total Owing	Current	Days Past Due		Over 90	Current Month	
				31-60	61-90		Debits	Credits
V. Aviero	449-3345	1000.00	1000.00				1000.00	
M. Brown	240-8463	5.00	5.00				55.00	50.00
B. Campbell	489-7772	50.00	50.00				50.00	
H. Chan	457-8976	951.00	951.00				1 251.00	300.00
R. Diloreto	324-0090	103.00	103.00				235.00	132.00
A. Gomes	443-1177	550.00	550.00				750.00	200.00
D. Garcia	678-0923	189.00	189.00				254.00	65.00
C. Lee	432-0987	115.00	115.00				115.00	
S. Lesniak	323-4356	103.00	103.00				103.00	
G. Tuck	679-9834	567.00	567.00				567.00	
C. Zander	299-0093	492.00	492.00				692.00	200.00

other businesses) often send statements only to those customers whose accounts are past due.

The type of statement of account prepared will vary with management's methods of keeping costs down. The simplest shows only the balance due at the end of the month. This type of statement is used by some professional people. For example, an accountant may prepare a statement of account as shown below.

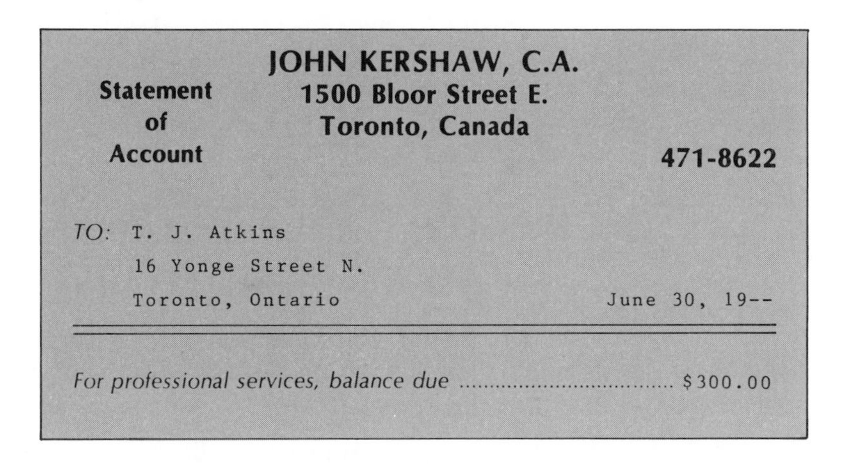
Statement of Account

JOHN KERSHAW, C.A.
1500 Bloor Street E.
Toronto, Canada

471-8622

TO: T. J. Atkins
16 Yonge Street N.
Toronto, Ontario

June 30, 19--

For professional services, balance due $300.00

Many businesses, including professional practices, prefer to make a photocopy of the customer's (patient's) ledger card once this card is completely posted for the month. In the case of Dr. Johnson's dental practice, the copy of Mr. D. Garcia's ledger card would appear as shown on the opposite page.

STATEMENT

JOHN H. JOHNSON, D.D.S.
Dental Surgeon
ANY STREET – ANY TOWN, CANADA
TELEPHONE 576-5950

MR.
MRS.
ANITA
DON

Mr. D. Garcia
Any Street
Any Town, Canada

NUMERO NUMBER	DATE	DESCRIPTION	HONORAIRES CHARGE	PAIEMENT PAYMENT	SOLDE COURANTE CUR. BAL
2982	19-8 Jan. 2	ECL XR (Mrs.) FEJ1	103 —		103 —
2984	3	ECLXR $73 (Anita) 2WF $78 (Mr.) FEJ1	151 —		254 —
3015	31	ROA CRJ1		65 —	189 —

S.V.P. PAYEZ LE DERNIER MONTANT DANS CETTE COLONNE
PLEASE PAY THE LAST AMOUNT IN THIS COLUMN

A – One Surface Amalgam
AA – Two Surface Amalgam
AAA – Three Surface Amalgam
BR – Bridge
CB – Cosmetic Bonding
CL – Cleaning
CR – Crown
DR – Denture Repair
E – Exam
EN – Endodontic Treatment
FD – Full Denture
FL – Fluoride Treatment
LAB – Laboratory Fee
MA – Missed Appointment
NC – No Charge
OR – Orthodontics
OS – Oral Surgery
PCC – Previously Charged on Account
PD – Partial Denture
PT – Periodontal Treatment
REC – Recall Exam
REL – Reline
TF – Temporary Filling
TT – Tissue Treatment
WF – White Filling
X – Extraction
XR – X-Ray

THIS IS A COPY OF YOUR ACCOUNT AS IT APPEARS ON YOUR LEDGER CARD

Where computers are used to process the accounts receivable application, it is common to prepare an aged monthly statement of account.

This statement shows the amounts currently due and the ones past due in ages of 31–60 days, 61–90 days, and over 90 days.

USING THE ONE-WRITE SYSTEM FOR THE ACCOUNTS RECEIVABLE APPLICATION

Traditional bookkeeping method: journalizing and posting data in separate steps.

So far you have learned the accounting of the accounts receivable application using the traditional bookkeeping method. The steps of this method are

- preparing a fee bill
- recording the amount in the Fees Earned Journal
- posting the amount to the patient's account in three separate steps
- preparing at month-end a statement of the patient's (or customer's) account

This method can give rise to several problems:

- Errors are often made when a clerk copies data incorrectly from one accounting form to another. For example, he or she may post the wrong debit figure from the Revenue Journal to the patient's account.
- Extra time is required to record the same information repeatedly. For example, the charge is recorded on the fee bill and is then copied to the journal, and again to the patient's account. This time could have been used for other accounting tasks.
- When the volume of transactions grows, there may not be time to post debits and credits to each customer's account for one or two days or perhaps not until month-end. Consequently, the true balance of an account cannot be determined for some time, perhaps a long time, after the transaction takes place.

To eliminate these shortcomings, many dental firms, as well as other small businesses, use shortcuts. One shortcut is to use one of the many computerized accounting systems available that are programmed to complete the steps in recording revenue and receipt transactions with one entry. However, not all businesses can afford to computerize and therefore use another manual shortcut which combines the separate steps. This manual system is known as the one-write system.

One-write system: a system of preparing more than one accounting document and record in a single step.

The user of the one-write system uses carbon paper to prepare the source documents and accounting entries at the same time. Refer to the illustration on the opposite page. You can see that by placing the patient's account underneath the fee bill and both on top of the Fees Earned Journal, the entries made on the fee bill by the bookkeeper are transferred directly to the patient account and the Fees Earned Journal. This means that the source document (fee bill), the journal entry (Fees Earned Journal), and the posting to the ledger (patient's account) are completed all in one writing. The Fees Earned Journal in this system is also the Cash Receipts Journal and therefore the cash receipt transactions can be recorded in one step by aligning the forms in a similar way.

If you had the available forms, you could complete the problems assigned in Topics 1 through 5 using the one-write system. You would find that the time required to complete each problem would be reduced and that your records would balance each time.

We have discussed the use of the one-write system as it may be used by a dental firm. However, it is not the only type of business which uses this system. Many other professional and service businesses which have one source of revenue also use a one-write system. In addition, there are one-write systems for the accounts payable and payroll applications.

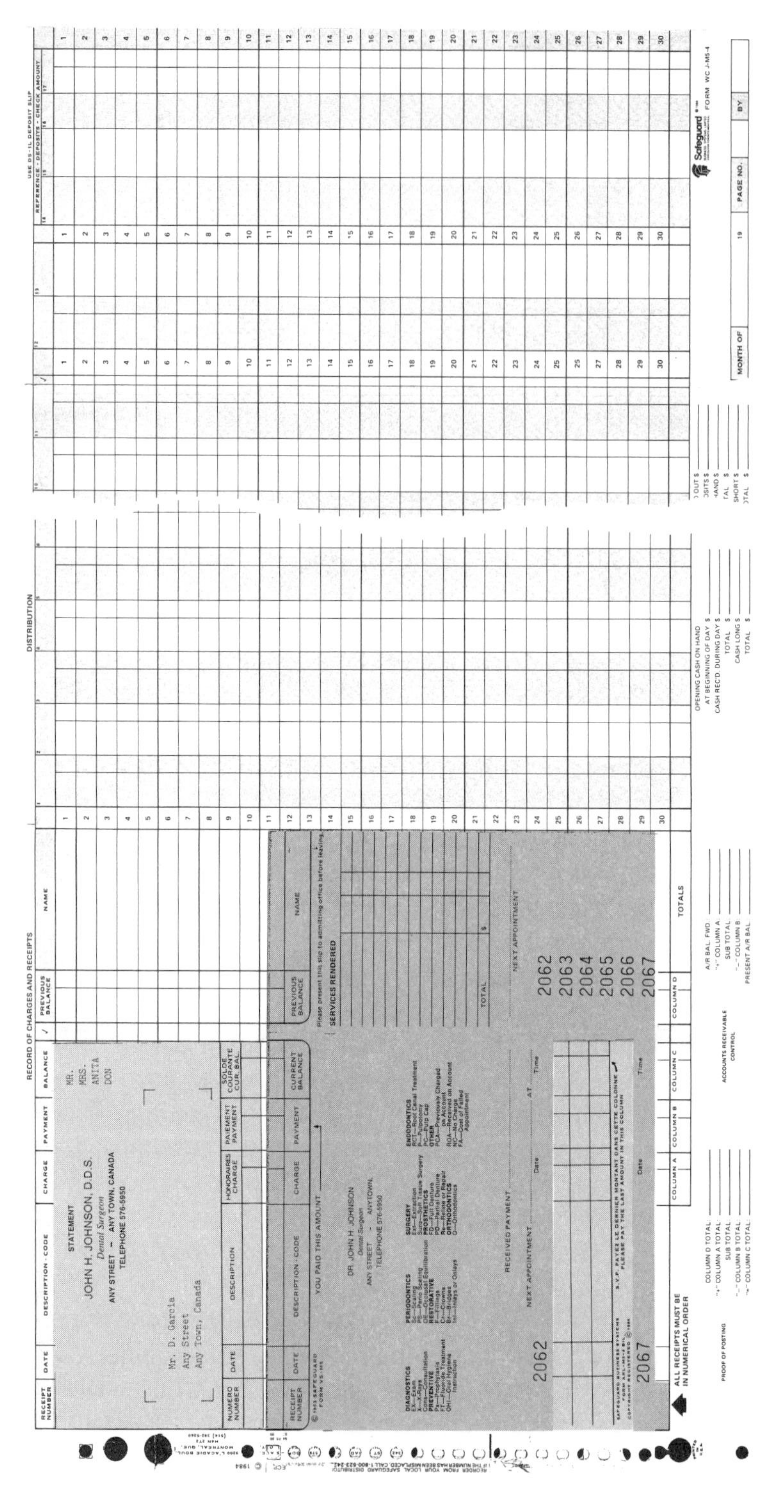

RECORD OF CHARGES AND RECEIPTS — DISTRIBUTION — USE DS-1L DEPOSIT SLIP

RECEIPT NUMBER	DATE	DESCRIPTION - CODE	CHARGE	PAYMENT	BALANCE	✓	PREVIOUS BALANCE	NAME

STATEMENT

JOHN H. JOHNSON, D.D.S.
Dental Surgeon
ANY STREET — ANY TOWN, CANADA
TELEPHONE 576-5950

MR.
MRS.
ANITA
DON

Mr. D. Garcia
Any Street
Any Town, Canada

NUMERO NUMBER	DATE	DESCRIPTION	HONORAIRES CHARGE	PAIEMENT PAYMENT	SOLDE COURANTE CUR. BAL.

RECEIPT NUMBER	DATE	DESCRIPTION - CODE	CHARGE	PAYMENT	CURRENT BALANCE	PREVIOUS BALANCE	NAME

YOU PAID THIS AMOUNT

Please present this slip to admitting office before leaving.

SERVICES RENDERED

TOTAL $

DR. JOHN H. JOHNSON
Dental Surgeon
ANY STREET — ANYTOWN,
TELEPHONE 576-5950

RECEIVED PAYMENT

NEXT APPOINTMENT .... Date .... AT .... Time

NEXT APPOINTMENT

2062
2063
2064
2065
2066
2067

S.V.P. PAYEZ LE DERNIER MONTANT DANS CETTE COLONNE
PLEASE PAY THE LAST AMOUNT IN THIS COLUMN

ALL RECEIPTS MUST BE IN NUMERICAL ORDER

COLUMN A | COLUMN B | COLUMN C | COLUMN D | TOTALS

PROOF OF POSTING: COLUMN D TOTAL; "+" COLUMN A TOTAL; SUB TOTAL; "−" COLUMN B TOTAL; "+" COLUMN C TOTAL

ACCOUNTS RECEIVABLE CONTROL: A/R BAL. FWD.; "+" COLUMN A; SUB TOTAL; "−" COLUMN B; PRESENT A/R BAL.

OPENING CASH ON HAND AT BEGINNING OF DAY $; CASH REC'D. DURING DAY $; TOTAL $; CASH LONG $; TOTAL $

MONTH OF .... 19 .... PAGE NO. .... BY ....

Safeguard FORM WC J-MS-4

TOPIC 5 PROBLEMS

Setting up the books for a new dental practice.

P 8-13 Challenge Problem On March 1, Dr. Robert Wong, D.D.S., acquired a dental practice from a retired dentist. Dr. Wong's opening balance sheet revealed the following: Cash, $50 000; Accounts Receivable, $2400; Dental Supplies on Hand, $5000; Dental Equipment, $70 000; Office Equipment, $5000; Furniture, $2600; Bank Loan Payable, $35 000.

a. In a General Journal, page 1, make the opening entry to record the assets, liabilities, and owner's equity reported in the opening balance sheet of March 1.

b. Open the following General Ledger accounts with account numbers as indicated in parentheses: Cash (101), Accounts Receivable (103), Dental Supplies on Hand (105), Dental Equipment (110), Office Equipment (112), Furniture (114), Bank Loan Payable (201), Robert Wong, Capital (301), Professional Fees Earned (401).

c. Post the opening entry from the General Journal to the appropriate accounts in the General Ledger.

d. Set up separate patient accounts receivable cards to make up the Accounts Receivable Ledger for the following patients (names in parentheses represent **the other family members**): Mr. J.M. Boersema (Mrs.), Ms. H. Cheng, Mrs. Helen Dye, Mr. H. Fisher (Mrs., Terry), Ms. Janet Gamble (new patient), Mr. R. Green (Mrs., Linda, Jim), Mrs. Jane Kaplan, Mr. John Lee (new patient), Mr. R. Mandel (Mrs., Betty, Barbara), Ms. Pat Nash (new patient). For each patient, invent appropriate street and city or town addresses.

e. For each old patient account acquired by the business, record the following balance forward as of March 1: Mr. J.M. Boersema, balance of $100; Ms. H. Cheng, balance of $200; Mrs. Helen Dye, balance of $250; Mr. H. Fisher, balance of $500; Mr. R. Green, balance of $175; Mrs. Jane Kaplan, balance of $450; Mr. R. Mandel, balance of $725.

Note: Keep all forms for use in the next question.

Completing all the steps in the accounts receivable application.

P 8-14 Challenge Problem The transactions below represent the dental fees charged and the cash received from the various patients of Dr. Robert Wong's dental practice for the month of March, 19-7.

Mar. 2 1001 Mr. John Lee. E CL, total fee of $103. No payment received.

3	1002	Received cheque for $100 from Mr. J.M. Boersema in full settlement of account.
6	1003	Mr. R. Mandel. E CL, total fee of $103. No payment received.
7	1004	Ms. Janet Gamble. Total fee of $115 for XR, E, and CL. Received $20 cash in part payment of account.
9	1005	Ms. Pat Nash. EX PRO, total fee of $103. Received $55 cash on account.
10	1006	Received cheque for $175 from Mr. R. Green in full settlement of account.
13	1007	Received cheque for $100 from Mrs. Helen Dye, in part payment of account.
14	1008	Total charge of $900 to Mrs. Boersema, wife of Mr. J.M. Boersema, for a bridge. No payment was received.
15	1009	Total charge of $650 to Mr. John Lee for a crown. Received a cheque for $100 in part payment of account.
16	1010	Received a cheque for $500 from Mr. H. Fisher in full settlement of account.
17	1011	Received a cheque for $150 from Mrs. Jane Kaplan in part payment of account.
20	1012	Received a cheque for $48 from Ms. Pat Nash in full settlement of account.
21	1013	Total fee charged to Mr. R. Green for dental services rendered to Linda, his daughter, $90 for a white filling. No payment received.
22	1014	Received a cheque for $150 from Mrs. Helen Dye in full settlement of account.
23	1015	Ms. Pat Nash, total fee of $400 charged for gold inlay. No payment received.
24	1016	Received a cheque for $95 from Ms. Janet Gamble in full settlement of account.
27	1017	Received a cheque for $500 from Mr. R. Mandel in part settlement of account.
28	1018	Received a cheque for $200 from Ms. H. Cheng in full settlement of account.
29	1019	Ms. Janet Gamble. Total fee of $1600 charged for root canal treatment. No payment received.
30	1020	Received a cheque for $100 from Mr. J.M. Boersema on account.
31	1021	To Terry, son of Mr. H. Fisher, total fee of $45 charged for tooth extraction. No payment received.

31 1022 Received from Mrs. Jane Kaplan a cheque for $50, on account.

a. Analyze each of the dental transactions summarized above. Then record each **charge** in a Fees Earned Journal, page 1. Also record each **payment** in a Cash Receipts Journal, page 1.

b. On a **daily basis**, post the information from the special journals to appropriate patient accounts receivable cards. (Use the Accounts Receivable Ledger established in Problem 8-13.)

c. Total the Fees Earned Journal and the Cash Receipts Journal and show each total **journalized** for the month of March.

d. Post the total from each special journal to appropriate accounts in the General Ledger. Use the General Ledger prepared for Problem 8-13.

e. Prepare a trial balance of both the General Ledger and the Accounts Receivable Ledger.

MINI-CASES

Analyzing errors made at month-end.

MC 8-11 You are the bookkeeper for Dr. Rejean Seguin, Orthodontist. You are completing the month-end procedures and find the Schedule of Accounts Receivable does not agree with the Accounts Receivable account in the General Ledger.

a. List five reasons why this situation might arise.

b. What procedures would you follow to discover the reason for the discrepancy?

Analyzing the effect of posting errors.

MC 8-12 A dental fee of $375, paid in cash, was recorded correctly in the Cash Receipts Journal but posted manually to the debit side of the Fees Earned account.

a. By how much would the trial balance be out of balance? Show your calculation.

b. What type of error has been made?

c. If this were the only error, what test would indicate that this type of error has been made?

Discussing the one-write system.

MC 8-13 Mary has just been hired as a receptionist/clerk in the Town Centre Dental Office. Among her duties, Mary will be required to bill patients and to record accounts receivable transactions in a one-write system.

Although Mary has studied some accounting at high school, she admits to no knowledge of the one-write system.

Assume that she approaches you to obtain an introduction to the accounting of patients' accounts receivable on a one-write system.

a. Briefly explain in words Mary can understand the meaning of a one-write system.

b. ''Walk'' Mary through a typical dental service for a new patient. Briefly explain the setting up of a new patient's ledger card, the forms required and the order of placing those forms on the one-write board, and how the bill is made out.

c. Explain two advantages offered by the one-write system over the traditional manual method of accounting for the same transaction.

d. Explain two limitations of the one-write system.

Note: The Comprehensive Case Study for Chapter 8 is at the end of Chapter 11. It is part of a large exercise which reviews all the systems discussed in Part 2.

CHAPTER 9

THE ACCOUNTS PAYABLE APPLICATION

Topic 1
Originating and Analyzing Accounts Payable Transactions

Topic 2
Journalizing and Posting the Transactions

Topic 3
Controlling and Accounting for Cash Payments

Topic 4
Reviewing Month-End Procedures

The accounts payable application deals with two related transactions: (1) the purchase of assets or services on account or credit, and (2) the cash payment to creditors to eliminate the accounts payable.

Many firms purchase all of their assets and expenses on a credit basis. This means that for every debit to an asset account or an expense account there will be a credit to accounts payable. These transactions are, therefore, part of the accounts payable application —accounting of supplier accounts.

TOPIC 1 ORIGINATING AND ANALYZING ACCOUNTS PAYABLE TRANSACTIONS

Invoice: a bill of sale made out by the vendor (seller).

To carry on his dental practice, Dr. Johnson must acquire goods and services, for example, dental supplies and telephone services, from various suppliers. The supplier will provide Dr. Johnson with an invoice which is the source document for the purchase transaction. This invoice represents the sales invoice for the preparer/supplier and a purchase invoice for the receiver/purchaser.

We will review three transactions to illustrate the purchase of assets and expenses.

Transaction 1

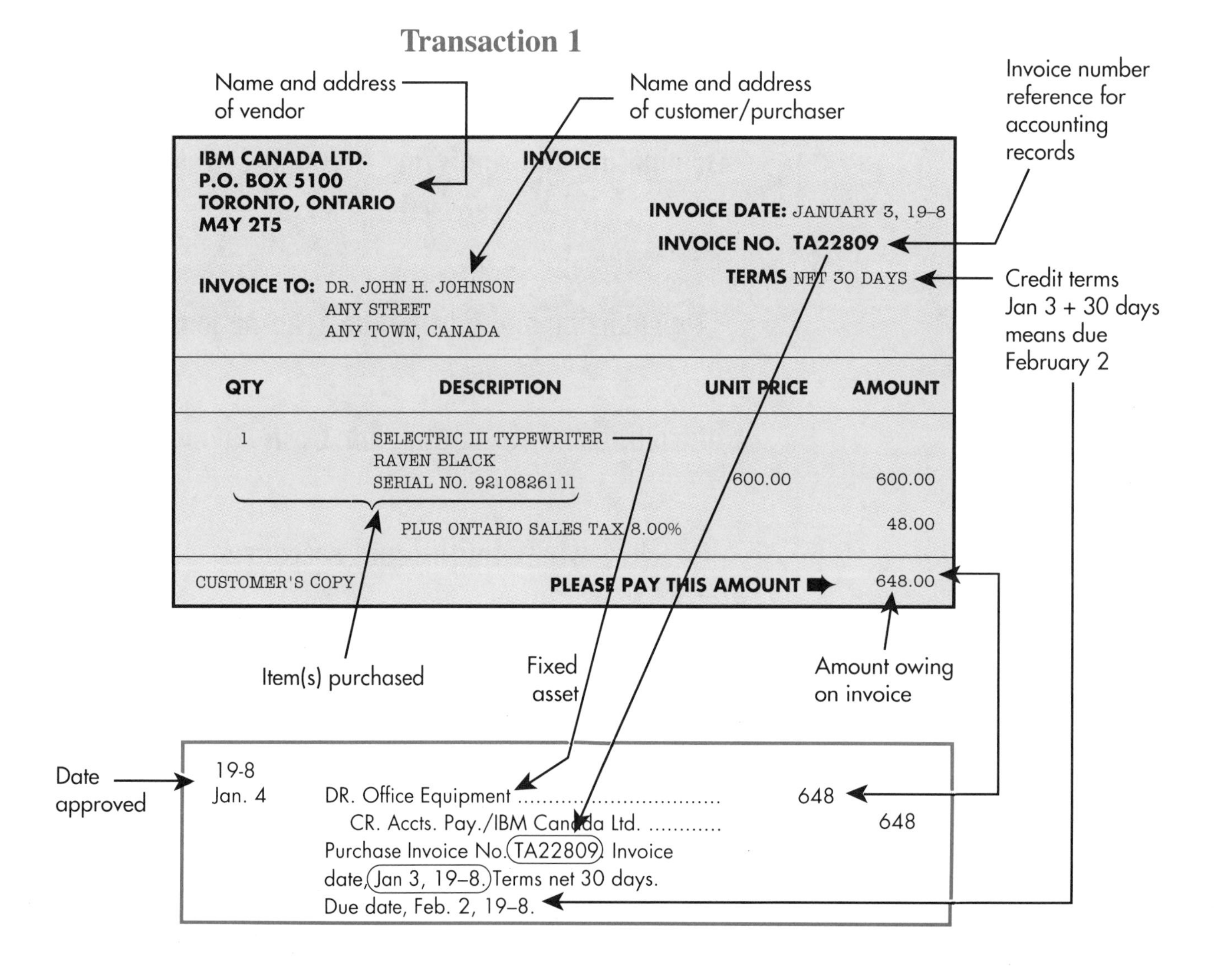

We can apply three GAAPs to this transaction.

- The **objectivity principle** states that all transactions must be supported by proof. The purchase invoice provides the "proof" of the purchase of a fixed asset and establishes the date for the transaction.

Cost as defined in the cost principle: the cash equivalent price on the invoice as of the day of receiving and approving that invoice.

- The **cost principle** states that the transaction must be recorded at the business's "laid-down cost." The laid-down cost is the cost incurred by the business to put the asset into service. Therefore, it can include such costs as transportation charge, excise tax, duty, or installation charge. The amount recorded for cost should be the cash equivalent price on the invoice(s) as of the day of receiving and approving the invoice. The meaning of cash equivalent price is explained in Transaction 3.
- The **cost principle** states that the asset must remain on the books at the originally recorded cost known as the "historical cost." For this reason you will see fixed assets disclosed on financial statements with the term "at cost" beside the heading. See the marginal note for an illustration.

John H. Johnson, D.D.S.
Partial Balance Sheet
As at January 2, 19-8

FIXED ASSETS (at cost):	
Dental Equipment	$70 000
Office Equipment	4 000

Transaction 2

Another invoice received and approved by Dr. Johnson on January 5 is illustrated on page 348.

This invoice shows the application of the objectivity principle and the cost principle, as well as the expense principle.

Expired cost: expenditure for an item used to earn revenue.

The **expense principle** states that expenses should be recognized when incurred. This means that the cost is recorded as an expense when the item has been used to earn revenue (expired) and not when the cash is paid. Although the dental supplies are not used up on the day they are purchased, they have been recorded as an expense. This would seem to violate the expense principle. However, the cost of the dental supplies can be correctly recorded as an expense even though they have not been used up, because by the end of the accounting period they will have been used. If some of the supplies are still on hand, an adjusting entry will be made to correct the ledger. These entries will be discussed in Part 3 of the textbook.

Transaction 3

Assume Dr. Johnson receives a third purchase invoice on January 6. This invoice is illustrated on page 349.

The objectivity principle and expense principle are illustrated in this entry as they were in the prior two transactions.

The amount that is recorded as the cost of the utility expense represents a different application of the cost principle. This principle states that the amount to be recorded should be equal to the cash equivalent price on the invoice as of the day of receiving and approving the invoice. The invoice states that if it is paid before January 18

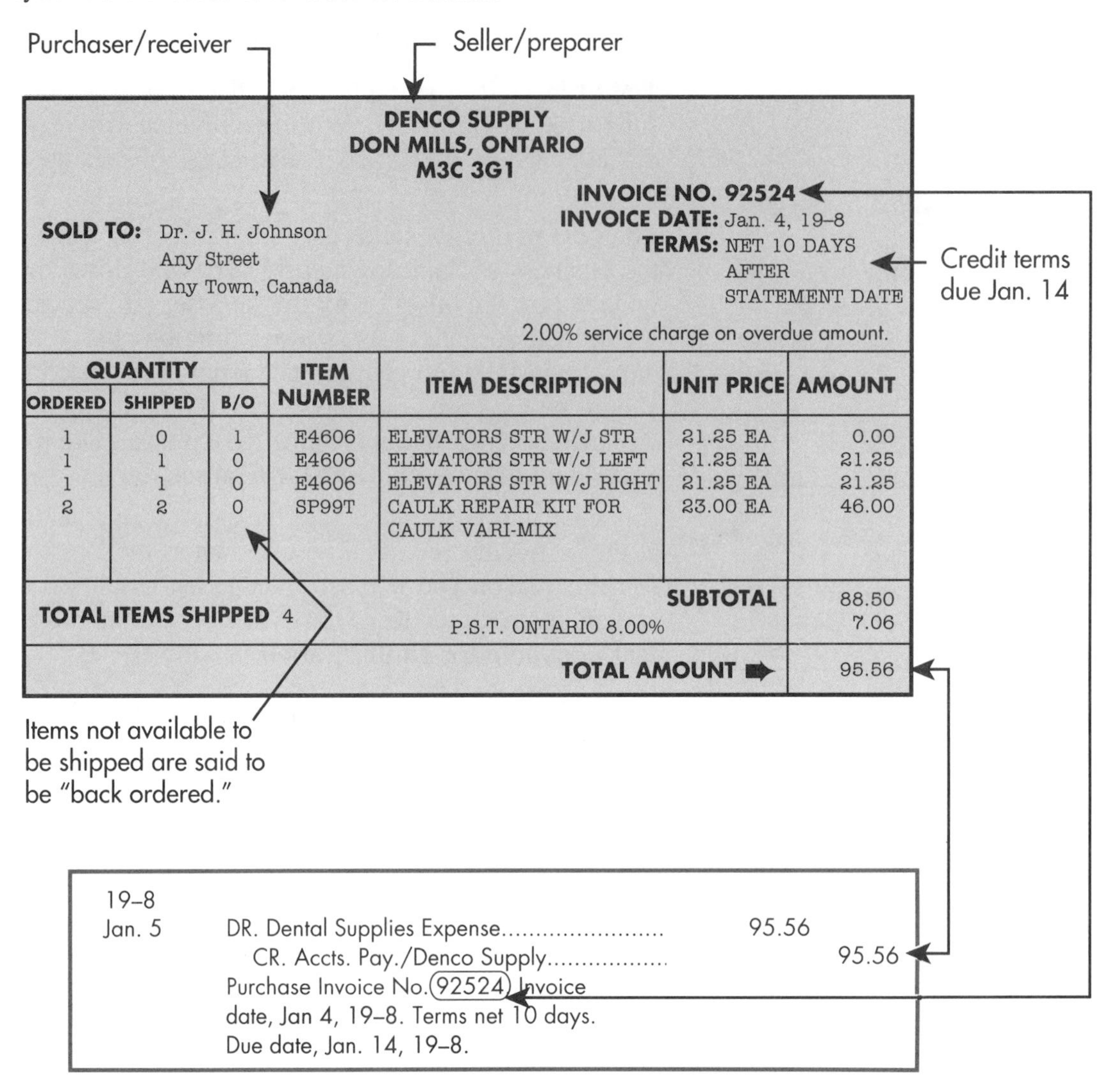
DENCO SUPPLY
DON MILLS, ONTARIO
M3C 3G1

INVOICE NO. 92524
INVOICE DATE: Jan. 4, 19–8
TERMS: NET 10 DAYS AFTER STATEMENT DATE

SOLD TO: Dr. J. H. Johnson
Any Street
Any Town, Canada

2.00% service charge on overdue amount.

QUANTITY			ITEM NUMBER	ITEM DESCRIPTION	UNIT PRICE	AMOUNT
ORDERED	SHIPPED	B/O				
1	0	1	E4606	ELEVATORS STR W/J STR	21.25 EA	0.00
1	1	0	E4606	ELEVATORS STR W/J LEFT	21.25 EA	21.25
1	1	0	E4606	ELEVATORS STR W/J RIGHT	21.25 EA	21.25
2	2	0	SP99T	CAULK REPAIR KIT FOR CAULK VARI-MIX	23.00 EA	46.00
TOTAL ITEMS SHIPPED 4					SUBTOTAL	88.50
					P.S.T. ONTARIO 8.00%	7.06
					TOTAL AMOUNT	95.56

19–8			
Jan. 5	DR. Dental Supplies Expense	95.56	
	CR. Accts. Pay./Denco Supply		95.56
	Purchase Invoice No. 92524 Invoice date, Jan 4, 19–8. Terms net 10 days. Due date, Jan. 14, 19–8.		

Discounts lost expense: additional amount paid for an expense because payment was made too late to take advantage of a lower cost.

the amount due is $61.75 and not the gross amount of $65.00. Therefore, the correct amount, or the discounted price, is $61.75. What if Dr. Johnson did not pay in time and was subsequently forced to pay the amount due after January 18, that is, the gross amount? The credit to Cash would be greater than the debit to the account payable. This difference would be recorded as a debit to an account called Discounts Lost Expense This account accumulates the extra amounts

PUBLIC UTILITIES COMMISSION
BOX 3060 ANY TOWN, CANADA **01 095 08184 02**

Inquiries – 8:15 to 4:30 – Monday to Friday Telephone: 679-5503

DR. J.H. JOHNSON **ANY STREET** **ANY TOWN, CANADA**

READING DATE	JAN 03, 19–8	
ELECTRIC READING	0000	
WATER READING	0000	
ELECTRIC	0000 KWH	0.00
WATER	0000 CU FT	0.00
INSTALLATION CHARGES		65.00
AMOUNT DUE IF PAID AFTER JAN. 18		65.00 E & O E
AMOUNT DUE IF PAID BY JAN. 18		61.75

Cost equivalent if paid date approved January 6

19–8			
Jan. 6	DR. Utilities Expense..................................	61.75	
	CR. Accts. Pay./Public Utilities Commission..		61.75
	Utility bill No. 01 095 08184 02. Date of bill, Jan. 3, 19–8. Due date, Jan. 18, 19–8.		

paid for expenses — the differences between the gross prices and the discounted prices. Of course, not taking advantage of discounted prices will reduce the business's net income and therefore the owner should take steps to ensure that payments are made in time to take advantage of the cost savings.

Journal Entry for Payment After January 18th

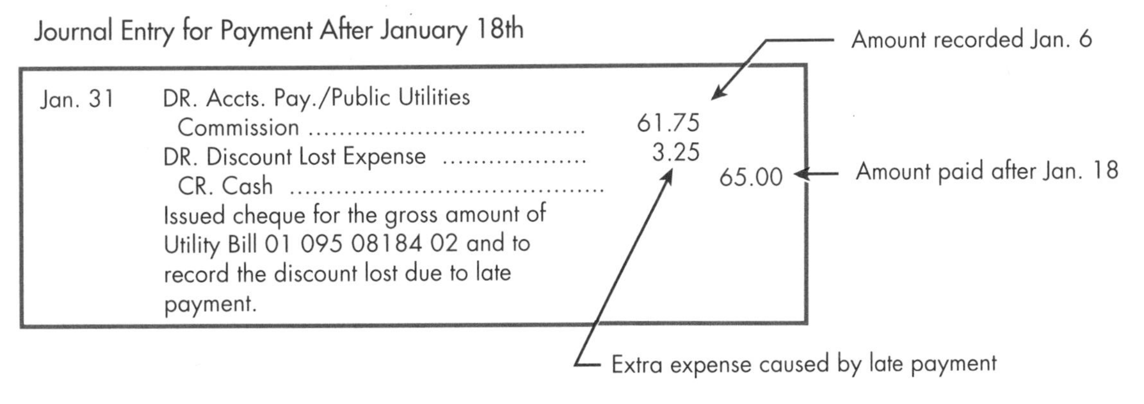

Jan. 31	DR. Accts. Pay./Public Utilities Commission	61.75	
	DR. Discount Lost Expense	3.25	
	CR. Cash		65.00
	Issued cheque for the gross amount of Utility Bill 01 095 08184 02 and to record the discount lost due to late payment.		

ANSWERING IMPORTANT QUESTIONS ON GAAPs

You have learned how accounts payable transactions originate through various ''purchase'' invoices received. But it is also important to know how to relate basic GAAPs to each invoice received and approved by the buyer. The following questions and answers will serve as a useful review.

- *What GAAP is recognized with the receipt of any purchase invoice?*
  The objectivity principle.
- *Suppose an invoice is received for the purchase of some office equipment on credit. What GAAP can be identified in addition to the objectivity principle?*
  The cost principle.
- *What is the meaning of cost in the term ''cost principle''?*
  Cost is the net amount payable on the invoice as at the day of receiving and approving it. This means the total cost in cases where a sales tax or any other amount like a shipping charge is added to the price of the office equipment. (*Note:* Amounts charged for the new GST would be excluded from the total cost. GST is examined in Part 3 of the textbook.)
- *What other meaning can you give to the cost principle?*
  Once the cost of the asset is recorded, this value remains on the books even if later prices for that asset go up.
- *How do accountants tell readers of financial statements that assets acquired were recorded and remain at their original cost?*
  On all balance sheets, the words ''at cost'' are placed opposite the title Fixed Assets.
- *Suppose a utility bill for electrical and water service is received. It offers 30 days' credit for the gross amount and 15 days' credit for the net amount. What GAAP decides which ''cost'' to use in recording the entry?*
  The cost principle. ''Cost'' is always the *cash equivalent price* (net amount payable) on the invoice as of the day the invoice is received and approved.
- *What other GAAP is related to the analysis of this utility bill?*
  The expense principle.
- *What two things does the expense principle say when applied to the utility bill?*
  (1) It defines expense as a cost amount used up in the process of earning revenue (that is, expired cost). (2) It requires the accounting entry for the expense to be made on the day the invoice is received and approved.

- *Suppose an invoice is received and approved for the purchase of dental supplies. What GAAPs may be used in analyzing the accounting of this purchase invoice?*

  Three are possible. (1) If management decides to record the supplies as an asset, then the **cost principle** must be used to record the correct ''cost value.'' This means the cash equivalent price on the invoice—the amount payable on the invoice on the day the invoice is received and approved. (2) If management believes that the cost of the supplies will be completely used up during the current accounting period, the **expense principle** requires that an appropriate expense account be selected for the debit entry. (3) The **objectivity principle** can be identified, because the purchase invoice gives evidence of the accounting transaction.

PROBLEMS

Analyzing a bill and preparing the journal entry.

P 9-1 Assume that the invoice on page 352 has been received and approved by Dr. Lien Chang's dental practice on December 5, 19-7.

a. By what date must this bill be paid? Show how you arrive at your answer.

b. On what date should an accounting entry be recorded for this invoice? Why?

c. Show the analysis of this invoice in General Journal form.

d. What type of account did you use for the debit entry? Why?

e. What type of account did you use for the credit entry? Why?

f. What GAAP helped you to choose the correct dollar amount in your double entry? Explain the full meaning of this principle.

g. What other GAAP can be related to the analysis of this purchase invoice? Briefly explain the meaning of this principle.

Analyzing a bill and preparing the journal entry.

P 9-2 Dr. R.B. Cousins, Orthodontist, operates a dental firm in Regina, Saskatchewan. On June 14, 19–8, Dr. Cousins received and approved a utility bill from Saskatchewan Power Corp. It showed the following information: Invoice No. 14896701; Reading Date, June 10, 19-8; Amount Due If Paid after June 25, 19-8, $74.00; Amount Due If Paid by June 25, 19-8, $70.30.

a. By what date must this bill be paid? Explain your answer.

b. On what date should an accounting entry be recorded for this bill? Explain your answer.

c. Show the analysis of this bill in General Journal form.

EXPRESS DENTAL INC.
DOWNSVIEW, ONTARIO

INVOICE NO. 748960

SOLD TO: Dr. Lien Chang
Any Street
Any Town, Canada

INVOICE DATE: DEC. 2, 19–7

TERMS: NET 30 DAYS

QUANTITY	DESCRIPTION	UNIT PRICE	AMOUNT
1	TRANSLUX VISIBLE LIGHT CURING UNIT	875.00	875.00
1	#2001 PULP TESTER	340.00	340.00
3	RIMLOCK CAULK TRAYS	10.50	31.50
2	RUBBER DAM CLAMP FORCEP	37.50	75.00
Note: A 2% late charge will be added to all accounts over 30 days.		**SUBTOTAL**	1 321.50
		ONTARIO SALES TAX 8.00%	105.72
		AMOUNT PAYABLE ➡	1 427.22

d. What dollar amount did you use in the double entry for **c** above? What GAAP helped you decide on your amount? Explain the full meaning of this principle.

e. What other GAAP can be related to the analysis of this utility bill? Briefly explain the meaning of this principle.

f. Suppose this dental practice paid the bill by issuing a cheque on June 30, 19-8. Show the required accounting of this cheque.

Analyzing a bill and preparing the journal entry.

P 9-3 On February 13 of the current year, MacPherson Plumbing & Heating of Fredericton, New Brunswick received and approved the monthly telephone bill from New Brunswick Telephone Co. The bill contained the following information: Date of Bill, February 10; Bill No. 1689480; Monthly Rate, $18.00; Tax (11%), $1.98; Chargeable Messages, $56.40; Tax (11%), $6.20; Total Now Due, $82.58.

a. What **basic** GAAP is immediately involved in this bill? Briefly explain the meaning of this principle.

b. By what date must the bill be paid? Explain your answer.

c. Show the required double entry in General Journal form.

d. What GAAP helped you to select the account title for the debit side of the entry? Explain the full meaning of this principle.

e. What GAAP helped you to choose the correct dollar amount in your double entry? Explain the full meaning of this principle.

Classifying and recording purchases.

P 9-4 Challenge Problem Dr. E.M. Sawchuck, Dental Surgeon, operates a dental firm in Winnipeg, Manitoba. Assume that the invoice below has been approved by Dr. Sawchuck on July 5, 19–7. *Note:* Dr. Sawchuck's accounting policy is to treat the cost of all dental supplies received as expenses. At the end of the accounting period, an adjustment is made to record dental supplies on hand.

Telephone
(204) 875-9000

LARR DENTAL PRODUCTS
2020 PORTAGE AVE.
WINNIPEG, MANITOBA
R3J 0K0

INVOICE NO. 168470

SOLD TO: Dr. E. M. SAWCHUCK
2799 Roblin Blvd.
Winnipeg, Manitoba
R3J 0B8

INVOICE DATE: July 2, 19–7

TERMS: Net 30 Days

QUANTITY	DESCRIPTION	UNIT PRICE	AMOUNT
1 only	POLY-F PLUS SUPPLY KIT	34.50	34.50
10 bottles	*GERMICIDAL CONCENTRATE (SULTAN)	12.00 *	120.00 *
1 PKG	IMPRESSION COMPOUND (KERR)	205.00	205.00
1 PKG	*FACIAL TISSUE	39.95 *	39.95 *
1 only	*INSTRUMENT STERILIZATION TRAY (BARD PARKER)	133.60 *	133.60 *
1 set	*AIR TWIST DENTAL DRILLS	795.00 *	795.00 *
*All items starred are subject to provincial sales tax.		**SUBTOTAL**	1 328.05
		MANITOBA SALES TAX 7.00%	92.96
A CHARGE OF 2% PER MONTH IS LEVIED ON OVERDUE AMOUNTS		**NET AMOUNT OWING**	1 421.01

a. The items shown on the purchase invoice may be classified under the headings Dental Supplies and Dental Equipment. What items would you list under each of these headings?

b. By what date must this invoice be paid? Show your calculation.

c. Check the accuracy of the provincial sales tax reported on the invoice. Show your calculation.

d. On what date would an accounting entry be made for this source document? Why?

e. Show the required accounting entry in General Journal form. Include all necessary calculations for the entry.

f. What GAAPs can you identify in the complete analysis of the source document? Briefly explain the meaning of each principle as related to the document.

MINI-CASES

Applying the cost principle.

MC 9-1 You are the accounting supervisor for a law office. One day you are reviewing entries made by one of your clerks. The law office has received an invoice for stationery on June 10, 19— for $560. If the bill is paid within ten days, the stationer will deduct $11.20 from the bill. Otherwise, the bill must be paid within 30 days. The clerk has made the following journal entry:

June 12	Office Supplies Expense	560.00	
	Accounts Payable/Hay Stationery		560.00
	To record invoice No. 3456.		

a. Explain to the clerk why the journal entry is incorrect using GAAPs.

b. Explain the GAAPs that would support the recording of the amount in the expense account instead of in the asset Supplies account.

Applying GAAPs to business expenses paid personally by the owner.

MC 9-2 You are the bookkeeper for Dr. Peter Metcalfe. Dr. Metcalfe uses personal funds to pay for different business expenses and then requests that you write a cheque for the amount of expenses. When you ask the doctor for the invoices, he explains that he lost them and cannot be expected to keep track of every piece of paper.

a. What GAAPs are being violated by Dr. Metcalfe? Explain.

Classifying the discounts lost expense.

MC 9-3 The Discounts Lost Expense account is used to record the difference between the gross amount and the discounted price. For example, a supplier's invoice shows a gross amount of $100. The invoice is dated July 1 and is paid July 31. The business would have had to pay only $90 up to July 11, but because the bill was paid on July 31 the gross amount remains at $100.

a. Is the Discounts Lost Expense of $10 an expense incurred in operating the business or is it an interest expense?

JOURNALIZING AND POSTING THE TRANSACTIONS

Once a purchase invoice on credit is received and approved by accounting as a valid source document, accounting must journalize and post the results of that invoice in the accounting records.

JOURNALIZING ACCOUNTS PAYABLE TRANSACTIONS

The method of recording debits and credits for accounts payable differs from one type of business to another. Some firms use a special Purchases Journal to record all purchase invoices on credit. This type of special journal is common among merchandising businesses and it will be discussed in detail in Part 3.

Many businesses, particularly those in the health science field, will not use a special journal for purchase invoices. For example, many dental businesses prefer to store all invoices to be paid in an accounts payable file. When a bill comes due for payment, these businesses often use a special Cash Payments Journal to record the cash disbursement side of the accounts payable application.

Other businesses prefer to record the initial accounts payable transactions in the General Journal and keep a separate ledger for individual creditor accounts. The General Journal is often preferred when very few purchase invoices on credit are received during any month. Cheques for payment of those invoices can then be recorded in a special Cash Payments Journal because cash disbursements occur very frequently in every month.

The dental practice of Dr. Johnson uses (1) a General Journal for recording all credit purchases of assets and services, (2) a subsidiary ledger to keep track of individual creditor accounts, and (3) a special Cash Payments Journal to record all issued cheques. To illustrate the initial accounts payable transactions for Dr. Johnson's practice, assume several entries were made in the General Journal for January. The GJ is illustrated at the top of page 356.

Accounts Payable Ledger: a subsidiary ledger storing individual creditor (vendor) accounts.

Accounts Payable: a controlling account in the General Ledger.

POSTING ACCOUNTS PAYABLE TRANSACTIONS

Many businesses have a separate Accounts Payable Ledger to control amounts owed to vendors so that all creditor accounts are removed from the General Ledger. When such a transfer occurs, a controlling account called Accounts Payable must replace all creditor accounts.

GENERAL JOURNAL Page 2

DATE 19-8		ACCOUNT TITLE AND EXPLANATION	POST. REF.	DEBIT		CREDIT	
Jan.	4	Office Equipment		648	—		
		Accts. Pay./IBM Canada Ltd.				648	—
		Purchase Invoice TA22809. Invoice date, Jan. 3, 19-8. Terms net 30 days. Due date, Feb. 2, 19-8.					
Jan.	5	Dental Supplies Expense		95	56		
		Accts. Pay./Denco Supply				95	56
		Purchase Invoice 92524. Invoice date, Jan. 4, 19-8. Terms net 10 days. Due date, Jan. 14, 19-8.					
Jan.	6	Utilities Expense		61	75		
		Accts. Pay./Public Utilities Commission ...				61	75
		Utility Bill No. 01 095 08184 02. Date of bill, Jan. 3, 19-8. Due date, Jan. 18, 19-8.					

Dr. Johnson's original Chart of Accounts shows two creditor accounts. The transfer of those accounts to a subsidiary ledger for accounts payable may be shown as follows:

General Ledger

Accounts Payable 202

	19-8 Jan. 2 Bal. 10 000*

*The balance in this controlling account must agree with the total of all individual creditor account balances in the subsidiary ledger.

Accounts Payable Ledger

Denco Supply

	19-8 Jan. 2 Bal. 8 000

Mardan Business Systems Ltd.

	19-8 Jan. 2 2 000

If formal ledger account forms were used, the above information would appear as follows:

GENERAL LEDGER

Accounts Payable — Account No. 202

DATE		EXPLANATION	POST. REF.	DEBIT	CREDIT	BALANCE
19-8						CR.
Jan.	2	Balance forward	✓			10000 –

ACCOUNTS PAYABLE LEDGER

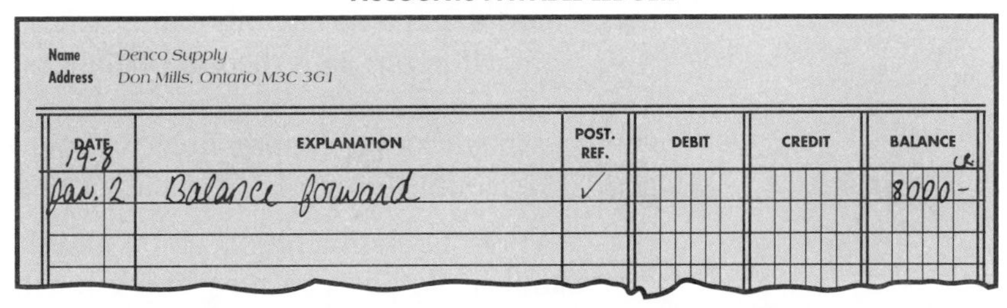

Name Denco Supply
Address Don Mills, Ontario M3C 3G1

DATE		EXPLANATION	POST. REF.	DEBIT	CREDIT	BALANCE
19-8						CR.
Jan.	2	Balance forward	✓			8000 –

Name Mardan Business Systems Ltd.
Address 48 Preston Street, Kitchener, Ontario N2G 3W4

DATE		EXPLANATION	POST. REF.	DEBIT	CREDIT	BALANCE
19-8						CR.
Jan.	2	Balance forward	✓			2000 –

Remember the following points about the creation of the Accounts Payable controlling account in the GL and the individual creditor accounts in the subsidiary ledger:

- The General Ledger account for Accounts Payable has a credit balance equal to the total of the account balances of the individual creditor accounts in the subsidiary ledger. This means that the GL account **controls by total** the individual balances of the related creditor accounts in the subsidiary ledger.
- The word "control" or "controlling" is rarely used in the name of the GL account—the word is understood.
- The form of each individual creditor account varies with the need for information. We have shown a three-column form with more information in the heading lines of the account.

- The accounts in the subsidiary ledger are listed in alphabetical order so there is no need to use account numbers.
- Notice how a balance is forwarded as at a particular date. The date of carrying forward the balance is shown. **Balance forward** is placed in the Explanation column. Because there is no posting, a check mark is placed in the Post. Ref. column. Finally, the balance forwarded is placed only in the Balance column.
- The Accounts Payable account in the GL will always supply the amount to report under Current Liabilities when a future balance sheet is prepared.
- The Accounts Payable Ledger will always be used to find out how much is owing to any individual creditor at any time.
- At the end of each month, the balance in the controlling account must agree with the total balances taken from the individual creditor accounts in the subsidiary ledger. Financial statements should never be prepared without first checking that the control account ''controls'' the balances in the related subsidiary ledger.

After the controlling account and the Accounts Payable Ledger are established, you can turn to the mechanics of posting accounts payable transactions. Refer to the General Journal illustrated on page 356. The transactions would be posted in this order:

(1) Post the information affecting individual creditor accounts on a daily basis. Then management can control the amounts owing to individual creditors on any given day. Refer to the posted General Journal illustrated next. Notice how a check mark is placed in the Post. Ref. column to indicate that posting has occurred to the individual creditor account in the subsidiary ledger.

(2) Post information affecting GL accounts at the end of the month. Posting every day to the GL is not necessary because financial statements are normally prepared at the end of the month. Notice in the posted General Journal that the GL account number is shown to indicate that posting has been completed to this GL account. The credit line, therefore, of an accounts payable entry in the General Journal must be posted once to the individual creditor account in the subsidiary ledger and once to the controlling account in the GL.

The General Journal and the two ledgers would appear after all postings have been completed as illustrated on pages 359 and 360.

The GL account shows posting for each date of entry in the General Journal. Posting dates are the dates of transactions and not the day on which the transfer occurs. The GL account also shows the posting reference—the GJ page from which the information was posted.

GENERAL JOURNAL **Page** 2

DATE 19-8		ACCOUNT TITLE AND EXPLANATION	POST. REF.	DEBIT		CREDIT	
Jan.	4	Office Equipment	112	648	–		
		*Accts. Pay./IBM Canada Ltd.	202/✓			648	–
		Purchase Invoice TA22809. Invoice date, Jan. 3, 19-8. Terms net 30 days. Due date, Feb. 2, 19-8.					
Jan.	5	Dental Supplies Expenses	503	95	56		
		*Accts. Pay./Denco Supply	202/✓			95	56
		Purchase Invoice No. 92524. Invoice date, Jan. 4, 19-8. Terms net 10 days. Due date, Jan. 14, 19-8.					
Jan.	6	Utilities Expense	506	61	75		
		*Accts. Pay./Public Utilities Commission	202/✓			61	75
		Utility Bill No. 01 095 08184 02. Date of bill, Jan. 3, 19-8. Due date, Jan. 18, 19-8.					

* Notice that this credit line is posted twice: once to Accounts Payable No. 202 in the GL; and once to the individual creditor account in the Accounts Payable Ledger. Posting references to the individual creditor account are shown by a check mark because these accounts are filed in alphabetical order.

GENERAL LEDGER

Accounts Payable Account No. 202

DATE 19-8		EXPLANATION	POST. REF.	DEBIT	CREDIT	BALANCE CR.
Jan	2	Balance forward	✓			10000 –
	4	G.J.	2		648 –	10648 –
	5	G.J.	2		95 56	10743 56
	6	G.J.	2		61 75	10805 31

Explanation columns are usually completed for the subsidiary ledger accounts. This is true for any subsidiary ledger account. Why? The subsidiary ledger supplies complete information about any individual account. Here, management can look to any creditor account to find out when payments are required to eliminate a debt.

ACCOUNTS PAYABLE LEDGER

Name: Denco Supply
Address: Don Mills, Ontario M3C 3G1

DATE 19-8		EXPLANATION	POST. REF.	DEBIT	CREDIT	BALANCE (Cr.)
Jan.	2	Balance forward	✓			8000 –
	5	Inv. 92524, due Jan. 14 G.J.	2		95 56	8095 56

Name: IBM Canada Ltd.
Address: Toronto, Ontario M4Y 2T5

DATE 19-8		EXPLANATION	POST. REF.	DEBIT	CREDIT	BALANCE
Jan.	4	Inv. TA22809; due Feb. 2 G.J.	2		648 –	648 –

Name: Mardan Business Systems Ltd.
Address: 48 Preston Street, Kitchener, Ontario N2G 3W4

DATE 19-8		EXPLANATION	POST. REF.	DEBIT	CREDIT	BALANCE (Cr.)
Jan.	2	Balance forward	✓			2000 –

Name: Public Utilities Commission
Address: Box 3060, Any Town, Canada

DATE 19-8		EXPLANATION	POST. REF.	DEBIT	CREDIT	BALANCE
Jan.	6	Bill 010950818402; due Jan. 18 G.J.	2		61 75	61 75

PROBLEMS

Setting up the books, journalizing, and posting purchases.

P 9-5 As outlined in problems for Chapter 8, Dr. Lien Chang's dental practice began business on Dec. 1, 19-7 with the following General Ledger account balances: Cash (101), \$10 000; Government of Canada Bonds (102), \$50 000; Dental Equipment (110), \$80 000; Office Equipment (112), \$4000; Furniture (114), \$6000;

Bank Loan Payable (201), $5000; Accts. Pay./Denco Equipment & Supply (202) (Don Mills, Ontario M3C 3G1), $10 000; Accts. Pay./ Mardan Business Systems Ltd. (203) (48 Preston Street, Kitchener, Ontario N2G 3W4), $3000; 5-Year Note Payable (220), $38 000; L. Chang, Capital (301), $94 000.

During December, 19-7 Dr. Lien Chang's practice received and approved several accounts payable invoices as summarized below. Dr. Chang accepted the advice of her accountant to introduce the following accounting policies: (1) the cost of all dental and office supplies will be expired in the belief that all such supplies will be used up completely by the end of the accounting period; (2) all purchase invoices on credit will be recorded in the General Journal; (3) all purchase invoices will be recorded in accordance with GAAPs; and (4) a separate Accounts Payable Ledger will be used to control amounts owing to individual creditors.

A summary of purchase invoices received and approved is as follows:

Dec. 5 From Express Dental Inc., Downsview, Ont.; Invoice No. 748960; Invoice Date, Dec. 2, 19-7; Terms Net 30 Days; dental equipment, $1321.50; Ontario Sales Tax, $105.72; Amount Payable, $1427.22.

7 From Mardan Business Systems Ltd.; Invoice No. 67891; Invoice Date, Dec. 4, 19-7; Terms Net 30 Days; accounting supplies, $300; Ontario Sales Tax, $24; Net Amount Payable, $324.

12 From Public Utilities Commission, Box 3060, Any Town, Canada; Bill No. 16250; Reading Date, Dec. 10, 19-7; Total Amount Due, after Dec. 27 for installation of electricity and water, $50; Amount Due If Paid by Dec. 27, $147.50.

29 From Denco Equipment & Supply; Invoice 84762; Invoice Date, Dec. 27; Terms Net 10 Days; dental supply kits, $400; dental equipment, $600; Applicable Ontario Sales Tax, $80; Total Amount, $1080.

a. Set up a General Ledger showing the beginning balances of GL accounts as at December 1, 19-7. Include a controlling account for Accounts Payable (202).

b. Transfer the beginning balances of the two accounts payable accounts to the subsidiary ledger.

c. Analyze each purchase invoice. Then record each invoice in the General Journal, beginning on page 2.

d. Post the accounts payable information from the General Journal to the individual creditor accounts in the subsidiary ledger.

e. Post all entries affecting the GL from the General Journal to appropriate accounts in the GL.

Setting up the books, journalizing, and posting purchases.

P 9-6 MacPherson Plumbing & Heating of Fredericton, New Brunswick, approved purchase invoices on credit as summarized below. The business supported the following accounting policies: (1) all supplies are to be expired immediately; (2) all purchase invoices on credit are to be recorded in the General Journal; (3) all purchase invoices are to be recorded in accordance with GAAPs; and (4) a separate Accounts Payable Ledger is to be used to control amounts owing to individual vendors.

On February 1, current year, the Accounts Payable account in the GL (No. 202) showed a credit balance forward of $18 000. The related subsidiary ledger showed the following individual accounts: Maritime Truck Centre, 442 Canada Street, Fredericton, New Brunswick, E3A 4A6, $10 000; Newcastle Manufacturing Co. Ltd., 102 Main Street, Newcastle, New Brunswick, E1V 3E7, $6000; Smith Business Equipment, 124 George St., Fredericton, New Brunswick, E3A 4E2, $2000.

A summary of approved purchase invoices on credit is as follows:

Feb. 8 Newcastle Manufacturing Co. Ltd.; Invoice No. 148012; Invoice Date, Feb. 5; Terms Net 30 Days; small tools costing $1000; Provincial Sales Tax, 11%, Net Amount Payable, $1110. (Charge Account No. 116, Small Tools.)

12 Smith Business Equipment; Invoice No. 35418; Invoice Date, Feb. 10; Terms Net 15 Days; total cost of office supplies, $80; Provincial Sales Tax, 11%, Net Amount Owing, $88.80.

18 Maritime Truck Centre; Invoice No. 8045; Invoice Date, Feb. 18; Terms Net EOM (end of current month); repairs and tune-up of truck, $450; Provincial Sales Tax, $49.50; Total Amount, $499.50. (Charge Truck Expense, Account No. 515.)

20 New Brunswick Electric Power Commission; Utility Bill No. 2A4747; Reading Date, Feb. 16; Amount Due If Paid by Feb. 28, $85.50; Amount Due If Paid after Feb. 28, $90.

25 St. John Wholesale Plumbing Supplies Ltd., 287 Duke St., St. John, NB, E2L 1P4; plumbing supplies, $600; Special Delivery Charge, $50; Total Owing, $650; Invoice No. A41217; Invoice Date, Feb. 24; Terms Net 30 Days.

a. Analyze each approved purchase invoice. Then record each in the General Journal, beginning on page 15.

b. Set up an Accounts Payable Ledger with the following creditor accounts: Maritime Truck Centre; New Brunswick Electric Power Commission; Newcastle Manufacturing Co. Ltd.; Saint John Wholesale Plumbing Supplies Ltd.; Smith Business Equipment. Show beginning balances for appropriate accounts as at February 1, current year.

c. Post all recorded entries from the General Journal to creditors in the Accounts Payable Ledger.

d. Open General Ledger accounts for all GL accounts involved in this problem. Show any required balances forward as of May 1, current year.

e. Post information from the General Journal to the General Ledger.

Setting up the books, journalizing, and posting purchases.

P 9-7 Challenge Problem Dr. John Reddon, Dental Surgeon, began his dental practice in Red Deer, Alberta on September 1 with the following assets and liabilities: Cash $50 000; Land, $50 000; Building, $150 000; Dental Equipment, $200 000; Bank Loan Payable (on demand), $20 000; Accounts Payable, $15 000 (to Edmonton Dental Supply, 3911 – 126th St., Edmonton, Alberta T6J 2A5); Mortgage Payable, $100 000.

a. Record the opening entry in the General Journal.

b. Set up a General Ledger with the following accounts: Cash (101); Dental Supplies on Hand (105); Office Supplies on Hand (106); Land (110); Land Improvements (111); Building (113); Dental Equipment (115); Office Equipment (117); Bank Loan Payable (201); Accounts Payable (202); Mortgage Payable (220); John Reddon, Capital (301); Utilities Expense (501); Lab Fees Expense (502).

c. Post the opening entry to the General Ledger.

d. Open an Accounts Payable Ledger with the following creditor accounts: Alberta Power Ltd., 4700 – 26th Ave. SW, Calgary, Alberta T3E 0R3; Edmonton Dental Supply; HealthCo. (Canada) Ltd., 511 North Railway St., Medicine Hat, Alberta T1A 2Z4; Mardan Business Systems Ltd., 3000 Elbow Dr. SW, Calgary, Alberta T2S 2J3; Pratt Dental Laboratory, 5701 West Park Cres., Red Deer, Alberta T4N 1E4; Western Construction Ltd., Box 5000, Lethbridge, Alberta T1K 1L7.

e. Post the opening entry affecting the individual creditor accounts from the General Journal to the subsidiary ledger.

f. During September, Dr. Reddon received and approved the following purchase invoices on credit:

Sept.	4	From Mardan Business Systems Ltd.; Invoice A7489; Invoice date, Sept. 3; Terms Net 30 Days; cost of office supplies, $300; one file cabinet, $1200; one reception desk, $1000; one conference table, $800; four office chairs at $100 each, $400; Total Amount Payable, $3700.
	5	Returned one office chair (wrong colour) to Mardan Business Systems Ltd. on Invoice No. A7489. Permission granted to ship the chair back on a collect basis.
	8	From HealthCo (Canada) Ltd.; Invoice No. 78989; Invoice date, Sept. 6; Terms Net 30 Days; dental supply kits, $500; dental equipment, $800; Total Amount Owing, $1300.
	9	From Alberta Power Ltd., Bill No. AB24890; Reading Date, Sept. 7; installation charges for electricity and water system, $65 if paid by Sept. 17, $70 if paid after Sept. 17.
	20	From Edmonton Dental Supply; Invoice No. 162480; Invoice Date, Sept. 19; dental equipment, $1500; special shipping charge of $150 for delivery of equipment; Terms Net 30 Days.
	21	From Edmonton Dental Supply; Invoice No. 162485; Invoice Date, Sept. 20; charge for installing dental equipment on Invoice No. 162480; Total Charge, $125; Terms Net 30 Days.
	30	From Pratt Dental Laboratory; Invoice No. 7580; Invoice Date, Sept. 30; lab fees to date, $700; Terms Net 15 Days.
	30	From Western Construction Ltd.; Invoice No. WA64891; Invoice Date, Sept. 30; for completion of needed parking lot, $4500 (use fixed asset account No. 111, Land Improvements); Terms Net 30 Days.

Also, management has approved the following accounting policies regarding the accounting of the accounts payable application: (1) all dental supplies and office supplies are to be charged to asset accounts Nos. 105 and 106, respectively; (2) all expired costs of dental supplies and office supplies will be charged to expenses at the end of the accounting period as part of the required adjusting entries; (3) all purchase invoices on credit are to be recorded in the General Journal; (4) all purchase invoices are to be recorded in accordance with

GAAPs; (5) a separate subsidiary ledger for vendor accounts is to be maintained.

Analyze each approved purchase invoice. Then record each in the General Journal immediately after the opening entry.

g. Post all recorded entries from the General Journal to creditors in the Accounts Payable Ledger.

h. Post the required information from the General Journal to appropriate General Ledger accounts.

MINI-CASES

Calculating cash discounts under two accounting systems.

MC 9-4 One business uses only a General Ledger for recording its purchase transactions. A second business uses an Accounts Payable Ledger and a General Ledger for recording these transactions. Both businesses take advantage of purchase discounts.

a. If you were an accounts payable clerk and had to calculate the purchase discounts, which business would you prefer to work for? Explain how you arrived at this decision.

Analyzing a purchase invoice.

MC 9-5 You have received a purchase invoice for office supplies. The gross amount of the invoice is $80. If the invoice is paid within 10 days, the supplier deducts $1.60 from the bill. The bill must be paid within 30 days.

a. Where should you record this transaction?

b. What dollar amount should be used?

c. You have journalized the transaction for the amount of $78.40, but posted it to the supplier's account in the Accounts Payable Ledger for the gross amount. Will your books balance? What other problem might arise because of the error?

Classifying accounts payable on the balance sheet.

MC 9-6 You are asked to prepare a classified balance sheet for a business.

a. In which section of the balance sheet would you put accounts payable?

b. Give reasons for your choice.

CONTROLLING AND ACCOUNTING FOR CASH PAYMENTS

In setting up an efficient system for cash payments, there are nine measures that may be used for controlling cash payments. These measures may be adapted or expanded to suit a firm's particular needs. These measures are:

- Checking the invoice.
- Using a tickler filing system.
- Pay all invoices by cheque.
- Use pre-numbered cheques.
- Preparing a cheque record for every payment.
- Voiding and keeping all spoiled cheques.
- Cancelling all bills and invoices after they have been paid.
- Dividing responsibilities.
- Using a special journal for cash payments.

CHECKING THE INVOICE

It is important to check that (1) the goods or services in the invoice were actually ordered and received and (2) the invoice has been accurately prepared. The first check ensures that the business is paying only for services and expenses used by the business and not for expenses of an employee or for services never received. The second check ensures that the amount on the invoice is correct. The person authorizing a cheque in payment of the invoice should ensure these checks have been made before the cheque is issued.

USING A TICKLER FILE SYSTEM

Tickler file: a reminder file arranged by date.

A tickler file categorizes invoices by the date of payment. For example, all invoices which should be paid by January 3 would be in one folder, those for January 4 would be in the next folder, and so on. In this way the file "tickles" the accounts payable clerk's memory to pay invoices on time. The invoices that allow discounts for early payment should always be filed so that they will be paid in time to take advantage of the discount.

The advantage of a tickler file system is evident in computerized accounts payable systems. The computer will prepare cheques automatically to allow a business to mail the cheque in time to meet the discount date.

Card Tickler File

January 12, 19-8

Issue cheque dated Jan. 14 to Denco Supply in payment of Invoice No. 92524.

PAYING BY PRE-NUMBERED CHEQUE

Why is it a good control measure to pay by cheques which are pre-numbered?

- The need for handling large amounts of money is eliminated.
- Proof of each payment is provided, because the bank returns each cancelled (paid) cheque to the business with the monthly bank statement.
- An independent record of each payment will be shown on the monthly bank statement.
- The owner is provided with the opportunity to ensure that all the payments are for business expenses, since it is likely that the owner will sign all cheques.
- With pre-numbered cheques, the owner may ensure that all cheques are accounted for and recorded, and that none of them have fallen into the wrong hands.

PREPARING A CHEQUE RECORD FOR EVERY PAYMENT

A cheque record is an important accounting document, because it is the source document for the accounting entry recording the payment. This is an application of the objectivity principle.

The cheque record is a stub which may be a part of the business's cheque book. The cheque portion can be detached.

Payee: the person/business to whom the cheque is made out

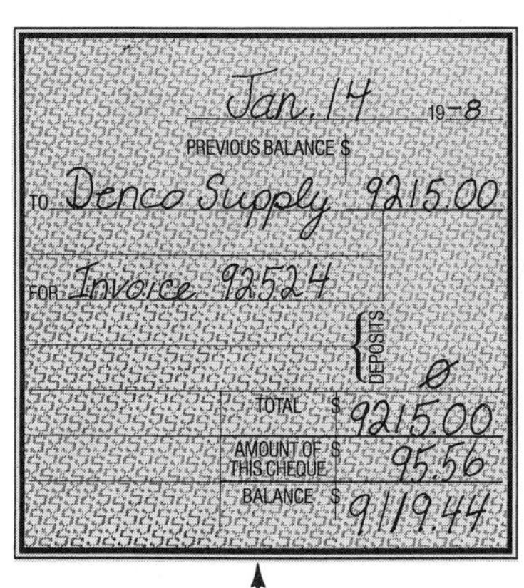
Jan. 14 19-8
PREVIOUS BALANCE $ 9215.00
TO Denco Supply
FOR Invoice 92524
DEPOSITS ø
TOTAL $ 9215.00
AMOUNT OF THIS CHEQUE $ 95.56
BALANCE $ 9119.44

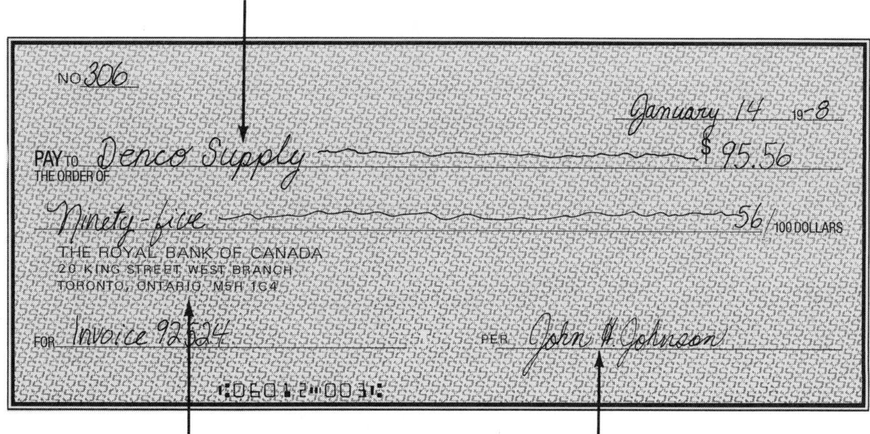
NO 306
January 14 19-8
PAY TO THE ORDER OF Denco Supply $ 95.56
Ninety-five 56/100 DOLLARS
THE ROYAL BANK OF CANADA
20 KING STREET WEST BRANCH
TORONTO, ONTARIO M5H 1C4
FOR Invoice 92524
PER John H. Johnson

Cheque Record (stub)

Drawee: the bank on which the cheque is drawn

Drawer: the person who signs the cheque

The cheque record may also be a duplicate or carbon copy of the cheque. The duplicate is kept in the cheque book and the original cheque is detached and issued.

VOIDING AND KEEPING ALL SPOILED CHEQUES

To void a cheque: to mark it so it cannot be cashed.

If a cheque is spoiled, it is important to void both the cheque and its record. By writing ''void'' on the cheque, you ensure that the cheque cannot be cashed. By keeping all spoiled or void cheques, you can check the continuity of the cheques issued as outlined above.

CANCELLING ALL BILLS PAID BY CHEQUE

By marking an invoice ''paid,'' you limit the chance of the invoice being paid more than once. It is also good practice to record the date of payment and the cheque number used for the payment of the invoice. In this way, if there are any discrepancies later the cheque number will help the clerk find the cheque record or the cheque itself.

DIVIDING THE RESPONSIBILITIES

As mentioned previously the owner of a small business usually controls all cash payments by signing all cheques. If this is not possible, the employees should be organized to ensure that no one employee has responsibility for more than a part of the cash payments system. The responsibility for handling the cheques and recording the payments should be divided so the work of one employee can be checked against that of another. This can be achieved in the following ways:

- The purchasing department should be separated from the accounting, receiving, and shipping departments.
- The responsibilities for verifying and for approving invoices should be separated. The purchasing clerk checks the bill; the head of purchasing approves the bill; the accounting clerk double-checks the bill before making the accounting entry.
- All documents associated with accounts payable should be controlled in that they go directly to accounting once they are received. This includes copies of purchase orders and receiving documents. Unauthorized persons should never have access to blank forms.
- Once the invoice has been approved, the accounting clerk prepares the cheque for signature; however, some other authorized person does the actual signing. Those authorized to sign cheques should not prepare the cheques or maintain accounting records for cash receipts and cash payments. The person who signs the

cheques should not return them to the clerk who prepared the cheque for mailing.

USING A SPECIAL JOURNAL TO RECORD CASH PAYMENTS

Cash Payments Journal (also known as Cash Disbursements Journal): a special journal in which all cheques are recorded.

A special journal should be used to record all cash payments transactions. This is known as the Cash Payments Journal or Cash Disbursements Journal. Before we examine this special journal, here's an important note on the mailing of signed cheques.

MAILING SIGNED CHEQUES

Voucher cheque: a two-part cheque with a detachable statement form.

In small businesses, a cheque in payment of accounts payable is mailed together with a short note or letter of explanation. This becomes the **remittance advice** — a statement advising the payee of the item or items covered by the cheque. In large businesses, a special cheque form known as a voucher cheque is commonly used. The most common voucher cheque has a perforated rider attached. The rider is removed by the recipient before the cheque is presented for payment. See the illustration below.

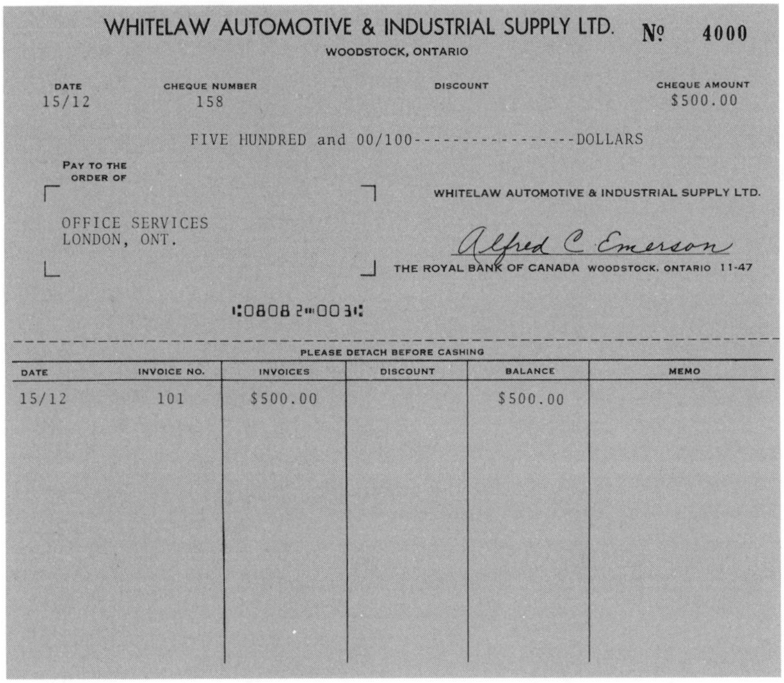

WHITELAW AUTOMOTIVE & INDUSTRIAL SUPPLY LTD. № 4000
WOODSTOCK, ONTARIO

DATE	CHEQUE NUMBER	DISCOUNT	CHEQUE AMOUNT
15/12	158		$500.00

FIVE HUNDRED and 00/100----------------DOLLARS

PAY TO THE ORDER OF
OFFICE SERVICES
LONDON, ONT.

WHITELAW AUTOMOTIVE & INDUSTRIAL SUPPLY LTD.
Alfred C Emerson
THE ROYAL BANK OF CANADA WOODSTOCK, ONTARIO 11-47

⑆08082⑈003⑆

PLEASE DETACH BEFORE CASHING

DATE	INVOICE NO.	INVOICES	DISCOUNT	BALANCE	MEMO
15/12	101	$500.00		$500.00	

JOURNALIZING CASH PAYMENTS TRANSACTIONS

The most common reasons for issuing cheques are to pay for assets purchased, to pay for operating expenses, to pay creditors, and to pay the owner when he or she makes regular withdrawals of cash for personal use.

To save time in journalizing and posting, many businesses use a Cash Payments Journal to record all cash payments transactions. In this way only one line is required to record a transaction. Furthermore, only the total need be posted to the credit side of the Cash account at the end of the month.

To illustrate how cash payments may be recorded in a Cash Payments Journal, suppose Dr. Johnson's dental practice issued the cheques as summarized on the next page for the month of January, 19–8. In all cases, assume that the basic measures to control all cash payments have been followed.

Summary of Cash Payments Transactions

19–8

Jan. 2 Issued Cheque No. 301 for $5000.00 to Central Realty Ltd. for January's rent of the office building.

3 Issued Cheque No. 302 to Denco Supply for $8000.00 in full settlement of account.

4 Issued Cheque No. 303 to Mardan Business Systems Ltd. for $2000.00 in full settlement of account.

5 Issued Cheque No. 304 for $200.00 to Dr. J.H. Johnson for his personal use.

14 Cheque No. 305 was spoiled and promptly voided.

14 Issued Cheque No. 306 for $95.56 to Denco Supply in payment of Invoice No. 92524.

18 Issued Cheque No. 307 for $61.75 to Public Utilities Commission in payment of utility bill number 01 095 08184 02.

18 Issued Cheque No. 308 for $285.33 to Bell Canada in payment of telephone bill 981390 due "Now."

20 Issued Cheque No. 309 for $200.00 to Dr. J.H. Johnson for his personal use.

22 Issued Cheque No. 310 to The Royal Trust Co. for $500 in part payment of the 5-Year Note Payable.

30 Issued cheques to pay monthly salaries as follows: Cheque No. 311 for $1000.00 to Lynn Fortier, front-office person; Cheque No. 312 for $1200.00 to Kathy Lewis, dental assistant/hygienist.

31 Received a lab fee bill, number 68741, from Edwards Laboratory, dated January 30; total lab fees, $700.00; terms: "Now Due." Issued Cheque No. 313 in full payment.

31 Purchased an office copier from Office Products Ltd. Special exhibition price of $1800.00 if purchased for cash. Issued Cheque No. 314 in full payment.

31 Issued Cheque No. 315 for $75.00 to A. Gilmore for delivery and installation charges to the new office copier purchased from Office Products Ltd.

Analysis: Look at how the cheques have been recorded in the Cash Payments Journal illustrated below. Are the cheque numbers in sequence? Here are other key points to remember in a careful analysis of the recorded transactions:

- The name of the special journal appears on the top line along with the journal page number.

CASH PAYMENTS JOURNAL Page 1

			ACCOUNTS PAYABLE		OTHER GENERAL LEDGER ACCOUNTS			
DATE 19-8	CHEQUE NO.	CHEQUE PAID TO	POST. REF.	AMOUNT DR.	ACCOUNT TITLE	POST. REF.	AMOUNT DR.	CASH CR.
Jan. 2	301	Central Realty Ltd.			Rent Expense		5 000 00	5 000 00
3	302	Denco Supply		8 000 00				8 000 00
4	303	Mardan Business Systems Ltd.		2 000 00				2 000 00
5	304	Dr. J.H. Johnson			J.H. Johnson, Drawing		200 00	200 00
14	305	VOID		—			—	—
14	306	Denco Supply		95 56				95 56
18	307	Public Utilities Commission		61 75				61 75
18	308	Bell Canada			Telephone Expense		285 33	285 33
20	309	Dr. J.H. Johnson			J.H. Johnson, Drawing		200 00	200 00
22	310	The Royal Trust Co.			5-Year Note Payable		500 00	500 00
30	311	Lynn Fortier			Salaries Expense		1 000 00	1 000 00
30	312	Kathy Lewis			Salaries Expense		1 200 00	1 200 00
31	313	Edwards Laboratory			Lab Fees Expense		700 00	700 00
31	314	Office Products Ltd.			Office Equipment		1 800 00	1 800 00
31	315	A. Gilmore			Office Equipment		75 00	75 00

Note: In practice, the number of columns will vary with the needs of the accounting system.

- Journal page numbers are numbered consecutively beginning with "1."
- The main headings for each column in this special journal are: (1) a **Date** column to record the transaction date appearing on the source document (in this case the date would be the date of the cheque, because the cheque stub would also have this date); (2) a **Cheque No.** column to record the pre-numbered cheque; (3) a **Cheque Paid To** column to record the name of the payee named on the cheque; (4) an **Accounts Payable** column for checking off future posting references and the amount debited to Accounts Payable; (5) a section to identify those General Ledger accounts other than Accounts Payable. Here, there is a GL **Account Title** column, a **Post. Ref.** column for future posting, and an **Amount DR.** column.

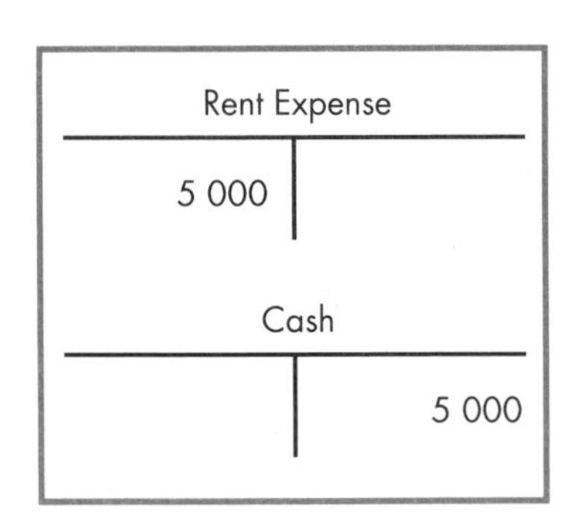

- Before recording any transaction in this special journal, analyze the transaction in either T-account form or General Journal form. For example, on January 2, Cheque No. 301 was issued in payment of the monthly rent so you would debit Rent Expense and credit Cash. Use appropriate account titles as offered from the business's Chart of Accounts. If no account name is available, use one that would be added in support of the accounting policies followed by the firm. Since the Cash account is credited, the transaction must be recorded in the Cash Payments Journal. And since no Accounts Payable is involved, Rent Expense is shown in the space for other GL account titles. Of course, the cheque amount is placed in the **Cash CR.** column. You have recorded the complete double entry across one line.
- Look at how an accounts payable transaction is recorded. For example, on January 3, Cheque No. 302 has been issued to Denco Supply in full settlement of account. Before recording this payment, think of the entry in T-account form or General Journal form as follows:

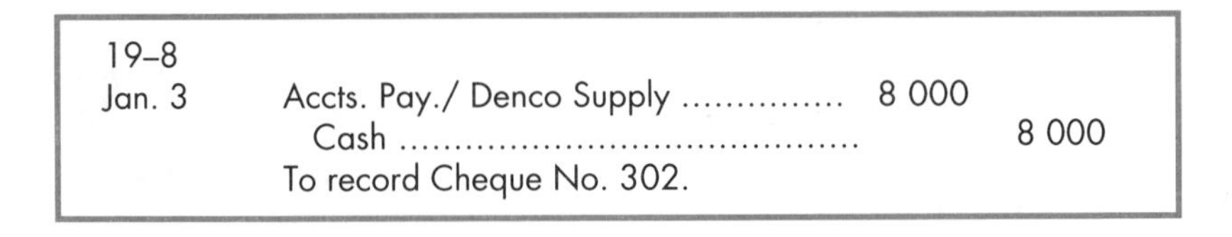

Since Denco Supply is an account payable, enter the amount in the Accounts Payable DR. column. Of course, the cheque amount goes to the Cash CR. column. Once again, the complete double entry has been recorded on one line.

- The transaction to record Cheque 304 on January 5 is easy. The owner of a business is allowed to withdraw cash for personal use, but good internal control requires that a cheque be issued even to the owner. Remember, all personal withdrawals must be debited to the owner's Drawing account rather than to an expense account.
- On January 14, a solid line is shown under appropriate columns to illustrate how a voided cheque is recorded. A sound measure of internal control requires that all cheques be accounted for; thus, show a recording of every spoiled cheque to account for all cheque numbers.
- The last two cheques issued have been recorded in accordance with the **cost principle**. (To ready the photocopier for its intended use, the firm had to pay the cost of the machine plus delivery and installation charges.) The cost principle requires you to debit both these ''costs'' to the Office Equipment account.
- On any line, the debit amount equals the credit amount. Thus, the double entry is recorded on one line only.

POSTING FROM THE CASH PAYMENTS JOURNAL

As with any special journal, postings from the Cash Payments Journal occur in two stages: one during the month, and a second at the end of the month.

During the Month All accounts that appear in a subsidiary ledger should be posted **daily**. Since the subsidiary ledger to be posted from the Cash Payments Journal deals with individual creditor accounts, all postings to these accounts must come from the **Accounts Payable DR.** money column. Because the individual creditor accounts are filed alphabetically, a check mark is placed in the **Post. Ref.** column of the Cash Payments Journal next to the **Accounts Payable** column. This shows that the amount has been transferred to the subsidiary ledger. The source of posting also appears in the **Post. Ref.** column of each individual creditor's account. Examine the illustrations on page 374.

At Month-End Post information to all **General Ledger accounts** only at the end of the month. Why? The GL provides the balances of accounts needed for the future of financial statements. Since financial statements are prepared monthly, postings to the GL occur monthly.

CASH PAYMENTS JOURNAL Page 1

DATE 19-8		CHEQUE NO.	CHEQUE PAID TO	ACCOUNTS PAYABLE POST. REF.	ACCOUNTS PAYABLE AMOUNT DR.	OTHER GENERAL LEDGER ACCOUNTS ACCOUNT TITLE	POST. REF.	AMOUNT DR.	CASH CR.
Jan.	2	301	Central Realty Ltd.			Rent Expense		5 000 00	5 000 00
	3	302	Denco Supply	✓	8 000 00				8 000 00
	4	303	Mardan Business Systems Ltd.	✓	2 000 00				2 000 00

ACCOUNTS PAYABLE LEDGER

Name Denco Supply
Address Don Mills, Ontario M3C 3G1

DATE 19-8		EXPLANATION	POST. REF.	DEBIT	CREDIT	BALANCE Cr.
Jan	2	Balance forward	✓			8000 –
	3	Cheque 302 CPJ	1	8000 –		–0–
	5	Inv. 92524; due Jan. 14 GJ	2		95 56	95 56

Name Mardan Business Systems Ltd.
Address 48 Preston Street, Kitchener, Ontario N2G 3W4

DATE 19-8		EXPLANATION	POST. REF.	DEBIT	CREDIT	BALANCE Cr.
Jan	2	Balance forward	✓			2000 –
	4	Cheque 303 CPJ	1	2000 –		–0–

Before such postings occur, these actions should be taken:

- Total the Cash Payments Journal.
- Double-check the totals (use the footing procedure or an adding-machine check).
- Prove the double-entry theory within the special journal: **The total debits must be equal to the total credits.**

The illustration below shows how this double entry works.

Total of Accounts Payable DR. column	$10 157.31
Total of Other GL Accounts DR. column	10 960.33
Total of All Debits	$21 117.64
Total of Cash CR. Column	$21 117.64

← These totals must agree. →

Remember this important point: Never post to the GL until the columns are proved to show that the total debits are equal to the total credits. Once this proof is obtained, postings can occur as illustrated below. The total of Accounts Payable DR. is posted from the Cash Payments Journal to the controlling account and the total of Cash CR. is transferred to the Cash account. Then the journal is ruled off for the month.

CASH PAYMENTS JOURNAL Page 1

DATE 19-8		CHEQUE NO.	CHEQUE PAID TO	ACCOUNTS PAYABLE POST. REF.	ACCOUNTS PAYABLE AMOUNT DR.		OTHER GENERAL LEDGER ACCOUNTS ACCOUNT TITLE	POST. REF.	AMOUNT DR.		CASH CR.	
Jan.	2	301	Central Realty Ltd.				Rent Expense	501	5 000	00	5 000	00
	3	302	Denco Supply	✓	8 000	00					8 000	00
	4	303	Mardan Business Systems Ltd.	✓	2 000	00					2 000	00
	31	314	Office Products Ltd.				Office Equipment	112	1 800	00	1 800	00
	31	315	A. Gilmore				Office Equipment	112	75	00	75	00
	31				10 157	31			10 960	33	21 117	64
					(202)				(✓)		(101)	

Double line to rule off the journal for the month.

GL account number shows the total posted to the controlling account.

Check mark indicates this total is not to be posted.

GL account number shows the total posted to the Cash account.

GENERAL LEDGER

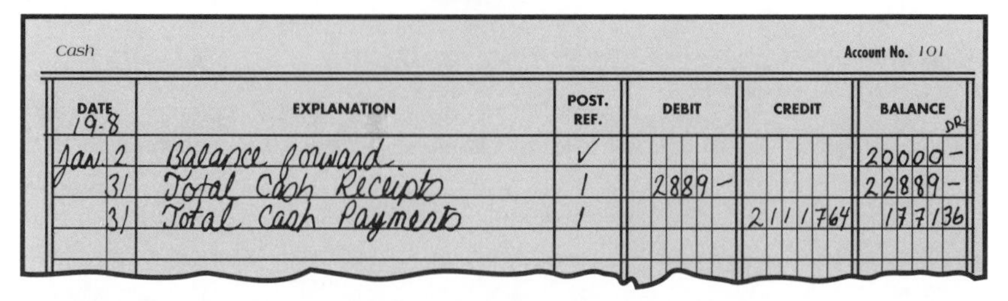

Cash — Account No. 101

DATE 19-8		EXPLANATION	POST. REF.	DEBIT	CREDIT	BALANCE DR
Jan.	2	Balance forward	✓			20000 —
	31	Total Cash Receipts	1	2889 —		22889 —
	31	Total Cash Payments	1		21117 64	1771 36

Accounts Payable — Account No. 202

DATE 19-8		EXPLANATION	POST. REF.	DEBIT	CREDIT	BALANCE CR.
Jan.	2	Balance forward	✓			10000 —
	4	G.J.	2		648 —	10648 —
	5	G.J.	2		95 56	10743 56
	6	G.J.	2		61 75	10805 31
	31	C.P.J.	1	10157 31		648 —

John H. Johnson, Drawing — Account No. 302

DATE 19-8		EXPLANATION	POST. REF.	DEBIT	CREDIT	BALANCE
Jan.	5	CPJ	1	200 —		200 —
	20	CPJ	1	200 —		400 —

ADVANTAGES OF A CASH PAYMENTS JOURNAL

The main advantages of using a special journal to record all cash payments may be summarized as follows:

- Most entries require one line instead of three or four lines.
- A special column for recording cheque numbers helps to account for all cheques issued. This special journal also helps to strengthen the internal control of cash payments.
- Since only the monthly total is posted to the credit of Cash, much time is saved. Also, the frequency of human error in posting is automatically reduced when only the total is transferred to the Cash account.
- The task of maintaining the Cash Payments Journal may be assigned to a single clerk. This is also in accordance with the control measure called division of responsibility.

SUMMARIZING THE CASH PAYMENTS SYSTEM

Seven of the nine measures we discussed for controlling cash payments in any firm may be summarized in the form of an accounting systems flowchart. Examine the flowchart below. Can you identify those control measures?

FLOWCHART OF A CASH PAYMENTS SYSTEM

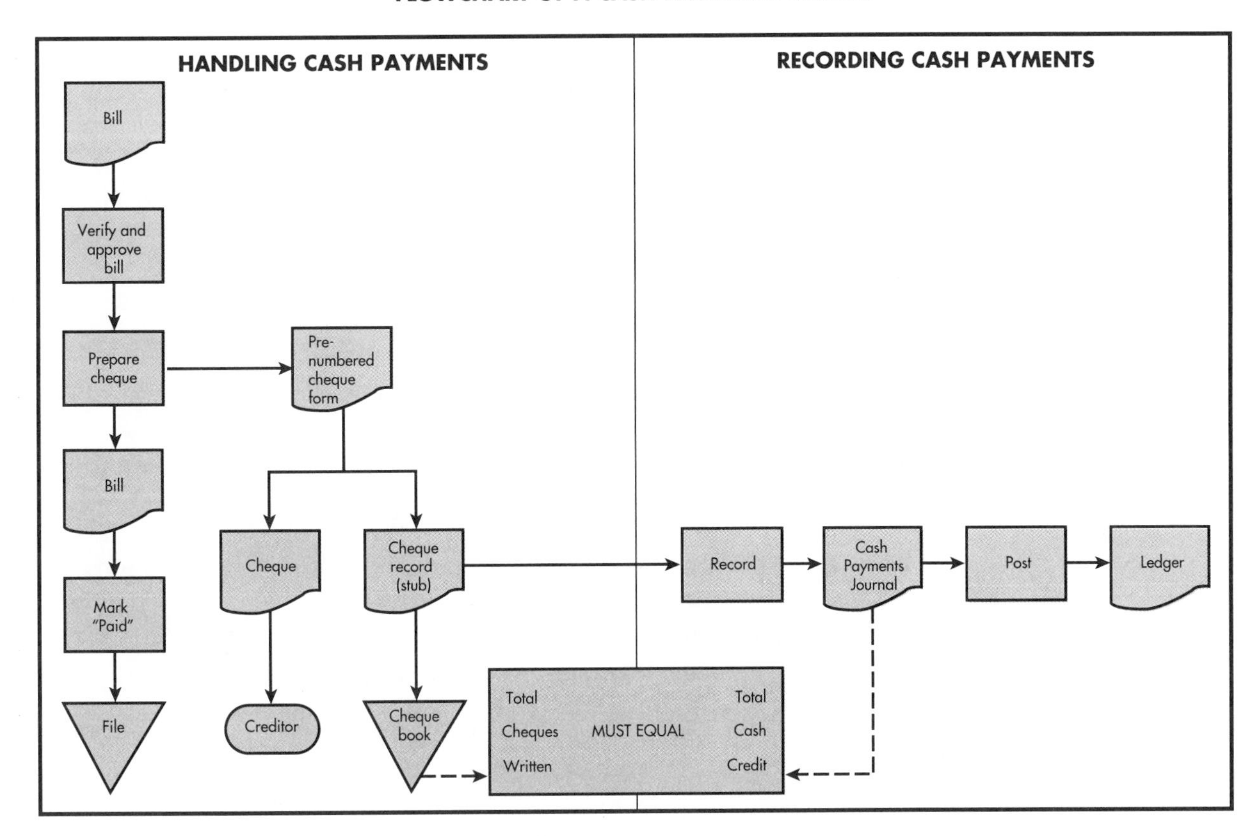

TOPIC 3 PROBLEMS

Setting up the books, preparing cheques, journalizing, and posting cash payments.

P 9-8 The following cheques were issued by Dr. Lien Chang's dental practice for the month of December, 19–7:

Dec. 1 Cheque No. 001 issued to City Realty Co. for $900 for rent of office and dental examining room.

3 Cheque No. 002 issued to Denco Equipment Supply for $500 on account.

4 Cheque No. 003 issued to Mardan Business Systems Ltd. for $200 on account.
8 Cheque No. 004 issued to Bell Canada for Invoice No. 4987 (installation of telephone) now due for $65.
9 Cheque No. 005 was spoiled and voided.
9 Cheque No. 006 was issued to City Dry Cleaners for $86 for cleaning of uniforms (Cleaning Expense, No. 510).
12 Cheque No. 007 issued to Wright Office Ltd. for $1500 (special cash price for purchase of office equipment, exclusive of installation).
13 Cheque No. 008 to A.J. Holt for $100 for installing office equipment obtained on December 12.
15 Cheque No. 009 issued to Dr. Lien Chang for personal use, $500.
16 Cheque No. 010 issued to Denco Equipment Supply for $500 on account.
17 Cheque No. 011 issued to Mardan Business Systems Ltd., $200 on account.
18 Cheque No. 012 was spoiled and voided.
22 Cheque No. 013 issued to Dr. Lien Chang for $1000 for personal use.
27 Cheque No. 014 to Public Utilities Commission for $147.50 in payment of Bill 16250 due today. *Note:* Recorded as an account payable on December 12.
30 Cheque No. 015 to Pat Davis, front-office person, monthly salary, $1500.
31 Cheque No. 016 to the Royal Bank of Canada, $500, in part payment of demand loan.
31 Cheque No. 017 to Central Finance Co., $635, for monthly payment of Five-Year Note Payable.

a. Use appropriate working forms to demonstrate how Cheques Nos. 001 and 002 would be issued. What action must be taken immediately after issuing each cheque? Why is this action required?

b. Record the above cheques in a Cash Payments Journal, page 1. Use a form similar to the one illustrated on page 371.

c. Set up individual accounts payable accounts as follows: Denco Equipment Supply, Don Mills, Ontario, M3C 3G1 (Balance Forward, Dec. 29, $11 070); Express Dental Inc., Downsview, Ontario (Balance Forward, Dec. 5, $1414.01); Mardan Business Systems Ltd., 48 Preston Street, Kitchener, Ontario, N2G 3W4 (Balance Forward, Dec. 7, $3321); Public Utilities

Commission, Box 3060, Any Town, Canada (Balance Forward, Dec. 12, $147.50).

d. Post the data from the Cash Payments Journal to the individual accounts set up for the Accounts Payable Ledger.

e. Total the money columns in the Cash Payments Journal. Then check the double-entry theory from these totals.

f. Post the data from the Cash Payments Journal to those General Ledger accounts affected by the special journal. Show balances forwarded in the following accounts: Cash (101), December 31, $10 874; Office Equipment (112), December 1, $4000; Bank Loan Payable (201), December 1, $5000; Accounts Payable (202), December 29, $15 852.51; Five-Year Note Payable (220), December 1, $38 000. Set up appropriate account titles and numbers for all other accounts affected by the special journal.

g. Rule off the Cash Payments Journal for the month.

Setting up the books, journalizing, posting cash payments, and calculating month-end totals in cash payments journal.

P 9-9 Bernice Obierski is the owner-manager of a mailing service. A cash register system is used to control cash receipts. This firm follows the accounting policy of debiting Supplies Expense for all supplies purchased. You have been asked to perform the following:

a. Open General Ledger accounts and record March 1 balances as follows: Cash (101), $8500; Equipment (110), $2500; Bank Loan Payable (201), $1000; Accounts Payable (202), $1400; Bernice Obierski, Capital (301), $8600; Bernice Obierski, Drawing (302); Rent Expense (501); Telephone Expense (502); Utilities Expense (503); Salaries Expense (504); Supplies Expense (505); Cash Short and Over (506).

b. Open an Accounts Payable Ledger with the following accounts and their balances forward as of March 1: Maritime Supply Co., 17 Upper Queen St., Charlottetown, Prince Edward Island, C1A 4C1 ($400); Jane Sands, 27 Central St., Summerside, P.E.I., C1N 3K8 ($1000).

c. Make the appropriate entries for the following transactions in a Cash Payments Journal similar to the one illustrated on page 371. You are starting on page 2 of the journal.

Mar. 1 Issued Cheque No. 28 for $800 for March rent to City Realty Co.
10 Issued Cheque No. 29 for $400 to Jane Sands on account.
15 Issued Cheque No. 30 for $1500 to Northern Equipment Co. for cash purchase of additional equipment.

18 Issued Cheque No. 31 for $150 to Maritime Supply Co., on account.
22 Issued Cheque No. 32 for $100 to Bernice Obierski, the owner, for personal use.
24 Issued Cheque No. 33, but later voided it.
25 Issued the following cheques: No. 34 to Maritime Telephone, $78 for March telephone bill; and No. 35 to City Stationery, $80 for office supplies.
27 Issued Cheque No. 36 for $280 to Public Utilities Commission for March utilities.
28 Issued Cheque No. 37 for $700 in part payment of the bank loan to the Royal Bank of Canada.
31 Issued Cheque No. 38 to Marjorie Ross for $2500 for monthly salary.

d. Post the appropriate entries from the Cash Payments Journal to the Accounts Payable Ledger.

e. Check the addition (using an adding machine tape or the footing procedure) and prove the double-entry theory against the totals of the journal.

f. Post the entries from the Cash Payments Journal to the General Ledger.

g. Rule the special journal for the month.

Journalizing and posting cash payments, calculating month-end totals in cash payments journal.

P 9-10 Challenge Problem The following cheques were issued by Dr. John Reddon's dental practice for the month of September:

Sept. 1 Cheque No. 001 issued to Alberta Telephones, $70 for installation of telephone.
5 Cheque No. 002 issued to City Dry Cleaners, $96 for cleaning of uniforms.
7 Cheque No. 003 was spoiled and promptly voided.
7 Cheque No. 004 issued to Edmonton Dental Supply, $500 on account.
8 Cheque No. 005 issued to Wright Dental Ltd., $7000 for new dental equipment acquired for cash.
9 Cheque No. 006 to Dr. John Reddon, $100 for personal use.
10 Cheque No. 007 to Office Specialty Co. for $170 for office supplies. *Note:* Refer to Problem 9-7 for accounting policy.
13 Cheque No. 008 was spoiled and promptly voided.

14 Issued the following bimonthly salary cheques: No. 009 to Pamela Brown, dental hygienist, $1250; No. 010 to Jill Murray, front-office person, $750.

17 Issued Cheque No. 011 for $65 to Alberta Power Ltd. in full settlement of account balance due today.

18 Issued Cheque No. 012 to Dr. John Reddon, $100 for personal use.

19 Cheque No. 013 to City Dental Supplies, $280 for dental supplies. *Note:* Check back to Problem 9-7 for accounting policy.

21 Cheque No. 014 to City Treasurer, $175 for business licence fee.

23 Cheque No. 015 to Edmonton Dental Supply, $500 on account.

26 Cheque No. 016 to Dr. John Reddon, $100 for personal use.

28 Cheque No. 017 issued to Edmonton Dental Supply, $500, on account.

30 Issued the following bimonthly salary cheques: No. 018 to Pamela Brown, $1250; No. 019 to Jill Murray, $750.

30 Issued Cheque No. 020 to the Royal Bank of Canada, $2000, in part payment of the demand loan.

30 Issued Cheque No. 021 to City Properties Ltd., $1200 for the monthly payment of the mortgage as follows: $500 applied to the principal (chief part) of the mortgage payable; the remaining $700 to be charged to Mortgage Interest Expense.

a. Record the above cheques in a Cash Payments Journal, beginning on page 1.

b. Post the data from the Cash Payments Journal to the Accounts Payable Ledger used in Problem 9-7. *Note:* No new accounts are required.

c. Total the money columns in the Cash Payments Journal. Then check the double-entry theory from these totals.

d. Post the data from the Cash Payments Journal to those General Ledger accounts affected by this special journal. Use the GL solved for Problem 9-7 and add the following accounts: Telephone Expense (503); Cleaning Expense (504); John Reddon, Drawing (302); Salaries Expense (505); Licence Fees Expense (506); Mortgage Interest Expense (520).

e. Rule off the Cash Payments Journal for the month.

MINI-CASES

Identifying weaknesses in cash payment controls and suggesting solutions.

MC 9-7 Dr. Barbara Teal's bookkeeper prepares the accounting records for her medical practice. Since Dr. Teal knows nothing about accounting, the bookkeeper orders all the supplies, records all purchases, and writes and authorizes all cheques.

Dr. Teal hires a local chartered accountant to prepare her annual financial statements and personal income tax return.

a. Explain any control weaknesses you detect in this system.

b. Is Dr. Teal at risk of losing any money? If so, how could this happen?

c. Suggest measures that would improve Dr. Teal's system of cash payment.

Identifying weaknesses in cash payment controls and suggesting solutions.

MC 9-8 Chad Stevenson operates a house-painting business. Chad purchases all his supplies from a local paint store where he has an account. When Chad purchases supplies, he receives an invoice for the amount of the purchase. Once he has collected the fee from the homeowner, Chad pays as many invoices as possible with cash on hand. He then files the invoice in a shoe box to be used in preparing his yearly financial statement. At the end of each month, the paint store sends Chad a statement of his account. Chad then writes a cheque for the balance on the account.

a. Explain any control weaknesses you detect in this system.

b. Could Chad be paying twice for supplies? If so, how could this happen?

c. Suggest some measures that would improve Chad's system of cash payments.

Identifying control measures and cash discounts.

MC 9-9 Carlton Dry Cleaners is a laundry and dry-cleaning business owned and operated by Vina Aveiro. The operation of the business is handled by Vina, but the bookkeeping is done by Martin, a part-time employee.

When an invoice is received, Martin ensures the goods have been received and checks the accuracy of the invoice. He then records the invoice in the General Journal using the total amount on the invoice. Finally, Martin files the invoice in his tickler file under the date which is one week in advance of the due date on the invoice.

On this date, the invoice, an addressed envelope, and a prepared cheque are given to Vina for her approval. Vina then mails the cheque to the supplier.

For example, an invoice for cleaning supplies was received December 16. The total amount of the invoice was $700 on credit.

If the bill is paid in ten days, $14 will be deducted from the amount. The bill must be paid within thirty days. The invoice was checked and recorded in the journal on December 17 and then placed in the tickler file dated January 8.

a. Explain any strengths and/or weaknesses you detect in this system.

TOPIC 4 REVIEWING MONTH-END PROCEDURES

So far, you have learned these important parts of the accounts payable application:

- originating accounts payable data through various purchase invoices
- journalizing and posting accounts payable data in appropriate journals and ledgers
- issuing cheques for appropriate payments
- journalizing and posting cheque record information in appropriate journals and ledgers

This final topic involves the last part of the accounts payable application—preparing monthly trial balances.

PREPARING MONTHLY TRIAL BALANCES

The preparation of monthly trial balances is similar to the preparation of the ones introduced in Chapter 8. The only difference here is that the subsidiary ledger is for accounts payable.

In a large firm with an efficient division of responsibility, a General Ledger clerk prepares the monthly trial balance for the General Ledger. The accounts payable clerk, a person not connected with direct work with the General Ledger, prepares the monthly schedule of accounts payable. With this division of responsibility, the General Ledger balance of accounts payable controls the listing of individual creditor account balances. How is this control achieved? The accountant responsible for the General Ledger has the balance of accounts payable. He or she asks for the total of the accounts payable subsidiary ledger as provided by the Schedule of Accounts Payable. If this total does not agree with the balance of Accounts Payable in the General Ledger, the accounts payable clerk must recheck posting information to come up with the right answer.

Schedule of Accounts Payable: a list of individual creditors with their month-end balances.

If trial balances for Dr. Johnson's dental practice were taken from the combined accounts receivable and accounts payable applications covered in Chapters 8 and 9, they would appear as follows:

John H. Johnson, D.D.S.
Trial Balance
January 31,19–8

Account	No.	Debit	Credit
Cash	101	$ 1 771.36	
Bank Deposit Receipts	102	15 680.00	
Accounts Receivable	103	4 125.00	
Dental Equipment	110	70 648.00	
Office Equipment	112	5 875.00	
Accounts Payable	202		$ 648.00
5-Year Note Payable	210		29 500.00
John H. Johnson, Capital	301		70 000.00
John H. Johnson, Drawing	302	400.00	
Professional Fees Earned	401		6 694.00
Rent Expense	501	5 000.00	
Salaries Expense	502	2 200.00	
Dental Supplies Expense	503	95.56	
Telephone Expense	505	285.33	
Utilities Expense	506	61.75	
Lab Fees Expense	507	700.00	
		$106 842.00	$106 842.00

John H. Johnson, D.D.S.
Schedule of Accounts Payable
January 31, 19–8

IBM Canada Ltd.	$648.00
Total of Accounts Payable	$648.00

John H. Johnson, D.D.S.
Schedule of Accounts Receivable
January 31, 19–8

V. Aviero	$1 000.00
M. Brown	5.00
B. Campbell	50.00
H. Chan	951.00
R. Diloreto	103.00
A. Gomes	550.00
D. Garcia	189.00
C. Lee	115.00
S. Lesniak	103.00
G. Tuck	567.00
C. Zander	492.00
Total of Accounts Receivable	$4 125.00

PROBLEMS

Preparing a subledger trial balance.

P 9-11 Refer to Problems 9-5 and 9-8 (Dr. Lien Chang's practice).

a. Prepare the General Ledger trial balance as at December 31 from the solutions for these problems. You will need two more accounts for this trial balance: Accounts Receivable (103), balance $1614; Professional Fees Earned (401), balance $2488.

b. Prepare the Schedule of Accounts Payable from the subsidiary ledger solved for Problem 9-8.

MINI-CASES

Analyzing posting errors.

MC 9-10 You have completed your month-end procedures for the purchases payables payments system. When you compare the Accounts Payable ledger account with your Schedule of Accounts Payable, you discover a discrepancy.

a. List the reasons why this discrepancy could occur.

b. What steps would you take to find the cause of the discrepancy?

Using the accounting equation to determine Accounts Payable amount at year-end.

MC 9-11 An accounting clerk supplied the following general listing as at January 31, current year:

Cash	$ 5 000
Accounts Receivable	6 500
Equipment	20 000
Accounts Payable	?
Benson Lee, Drawing	1 500
Benson Lee, Capital	20 000
Fees Earned	9 000
Salary Expense	1 500
Supplies Expense	800
Miscellaneous Expense	200

The clerk could not proceed to the trial balance because the account balance for Accounts Payable as at January 31 could not be located.

a. Assume that all listed amounts are correct and support normal account balances. Determine which accounts listed have normal debit and credit balances. Prepare a trial balance that includes Accounts Payable.

Note: The Comprehensive Case Study for Chapter 9 is found at the end of Chapter 11. It is part of a large exercise which reviews all the systems discussed in Part 2.

CHAPTER 10

INTRODUCING PETTY CASH AND BANKING APPLICATIONS

Topic 1

Establishing and Maintaining the Petty Cash System

Topic 2

Preparing a Bank Reconciliation Statement and Discussing Personal Banking Applications

Topic 3

Preparing the Statement of Cash Flows and Accounting for Cash Short and Over Transactions

In explaining the accounts receivable and accounts payable applications, we took great care to point out the importance of internal measures to control cash. This chapter presents other measures taken to control petty (small) expenditures of cash, preparation of a monthly bank reconciliation statement and its role in controlling cash, and preparation of a Statement of Cash Flows. With this background, you should be able to apply your knowledge to personal banking.

TOPIC 1 ESTABLISHING AND MAINTAINING THE PETTY CASH SYSTEM

Petty cash system: a system designed to control small (petty) expenditures.

In Chapter 9 you learned that making payments by cheque helps businesses control the outflow of cash. However, writing cheques for very small expenditures is not practical because it is time-consuming and costly. To pay for and maintain control over these small expenditures many firms set up a petty cash system. The main features of this system are illustrated below.

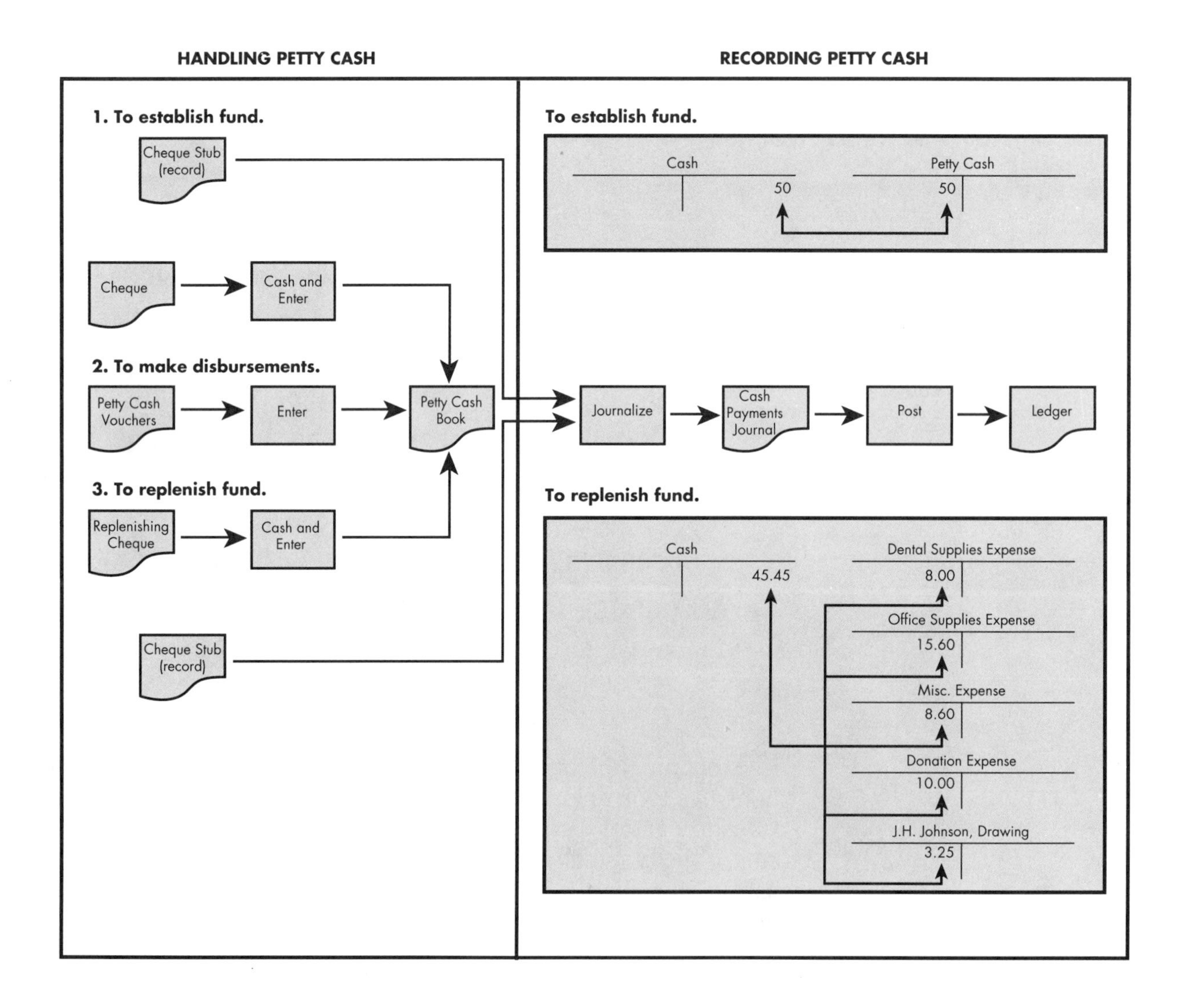

On the left side, the flowchart shows that the system for handling petty cash is divided into three main parts: (1) establishing the petty cash fund, (2) making petty cash disbursements, and (3) replenishing the petty cash fund. A petty cash system, like any other cash system, should include some control features. You will notice that the handling of petty cash is separate from recording. Another control measure is to set the amount of the petty cash fund. The amount should be small enough so that if it were lost or stolen, the loss would be minimal. On the other hand, the fund should be large enough so that there is enough money to cover the typical amount of petty cash expenditures made between each replenishment. Finally, the amount is generally a round number to make recordkeeping easier.

Chart of Accounts
CURRENT ASSETS
101 Cash
102 Petty Cash
103 Bank Deposit Receipts
104 Accounts Receivable

ESTABLISHING THE PETTY CASH FUND

To establish the petty cash fund the flowchart shows that a cheque is issued. The cheque should be issued to the employee who will be the custodian of the fund. The cheque is not issued to Petty Cash because if it were lost anyone could cash the cheque and the business would lose the money. Once the cheque is cashed, the money is kept in a locked money box or drawer and the key is kept by the custodian.

The cheque is recorded as follows:

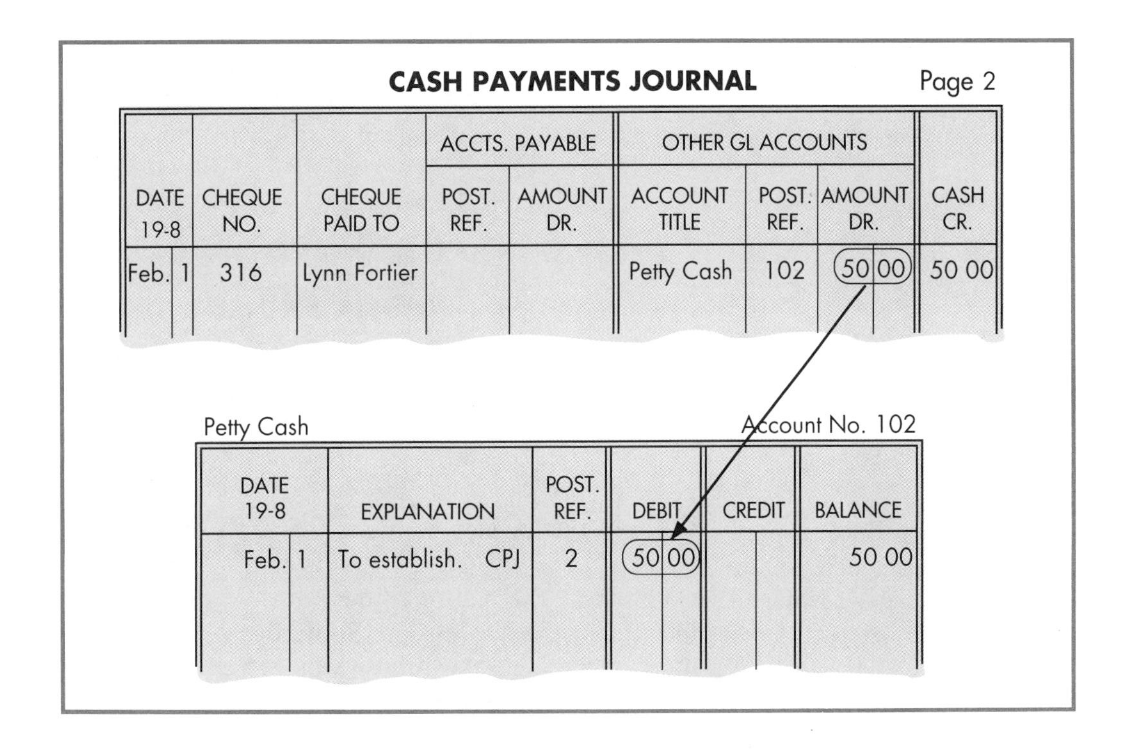

CASH PAYMENTS JOURNAL Page 2

DATE 19-8		CHEQUE NO.	CHEQUE PAID TO	ACCTS. PAYABLE POST. REF.	ACCTS. PAYABLE AMOUNT DR.	OTHER GL ACCOUNTS ACCOUNT TITLE	OTHER GL ACCOUNTS POST. REF.	OTHER GL ACCOUNTS AMOUNT DR.	CASH CR.
Feb.	1	316	Lynn Fortier			Petty Cash	102	50 00	50 00

Petty Cash Account No. 102

DATE 19-8		EXPLANATION	POST. REF.	DEBIT	CREDIT	BALANCE
Feb.	1	To establish.	CPJ 2	50 00		50 00

Petty Cash (account): a current asset.

The Cash or Bank ledger account is credited or reduced by the amount of the fund. The Petty Cash account is debited. The balance in the Petty Cash account remains unchanged unless one of the following two transactions takes place:

- When the fund is insufficient to pay for the small expenses. The balance is increased.
- The fund is closed and the cash is deposited back into the bank account.

Petty Cash is a current asset and for most businesses is one of the first accounts in the General Ledger.

MAKING PETTY CASH DISBURSEMENTS

Petty cash vouchers: prenumbered documents showing evidence of a petty cash payment.

Individual petty cash payments do not go through the accounting records. As the flowchart clearly shows, petty cash vouchers must be issued for all disbursements. An example of a petty cash voucher is illustrated below. This voucher represents the source document, providing proof of the transaction. If an invoice is received for an expenditure, it would be stapled to the voucher, providing additional proof of the transaction.

No. 1 Amount $ 1.85

PETTY CASH VOUCHER

Date Feb. 4, 19-8

Paid to C.P. Telecommunications

For Collect courier

Charge to Misc. Expense

JOHN H. JOHNSON, D.D.S.

Approved by J.H.J. Received by J.C. Forest

Petty Cash Book: a non-accounting record for the use of the petty cashier to summarize petty cash transactions.

Some businesses will record each expenditure in a Petty Cash Book. The Petty Cash Book is not a journal but a summary of the expenditures. Because all the information is in one book, journalizing the transactions is easier. Some businesses summarize the expenditures at the time the fund needs replenishing. A Petty Cash Book is illustrated on the opposite page.

PETTY CASH BOOK Page 1

DATE		EXPLANATION	VO. NO.	PETTY CASH FUND RECEIVED	PETTY CASH FUND PAID OUT	DISTRIBUTION OF PAYMENTS DENTAL SUPPLIES EXPENSE	OFFICE SUPPLIES EXPENSE	MISC. EXPENSE	NAME OF OTHER ACCOUNT	AMOUNT
Feb.	1	Chq. 316 to establish fund	—	50 00						
	4	Collect courier	1		1 85			1 85		
	5	No. 2 liquid cement	2		4 00	4 00				
	6	Window washing	3		4 50			4 50		
	7	Postage stamps	4		1 60		1 60			
	8	United Way	5		10 00				Donation Expense	10 00
	11	Refills for writing pens	6		7 50		7 50			
	12	Paper clips	7		75		75			
	13	Finishing burs	8		4 00	4 00				
	14	Proprietor's lunch	9		3 25				J.H. Johnson, Drg.	3 25
	15	Envelopes	10		5 75		5 75			
	15	Messenger service	11		2 25			2 25		
				50 00	45 45	8 00	15 60	8 60		13 25
	15	Totals		50 00	45 45	8 00	15 60	8 60		13 25
	15	Cash on hand			4 55					
				50 00	50 00					
Feb.	15	Cash on hand	—	4 55						
	15	Chq. 325 to replenish	—	45 45						

REPLENISHING THE PETTY CASH FUND

When the petty cash fund gets low and it is time to replenish it, the petty cashier:

(1) totals the amount of expenditures paid for with petty cash

(2) proves the cash by ensuring the expenditures plus the cash left in the box together are equal to the original amount of the fund

(3) submits the cash proof to the person responsible for issuing the cheque to replenish the fund

(4) cashes the cheque and deposits the cash in the locked box

At the time the fund is replenished, the accounting records are updated. Since a cheque has been issued, the entry is recorded in the

Cash Payments Journal. The amount of the cheque to replenish the fund is credited to the bank account and the individual expenditures are recorded in various expense accounts. Look at the journal below in which the items on the petty cash requisition are recorded.

JOHN H. JOHNSON, D.D.S.
Petty Cash Requisition

REQUEST TO REPLENISH PETTY CASH

FOR PERIOD: Feb. 1 to Feb. 15, 19-8

Petty Cash Summary:

Dental Supplies Expense	$ 8.00
Office Supplies Expense	15.60
Miscellaneous Expense	8.60
Donation Expense	10.00
J.H. Johnson, Drawing	3.25
Total Disbursements	$45.45
Cash on Hand	4.55
Amount of Petty Cash Fund	$50.00

Lynn Fortier
(Petty Cashier)

CASH PAYMENTS JOURNAL Page 2

DATE 19-8	CHEQUE NO.	CHEQUE PAID TO	ACCOUNTS PAYABLE POST. REF.	ACCOUNTS PAYABLE AMOUNT DR.	OTHER GENERAL LEDGER ACCOUNTS ACCOUNTS TITLE	OTHER GENERAL LEDGER ACCOUNTS POST. REF.	OTHER GENERAL LEDGER ACCOUNTS AMOUNT DR.	CASH CR.
Feb. 15	325	Lynn Fortier			Dental Supplies Exp.		8 00	
					Office Supplies Exp.		15 60	
					Misc. Expense		8 60	
					Donation Expense		10 00	
					J.H. Johnson, Drg.		3 25	45 45

DESCRIBING THE PETTY CASH SYSTEM AS AN IMPREST SYSTEM

Imprest system: a loan or advance of money from the main Cash (chequing) account.

The petty cash fund is a fixed sum loaned or set aside from the cash in the bank. Accountants call this system of lending money the imprest system of petty cash. The imprest system is widely used because the amount borrowed can be redeposited at any time into the bank account. As a way to control cash, accountants support the imprest system because a cheque payment is required both to create the fund and also to replenish it.

REPORTING PETTY CASH ON THE BALANCE SHEET

Although the Petty Cash account is classified separately as a current asset in a firm's Chart of Accounts, the question usually arises: Why is petty cash not given its own heading in the balance sheet?

To answer that question, you must first learn the meaning of cash to an accountant. In accounting, cash:

Cash (as defined in accounting): any item acceptable for deposit in the firm's chequing account.

(1) can be deposited in the business's chequing account, for example, coins or cheques received on account; and

(2) is readily available to meet current operating expenses and to pay off current liabilities.

The petty cash fund could be deposited in the business's chequing account at any time and it is used to pay for small operating expenses. Since it is acceptable and available as cash, the fund is added to the cash balance in the chequing account and the total figure is recorded as the Cash or Bank balance on the balance sheet.

PROBLEMS

Completing all steps involved with establishing, reimbursing, and recording petty cash.

P 10-1 The transactions below represent the petty cash events of Dr. P. Mazzone's dental practice.

19--

Jan. 2 Issued Cheque No. 150 for $100.00 to establish the petty cash fund. Miss M. Toth is the front-office clerk who handles the petty cash fund.

3 Paid $4.40 to City Stationery Co. for office stationery.

4 Paid $16.50 to City Dry Cleaners for dry cleaning of uniforms. (Dry cleaning Expense.)

5 Paid $4.25 to Unitel for collect courier.

8 Paid $9.65 to City Drug Supplies for cotton pellets. (Dental Supplies Expense.)
9 Paid to City Stationery Co. $7.25 for paper clips.
10 Paid $8 for tickets to Community Church Fair. (Donation Expense.)
11 Paid $18.60 to City Drug Supplies for denture paste.
12 Paid $4.50 to Dr. Mazzone for personal use.
12 Paid $15.00 to Tom Smith for window washing. (Miscellaneous Expense.)

a. Illustrate how the cheque on January 2 would be issued to establish the fund. Assume the dental practice has a current account with the Royal Bank of Canada. Also assume that the balance on Cheque Stub 150 is $2496.40.

b. Show how the entry to establish the petty cash fund would appear in the Cash Payments Journal, page 28.

c. Assume that the petty cashier is required to use petty cash vouchers (beginning with Vo. No. 1) and a Petty Cash Book similar to the ones illustrated in this chapter. Show how the petty cash transactions would appear on the vouchers and in the Petty Cash Book. Print the following account titles in the three special Distribution of Payments money columns: Dental Supplies Expense, Office Supplies Expense, and Misc. Expense. Assume that Dr. Mazzone is to approve each voucher. Invent a second personal name for the other signature.

d. Assume that petty cash is to be replenished on January 12. Show a proof of the Petty Cash Book. Then illustrate how the petty cash requisition form would look.

e. Assume that Cheque No. 175 is issued to replenish the fund. Show how the cheque would look. Assume the balance on the stub is $2850.75.

f. Show how the entry to replenish the fund would look in the Cash Payments Journal.

g. Complete the Petty Cash Book for the petty cash period. Then show the cash on hand and the cheque to replenish in order to begin the new period.

Using a Petty Cash Book to record expenses.

P 10-2 The events summarized below are more petty cash transactions for Dr. Mazzone's dental practice.

Jan. 15 Paid $4.85 for office envelopes.
16 Paid $7.80 for postage stamps.
18 Paid $8.00 for dry cleaning of uniform.

19 Paid $3.25 for collect courier.
22 Paid $16.40 for amalgam vibrator tips.
24 Paid $3.85 for pencils for the office.
26 Paid $8.00 for Dr. Mazzone's personal use.
28 Paid $0.40 for postage due. (Miscellaneous Expense.)
31 Paid $5.95 for cotton-tip applicators.

a. Assume that petty cash vouchers have been issued correctly for each petty cash transaction. Use the Petty Cash Book for Problem 10-1. Leave one blank line near the bottom, to show Total Forward. Then continue the record on a second page.

b. Assume that the fund is to be replenished on January 31 through the issue of Cheque No. 201. Show a petty cash requisition to replenish the fund. Complete the Petty Cash Book for the period, bring down the balance of the cash on hand, and record the replenishing cheque for the new period.

c. Record the replenishing cheque in the Cash Payments Journal. Continue on the journal form from Problem 10-1.

Applying the accountant's definition of cash.

P 10-3 Explain briefly why each of the separate items listed below would or would not be included in the accountant's definition of cash.

a. postage stamps
b. a bank money order
c. a retail credit card
d. a cheque received from a customer
e. a stock (share) certificate
f. a valuable diamond
g. a $500-dollar bill
h. a $1000-dollar bill
i. a bank's "pure" savings account
j. a petty cash fund
k. a Canada Savings Bond interest coupon now due

Recording petty cash when cash and vouchers do not total the fund balance.

P 10-4 Challenge Problem Frank Joyce Co. established a petty cash fund and appointed Elizabeth Condos petty cashier. The company then completed the transactions summarized below.

Oct. 1 Received, cashed, and placed into the petty cash box the $100 proceeds of Cheque No. 71.
2 Paid $5 to have the office windows washed.

3 Bought carbon paper and paper clips, $15.65.
4 Paid $18.30 for an advertisement in the local newspaper.
5 Bought postage stamps, $15.60.
8 Paid $15.95 for minor repairs to an office chair.
9 Paid the proprietor, Frank Joyce, $2.00 for his own use.
12 Gave $15.00 to the United Way Campaign.
12 After giving the donation to the United Way canvasser, the petty cashier found that she had only $10.50 in money in her petty cash box. Her cash proof of the petty cash box, however, showed that she should have had $12.50. The cashier found that the difference of $2 was spent by the owner on lunch. She then prepared a petty cash requisition and exchanged this form together with the paid vouchers for the replenishing Cheque No. 84.

a. Record the above transactions in the appropriate journal and in the Petty Cash Book. For the Distribution of Payments section, show Adv. Expense, Office Expense, and Misc. Expense.

b. Prepare the Petty Cash Book for the next petty cash period.

MINI-CASES

Identifying weaknesses in petty cash control.

MC 10-1 A friend of yours, the owner of a medium-sized company, learns that you have studied some important measures of controlling cash. He invites you to spend a few days studying the application of these control measures in his business. You found the following:

(i) A petty cash fund of $1000 had been established to take care of small payments. Instead of a regular voucher form, people were allowed to submit their own forms. Many of the forms were a variety of store receipts; some were short pieces of paper with some explanation by the user of the petty cash. The Petty Cash Book revealed the fund was replenished weekly.

(ii) The petty cashier was permitted to issue the replenishing cheque, sign the cheque, and make the accounting record for all petty cash payments.

(iii) The petty cashier was also permitted to approve payments of any amount up to and including $100.

(iv) Personal cheques of customers and employees were cashed from the petty cash fund.

(v) One person was given the responsibility to act as the cashier and bookkeeper. Among other duties, he handled cash receipts, deposited all cash in the bank, issued and signed all cheques, and maintained the accounting records for all cash transactions other than those of a petty cash nature.

(vi) A cheque for $855 issued in payment of an account payable was erroneously listed in the Cash Payments Journal as $585. The error was not corrected until the next month when the cancelled cheque was received from the bank.

a. Identify the cash control weaknesses for each of the above.

b. What changes in the overall cash control system would you recommend to improve the problem areas?

Identifying weaknesses in petty cash control.

MC 10-2 After completing an introductory accounting course, Kim Chiu offered to tutor a school friend who needed help with the topic of petty cash. Kim instructs his friend that to establish the petty cash fund a cheque payable to the order of ''Petty Cash'' is made out.

a. Do you agree with Kim's instruction? Explain why or why not.

Identifying petty cash control weaknesses and suggesting an improved system.

MC 10-3 You are a lawyer with a small local practice. Your bookkeeping is done on a part-time basis by Daniel So, who comes to your office on Mondays and Thursdays to do all the bookkeeping and also banking. In order for you and your staff to make small expenditures during the entire week, Daniel has placed a petty cash fund in the top drawer of his desk. Anyone requiring a reimbursement for a small expense will take the appropriate amount from the drawer. If this person has a receipt, he or she will drop it in the drawer.

a. Do you detect any cash control weaknesses in this system?

b. Suggest a system to avoid the problems you indicated in **a**.

PREPARING A BANK RECONCILIATION STATEMENT AND DISCUSSING PERSONAL BANKING APPLICATIONS

In Chapters 8 and 9 you learned several important measures for controlling cash receipts and cash payments. The two most important are:

- All cash receipts should be deposited intact into the business's bank account.
- All cash payments should be made by cheque.

Both measures imply the use of a bank current (chequing) account. In Chapter 8 you learned that a bank provides current account depositors with a monthly statement, which is an accounting record of withdrawals and deposits. The bank statement allows information to be checked against the business's records to make sure the statement and the records agree. With this separate accounting, the business can make one more check on the accuracy of its accounting records.

ILLUSTRATING THE BANK STATEMENT

Banks prepare monthly statements, which are mailed to the business on a monthly basis. An example is illustrated below:

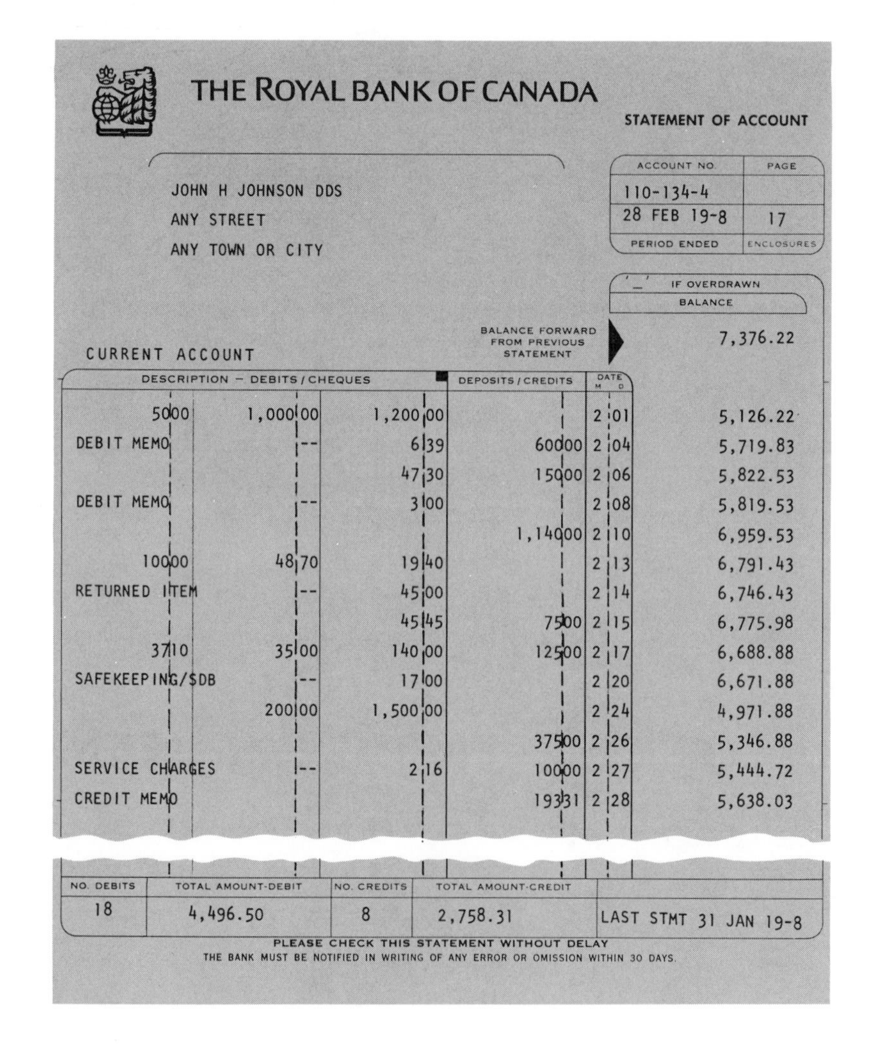

THE ROYAL BANK OF CANADA

STATEMENT OF ACCOUNT

JOHN H JOHNSON DDS
ANY STREET
ANY TOWN OR CITY

ACCOUNT NO.	PAGE
110-134-4	
28 FEB 19-8	17
PERIOD ENDED	ENCLOSURES

IF OVERDRAWN

BALANCE

CURRENT ACCOUNT

BALANCE FORWARD FROM PREVIOUS STATEMENT 7,376.22

DESCRIPTION – DEBITS / CHEQUES			DEPOSITS / CREDITS	DATE M D	BALANCE
50.00	1,000.00	1,200.00		2 01	5,126.22
DEBIT MEMO	--	6.39	600.00	2 04	5,719.83
		47.30	150.00	2 06	5,822.53
DEBIT MEMO	--	3.00		2 08	5,819.53
			1,140.00	2 10	6,959.53
100.00	48.70	19.40		2 13	6,791.43
RETURNED ITEM	--	45.00		2 14	6,746.43
		45.45	75.00	2 15	6,775.98
37.10	35.00	140.00	125.00	2 17	6,688.88
SAFEKEEPING/$DB	--	17.00		2 20	6,671.88
	200.00	1,500.00		2 24	4,971.88
			375.00	2 26	5,346.88
SERVICE CHARGES	--	2.16	100.00	2 27	5,444.72
CREDIT MEMO			193.31	2 28	5,638.03

NO. DEBITS	TOTAL AMOUNT-DEBIT	NO. CREDITS	TOTAL AMOUNT-CREDIT	
18	4,496.50	8	2,758.31	LAST STMT 31 JAN 19-8

PLEASE CHECK THIS STATEMENT WITHOUT DELAY
THE BANK MUST BE NOTIFIED IN WRITING OF ANY ERROR OR OMISSION WITHIN 30 DAYS.

Identify this information contained in the bank statement:

- The top portion identifies the depositor, the account number, and the period-end date of the statement.

- The balance forward ($7376.22) represents the bank balance at the end of the last statement (January 31, 19-8), listed at the bottom.
- The body of the statement records: the cheques that have been cashed by the bank in the debit column; the deposits made to the account in the credit column; and the running balance in the account.

At first glance, you may think that the bank records transactions in a manner that is backward to normal accounting practices but this is not the case. From the banker's viewpoint, the depositor's account is a current liability payable on demand. If the depositor's bank balance goes down, the bank owes the depositor less money. Therefore, cheques which reduce the depositor's balance are recorded as debits in the bank's records. On the other hand, deposits increase the current liability of the banker. Therefore, they are recorded as credits on all bank statements.

Bank statement (in accounting language): a copy of a current liability on the banker's books.

Notice that the entries in the body of the bank statement are sometimes accompanied by phrases which describe the kind of transaction. We will discuss the meaning of these phrases.

- **Service charges** represent cash withdrawn from your account to pay the bank for the services it provides. For example, a service charge is levied to the depositor and also the writer of an NSF cheque.

Bank debit memo: a source document decreasing (debiting) the depositor's account on the banker's books.

- A bank debit memo refers to an enclosed note explaining why an amount has been deducted from the depositor's account. Two transactions that would result in a debit memo being issued are: (1) bank charges for preparing addressed and coded cheques; and (2) bank loan repayments or interest charges on a bank loan.

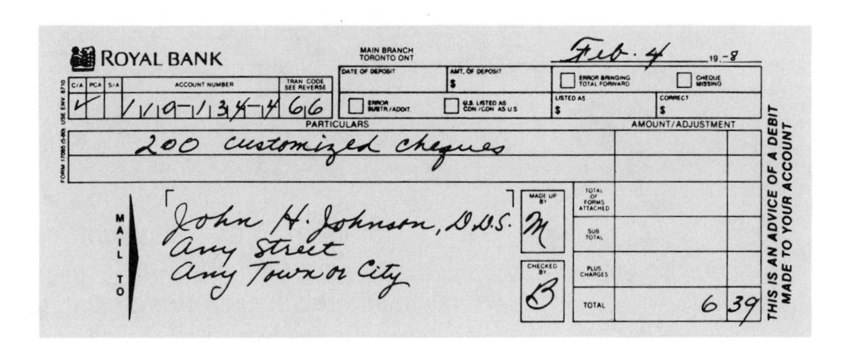
ROYAL BANK
MAIN BRANCH TORONTO ONT
Feb. 4 19-8

C/A	PCA	S/A	ACCOUNT NUMBER	TRAN CODE SEE REVERSE
✓			1119-1134-14	66

DATE OF DEPOSIT | AMT. OF DEPOSIT $ | ERROR BRINGING TOTAL FORWARD | CHEQUE MISSING
ERROR SUBTR./ADDIT. | U.S. LISTED AS CDN/CDN AS U.S. | LISTED AS $ | CORRECT $

PARTICULARS	AMOUNT/ADJUSTMENT	
200 customized cheques		

MAIL TO
John H. Johnson, D.D.S.
Any Street
Any Town or City

MADE UP BY M
CHECKED BY B

TOTAL OF FORMS ATTACHED		
SUB TOTAL		
PLUS CHARGES		
TOTAL	6	39

THIS IS AN ADVICE OF A DEBIT MADE TO YOUR ACCOUNT

NSF cheque: a cheque marked "Not Sufficient Funds."

- **Returned Item** or NSF (not sufficient funds) cheque refers to a cheque that the depositor has received (as payment) and subsequently deposited into the bank account. However, the issuer of the cheque does not have sufficient funds to cover the cheque. Since this amount was added to the bank balance, it must then be shown as a reduction to correct the discrepancy. Generally, the bank will levy a service charge to cover the costs of processing and to discourage such cheques.

- **Safekeeping/SDB** shows the amount withdrawn from the account by the bank for rental fees on a safety deposit box. These boxes are used by depositors to store valuable documents and are kept in a locked facility in the bank. Sometimes this charge is recorded on a debit memo.

Bank credit memo: a source document increasing (crediting) the depositor's account on the banker's books.

Term deposit receipt: a source document issued by the bank, giving evidence of a short-term investment.

- A bank credit memo refers to an enclosed note explaining why an amount has been deposited in the account. An example of such a transaction might be the deposit of interest earned on a term deposit receipt which is a short-term investment taken out by the depositor.

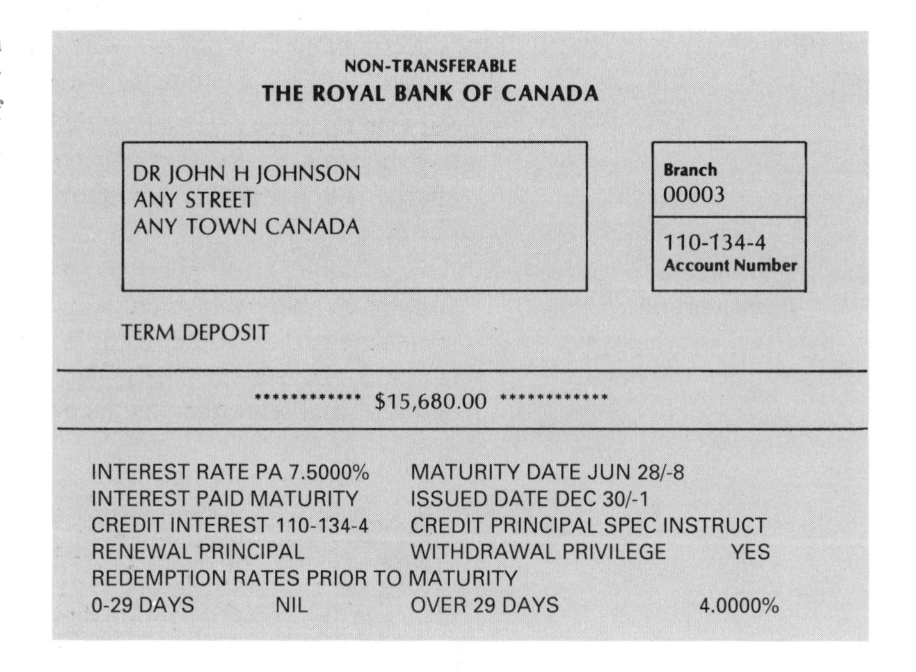
NON-TRANSFERABLE
THE ROYAL BANK OF CANADA

DR JOHN H JOHNSON
ANY STREET
ANY TOWN CANADA

Branch
00003

110-134-4
Account Number

TERM DEPOSIT

************ $15,680.00 ************

INTEREST RATE PA 7.5000%		MATURITY DATE JUN 28/-8	
INTEREST PAID MATURITY		ISSUED DATE DEC 30/-1	
CREDIT INTEREST 110-134-4		CREDIT PRINCIPAL SPEC INSTRUCT	
RENEWAL PRINCIPAL		WITHDRAWAL PRIVILEGE	YES
REDEMPTION RATES PRIOR TO MATURITY			
0-29 DAYS	NIL	OVER 29 DAYS	4.0000%

- The bottom of the statement provides information that can be used to prove the accuracy of accounting records. The depositor should check each item listed. It also provides the balance in the account at the end of the period covered by the statement.

EXPLAINING THE NEED FOR A BANK RECONCILIATION

In theory, the balance in the ledger should match the balance on the bank statement, since both the business and the bank are keeping track of the same bank account. In practice, however, this does not happen for the following reasons:

Outstanding cheques: cheques issued but not as yet "cashed" (cancelled) by the bank.

(1) The business has issued one or more cheques that have yet to be received and processed or cancelled by the bank. These outstanding cheques will make the bank statement balance larger than the firm's cash account balance.

Deposit in transit: a deposit not yet credited by the bank on the books of the banker.

(2) The business may have deposited an amount which is shown in the business's records but has yet to appear on the bank statement. This generally happens if a deposit is made late on the same day the bank statement is prepared. This late deposit is called an outstanding deposit or deposit in transit, and it will cause the bank balance to be lower than the business's balance. The outstanding deposits are a result of a timing difference.

(3) The bank may have enclosed one or more debit or credit memos. Until the bank statement has been received, the business has no knowledge of these transactions and therefore cannot record them in the ledger. Once the memos are received, they are journalized and posted.

(4) The bank may have deducted items such as service charges on the bank statement. These charges are similar to those discussed in point (3).

(5) There may be errors in or omissions from the bank statement or the business's records. These errors can only be discovered by carefully comparing the bank's records with the business's records. If the error was made by the business, then a journal entry can be made to correct the mistake. If the bank is at fault, then the business must notify the bank and then check the next bank statement to ensure the correction has been recorded by the bank.

The process of adjusting the ledger and bank balance to account for these discrepancies is called **reconciling the bank**. The steps involved in the procedure will be discussed on pages 402 to 406.

PREPARING A BANK RECONCILIATION STATEMENT

Bank reconciliation statement: a statement detailing the items that cause the balance on the bank statement to be different from the balance in the Cash account.

A bank reconciliation statement lists all of the items discussed on the previous page and shows how they adjust the cash account balance or the bank balance so they are equal. The statement also provides a permanent record of the reconciliation that may be checked by the owner. Bank statements should be reconciled (made to agree) by an employee who does not handle cash or cash records. This person in fact might be the owner who has no day-to-day accounting responsibilities. By preparing the bank reconciliation statement, the owner is able to review all the cash receipts and disbursements. This review is a very good internal control measure over the business's most valuable asset, **Cash**.

There are many ways of preparing a bank reconciliation statement: only one will be illustrated in this chapter.

The bank reconciliation statement for Dr. Johnson's practice is illustrated, in addition to other documents. The steps that follow describe how to prepare this bank statement.

Step 1 Collect the following documents: prior month's bank reconciliation statement, Cash Payments Journal, Cash Receipts Journal, GL Cash account, and current bank statement.

John H. Johnson, D.D.S.
Bank Reconciliation Statement
As at January 31, 19–8

Balance as per bank statement, Jan. 31		$7 376.22
Deduct Outstanding Cheques:		
No. 319	$ 50.00 ✓	
No. 320	1 000.00 ✓	
No. 321	1 200.00 ✓	2 250.00
Deduct: Error made by bank		47.30
Adjusted bank statement balance		$5 078.92
Balance as per Cash account, Jan. 31		$4 951.82
Add: Bank credit memo for interest earned from bank deposit receipts		205.60
		5157.42
Deduct:		
Service Charges	$ 3.50	
NSF Cheque of Mr. Mennill	75.00	78.50
Adjusted book balance of cash		$5 078.92

CASH PAYMENTS JOURNAL Page 2

DATE 19-8		CHEQUE NO.	CHEQUE PAID TO	ACCOUNTS PAYABLE POST. REF.	ACCOUNTS PAYABLE AMOUNT DR.	OTHER GENERAL LEDGER ACCOUNTS ACCOUNT TITLE	POST. REF.	AMOUNT DR.	CASH CR.	
Feb.	2	322	Dr. Johnson			Drawing	302	100 00	100 00	✓
	5	323	Central Lab		48 70				48 70	✓
	6	324	Central Lab		19 40				19 40	✓
	7	325	Telephone–Bell			Telephone	505	45 45	45 45	✓
	10	326	Time Magazine		37 10				37 10	✓
	11	327	Canada Post		35 00				35 00	✓
	12	328	Union Gas		140 00				140 00	✓
	17	329	Public Utilities		200 00				200 00	✓
	18	330	Central Realty			Rent Expense	501	1500 00	1500 00	✓
	25	331	Denco Supply		50 00				50 00	Outstanding cheques
	26	332	Lynn Fortier			Salaries	502	1000 00	1000 00	Outstanding cheques
	27	333	Kathy Lewis			Salaries	502	1200 00	1200 00	Outstanding cheques
					530 20			3845 45	4375 65	
					(202)			✓	(101)	

CASH RECEIPTS JOURNAL Page 2

RECEIPT NO.	DATE 19-8		ACCOUNT CREDITED	DESCRIPTION	POST. REF.	AMOUNT	
2657	Feb.	4	Miss Hewitt	Full Settlement	✓	250 00	$600✓
2658		4	Mrs. Brown	Full Settlement	✓	150 00	$600✓
2659		4	Mrs. Sweeney	Full Settlement	✓	300 00	$600✓
2660		6	Mrs. Caldwell	Full Settlement	✓	150 00	✓
2661		10	Mr. Tomaszewski	ROA	✓	600 00	$1140✓
2662		10	Mr. Maronets	ROA	✓	540 00	$1140✓
2663		15	Ms. Graham	ROA	✓	75 00	✓
2664		17	Ms. Pritchard	Full Settlement	✓	125 00	✓
2665		26	Ms. Snider	ROA	✓	175 00	$375✓
2666		26	Mr. Weicker	Full Settlement	✓	200 00	$375✓
2667		27	Mrs. Brown	Full Settlement	✓	100 00	✓
2668		28	Mrs. Harries	Full Settlement		512 00	← Outstanding deposit
		28	Cash DR./Accounts Receivable CR.		101/103	3077 00	
						(101)	

DATE	No. 334
ORDER OF	
	$

DEPOSITS		JOURNAL		
		BALANCE	3780	27
		ADD DEPOSIT(S)		
		BALANCE		
		DEDUCT CHEQUE		
TOTAL		BALANCE		

DR. JOHNSON'S RECORDS

Bank statement balance as of February 28 reports $5 638.03.

GENERAL LEDGER

Cash — Account No. 101

DATE 19-8		EXPLANATION	POST. REF.	DEBIT	CREDIT	BALANCE
Feb	28	Balance forward				3 780 27

The Cash and bank statement balances do not agree.

Balance per Cash account

Step 2 Complete the three-line heading: Line 1 shows the name of the business; Line 2, the name of the statement; and Line 3, the date on the bank statement.

Step 3 Record the bank statement balance as per February 28 and the balance per the Cash account.

Step 4 Find the discrepancies using the following process.

(1) Compare the **prior** bank reconciliation statement to the current bank statement to ensure that all discrepancies have now been recorded by the bank and the business. Place a small check mark beside each item on the bank reconciliation statement and on the bank statement or journal. This ensures that all items are accounted for from the previous month.

(2) Check that all the cheques on the Cash Payments Journal have been cancelled by the bank and that the bank and the ledger agree on the cheque amount. Place a small check mark beside the cheque in the journal and on the bank statement. If a cheque has been cashed or recorded incorrectly, place the correct figure in pencil above the error.

(3) Repeat the above procedure for all the deposits in the Cash Receipts Journal.

(4) Any items on the prior bank reconciliation statement which are not checked off should be recorded on the reconciliation statement in a manner identical to the prior month's statement. Any items

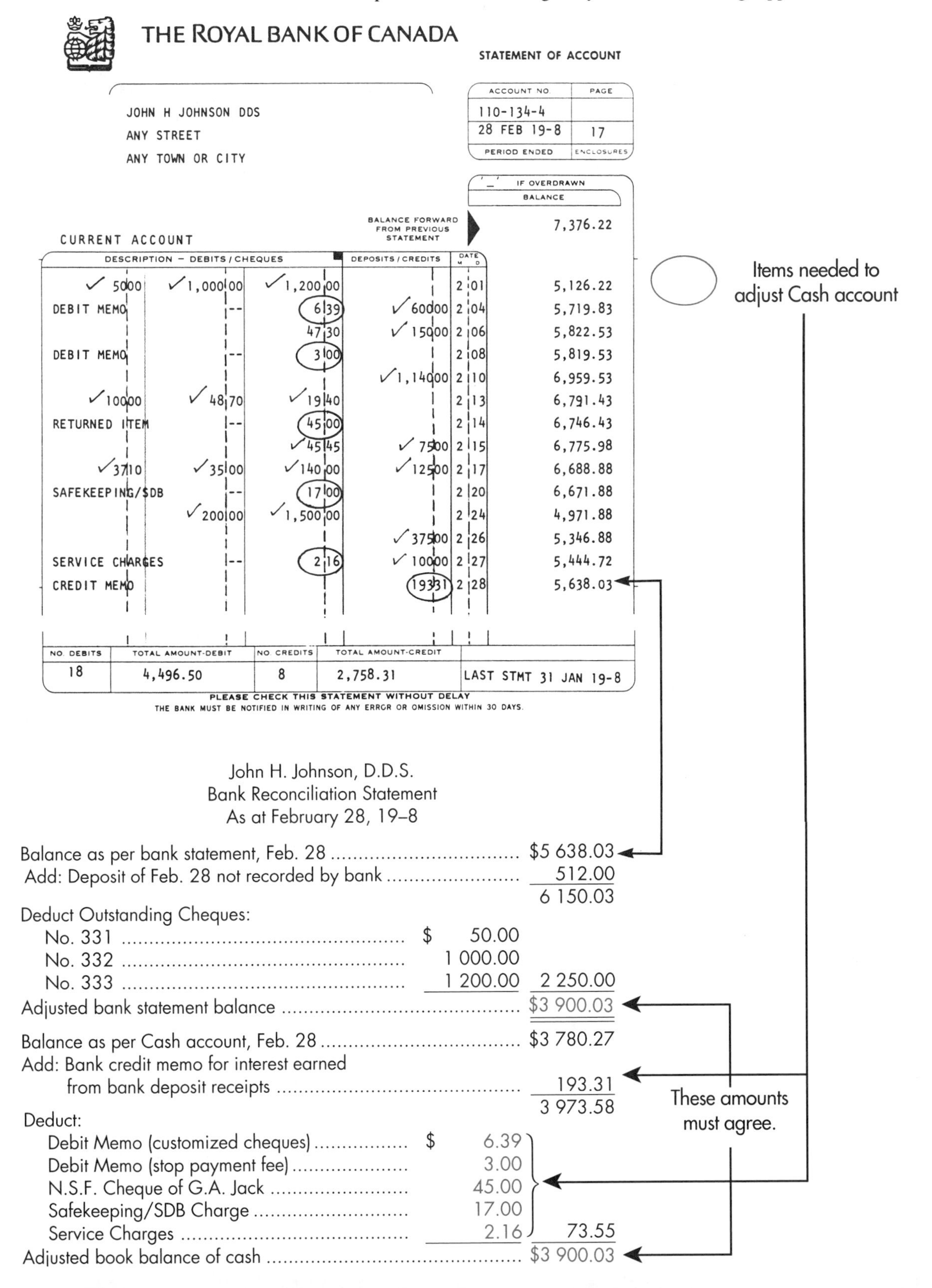

THE ROYAL BANK OF CANADA

STATEMENT OF ACCOUNT

JOHN H JOHNSON DDS
ANY STREET
ANY TOWN OR CITY

ACCOUNT NO.	PAGE
110-134-4	
28 FEB 19-8	17
PERIOD ENDED	ENCLOSURES

IF OVERDRAWN — BALANCE

CURRENT ACCOUNT

BALANCE FORWARD FROM PREVIOUS STATEMENT 7,376.22

DESCRIPTION – DEBITS / CHEQUES			DEPOSITS / CREDITS	DATE M D	BALANCE
✓ 50.00	✓ 1,000.00	✓ 1,200.00		2 01	5,126.22
DEBIT MEMO	--	6.39	✓ 600.00	2 04	5,719.83
		47.30	✓ 150.00	2 06	5,822.53
DEBIT MEMO	--	3.00		2 08	5,819.53
			✓ 1,140.00	2 10	6,959.53
✓ 100.00	✓ 48.70	✓ 19.40		2 13	6,791.43
RETURNED ITEM	--	45.00		2 14	6,746.43
		✓ 45.45	✓ 75.00	2 15	6,775.98
✓ 37.10	✓ 35.00	✓ 140.00	✓ 125.00	2 17	6,688.88
SAFEKEEPING/SDB	--	17.00		2 20	6,671.88
	✓ 200.00	✓ 1,500.00		2 24	4,971.88
			✓ 375.00	2 26	5,346.88
SERVICE CHARGES	--	2.16	✓ 100.00	2 27	5,444.72
CREDIT MEMO			193.31	2 28	5,638.03

NO. DEBITS	TOTAL AMOUNT-DEBIT	NO. CREDITS	TOTAL AMOUNT-CREDIT	
18	4,496.50	8	2,758.31	LAST STMT 31 JAN 19-8

PLEASE CHECK THIS STATEMENT WITHOUT DELAY
THE BANK MUST BE NOTIFIED IN WRITING OF ANY ERROR OR OMISSION WITHIN 30 DAYS.

John H. Johnson, D.D.S.
Bank Reconciliation Statement
As at February 28, 19–8

Balance as per bank statement, Feb. 28		$5 638.03
Add: Deposit of Feb. 28 not recorded by bank		512.00
		6 150.03
Deduct Outstanding Cheques:		
No. 331	$ 50.00	
No. 332	1 000.00	
No. 333	1 200.00	2 250.00
Adjusted bank statement balance		$3 900.03
Balance as per Cash account, Feb. 28		$3 780.27
Add: Bank credit memo for interest earned from bank deposit receipts		193.31
		3 973.58
Deduct:		
Debit Memo (customized cheques)	$ 6.39	
Debit Memo (stop payment fee)	3.00	
N.S.F. Cheque of G.A. Jack	45.00	
Safekeeping/SDB Charge	17.00	
Service Charges	2.16	73.55
Adjusted book balance of cash		$3 900.03

in the journals which are not checked off must be used to adjust the bank's balance. Any items found to be in error must be reconciled as follows: if the business has made the error, correct the Cash account; if the bank has made the error, correct the balance as per the bank statement.

(5) Check the bank statement. Any item which is not checked off must be used to correct the business's Cash account.

Step 5 Calculate the adjusted bank balance and the adjusted book balance by adding or subtracting the discrepancies. These two adjusted balances must agree.

ADJUSTING THE CASH RECORDS AFTER RECONCILIATION

From the depositor's point of view, two cash records must be adjusted after the bank reconciliation:

- The balance on the latest cheque stub must agree with the adjusted book balance of cash, on the bank reconciliation statement.
- The Cash account in the General Ledger must be updated by journalizing and posting the discrepancies. These items make the Cash account agree with the adjusted bank balance. These are the items that cannot be determined until the bank statement is received. The bank statement and/or the enclosed memos provide the proof of the entries. Therefore, the objectivity principle is properly applied.

The corrections to the cheque stub and the General Ledger are shown in the margin and on the opposite page, respectively.

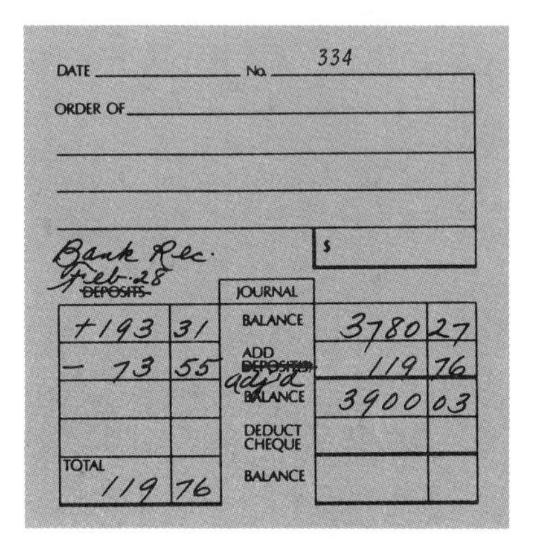

DATE ______ No. 334

ORDER OF ______

$

Bank Rec. Feb. 28

~~DEPOSITS~~		JOURNAL		
+193	31	BALANCE	3780	27
−73	55	ADD ~~DEPOSITS~~ adj'd	119	76
		BALANCE	3900	03
		DEDUCT CHEQUE		
TOTAL 119	76	BALANCE		

APPLYING BANK RECONCILIATION PROCEDURES TO PERSONAL BANKING

Bank reconciliation can also be applied to any individual's need to control personal cash. Here's a brief summary of the key measures to control anyone's most valuable asset.

- Open a personal chequing account or business current account at a nearby bank or trust company. (You do not have to be in business to open a business account.) A chequing account provides you with the return of **all** cancelled cheques and a monthly bank statement.
- Open a pure (true) savings account. This will earn a higher rate of interest than you can receive from a combination chequing

GENERAL JOURNAL Page 55

DATE 19-8		ACCOUNT TITLE AND EXPLANATION	POST. REF.	DEBIT	CREDIT
Feb	28	Cash		19331	
		Interest Revenue			19331
		To record the bank credit			
		memo for interest earned			
		from bank deposit receipts			
	28	Miscellaneous Expense		939	
		Cash			939
		To record the bank debit			
		memos for customized			
		cheques ($6.39) and the			
		stop payment fee ($3.00).			
	28	Accts. Rec./G.A. Jack		4500	
		Cash			4500
		To record the NSF cheque			
		of G.A. Jack.			
	28	Safety Deposit Box Rental Expense		1700	
		Cash			1700
		To record the annual			
		rental charge on the SDB.			
	28	Bank Service Charges Expense			
		Cash			
		To record the service		216	
		charges reported on the bank			216
		statement of Feb. 28.			

Cash **GENERAL LEDGER** Account No. 101

DATE 19-8		EXPLANATION	POST. REF.	DEBIT	CREDIT	BALANCE
Feb	28	Balance forward	✓			378027
	28		G.J. 55	19331		397358
	28		G.J. 55		939	396419
	28		G.J. 55		4500	391919
	28		G.J. 55		1700	390219
	28		G.J. 55		216	390003

and savings account. Also, you can better control your cash if you have only *one* chequing account.

- Deposit intact **all** cash receipts into your chequing account. Arrange to have your main source of cash receipts—your pay—deposited directly into this chequing account. When you get paid by cheque, always endorse the cheque "For Deposit Only" to the credit of your chequing account.
- Leave only enough cash in the chequing account to pay your bills. Any extra amounts should always be transferred to your savings account for later investments such as bank deposit receipts, bonds, long-term guaranteed savings certificates, and stocks of business corporations.
- Rent a safety deposit box to store your valuable documents.
- Check all bills before making payment.
- Use consecutively pre-numbered cheques to pay all bills. You can order customized cheques from your banker for a very reasonable fee.
- Always record every cheque **before** completing the main cheque form. Bankers provide cheque stub forms or records in booklet form.
- Void all spoiled cheques and keep these cancelled cheques in a Cheques Returned file.
- Avoid carrying large amounts of cash on your person. Instead, obtain a recognized credit card for your personal expenditures. That way your purchases will eventually be controlled by a cheque payment. Where it is necessary to have actual currency, make out the cheque to **Cash** only at your bank so you won't lose it.
- Always pay your bills on time and avoid paying interest on overdue bills. Use a tickler file system if necessary.
- Always cancel every bill after issuing the cheque. Keep all cancelled bills in a file. These papers should be kept for at least **six** years. That's the length of time Revenue Canada—Taxation expects individual Canadians to keep documents just in case the individual has to have a tax audit of his or her personal income tax return.
- Always prepare a bank reconciliation statement immediately after receiving your monthly bank statement.
- Keep on file for **six** years all bank statements, cancelled cheques, and bank memos.

TOPIC 2 PROBLEMS

Preparing a bank reconciliation statement and necessary journal entries.

P 10-5 Assume that the bank statement as of February 28, prepared for Paul W. Black, D.D.S. shows a final balance of $384.00, while Black's Cash account (and cheque book balance) as of February 28 shows $399.20. After having compared all items shown on the bank statement with the accounting records, Black writes down the following information:

Outstanding cheques: No. 110, $25.40; No. 115, $67.10; No. 123, $125.80; No. 140, $18.50

Deposit of February 28 not recorded by bank: $250

Bank service charges reported on the bank statement: $2

a. Prepare a bank reconciliation statement from the above information.

b. Prepare in the General Journal any entries that the depositor should make as a result of having prepared the bank reconciliation.

Preparing a bank reconciliation statement and necessary journal entries.

P 10-6 Assume that the bank statement as of March 31, prepared for Bonnie Flood, D.D.S. shows a final balance of $596.12, while Flood's Cash account (and cheque book balance) as of March 31 shows $1758.42. Assume Flood writes down the following information after comparing all items shown on the bank statement with the accounting records.

(i) Outstanding cheques: No. 45, $35.80; No. 47, $76.10; No. 50, $225.80

(ii) Deposit in transit, March 31: $1485

(iii) Debit memo for annual safety deposit box rental: $12

(iv) Bank service charges: $3

a. Prepare a bank reconciliation statement from the above information.

b. Prepare General Journal entries that the depositor should make after preparing the bank reconciliation.

Preparing a bank reconciliation statement and necessary journal entries.

P 10-7 The information below results from identifying and listing the discrepancy items for L.M. Munro, D.D.S. as of the February 28 bank statement.

Bank statement balance, February 28	$1 263
Cash account balance, February 28	1 510
Deposit in transit, February 28	425

Outstanding Cheques:	
No. 210	50
No. 212	65
No. 219	85
Bank service charges	4

Cheque No. 218, returned with the cancelled cheques, was correctly drawn for $42 in payment of the telephone bill. However, this cheque was accidentally recorded on the cheque record and in the Cash Payments Journal as $24.

a. Prepare a bank reconciliation statement from the above information.

b. Prepare General Journal entries to adjust the Cash account following a bank reconciliation.

Journalizing transactions in the bank's books.

P 10-8 Challenge Problem Assume that you work in the accounting department of a local bank. The separate transactions below, pertaining to a current depositor called Dolly's Flowers, have come to your attention for a complete analysis.

(i) Dolly's Flowers, a current account depositor, deposits cash receipts totalling $500.

(ii) The bank cashes cheques drawn by Dolly's Flowers to the amount of $200.

(iii) The bank agrees to a demand loan for Dolly's Flowers in the amount of $1000. In turn, Dolly's Flowers deposits the amount of the loan into its current account.

(iv) The bank receives a cheque for $200 from Dolly's Flowers in part payment of the demand loan.

(v) The bank issues a debit memo to Dolly's Flowers showing $5 interest on the demand loan for one month.

(vi) The bank issues a debit memo to Dolly's Flowers showing that $7.50 had been charged against the depositor's account for the rental of a safety deposit box.

(vii) Dolly's Flowers has a cheque for $1200 certified at the bank. The certified cheque is promptly mailed to the payee.

Note: A certified cheque is first made out by the depositor in the regular way. It is then presented at the depositor's bank where the banker checks the chequing account to see if there is sufficient cash to certify the cheque. If there is, the banker immediately takes out the amount from the depositor's account and keeps the funds in a special account. When the certified cheque is cashed, the bank uses the funds from this special account and not from the depositor's account. Remember, the banker has already debited the depositor's account with the amount of the certified cheque immediately after certifying it. For this service, most bankers now charge a small amount which is shown as part of the regular bank service charges on the monthly bank statement.

(viii)The bank prepares a debit memo informing Dolly's Flowers that its current account has been decreased by $100 as a result of an NSF cheque drawn by H. Hunt, an accounts receivable customer of the depositor.

(ix)The bank prepares a credit memo notifying Dolly's Flowers that its current account has been credited for $46.50 interest on Canada Savings Bonds held for the depositor.

(x)The bank deducts $12.40 from the current account of Dolly's Flowers for monthly bank service charges.

Show your analysis of each transaction in General Journal form. Remember to do this from the bank's viewpoint. Make up appropriate General Ledger titles for each entry. *Hint:* Think of the effects of each event on the bank's accounting equation before you show the double entry in General Journal form.

Journalizing transactions in the depositor's books.

P 10-9 Rewrite the accounting entries for each transaction in Problem 10-8, but analyze each transaction from the viewpoint of the **depositor's** records. Use the two-column General Journal form. Suggest appropriate titles for each accounting entry.

Preparing a bank reconciliation statement and necessary journal entries.

P 10-10 The following information was available to reconcile the business of Mary R. Macdonald:

(i)The ledger account for Cash showed a balance on June 30 of $4252.90.

(ii)The June bank statement showed a closing balance of $3918.70.

(iii)The cash received on June 30 amounted to $490.75. This amount was deposited intact at the bank into the night depository chute after banking hours on June 30, so the deposit was not recorded by the bank on the June statement.

(iv)Among the cancelled cheques returned by the bank with the June bank statement was one issued by an "R. Mary McDonald" for $270. The bank erroneously charged this cheque to the account of "Mary R. Macdonald."

(v)Also included with the June bank statement was a debit memo from the bank for $10.75 representing the bank charge for renting a safety deposit box to the depositor.

(vi) Examination of the paid cheques revealed that these cheques, all issued in June, had not been cancelled by the bank: No. 540 for $187.50; No. 561 for $43.80; No. 570 for $195.25; No. 574 for $99.25; a certified cheque No. 580 for $750.

(vii) Included with the bank statement was a $75.00 cheque drawn by Judy White, a customer of Mary R. Macdonald. This cheque was marked NSF. It has been included in the deposit of June 27, but had been charged back on the bank statement on June 30.

(viii) The bank statement showed a service charge of $4.50 for operating the account during June.

(ix) Cheque No. 510, issued and cancelled correctly for $43.75, had been erroneously recorded as $34.75 on the cheque record and in the cash payments journal. This cheque was issued in payment of Utilities Expense.

a. Prepare a bank reconciliation statement for Mary R. Macdonald.

b. After completing the bank reconciliation, prepare adjusting entries to correct the Cash account as at June 30.

Preparing a bank reconciliation statement and necessary journal entries when reconciling items are not given.

P 10-11 Challenge Problem Martin Flowers Ltd. has a current account with the Northern Bank of Canada. The business last reconciled its book and bank statement balances on July 31 with two cheques, No. 310 for $118 and No. 311 for $265, outstanding. The July 31 reconciliation showed that a deposit in transit on July 31 for $298.75 had not been recorded by the bank. The following information (page 413) has been supplied in order to do the August 31 reconciliation.

Included with the bank statement was an NSF cheque drawn by a customer, Peter Gruhn. The cheque was charged back to the depositor's account on August 30. Its return is unrecorded.

Cheque No. 318 was correctly issued for $402 in payment of Office Equipment. An examination of the cash records showed that the accounting clerk entered it as $420.

The credit memo resulted from the banker's clipping of bond interest coupons on Canada Savings Bonds held for the depositor at the bank.

Two debit memos were included with the bank statement: one for the monthly interest charged on the bank loan of August 2, the other for the annual fee for renting a safety deposit box.

a. Compare the bank statement with the depositor's cash records; then locate and list all discrepancy items.

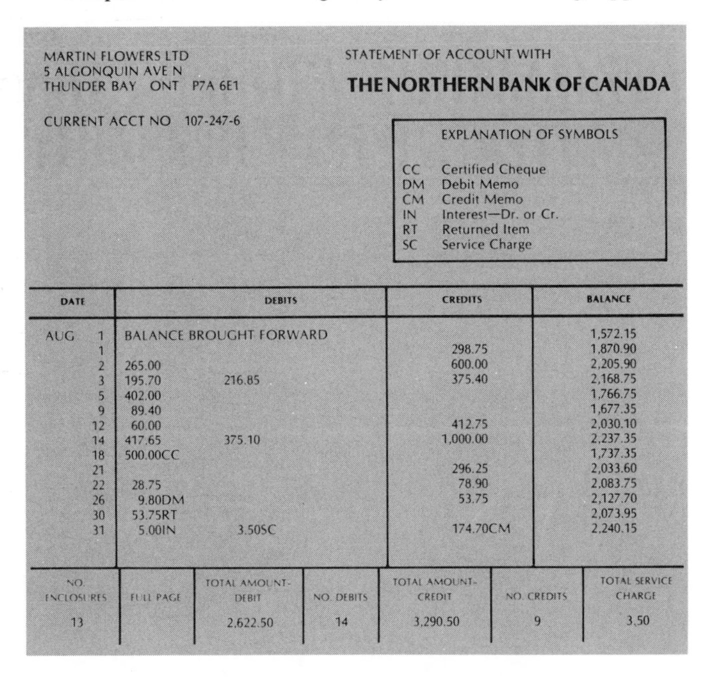

MARTIN FLOWERS LTD
5 ALGONQUIN AVE N
THUNDER BAY ONT P7A 6E1

STATEMENT OF ACCOUNT WITH
THE NORTHERN BANK OF CANADA

CURRENT ACCT NO 107-247-6

EXPLANATION OF SYMBOLS

CC Certified Cheque
DM Debit Memo
CM Credit Memo
IN Interest—Dr. or Cr.
RT Returned Item
SC Service Charge

DATE	DEBITS		CREDITS	BALANCE
AUG 1	BALANCE BROUGHT FORWARD			1,572.15
1			298.75	1,870.90
2	265.00		600.00	2,205.90
3	195.70	216.85	375.40	2,168.75
5	402.00			1,766.75
9	89.40			1,677.35
12	60.00		412.75	2,030.10
14	417.65	375.10	1,000.00	2,237.35
18	500.00CC			1,737.35
21			296.25	2,033.60
22	28.75		78.90	2,083.75
26	9.80DM		53.75	2,127.70
30	53.75RT			2,073.95
31	5.00IN	3.50SC	174.70CM	2,240.15

NO. ENCLOSURES	FULL PAGE	TOTAL AMOUNT-DEBIT	NO. DEBITS	TOTAL AMOUNT-CREDIT	NO. CREDITS	TOTAL SERVICE CHARGE
13		2,622.50	14	3,290.50	9	3,50

CASH RECEIPTS JOURNAL Page 16

DATE		POST. REF.	AMOUNT
Aug.	2	201	600.00
	3	401	375.40
	12	401	412.75
	14	301	1 000.00
	21	401	296.25
	22	103	78.90
	26	105	53.75
	31	401	448.95
	31	101	3 266.00

CASH PAYMENTS JOURNAL Page 21

CHEQUE NO.	POST. REF.	AMOUNT
315	202	195.70
316	519	216.85
317	203	89.40
318	112	420.00
319	520	217.40
320	302	60.00
321	104	127.90
322	516	417.65
323	107	500.00
324	110	375.10
325	205	59.40
326	505	28.75
327	502	17.90
	101	2 726.05

Cash **ACCOUNT NO.** 101

DATE		EXPLANATION	POST. REF.	DEBIT	CREDIT	BALANCE	
Aug.	1	Balance	✓			1 487.90	DR.
	31	Total Cash Receipts	CR 16	3 266.00		4 753.90	
	31	Total Cash Payments	CP 21		2 726.05	2 027.85	

b. Prepare an August 31 bank reconciliation for the company.

c. Prepare the General Journal entries needed to adjust the book balance of cash to the reconciled balance.

Using bank reconciliation procedures to prove a balance owing.

P 10-12 Personal-Use Application A London, Ontario couple recently received their electricity and water bill from that city's Public Utilities Commission (PUC) as shown below.

PUBLIC UTILITIES COMMISSION D
BOX 3060 LONDON, ONT N6A 4J8

INQUIRIES - 8:15 TO 4:30 - MONDAY TO FRIDAY
TELEPHONE 679-5503

01 905 08184 02 843 DRIFTWOOD RD

READING DATE 29 AUG 19-3
ELECTRIC READING 1994
WATER READING 1283

29	ELECTRIC	4322 KWH	181.38
	WATER	3919 CU FT	31.40

THIS BILL MAY BE PAID ON OR BEFORE THE DUE
DATE AT ANY LONDON BANK OR TRUST COMPANY.

AMOUNT DUE IF PAID AFTER 22 SEP .... 223.43 E & OE

AMOUNT DUE IF PAID BY 22 SEP 19-3 .. 212.78

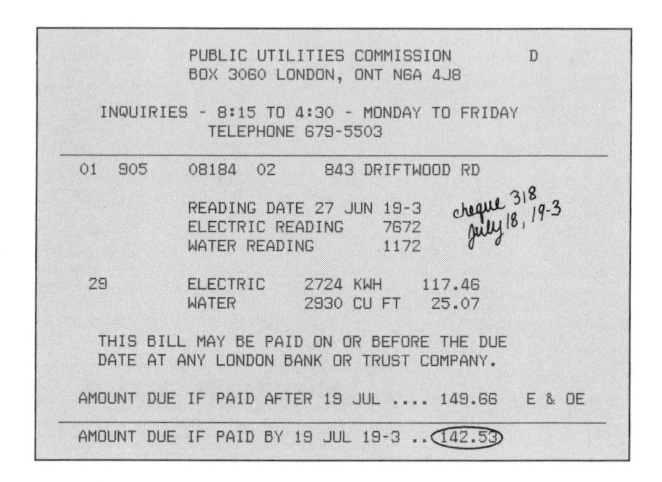

PUBLIC UTILITIES COMMISSION D
BOX 3060 LONDON, ONT N6A 4J8

INQUIRIES - 8:15 TO 4:30 - MONDAY TO FRIDAY
TELEPHONE 679-5503

01 905 08184 02 843 DRIFTWOOD RD

READING DATE 27 JUN 19-3
ELECTRIC READING 7672
WATER READING 1172

cheque 318
July 18, 19-3

29	ELECTRIC	2724 KWH	117.46
	WATER	2930 CU FT	25.07

THIS BILL MAY BE PAID ON OR BEFORE THE DUE
DATE AT ANY LONDON BANK OR TRUST COMPANY.

AMOUNT DUE IF PAID AFTER 19 JUL .... 149.66 E & OE

AMOUNT DUE IF PAID BY 19 JUL 19-3 .. 142.53

Before issuing the cheque, the couple checked the accuracy of the bill. They could not believe that $70.25 more was needed over the last bill, as shown in the second illustration.

A close look at the electricity reading showed 7672 on reading date June 27, 19-3, while the reading on August 29, 19-3 showed a lower number, 1994. How could it go from a higher to a lower number? They agreed there must be a computer error.

They also looked at the water reading. The June 27 bill showed a reading of 1172, while the current bill showed 1283—a difference of only one hundred eleven. But the current bill shows 3919 cubic feet of water used.

Before calling to make an inquiry, the couple checked the Bills Paid file for Sept. 19-2. The total electricity and water bill for a similar period one year ago showed $167.85. They were convinced errors were made in the current bill.

A call to the PUC office revealed the following:

(i) The maximum reading on all electric meters in the city is 9999; after that, the meter begins again at 0000.

(ii) The current rate for electricity is: (a) for the first 500 kW·h (kilowatt hours), $0.0570 per kW·h (5.70 cents per KW·h (b) the remainder at $0.04 per kW·h.

(iii) Water meters are to be read in cubic **metres**.

(iv) Water rates are based on cubic feet, so you must convert the water readings to cubic feet (the conversion is 35.31 cubic feet = 1 cubic metre).

(v) Current water rates: (a) for the first 200 cubic feet, $3.80 per 100 cubic feet; (b) for the next 5000 cubic feet, $0.64 per 100 cubic feet.

(vi) According to the PUC representative, the commission's computer is correct.

You have been asked to verify the accuracy of the current bill. Would you advise the London couple to issue the cheque or to file a letter of protest? Show calculations to support your answer.

Maintaining personal banking records.

P 10-13 Personal Banking Application Assume that you have acquired a full-time position after completing your education. You have also taken out a current account with a nearby branch of the Royal Bank of Canada. The transactions that follow represent your personal banking for the month of July.

July 1 Deposited $3000 into the current account.
1 Issued Cheque No. 001 to City Properties Ltd. for $800 for one month's rent.
3 Issued Cheque No. 002 to *Sports Illustrated* for $78.00 for one year's subscription.
6 Issued Cheque No. 003 for $90 to Bell Canada for installation of telephone.
7 Issued Cheque No. 004 for $65 to A & P Foods Ltd. for weekly groceries.
9 Received a cheque from J. Young for $100 in part payment of a loan transacted in June. Endorsed the cheque "For Deposit Only."
12 Issued Cheque No. 005 for $73 to Dr. R.B. Biesenthal, D.D.S. for exam, X-ray, and cleaning of teeth.
14 Issued Cheque No. 006 for $70.80 to A & P Foods Ltd. for weekly groceries.
15 Received pay slip from employer stating that the net pay for two weeks, $700, was deposited to the credit of the current account.
18 Issued Cheque No. 007 to Cash for $50 for entertainment.

SUGGESTIONS FOR USING YOUR CHEQUE REGISTER

THE CHEQUE REGISTER IS DESIGNED TO GIVE YOU AN ACCURATE, COMPACT, AND THOROUGH RECORD OF YOUR CHEQUES AND DEPOSITS. HERE ARE SOME SUGGESTIONS FOR USE.

1. BE SURE THAT ALL INFORMATION IS INCLUDED AND ACCURATE.

2. KEEP A CURRENT RUNNING BALANCE BY SUBTRACTING THE CHEQUE OR ADDING THE DEPOSIT TO THE PREVIOUS BALANCE. DO THIS WITH EACH TRANSACTION OR AS OFTEN AS NECESSARY IN ORDER TO BE CURRENT.

3. THE ✓ COLUMN CAN BE USED FOR ONE OF TWO THINGS.

   A. TO RECONCILE BANK STATEMENTS. THE ✓ COLUMN MAY BE USED TO MARK EACH CHEQUE PAID BY THE BANK. ITEMS NOT MARKED ARE OUTSTANDING AND HAVE NOT BEEN PAID BY THE BANK AS OF STATEMENT DATE.

   B. TO INDICATE TAX DEDUCTIBLE ITEMS. THIS LETS YOU EASILY IDENTIFY THESE ITEMS AT TAX TIME.

4. WHEN THE REGISTER IS FULL, WRITE THE STARTING AND ENDING CHEQUE NUMBERS AND DATES ON THE FRONT AND FILE AWAY FOR FUTURE REFERENCE.

5. LIST AUTOMATIC DEPOSITS AND WITHDRAWALS ON THE PREAUTHORIZED CHARGES AND DEPOSITS PAGE AS A REMINDER TO RECORD THESE AT THE PROPER TIME.

DATE	CHEQUE NO	CHEQUES ISSUED TO OR DESCRIPTION OF DEPOSIT	AMOUNT	✓		BALANCE FORWARD ✓	
						✓	1,000 00
		To Bank	175 00		DEDUCT CHEQUE − ADD DEPOSIT +		175 00
		For Car Loan			BALANCE		825 00
		To Visa	50 00		DEDUCT CHEQUE − ADD DEPOSIT +		50 00
		For Payment			BALANCE		775 00
		To Deposit	250 00		DEDUCT CHEQUE − ADD DEPOSIT +		250 00
		For			BALANCE		1025 00
		To Mortgage	300 00		DEDUCT CHEQUE − ADD DEPOSIT +		300 00
		For Payment			BALANCE		725 00
		To Cancer Society	20 00		DEDUCT CHEQUE − ADD DEPOSIT +		20 00
		For Donation			BALANCE		705 00
		To			DEDUCT CHEQUE − ADD DEPOSIT +		
		For			BALANCE		

DATE	CHEQUE NO.	CHEQUES ISSUED TO OR DESCRIPTION OF DEPOSIT	AMOUNT	✓		BALANCE FORWARD ✓	
		To			DEDUCT CHEQUE − ADD DEPOSIT +		
		For			BALANCE		
		To			DEDUCT CHEQUE − ADD DEPOSIT +		
		For			BALANCE		
		To			DEDUCT CHEQUE − ADD DEPOSIT +		
		For			BALANCE		
		To			DEDUCT CHEQUE − ADD DEPOSIT +		
		For			BALANCE		
		To			DEDUCT CHEQUE − ADD DEPOSIT +		
		For			BALANCE		
		To			DEDUCT CHEQUE − ADD DEPOSIT +		
		For			BALANCE		

20 Issued Cheque No. 008 to L & X TV and Stereo Ltd., $100 as a down payment on a new TV set.

21 Issued Cheque No. 009 for $93.72 to A & P Foods Ltd. for weekly groceries.

25 Received a bill from Esso Canada Ltd. for $55.55 for credit card purchases to date. Payment was due immediately. Issued Cheque No. 010 in full payment.

26 Issued Cheque No. 011 to L & X TV and Stereo Ltd. for $800 for FM/AM stereo cassette recorder.

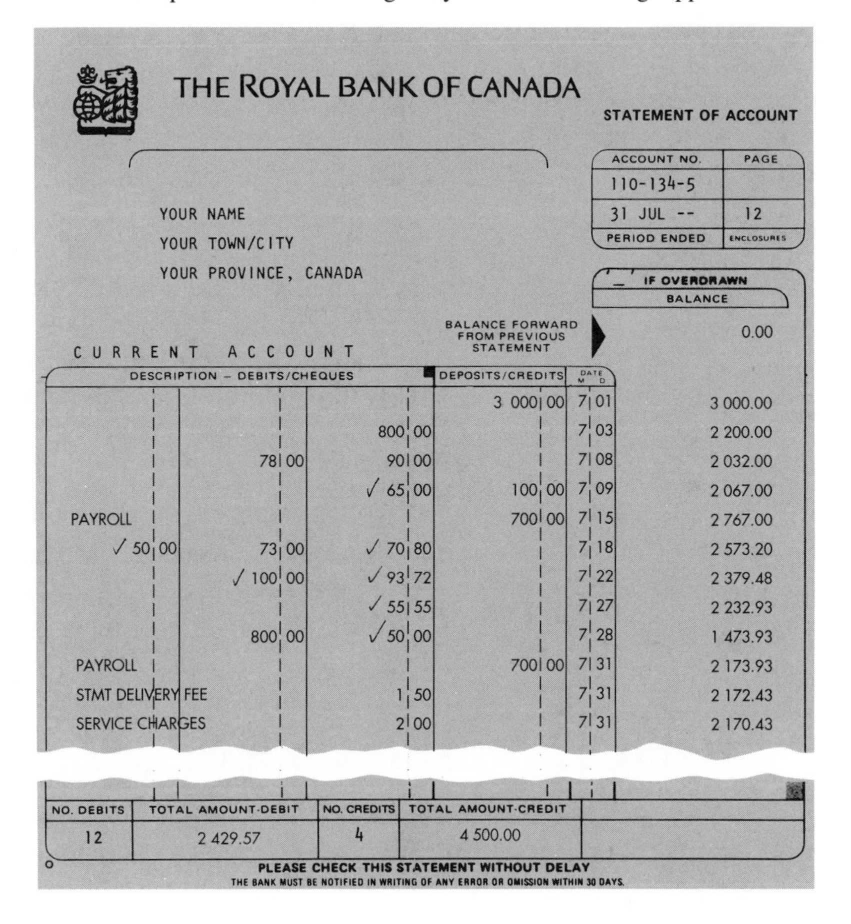

THE ROYAL BANK OF CANADA

STATEMENT OF ACCOUNT

ACCOUNT NO.	PAGE
110-134-5	
31 JUL --	12
PERIOD ENDED	ENCLOSURES

YOUR NAME
YOUR TOWN/CITY
YOUR PROVINCE, CANADA

– IF OVERDRAWN

CURRENT ACCOUNT

BALANCE FORWARD FROM PREVIOUS STATEMENT: 0.00

DESCRIPTION – DEBITS/CHEQUES				DEPOSITS/CREDITS	DATE M D	BALANCE
				3 000.00	7 01	3 000.00
			800.00		7 03	2 200.00
		78.00	90.00		7 08	2 032.00
			✓ 65.00	100.00	7 09	2 067.00
PAYROLL				700.00	7 15	2 767.00
	✓ 50.00	73.00	✓ 70.80		7 18	2 573.20
		✓ 100.00	✓ 93.72		7 22	2 379.48
			✓ 55.55		7 27	2 232.93
		800.00	✓ 50.00		7 28	1 473.93
PAYROLL				700.00	7 31	2 173.93
STMT DELIVERY FEE			1.50		7 31	2 172.43
SERVICE CHARGES			2.00		7 31	2 170.43

NO. DEBITS	TOTAL AMOUNT-DEBIT	NO. CREDITS	TOTAL AMOUNT-CREDIT
12	2 429.57	4	4 500.00

PLEASE CHECK THIS STATEMENT WITHOUT DELAY
THE BANK MUST BE NOTIFIED IN WRITING OF ANY ERROR OR OMISSION WITHIN 30 DAYS.

27 Received a VISA account statement showing a total owing of $138.70. Payment is due by August 15.

28 Issued the following cheques: No. 012 for $68.23 to A & P Foods Ltd. for weekly groceries; No. 013 for $50 to Cash for entertainment.

30 Issued Cheque No. 014 for $100 to L & X TV and Stereo Ltd. on account.

31 Received pay slip from employer showing $700 net pay being deposited into the bank's current account under your name.

31 Issued Cheque No. 015 for $120 to Eastown Chev Ltd. for car repairs.

31 Received cheque for $100 from J. Young as the final payment on loan due today. Deposited the cheque into the overnight depository.

a. Assume that the Royal Bank of Canada supplied you with a current account cheque register as illustrated opposite. Show how the transactions above would be recorded in this cheque record. Remember that the cheque register records cheques issued as well as your deposits.

b. Assume that the bank has mailed you the statement on page 417. The following cheques were enclosed: 001, 002, 003, 004, 005, 006, 007, 008, 009, 010, 011, 013. No bank debit memos or bank credit memos were enclosed.

Check the accuracy of the final balance by using the various proofs at the bottom of the statement. Thus, compare the cheque register with the bank statement given and make a note of any differences.

c. Prepare a bank reconciliation statement.

d. Update your cheque record with any adjustments.

TOPIC 2 MINI-CASES

Understanding accounting from the bank's viewpoint.

MC 10-4 After studying the debits and credits on a monthly bank statement, Tawiah addresses this question to a friend: ''I still don't understand why the bank has credited the customer's account for increases and debited the account for decreases. Is bank accounting backward?''

a. How would you reply to Tawiah's friend's question?

Describing the bank reconciliation statement as a cash control measure.

MC 10-5 In preparing for a test on the theory of business banking and bank reconciliation, Tyler expressed great difficulty in understanding the relationship between the monthly bank statement and the business's Cash account. Also, Tyler did not know why the regular preparation of a bank reconciliation statement was such an important control measure over the business's most valuable asset—Cash.

a. What explanation would you give to help Tyler?

Explaining why a reconciliation doesn't work.

MC 10-6 Your friend is trying to reconcile his personal chequing account but can never get the bank balance and his records to match.

When you ask how he goes about doing the reconciliation, he says, "First I look down the bank statement for any service charges, then I adjust my records. Next, I look at the last three cheques I have written to see if they are on the bank statement. After that I figure the two should balance."

a. Suggest additional procedures that will help your friend complete his bank reconciliation.

TOPIC 3 PREPARING THE STATEMENT OF CASH FLOWS AND ACCOUNTING FOR CASH SHORT AND OVER TRANSACTIONS

Statement of Cash Flows: a financial statement reporting the main sources of cash, the main uses of cash, and the net increase or decrease of cash over a specific time period.

Cash is a business or person's most valuable asset. To effectively manage this asset, it is useful for owners of businesses to know the main sources of cash receipts and cash payments. This information is summarized in the Statement of Cash Flows.

The Statement of Cash Flows can take several forms because it is prepared for different reasons:

- to show how cash was spent or collected during a specific accounting period that has ended
- to report what cash the business hopes to receive and anticipates paying out for an accounting period in the future.

In accounting, cash flow statements based on a period that has **ended** are described as **historic**, while those statements based on a period that is **ending** are **prospective**. Only the historic perspective will be illustrated in this text.

Examine the illustration on page 420. It shows how a Statement of Cash Flows is prepared for Dr. Johnson's dental practice.

Analysis:

- As in all financial statements, two main parts are the heading and the body.

John H. Johnson, D.D.S.
Statement of Cash Flows
For the Month Ended January 31, 19–8

CASH WAS PROVIDED BY:		
Remittances from accounts receivable.............	$ 2 889.00	
Total Sources of Cash...............................		$ 2 889.00
CASH WAS USED FOR:		
Monthly office rent.......................................	$ 5 000.00	
Telephone calls...	285.33	
Personal withdrawals...................................	400.00	
Part payment on 5-Year Note Payable............	500.00	
Salaries...	2 200.00	
Lab fees...	700.00	
New office equipment.................................	1 875.00	
Payment to creditors for utilities service, dental equipment, and office and dental supplies...	10 157.31	
Total Uses of Cash..................................		21 117.64
Net Increase (Decrease) in Cash for January...		($18 228.64)
Cash balance at beginning of January............		20 000.00
Cash balance at end of January.....................		$ 1771.36

Cash — GENERAL LEDGER — Account No. 101

DATE 19-8		EXPLANATION	POST. REF.	DEBIT	CREDIT	BALANCE DR.
Jan	2	Balance forward	✓			20000 –
	31	Total Cash Receipts CRJ.	1	2889 –		22889 –
	31	Total Cash Payments CPJ.	1		21117 64	1771 36

- The heading consists of three lines: Line 1 reports the name of the firm; Line 2, the name of the statement; Line 3, the time period for reporting the inflow and outflow of cash.
- The time period in our example is one month. Although this is unusual for a financial statement, which is usually prepared once a year, it is important for the manager or owners to have timely information about the cash balance. Therefore, a monthly statement provides much better information for making day-to-day

business decisions. Some businesses will actually prepare a less formal statement on a daily basis so that they have the most current information to manage this crucial asset.

- The body contains these important subsections: the sources of cash as reported under the subheading Cash Was Provided By; the main uses of cash as reported under Cash Was Used For; and the calculation of the cash balance under the head Net Increase (Decrease) in Cash (for the period). These heads may be different for different statements.
- Only one source of cash is shown in Dr. Johnson's statement—the cash received from patients during January. This information was obtained from the Cash Receipts Journal. There may be several different sources of cash receipts.
- Eight different uses of cash are reported in the statement. This information is obtained by analyzing the data in the Cash Payments Journal.
- Since more cash was used than received, the statement shows a net decrease in cash flow during the month. This decrease is reported in parentheses to indicate a negative figure.
- The beginning balance of Cash for January is added to the net decrease to report the Cash balance at the end of the month. This balance must agree with the Cash account in the GL.
- The double line below the final figure indicates the end of a statement.
- Since the Statement of Cash Flows is a formal report, dollar signs and completeness in reporting are required.

Why prepare the Statement of Cash Flows when the same information is available from two special journals *and the General Ledger accounts?* The statement combines the information in one document so it may be used by the owner and other interested parties outside the business. For example, a bank manager may request such a statement before granting a loan. You must pay for assets, expenses, and debts with cash, and therefore how much cash you have is of interest to many people involved with the business.

Accounting for Cash Short and Over Transactions No matter how well a system is set up, mistakes are made in handling and recording cash. When this happens, the cash on hand is either "short" or "over" the amount recorded. These discrepancies are known as cash shortages or cash overages.

ANALYZING CASH SHORTAGES

If a comparison of the accounting entries and the actual cash indicates that less cash was collected than was recorded, there is said to be a **cash shortage**. In order to reduce the cash amount recorded, you must make a credit entry to Cash and a debit entry to some other account. But which account? This discrepancy does not represent an expense — an expenditure made to generate revenue — and therefore an expense account would be inappropriate. Instead a separate account called Cash Short and Over is debited. Since there is a credit to cash, the Cash Payments Journal is used.

Cash Short and Over: a GL account whose DR. balance is a miscellaneous expense and whose CR. balance is miscellaneous revenue.

Assume that the cash register tape indicated $600 cash was collected but the cash drawer only contained $595. The entry in the General Journal is illustrated below.

DR. Cash Short and Over	5	
CR. Cash		5

To record the cash shortage as per cash proof for Register 2, Feb. 21.

(Since Cash is credited, the entry would be recorded in the Cash Payments Journal.)

ANALYZING CASH OVERAGES

If a comparison of the accounting records to the cash indicates that more cash was collected than was recorded, there is said to be a **cash overage**. In order to adjust or increase the cash account, a debit entry is required. The offsetting credit cannot be considered a revenue because it is not cash paid for services rendered. Therefore, the credit is made to the Cash Short and Over account. This entry is recorded in the Cash Receipts Journal.

For example, if cash collected was $499 and sales per the cash registered were only $497 the entry in General Journal form would be as follows.

DR. Cash ($497 + $2)	499	
CR. Sales Revenue		497
CR. Cash Short and Over		2

To record the sales from Register 2 on Feb. 22 and the $2 cash overage as per the cash proof of Register 2.

ANALYZING THE BALANCE

After the cash overages and shortages have been posted to the Cash Short and Over account at month-end, the balance in the account will be a net cash overage or a net cash shortgage. Because of the above discussion, this balance is not a true revenue or an expense. However, since the balance is small, a net cash overage — credit balance — is considered a miscellaneous revenue and a net cash shortage — debit balance — is considered a miscellaneous expense. Generally, the account has a debit balance and so the account is listed in the Chart of Accounts along with the expenses.

It is important to realize that any discrepancy should be investigated so that its cause can be determined. If there is no apparent reason found, then the entry to the Cash Short and Over account is made.

PROBLEMS

Accounting for Cash Short and Over.

P 10-14 Deirdre Doxtator is the manager and bookkeeper of Muffy's, a muffin and croissant store at the food court in a mall. Each night the employee counts out a $100-dollar float. The remaining cash is counted and recorded on a bank deposit slip, then the cash and deposit slip are placed in the night deposit at the bank. A duplicate deposit is left on Deirdre's desk. When Deirdre comes in, she takes a reading from the cash register which shows the total sales from the prior day. The following is a summary of a week's data:

Dec. 27 Total sales per register, $250.00 amount per duplicate deposit slip, $247.85.

28 Total sales per register, $387.95; amount per duplicate deposit slip, $385.63; petty cash vouchers for items paid out of the til, $4.85.

29 Total sales per register, $267.84; amount per duplicate deposit slip, $269.81.

30 Total sales per register, $563.86; amount per duplicate deposit slip, $561.27. The banker called to say there were only eleven $5-dollar bills in the bag instead of the twelve recorded on the deposit slip.

31 Total sales per register, $863.52; amount per duplicate deposit slip, $866.12.

a. Record the five transactions in the General Journal on page 23.

b. Post the entries to the General Ledger.

c. Assume the balance forward in the Cash Short and Over account is $1.63 debit. What is the balance at December 31?

d. The business has a December 31 year-end. Explain where the balance in the Cash Short and Over would appear on the financial statements.

Preparing a Statement of Cash Flows.

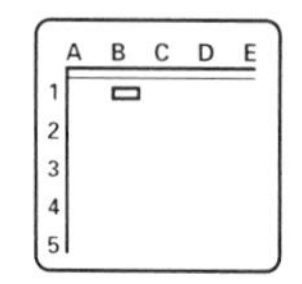

It is possible to use an electronic spreadsheet to solve Problems 10-15 and 10-16.

P 10-15 The Cash Receipts and Cash Payments Journals, along with General Ledger information, for MacPherson Plumbing & Heating of Fredericton, New Brunswick revealed the following data:

(i)Total cash received from customers during the year: $58 750.80

(ii)Cash received from sale of Government of Canada Bonds: $20 000.00

(iii)Cash received from sale of an old office desk: $150.00

(iv)Total cash paid to creditors for purchases of heating and plumbing supplies: $19 680.70

(v)Total cash paid for salaries and wages: $30 120.40

(vi)Total cash paid for rent of building: $7200.00

(vii)Total cash paid for telephone: $604.08

(viii)Total cash paid for utilities: $812.80

(ix)Total cash paid for truck repairs: $920.10

(x)Beginning year's balance (January 1, 19-8) in Cash account: $4870.10

a. Prepare a Statement of Cash Flows for MacPherson Plumbing and Heating for the year.

Preparing a Statement of Cash Flows.

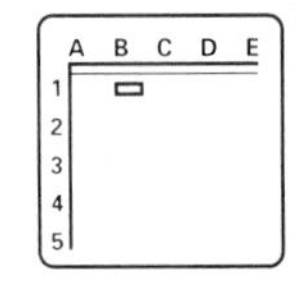

P 10-16 Dr. John Reddon (Problem 9-10) asks you to prepare a Statement of Cash Flows for the month ended September 30, 19-1. Assume that the Cash Receipts Journal reported total cash received from patients during September of $12 480.

a. From the above information and the solutions for Problem 9-10, prepare a Statement of Cash Flows in good form.

MINI-CASES

Following up on cash overages or shortages.

MC 10-7 You are the owner of a small business. The debit balance in the Cash Short and Over account is increasing at a steady pace.

When you ask your accountant why, he replies that he has not looked into the causes for the discrepancy, but has just entered the amounts according to the records kept by the part-time employees who work in the evening.

a. Are you satisfied with your accountant's response? Explain why or why not.

b. What steps should be taken to address this problem?

c. If you can trace the problem to one employee, can you make that employee financially responsible for the lost cash?

Explaining the purpose of a Cash Budget Statement.

MC 10-8 Your parents own a small business and wish to expand it in the next few months. One evening at the dinner table, your parents mention that the bank manager would not consider loaning the business money unless a Cash Budget Statement was prepared for the next fiscal year. Your father went on to say, ''We pay a good portion of our hard-earned money each year to have our accountant prepare financial statements. The bank manager gets a copy of these statements. Why can't she use this information to assess the loan application?''

a. Explain to your parents why historical financial statements are not as useful to the bank manager for assessing a loan application and why the accountant has specifically requested a Cash Budget Statement.

b. Explain to your parents how they might find this statement useful for the day-to-day management of the business.

Explaining the purpose of a Statement of Cash Flows.

MC 10-9 You want to start your own business this summer to earn some extra money. You decide that performing as a clown at children's parties would be fun and profitable. You plan to advertise at the local grocery store. Your posters say you will entertain at children's parties, perform magic tricks, and give out small favours to the children.

a. Why might you need to prepare a Cash Flow Statement during the months you operate your business?

b. Is there any other statement which might help you with your business?

Note: The Comprehensive Case Study for Chapter 10 is found at the end of Chapter 11. It is part of a large exercise which reviews all the systems discussed in Part 2.

CHAPTER 11

EXAMINING THE PAYROLL APPLICATION

Topic 1
Collecting Payroll Data

Topic 2
Recording Payroll Data

Topic 3
Explaining Payroll Remittances and Annual Tax Statements

Employee: a person hired to work for a person or business.

Every business that hires one or more employees is required by federal and provincial laws to keep payroll records. The system for collecting payroll data, recording payroll data, accounting for payroll remittances, and preparing annual tax makes up the payroll application.

This chapter will introduce the payroll application for only employees who work for a salary (or salaried employees). A small dental practice with two employees will be used as an example. The more complicated aspects of a salaried payroll together with the payroll accounting for personnel who are employed on an hourly basis are dealt with in Chapter 14.

COLLECTING PAYROLL DATA

A payroll application begins with the collection of important data on each employee. This data consists of:

(1) the employee's social insurance number
(2) the information that appears in the income tax form called form TD1 or the Personal Tax Credit Return
(3) details about the salaried payroll plan
(4) information regarding the time worked
(5) employee payroll deductions

Social Insurance Number All employees must have a card which contains a **social insurance number** (SIN). This number is important since you need it to do any of the following:

- Open a bank account.
- Complete your first income tax form (form TD1).
- Receive your first pay cheque.
- File your personal income tax returns.
- Receive unemployment insurance if eligible.
- Start your first pension plan (the Canada Pension Plan).

If you do not have a SIN, the nearest Canada Employment Centre has application forms; you do not have to be employed to apply.

The TD1 Form (Personal Tax Credit Return) The TD1 form is the first income tax form normally completed by employees at the start of a new job. The employer uses this form to determine the amount of income tax that should be deducted from an employee's pay. The form calculates a net claim code for the employee which is used in conjunction with government-published tax tables to calculate the income tax deduction.

Tax credits: allowances given by the federal government to reduce taxes otherwise payable.

The net claim code is determined by the total tax credits available to an employee. A tax credit represents an allowance given by the government to enable a taxpayer to, in effect, earn money that will not be taxed. For example, the Amount for Dependent Children (item 4) recognizes that a taxpayer with children needs to pay less tax so that he or she has more money to support his or her children. The Tuition Fee credit allows students to pay less tax so more of their earnings can be spent on their education. The higher the total tax credits, the higher the net claim code and the less taxes that will be deducted from the employee's pay.

Revenue Canada Taxation / Revenu Canada Impôt

page 1
TD1 (E) Rev. 1990

1990 PERSONAL TAX CREDIT RETURN

FAMILY NAME (Please Print) LEWIS	USUAL FIRST NAME AND INITIALS Kathy	EMPLOYEE NUMBER
ADDRESS Any Town / City	For NON-RESIDENTS ONLY Country of Permanent Residence	SOCIAL INSURANCE NUMBER 473 621 459
Province — Postal Code N6H 4H9		DATE OF BIRTH Day 14 Month 01 Year 19—

Instructions

- Please fill out this form so your employer or payer will know how much tax to deduct regularly from your pay. Regular deductions will help you avoid having to pay when you file your income tax return.
- **You must complete this form if you receive** • salary, wages, commissions or any other remuneration;
  - superannuation or pension benefits including an annuity payment made under a superannuation or pension fund or plan;
  - Unemployment Insurance benefits including training allowances.
- You may also complete this form if you receive annuity payments under registered retirement income funds and registered retirement savings plans.
- Give the completed form to your employer or payer. Otherwise, you will be allowed **only** the basic personal amount of $6,169.
- All amounts on this form should be rounded to the nearest dollar.
- **Need Help?** If you need help to complete this form, you may ask your employer or payer, or call the Source Deductions Section of your local Revenue Canada district taxation office. Before you do this, please refer to the additional information on page 2 under "Notes to Employees and Payees."

1. **Are you a non-resident of Canada?** (see note 1 on page 2). If so, and **less than** 90 per cent of your 1990 total world income will be included when calculating taxable income earned in Canada, enter 0 in the box on line 17 and sign the form. If you are a resident of Canada, go to item 2.

2. **Basic personal amount.** (everyone may claim $6,169) ▶ $6,169 2.

3. (a) **Are you married and supporting your spouse?** (see notes 4 and 5 on page 2)
   or
   (b) **Are you single, divorced, separated or widowed and supporting a relative who lives with you who is either your parent or grandparent, OR who is under 19 at the end of 1990, OR 19 or older and infirm?** (see notes 2, 3 and 4 on page 2)
   Note: A spouse or dependant claimed here cannot be claimed again on lines 4 or 5.
   If you answered yes to either (a) or (b) and your spouse's or dependant's 1990 net income will be
   - under $514, CLAIM $5,141
   - between $514 and $5,655, CLAIM (e)
   - over $5,655, CLAIM $0

	$ 5,655	(c)
Minus: spouse or dependant's net income	______	(d)
Claim (c minus d)	______	(e)

   ▶ ______ 3.

4. **Do you have any dependants who will be under 19 at the end of 1990?** (see notes 2 and 4 on page 2). If so, and your 1990 net income will be **higher** than your spouse's, calculate the amount to claim for **each** dependant. If you are not married, please refer to notes 2, 3 and 4 on page 2.
   Note: If you have three or more dependants who will be under 19 years old at the end of the year, you do not have to claim them in the order they were born. You may claim them in the **most benefical** order. For example, a dependant who is 16 years old with a net income of $3,500 could be claimed as the first dependant (claim 0) while the other two, with no income, could be claimed as second and third dependants.

   First and second dependant:
   If your dependant's 1990 net income will be
   - under $2,570, CLAIM $399
   - between $2,570 and $2,969, CLAIM (e)
   - over $2,969, CLAIM $0

	$ 2,969	(c)
Minus: dependant's net income	______	(d)
Claim (c minus d)	______	(e)

   Third and each additional dependant:
   If your dependant's 1990 net income will be
   - under $2,570, CLAIM $798
   - between $2,570 and $3,368, CLAIM (e)
   - over $3,368, CLAIM $0

	$ 3,368	(c)
Minus: dependant's net income	______	(d)
Claim (c minus d)	______	(e)

   dependants: 1st ______ 2nd ______ 3rd ______ 4th ______ 5th ______
   Total ______ ▶ ______ 4.

5. **Do you have any infirm dependants who will be 19 or older at the end of 1990?** (see notes 2 and 4 on page 2). If so, and your dependant's net income will be
   - under $2,570, CLAIM $1,512
   - between $2,570 and $4,082, CLAIM (e)
   - over $4,082, CLAIM $0

	$ 4,082	(c)
Minus: dependant's net income	______	(d)
Claim (c minus d)	______	(e)

   dependants: 1st ______ 2nd ______ 3rd ______
   Total ______ ▶ ______ 5.

6. **Do you receive eligible pension income?** (see note 6 on page 2). If so, claim your pension income amount or $1,000, **whichever is less.** ▶ ______ 6.

7. **Will you be 65 or older at the end of 1990?** If so, claim $3,327. ▶ ______ 7.

8. **Are you disabled?** (see note 7 on page 2). If so, claim $3,327. ▶ ______ 8.

9. **Are you a student?** If so, claim
   - **tuition fees** paid for courses you take in 1990 to attend either a university, college or a certified educational institution. If you receive any scholarships, fellowships or bursaries in 1990, subtract the amount over $500 from your tuition fees before you claim them. 320
   - $60 for each month in 1990 that you will be in **full-time attendance** in a qualifying program, at either a university, college or a school offering job re-training courses. ______

   Total 320 ▶ 320 9.

10. Total (add lines 2 to 9 - please enter this amount on line 11 on page 2) 6 489 10.

(See reverse)

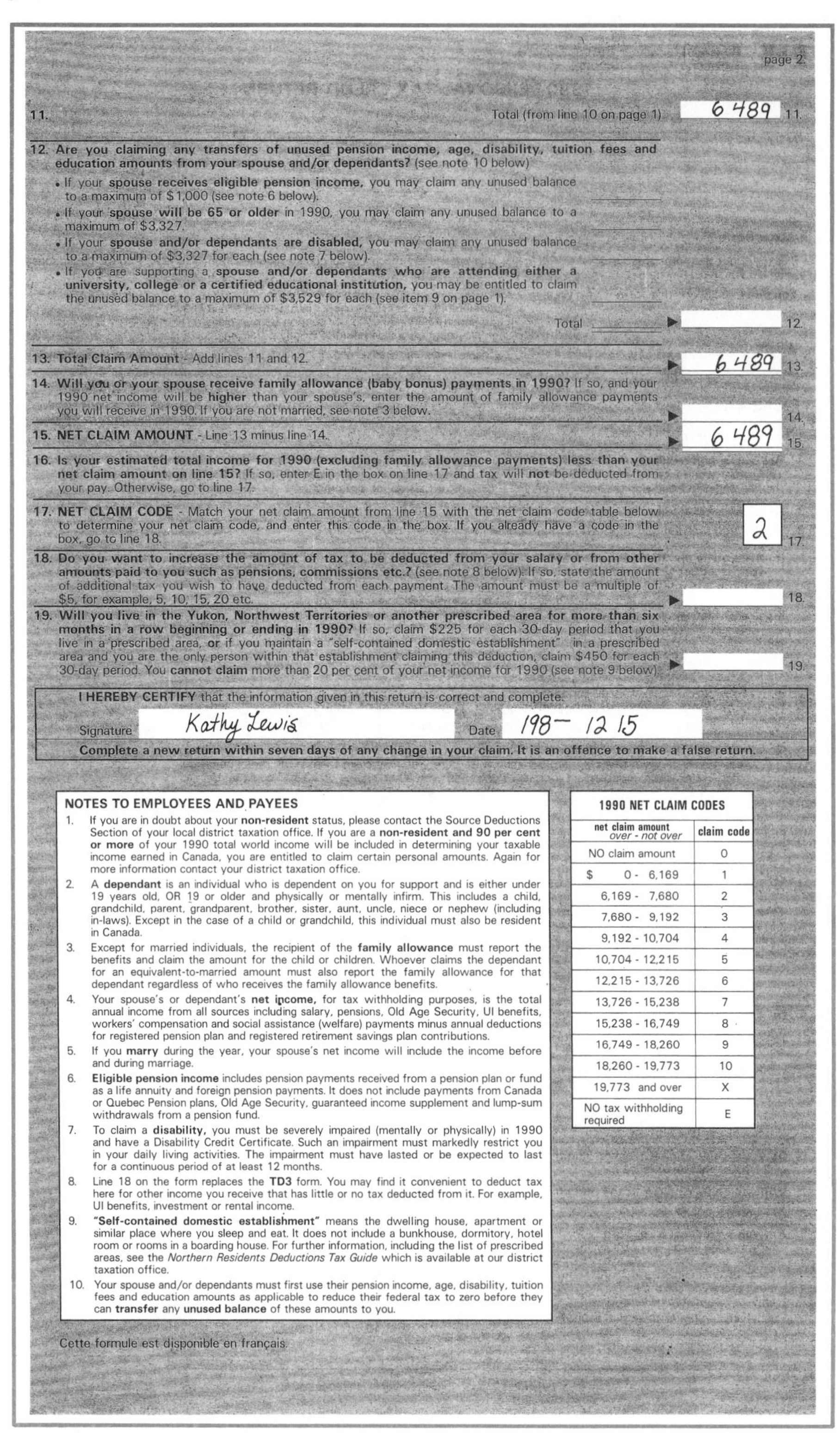

page 2

11. Total (from line 10 on page 1) 6 489 11.

12. **Are you claiming any transfers of unused pension income, age, disability, tuition fees and education amounts from your spouse and/or dependants?** (see note 10 below)
- If your **spouse receives eligible pension income,** you may claim any unused balance to a maximum of $1,000 (see note 6 below).
- If your **spouse will be 65 or older** in 1990, you may claim any unused balance to a maximum of $3,327.
- If your **spouse and/or dependants are disabled,** you may claim any unused balance to a maximum of $3,327 for each (see note 7 below).
- If you are supporting a **spouse and/or dependants who are attending either a university, college or a certified educational institution,** you may be entitled to claim the unused balance to a maximum of $3,529 for each (see item 9 on page 1).

Total ▶ 12.

13. **Total Claim Amount** - Add lines 11 and 12. ▶ 6 489 13.

14. **Will you or your spouse receive family allowance (baby bonus) payments in 1990?** If so, and your 1990 net income will be **higher** than your spouse's, enter the amount of family allowance payments you will receive in 1990. If you are not married, see note 3 below. ▶ 14.

15. **NET CLAIM AMOUNT** - Line 13 minus line 14. ▶ 6 489 15.

16. **Is your estimated total income for 1990 (excluding family allowance payments) less than your net claim amount on line 15?** If so, enter E in the box on line 17 and tax will **not** be deducted from your pay. Otherwise, go to line 17.

17. **NET CLAIM CODE** - Match your net claim amount from line 15 with the net claim code table below to determine your net claim code, and enter this code in the box. If you already have a code in the box, go to line 18. 2 17.

18. **Do you want to increase the amount of tax to be deducted from your salary or from other amounts paid to you such as pensions, commissions etc.?** (see note 8 below). If so, state the amount of additional tax you wish to have deducted from each payment. The amount must be a multiple of $5, for example, 5, 10, 15, 20 etc. ▶ 18.

19. **Will you live in the Yukon, Northwest Territories or another prescribed area for more than six months in a row beginning or ending in 1990?** If so, claim $225 for each 30-day period that you live in a prescribed area, **or** if you maintain a "self-contained domestic establishment" in a prescribed area and you are the only person within that establishment claiming this deduction, claim $450 for each 30-day period. You **cannot claim** more than 20 per cent of your net income for 1990 (see note 9 below). ▶ 19.

I HEREBY CERTIFY that the information given in this return is correct and complete.

Signature Kathy Lewis Date 198– 12 15

Complete a new return within seven days of any change in your claim. It is an offence to make a false return.

NOTES TO EMPLOYEES AND PAYEES

1. If you are in doubt about your **non-resident** status, please contact the Source Deductions Section of your local district taxation office. If you are a **non-resident and 90 per cent or more** of your 1990 total world income will be included in determining your taxable income earned in Canada, you are entitled to claim certain personal amounts. Again for more information contact your district taxation office.
2. A **dependant** is an individual who is dependent on you for support and is either under 19 years old, OR 19 or older and physically or mentally infirm. This includes a child, grandchild, parent, grandparent, brother, sister, aunt, uncle, niece or nephew (including in-laws). Except in the case of a child or grandchild, this individual must also be resident in Canada.
3. Except for married individuals, the recipient of the **family allowance** must report the benefits and claim the amount for the child or children. Whoever claims the dependant for an equivalent-to-married amount must also report the family allowance for that dependant regardless of who receives the family allowance benefits.
4. Your spouse's or dependant's **net income,** for tax withholding purposes, is the total annual income from all sources including salary, pensions, Old Age Security, UI benefits, workers' compensation and social assistance (welfare) payments minus annual deductions for registered pension plan and registered retirement savings plan contributions.
5. If you **marry** during the year, your spouse's net income will include the income before and during marriage.
6. **Eligible pension income** includes pension payments received from a pension plan or fund as a life annuity and foreign pension payments. It does not include payments from Canada or Quebec Pension plans, Old Age Security, guaranteed income supplement and lump-sum withdrawals from a pension fund.
7. To claim a **disability,** you must be severely impaired (mentally or physically) in 1990 and have a Disability Credit Certificate. Such an impairment must markedly restrict you in your daily living activities. The impairment must have lasted or be expected to last for a continuous period of at least 12 months.
8. Line 18 on the form replaces the **TD3** form. You may find it convenient to deduct tax here for other income you receive that has little or no tax deducted from it. For example, UI benefits, investment or rental income.
9. **"Self-contained domestic establishment"** means the dwelling house, apartment or similar place where you sleep and eat. It does not include a bunkhouse, dormitory, hotel room or rooms in a boarding house. For further information, including the list of prescribed areas, see the *Northern Residents Deductions Tax Guide* which is available at our district taxation office.
10. Your spouse and/or dependants must first use their pension income, age, disability, tuition fees and education amounts as applicable to reduce their federal tax to zero before they can **transfer** any **unused balance** of these amounts to you.

1990 NET CLAIM CODES

net claim amount *over - not over*	claim code
NO claim amount	0
$ 0 - 6,169	1
6,169 - 7,680	2
7,680 - 9,192	3
9,192 - 10,704	4
10,704 - 12,215	5
12,215 - 13,726	6
13,726 - 15,238	7
15,238 - 16,749	8
16,749 - 18,260	9
18,260 - 19,773	10
19,773 and over	X
NO tax withholding required	E

Cette formule est disponible en français.

Look closely at the TD1 form shown on pages 429 and 430.

Analysis: Here are the important points to remember about completing the TD1 form.

- The first boxes are for personal data, such as name, address, SIN, and so on.
- Following the instructions, the return lists the different tax credits and the amount of each credit. The total (or net) credits establishes the **net claim code**. This code is the basis for the calculation of the income taxes payable by the employee. The calculation is discussed in more detail in Topic 2.
- Anyone who is required to pay income taxes in Canada receives the first credit, the Basic Personal Amount. The amount of $6169 is for the 1990 taxation year. The basic amount represents income that is tax free. In other words, if an employee earns less than $6169 in a year, he or she does not pay income tax.

Basic Personal Amount: a tax credit available to all taxpayers.

- The rest of the credits may be claimed by an employee depending on circumstances.
- The larger the total credits, the **smaller** the income tax that will be deducted from the employee's pay. For Kathy Lewis, the credit total is $6489. By looking at the table at the bottom of page 2 of the TD1, we see that the corresponding net claim code is 2. This code appears in the box for item 17.
- The form must be signed by the employee to certify that the information that the employee gives in the form is correct.

The Salaried Payroll Plan A payroll system based on a salary is a fixed sum payable after an employee works a certain length of time. This fixed sum becomes the employee's earned gross pay unless that person loses some pay because of non-excused time off. The payroll plan pays each employee a predetermined amount at the end of a specific, fixed payroll period. This amount is a **salary**. All salaried payrolls are organized around a variety of fixed payroll periods. Study the following table of common salary pay periods.

Gross pay: amount before payroll deductions.

Type of Pay Period	Duration of Pay Period	Number of Pay Periods Per Year (= Number of Pay Days)
weekly	**at the end of one work week**, usually ending Friday.	52
biweekly	**at the end of two work weeks**, usually every second Friday.	26
semi-monthly	**twice a month**, at the half-point and at the end of each month.	24
monthly	**once a month**, for example, the 28th if this is chosen as the pay day.	12

For Dr. Johnson's dental practice, beginning in March of 1990, two employees have been hired on a biweekly salaried plan as follows:

(1) Kathy Lewis, dental hygienist, at $600 per week; biweekly salary, $1200

(2) Lynn Fortier, receptionist/bookkeeper, at $400 per week; biweekly salary $800

Employee's individual earnings record: a payroll record showing an individual employee's payroll details for each pay period.

Once an employee's salary and pay period are established, this information and other important employee data are recorded in the top portion of an employee's individual earnings record. This may be in the form of a card or a computer printout. An example of a record card is shown below for Kathy Lewis.

EMPLOYEE'S INDIVIDUAL EARNINGS RECORD FOR THE YEAR 1990

Employee's Name: Lewis, Kathy SIN: 473 621 459 Tel. No.: 679-3734

Address: Any Town/City Canada N6H 4H9

Date of Birth: January 14, 19– Date Employed: June 15, 19– Date of Termination:

Position: Dental Hygienist Salary Plan: biweekly Rate of Pay: $600 per week

Net Claim Code per TD1: 2 UI Insurable Earnings: Minimum: $256 biweekly Maximum: $1280 biweekly Maximum UI Yearly Premium: $748.80

CPP Year's Maximum Earnings	Year's Basic Exemption	Maximum Earnings for Contributions	Maximum Yearly CPP
$28 900.00	$2 800.00	$26 100.00	$574.20

Pay Period Ending	Time Worked		Rate /Wk.	Earnings			Deductions				Net Pay	Year-to-Date			
	Weeks	OT Days		Regular	OT Excess	Gross Pay	CPP	UI	Inc. Tax	Total		Gross Pay	CPP	UI	Inc. Tax

Attendance Record Small businesses usually allow each salaried person to keep track of his or her own days worked. Toward the end of a payroll period, the payroll accounting clerk checks with each employee to verify the time worked. In many businesses, employees lose a day's pay for each day off work without a reasonable explanation. For example, if a salaried person earns $500 per week for working five days, a day off without permission means a pay loss of the $100 for that day. In disputed cases the owner makes all final decisions on each person's salary **before** the payroll application is processed.

In businesses with several offices and many employees, management may use a formal payroll and absentee report to keep track of the attendance of salaried employees. The office manager signs this record before sending it to payroll accounting. An example of a payroll and absentee report used by one large business is shown below.

Department Gregg
Completed by L. Taylor
From Monday 23 April 1990 (day, date, month)
To Friday 27 April 1990 (day, date, month)

NAME	MONDAY absent	TUESDAY absent	WEDNESDAY absent	THURSDAY absent	FRIDAY absent	SATURDAY absent	TOTAL DAYS ABSENT	EXPLANATIONS Reasons for absence, vacations etc.
Scott Aplin	x						1	Virus cold
Ray Butler								
Henry Conway								
John Davis	x	x	x	x	x		5	Vacation

The attendance record shows only the days on which the employee is absent. Reasons for absence are written in the Explanations column. Any 'clean' record would indicate to payroll accounting that the person's regular salary should be processed. Thus, accounting for the time worked for salaried employees is quite simple: payroll accounting assumes the regular salary is to be paid unless management instructs the payroll department to deduct an amount from the employee's regular salary.

In this chapter, we will assume for Dr. Johnson's salaried biweekly payroll that his employees have had a perfect attendance record.

CALCULATING PAYROLL DEDUCTIONS

After an employee's gross pay is calculated, payroll accounting must determine and then subtract the deductions from gross pay. This

Net (or take-home) pay: amount after payroll deductions.

leaves the employee with net pay, sometimes called ''take-home pay.'' The three most common payroll deductions are for the Canada Pension Plan, Unemployment Insurance, and income tax. These deductions will be studied in the sections that follow. Other payroll deductions are discussed in Topic 2, Chapter 14.

Canada Pension Plan (CPP): a compulsory employee's pension plan administered by the federal government.

Pensionable employment: employment for which CPP contributions are required.

Canada Pension Plan In most provinces, except Quebec, if you are 18 years old and an employee, the employer must deduct from each payroll the employee's contribution to the Canada Pension Plan (CPP). Employers in Quebec must deduct a similar amount but the contribution goes into the Quebec Pension Plan.

The Canada Pension Plan is a fund set up by the federal government for all employees who have pensionable employment. Employees must make contributions to this fund as long as they work, up to the age of 69. No deductions are made after an employee reaches 70 years of age. Employees are eligible to start collecting at age 65 which is when most employees retire. If employees do not retire at this age, they may continue to contribute until their 70th birthday, but they may not receive the Canada pension during this time. *Note:* An employee must make CPP contributions up to the month before the month he or she begins to collect.

The employer must match the amount deducted from the employee's salary. For example, if $5.00 were deducted from the employee's pay, the employer must also contribute $5.00. The $10.00 is remitted to Revenue Canada—Taxation, and it is this government department that administers the fund.

Calculating the CPP Deduction To help employers calculate the correct deduction, Revenue Canada—Taxation publishes each January a booklet of CPP contribution tables called *Canada Pension Plan Contributions and Unemployment Insurance Premiums*. As the name suggests, this booklet also helps employers calculate the Unemployment Insurance premiums.

The CPP contribution tables are set up according to the type of pay period. There is also a special section explaining how to calculate the employee's contribution when the table method cannot be used. Portions of the CPP tables are illustrated opposite. We will calculate the CPP contributions or deductions for Dr. Johnson's two employees.

Calculating the amount of the contribution is easy with the tables. Examine the following examples for Dr. Johnson's dental practice.

Kathy Lewis, biweekly salary $1200: Select the table corresponding to the pay period. In this example the correct choice is the table for a biweekly salary range of $1023.83—$2052.00 under the heading 1048.83—2052.00. A portion of this table is shown below. Look down the Remuneration column for the pay category which includes the employee's pay, in this case, $1192.01—$1202.00. The corresponding amount of $23.96 in the CPP column is the amount of contribution to deduct from the employee's pay. To this amount, add the employer's contribution, which is also $23.96. The amount to remit to Revenue Canada Taxation is then $47.92.

Lynn Fortier, biweekly salary $800: If the steps above are followed, the deduction is $15.23. The amount to remit to Revenue Canada Taxation is $30.46 (or twice the amount deducted from the employee).

26 CANADA PENSION PLAN CONTRIBUTIONS COTISATIONS AU RÉGIME DE PENSIONS DU CANADA

BI-WEEKLY PAY PERIOD — *PÉRIODE DE PAIE DE DEUX SEMAINES*

762.01 — 892.91

Remuneration *Rémunération* From-*de*	To-*à*	C.P.P. *R.P.C.*	Remuneration *Rémunération* From-*de*	To-*à*	C.P.P. *R.P.C.*	Remuneration *Rémunération* From-*de*	To-*à*	C.P.P. *R.P.C.*	Remuneration *Rémunération* From-*de*	To-*à*	C.P.P. *R.P.C.*
762.01 -	762.46	14.40	794.74 -	795.18	15.12	827.47 -	827.91	15.84	860.19 -	860.64	16.56
762.47 -	762.91	14.41	795.19 -	795.64	15.13	827.92 -	828.37	15.85	860.65 -	861.09	16.57
762.92 -	763.37	14.42	795.65 -	796.09	15.14	828.38 -	828.82	15.86	861.10 -	861.55	16.58
763.38 -	763.82	14.43	796.10 -	796.55	15.15	828.83 -	829.28	15.87	861.56 -	862.00	16.59
763.83 -	764.28	14.44	796.56 -	797.00	15.16	829.29 -	829.73	15.88	862.01 -	862.46	16.60
764.29 -	764.73	14.45	797.01 -	797.46	15.17	829.74 -	830.18	15.89	862.47 -	862.91	16.61
764.74 -	765.18	14.46	797.47 -	797.91	15.18	830.19 -	830.64	15.90	862.92 -	863.37	16.62
765.19 -	765.64	14.47	797.92 -	798.37	15.19	830.65 -	831.09	15.91	863.38 -	863.82	16.63
765.65 -	766.09	14.48	798.38 -	798.82	15.20	831.10 -	831.55	15.92	863.83 -	864.28	16.64
766.10 -	766.55	14.49	798.83 -	799.28	15.21	831.56 -	832.00	15.93	864.29 -	864.73	16.65
766.56 -	767.00	14.50	799.29 -	799.73	15.22	832.01 -	832.46	15.94	864.74 -	865.18	16.66
767.01 -	767.46	14.51	799.74 -	800.18	15.23	832.47 -	832.91	15.95	865.19 -	865.64	16.67
767.47 -	767.91	14.52	800.19 -	800.64	15.24	832.92 -	833.37	15.96	865.65 -	866.09	16.68
767.92 -	768.37	14.53	800.65 -	801.09	15.25	833.38 -	833.82	15.97	866.10 -	866.55	16.69
768.38 -	768.82	14.54	801.10 -	801.55	15.26	833.83 -	834.28	15.98	866.56 -	867.00	16.70
768.83 -	769.28	14.55	801.56 -	802.00	15.27	834.29 -	834.73	15.99	867.01 -	867.46	16.71
769.29 -	769.73	14.56	802.01 -	802.46	15.28	834.74 -	835.18	16.00	867.47 -	867.91	16.72
769.74 -	770.18	14.57	802.47 -	802.91	15.29	835.19 -	835.64	16.01	867.92 -	868.37	16.73

1048.83 — 2052.00

From-*de*	To-*à*	C.P.P. *R.P.C.*	From-*de*	To-*à*	C.P.P. *R.P.C.*	From-*de*	To-*à*	C.P.P. *R.P.C.*	From-*de*	To-*à*	C.P.P. *R.P.C.*
1048.38 -	1048.82	20.70	1081.10 -	1081.55	21.42	1152.01 -	1162.00	23.08	1872.01 -	1882.00	38.92
1048.83 -	1049.28	20.71	1081.56 -	1082.00	21.43	1162.01 -	1172.00	23.30	1882.01 -	1892.00	39.14
1049.29 -	1049.73	20.72	1082.01 -	1082.46	21.44	1172.01 -	1182.00	23.52	1892.01 -	1902.00	39.36
1049.74 -	1050.18	20.73	1082.47 -	1082.91	21.45	1182.01 -	1192.00	23.74	1902.01 -	1912.00	39.58
1050.19 -	1050.64	20.74	1082.92 -	1083.37	21.46	1192.01 -	1202.00	23.96	1912.01 -	1922.00	39.80
1050.65 -	1051.09	20.75	1083.38 -	1083.82	21.47	1202.01 -	1212.00	24.18	1922.01 -	1932.00	40.02
1051.10 -	1051.55	20.76	1083.83 -	1084.28	21.48	1212.01 -	1222.00	24.40	1932.01 -	1942.00	40.24
1051.56 -	1052.00	20.77	1084.29 -	1084.73	21.49	1222.01 -	1232.00	24.62	1942.01 -	1952.00	40.46
1052.01 -	1052.46	20.78	1084.74 -	1085.18	21.50	1232.01 -	1242.00	24.84	1952.01 -	1962.00	40.68
1052.47 -	1052.91	20.79	1085.19 -	1085.64	21.51	1242.01 -	1252.00	25.06	1962.01 -	1972.00	40.90
1052.92 -	1053.37	20.80	1085.65 -	1086.09	21.52	1252.01 -	1262.00	25.28	1972.01 -	1982.00	41.12
1053.38 -	1053.82	20.81	1086.10 -	1086.55	21.53	1262.01 -	1272.00	25.50	1982.01 -	1992.00	41.34
1053.83 -	1054.28	20.82	1086.56 -	1087.00	21.54	1272.01 -	1282.00	25.72	1992.01 -	2002.00	41.56
1054.29 -	1054.73	20.83	1087.01 -	1087.46	21.55	1282.01 -	1292.00	25.94	2002.01 -	2012.00	41.78
1054.74 -	1055.18	20.84	1087.47 -	1087.91	21.56	1292.01 -	1302.00	26.16	2012.01 -	2022.00	42.00
1055.19 -	1055.64	20.85	1087.92 -	1088.37	21.57	1302.01 -	1312.00	26.38	2022.01 -	2032.00	42.22
1055.65 -	1056.09	20.86	1088.38 -	1088.82	21.58	1312.01 -	1322.00	26.60	2032.01 -	2042.00	42.44
1056.10 -	1056.55	20.87	1088.83 -	1089.28	21.59	1322.01 -	1332.00	26.82	2042.01 -	2052.00	42.66

These deductions are made from each pay cheque until a certain limit is reached. The maximum contribution varies with each calendar year. This and other information is given at the beginning of the booklet in Schedule I — Canada Pension Plan. As you see below, in 1990 the maximum contribution is $574.20.

SCHEDULE I—CANADA PENSION PLAN		
Year's maximum pensionable earnings		$28,900
Year's basic exemption		$2,800
Maximum earnings on which contributions are based		$26,100
Maximum Employee Contribution	2.2% of $26,100	$574.20
Maximum Employer Contribution	2.2% of $26,100	$574.20

Schedule I also shows how the maximum contribution per employee —and the employer's matching contribution—is calculated. The maximum amount of pensionable earnings is $28 900 and the basic exemption is $2800. The difference between the two is $26 100 and represents the maximum earnings. Thus, the contribution is calculated as a percentage of this amount: 2.2% of $26 100 or $574.20. It is very important to note that these figures change from year to year. This data is provided by the tax department.

The employer must ensure that the payroll system keeps track of the employee contributions so that deductions from the employee's salary stop when the total deductions equal the maximum amount. The employee's earnings record card illustrated earlier is one way of recording deductions. Many employees will not reach the maximum because their annual gross income does not exceed the $26 100 limit.

By law, the employer must keep records and books of account for CPP contributions. These records must include enough information to determine the correct deductions from each employee's pay. Payroll accounting must keep records of each employee's total earnings, or contributory earnings if different from total earnings, and CPP contributions for the year. Thus, the individual employee's earnings record becomes an important document in every payroll application. By law, the employer must keep payroll records for six years.

Legal time limit for keeping payroll records: six years.

Unemployment Insurance

Most Canadian workers are required to contribute premiums to unemployment insurance. This entitles them to collect UI benefits when they're out of work.

UI: unemployment insurance.

There are some exceptions. Workers reaching their 65th birthday do not pay for unemployment insurance. Also, some part-time and a few classes of other full-time workers do not pay. Nor do those who are self-employed pay. Of course, if you do not contribute, you cannot collect UI benefits.

UI premiums: the required contributions to unemployment insurance.

UI premiums are not like deposits in a bank account where you deposit in and withdraw money whenever you wish. It is more like fire insurance: you pay a premium for protection against a fire in your home or business. If you do have a fire, you collect money to replace the items lost. If you do not have a fire, you do not collect anything. Your premiums help pay for the person who does have a fire and qualifies to receive some money. Insurance involves sharing the risk. It is the same with UI. If you qualify, you can collect. If you do not qualify, you cannot collect.

Insurable earnings: the amount of earnings upon which UI premiums are calculated.

Every year, the minimum and maximum limits of insurable earnings are set by the Canada Employment and Immigration Commission. Premiums are calculated on insurable earnings.

In Schedule II — Unemployment Insurance, shown below, you can see that the biweekly minimum amount of insurable earnings is $256. This means that any employee who worked two weeks and earned at least $256 must have an amount — or premium — deducted from his or her pay for UI. However, an employee who did not earn $256 in a biweekly pay period but worked at least 15 hours in one of those weeks must also contribute to UI (condition 2 in the first paragraph of Schedule II).

SCHEDULE II–UNEMPLOYMENT INSURANCE

Schedule of Minimum Hours and Insurable Earnings and Maximum Insurable Earnings and Premiums for Various Pay Periods

Under Regulation 13 an employee is in insurable employment when one of the two following conditions is met; (1) the employee has cash earnings of at least 20 percent of the maximum weekly insurable earnings or (2) worked at least 15 hours in a week. As long as an employee has worked in each week or part week of the pay period and the cash earnings or hours worked in the pay period are equal to or exceed the minimum for the pay period as in the table below, earnings for the whole pay period are insurable. IMPORTANT: Please read the text "Employment and Earnings Subject and Not Subject to UI Premiums," contained in this publication.

Pay Period (PP)	Note*: It is necessary to fall below **both** of the minimum requirements specified in UI Regulation 13 in order to be in EXCEPTED employment for UI purposes.	Minimum*		Maximum Insurable Earnings ($)	Maximum Premium ($)	
		Hours	Earnings		Per Period @ 2.25%	Per Annum see **Note(1)**
Weekly	(52 P.P.)	15	128.00	640.00	14.40	748.80(1)
Bi-Weekly	(26 P.P.)	30	256.00	1,280.00	28.80	748.80(1)
Semi-Monthly	(24 P.P.)	33	277.33	1,386.66	31.20	748.80
Monthly	(12 P.P.)	65	554.66	2,773.33	62.40	748.80
10 Pay Periods Per Year		78	665.60	3,328.00	74.88	748.80
13 Pay Periods Per Year		60	512.00	2,560.00	57.60	748.80
22 Pay Periods Per Year		35	302.54	1,512.72	34.04	748.88
Yearly (commission)			6,656.00	33,280.00		748.80

Employee Premium Rate 2.25%

Note(1): See "Additional Weekly or Bi-weekly Premiums."

Employer Premium Rate 1.4 times employee's premium unless a reduced rate applies. See "Employer's Premium Rate Reduction".

The schedule also shows that the maximum insurable earnings for those working on a biweekly basis is $1280.00. (Remember, this amount changes from year to year.) Based on this amount, the maximum premium is $28.80. Other types of pay periods are also listed in the schedule.

How much does an employee pay for UI? The premium is a rate or percentage and in this case is 2.25% of insurable earnings. Thus, the premium is $2.25 for every $100 of insurable earnings.

By law, the employer is also required to pay an employer's premium on behalf of each employee. It is set at a fixed rate of 1.4 times the employee's premium. In other words, for every dollar contributed by the employee, the employer must contribute $1.40.

Calculating the UI Deduction The following examples illustrate how to calculate UI deductions for the employees of Dr. Johnson's dental practice.

Kathy Lewis, biweekly salary $1200: Using the Unemployment Insurance Premiums table opposite, locate under the Remuneration column a salary of $1200. The corresponding amount in the U.I. Premium column is $27.00. Since this amount is **less** than the biweekly maximum of $28.80, $27.00 is deducted from Kathy's pay. If the premium in the table was **greater** than the maximum, then $28.80 would be deducted. Dr. Johnson must contribute 1.4 × $27.00 or $37.80. The total amount to be remitted to the federal government is $27.00 + $37.80 or $64.80.

Lynn Fortier, biweekly salary $800: The UI premium deduction is $18.00 as shown in the table opposite. The employer's contribution is $25.20 and the remittance to Revenue Canada Taxation is $18.00 + $25.20 or $43.20.

The UI tables simply list the salary ranges, which are not segregated, as in the CPP tables, by type of pay period. Therefore, it is important for the payroll clerk to always check that the amount shown in the table does not exceed the premium for the type of pay period used by the employer. The maximums are listed at the bottom of each page, as shown here.

Maximum Premium Deduction for a Pay Period of the stated frequency. Déduction maximale de prime pour une période de paie d'une durée donnée.				
Weekly - Hebdomadaire	14.40	10 pp per year - 10 pp par année	74.88
Bi-Weekly - Deux semaines	28.80	13 pp per year - 13 pp par année	57.60
Semi-Monthly - Bi-mensuel	31.20	22 pp per year - 22 pp par année	34.04
Monthly - Mensuellement	62.40		

Record of Employment: a key document proving work in insurable employment.

Under the Unemployment Insurance Act, a Record of Employment must be given to you by your employer within five days after an interruption of earnings, for example, termination of employment. This form is the piece of paper that gets the unemployed person into the UI system and starts his or her payments. A guide to filling out

UNEMPLOYMENT INSURANCE PREMIUMS

For minimum and maximum insurable earnings amounts for various pay periods see Schedule II. For the maximum premium deduction for various pay periods see bottom of this page.

Remuneration *Rémunération* From-*de*	To-*à*	U.I. Premium *Prime d'a.-c.*	Remuneration *Rémunération* From-*de*	To-*à*	U.I. Premium *Prime d'a.-c.*
796.23 -	796.66	17.92	828.23 -	828.66	18.64
796.67 -	797.11	17.93	828.67 -	829.11	18.65
797.12 -	797.55	17.94	829.12 -	829.55	18.66
797.56 -	797.99	17.95	829.56 -	829.99	18.67
798.00 -	798.44	17.96	830.00 -	830.44	18.68
798.45 -	798.88	17.97	830.45 -	830.88	18.69
798.89 -	799.33	17.98	830.89 -	831.33	18.70
799.34 -	799.77	17.99	831.34 -	831.77	18.71
799.78 -	800.22	18.00	831.78 -	832.22	18.72
1152.23 -	1152.66	25.93	1184.23 -	1184.66	26.65
1152.67 -	1153.11	25.94	1184.67 -	1185.11	26.66
1153.12 -	1153.55	25.95	1185.12 -	1185.55	26.67
1153.56 -	1153.99	25.96	1185.56 -	1185.99	26.68
1154.00 -	1154.44	25.97	1186.00 -	1186.44	26.69
1154.45 -	1154.88	25.98	1186.45 -	1186.88	26.70
1154.89 -	1155.33	25.99	1186.89 -	1187.33	26.71
1155.34 -	1155.77	26.00	1187.34 -	1187.77	26.72
1155.78 -	1156.22	26.01	1187.78 -	1188.22	26.73
1156.23 -	1156.66	26.02	1188.23 -	1188.66	26.74
1156.67 -	1157.11	26.03	1188.67 -	1189.11	26.75
1157.12 -	1157.55	26.04	1189.12 -	1189.55	26.76
1157.56 -	1157.99	26.05	1189.56 -	1189.99	26.77
1158.00 -	1158.44	26.06	1190.00 -	1190.44	26.78
1158.45 -	1158.88	26.07	1190.45 -	1190.88	26.79
1158.89 -	1159.33	26.08	1190.89 -	1191.33	26.80
1159.34 -	1159.77	26.09	1191.34 -	1191.77	26.81
1159.78 -	1160.22	26.10	1191.78 -	1192.22	26.82
1160.23 -	1160.66	26.11	1192.23 -	1192.66	26.83
1160.67 -	1161.11	26.12	1192.67 -	1193.11	26.84
1161.12 -	1161.55	26.13	1193.12 -	1193.55	26.85
1161.56 -	1161.99	26.14	1193.56 -	1193.99	26.86
1162.00 -	1162.44	26.15	1194.00 -	1194.44	26.87
1162.45 -	1162.88	26.16	1194.45 -	1194.88	26.88
1162.89 -	1163.33	26.17	1194.89 -	1195.33	26.89
1163.34 -	1163.77	26.18	1195.34 -	1195.77	26.90
1163.78 -	1164.22	26.19	1195.78 -	1196.22	26.91
1164.23 -	1164.66	26.20	1196.23 -	1196.66	26.92
1164.67 -	1165.11	26.21	1196.67 -	1197.11	26.93
1165.12 -	1165.55	26.22	1197.12 -	1197.55	26.94
1165.56 -	1165.99	26.23	1197.56 -	1197.99	26.95
1166.00 -	1166.44	26.24	1198.00 -	1198.44	26.96
1166.45 -	1166.88	26.25	1198.45 -	1198.88	26.97
1166.89 -	1167.33	26.26	1198.89 -	1199.33	26.98
1167.34 -	1167.77	26.27	1199.34 -	1199.77	26.99
1167.78 -	1168.22	26.28	1199.78 -	1200.22	27.00
1168.23 -	1168.66	26.29	1200.23 -	1200.66	27.01
1168.67 -	1169.11	26.30	1200.67 -	1201.11	27.02
1169.12 -	1169.55	26.31	1201.12 -	1201.55	27.03
1169.56 -	1169.99	26.32	1201.56 -	1201.99	27.04
1170.00 -	1170.44	26.33	1202.00 -	1202.44	27.05
1170.45 -	1170.88	26.34	1202.45 -	1202.88	27.06
1170.89 -	1171.33	26.35	1202.89 -	1203.33	27.07
1171.34 -	1171.77	26.36	1203.34 -	1203.77	27.08
1171.78 -	1172.22	26.37	1203.78 -	1204.22	27.09

the form is published by the Employment and Immigration Commission and is called *How to complete the Record of Employment.* This booklet gives information for each type of pay period. One example given in the booklet covering biweekly pay periods is shown below.

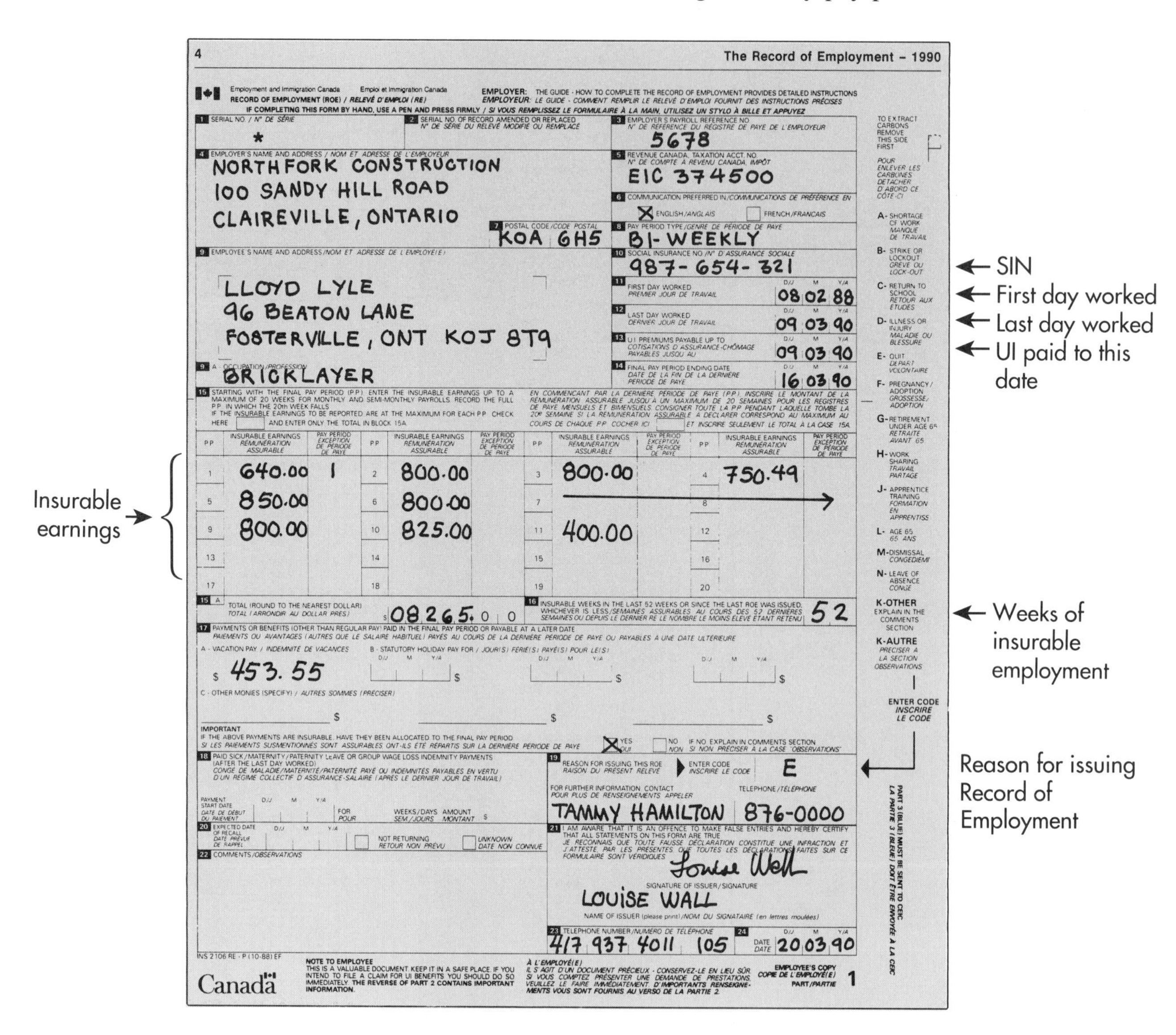
4 The Record of Employment – 1990

Employment and Immigration Canada / Emploi et Immigration Canada
RECORD OF EMPLOYMENT (ROE) / *RELEVÉ D'EMPLOI (RE)*
EMPLOYER: THE GUIDE - HOW TO COMPLETE THE RECORD OF EMPLOYMENT PROVIDES DETAILED INSTRUCTIONS
EMPLOYEUR: LE GUIDE - COMMENT REMPLIR LE RELEVÉ D'EMPLOI FOURNIT DES INSTRUCTIONS PRÉCISES
IF COMPLETING THIS FORM BY HAND, USE A PEN AND PRESS FIRMLY / *SI VOUS REMPLISSEZ LE FORMULAIRE À LA MAIN, UTILISEZ UN STYLO À BILLE ET APPUYEZ*

1 SERIAL NO. / *Nº DE SÉRIE*: *
2 SERIAL NO. OF RECORD AMENDED OR REPLACED / *Nº DE SÉRIE DU RELEVÉ MODIFIÉ OU REMPLACÉ*
3 EMPLOYER'S PAYROLL REFERENCE NO. / *Nº DE RÉFÉRENCE DU RÉGISTRE DE PAYE DE L'EMPLOYEUR*: 5678
4 EMPLOYER'S NAME AND ADDRESS / *NOM ET ADRESSE DE L'EMPLOYEUR*:
NORTHFORK CONSTRUCTION
100 SANDY HILL ROAD
CLAIREVILLE, ONTARIO
5 REVENUE CANADA, TAXATION ACCT. NO. / *Nº DE COMPTE À REVENU CANADA, IMPÔT*: EIC 374500
6 COMMUNICATION PREFERRED IN / *COMMUNICATIONS DE PRÉFÉRENCE EN*: [X] ENGLISH/*ANGLAIS* [ ] FRENCH/*FRANCAIS*
7 POSTAL CODE / *CODE POSTAL*: KOA 6H5
8 PAY PERIOD TYPE / *GENRE DE PÉRIODE DE PAYE*: BI-WEEKLY
9 EMPLOYEE'S NAME AND ADDRESS / *NOM ET ADRESSE DE L'EMPLOYÉ(E)*:
LLOYD LYLE
96 BEATON LANE
FOSTERVILLE, ONT KOJ 8T9
10 SOCIAL INSURANCE NO. / *Nº D'ASSURANCE SOCIALE*: 987-654-321
11 FIRST DAY WORKED / *PREMIER JOUR DE TRAVAIL* (D/J M Y/A): 08 02 88
12 LAST DAY WORKED / *DERNIER JOUR DE TRAVAIL* (D/J M Y/A): 09 03 90
13 U.I. PREMIUMS PAYABLE UP TO / *COTISATIONS D'ASSURANCE-CHÔMAGE PAYABLES JUSQU'AU* (D/J M Y/A): 09 03 90
9A OCCUPATION / *PROFESSION*: BRICKLAYER
14 FINAL PAY PERIOD ENDING DATE / *DATE DE LA FIN DE LA DERNIÈRE PÉRIODE DE PAYE* (D/J M Y/A): 16 03 90

15 STARTING WITH THE FINAL PAY PERIOD (P.P.) ENTER THE INSURABLE EARNINGS UP TO A MAXIMUM OF 20 WEEKS. FOR MONTHLY AND SEMI-MONTHLY PAYROLLS RECORD THE FULL P.P. IN WHICH THE 20th WEEK FALLS.
IF THE INSURABLE EARNINGS TO BE REPORTED ARE AT THE MAXIMUM FOR EACH P.P. CHECK HERE [ ] AND ENTER ONLY THE TOTAL IN BLOCK 15A.
EN COMMENCANT PAR LA DERNIÈRE PÉRIODE DE PAYE (P.P.) INSCRIRE LE MONTANT DE LA RÉMUNÉRATION ASSURABLE JUSQU'À UN MAXIMUM DE 20 SEMAINES. POUR LES REGISTRES DE PAYE MENSUELS ET BIMENSUELS CONSIGNER TOUTE LA P.P. PENDANT LAQUELLE TOMBE LA 20e SEMAINE. SI LA RÉMUNÉRATION ASSURABLE À DECLARER CORRESPOND AU MAXIMUM AU COURS DE CHAQUE P.P. COCHER ICI [ ] ET INSCRIRE SEULEMENT LE TOTAL À LA CASE 15A.

P.P.	INSURABLE EARNINGS / *RÉMUNÉRATION ASSURABLE*	PAY PERIOD EXCEPTION / *DE PÉRIODE DE PAYE*	P.P.	INSURABLE EARNINGS / *RÉMUNÉRATION ASSURABLE*	PAY PERIOD EXCEPTION / *DE PÉRIODE DE PAYE*	P.P.	INSURABLE EARNINGS / *RÉMUNÉRATION ASSURABLE*	PAY PERIOD EXCEPTION / *DE PÉRIODE DE PAYE*	P.P.	INSURABLE EARNINGS / *RÉMUNÉRATION ASSURABLE*	PAY PERIOD EXCEPTION / *DE PÉRIODE DE PAYE*
1	640.00	1	2	800.00		3	800.00		4	750.49	
5	850.00		6	800.00		7	→		8	→	
9	800.00		10	825.00		11	400.00		12		
13			14			15			16		
17			18			19			20		

15A TOTAL (ROUND TO THE NEAREST DOLLAR) / *TOTAL (ARRONDIR AU DOLLAR PRÈS)*: $08265.00
16 INSURABLE WEEKS IN THE LAST 52 WEEKS OR SINCE THE LAST ROE WAS ISSUED, WHICHEVER IS LESS / *SEMAINES ASSURABLES AU COURS DES 52 DERNIÈRES SEMAINES OU DEPUIS LE DERNIER RE LE NOMBRE LE MOINS ÉLEVÉ ÉTANT RETENU*: 52

17 PAYMENTS OR BENEFITS (OTHER THAN REGULAR PAY) PAID IN THE FINAL PAY PERIOD OR PAYABLE AT A LATER DATE
PAIEMENTS OU AVANTAGES (AUTRES QUE LE SALAIRE HABITUEL) PAYÉS AU COURS DE LA DERNIÈRE PÉRIODE DE PAYE OU PAYABLES À UNE DATE ULTÉRIEURE
A - VACATION PAY / *INDEMNITÉ DE VACANCES*: $ 453.55
B - STATUTORY HOLIDAY PAY FOR / *JOUR(S) FÉRIÉ(S) PAYÉ(S) POUR LE(S)* (D/J M Y/A) $ (D/J M Y/A) $ (D/J M Y/A) $
C - OTHER MONIES (SPECIFY) / *AUTRES SOMMES (PRÉCISER)* $ $ $
IMPORTANT
IF THE ABOVE PAYMENTS ARE INSURABLE, HAVE THEY BEEN ALLOCATED TO THE FINAL PAY PERIOD
SI LES PAIEMENTS SUSMENTIONNÉS SONT ASSURABLES ONT-ILS ÉTÉ RÉPARTIS SUR LA DERNIÈRE PÉRIODE DE PAYE
[X] YES / *OUI* [ ] NO / *NON* IF NO EXPLAIN IN COMMENTS SECTION / *SI NON PRÉCISER À LA CASE "OBSERVATIONS"*

18 PAID SICK/MATERNITY/PATERNITY LEAVE OR GROUP WAGE LOSS INDEMNITY PAYMENTS (AFTER THE LAST DAY WORKED)
CONGÉ DE MALADIE/MATERNITÉ/PATERNITÉ PAYÉ OU INDEMNITÉS PAYABLES EN VERTU D'UN RÉGIME COLLECTIF D'ASSURANCE-SALAIRE (APRÈS LE DERNIER JOUR DE TRAVAIL)
PAYMENT START DATE / *DATE DE DÉBUT DU PAIEMENT* (D/J M Y/A) FOR / *POUR* WEEKS/DAYS / *SEM./JOURS* AMOUNT / *MONTANT* $
19 REASON FOR ISSUING THIS ROE / *RAISON DU PRÉSENT RELEVÉ* ▶ ENTER CODE / *INSCRIRE LE CODE*: E
FOR FURTHER INFORMATION CONTACT / *POUR PLUS DE RENSEIGNEMENTS APPELER*: TAMMY HAMILTON
TELEPHONE / *TÉLÉPHONE*: 876-0000
20 EXPECTED DATE OF RECALL / *DATE PRÉVUE DE RAPPEL* (D/J M Y/A) [ ] NOT RETURNING / *RETOUR NON PRÉVU* [ ] UNKNOWN / *DATE NON CONNUE*
21 I AM AWARE THAT IT IS AN OFFENCE TO MAKE FALSE ENTRIES AND HEREBY CERTIFY THAT ALL STATEMENTS ON THIS FORM ARE TRUE
JE RECONNAIS QUE TOUTE FAUSSE DÉCLARATION CONSTITUE UNE INFRACTION ET J'ATTESTE PAR LES PRÉSENTES QUE TOUTES LES DÉCLARATIONS FAITES SUR CE FORMULAIRE SONT VÉRIDIQUES
Louise Wall
SIGNATURE OF ISSUER / SIGNATURE
LOUISE WALL
NAME OF ISSUER (please print) / *NOM DU SIGNATAIRE (en lettres moulées)*
22 COMMENTS / *OBSERVATIONS*
23 TELEPHONE NUMBER / *NUMÉRO DE TÉLÉPHONE*: 417 937 4011 105
24 DATE / *DATE* (D/J M Y/A): 20 03 90

TO EXTRACT CARBONS REMOVE THIS SIDE FIRST / *POUR ENLEVER LES CARBONES DETACHER D'ABORD CE CÔTE-CI*
A - SHORTAGE OF WORK / *MANQUE DE TRAVAIL*
B - STRIKE OR LOCKOUT / *GREVE OU LOCK-OUT*
C - RETURN TO SCHOOL / *RETOUR AUX ETUDES*
D - ILLNESS OR INJURY / *MALADIE OU BLESSURE*
E - QUIT / *DEPART VOLONTAIRE*
F - PREGNANCY/ADOPTION / *GROSSESSE/ADOPTION*
G - RETIREMENT UNDER AGE 65 / *RETRAITE AVANT 65*
H - WORK SHARING / *TRAVAIL PARTAGE*
J - APPRENTICE TRAINING / *FORMATION EN APPRENTISS*
L - AGE 65 / *65 ANS*
M - DISMISSAL / *CONGEDIEMI*
N - LEAVE OF ABSENCE / *CONGE*
K - OTHER EXPLAIN IN THE COMMENTS SECTION
K - AUTRE *PRECISER A LA SECTION OBSERVATIONS*
ENTER CODE / *INSCRIRE LE CODE*

PART 3 (BLUE) MUST BE SENT TO CEIC / *LA PARTIE 3 (BLEUE) DOIT ÊTRE ENVOYÉE À LA CEIC*

INS 2106 RE - P (10-88) EF
Canada
NOTE TO EMPLOYEE
THIS IS A VALUABLE DOCUMENT. KEEP IT IN A SAFE PLACE. IF YOU INTEND TO FILE A CLAIM FOR UI BENEFITS YOU SHOULD DO SO IMMEDIATELY. **THE REVERSE OF PART 2 CONTAINS IMPORTANT INFORMATION.**
À L'EMPLOYÉ(E)
IL S'AGIT D'UN DOCUMENT PRÉCIEUX - CONSERVEZ-LE EN LIEU SÛR. SI VOUS COMPTEZ PRÉSENTER UNE DEMANDE DE PRESTATIONS, VEUILLEZ LE FAIRE IMMÉDIATEMENT. ***D'IMPORTANTS RENSEIGNEMENTS VOUS SONT FOURNIS AU VERSO DE LA PARTIE 2.***
EMPLOYEE'S COPY / *COPIE DE L'EMPLOYÉ(E)* PART/*PARTIE* 1

The essential information in this important record are: the employee's SIN, the employee's first day of work, the employee's last day of work, the last day for which the employer paid UI premiums for this employee, the number of weeks of insurable employment based on a biweekly pay period, the reason for issuing the Record of Employment, and a list of insurable earnings by pay period.

Finally, by law, the employer must keep records and books of account for all UI premiums. These records must be kept for **six years**, unless the tax department grants permission to destroy them earlier.

Income Tax Since 1917, all Canadians have had to pay income tax on their earnings. Employers must deduct income tax from each employee's salary, wages and commissions, bonuses, vacation pay, and any other type of earnings. Such deductions are called income tax deductions at source.

Income tax deductions at source: income tax taken off employee's pay.

Both the federal and the provincial governments enforce income tax acts which require income taxes to be deducted.

To simplify collection and remittances, all the provinces, with the exception of Quebec, have agreed to allow the Canadian government to collect from employers both federal and provincial income taxes as a lump sum. In Quebec, separate collections and remittances are required, one to the Receiver General for Canada for federal tax and one to the Treasurer of Quebec for provincial tax.

Both levels of government set their own rates of income tax. For that reason, Revenue Canada — Taxation publishes each year a separate booklet of tax tables for each province. Booklets are available for people who report for work to an employer in Ontario, Nova Scotia, and every other province.

Except in Quebec, the booklet of tables combines the income taxes to be collected for the federal government and for the province. Payroll clerks must be sure to use the correct booklet of tax tables; otherwise, incorrect **deductions at source** will be made.

If an employer uses a computer to process the payroll, Revenue Canada Taxation allows him or her to use a specific formula adaptable for use on the equipment rather than the tax tables. However, most employers across Canada still use the booklet of tax tables.

To find out how much a payroll clerk should deduct from each employee for income tax, check the employee's net claim code on the TD1 form.

If the employee has not completed the TD1 form, Revenue Canada Taxation requires that the employee be treated as having net claim code 1 (the code for deducting the highest amount from the employee's pay). No deductions are made if the employee certifies that the total remuneration received, and also receivable, during the calendar year will not exceed the tax credit claimed (this means a net claim code of E). For example, in the 1990 taxation year if an employee is only eligible for the basic personal amount and certifies that he or she will earn less than $6169, then the net claim code is E and the employee will not pay any income tax for that calendar year. See the illustration on pages 429 and 430.

Most employees will earn more than the basic amount. Therefore, payroll will use the booklet of tables and the net claim codes as shown in the TD1 form. Like the CPP booklet, the tax booklet has separate tables for the type of pay period used by the employer.

Calculating Income Tax Deductions Table 2 opposite shows the biweekly tax deductions. We will illustrate the tax deductions for Dr. Johnson's two employees.

(1) Kathy Lewis, biweekly salary $1200: Look down the biweekly pay column. Kathy's salary is above $1189, but below $1205. Since her net claim code is 2, the corresponding tax deduction is $252.35.

(2) Lynn Fortier, biweekly salary $800: Lynn's net claim code is 1. The amount of income tax to withhold, as per the table, is $142.50.

Unlike CPP and UI deductions, income taxes are paid by the employee only, and therefore the amount deducted from the employee's pay is remitted directly to Revenue Canada—Taxation.

After deductions for CPP, UI, and employee's income taxes are subtracted from the employee's salary, the result is the employee's net or take-home pay. The calculation of net pay for Dr. Johnson's two employees may be summarized as follows:

Employee	Gross Pay	Deductions				Net Pay
		CPP	UI	Income Tax	Total	
Kathy Lewis	1200.00	23.96	27.00	252.35	303.31	896.69
Lynn Fortier	800.00	15.23	18.00	142.50	175.73	624.27

TOPIC 1 PROBLEMS

Calculating net pay when deductions are given.

P 11-1 Dr. F. Greco, D.D.S. has three employees in his dental practice, located in Ontario. Dr. Greco pays his salaried employees monthly. At the end of the month, the payroll clerk provided the following data: Sally Anderson, SIN 458 211 896, net claim code 4, monthly gross pay of $1800, CPP contribution of $34.47, UI premium of $40.50, and income tax deduction of $240.95; Jane Haney, SIN 321 365 333, net claim code 1, monthly gross pay of $3000, CPP contribution of $60.94, UI premium of $62.40, and income tax deduction of $725.90; and Wayne Tse, SIN 425 555 896, net claim code 2, monthly gross pay of $2600, CPP

ONTARIO

BI-WEEKLY TAX DEDUCTIONS
Basis — 26 Pay Periods per Year

TABLE 2

ONTARIO

RETENUES D'IMPÔT DE DEUX SEMAINES
Base — 26 périodes de paie par année

BI-WEEKLY PAY Use appropriate bracket — PAIE DE DEUX SEMAINES *Utilisez le palier approprié*		IF THE EMPLOYEE'S "NET CLAIM CODE" ON FORM TD1 IS — *SI LE CODE DE DEMANDE NETTE DE L'EMPLOYÉ SELON LA FORMULE TD1 EST DE*										
		0	1	2	3	4	5	6	7	8	9	10
From - *De*	Less than *Moins que*	DEDUCT FROM EACH PAY — *RETENEZ SUR CHAQUE PAIE*										
781.-	789.	202.10	138.35	130.55	114.95	99.35	83.70	68.30	52.50	36.90	16.30	3.75
789.-	797.	204.15	140.45	132.60	117.00	101.40	85.75	70.35	54.55	38.95	19.75	5.10
797.-	805.	206.20	142.50	134.70	119.05	103.45	87.85	72.40	56.60	41.00	23.15	6.50
805.-	813.	208.25	144.55	136.75	121.10	105.50	89.90	74.50	58.65	43.05	26.60	7.85
813.-	821.	210.30	146.60	138.80	123.15	107.55	91.95	76.55	60.70	45.10	29.50	9.20
821.-	829.	212.35	148.65	140.85	125.20	109.60	94.00	78.60	62.75	47.15	31.55	10.60
829.-	837.	214.40	150.70	142.90	127.25	111.65	96.05	80.65	64.80	49.20	33.60	11.95
837.-	845.	216.50	152.75	144.95	129.35	113.70	98.10	82.70	66.85	51.25	35.65	14.20
845.-	853.	218.55	154.80	147.00	131.40	115.75	100.15	84.75	68.90	53.30	37.70	17.65
853.-	861.	220.60	156.85	149.05	133.45	117.80	102.20	86.80	70.95	55.35	39.75	21.10
861.-	869.	222.65	158.90	151.10	135.50	119.85	104.25	88.85	73.05	57.40	41.80	24.50
869.-	877.	224.70	160.95	153.15	137.55	121.90	106.30	90.90	75.10	59.45	43.85	27.95
877.-	885.	226.75	163.00	155.20	139.60	123.95	108.35	92.95	77.15	61.50	45.90	30.30
885.-	893.	228.80	165.05	157.25	141.65	126.05	110.40	95.00	79.20	63.55	47.95	32.35
893.-	901.	230.85	167.10	159.30	143.70	128.10	112.45	97.05	81.25	65.60	50.00	34.40
901.-	917.	233.95	170.20	162.40	146.80	131.15	115.55	100.15	84.30	68.70	53.10	37.45
917.-	933.	238.05	174.30	166.50	150.90	135.25	119.65	104.25	88.40	72.80	57.20	41.60
933.-	949.	242.15	178.40	170.60	155.00	139.35	123.75	108.35	92.55	76.90	61.30	45.70
949.-	965.	246.25	182.50	174.70	159.10	143.50	127.85	112.45	96.65	81.00	65.40	49.80
965.-	981.	250.35	186.60	178.80	163.20	147.60	131.95	116.55	100.75	85.15	69.50	53.90
981.-	997.	254.45	190.75	182.90	167.30	151.70	136.05	120.65	104.85	89.25	73.65	58.00
997.-	1013.	258.55	194.85	187.05	171.40	155.80	140.20	124.80	108.95	93.35	77.75	62.10
1013.-	1029.	262.65	198.95	191.15	175.50	159.90	144.30	128.90	113.05	97.45	81.85	66.20
1029.-	1045.	266.80	203.05	195.25	179.65	164.00	148.40	133.00	117.15	101.55	85.95	70.30
1045.-	1061.	270.90	207.15	199.35	183.75	168.10	152.50	137.10	121.30	105.65	90.05	74.45
1061.-	1077.	275.00	211.25	203.45	187.85	172.20	156.60	141.20	125.40	109.75	94.15	78.55
1077.-	1093.	279.10	215.35	207.55	191.95	176.35	160.70	145.30	129.50	113.85	98.25	82.65
1093.-	1109.	285.10	221.40	213.55	197.95	182.35	166.70	151.30	135.50	119.90	104.25	88.65
1109.-	1125.	291.50	227.80	220.00	204.35	188.75	173.15	157.75	141.90	126.30	110.70	95.05
1125.-	1141.	298.00	234.25	226.45	210.85	195.25	179.60	164.20	148.40	132.75	117.15	101.55
1141.-	1157.	304.50	240.75	232.95	217.35	201.70	186.10	170.70	154.85	139.25	123.65	108.00
1157.-	1173.	310.95	247.20	239.40	223.80	208.20	192.55	177.15	161.35	145.75	130.10	114.50
1173.-	1189.	317.45	253.70	245.90	230.30	214.65	199.05	183.65	167.80	152.20	136.60	120.95
1189.-	1205.	323.90	260.15	252.35	236.75	221.15	205.50	190.10	174.30	158.70	143.05	127.45
1205.-	1221.	330.40	266.65	258.85	243.25	227.60	212.00	196.60	180.75	165.15	149.55	133.90

contribution of $52.14, UI premium of $58.50, and income tax deduction of $556.30

a. How much is each employee's gross pay?

b. Calculate and show the net pay for each employee.

c. How much is the total gross pay for this payroll?

d. How much is the total net pay for this payroll?

e. How much is Dr. Greco's total CPP contribution for this payroll?

f. How much is Dr. Greco's total UI premium for this payroll?

g. Does Dr. Greco pay income taxes on behalf of his employees?

For the remaining problems use the tables provided on the next two pages or the latest tables provided by Revenue Canada Taxation.

Calculating employer and employee CPP contributions.

P 11-2 Record the following employees' names and their weekly earnings in columns (1) and (2), respectively: Anne Attridge, $450; Ross Geimer, $530; James Jessup, $560; and Marg Ryan, $710.

Employee (1)	Weekly Gross Earnings (2)	Employee Contribution to CPP (3)	Employer Contribution to CPP (4)	Combined Contribution to CPP (5)
Anne Attridge	$460			

Now calculate and record the CPP contribution for each employee (column 3) and for the employer (column 4) and also the total CPP contribution to be remitted (column 5). Complete the table by totalling each column, and list the totals at the bottom of the table.

Calculating employer and employee UIC premiums.

P 11-3 Using the information provided in Problem 11-2 and a similar table, calculate the UI premium for each employee, the employer's premium for each employee, and the total premium to be remitted to Revenue Canada—Taxation.

Calculating income tax deductions.

P 11-4 Assume the following net claim codes for the employees named in Problems 11-2 and 11-3: Attridge, 2; Geimer, 3; Jessup, 1; and Ryan, 8.

Show the amount of income tax to be withheld from each employee's pay.

Calculating net pay using data in above problems.

P 11-5 Using a summary table similar to the one illustrated at the end of Topic 1, calculate the net pay for each employee in the above problems.

CANADA PENSION PLAN CONTRIBUTIONS — COTISATIONS AU RÉGIME DE PENSIONS DU CANADA 19

WEEKLY PAY PERIOD — *PÉRIODE HEBDOMADAIRE DE PAIE*

446.34 — 1016.33

Remuneration *Rémunération* From-*de*	To-*à*	C.P.P. *R.P.C.*	Remuneration *Rémunération* From-*de*	To-*à*	C.P.P. *R.P.C.*	Remuneration *Rémunération* From-*de*	To-*à*	C.P.P. *R.P.C.*	Remuneration *Rémunération* From-*de*	To-*à*	C.P.P. *R.P.C.*
446.34 -	446.79	8.64	479.07 -	479.52	9.36	511.80 -	512.24	10.08	544.53 -	544.97	10.80
446.80 -	447.24	8.65	479.53 -	479.97	9.37	512.25 -	512.70	10.09	544.98 -	545.43	10.81
447.25 -	447.70	8.66	479.98 -	480.43	9.38	512.71 -	513.15	10.10	545.44 -	545.88	10.82
447.71 -	448.15	8.67	480.44 -	480.88	9.39	513.16 -	513.61	10.11	545.89 -	546.33	10.83
448.16 -	448.61	8.68	480.89 -	481.33	9.40	513.62 -	514.06	10.12	546.34 -	546.79	10.84
448.62 -	449.06	8.69	481.34 -	481.79	9.41	514.07 -	514.52	10.13	546.80 -	547.24	10.85
449.07 -	449.52	8.70	481.80 -	482.24	9.42	514.53 -	514.97	10.14	547.25 -	547.70	10.86
449.53 -	449.97	8.71	482.25 -	482.70	9.43	514.98 -	515.43	10.15	547.71 -	548.15	10.87
449.98 -	450.43	8.72	482.71 -	483.15	9.44	515.44 -	515.88	10.16	548.16 -	548.61	10.88
450.44 -	450.88	8.73	483.16 -	483.61	9.45	515.89 -	516.33	10.17	548.62 -	549.06	10.89
450.89 -	451.33	8.74	483.62 -	484.06	9.46	516.34 -	516.79	10.18	549.07 -	549.52	10.90
451.34 -	451.79	8.75	484.07 -	484.52	9.47	516.80 -	517.24	10.19	549.53 -	549.97	10.91
451.80 -	452.24	8.76	484.53 -	484.97	9.48	517.25 -	517.70	10.20	549.98 -	550.43	10.92
452.25 -	452.70	8.77	484.98 -	485.43	9.49	517.71 -	518.15	10.21	550.44 -	550.88	10.93
452.71 -	453.15	8.78	485.44 -	485.88	9.50	518.16 -	518.61	10.22	550.89 -	551.33	10.94
453.16 -	453.61	8.79	485.89 -	486.33	9.51	518.62 -	519.06	10.23	551.34 -	551.79	10.95
453.62 -	454.06	8.80	486.34 -	486.79	9.52	519.07 -	519.52	10.24	551.80 -	552.24	10.96
454.07 -	454.52	8.81	486.80 -	487.24	9.53	519.53 -	519.97	10.25	552.25 -	552.70	10.97
454.53 -	454.97	8.82	487.25 -	487.70	9.54	519.98 -	520.43	10.26	552.71 -	553.15	10.98
454.98 -	455.43	8.83	487.71 -	488.15	9.55	520.44 -	520.88	10.27	553.16 -	553.61	10.99
455.44 -	455.88	8.84	488.16 -	488.61	9.56	520.89 -	521.33	10.28	553.62 -	554.06	11.00
455.89 -	456.33	8.85	488.62 -	489.06	9.57	521.34 -	521.79	10.29	554.07 -	554.52	11.01
456.34 -	456.79	8.86	489.07 -	489.52	9.58	521.80 -	522.24	10.30	554.53 -	554.97	11.02
456.80 -	457.24	8.87	489.53 -	489.97	9.59	522.25 -	522.70	10.31	554.98 -	555.43	11.03
457.25 -	457.70	8.88	489.98 -	490.43	9.60	522.71 -	523.15	10.32	555.44 -	555.88	11.04
457.71 -	458.15	8.89	490.44 -	490.88	9.61	523.16 -	523.61	10.33	555.89 -	556.33	11.05
458.16 -	458.61	8.90	490.89 -	491.33	9.62	523.62 -	524.06	10.34	556.34 -	566.33	11.16
458.62 -	459.06	8.91	491.34 -	491.79	9.63	524.07 -	524.52	10.35	566.34 -	576.33	11.38
459.07 -	459.52	8.92	491.80 -	492.24	9.64	524.53 -	524.97	10.36	576.34 -	586.33	11.60
459.53 -	459.97	8.93	492.25 -	492.70	9.65	524.98 -	525.43	10.37	586.34 -	596.33	11.82
459.98 -	460.43	8.94	492.71 -	493.15	9.66	525.44 -	525.88	10.38	596.34 -	606.33	12.04
460.44 -	460.88	8.95	493.16 -	493.61	9.67	525.89 -	526.33	10.39	606.34 -	616.33	12.26
460.89 -	461.33	8.96	493.62 -	494.06	9.68	526.34 -	526.79	10.40	616.34 -	626.33	12.48
461.34 -	461.79	8.97	494.07 -	494.52	9.69	526.80 -	527.24	10.41	626.34 -	636.33	12.70
461.80 -	462.24	8.98	494.53 -	494.97	9.70	527.25 -	527.70	10.42	636.34 -	646.33	12.92
462.25 -	462.70	8.99	494.98 -	495.43	9.71	527.71 -	528.15	10.43	646.34 -	656.33	13.14
462.71 -	463.15	9.00	495.44 -	495.88	9.72	528.16 -	528.61	10.44	656.34 -	666.33	13.36
463.16 -	463.61	9.01	495.89 -	496.33	9.73	528.62 -	529.06	10.45	666.34 -	676.33	13.58
463.62 -	464.06	9.02	496.34 -	496.79	9.74	529.07 -	529.52	10.46	676.34 -	686.33	13.80
464.07 -	464.52	9.03	496.80 -	497.24	9.75	529.53 -	529.97	10.47	686.34 -	696.33	14.02
464.53 -	464.97	9.04	497.25 -	497.70	9.76	529.98 -	530.43	10.48	696.34 -	706.33	14.24
464.98 -	465.43	9.05	497.71 -	498.15	9.77	530.44 -	530.88	10.49	706.34 -	716.33	14.46
465.44 -	465.88	9.06	498.16 -	498.61	9.78	530.89 -	531.33	10.50	716.34 -	726.33	14.68
465.89 -	466.33	9.07	498.62 -	499.06	9.79	531.34 -	531.79	10.51	726.34 -	736.33	14.90
466.34 -	466.79	9.08	499.07 -	499.52	9.80	531.80 -	532.24	10.52	736.34 -	746.33	15.12

70 UNEMPLOYMENT INSURANCE PREMIUMS — COTISATIONS À L'ASSURANCE-CHÔMAGE

For minimum and maximum insurable earnings amounts for various pay periods see Schedule II. For the maximum ... periods see bott...

...montants minimum et maximum des gains assurables ... rses périodes de paie figurent en annexe II. La dé- ... rses périodes de

From-*de*	To-*à*	U.I. Premium *Prime d'a.-c.*	From-*de*	To-*à*	U.I. Premium *Prime d'a.-c.*	Remuneration *Rémunération* From-*de*	To-*à*	*Prime d'a.-c.*	From-*de*	To-*à*	*d'a.-c.*
456.23 -	456.66	10.27	528.23 -	528.66	11.89	556.23 -	556.66	12.52	708.23 -	708.66	15.94
456.67 -	457.11	10.28	528.67 -	529.11	11.90	556.67 -	557.11	12.53	708.67 -	709.11	15.95
457.12 -	457.55	10.29	529.12 -	529.55	11.91	557.12 -	557.55	12.54	709.12 -	709.55	15.96
457.56 -	457.99	10.30	529.56 -	529.99	11.92	557.56 -	557.99	12.55	709.56 -	709.99	15.97
458.00 -	458.44	10.31	530.00 -	530.44	11.93	558.00 -	558.44	12.56	710.00 -	710.44	15.98
458.45 -	458.88	10.32	530.45 -	530.88	11.94	558.45 -	558.88	12.57	710.45 -	710.88	15.99
458.89 -	459.33	10.33	530.89 -	531.33	11.95	558.89 -	559.33	12.58	710.89 -	711.33	16.00
459.34 -	459.77	10.34	531.34 -	531.77	11.96	559.34 -	559.77	12.59	711.34 -	711.77	16.01
459.78 -	460.22	10.35	531.78 -	532.22	11.97	559.78 -	560.22	12.60	711.78 -	712.22	16.02

ONTARIO

WEEKLY TAX DEDUCTIONS
Basis — 52 Pay Periods per Year

TABLE 1

ONTARIO

RETENUES D'IMPÔT PAR SEMAINE
Base — 52 périodes de paie par année

WEEKLY PAY Use appropriate bracket — PAIE PAR SEMAINE: *Utilisez le palier approprié*		IF THE EMPLOYEE'S "NET CLAIM CODE" ON FORM TD1 IS — *SI LE CODE DE DEMANDE NETTE DE L'EMPLOYÉ SELON LA FORMULE TD1 EST DE*										
From - *De*	Less than *Moins que*	0	1	2	3	4	5	6	7	8	9	10
			DEDUCT FROM EACH PAY — *RETENEZ SUR CHAQUE PAIE*									
451.-	459.	117.10	85.25	81.30	73.50	65.70	57.90	50.20	42.30	34.50	26.70	18.85
459.-	467.	119.15	87.30	83.40	75.55	67.75	59.95	52.25	44.35	36.55	28.75	20.90
467.-	475.	121.20	89.35	85.45	77.60	69.80	62.00	54.30	46.40	38.60	30.80	22.95
475.-	483.	123.25	91.40	87.50	79.70	71.85	64.05	56.35	48.45	40.65	32.85	25.00
483.-	491.	125.30	93.45	89.55	81.75	73.90	66.10	58.40	50.50	42.70	34.90	27.10
491.-	499.	127.35	95.50	91.60	83.80	75.95	68.15	60.45	52.55	44.75	36.95	29.15
499.-	507.	129.40	97.55	93.65	85.85	78.05	70.20	62.50	54.60	46.80	39.00	31.20
507.-	515.	131.45	99.60	95.70	87.90	80.10	72.25	64.55	56.65	48.85	41.05	33.25
515.-	523.	133.50	101.65	97.75	89.95	82.15	74.35	66.60	58.70	50.90	43.10	35.30
523.-	531.	135.55	103.70	99.80	92.00	84.20	76.40	68.70	60.75	52.95	45.15	37.35
531.-	539.	137.60	105.75	101.85	94.05	86.25	78.45	70.75	62.80	55.00	47.20	39.40
539.-	547.	139.70	107.80	103.90	96.10	88.30	80.50	72.80	64.85	57.05	49.25	41.45
547.-	555.	142.75	110.90	107.00	99.20	91.35	83.55	75.85	67.95	60.15	52.35	44.55
555.-	563.	145.95	114.10	110.20	102.40	94.60	86.75	79.05	71.15	63.35	55.55	47.75
563.-	571.	149.20	117.35	113.45	105.65	97.80	90.00	82.30	74.40	66.60	58.80	50.95
571.-	579.	152.45	120.55	116.65	108.85	101.05	93.25	85.55	77.65	69.85	62.00	54.20
579.-	587.	155.70	123.80	119.90	112.10	104.30	96.50	88.80	80.85	73.05	65.25	57.45
587.-	595.	158.90	127.05	123.15	115.35	107.55	99.70	92.00	84.10	76.30	68.50	60.70
595.-	603.	162.15	130.30	126.40	118.60	110.75	102.95	95.25	87.35	79.55	71.75	63.95
603.-	611.	165.40	133.55	129.60	121.80	114.00	106.20	98.50	90.60	82.80	74.95	67.15
611.-	619.	168.65	136.75	132.85	125.05	117.25	109.45	101.75	93.85	86.00	78.20	70.40
619.-	627.	171.85	140.00	136.10	128.30	120.50	112.70	104.95	97.05	89.25	81.45	73.65
627.-	635.	175.10	143.25	139.35	131.55	123.70	115.90	108.20	100.30	92.50	84.70	76.90
635.-	643.	178.35	146.50	142.60	134.75	126.95	119.15	111.45	103.55	95.75	87.95	80.10
643.-	651.	181.60	149.75	145.85	138.05	130.25	122.45	114.75	106.80	99.00	91.20	83.40
651.-	659.	184.90	153.05	149.15	141.35	133.55	125.70	118.00	110.10	102.30	94.50	86.70
659.-	667.	188.20	156.35	152.45	144.60	136.80	129.00	121.30	113.40	105.60	97.80	89.95
667.-	675.	191.50	159.60	155.70	147.90	140.10	132.30	124.60	116.70	108.85	101.05	93.25
675.-	683.	194.75	162.90	159.00	151.20	143.40	135.60	127.90	119.95	112.15	104.35	96.55
683.-	691.	198.05	166.20	162.30	154.50	146.65	138.85	131.15	123.25	115.45	107.65	99.85
691.-	699.	201.35	169.50	165.60	157.75	149.95	142.15	134.45	126.55	118.75	110.95	103.10
699.-	707.	204.65	172.75	168.85	161.05	153.25	145.45	137.75	129.80	122.00	114.20	106.40
707.-	715.	207.90	176.05	172.15	164.35	156.55	148.70	141.00	133.10	125.30	117.50	109.70
715.-	723.	211.20	179.35	175.45	167.65	159.80	152.00	144.30	136.40	128.60	120.80	112.95
723.-	731.	214.50	182.60	178.70	170.90	163.10	155.30	147.60	139.70	131.90	124.05	116.25
411.-	415.	106.30	74.45	70.55	62.75	54.95	47.10	39.40	31.50	23.70	15.90	5.35
415.-	419.	107.35	75.45	71.55	63.75	55.95	48.15	40.45	32.55	24.75	16.90	6.05
419.-	423.	108.35	76.50	72.60	64.80	57.00	49.15	41.45	33.55	25.75	17.95	7.35
423.-	427.	109.40	77.55	73.65	65.80	58.00	50.20	42.50	34.60	26.80	19.00	9.05
427.-	431.	110.40	78.55	74.65	66.85	59.05	51.25	43.55	35.60	27.80	20.00	10.75
431.-	435.	111.45	79.60	75.70	67.85	60.05	52.25	44.55	36.65	28.85	21.05	12.45
435.-	439.	112.45	80.60	76.70	68.90	61.10	53.30	45.60	37.65	29.85	22.05	14.20
439.-	443.	113.50	81.65	77.75	69.90	62.10	54.30	46.60	38.70	30.90	23.10	15.25
443.-	447.	114.55	82.65	78.75	70.95	63.15	55.35	47.65	39.70	31.90	24.10	16.30
447.-	451.	115.55	83.70	79.80	72.00	64.15	56.35	48.65	40.75	32.95	25.15	17.35

MINI-CASES

Analyzing the purpose of the TD1 form.

MC 11-1 You have just been hired for a part-time job in a local bookstore. The job requires you to work 15 hours per week after classes and on the weekend. You have not completed any government forms before you get your first pay cheque.

a. Why is it in your best interest to complete the TD1 form (or Personal Tax Credit Return) when you start a new job?

b. Looking at the illustration of this form on pages 429 and 430, what are some of the credits for which you may qualify?

Explaining the rules concerning UI premiums.

MC 11-2 You and some friends are talking in the cafeteria at school about your part-time jobs. One friend, Wanita Newton, says that she never has UI premiums deducted from her pay cheque. Your other friend, Bill Chin, gets upset and replies that UI premiums are always deducted from his pay cheque. Bill turns to you and says, ''You take accounting, don't you? Why are UI premiums deducted from my pay and not from Wanita's?

After asking them some questions, you discover that Wanita's parents only allow her to work 10 hours a week because she is also on the school volleyball team. Bill on the other hand usually works 20 hours one week and 10 the next on an alternating basis. Both Bill and Wanita are paid on a biweekly basis.

a. Explain to your friends why there is a difference in their payroll deductions.

Analyzing the importance of a correct TD1 form.

MC 11-3 You have started your first part-time job and were asked to complete a TD1 form. You were unsure how to complete the form and so you just put down a net claim code of 1.

a. Will you have income tax deducted from your pay cheque?

b. If you will earn approximately $4500 over the year, will you have too much or too little tax deducted?

c. If too much tax is deducted, will you be able to get it back? When will this happen?

d. Have you lost anything because of your mistake?

RECORDING PAYROLL DATA

The next part of any payroll application is to make an accounting record of the pay period. Actually, this accounting record is divided into three parts:

- preparing a payroll summary known as the payroll register
- preparing the employee's individual earnings record
- journalizing and posting the payroll so that ledger accounts affected by the payroll can be updated

PREPARING THE PAYROLL REGISTER

Payroll register: an accounting record summarizing the details of a pay period.

After calculating the details of gross earnings, deductions, and the net pay for each employee and for a particular payroll period, the complete payroll is summarized in an accounting record. This record is called the payroll summary or payroll register.

In some accounting systems, a payroll register is prepared for each different payroll plan. Thus, separate hourly payroll registers are used to summarize the payroll for hourly rated employees and for salaried employees. Other accounting systems combine the payroll summaries. In this topic, a basic salary payroll register will be used to summarize the payroll for Dr. Johnson's dental firm.

The design and form of payroll registers will vary from one business to another and with the actual method of processing the payroll. For example, a register prepared by hand requires a design quite different from that of one prepared with a computer. Every payroll register, however, will contain columns to record at least:

- the names and SINs of employees
- the details of the employees' gross earnings
- the details of the employees' payroll deductions
- the employees' net pay

The payroll register opposite shows how Dr. Johnson's payroll is summarized for the payroll data collected in Topic 1. Study this illustration closely. Then read the analysis.

Analysis: These are the main points to remember about the contents and preparation of any payroll register:

- The pay-ending period is found in the heading of the payroll register. Since payroll is handled on a biweekly basis, the heading is For the Two Weeks Ending March 9, 1990.
- Record in the heading the date of the employees' cheques. This date will always be the date of the payday.

SALARY PAYROLL REGISTER For the Two Weeks Ending March 9, 1990 Paid ________ 19__

Employee Data			Time Worked			Earnings			Deductions					
SIN	Name	NC Code	Weeks	OT Days	Rate Per Wk.	Regular	OT Excess	Gross Pay	CPP	UI	Income Tax	Total	Net Pay	Cheque No.
473-621-459	Lewis, Kathy	2	2	–	600 00	1200 00		1200 00	23 96	27 00	252 35	303 31	896 69	
447-231-135	Fortier, Lynn	1	2	–	400 00	800 00		800 00	15 23	18 00	142 50	175 73	624 27	
						2000 00		2000 00	39 19	45 00	394 85	479 04	1520 96	

Proof of Salary Payroll Register

Earnings:		
Regular	$2 000.00	
Overtime	—	
Total Gross Pay		$2 000.00
Deductions:		
CPP	$ 39.19	
UI	45.00	
Income Tax	394.85	
Total		479.04
Net Pay		$1 520.96

- The body of the register contains the columns Employee Data, Earnings, Deductions, and Net Pay. Of course, the information entered into these columns has already been collected and checked in Topic 1.
- The deductions are added and the total is entered into the Total column of the Deductions section. This step is important for calculating the net pay for each employee.
- There is a special column at the far right where the number of the cheque paid to the employee is later recorded.

Observe above how the payroll is proved. After the data for every employee is entered and **before the employees are paid**, the various columns must be totalled. Payroll registers are proved by adding and subtracting the appropriate column totals across the register. In some methods of data processing, the proof is done automatically by means of a computer. In manual methods, it is done with an adding machine or a calculator.

PREPARING THE EMPLOYEE'S EARNINGS RECORD

Employee's individual earnings record: a payroll record showing the details of an employee's pay periods.

After the payroll register has been prepared and proved, the details of each employee's earnings may be posted to the employee's individual earnings record. This individual record is especially important for the following reasons.

- For each employee it shows in one place a full year's summary of his or her pay periods, gross earnings, deductions, net pay, and important year-to-date totals.
- It serves as a basis for preparing tax slips so that the employer may complete an income tax return.
- It helps determine when the employer has reached the maximum contributions to UI and CPP.

Below is an example of how Kathy Lewis's individual earnings would be prepared. Remember that the individual earnings record for a given pay period must agree with the payroll register for the same period.

EMPLOYEE'S INDIVIDUAL EARNINGS RECORD FOR THE YEAR 1990

Employee's Name: Lewis, Kathy SIN: 473 621 459 Tel. No.: 679-3734

Address: Any Town/City Canada N6H 4H9

Date of Birth: January 14, 19– Date Employed: June 15, 19– Date of Termination:

Position: Dental Hygienist Salary Plan: biweekly Rate of Pay: $600 per week

Net Claim Code per TD1: 2 UI Insurable Earnings: Minimum: $256 biweekly Maximum: $1280 biweekly Maximum UI Yearly Premium: $748.80

CPP Year's Maximum Earnings	Year's Basic Exemption	Maximum Earnings for Contributions	Maximum Yearly CPP
$28 900.00	$2 800.00	$26 100.00	$574.20

Pay Period Ending	Time Worked		Rate /Wk.	Earnings			Deductions				Net Pay	Year-to-Date			
	Weeks	OT Days		Regular	OT Excess	Gross Pay	CPP	UI	Inc. Tax	Total		Gross Pay	CPP	UI	Inc. Tax
Mar. 9	2	–	600	1 200	–	1 200	23.96	27.00	252.35	303.31	869.69	6 000	119.80	135.00	1 261.75

Three final points are worth noting:

- The Earnings, Deductions and Net Pay sections are in the same order as they appear on the payroll register. This is so that the amounts can be posted easily to the employee's individual earnings record. In some short-cut methods of processing the payroll, this order is important because the payroll register and the individual employee's earnings record are both prepared in one writing.
- An additional section, Year-To-Date, has been added to the earnings record. This contains columns to show the total gross pay, the total CPP, the total UI, and the total income tax to the date of posting the latest entry. From these columns, the payroll clerk can easily see when the employee has reached the maximum amount for CPP and UI, and can prepare a tax summary known as the T4 tax slip. (The T4 slip will be examined in Topic 3 of this chapter.)
- The employee's individual record becomes a payroll subsidiary ledger account. This means that each individual's earnings are accounted for in a separate Payroll Ledger. The total of the individual employees' gross pays will be added to show a total which must agree with the balance shown for Salaries Expense in the General Ledger. The same idea applies to each employee's deduction. The totals of the individual employees' deductions for UI, CPP, and income tax must agree with the amount recorded in the General Ledger accounts for UI Payable, CPP Payable, and Employees' Income Tax Payable. And the total of each employee's net pay must add up to the balance shown in the General Ledger for Salaries Payable. Each General Ledger account, then, becomes the control account to control by one figure the total of all employees' amounts shown in the payroll subsidiary ledger.

Payroll Ledger: a subsidiary ledger containing individual employees' earnings records.

JOURNALIZING AND POSTING TO THE GENERAL LEDGER

The payroll data is now ready to be recorded and posted to appropriate accounts in the General Ledger.

In some accounting systems, the totals of the payroll register are posted directly. This means that account numbers are placed beneath each total posted to show that the transfer has occurred. Under this system, the payroll register becomes the **book of original entry**. Since any book of original entry is a journal, the "book" showing the original payroll entries is known as the Payroll Journal. Most

Payroll Journal: the payroll register used as the book of original entry.

payroll applications using the one-write system use a Payroll Journal.

On the other hand, many accounting systems prefer to journalize the various totals of the payroll summary in the General Journal. In this case, the payroll summary is known as the **payroll register** because no postings occur from a register. Most computer systems print payroll registers. The totals of the payroll register are summarized in the form of a compound entry and recorded in the General Journal. In this chapter, assume that the totals of the payroll register are recorded in the General Journal.

Two classes of entries must be recorded in the General Journal:

- a compound entry recording the totals of the payroll register
- another compound entry recording the employer's additional expenses resulting from each payroll.

Let us examine each of these entries separately.

The Payroll Register Totals It is useful to return to the proof of the payroll register and analyze the key figures reported. Examine the proof below.

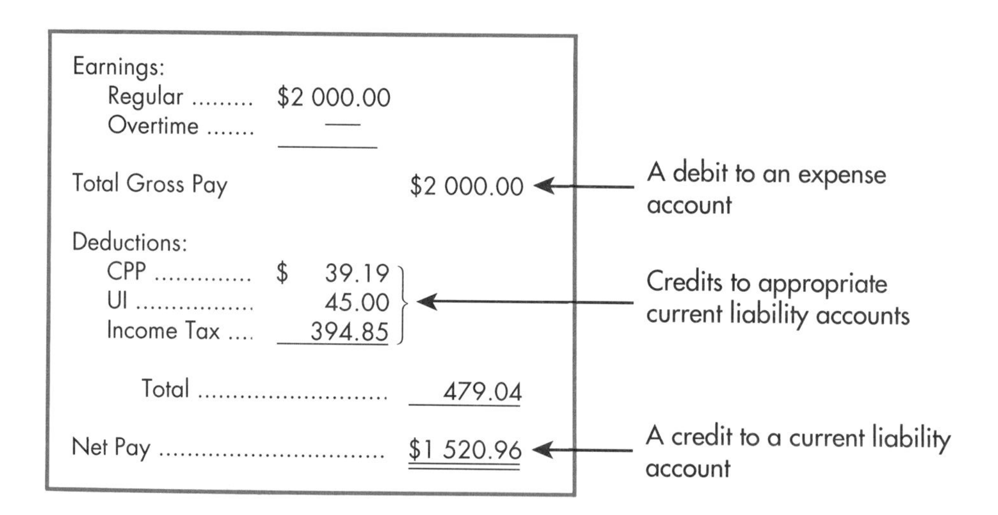

Earnings:			
Regular	$2 000.00		
Overtime	—		
Total Gross Pay		$2 000.00	← A debit to an expense account
Deductions:			
CPP	$ 39.19		← Credits to appropriate current liability accounts
UI	45.00		
Income Tax	394.85		
Total		479.04	
Net Pay		$1 520.96	← A credit to a current liability account

Analysis:

- The total of gross earnings from the payroll register must be debited to an appropriate expense account. Since this register records a salary payroll, the total of the Gross Pay column may be debited to an expense called Salaries Expense.
- For each of the payroll deductions, an appropriate current liability account must be credited, because the amounts withheld do not belong to the employer; they must be paid to the federal gov-

John H. Johnson, D.D.S.
Chart of Accounts

CURRENT LIABILITIES
205 Salaries Payable
206 CPP Contributions Payable
207 UI Premium Payable
208 Income Tax Deductions Payable

EXPENSES
502 Salaries Expense
510 Payroll Taxes Expense

ernment. Until these amounts are paid, they must be treated as current liabilities on the books of the employer.

- The total amount in the Net Pay column is also a current liability until the employees are paid. An appropriate liability account in this case would be Salaries Payable.

The entry to record the payroll register for Dr. Johnson's dental practice is shown next. After this entry is posted to the General Ledger, the various liability accounts will show the amounts owed to the federal government and the employees.

Mar. 9	Salaries Expense	2 000.00	
	CPP Contributions Payable		39.19
	UI Premium Payable		45.00
	Income Tax Deductions Payable		394.85
	Salaries Payable		1 520.96
	To record the biweekly payroll for salaried employees for the two weeks ended on March 9.		

The Employer's Additional Payroll Expenses All employers are obliged by law to contribute to the Canada Pension Plan and to unemployment insurance. To the CPP they must contribute dollar amounts equal to the employees' contribution, and they must also contribute 1.4 times the employee's share of UI. These represent additional expenses resulting from the payroll, and so they must be journalized and posted to appropriate General Ledger accounts. Study the General Journal entry shown below.

Mar. 9	Payroll Taxes Expense	102.19	
	CPP Contributions Payable		39.19
	UI Premium Payable		63.00
	To record payroll taxes resulting from the biweekly payroll ended March 9.		

Payroll Taxes Expense: an account used to record the additional employer's expense resulting from the payroll.

An account called Payroll Taxes Expense is commonly used to record the total debit of the employer's various additional payroll expenses. Do not misunderstand the word "taxes" in this account title; it does not mean the income taxes are withheld from employees and accounted for in the current liability account. Here the word is used to suggest that the additional amounts are regarded as levies against the employer by the government, like property taxes or licence fees required for doing business — "taxes" related to payroll expense.

To complete the double entry, separate current liability accounts are used to show the dollar amounts that must be paid on behalf of the employer for the Canada Pension Plan and unemployment insurance. Once these amounts are posted, the balance in the current liability accounts will show how much must be paid to the federal government. This remittance will be examined in Topic 3.

PROBLEMS

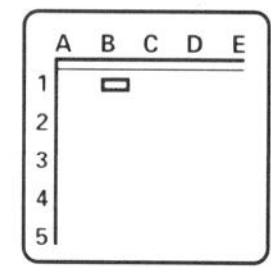

These problems may be completed using electronic spreadsheet software to prepare the payroll register.

Preparing and proving a payroll register.

Journalizing the payroll.

P 11-6 Refer to your solution for Problem 11-1. Assume the end of the payroll period is February 14 of this year.

a. Prepare a salary payroll register similar to the one illustrated on page 449.

b. Total and prove the register.

c. Show how the payroll entries would appear in the General Journal.

Preparing and proving a payroll register.

Journalizing the payroll.

P 11-7 You will require the information for Problems 11-3, 11-4 and 11-5. Assume the payroll period ends February 10. Make up appropriate SINs.

a. Prepare a salary payroll register similar to the one illustrated on page 449.

b. Total and prove the register.

c. Show how the payroll entries would appear in the General Journal.

Preparing an employee's earnings record.

Posting amounts to payroll register.

P 11-8 Anne Attridge has been employed as a dental assistant since the beginning of this year. She resides at 400 Main Street, Any City/Town, Canada. Her telephone number is 587-4000. Her TD1 form shows her date of birth as June 4, 19—. At the top of the opposite page are her past payroll periods to February 3.

Pay Period Ending	Regular	Earnings OT	Gross Pay	CPP	Deductions UI	Inc. Tax
Jan. 6	460.00	—	460.00	8.94	10.35	83.40
Jan. 13	460.00	—	460.00	8.94	10.35	83.40
Jan. 20	460.00	100	560.00	11.16	12.60	110.20
Jan. 27	460.00	—	460.00	8.94	10.35	83.40
Feb. 3	460.00	50	510.00	10.26	11.70	97.75

a. From the information given in Problems 11-4 and 11-5, and from the additional information above, complete an individual employee's earnings record for Anne Attridge to the end of February 3.

b. Post the current payroll from the register prepared in Problem 11-7 to Attridge's account in the subsidiary payroll ledger.

MINI-CASES

Calculating a journal entry from incomplete payroll records.

MC 11-4 A payroll clerk was rushed to hospital for an emergency operation. Before he became ill, he had collected the following information on the payroll for the New Brunswick Manufacturing Company, not yet completed:

(i) The Payroll period is for the month ending September 30, current year.

(ii) Total gross pay for the month of September is $550 000. Of this amount $325 000 represented amounts paid in excess of $26 100 (year to date) to certain employees.

(iii) The amount paid to employees in excess of $2773.33 (the maximum monthly insurable earnings for unemployment insurance) was $300 000.

(iv) Income taxes totalling $165 000 are to be withheld from employee's earnings.

(v) Union dues totalling $19 000 are to be deducted from employee's earnings.

(vi) UI premiums related to insurable earnings are 2.25%. The employer is required to contribute 1.4 times the employee's premium.

(vii) The current CPP contribution rate on pensionable earnings is 2.2%. The employer is required to match the employee's contribution.

(viii) The company's Chart of Accounts shows General Ledger accounts for: Salaries and Wages Payable, 210; CPP Contributions Payable, 211; UI Premiums Payable, 212; Income Tax Deductions Payable, 213; Union Dues Payable, 214; Salaries and Wages Expense, 515; and Payroll Taxes Expense, 516.

You have been called in to complete the accounting entries for the September payroll.

a. Record the salaries and wages expense in the General Journal.

b. Prepare the employer's additional expense resulting from the September payroll.

Classifying payroll deductions.

MC 11-5 The payroll clerk for Angus Art Suppliers, Ryan Laing, prepares the cheque for the monthly payroll remittances to the federal government and other organizations for each monthly pay period. He notices that some of the items are deductions from only the employees' pay, some are paid only by the business, and some are partly deducted from the employees' pay and partly paid by the business.

The remittances are for the following payroll items:

- CPP contributions
- UI premiums
- employee income tax
- union dues
- life insurance premiums (80% is paid by the employer)
- disability insurance premiums (80% is paid by the employer)
- charitable donations made through payroll deductions
- Canada Savings Bonds purchased through payroll deductions
- professional association dues

a. Using the categories described by Ryan, segregate these items into the three groups. Explain why you placed each item in each group.

Discussing the paper work required when an employee resigns.

MC 11-6 One of your employees has just resigned to return to school full-time. The person had been working for you for four months.

a. Other than the final pay cheque, are there any other records that must be completed at this time?

b. What is the purpose of these records?

EXPLAINING PAYROLL REMITTANCES AND ANNUAL TAX STATEMENTS

As a result of journalizing the payroll, several current liabilities have been recorded in appropriate ledger accounts, and represent the amounts owing to the employees and to the federal government. All payroll applications must include procedures for paying off these current liabilities. These payments are called payroll remittances.

Payroll remittances: payments to employees and the federal government resulting from journalizing a payroll.

The payroll application must also include procedures for preparing annual tax statements for the employees and the federal government.

PAYING THE EMPLOYEES

In a large business, paying employees on a regular payday involves important measures to control cash payments. This is especially true when the payroll involves both hourly-rated employees and salaried personnel. (These measures will be looked at in Chapter 14.)

For a small business such as Dr. Johnson's dental practice, employees are usually paid by issuing cheques drawn against the regular bank current account. Of course, these cheques would be recorded in the Cash Payments Journal as illustrated below.

CASH PAYMENTS JOURNAL Page 3

DATE 19-8		CHEQUE NO.	CHEQUE PAID TO	ACCOUNTS PAYABLE POST. REF.	ACCOUNTS PAYABLE AMOUNT DR.	OTHER GENERAL LEDGER ACCOUNTS ACCOUNT TITLE	POST. REF.	AMOUNT DR.	CASH CR.
Mar.	9	350	Kathy Lewis			Salaries Payable	205	896 69	896 69
	9	351	Lynn Fortier			Salaries Payable	205	624 27	624 27

Analysis: These points will help you understand the accounting of the separate cheques issued to the employees:

- Each cheque must be analyzed as a debit to Salaries Payable and a credit to Cash.
- After the entries are posted to the GL, the Salaries Payable account would show **no balance** as follows:

Salaries Payable — GENERAL LEDGER — Account No. 205

DATE 19-8		EXPLANATION	POST. REF.	DEBIT	CREDIT	BALANCE
Mar.	9		GJ. 5		1520.96	1520.96
	9		CPJ. 3	896.69		624.27
	9		CPJ. 3	624.27		-0-

Pay statement: an employee's statement of earnings and deductions for a pay period.

There's one more step involved in making payroll remittances to employees—preparing the employee's pay statement. This statement may be attached to a special payroll cheque or it may be a separate form. In the case of Dr. Johnson's practice, assume that the employee's pay statement is done on a separate form:

Name	Pay Period Ending	Time Worked: Weeks	Time Worked: OT Days	Per Week	Earnings: Regular	Earnings: OT Excess	Earnings: Gross Pay	Deductions: CPP	Deductions: UI	Deductions: Inc. Tax	Deductions: Total	Net Pay
Kathy Lewis	Mar. 9	2	–	600.00	1200.00	–	1200.00	23.96	27.00	252.35	303.31	896.69

PAY STATEMENT

Retain this statement. It is a record of your earnings and deductions.

Analysis:

- All pay statements show the important details of the employee's pay period.
- Compare the main columns of the pay statement with those on

the payroll register and the individual employee's earnings record. Do you see any similarities?

- The arrangement of columns for Earnings, Deductions, and Net Pay is identical to that for the form shown on both the payroll register and the employee's individual earnings record. Since the order is identical, some payroll applications will prepare all three payroll forms in one writing similar to the accounts receivable application discussed in Chapter 8.

PAYING THE FEDERAL GOVERNMENT

Before the payroll remittance to the federal government is examined, it is useful to study the liability accounts created by the payroll. This study will determine how much should be paid. Consider, for example, the General Ledger in T-account form of Dr. Johnson's practice immediately after the payment of the employees' salaries, shown here.

General Ledger in T-Account Form

Cash 101

		Mar. 9	1 520.96

Salaries Payable 205

Mar. 12	896.69	Mar. 9	1 520.96
12	624.27		
	Ø		

CPP Contributions Payable 206

		Mar. 9	39.19
		9	39.19
		Balance	78.38

UI Premium Payable 207

		Mar. 9	45.00
		9	63.00
		Balance	108.00

Income Tax Deductions Payable 208

		Mar. 9	394.85

Salaries Expense 502

Mar. 9	2 000.00		

Payroll Taxes Expense 510

Mar. 9	102.19		

Analysis:

- The GL shows three current liability accounts with balances. These are CPP Contributions Payable for $78.38, UI Premium Payable for $108.00; and Income Tax Deductions Payable for $394.85.
- Under federal law, the balances shown by these three liability accounts must be remitted on form PD7AR, called ''Tax Deduction/Canada Pension Plan/Unemployment Insurance Remittance Return.''
- Form PD7AR, along with a certified cheque or money order made payable to the Receiver General for Canada, must be paid at the bank where the business has an account, or mailed to the appropriate Taxation Centre, by the 15th of the month following that in which the payroll is recorded. Look closely at form PD7AR, illustrated opposite.

Analysis:

- The data to complete the necessary blocks is obtained from the balances of the General Ledger accounts.
- As the individual blocks require, the payroll clerk must show the amounts for CPP Contributions Payable (employer's and employees' combined), the UI Premium Payable (employer's and employees' combined), and Income Tax Deductions Payable.
- The total of all these account balances represents the amount to be remitted to the federal government.

In the case of Dr. Johnson's practice, a cheque for $581.23 would be issued, recorded, and analyzed as shown below.

Apr. 15	CPP Contributions Payable	78.38	
	UI Premium Payable	108.00	
	Income Tax Deductions Payable	394.85	
	Cash		581.23
	To record cheque issued to Receiver General for Canada as per form PD7AR.		
	(This entry would be recorded in the Cash Payments Journal.)		

After the remittance is received, the bank teller or the Taxation Centre returns:

Revenue Canada Taxation | Revenu Canada Impôt

PD7AR
REV 87

REMITTANCE FORM - *FORMULE DE VERSEMENT*

COMPLETE THE UNSHADED BOXES ONLY
NE REMPLIR QUE LES CASES NON OMBRAGÉES

NAME, ADDRESS AND OWNERSHIP CHANGES Please enter any changes not reported previously	*CHANGEMENTS DE NOM, D'ADRESSE ET DE PROPRIÉTAIRE Prière d'indiquer le détail des changements non signales anterieurement*
New name *Nouveau nom*	
Care of Address *Adresse aux soins de*	
New Address *Nouvelle adresse*	
City, Province, Postal Code *Ville, province, code postal*	
If ownership of business has changed enter effective date. (Day, Month, Year) *Si la propriété de l'entreprise a changé en indiquer la date de prise d'effet. (Jour, Mois, Année)*	

DEDUCTIONS WITHHELD DURING THE MONTH OF *RETENUES DU MOIS DE*	March 1990
C.P.P. CONTRIBUTIONS *COTISATIONS AU RPC*	78.38
U.I. PREMIUMS *PRIMES D'A.-C.*	108.00
TAX DEDUCTIONS *RETENUES D'IMPÔT*	394.85
CURRENT PAYMENT *PAIEMENT COURANT*	581.23

1

JOHN H JOHNSON, D.D.S.
ANY TOWN/CITY
PROVINCE CANADA

N6H 4H9

ACCOUNT NUMBER
NUMÉRO DE COMPTE
BAC 12345 6

6

Sub-code *Sous-code*	NO OF PAYTS *NBRE VERS*	MONTH *MOIS*	YEAR *ANNÉE*

Revenue Canada Taxation | Revenu Canada Impôt

PD7A REV 87

2 EMPLOYER NUMBER *N° DE L'EMPLOYEUR* BAC 12345 6 EMPLOYER NAME *NOM DE L'EMPLOYEUR* JOHN H JOHNSON D.D.S.

Your payment may be made where you bank or to
Vous pouvez faire le paiement à votre institution financière ou à
Taxation Centre - *Centre fiscal*

SUDBURY
P3A 5C3

See reverse *Voir au verso*

- If payment is made where you bank, detach and present parts 1 and 2 to the teller. Retain part 2 for your record of payment after it is receipted by the teller. See reverse.

- *Si le paiement est fait à votre institution financière, détachez les parties 1 et 2 et présentez-les au caissier. Gardez le partie 2 comme preuve de votre paiement, après qu'elle a été quittancée par le caissier. Voir au verso.*

C.P.P. CONTRIBUTIONS *COTISATIONS AU RPC*	78.38
U.I. PREMIUMS *PRIMES D'A.-C.*	108.00
TAX DEDUCTIONS *RETENUES D'IMPÔT*	394.85
CURRENT PAYMENT *PAIEMENT COURANT*	581.23

(1) the lower part of form PD7AR as a receipt, and
(2) a blank remittance form to process next month's returns.

PREPARING ANNUAL PAYROLL TAX STATEMENTS

All payroll applications must include the preparation of annual payroll tax statements.

On or before the last day of February of each year, employers must submit two important returns:

1. Annual Tax Statements to Employees Employers must give their employees a report of their yearly earnings and deductions

Statement of Remuneration Paid (T4 slip): a yearly statement of earnings and deductions for income tax purposes.

on a form known as the T4 Supplementary, the Statement of Remuneration Paid, or simply the **T4 slip**.

This is Kathy Lewis's T4 slip.[1]

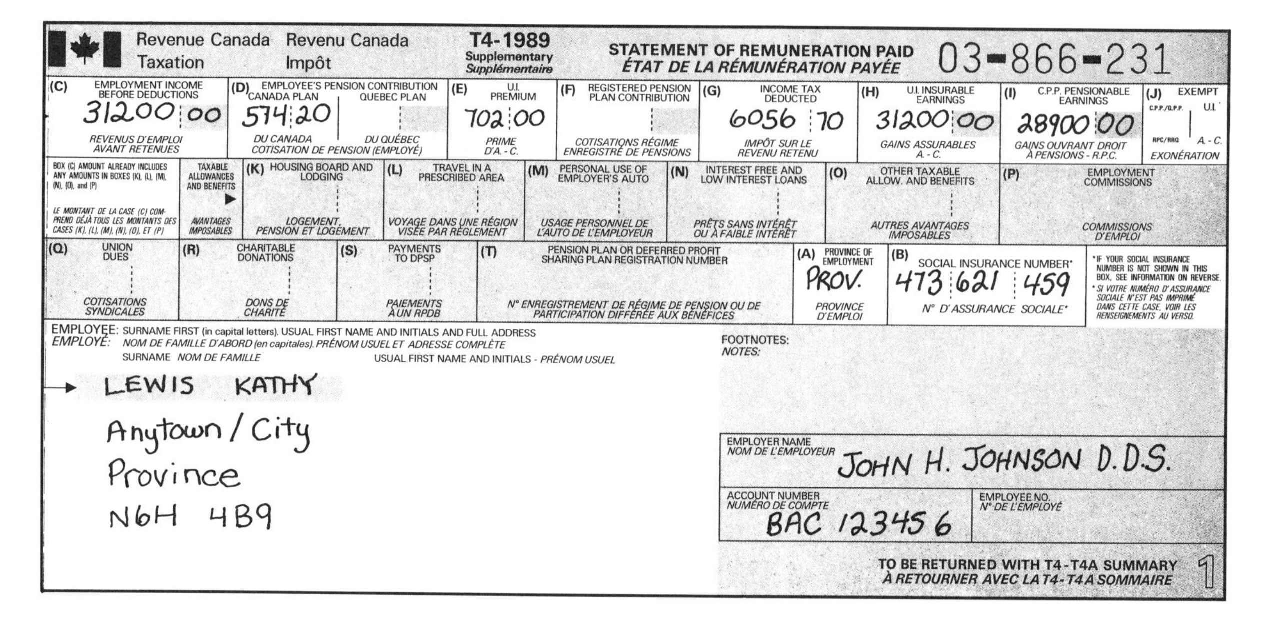

Revenue Canada Taxation | Revenu Canada Impôt | T4-1989 Supplementary *Supplémentaire* | STATEMENT OF REMUNERATION PAID | *ÉTAT DE LA RÉMUNÉRATION PAYÉE* | 03-866-231

(C) EMPLOYMENT INCOME BEFORE DEDUCTIONS — 31200 00 — *REVENUS D'EMPLOI AVANT RETENUES*

(D) EMPLOYEE'S PENSION CONTRIBUTION — CANADA PLAN 574 20 — QUEBEC PLAN — *DU CANADA — DU QUÉBEC — COTISATION DE PENSION (EMPLOYÉ)*

(E) U.I. PREMIUM — 702 00 — *PRIME D'A. - C.*

(F) REGISTERED PENSION PLAN CONTRIBUTION — *COTISATIONS RÉGIME ENREGISTRÉ DE PENSIONS*

(G) INCOME TAX DEDUCTED — 6056 70 — *IMPÔT SUR LE REVENU RETENU*

(H) U.I. INSURABLE EARNINGS — 31200 00 — *GAINS ASSURABLES A. - C.*

(I) C.P.P. PENSIONABLE EARNINGS — 28900 00 — *GAINS OUVRANT DROIT À PENSIONS - R.P.C.*

(J) EXEMPT — C.P.P./Q.P.P. — U.I. — RPC/RRQ — *A. - C.* — *EXONÉRATION*

BOX (C) AMOUNT ALREADY INCLUDES ANY AMOUNTS IN BOXES (K), (L), (M), (N), (O), and (P) — *LE MONTANT DE LA CASE (C) COMPREND DÉJÀ TOUS LES MONTANTS DES CASES (K), (L), (M), (N), (O), ET (P)*

TAXABLE ALLOWANCES AND BENEFITS ▶ *AVANTAGES IMPOSABLES*

(K) HOUSING BOARD AND LODGING — *LOGEMENT, PENSION ET LOGEMENT*

(L) TRAVEL IN A PRESCRIBED AREA — *VOYAGE DANS UNE RÉGION VISÉE PAR RÈGLEMENT*

(M) PERSONAL USE OF EMPLOYER'S AUTO — *USAGE PERSONNEL DE L'AUTO DE L'EMPLOYEUR*

(N) INTEREST FREE AND LOW INTEREST LOANS — *PRÊTS SANS INTÉRÊT OU À FAIBLE INTÉRÊT*

(O) OTHER TAXABLE ALLOW. AND BENEFITS — *AUTRES AVANTAGES IMPOSABLES*

(P) EMPLOYMENT COMMISSIONS — *COMMISSIONS D'EMPLOI*

(Q) UNION DUES — *COTISATIONS SYNDICALES*

(R) CHARITABLE DONATIONS — *DONS DE CHARITÉ*

(S) PAYMENTS TO DPSP — *PAIEMENTS À UN RPDB*

(T) PENSION PLAN OR DEFERRED PROFIT SHARING PLAN REGISTRATION NUMBER — *N° ENREGISTREMENT DE RÉGIME DE PENSION OU DE PARTICIPATION DIFFÉRÉE AUX BÉNÉFICES*

(A) PROVINCE OF EMPLOYMENT — PROV. — *PROVINCE D'EMPLOI*

(B) SOCIAL INSURANCE NUMBER* — 473 621 459 — *N° D'ASSURANCE SOCIALE**

*IF YOUR SOCIAL INSURANCE NUMBER IS NOT SHOWN IN THIS BOX, SEE INFORMATION ON REVERSE. **SI VOTRE NUMÉRO D'ASSURANCE SOCIALE N'EST PAS IMPRIMÉ DANS CETTE CASE, VOIR LES RENSEIGNEMENTS AU VERSO.*

EMPLOYEE: SURNAME FIRST (in capital letters). USUAL FIRST NAME AND INITIALS AND FULL ADDRESS
EMPLOYÉ: NOM DE FAMILLE D'ABORD (en capitales). PRÉNOM USUEL ET ADRESSE COMPLÈTE
SURNAME *NOM DE FAMILLE* — USUAL FIRST NAME AND INITIALS - *PRÉNOM USUEL*

LEWIS KATHY
Anytown / City
Province
N6H 4B9

FOOTNOTES: *NOTES:*

EMPLOYER NAME *NOM DE L'EMPLOYEUR* — JOHN H. JOHNSON D.D.S.

ACCOUNT NUMBER *NUMÉRO DE COMPTE* — BAC 123456

EMPLOYEE NO. *N° DE L'EMPLOYÉ*

TO BE RETURNED WITH T4-T4A SUMMARY *À RETOURNER AVEC LA T4-T4A SOMMAIRE* 1

- The employer must fill out the Total Earnings Before Deductions, the Employee's Pension Contribution—Canada Plan, the UI Premium, the Income Tax Deducted, and the UI Insurable Earnings sections. To do this, the payroll clerk refers to the individual employee's earnings record.
- After completing the four-copy set of T4 slips for all employees, the employer must mail or deliver copy 1 of each T4 Supplementary to Revenue Canada Taxation by no later than February 28 of each year.
- Copies 2 and 3 must also be given to the employee by no later than February 28. Copy 2 is attached to the employee's income tax return, which must be mailed by no later than April 30. Copy 3 is kept by the employee for his or her income tax records.
- Copy 4 is retained by the employer and must be kept on file, together with all other payroll records, for at least six years.

[1]At the time of writing the T4-T4A Summary for 1990 was not available.

2. Annual Tax Statement to Revenue Canada Employers must also submit a detailed payroll summary to Revenue Canada Taxation. This summary is called the T4-T4A Summary.[2]

Revenue Canada Taxation   Revenu Canada Impôt

T4-T4A SUMMARY - 1989
SUMMARY OF REMUNERATION PAID
FOR THE YEAR ENDING DECEMBER 31, 1989

copy 1

1989 THIS RETURN SHOULD BE COMPLETED IN CONJUCTION WITH THE INSTRUCTIONS OUTLINED IN THE "EMPLOYER'S AND TRUSTEES GUIDE" OR THE "SOURCE DEDUCTIONS FOR SMALL BUSINESS EMPLOYERS GUIDE".

IF YOUR T4-T4A RETURN IS FILED ON MAGNETIC TAPE PLACE TICK MARK (✓) INSIDE THE SYMBOL AT LEFT AND ENSURE THAT TAPE(S) AND PAPER RETURNS ARE SHIPPED TO THE TAPE FILER ADDRESS IN THE BOOKLET ENTITLED, "COMPUTER SPECIFICATIONS FOR T4,T4A AND T4A-NR DATA FILED ON MAGNETIC TAPE".

IMPORTANT
Employer name and number must correspond to that shown on your Tax Deduction - Canada Pension Plan - Unemployment Insurance Remittance Return, form P D 7 A.

EMPLOYER NO. (Per Remittance Return)

NAME AND ADDRESS OF EMPLOYER

TAXATION OFFICE   D.O. CODE

AMOUNTS MUST BE REPORTED IN CANADIAN FUNDS

T4 SUPPLEMENTARY TOTALS

TOTAL NUMBER OF T4 SLIPS FILED * ① △
EMPLOYMENT INCOME BEFORE DEDUCTIONS - BOX (C), T4 SLIPS ② △
REGISTERED PENSION PLAN CONTRIBUTIONS - BOX (F), T4 SLIPS ③ △

Number of T4 Slips included in the Total at the left, where the address of the employee is in the U.S.A.

EMPLOYEES' PENSION CONTRIBUTIONS - CANADA PLAN - BOX (D), T4 SLIPS ④ △
EMPLOYER'S PENSION CONTRIBUTIONS - CANADA PLAN ⑤ △
EMPLOYEES' UNEMPLOYMENT INSURANCE PREMIUMS - BOX (E), T4 SLIPS ⑥ △
EMPLOYER'S UNEMPLOYMENT INSURANCE PREMIUMS ⑦ △
T4 INCOME TAX DEDUCTED - BOX (G), T4 SLIPS ⑧ △

* FOR RETURNS OVER 300 T4 SLIPS PLEASE REFER TO INSTRUCTIONS IN EMPLOYER'S AND TRUSTEE'S GUIDE RELATING TO THE BREAKDOWN OF LARGE RETURNS

T4A / T4A-NR SUPPLEMENTARY TOTALS

TOTAL NUMBER OF T4A SLIPS FILED ** 9 △
TOTAL NUMBER OF T4A-NR SLIPS FILED 10 △
TOTAL T4A PENSION OR SUPERANNUATION TOTALS - BOX (C), T4A SLIPS 11 △

Number of T4A Slips included in the Total at the left, where the address of the payee is in the U.S.A.

TOTAL T4A INCOME TAX DEDUCTED - BOX (J), T4A SLIPS ⑫ △
TOTAL T4A-NR INCOME TAX DEDUCTED - BOX (D), T4A-NR SLIPS ⑬ △

** FOR RETURNS OVER 300 T4A SLIPS PLEASE REFER TO INSTRUCTIONS IN EMPLOYER'S AND TRUSTEE'S GUIDE RELATING TO THE BREAKDOWN OF LARGE RETURNS

TOTAL DEDUCTIONS REPORTED ④+⑤+⑥+⑦+⑧+⑫+⑬ ⑭
REMITTANCES FOR THE YEAR ⑮
DIFFERENCE

If you have not remitted the total deductions reported, the balance should be forwarded with this T4-T4A Summary. Any balance owing may be subject to penalty for late remitting.

A difference of less than $ 1.00 is neither charged nor refunded.

OVERPAID ⑯   BALANCE DUE ⑰

CANADIAN CONTROLLED PRIVATE CORPORATIONS OR UNINCORPORATED EMPLOYERS: ENTER THE SOCIAL INSURANCE NUMBER OF THE PROPRIETOR OR PRINCIPAL OWNERS. ⑱ ⑲

PERSON FROM WHOM FURTHER INFORMATION MAY BE OBTAINED REGARDING THE T4-T4A RETURN:
Name   Usual First Name   Surname   Telephone Number   Area Code

CERTIFICATION

I HEREBY CERTIFY that the information given in the T4-T4A Return - Form T4-T4A Summary and related forms T4 Supplementary, T4A Supplementary and T4A-NR Supplementary - is true, correct and complete in every respect.

Date   Signature of authorized person   Position or Office

FOR DEPARTMENTAL USE ONLY - PLEASE DO NOT WRITE IN THIS AREA

⑳ Transfer Action: 1 LAST TO CURR. 2 NO ACTION 3 OTHER
MANUALLY CALCULATED: ㉑ T4A TD ㉒ T4A-NR TD
㉓ Proforma Return: 1 NO 2 YES   Type ORIG. 1
MEMO   LFP   DATE   PREPARED BY
REJECT CORRECTIONS ONLY
T4 BAL 1   OVERRIDE 1   DELETE 3   REJECT NUMBER

		CODE 2	CORR.	INC.	EMP. C.	DRESSED	REV.	FICHE
INITIALS								
DATE								

Retain the Working Copy of this T4-T4A Summary for your records. Forward Copies 1 and 2 of this T4-T4A Summary, Copy 1 of related forms T4 Supplementary and/or Copies 1 and 2 of related forms T4A and/or T4A-NR Supplementary to your local taxation centre. See the Employer's and Trustee's Guide or the Source Deductions for Small Business Employers Guide for the applicable address.

CANADIAN HUMAN RIGHTS ACT FEDERAL INFORMATION BANK NUMBER 15615 - FORM AUTHORIZED AND PRESCRIBED BY ORDER OF THE MINISTER OF NATIONAL REVENUE
THIS FORM IS AVAILABLE IN FRENCH AT YOUR NEAREST DISTRICT TAXATION OFFICE - CETTE FORMULE EST DISPONIBLE EN FRANÇAIS À VOTRE BUREAU DE DISTRICT D'IMPÔT

[2]At the time of writing the T4-T4A Summary for 1990 was not available.

This summary reports the following for the preceding calendar year:

- the total gross earnings of all employees
- the total employer's and employees' contributions to the Canada Pension Plan
- the total employer's and employees' unemployment insurance premiums
- the total tax deducted from employees

These totals are obtained from appropriate accounts in the General Ledger.

PROBLEMS

Journalizing payroll accrual and payment.

Preparing a monthly government remittance slip.

P 11-9 The salary payroll register for Dr. R. Schenck's dental practice in Winnipeg, Manitoba showed the following totals for the biweekly payroll ending June 30:

Earnings		Deductions	
Regular	$3 516	CPP	$ 79.20
Overtime	84	UI	81.00
Gross Pay	3 600	Income Tax .	1 249.05
		Net Pay	2 190.75

a. Record the payroll in the General Journal.

b. The employees are paid by cheque on June 30. Show the payment to employees in General Journal form.

c. Form PD7AR is made out on July 15. Record the remittance to the Receiver General for Canada as per form PD7AR. Show the entry in General Journal form.

Journalizing salary payment and government remittance.

P 11-10 Refer to the solution for Problem 11-6 of this chapter. Using the information of Problem 11-6, prepare entries in General Journal form for the transactions summarized below. Show a brief explanation for each entry.

a. Feb. 14 Issued pay statements with salary cheques to all employees.

b. Mar. 15 Issued certified cheque to the Receiver General for Canada and enclosed form PD7AR to return the required amounts for Canada Pension Plan, unemployment insurance, and income taxes. *Note:* In this instance only, the payroll is to be treated as biweekly.

Journalizing salary payment and government remittance.

P 11-11 Refer to the solution for Problem 11-7 of this chapter. Using the information of Problem 11-7, prepare entries in General Journal form for the transactions summarized below. Show a brief explanation for each entry.

a. Mar. 17 Issued pay statements with salary cheques to all employees.

b. Apr. 15 Issued certified cheque to the Receiver General for Canada and enclosed form PD7AR to return the required amounts for Canada Pension Plan, unemployment insurance, and income taxes. *Note:* Reference to additional payrolls in March has been omitted to simplify this problem.

MINI-CASES

Discussing preparation of T4 slips and T4-T4A summary.

MC 11-7 The T4 slips and T4-4A Summary must be filed with the government and sent to a business's employees no later than the last day of February each year.

a. Why has the government set a deadline for filing these statements?

b. Why would the government choose the last day of February?

c. Why does the government require the employer to send them a copy of each T4 prepared?

Preparing a T4 slip.

MC 11-8 Vanessa Robinson is a nurse who works for Dr. Jane Cumming. Dr. Cumming uses a weekly pay period plan. Vanessa makes $465 per week.

a. Using the tables provided with the Topic 1 problems and assuming Vanessa does not work overtime during the year, calculate Vanessa's gross pay, total CPP contributions, UI premiums, and income tax deduction for the year. *Hint:* Calculate her weekly deductions and assume 52 pay periods in the year.

b. Prepare the T4 slip for Vanessa Robinson. Improvise a slip similar to the one illustrated in this chapter. Make up an address and SIN for Vanessa.

Understanding payroll deductions, remittances, and expenses.

MC 11-9 Ponytails by Jean Claude is a local beauty salon. The bookkeeper records the payroll deductions as a credit to three liability accounts when the weekly payroll is calculated. Then when the monthly remittance to Revenue Canada is made, the total CPP contributions, UI contributions, and income tax deductions are debited to the three liability accounts and credited to Cash.

a. After the monthly remittance is made, what kind of balance will be in the CPP Payable, UI Payable, and Income Tax Payable accounts?

b. What do these balances represent?

c. Instruct the bookkeeper how the entries should be made.

COMPREHENSIVE CASE STUDY 8

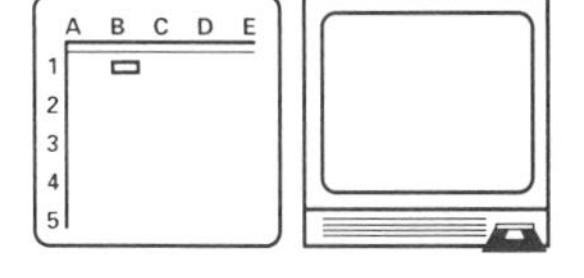

This case study has been separated into four parts that correspond with the four chapters of Part 2. The problems in the case study may be completed using a manual system or using a general accounting package that integrates Accounts Receivable, Accounts Payable, and General Ledger modules. An electronic spreadsheet may be used to complete the payroll register.

Note: The accounting of the Goods and Services Tax and any applicable provincial sales tax are omitted from this case study. These taxes are discussed in Part 3.

HARRY'S HORTICULTURAL SERVICES

Accounts Receivable Application (Chapter 8)

Harry Kwa has decided to start his own lawn-care business to earn extra money. He has never taken accounting so he has asked you to keep his books. You agree to teach Harry how to do his bookkeeping in return for some help in calculus.

Harry has the following economic resources to use in his business:

Savings account balance	$320
Lawnmower	800
Small tools	85

The lawnmower was purchased by Harry's mother, Katherine Kwa, on his behalf. The bank account was a savings account Harry opened when he was ten years old. He uses this account to buy small equipment.

Harry has lined up five customers for his business: S. Achim, G. Chliszczyk, O. Heine, J. Leung, and M. Ordower. Harry agrees to provide these people with lawn care services whenever necessary and collect for his services at the end of each month. The services were to be billed at an hourly rate of $8.

1. Set up a Chart of Accounts for Harry's Horticultural Services. Add appropriate data where necessary to complete this chart under the manual system or your computerized General Ledger system.

2. Set up a General Ledger and Accounts Receivable Ledger. Add appropriate data where necessary to complete both ledgers.

During the month of May, Harry's business had the following transactions:

May	1	Worked 3 hours for S. Achim.
	1	Worked 2 hours for O. Heine.
	1	Worked 4.5 hours for J. Leung.
	2	Worked 1 hour for M. Ordower.
	2	Purchased gasoline for $10 and oil for $8.
	2	Worked 9 hours for G. Chliszczyk.
	8	G. Chliszczyk recommended Harry to D. Tseng.
	8	Worked 8 hours for D. Tseng who paid cash.
	9	Worked 1 hour for M. Ordower.
	9	Purchased gasoline for $15. (Gasoline and oil Expense.)
	15	Worked 2 hours for O. Heine and then 4 hours for his neighbour L. Hinojosa.
	15	Worked 4 hours for S. Achim.
	16	Purchased gasoline for $20.
	16	Worked 1 hour for M. Ordower.
	16	Worked 4 hours for J. Leung and then went to Ms. Leung's business, J. Leung, C.A., and worked 2 hours.
	22	Worked 3 hours for S. Achim.
	22	Worked 2 hours for O. Heine.
	22	Worked 5 hours for G. Chliszczyk.
	23	Purchased gasoline for $20.
	23	Worked 6 hours for D. Tseng.
	29	Received cash for full payment on account from S. Achim, O. Heine, and G. Chliszczyk.
	29	Received $25 cash from J. Leung and $16 from J. Leung, C.A.
	30	Worked 1 hour for L. Hinojosa.
	30	Received cash for full payment on account from all customers who did not make a payment on April 29.

3. Journalize May's transactions in the Fees Earned Journal, Cash Receipts Journal, and the General Journal. Use appropriate transaction entry grids if you enter these transactions through your microcomputer's accounts receivable and General Ledger software packages. Print copies of all relevant journals.

4. Post the transactions to the customer accounts (Accounts Receivable Ledger).

5. Calculate the month-end totals in the special journals. Post the totals and the entries in the General Journal to the General Ledger accounts. Prepare a trial balance from the Accounts Receivable Ledger.
6. Do you detect any control weaknesses in this system?
7. Why must you have separate accounts for J. Leung and her business? Support your answer with the appropriate GAAPs.

Accounts Payable Application (Chapter 9)

As Harry begins to receive requests from his customers for work to be done in June, it becomes clear to him that he is going to need more supplies. The trouble is he will need the supplies during the month, but he is not going to get any cash until he collects his accounts at month-end. Harry's mother agrees to accompany him to various suppliers and co-sign invoices so that Harry is able to buy supplies on account. They arrange to get fertilizer, seed, and plants from Little Tree Farm and Godamunne's Nursery, any special equipment from Rayner Rentals, small tools from Lantaigne Hardware, and gasoline and oil from Stirling Fuels. All vendors offer credit terms of n/30.

8. Set up an Accounts Payable Ledger. Add the appropriate date to complete this ledger.

The following summarize the accounts payable transactions for the month of June.

June 6 Purchased $150 of small tools from Lantaigne Hardware.
6 Purchased $85 of fertilizer (Supplies Expense) and a $47 fertilizer spreader (Gardening Equipment) from Little Tree Farm.
6 Rented a rototiller from Rayner Rentals for the weekend for $53.
6 Purchased $40 gasoline and oil from Stirling Fuels.
7 Purchased shrubs costing $320 (Plants Expense) and planting soil costing $68 to be used exclusively at O. Heine's property from Godamunne's Nursery.
7 Purchased grass seed (Supplies Expense) for S. Achim from Little Tree Farm for $47.
13 Rented a weed eater from Rayner Rentals for the weekend for $23.
13 Purchased $45 gasoline and oil from Stirling Fuels.
14 Purchased fruit trees (Plant Expense) for M. Ordower's property from Little Tree Farm for $289.

14 Purchased evergreens for J. Leung's business from Little Tree Farm for $578.
20 Purchased bedding plants from Summertime Nurseries for the following customers:

S. Achim	$ 27
G. Chliszczyk	54
O. Heine	52
L. Hinojosa	76
J. Leung	32
J. Leung, C.A.	135
M. Ordower	63
D. Tseng	101

20 Purchased $42 gasoline and oil from Stirling Fuels.
21 Rented for $42 for the weekend a weed eater and hedge trimmers from Rayner Rentals.
22 Paid outstanding accounts in full as of May 21.
27 Purchased a weed eater from Lantaigne Hardware for $169.
27 Purchased $47 gasoline and oil from Stirling Fuels.
27 Purchased a used lawn mower from Rayner Rentals for $245.

A summary of the revenue transactions and cheques received for the month of June are as follows:

Customer	Hours Worked	Amount Paid	Date Paid
S. Achim	16	213.10	June 27
G. Chliszczyk	15	182.10	June 28
O. Heine	28	587.80	June 27
L. Hinojosa	11	151.40	June 31
M. Lalani	30	120.00	June 28
J. Leung	14	126.30	June 30
J. Leung, C.A.	23	722.95	June 28
M. Ordower	20	564.80	June 30
D. Tseng	13	118.15	June 27

Harry also charged a 15% mark-up on plants or supplies purchased specifically for any of his customers as a fee for his time spent purchasing the items.

9. Journalize June's purchase transactions in the Purchases Journal and the Cash Payments Journal. Use appropriate

transaction entry grids if you enter these transactions through your computer's accounts payable and General Ledger software packages. Print copies of all relevant journals.

10. Journalize June's revenue and receipts transactions.

11. Post the transactions to the subsidiary ledgers.

12. Calculate the month-end totals in the special journals. Take a trial balance off each subsidiary ledger.

13. What are the benefits of using these special journals? Are there any disadvantages?

Banking Application (Chapter 10)

While you were doing the May bookkeeping for Harry, you explained to him that doing business with cash was risky and did not provide him with important controls over his most valuable asset — Cash. Also, since his business was growing he did not have time to collect cash from his customers or deliver cash payment to all his suppliers. Harry agreed with you and decided to open a business account with the bank he dealt with for his savings account. The following transactions took place.

June 10	Opened a chequing account and transferred $650 from savings account.
22	Wrote cheques for Accounts Payable as indicated above. The cheques were written in the order the suppliers appear in the ledger (alphabetically) beginning with cheque number 101.
24 to 27	Mailed or delivered cheques written June 22.
27	Deposited all cheques received from customers.
30	Deposited all cheques received from customers.

14. Journalize the June 10 transaction.

15. Post the transactions totals from the special journals and any General Journal entries to the General Ledger.

16. Using the bank statement below, prepare a bank reconciliation statement.

17. Make any necessary journal entries and post them to the General Ledger.

18. Should the cheques be authorized by Harry or yourself? Give reasons for your answer.

19. What cash controls are provided when a bank account is used?

A Chartered Bank

Daily Interest Chequing Account

Harry Kwa,
459 Queen Street,
City, Province
A1B 2C3

Branch Address:
489 King Street,
City, Province
A1B 2C5

Account Number: 2504612

Statement Date: 19— 06 31

Date	Item description	Debit	Credit	Account balance
June 10	Transfer from 5502399		650.00	650.00
June 24	Cheque #101	388.00		262.00
June 25	Cheque #102	150.00		112.00
June 27	Deposit		919.05	1031.05
June 30	Cheque #104	118.00		913.05
June 31	Deposit		1025.05	1938.10
June 31	N.S.F. D. Tseng	118.15		1819.95
June 31	Debit memo	10.00		1809.95
June 31	Deposit		126.30	1936.25
June 31	Cheque #105	127.00		1809.25
June 31	Interest		289.03	2098.28
June 31	Service charge	4.25		2094.03

No. of cheques	Balance forward	− Total debits	+ Total credits	= Closing Balance
4	0.00	915.40	3009.43	2094.03

Payroll Application (Chapter 11)

As the work requests began to arrive for July, Harry realized he did not have the time to keep his own books and you would not be able to teach him how. Therefore, Harry decides to put you on the payroll and to hire a neighbour, Jacqueline Latella, to help with the lawn care services. It is agreed that Jacqueline will be paid $90 per week for 20 hours of work and you will be paid $75 per week for 5 hours of work.

You and Jacqueline fill out TD1 forms. Your net claim code is 3 and Jacqueline's is E. Both of you will make CPP contributions.

July's pay cheques are written on the 3rd, 10th, 17th, and 24th of the month.

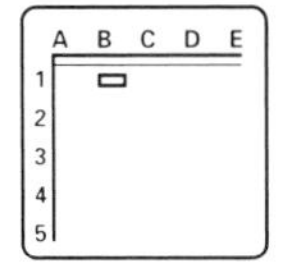

20. Complete the payroll register for each payday during the month of July. (This may be completed using an electronic spreadsheet.)

21. Journalize each payroll.

22. Post the month-end totals to the General Ledger.

23. When will the July deductions be remitted to Revenue Canada—Taxation?

24. Journalize the remittance payment in the General Journal.

25. All of the deductions (CPP, UIC, and Income Tax) were not made on all of the salary payments. Explain why.

Note: In order to avoid repetitions, the accounts receivable, cash receipts, accounts payable, cash payments, and banking transactions have been excluded for the month of July.

PART 3

THE ACCOUNTING CYCLE FOR A MERCHANDISING BUSINESS

In Part 1 of the textbook, you learned the basic accounting cycle, as well as basic adjusting entries for a service business. In Part 2, you looked in detail at the accounts receivable and accounts payable applications, cash control and banking, and payroll. In this part, you will study the financial transactions of a merchandising business and learn the following:

- how to prepare financial statements from a ten-column work-sheet, which includes more complex adjusting entries.
- how to use the multiple journal system, as well as the use of the combination journal.
- how to account for the Goods and Services Tax and provincial sales taxes.
- how to analyze the information presented by financial statements
- how to examine some further applications of the electronic spreadsheet and General Ledger software packages

CHAPTER 12

INTRODUCING ACCOUNTING CONCEPTS FOR MERCHANDISING BUSINESSES

Topic 1
Examining Changes to the Financial Statements for Merchandising Businesses

Topic 2
Analyzing Merchandising Transactions

Merchandising business: a business that buys finished goods and sells them at increased prices.

This chapter will explain the basic accounting concepts that apply to a business that sells a product. This type of business is called a merchandising business and the products it sells are called merchandise or goods.

A merchandising business buys finished products and sells them at higher prices to make a profit. A **wholesaler** is a merchandising business that buys goods from a manufacturer or producer, adds a mark-up, and sells them to a merchandising business known as the **retailer**. Both the wholesaler and the retailer add a mark-up (increase in price) to the goods, and sell them to the **consumer**, who is the final user of the goods.

EXAMINING CHANGES TO THE FINANCIAL STATEMENTS FOR MERCHANDISING BUSINESSES

The most important difference between a service business and a merchandising business is what is sold. A service business deals in only services, whereas a merchandising business sells products. Therefore, a merchandising business has an additional asset called merchandise inventory or **inventory**.

Merchandise inventory: merchandise or goods acquired for resale; a current asset on a balance sheet of a merchandising firm.

Merchandise inventory—a valuable asset—is reported in the Current Assets section of the balance sheet at year-end. Refer to the partial balance sheet shown below.

Any Merchandising Firm
Partial Balance Sheet
as at a Certain Date

ASSETS

Current Assets:	
Cash	$15 000
Accounts Receivable	20 000
Inventory (at cost)	40 000

Analysis:

- Any merchandise inventory on hand, that is, not sold, at the end of an accounting period (one month, three months, one year, etc.) is an asset of the business.
- Since the merchandise inventory is expected to be sold within a short time—within one year of the balance sheet date, if not sooner—it must be reported as a current asset.
- The current asset Inventory follows Accounts Receivable. Cash, as the most liquid asset, comes first. Accounts Receivable is

next, since most customers will pay their account within 30 days. Inventory is last, since it is usually sold on credit.

- If a business has excess[1] cash on hand, it often invests in marketable securities such as Canadian stocks, bonds, or treasury bills to generate additional revenue. Marketable Securities appear before Accounts Receivable in the balance sheet, since they can be converted to cash very quickly.

Current Assets:	
Cash	$15 000
Marketable Securities	50 000
Accounts Receivable	20 000
Inventory (at cost)	40 000

- Notice the phrase ''at cost'' after Inventory. This indicates that the asset is valued at **cost**—the original price of this asset—rather than at the selling price or replacement cost. Inventory is always qualified in this manner on the balance sheet. As with the reporting of fixed assets in earlier chapters, this presentation of the inventory is an application of the cost principle.

A merchandising business earns most of its revenue by selling merchandise from its stock of inventory. When goods are sold, the cost of those goods is then an expense which is matched against revenue to determine a profit (net income) or a net loss. This expense is called cost of goods sold.

Cost of goods sold: a large expense of any merchandising firm; represents the amount paid for the goods that were sold.

Some accountants include **cost of goods sold** with all of the operating expenses, such as rent, wages, and utilities in the income statement. Net income is then calculated by matching revenue earned for a definite accounting period with expenses incurred in that same period in accordance with the matching principle. This calculation is illustrated in the condensed income statement on page 480.

Analysis:

- The word ''condensed'' means that only the key parts of the statement are shown. Cost of Goods Sold and Operating Expenses are shown as totals; the detail is eliminated to focus attention on the important parts.
- The main source of revenue for any merchandising business is the sale of merchandise, reported under **Revenue** as Sales of Goods or Sales.

[1]Excess cash is more cash than is needed for the day-to-day operations of the business.

Any Merchandising Firm Condensed Income Statement For a Definite Accounting Period		
Revenue:		
Sales of Goods		$80 000
Expenses:		
Cost of Goods	$40 000	
Operating Expenses	20 000	
Total Expenses		60 000
Net Income		$20 000

- Cost of goods sold is an expense of the business because it represents the cost of buying the goods that are sold. This expense is usually the single largest expense of a merchandising business.

There is another way to report the income statement, as illustrated here.

Any Merchandising Firm Condensed Income Statement For a Definite Accounting Period	
Revenue:	
Sales	$80 000
Cost of Goods Sold	40 000
Gross Profit from Sales	40 000
Operating Expenses	20 000
Net Income	$20 000

Analysis:

Gross profit from sales: the result of matching sales revenue with the cost of goods sold.

- On the basis of the matching principle and a definite accounting period, revenue is matched against the expense of buying goods (cost of goods sold) to calculate the gross profit from sales. This is the profit earned before the regular operating expenses are deducted.

Important: In this textbook, report the result of matching sales revenue with cost of goods sold as the Gross Profit from Sales and not simply Gross Profit. Also, remember that the Cost of Goods Sold reported on any income statement is classified as an expense to support the application of the matching principle.

- Gross profit from sales is the **first level** of income, before operating expenses are deducted. The result of deducting operating expenses from gross profit is the **second level** of income: net income or net loss. This second level is also the final income because, as you will recall from Chapter 3, the word "net" means that **all** expenses have been matched with **all** revenue.
- When reporting the Gross Profit from Sales, use the complete term so that the difference between sales revenue and the expense cost of goods sold is clearly identified. Do not use abbreviations.
- Although cost of goods sold is matched with sales revenue, rather than being included in the expense section, it is still an expense. All income statements must follow the **matching principle**—revenues are matched with expenses for the same accounting period. If the sale of goods is revenue, then the cost of those goods is the expense to be matched against sales revenue. The cost of goods sold is an expense no matter where it is reported on the income statement.
- The cost of **unsold** goods, the inventory, is an unexpired cost. Therefore, Inventory is reported as a current asset on the balance sheet. As merchandise is sold, the unexpired cost becomes an expired cost, which is then added to the Cost of Goods Sold expense. In this way, the revenue for the period, generated by sales of inventory, is matched against the cost of those goods.

CALCULATING THE COST OF GOODS SOLD

Before calculating the cost of goods sold, you must understand inventory methods. We will examine two methods—perpetual inventory and periodic inventory.

Perpetual inventory: a system of calculating the cost of goods sold and of updating the Inventory account immediately after the sale of the inventory item.

Periodic inventory: a system of calculating the cost of all goods sold during the period, based on a physical count, at the end of the period.

Some businesses require an accurate and immediate count of inventory. What type of products might you count at the end of every day to ensure that all products sold have been recorded? If you answered "cars" or "diamond rings," you will understand the initial concept of perpetual inventory. As the name suggests, this type of inventory is tracked constantly, by recording all changes resulting from purchases and sales in the Inventory account. At any point in time, the business knows the quantity of inventory and also the cost of goods sold. Physical counts are taken periodically to check against amounts reported by inventory records. Any differences would be accounted for as inventory losses.

The second type of inventory system is called periodic inventory. Under this method, no changes are made to the Inventory account until the end of an accounting period. Similarly, no accounting of the cost of goods sold is made until the end of the accounting period. With the record of the beginning count of inventory carried forward from the end of the last accounting period, a record of all merchandise purchases made during the current period, and the actual count of inventory taken at the end of the current accounting period, accountants can determine the cost of goods sold and update the Inventory account. This system is generally used for low-cost, small items, for which it would be impractical to record every sale, for example, nuts and bolts in a hardware store.

Let's calculate the cost of goods sold using the periodic inventory. Suppose that the business records of Hawkeye's Medical Supply Wholesale shows the following information for the month of August:

1.	Cost of the goods on hand at the beginning of August (beginning inventory)	$ 50 000
2.	Cost of the goods purchased throughout the month	70 000
3.	Sale of medical supplies to various retailers throughout the month	130 000

Use the following formula to calculate the cost of goods available for sale:

Beginning Inventory	+	Purchases	=	Cost of Goods Available for Sale
$50 000	+	$70 000	=	$120 000

You now know how much was available for sale. But what is left? At the end of the period — August 31 in this example — the goods remaining in the store must be physically counted. A physical inventory is necessary because no records were kept of the cost of the items that were sold. After the inventory is counted, the cost of each item is calculated—or **valued**—by multiplying the number of that item by the price paid for each item. The prices are obtained from the purchase records. The total cost of all items is the cost value of remaining inventory, which is reported on the balance sheet. Assume that the physical count and valuation shows $65 000 of inventory in stock. Use this formula to calculate the cost of goods sold.

Physical inventory: the actual counting of inventory items at the end of an accounting period.

Cost of Goods Available for Sale	–	Ending Inventory	=	Costs of Goods Sold
$120 000	–	$65 000	=	$55 000

The results of these calculations are reported on the partial income statement below.

Hawkeye's Medical Supply Wholesale
Partial Income Statement
For the Month Ended August 31, 19–

Revenue from Sales		$130 000
Cost of Goods Sold:		
Inventory, August 1	$ 50 000	
Purchases	70 000	
Cost of Goods Available for Sale	120 000	
Less: Inventory, August 31	65 000	
Cost of Goods Sold		55 000
Gross Profit from Sales		$ 75 000

To summarize your calculation:

(1) Determine the beginning inventory.

(2) Determine what was purchased during the month.

(3) Add (1) and (2) to determine Cost of Goods Available for Sale.

(4) At the end of the period, physically count the goods, and value them by multiplying their cost by the number in stock. The cost figures are obtained from the purchase records. This value is Ending Inventory.

(5) Subtract Ending Inventory from Cost of Goods Available for Sale to get Cost of Goods Sold.

(6) Finally, subtract Cost of Goods Sold from Sales Revenue to get Gross Profit from Sales.

Beginning Inventory + Net Purchases = Goods Available for Sale – Ending Inventory
= Cost of Goods Sold

Sales Revenue – Cost of Goods Sold = Gross Profit from Sales

EXPLAINING THE FACTORS THAT AFFECT SALES REVENUE

There are three different factors that affect the reporting of the final or net sales figure on the income statement, especially for wholesalers:

- merchandise returned by customers
- allowances granted to customers
- sales discounts granted to customers for early payment

Usually, the first two factors are grouped under the heading Sales Returns and Allowances, and the third factor appears under the heading Sales Discounts.

Sales Returns and Allowances Most retail and wholesale businesses allow their customers to return merchandise that is unsatisfactory, that is, if the merchandise is damaged, broken, or is the wrong size, shape, or colour. The cost of the item or the sales return is deducted from the customer's outstanding balance. In some cases, the customer may be willing to keep the goods, if the seller will reduce the price. This reduction or sales allowance reduces the customer's account in the same way as the sales return does. If the goods were paid for with cash, a cash refund is made; otherwise, the customer's outstanding balance is reduced.

Sales return: return of goods by a customer to the seller.

Sales allowance: a reduction in the original sales price for slightly inferior or unsuitable goods.

Sales Discounts Businesses sometimes offer what is known as a sales discount to encourage customers to pay their accounts before the due date. For example, a wholesaler offers credit terms to its retailers of "1/10, n/30." These terms mean that 1% will be deducted from the purchase price if the bill is paid within 10 days of the invoice date; otherwise, the entire amount is due within 30 days of the invoice date.

Sales discount: cash discount deducted from the sales invoice.

Both sales returns and allowances, and also sales discounts decrease sales revenue. As you can see in the illustration, Net Sales (net revenue from sales) is calculated by subtracting Sales Returns and Allowances and Sales Discounts from Gross Sales.

Revenue from Sales:		
Gross Sales		$20 000
Less: Sales Returns		
and Allowances	$200	
Sales Discounts	100	300
Net Sales		$19 700

EXPLAINING THE FACTORS THAT AFFECT COST OF GOODS SOLD

Merchandising businesses that use the periodic inventory method face several factors that will affect the calculation of cost of goods sold. These factors are:

- transportation-in or freight-in charges for moving goods from the supplier to the merchandiser's place of business
- purchases returns to the supplier
- allowances granted by the supplier
- purchases discounts offered by the merchandiser for early payment of the purchase invoice

Note: Although perpetual inventory systems must account for the above costs as well, we will examine these factors from the viewpoint of the merchandiser who uses the periodic inventory method.

Transportation-in A merchandiser is often required to pay the cost of transporting the goods from the supplier's place of business to the buyer's. These costs, called **Transportation-in** or **Freight-in**, become part of the cost of the goods and are, therefore, added to the purchase price. The result is the **cost of delivered goods**. For example, if your business buys goods costing $8000 from St. John's, Newfoundland, and you must pay $600 to get them to your place of business, the cost of delivered goods is $8600.

Purchases	$5 000
Transportation-in	300
Cost of Delivered Goods	$5 300

Do not confuse these costs with the **delivery expense**, which is the cost of delivering the goods to **your** customers, once the goods are sold. This operating expense is called **Transportation-out**, **Freight-out**, or **Delivery Expense** and is completely different from transportation-in; the two expenses are **not** interchangeable.

Purchases Returns and Allowances A business inspects purchased goods when received, and may find that some are unsatisfactory. It may choose to either return these goods or negotiate for a lower price. Depending on what decision is made, the business will record either a purchases return or an allowance. Both decrease the cost of goods delivered.

Cost of Delivered Goods	$5 300
Purchases Returns and Allowances	200
Net Purchases	$5 100

Purchase Discounts Suppliers will often encourage their customers to pay their bills before the due date by offering a discount. This is common practice between manufacturers and wholesalers, and between wholesalers and retailers.

For example, a chemical business offers credit terms to its customers of 3/10, 1/15, n/60. In other words a 3% discount is allowed if payment is received within 10 days of the invoice date; a 1% discount is allowed if payment is received within 15 days of the invoice date; and the final gross amount must be paid within 60 days of the invoice date. For example, on a $1000 invoice, the supplier will deduct $30 if the bill is paid within the 10 days or $10 if the bill is paid between 10 and 15 days. The buyer must pay the full amount by day 60.

Cost of Delivered Goods		$5 300
Purchases Returns and Allowances ..	$200	
Purchases Discounts	300	500
Net Purchases		$4 800

The reporting of purchases returns and allowances and purchases discounts as part of the **Cost of Goods Sold** section of an income statement is illustrated above. Note that the final purchase cost is called **Net Purchases.**

The income statement and also the balance sheet for Redrock Paper Products are illustrated on the next two pages for a merchandising business that uses the periodic inventory method.

PROBLEMS

Calculating net sales, sales returns and allowances, and sales returns.

P 12-1 Calculate net sales under each of the following conditions. Prepare the Revenue section of the income statement for **d** and **e**. For all parts, Gross Sales = $8000.

a. Sales Returns and Allowances = 0, Sales Discounts = 0

b. Sales Returns and Allowances = $1200

c. Sales Discounts = $ 453

d. Sales R & A = $974, Sales Discounts = $413

e. Sales Returns = $388, Sales Allowances = $422, Sales Discounts = $298

Calculating the cost of goods sold.

P 12-2 During the year, Hughsie's Products Company purchased merchandise inventory costing $50 000. For each of the following assumptions, calculate the cost of goods sold. *Hint:* Use a format similar to the Cost of Goods Sold section of the income statement.

Redrock Paper Products
Income Statement
For the Year Ended December 31, 19–

Revenue from Sales:				
Sales			$65 500.00	
Less: Sales Returns and Allowances		$ 285.00		
Sales Discounts		215.00	500.00	
Net Sales				$65 000.00
Cost of Goods Sold:				
Inventory, January 1			$15 600.00	
Purchases		$48 870.00		
Add: Transportation-in		630.00		
Cost of Delivered Goods		49 500.00		
Less: Purchase Returns and Allowances	$1 250.00			
Purchases Discounts	500.00	1 750.00		
Net Purchases			47 750.00	
Cost of Goods Available for Sale			63 350.00	
Less: Inventory, December 31			14 860.00	
Cost of Goods Sold				48 490.00
Gross Profit from Sales				16 510.00
Operating Expenses:				
Advertising Expense			$ 150.00	
Salesperson's Salaries Expense			3 200.00	
Heat and Power Expense			4 000.00	
Telephone Expense			860.00	
Delivery Expense			1 110.00	
Payroll Tax Expense			630.00	
Total Operating Expenses				9 950.00
Net Income				$ 6 560.00

(Problem 12-2 continued.)

a. Beginning Inventory = 0, Ending Inventory = $120 000

b. Beginning Inventory = $57 000, Ending Inventory = $38 000

c. Beginning Inventory = $43 500, Ending Inventory = 0

d. Beginning Inventory = $37 000, Ending Inventory = $56 987

e. Beginning Inventory = $110 000, Ending Inventory = $132 000

Redrock Paper Products
Balance Sheet
as at December 31, 19–

ASSETS

Current Assets:		
Cash	$ 5 200.00	
Marketable Securities	2 500.00	
Accounts Receivable	8 000.00	
Inventory (at cost)	14 860.00	
Supplies on Hand	1 200.00	
Total Current Assets		$31 760.00
Fixed Assets (at cost):		
Land	$10 000.00	
Building (security for the mortgage)	35 000.00	
Equipment	8 000.00	
Delivery Truck	6 500.00	
Total Fixed Assets		59 500.00
Total Assets		$91 260.00

LIABILITIES AND OWNER'S EQUITY

Current Liabilities:		
Bank Loan Payable	$ 2 800.00	
Accounts Payable	4 050.00	
Current Portion of Mortgage Payable	5 000.00	
Total Current Liabilities		$11 850.00
Long-Term Liabilities:		
Mortgage Payable, due 2010 –(secured by building)	$25 000.00	
Less: Current Portion due within year	5 000.00	
Total Long-Term Liabilities		20 000.00
Total Liabilities		$31 850.00
Owner's Equity:		
R. Robturn, Capital	$55 350.00	
Add: Net Income	6 560.00	
	61 910.00	
Less: R. Robturn, Drawing	2 500.00	
Total Owner's Equity		59 410.00
Total Liabilities and Owner's Equity		$91 260.00

Calculating the cost of goods sold.

P 12-3 Calculate the cost of goods sold for ACME Widget Company given the following information:

(i) Beginning Inventory = $20 000
(ii) Purchases = $130 000; Freight-in = $1020
(iii) Purchases Returns and Allowances = $500
(iv) Ending Inventory = $22 000

Preparing a partial income statement.

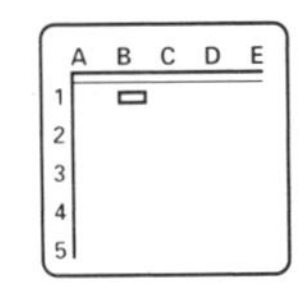

P 12-4 Prepare a partial income statement for the year ended December 31, 19— for the Mallory Paper Company Ltd., using electronic spreadsheet software or the manual method and the following information. Use proper format, including a three-line heading.

(i)Sales = $15 950
(ii)Sales Returns and Allowances = $482
(iii)Sales Discounts = $245
(iv)Inventory, January 1, 19— = $13 245
(v)Purchases: February $3400, June $5890, October $2876
(vi)Purchase Returns and Allowances = $236, Purchases Discounts = $150
(vii)Freight-in = $362
(viii)Inventory, December 31, 19— = $14 110

TOPIC 1 MINI-CASES

Preparing an income statement and classified balance sheet.

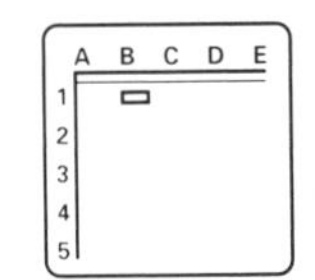

MC 12-1 Yukon Auto Sales and Service Company is owned and operated by Harold Beetont. He has collected the information given below and requested that you prepare the following.

a. an income statement for the year ended December 31, 19—

b. a classified balance sheet in report form as at December 31, 19—

(i) Sales, $280 500; **(ii)** Sales Returns and Allowances, $1535; **(iii)** Sales Discounts, $950; **(iv)** Purchases, $155 000; **(v)** Purchases Returns and Allowances, $2123; **(vi)** Purchases Discounts, $1240; **(vii)** Inventory, January 1, $47 000; **(viii)** Inventory, December 31, $52 500; **(ix)** Transportation-in, $2700; **(x)** Salesperson's Salary, $18 000; **(xi)** Office Salaries, $12 000; **(xii)** Utilities Expense, $550; **(xiii)** Telephone

Expense, $360; **(xiv)** Property Tax Expense, $1755; **(xv)** Payroll Tax Expense, $1255; **(xvi)** Insurance Expense, $1495; **(xvii)** Shop Supplies Expense, $4560; **(xviii)** Cash, $10 800; **(xix)** Accounts Receivable, $87 600; **(xx)** Office Supplies on Hand, $763; **(xxi)** Land, $21 000; **(xxii)** Building, $25 000; **(xxiii)** Equipment, $5675; **(xxiv)** Accounts Payable, $10 500; **(xxv)** Property Tax Payable, $480; **(xxvi)** Bank Loan Payable, $8 500; **(xxvii)** Mortgage Payable, $27 000; (current portion due within year, $7000; security: land and building); **(xxviii)** H. Beetont, Capital, January 1, $85 655; **(xxix)** H. Beetont, Drawing, $18 000.

Note: This mini-case may be solved using electronic spreadsheet software or the traditional manual method.

Calculating the missing amounts in income statement calculations.

MC 12-2 Determine the missing item and its value in each of the following sets of information.

a. Beginning Inventory = $23, Ending Inventory = $16, Cost of Goods Sold = $76, Freight-in = $7, Purchases = ?

b. Beginning Inventory = $437, Purchases = $2388, Purchase Returns and Allowances = $37, Ending Inventory = $378, Cost of Goods Sold = $649, Purchase Discounts = $24, Freight-in = ?

c. Cost of Goods Sold = $200, Purchases = $160, Purchases Returns and Allowances = $9, Sales Returns and Allowances = $10, Sales Discounts = $5, Beginning Inventory = $110, Ending Inventory = ?, Sales = ?, Gross Profit from Sales = $98

Analyzing an income statement for a merchandising business.

MC 12-3 Sam Taylor has just started his own mail-order business, which he operates from his home. He sells discount fishing equipment, which he imports from other countries. Because he imports most of his goods, he incurs many expenses in addition to the actual cost of the goods, such as transportation, insurance, currency exchange, and import duties. Sam doesn't know a lot about accounting, and has arranged his income statement as follows:

Sales	$15 000
Expenses:	
Purchases	10 000
Telephone	110
Supplies	672
Duties	2100
Freight-in	700
Exchange	2200
Insurance	300
Net Loss	$ 82

Sam cannot understand why his business has a net loss. "I buy these goods at a good price, and mark them up 50% over cost, which should be enough to allow me to earn a profit. My expenses are quite reasonable, yet I'm losing money. Why?"

a. Explain to Sam the errors he has made in arranging his income statement.

b. Suggest to Sam how to prepare a proper income statement.

c. Assume that Sam started with no inventory, and sold all the inventory purchased during this month. Prepare an income statement in proper format to assist Sam.

d. Examine the income statement you have prepared. What is Sam's main problem? Explain why Sam's approach to accounting has hidden this problem.

ANALYZING MERCHANDISING TRANSACTIONS

A = L + OE
Assets originate on the left side; liabilities and owner's equity on the right side.

Much of what you have learned about analyzing service business transactions also applies to merchandising businesses. In Chapter 3, Part 1, you learned that there are three rules for debiting and crediting accounts.

- To increase an account, record the increase on the same side as where the account is found in the accounting equation. To increase an **asset** account, record the increase on the left (DR.) side of the account, since assets are on the left side of the accounting equation. The same principle holds true for liability and owner's equity accounts. Since both types of accounts are found on the right side of the accounting equation, record an increase on the right (CR.) side of the account. Since (1) reve-

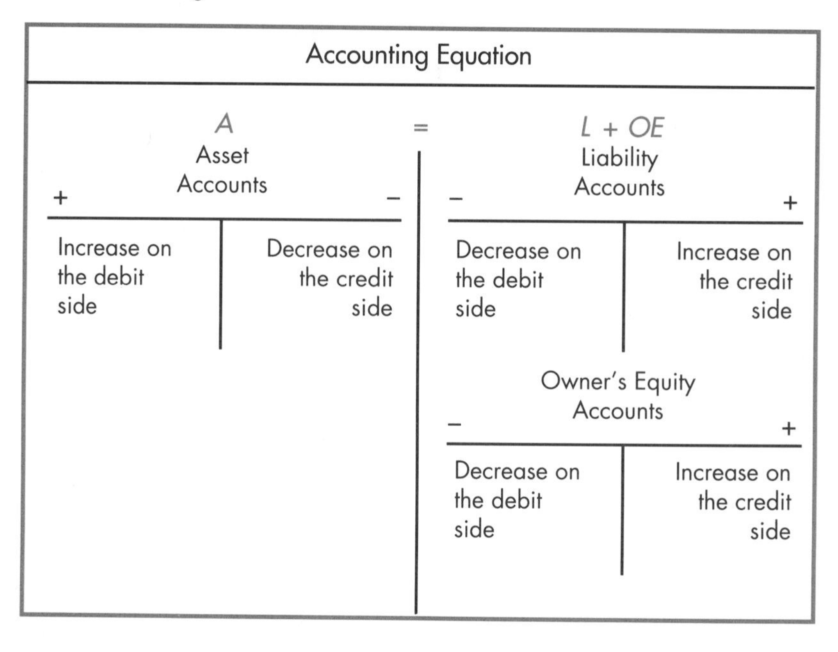

nue produces an increase in the Owner's Equity account and (2) Sales is a revenue account, all sales of merchandise (increase in sales) will be recorded on the right (CR.) side of the Sales account.

- A decrease to an account is recorded on the side opposite to the one where the account appears in the accounting equation. Therefore, record a decrease to an asset on the right (CR.) side of the account, since assets appear on the left side of the accounting equation. Record decreases to liabilities and owner's equity accounts on the left (DR.) side of the account, since the accounts are found on the right side of the accounting equation. Because expenses decrease owner's equity, expenses are recorded on the debit side (left side) of the account.
- Normal balances in the accounts are identified on the same side that the account appears in the accounting equation. Therefore, we would expect asset accounts to have a normal debit balance, since the account appears on the left side of the accounting equation. Liabilities would have a credit balance. Capital and revenue accounts and those owner's equity accounts that increase owner's equity have credit balances. Drawings and expense accounts and those owner's equity accounts that decrease owner's equity have debit balances.

With these concepts in mind, we can now analyze most merchandising business transactions. For this topic, we will ignore the effect of the Goods and Services Tax, which will be addressed in later chapters.

COMPARING CASH SALES TO CREDIT SALES

When a business sells goods for cash, one entry represents the entire transaction. But when the business sells goods on credit, several transactions occur. The first transaction records the sale on credit; the second, the receipt of cash.

May 4	Cash	500	
	Sales		500
	To record the day's cash sales.		

May 1	Accts. Rec./Eastside Variety	1 500	
	Sales		1 500
	To record the sale of goods to Eastside Variety on account. Terms 2/10, n/30.		
May 31	Cash	1 500	
	Accts. Rec./Eastside Variety		1 500
	To record payment in full.		

RECORDING SALES RETURNS AND ALLOWANCES

Sales Returns and Allowances: a contra revenue account.

Sales returns and allowances have the effect of decreasing revenue. This decrease is recorded in a combined account called Sales Returns and Allowances. Because this account is separate from the Sales account, management can then better analyze the number, type, and frequency of returns in an effort to reduce future returns. If a cash sale results in a return, cash is refunded to the customer. If the sale was on credit, the business will reduce the outstanding account receivable by the return or allowance. Examine the journal entry.

May 4	Sales Returns and Allowances	200	
	Accts. Rec./Eastside Variety		200
	The customer returned unsatisfactory goods.		

Sales returns and allowances decrease revenue; therefore, this account is in opposition to the Revenue account. In this case, Sales

Returns and Allowances is a **contra revenue** account, because it has the effect of decreasing revenue, and therefore the Owner's Equity account. Since any decrease to owner's equity must be recorded as a debit to the account that decreased, all sales returns and allowances are recorded as debits.

RECORDING SALES DISCOUNTS TRANSACTIONS

Study the entry for a credit sale. If there are **no returns** and the business pays according to credit terms of 2/10, n/30, then a cheque for $1470 pays the outstanding invoice in full. A 2% discount on $1500 is equal to $30, and this is recorded in the Sales Discounts account as a debit, because the discount reduces the total revenue earned.

Sales Discounts: a contra revenue account.

The total of the debits (Cash and Sales Discounts) equals the credit for Accounts Receivable/Eastside Variety. Since Sales Discounts reduce revenue, and therefore reduce owner's equity, Sales Discounts is also a **contra revenue** account. Since the customer is paying the account in full, the entire invoice amount of $1500 must be credited to Accounts Receivable/Eastside Variety to reduce the outstanding balance to zero. But only $1470 has been received in cash (debit to Cash); therefore, the difference of $30 between the two accounts must be debited to Sales Discounts.

May 10	Cash	1 470	
	Sales Discounts	30	
	Accts. Rec./Eastside Variety......		1 500
	To record payment of May 1 sales less 2% discount.		

Consider the accounting problem that is created when a customer, who purchased merchandise on credit, returns some of the merchandise or is granted an allowance on the sale. When it is time to pay the bill, how is the discount calculated? Let's examine the first transaction for Eastside Variety again. The initial sale was for $1500, but the customer returned $200 of goods. The net sale was therefore $1300. The sales discount is taken on the net sale **after** any returns or allowances are subtracted. The 2% discount then must be taken on the net amount of $1300; therefore, the discount is $26. The second entry dated May 10 shows the resulting entry.

May 10	Cash	1 274	
	Sales Discounts	26	
	Accts. Rec./Eastside Variety		1 300
	To record payment of the May 1 sale less the return and discount.		

Chart of Accounts
REVENUE
401 Sales
402 Sales Returns and Allowances
403 Sales Discounts

Both Sales Returns and Allowances and Sales Discounts are **contra revenue** accounts, and must show debit entries. Also, since both are related to revenue, their account numbers in a Chart of Accounts should follow the Revenue account, as shown in the margin.

RECORDING THE COST OF GOODS SOLD TRANSACTIONS

Let's review the concept of cost of goods sold before examining the entries that account for it.

In Topic 1, you learned that the cost of goods sold is matched with the related sales revenue over a specific accounting period to determine the gross profit from sales. In a service business, expenses are matched with revenue for a period to determine net income for that period. In a merchandising business, the matching of cost of goods sold with revenues must be regarded in the same way since the cost of goods sold is one of the main expenses in a merchandising business.

As shown in Topic 1, only the cost of goods sold should be matched with revenue to disclose the difference — called the **margin** — between the sale and the cost of that sale.

An analysis of a sales transaction and its effect on the accounting equation supports the concept that the cost of goods sold is an expense for a merchandising business. Assume a beginning accounting equation as follows:

Assets					=	Liabilities	+	Owner's Equity
Cash		Inventory		Equipment		Accounts Payable		J. Hill, Capital
$5 000	+	$20 000	+	$5 000	=	$12 000	+	$18 000
		$30 000			=		$30 000	

Consider the effects of selling some of the inventory that cost $1000 for $4000 cash. The inflow of cash resulting from the sale is shown below:

	Assets					=	Liabilities	+	Owner's Equity		
	Cash		Inventory		Equipment		Accounts Payable		J. Hill, Capital		Revenue (Sales)
	$5 000	+	$20 000	+	$5 000	=	$12 000	+	$18 000		
(1)	+ $4 000									+	$4 000
	$9 000	+	$20 000	+	$5 000	=	$12 000	+	$18 000	+	$4 000
	$34 000					=	$34 000				

The decrease in inventory is not recorded; so far we have only dealt with the cash inflow. Since $1000 of inventory was sold, the Inventory account is decreased, as illustrated below. You have learned that a decrease on the left side of the accounting equation must be equalled by a decrease on the right side, in order to keep the equation in balance. If the Inventory account is decreased, what account must also be decreased on the right side? Since liabilities are not affected, it must be an owner's equity account. Since both Capital and Revenue accounts **increase** owner's equity through investment and sales, an expense must have caused the $1000 decrease to owner's equity. The expense incurred is the cost of the asset Inventory which was sold to produce the revenue. This cost is called the **cost of goods sold**. The effect of the cost of goods sold on the accounting equation is shown below.

	Assets					=	Liabilities	+	Owner's Equity				
	Cash		Inventory		Equipment		Accounts Payable		J. Hill, Capital		Revenue		Cost of Goods Sold (Expense)
	$9 000	+	$20 000	+	$5 000	=	$12 000	+	$18 000	+	$4 000		
(2)		−	$ 1 000									−	$1 000
	$9 000	+	$19 000	+	$5 000	=	$12 000	+	$18 000	+	$4 000	−	$1 000
	$33 000					=	$33 000						

In order to match the cost of goods sold with revenue, the equation is rearranged in this way.

Assets			=	Liabilities	+	Owner's Equity		
Cash	Inventory	Equipment		Accounts Payable		J. Hill, Capital	$4 000	Sales Revenue
							−1 000	Cost of Goods Sold
$9 000 +	$19 000 +	$5 000	=	$12 000	+	$18 000 +	$3 000	Gross Profit from Sales
$33 000			=	$33 000				

If we replace the items in the accounting equation with account names, we can account for the cost of goods sold. The Cost of Goods Sold account is debited, and the Inventory account is credited. These are, in fact, the accounts used by merchandising businesses that use the perpetual inventory method, but not by businesses using the periodic inventory method. Under the periodic method, the cost of goods sold is calculated only once, that is, at the end of the accounting period. As we analyze transactions under the periodic method, follow through the examples in Topic 1.

ANALYZING INVENTORY CHANGES

Inventory is an asset under both periodic and perpetual inventory systems. In the perpetual system, the Inventory account is constantly changing, because it is updated as soon as a sale is made. In the periodic system, the Inventory account changes only at the end of the period, when a physical count is made.

Analysis:

- The **beginning inventory** is the same as the **ending inventory** from the last accounting period. This value can be obtained from the Inventory account in the General Ledger.

Inventory	
Beginning inventory is the cost of the unsold inventory carried forward from the last accounting period.	

- The beginning inventory is added to net purchases to calculate the **cost of goods available for sale** on the income statement of the accounting period.

- When the goods are physically counted and valued at the end of the accounting period, their cost value becomes a current asset on the balance sheet. This value replaces the beginning inventory, which is no longer accurate. In addition, the ending inventory is deducted from the cost of goods available for sale to calculate cost of goods sold.

> Beginning Inventory + Purchases = Goods Available for Sale − Ending Inventory
> = Cost of Goods Sold

- At the end of the accounting cycle, closing entries are made in the General Journal to replace the beginning inventory with the ending inventory, so that the correct inventory will then be shown in the General Ledger, and also on the balance sheet.

PURCHASING MERCHANDISE

Purchases: an expense account under the periodic inventory method.

Under the periodic inventory method, the cost of merchandise purchased for resale is not added directly to the Inventory account. Instead, it is accumulated in an account called Purchases. The Purchases account is debited whether the goods are bought on credit, or for cash. The purpose of the account is to keep track of all purchases of inventory in one account.

Jun. 15	Purchases	2 000	
	Accts. Pay./Yellow Paint Store *or* Cash		2 000
	Purchased merchandise on credit terms 1/10, n/30 (or buy for cash).		

Analysis: The following points must be stressed in the analysis of the debit entry to Purchases.

- The Purchases account is used only to record merchandise purchased for resale, that is, inventory. Assets such as trucks, supplies, or equipment that are not for resale, but for use in the business, are recorded in separate asset accounts.
- The Purchases account is neither an inventory nor an asset account. It does not show whether the goods have been sold, or if they are still in stock; this account indicates only the total value of goods acquired for resale during a specific period.

Chart of Accounts
COSTS AND EXPENSES
501 Purchases

- Since the only function of the Purchases account is to provide information for the calculation of the cost of goods sold, it must be regarded as part of cost of goods sold. The cost of goods sold is an expense; therefore, Purchases is also an expense and is placed under the heading **Costs and Expenses** in the Chart of Accounts.

Transportation-in (freight-in): an expense account under the periodic inventory method.

Transportation-in Freight charges must be added to the cost of purchases to determine the cost of delivered goods. The entry below shows what happens when a transport business is paid, or gives credit terms. It is important to classify transportation-in, or freight-in, as part of cost of goods sold. This makes the Transportation-in an expense account; entries should be debited to this account. Do not confuse this account with Delivery Expense, which is the cost of delivering the goods to **your** customers. This is also an expense, but **not** part of the Cost of Goods Sold.

Jun. 16	Transportation-in	55	
	Accts. Pay./CP Express *or* Cash		55
	To record freight charges on merchandise purchased on June 15.		

To import merchandise from other countries it may be necessary to pay a tax called **duty** before the merchandise can enter the country. Therefore, duty must also be added to the cost of purchases. It is common to debit only one account — **Transportation-in** or **Transportation-in and Duty-In** — with the cost of duties. If a business purchases large amounts of merchandise from other countries, it may use separate accounts to provide better information for decision making. *Note:* In the Chart of Accounts shown in the margin, Transportation-in is numbered very closely to the Purchases account since these expenses are connected.

Chart of Accounts
501 Purchases
502 Transportation-in

Purchases Returns and Allowances When merchandise received from suppliers is unsatisfactory, it may be returned or an allowance may be granted on the purchase price. In either case, the cost of purchases must decrease. The journal entry for such a transaction is shown.

Jun. 16	Accts. Pay./Yellow Paint Store	300	
	Purchases Returns and Allowances		300
	To record the return of defective merchandise bought on June 15 on account (or for cash).		

Analysis: The return or allowance causes the quantity and value of the purchase to decrease. In theory, this decrease could be credited to the Purchases account. Once again, better information for decision making can be obtained by keeping this transaction separate, in an account called Purchases Returns and Allowances, allowing more complete disclosure on the income statement. Management may clearly see the value of purchases returns and allowances. Since this account is in opposition to Purchases, it is a **contra** account. Purchases Returns and Allowances appears in the Chart of Accounts as shown in the margin.

Purchases Returns and Allowances: a contra expense account under the periodic inventory method.

Chart of Accounts
501 Purchases
502 Transportation-in
503 Purchases Returns and Allowances

Purchases Discounts When a supplier offers credit terms that include a discount for early payment, the buyer should take advantage of them, in order to reduce the cost of purchases. In our example, the credit terms offered by the Yellow Paint Store are 1/10, n/30. Taking advantage of the discount, the buyer pays the bill and writes a cheque for $1683. The journal entry is shown below.

Chart of Accounts
501 Purchases
502 Transportation-in
503 Purchases Returns and Allowances
504 Purchases Discounts

Jun. 16	Accts.Pay./Yellow Paint Store	1 700	
	Purchases Discounts		17
	Cash		1 683
	Cheque No. 417 in payment of the June 15 purchase, less a 1% cash discount.		

Purchases	$2 000
Less Return	300
Net Purchase	$1 700
Less Discount	17
Amount of Cheque	$1 683

Purchases Discounts is a contra expense account, and entries will cause owner's equity to increase. To increase an owner's equity account, a credit entry is required. Let's summarize the main points in calculating cost of goods sold under the periodic inventory method.

Purchases Discounts: a contra expense account under the periodic inventory account.

- The value for the cost of goods available at the beginning of the accounting period—the Beginning Inventory—is obtained from the inventory account. This inventory is equal to the ending inventory at the end of the last period.
- Add Net Purchases to the Beginning Inventory to calculate the Goods Available for Sale. Net purchases is calculated by adding Purchases, and then adjusting for Transportation-in or Freight-in, and the two contra accounts, Purchases Returns and Allowances and Purchases Discounts.
- At period-end, the inventory remaining is counted, and it is valued using cost figures. The Ending Inventory is then subtracted from Cost of Goods Available for Sale to determine the expense called Cost of Goods Sold.

- Finally, this expense is matched against revenue from sales to determine Gross Profit from Sales for the accounting period.

TOPIC 2 PROBLEMS

Journalizing merchandising transactions, including returns, allowances, and discounts.

P 12-5 Record the transactions below in General Journal form. Add a brief explanation for each entry.

Nov. 2 Cash sales for the day were $1392.
4 Purchased merchandise from Poag's Clocks Ltd. totalling $3000. Terms 2/10, n/30.
8 Sold $2359 of merchandise on account to Bronstein Construction Co. Terms 1/15, n/60.
10 Bought a new truck for $19 600. Paid $4583 down, remainder due in 30 days to Reid's Truck Sales.
14 Paid Poag's Clocks Ltd. in full. *Hint:* Do not forget to take the discount.
16 Bronstein Construction returned $788 of defective goods.
18 Purchased $1258 of merchandise from Treva's Paper Products on account. Terms 2/10, n/30.
20 Some of the merchandise from Treva's Paper Products was unsatisfactory, but was kept after negotiating an allowance of $65.
23 Received payment in full from Bronstein's Construction Co.
27 Paid the invoice from Treva's Paper Products in full.

Journalizing and posting of merchandising transactions.

P 12-6 The transactions for a merchandising business operating under the periodic inventory method are recorded.

Calculating the cost of goods sold.

Mar. 1 The beginning inventory is $9000. *Note:* No journal entry is required for this. Put a debit balance for this amount into the Inventory account.
4 Purchased merchandise for cash, $1200.
7 Purchased merchandise on account from Johnston Bros. Ltd. for $5400. Terms 2/10, n/60.
7 Paid Saint Hubert Express Co. freight charges of $73 on the above purchase. Used Cheque No. 217.
8 Purchased new equipment from Moncton Sales and Service for $18 399. Paid $6300 in cash, balance due in 30 days.
9 Returned for a full refund $672 of goods purchased from Johnston Bros. Ltd.

11 Purchased merchandise on credit from Fredericton Wholesalers for $8300. Terms 4/5, 2/15, n/30.
15 Purchased merchandise for cash from Ridgetown Manufacturers Ltd. for $4577.
17 Paid Johnston Bros. Ltd. in full with Cheque No. 218. *Note:* Do not forget the return and the discount.
22 Paid the monthly utility bill with Cheque No. 219 for $325.
26 Paid Fredericton Wholesalers in full with Cheque No. 220. (Remember the discount.)

a. Analyze each of the transactions in General Journal form. Briefly explain each entry.

b. Post each of the journal entries to T-accounts using the account names introduced in this chapter.

c. Assume that on March 31, month-end physical inventory is taken, and the value of unsold goods is $9300. From the information in the problem, and the T-accounts ledger, calculate the Cost of Goods Sold for the month of March. The name of the company is Halifax Mfg. Co.

Journalizing of merchandising transactions and posting to T-accounts.

P 12-7 M. Pittana owns and operates his own photography studio. The following information is provided about the transactions for the month of July.

Calculating cost of goods sold.

Preparing an income statement.

a. Journalize the entries in a General Journal, and then post to T-accounts.

b. Calculate the cost of goods sold.

c. Prepare an income statement in proper format for the month of July.

July 1 Purchased from Acme Photo Supply photographic paper and chemicals costing $800. Terms n/30.
2 Sold photo services to a customer for $400 which was paid in cash.
3 Purchased film from Adams Film Supply for $225, terms 2/10, n/30.
5 Printed photographs for a commercial customer, ABCA Services, for $2300, terms 2/10, n/30.
6 Returned $30 of film to Adams Film Supply because it was out-of-date. A credit memo was issued.
13 Sold photo mural to a corporate customer, SUTA Corp., for $3400. Terms 2/10, n/30.
16 Paid invoice from Adams Film Supply, taking full discount. *Hint:* Do not forget the credit memo.

19 Received payment in full from ABCA Services, with no discount taken.

21 Purchased photo frames for $210 for use in the business. Paid cash.

23 Received payment from SUTA Corp., for full amount less discount.

Other Information:

Pittana Photography had a photographic supplies inventory of $131 at the start of the month, and $276 at the end of the month. Operating expenses for the month of July totalled $2435.

MINI-CASES

Explaining the effects of inventory errors.

MC 12-4 The stock clerk at Burton's Electronics was given the task of counting the inventory for the year-end. In doing so, he failed to count the merchandise on one entire shelf. Consequently, the year-end financial statements were prepared with an incorrect valuation figure for the ending inventory. A few days afterward, the omission was discovered and reported to the manager. After analyzing the statement, the manager estimated that the value of inventory missed was $2000.

a. Explain the effect of this omission on each of the following:

(i) the cost of goods sold

(ii) gross income from sales

(iii) net income

(iv) the balance sheet.

b. Assume the manager did nothing to correct the error, and she permitted this error to be carried forward to the next accounting year. What would be the effect of this error:

(i) on the income statement?

(ii) on the balance sheet?

Examining the concept of cost of goods sold.

MC 12-5 Joan Jetts is a junior accounting student who wants to start her own business. She is somewhat confused by the concept of cost of goods sold, and its function in the income statement. "If I buy goods for $100, and sell them for more than that, I **have to** make a profit. Why bother with all these calculations?"

a. Is Joan right? Is it guaranteed that she will make a profit? Explain your answer.

COMPREHENSIVE CASE STUDY 9

Jim Mallory owns and operates a print shop called AAA Printers. He uses the periodic inventory method to calculate the cost of goods sold. The financial transactions for the month of January are listed below. On January 1, Jim Mallory's business had the following balances in these accounts: Cash, $5000; Inventory, $4500; Equipment, $3700; Bank Loan Payable, $4300; Accounts Payable/London Supply Co., $854. *Hint:* Calculate owner's equity.

Note: This comprehensive case study may be completed by using an appropriate general accounting package or by the traditional manual method. If the general accounting package is used, first prepare the initial data files for the General Ledger Chart of Accounts, the customers for the Accounts Receivable Ledger, and the vendors for the Accounts Payable Ledger.

Jan. 2 Paid rent on building for January $1500. Used Cheque No. 677.
3 Purchased $2300 of merchandise on credit from Best Paper Products. Terms 2/10, n/30.
5 Issued Cheque No. 678 to London Supply Co. for $600 on account.
6 Sold merchandise on credit to A. Hoffman for $1600. Terms n/30.
7 Cash sales for the week totalled $4200.
8 Purchased additional printing equipment from Boston Press Manufacturing Ltd. for $2100 with terms n/60.
10 Sold merchandise on credit to T. Horton for $756 with terms n/30.
11 Received a shipment of paper supplies from L. G. Paper Wholesalers at a cost of $5600. Terms 1/15, n/60.
11 Freight charges on the shipment received totalled $175. Paid CN Express with Cheque No. 679.
13 Issued Cheque No. 680 to Best Paper Products, taking the discount allowed.
14 Cash sales for the week totalled $4600.
15 Returned damaged goods received from L.G. Paper Wholesalers totalling $300.
16 J. Mallory invested $5000 cash in the business.

18 Bought a new cash register for the business by issuing Cheque No. 681 for $990.
19 Received payment in full from A. Hoffman.
21 Cash sales for the week were $4300.
22 Issued Cheque No. 682 for the monthly telephone bill of $112.
23 Received a supply of printer's ink from Graffix Ltd. costing $677 on terms 1/15, n/30.
24 Received an advertising bill from the Age-Dispatch for $266. Terms n/30.
25 Issued Cheque No. 683 in payment of an invoice with L. G. Paper Wholesalers, less return, less discount.
28 Paid for adjustment and repairs to the printing equipment. Issued Cheque No. 684 for $328.
29 J. Mallory withdrew $1200 for personal use. Issued Cheque. No. 685.
30 J. Mallory took home, for personal use, paper and envelopes valued at $130 cost. *Hint:* Do not use the Inventory account; the account that was originally debited must be changed.
30 Issued separate cheques (nos. 686, 687, and 688) for the following items: part payment of the bank loan, $1500; monthly hydro bill $148; part payment to Boston Press Manufacturing Ltd, $800.

Journalizing and posting to the GL.

a. Journalize each of the transactions in a General Journal, page 35. Include a brief explanation.

Using subsidiary ledgers.

b. Post to the three-column ledger. If you are not using the workbook, set aside 20 lines for Cash, 8 lines for Sales, and 15 lines for Accounts Payable control.

Preparing an income statement and balance sheet.

c. Post to the Accounts Receivable and Accounts Payable Ledgers. Prepare schedules for each to verify the control accounts in the General Ledger.

d. Physical inventory count on January 31 showed unsold goods of $3200. Prepare a month-end income statement and related balance sheet.

CHAPTER 13

INTRODUCING THE ACCOUNTING CYCLE FOR A MERCHANDISING BUSINESS

Topic 1
Journalizing and Posting Credit Sales Transactions

Topic 2
Journalizing and Posting Cost of Goods Sold Transactions

Topic 3
Journalizing and Posting Cash Transactions

Topic 4
Using the Combination Journal

In Part 1, you learned these four steps in the accounting cycle:

(1) originating transaction data from source documents
(2) making debit and credit entries to the journal
(3) posting entries from the journal to the ledger
(4) preparing a trial balance from a listing of all ledger accounts to prove that the debits equal credits.

After calculating the trial balance, you completed the worksheet. From the worksheet, you prepared the income statement and the balance sheet in proper form.

These four steps will now be applied to an accounting system that is used by a **merchandising** business.

Goods and Services Tax (GST): the federal government's consumption tax on the majority of goods and services consumed in Canada; to be implemented in January 1991.

This chapter incorporates some aspects of the Goods and Services Tax (GST) which replaces the Federal Sales Tax as of January 1, 1991. Under this proposed system, which at the time of this writing has yet to be declared law, the majority of goods and services will be taxed at a rate of 7%, payable at all business levels (manufacturing, wholesaling, and retail). The more complex accounting of the GST is treated in Topic 1 of Chapter 14. The accounting of provincial sales taxes for retail merchandising businesses will be discussed in a later topic.

TOPIC 1 JOURNALIZING AND POSTING CREDIT SALES TRANSACTIONS

Sales transactions in a business are completed on a cash or credit basis. This topic will examine journalizing and posting of only credit sales.

INTRODUCING THE CREDIT SALES SYSTEM

Sales invoice: a source document capturing the dollar results of a credit sale of merchandise.

When a business sells merchandise on account, that is, on credit, a source document called a sales invoice is prepared. This document is the starting point for all transactions. While it is most important in a credit sale, many transactions and documents are processed as a result. By studying the flowchart opposite, you will understand the flow of information and documents in a merchandising business. The specific procedures in a system will vary among businesses, but the basic pattern is similar.

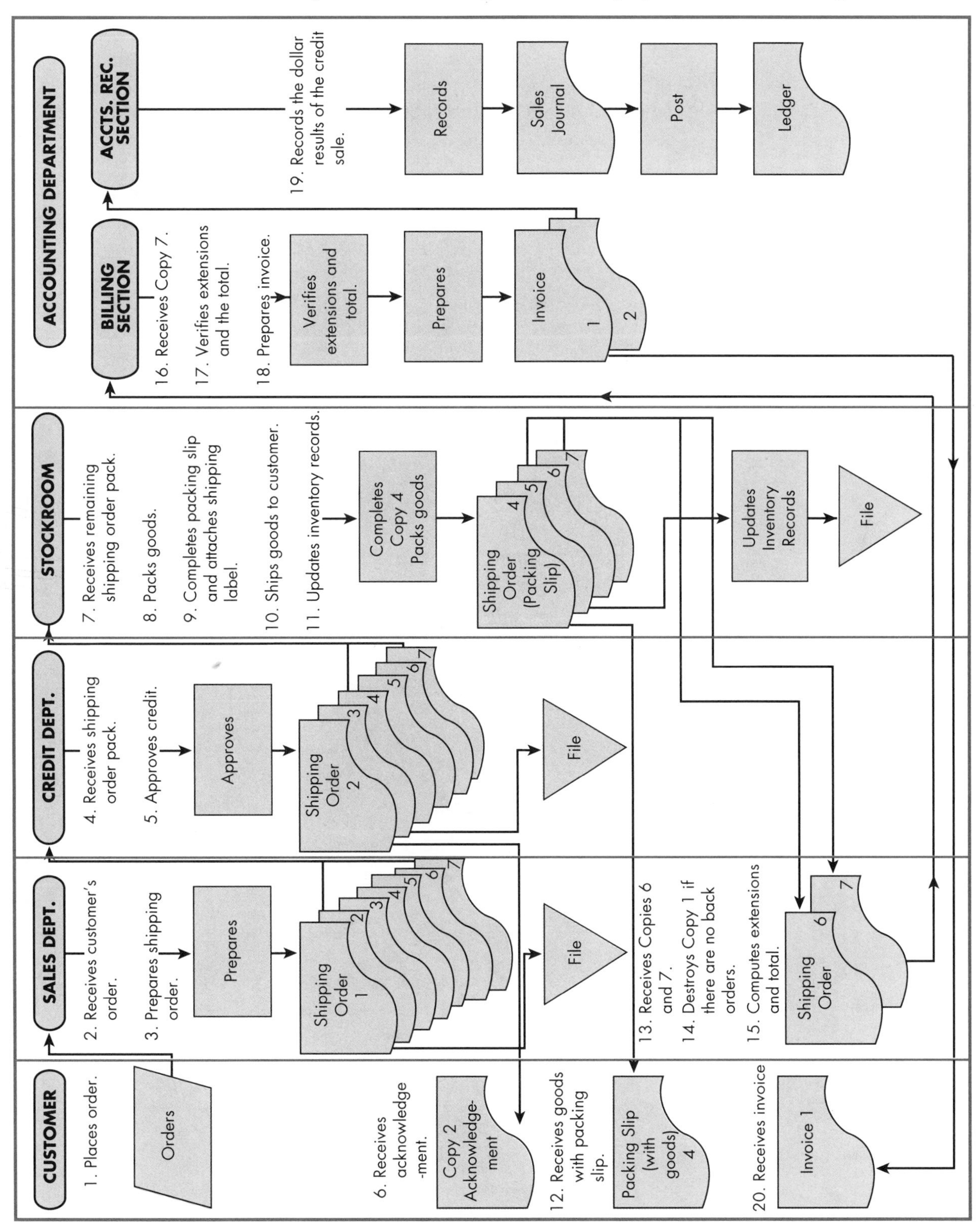
FLOWCHART OF A CREDIT SALES SYSTEM
CUSTOMER
1. Places order.
Orders
6. Receives acknowledge -ment.
Copy 2 Acknowledge- ment
12. Receives goods with packing slip.
Packing Slip (with goods) 4
20. Receives invoice
Invoice 1
SALES DEPT.
2. Receives customer's order.
3. Prepares shipping order.
Prepares
Shipping Order 1
2
3
4
5
6
7
File
13. Receives Copies 6 and 7.
14. Destroys Copy 1 if there are no back orders.
15. Computes extensions and total.
Shipping Order
6
7
CREDIT DEPT.
4. Receives shipping order pack.
5. Approves credit.
Approves
Shipping Order 2
3
4
5
6
7
File
STOCKROOM
7. Receives remaining shipping order pack.
8. Packs goods.
9. Completes packing slip and attaches shipping label.
10. Ships goods to customer.
11. Updates inventory records.
Completes Copy 4 Packs goods
Shipping Order (Packing Slip)
4
5
6
7
Updates Inventory Records
File
ACCOUNTING DEPARTMENT
BILLING SECTION
16. Receives Copy 7.
17. Verifies extensions and the total.
18. Prepares invoice.
Verifies extensions and total.
Prepares
Invoice
1
2
ACCTS. REC. SECTION
19. Records the dollar results of the credit sale.
Records
Sales Journal
Post
Ledger

As you can see, there are many documents and procedures in a credit sales system. This system is organized to receive and approve orders, pack and ship merchandise, bill customers, and account for transactions. The flowchart emphasizes the idea that responsibility for these tasks should be divided. This concept of internal accounting control is very important. For example, the person who sells the product should not be the same person who records or approves the sale. Similarly, the person who packs the goods must not also be the person who records the accounting transactions. Dividing responsibility reduces the possibility that a dishonest employee might commit fraud or theft.

Study these points as you follow the credit sales system in the flowchart:

Receiving the Customer's Order A sale begins when a **customer** places an order. The order may be received in several ways:

- a salesperson makes out a sales order after a successful visit to a customer
- an order department clerk takes a customer's order in person or over the telephone
- a customer sends a purchase order form in the mail

PURCHASE ORDER

EGLINTON HARDWARE CENTRE

1975 Eglinton Avenue East
Scarborough, Ontario

No **645839**

To: Scarborough Wholesale Hardware
330 Progress Avenue
Scarborough, Ontario M1P 2Z5

- GST Reg'n. No.: #34233
- Purchase order numbers must appear on all papers and packages. Packing slip must accompany shipments.
- Terms of discount must be shown on invoice.
- Delivery schedule as indicated must be held.

Date	Items Needed by	Terms	Via	FOB
19— 05 01	19— 05 10	2/10, n/30	Truck Transport	Scarborough

QUANTITY	DESCRIPTION	UNIT PRICE
30 sets	Wrench Set No. 53Y5197	3.59
20 sets	Socket Wrench Set No. 53Y1883	6.49
30 sets	Tool Boxes No. 53-R1755	14.89
10 only	Heavily Insulated Pliers No. 58-4628	2.10
10 only	450 g DeLuxe Claw Hammer No. 57-4121	3.79

- a customer sends a letter to place an order

A typical **purchase order** is illustrated opposite.

Preparing the Shipping Order The next step is preparing the **shipping order** in the **sales department**. The order is **standardized**. As explained above, an order may be placed in different ways with different information. However, the sales department requires specific information and the order is set up so that the information received for each and every order is in the same format. Since ship-

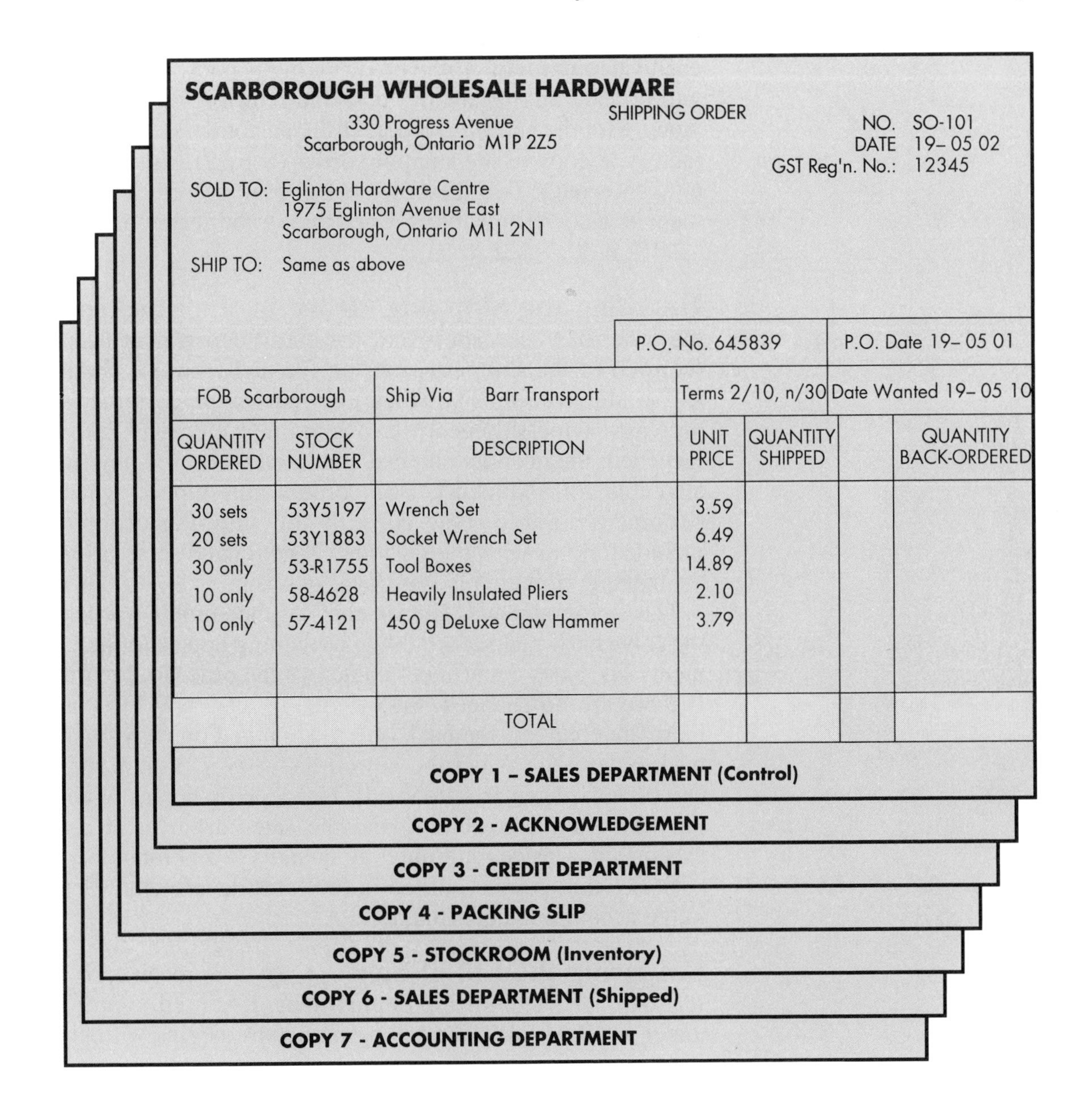

SCARBOROUGH WHOLESALE HARDWARE
330 Progress Avenue
Scarborough, Ontario M1P 2Z5

SHIPPING ORDER

NO. SO-101
DATE 19– 05 02
GST Reg'n. No.: 12345

SOLD TO: Eglinton Hardware Centre
1975 Eglinton Avenue East
Scarborough, Ontario M1L 2N1

SHIP TO: Same as above

P.O. No. 645839 | P.O. Date 19– 05 01

FOB Scarborough | Ship Via Barr Transport | Terms 2/10, n/30 | Date Wanted 19– 05 10

QUANTITY ORDERED	STOCK NUMBER	DESCRIPTION	UNIT PRICE	QUANTITY SHIPPED		QUANTITY BACK-ORDERED
30 sets	53Y5197	Wrench Set	3.59			
20 sets	53Y1883	Socket Wrench Set	6.49			
30 only	53-R1755	Tool Boxes	14.89			
10 only	58-4628	Heavily Insulated Pliers	2.10			
10 only	57-4121	450 g DeLuxe Claw Hammer	3.79			
		TOTAL				

COPY 1 – SALES DEPARTMENT (Control)
COPY 2 - ACKNOWLEDGEMENT
COPY 3 - CREDIT DEPARTMENT
COPY 4 - PACKING SLIP
COPY 5 - STOCKROOM (Inventory)
COPY 6 - SALES DEPARTMENT (Shipped)
COPY 7 - ACCOUNTING DEPARTMENT

ping orders will be used by several departments, especially in a large merchandising business, many copies of a shipping order are needed and the order itself is typically a multi-part form. The illustration of a shipping order on page 511 shows copies for seven departments. The actual number of copies depends on the needs of the business. As you examine the system flowchart in detail, be sure to follow the path of each of the seven copies.

Approving the Customer's Credit Rating Before merchandise can be sent to a customer, the customer's credit rating must be approved. In a large business, this task is usually handled by the **credit department**. If the credit rating is poor, the credit department will prepare an explanatory note and return it to the sales department along with the shipping order. If the customer's credit rating is satisfactory, a copy of the shipping order (copy 2) is sent to the customer to acknowledge that the order is being processed. The credit department is also responsible for approving the terms of credit, such as "2/10, n/30," and so on.

Handling the Shipping Order in the Stockroom Once the order has been approved, the credit department keeps one copy (copy 3) of the shipping order on file and forwards the other copies to the **stockroom**. The stockroom packs the customer's order and prepares it for shipment. Two important pieces of information are recorded: the quantity shipped and **back orders,** if any (items not yet available for shipment). Back orders are shipped when the goods become available. One copy of the shipping order (copy 4) is included along with the customer's merchandise as a **packing slip**, an example of which is illustrated opposite.

The stockroom will file its copy of the shipping order, copy 5 in the flowchart, and send the two remaining copies to the sales department. The sales department compares the order to the original order. If there are no changes, the original order (copy 1) is destroyed. If there are changes, the back orders are noted on copy 1 and put in the back-order file. When the new stock arrives, a new shipping order can be completed from copy 1. The process begins again at step 15 on the systems flowchart, and the sales department computes the **extensions**—price multiplied by quantity—and totals.

Notice that copy 6 is filed in the sales department. Copy 7 is sent to the accounting department.

Preparing the Bill of Sale Copy 7 is received by the billing section of the **accounting department**. It is used to prepare the customer's bill of sale. The billing procedure begins with checking cal-

SCARBOROUGH WHOLESALE HARDWARE

330 Progress Avenue
Scarborough, Ontario M1P 2Z5

SHIPPING ORDER

NO. SO-101
DATE 19– 05 02
GST Reg'n. No.: 12345

SOLD TO: Eglinton Hardware Centre
1975 Eglinton Avenue East
Scarborough, Ontario M1L 2N1

SHIP TO: Same as above

Shipped by J. Miller 5/2/--

Mass 40 Kg	No. of Packages 3
P.O. No. 645839	P.O. Date 19– 05 01

FOB Scarborough	Ship Via Barr Transport	Terms 2/10, n/30	Date Wanted 19– 05 10

QUANTITY ORDERED	STOCK NUMBER	DESCRIPTION		QUANTITY SHIPPED		QUANTITY BACK-ORDERED
30 sets	53Y5197	Wrench Set		30		0
20 sets	53Y1883	Socket Wrench Set		20		0
30 only	53-R1755	Tool Boxes		30		0
10 only	58-4628	Heavily Insulated Pliers		10		0
10 only	57-4121	450 g DeLuxe Claw Hammer		10		0
		TOTAL				

COPY 4 - PACKING SLIP

culations and ends with preparing the important document called the **sales invoice** or simply the **invoice.**

In practice, two or more copies of the invoice are produced. The original is sent to the customer; the second copy is the source document that proves that a credit sales transaction has occurred.

Accounting for the Sales Invoice Copy 2 of the invoice is used by the accounts receivable clerk to record the credit sale. This copy of the sales invoice is illustrated on page 514.

ANALYZING THE SALES INVOICE

The sales invoice is an important document in the sales credit system. In Part 1, you learned that two basic accounting principles are involved in the analysis of a source document. These are the **revenue principle** and the **objectivity principle**.

SCARBOROUGH WHOLESALE HARDWARE
330 PROGRESS AVENUE INVOICE NO. **101**
SCARBOROUGH, ONTARIO M1P 2Z5

SOLD TO: Eglinton Hardware Centre
1975 Eglinton Avenue East
Scarborough, Ontario M1L 2N1

SHIP TO: Same as above

INVOICE DATE: 19– 05 02
GST REGISTRATION NO.: 12345
TERMS: 2/10, n/30

Purchase Order No.	Date	Shipped Via	FOB	No. of Packages
645839	19– 05 01	Barr Transport	Scarborough	3

QUANTITY	STOCK NO.	DESCRIPTION	GST RATE	UNIT PRICE	AMOUNT
30 sets	53Y5197	Wrench Set	7%	3.59	107.70
20 sets	53Y1883	Socket Wrench Set	7%	6.49	129.80
30 only	53-R1755	Tool Boxes	7%	14.89	446.70
10 only	58-4628	Heavily Insulated Pliers	7%	2.10	21.00
10 only	57-4121	450 g DeLuxe Claw Hammer	7%	3.79	37.90
		TOTAL BEFORE TAXES			743.10
		GST 7%			52.02
		TOTAL AMOUNT OWING			795.12

COPY 2 - ACCOUNTING

The Revenue Principle Revenue may be defined as an inflow of assets, that is, accounts receivable or cash, resulting from the sale of merchandise. The total before taxes amount indicated on the invoice is revenue.

The invoice is dated May 2, 19—. Therefore, revenue is recognized as earned at the point of sale, for example, the date on the invoice.

The Objectivity Principle The sales invoice is a source document giving proof that a sale on account (credit sale) has taken place. This evidence supports the basic accounting principle of objectivity; once it is available, then the sale can be recorded.

In summary, a credit sales system results in the sales invoice, which is used to make accounting entries. As the systems flowchart shows, the accounting copy is recorded in a special journal, the Sales Journal.

INTRODUCING THE SALES JOURNAL

An efficient accounting system uses special journals to record groups of repetitive transactions. For example, all cash inflows (debits to Cash) are recorded in the Cash Receipts Journal. Similarly, all cash outflows (credits to Cash) are recorded in the Cash Payments Journal.

Sales Journal: a chronological record of credit sales.

If a business makes most of its sales of merchandise on credit, a special journal called the Sales Journal is used to record them. The information for entries in the Sales Journal comes from source documents, specifically sales invoices.

Columnar Sales Journal (multi-column sales journal): a sales journal with several money columns.

There are many forms of a Sales Journal. A very simple one records only credit sales as illustrated below. Since the Goods and Services Tax must now be tracked, the single-column Sales Journal is obsolete. This will be discussed in detail in Chapter 14. Most businesses now use a three-column Sales Journal, which is a simple columnar sales journal

SALES JOURNAL Page 1

DATE		INVOICE NO.	ACCOUNTS DEBITED	TERMS	POST. REF.	ACCOUNTS RECEIVABLE DR.	GST PAYABLE CR.	SALES CR.
19–								
May	2	101	Eglinton Hardware Centre......	2/10, n/30		795 12	52 02	743 10
	5	102	Plaza Home Hardware	2/10, n/30		687 80	45 00	642 80
	9	103	Woodbridge Hardware	1/20, n/30		1 043 57	68 27	975 30
	14	104	Summers Hardware Limited ...	1/15, n/60		1 540 00	100 75	1 439 25
	17	105	Markham Home Hardware	2/10, n/30		890 40	58 25	832 15
	24	106	Eglinton Hardware Centre	2/10, n/30		571 81	37 41	534 40
	27	107	Hyland Hardware	1/20, n/30		952 48	62 31	890 17
	30	108	Thornhill Home Hardware	2/10, n/30		789 97	51 68	738 29

Invoice No. 101

Total Before Tax	$743.10
GST 7%	52.02
Total Owing	$795.12

Copy 2 - Accounting

Analysis:

- The name of the journal and the page number are at the top.

- The date entered in the journal is the invoice date, which recognizes the revenue as earned at the time of sale.
- There are three money columns: Accounts Receivable DR., GST Payable CR., and Sales CR. The first of these is the total of the following two.
- There are separate columns to record the invoice number, the account debited, and the terms.
- Only credit sales (sales on account) are recorded in this sales journal.

The Goods and Services Tax is calculated on the **amount before taxes** at the rate of 7% on most goods and services. This tax replaces the Federal Sales Tax, which was applied at the manufacturing level and hidden in the retail price. The GST is explained in more detail in Chapter 14.

- Each sales invoice must be analyzed as a debit to Accounts Receivable for the entire amount owing, a credit to Sales for the sales price, and a credit to GST Payable CR. for the Goods and Services Tax.
- At period-end, the Sales CR. column is totalled, and the total is posted to the Sales account in the General Ledger. The total of the GST Payable CR. column is posted to the GST Payable account in the General Ledger. Finally, the total of the Accounts Receivable DR. column is posted to the Accounts Receivable control account. This procedure reduces the time needed for posting, since an entire page of transactions has been reduced to three posting entries.

ANALYZING THE NEED FOR THE ACCOUNTS RECEIVABLE LEDGER

A modern accounting system uses a separate or subsidiary Accounts Receivable Ledger to account for changes in individual customer accounts. This ledger was introduced in Chapter 8 for the accounts receivable application of a dental practice. The need for a separate ledger is equally important for a merchandising business. Let's examine the problems that may arise if an accounting system is restricted to using only one ledger.

- If a business were to list all its individual customer accounts in the General Ledger, the ledger would be overloaded with too many individual customer accounts mixed in with the other GL accounts, making the ledger cumbersome and unwieldy.

- Only one person could post at any one time.
- The trial balance would require several pages.
- If the trial balance did not balance, it could take a great deal of time to find the error in the GL, especially if there is a large number of accounts.
- The Current Assets section of the balance sheet would be extremely long.

Accounts Receivable Ledger: a subsidiary ledger in which are filed all customer accounts.

To eliminate these problems, most merchandising businesses remove the individual customer accounts from the General Ledger and replace them with one Accounts Receivable control account. Individual accounts are filed in the Accounts Receivable Ledger or Customer Ledger. The process of placing the individual customer accounts with the one control account is shown below.

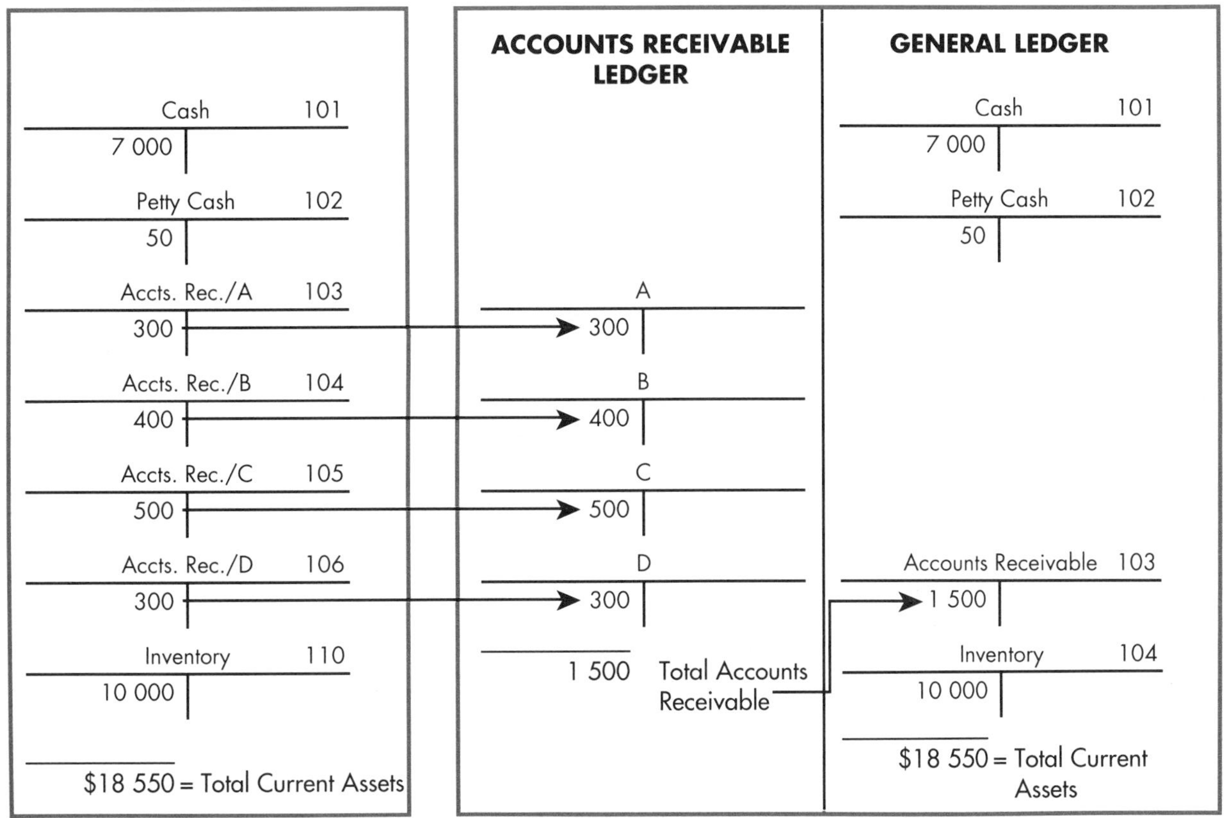

Analysis: Keep these points in mind as you study the illustration:

- A second ledger, the subsidiary **Accounts Receivable Ledger**, now contains all the individual accounts receivable. The individual accounts have been replaced by one controlling account called Accounts Receivable in the General Ledger.
- Note that the amount shown in the GL Accounts Receivable account is the sum of all individual accounts receivable which are now found in the Accounts Receivable Ledger.
- The word "control" is always understood to refer to the Accounts Receivable account in the General Ledger. This account is said to **control** all the individual accounts in the subsidiary ledger because the total of the individual customer accounts must always agree with the debit balance of this account. In this sense, Accounts Receivable in the GL controls all individual accounts filed in the subsidiary ledger.
- The term "subsidiary" also has a special meaning in accounting. The General Ledger controls **all** the business accounts for the purpose of preparing financial statements. The Accounts Receivable Ledger is then a secondary or subsidiary ledger. This concept also applies to other subsidiary ledgers, such as the Accounts Payable Ledger. Subsidiary ledgers contain only individual accounts making up specifically one class of account. They do not contain the accounts required to prepare financial statements. Although the majority of accounting systems will have a General Ledger, only larger businesses need one or more additional subsidiary ledgers.
- Subsidiary ledger accounts usually do not display account numbers as do GL accounts, but instead are arranged alphabetically by customer name.
- The use of subsidiary ledgers allows specialization and division of labour. In large companies there are several accounting departments and each specializes in one aspect such as accounts receivable, as illustrated in the flowchart on page 509. Within a department, one clerk would be responsible for a specific task, for example, posting to the Accounts Receivable Ledger. As well, this clerk may be responsible for other related tasks such as preparing monthly credit reports for the local credit bureau.

It is important to remember that this system of dividing work among different ledgers not only speeds up the processing of accounting information, but also supports the internal control concept of division of responsibility.

ACCOUNTING CLERK

A major law firm seeks qualified candidates for this entry level position.

A high school education is a must and typing experience is an asset. Some accounting background would be helpful, but is not necessary.

Forward your resume in confidence to:

Accounts Receivable Clerk

Required immediately for a fast-growing manufacturer. Necessary qualifications include one year of experience in accounts receivable and computer knowledge.

A non-smoking environment and good benefits as well as a competitive salary.

If you feel you are the person for this position, please apply to Mr. Jason Kelpin, 598-2231.

POSTING CREDIT SALES TO THE ACCOUNTS RECEIVABLE LEDGER

The posting of credit sales is done in two stages: (1) to the accounts receivable ledger on a daily basis; (2) to the General Ledger at the end of the month.

Daily Posting Study the illustration of how posting is done to the subsidiary ledger.

Analysis:

- Note that Eglinton Hardware Centre does not have an account number. Usually, all customer accounts are filed separately and in alphabetical order.
- There is additional information in the heading at the top for the customer's account in the subsidiary ledger: name and complete mailing address, telephone number, and the credit limit.

Stage 1: Post daily to individual accounts in the subsidiary Accounts Receivable Ledger.

SALES JOURNAL Page 1

DATE		INVOICE NO.	ACCOUNTS DEBITED	TERMS	POST. REF.	ACCOUNTS RECEIVABLE DR.		GST PAYABLE CR.		SALES CR.	
19– May	2	101	Eglinton Hardware Centre	2/10, n/30	✓	795	12	52	02	743	10
	5	102	Plaza Home Hardware	2/10, n/30		687	80	45	00	642	80
	9	103	Woodbridge Hardware	1/20, n/30		1 043	57	68	27	975	30
	14	104	Summers Hardware Limited ...	1/15, n/60		1 540	00	100	75	1 439	25
	17	105	Markham Home Hardware ...	2/10, n/30		890	40	58	25	832	15
	24	106	Eglinton Hardware Centre	2/10, n/30	✓	571	81	37	41	534	40
	27	107	Hyland Hardware	1/20, n/30		952	48	62	31	890	17
	30	108	Thornhill Home Hadware	2/10, n/30		789	97	51	68	738	29
						7 271	15	475	69	6 795	46

ACCOUNTS RECEIVABLE LEDGER

Name Eglinton Hardware Centre Credit Limit $5 000

Address 1975 Eglinton Ave. E., Scarborough, Ont. M1L 2N1 Telephone 293-1810

DATE		EXPLANATION	POST. REF.	DEBIT		CREDIT		BALANCE	
19– May	2	Inv. 101; 2/10, n/30	S1	795	12			795	12
	24	Inv. 106; 2/10, n/30	S1	571	81			1 366	93

- Posting is done on a **daily** basis. This is necessary to get accurate, up-to-date information concerning the account at any time. The amount posted is the total of the Accounts Receivable DR. column for each account. This column is the **total amount owing**, which is the total of the amount before tax (Sales CR.) and GST (GST Payable CR.) since this is what the customer really owes.

  Once the individual customer accounts are posted, a check mark (✓) is noted in the Post. Ref. column. The mark replaces the usual account number, since the accounts are filed alphabetically and not by account number. The illustration of the Sales Journal shows two check marks because the entries on May 2 and May 24 have been posted.
- The Explanation column lists the invoice number and terms. Unlike General Ledger accounts, individual customer accounts in the subsidiary ledger show detailed explanations of all entries. This information can be very important in checking the discount dates, and specifying a particular invoice.

Direct posting: transferring information from the source document directly to the subsidiary ledger account.

Some businesses use a direct posting system when transferring information to the Accounts Receivable Ledger. This means that these businesses will post **directly** from source documents to the Accounts Receivable Ledger. Under this short-cut system, one copy of the sales invoice goes to the accounts receivable department and is then posted to the control accounts in the General Ledger.

Stage 2: posting credit sales; posting the monthly total to the General Ledger accounts.

Month-end Posting

The month-end posting is slightly different because the GST must be tracked for remittance to the government. The posting is a compound entry: a debit to the Accounts Receivable control account for the total of the Accounts Receivable column, a credit in the amount of total sales to Sales, and a credit to GST Payable in the amount of GST Payable. Study the opposite illustration.

Analysis: The illustration shows the month-end posting to the General Ledger.

- The date (May 31), the posting reference (S1 standing for Sales Journal, Page 1), and the debit ($7271.15) are posted to the Accounts Receivable account in the GL. Finally, the new balance in the account is calculated. Since there is no previous balance, the new balance is the same as the total debit posted.
- Notice that the account number (103) is also recorded in the Sales Journal at the bottom of the Accounts Receivable DR. column.

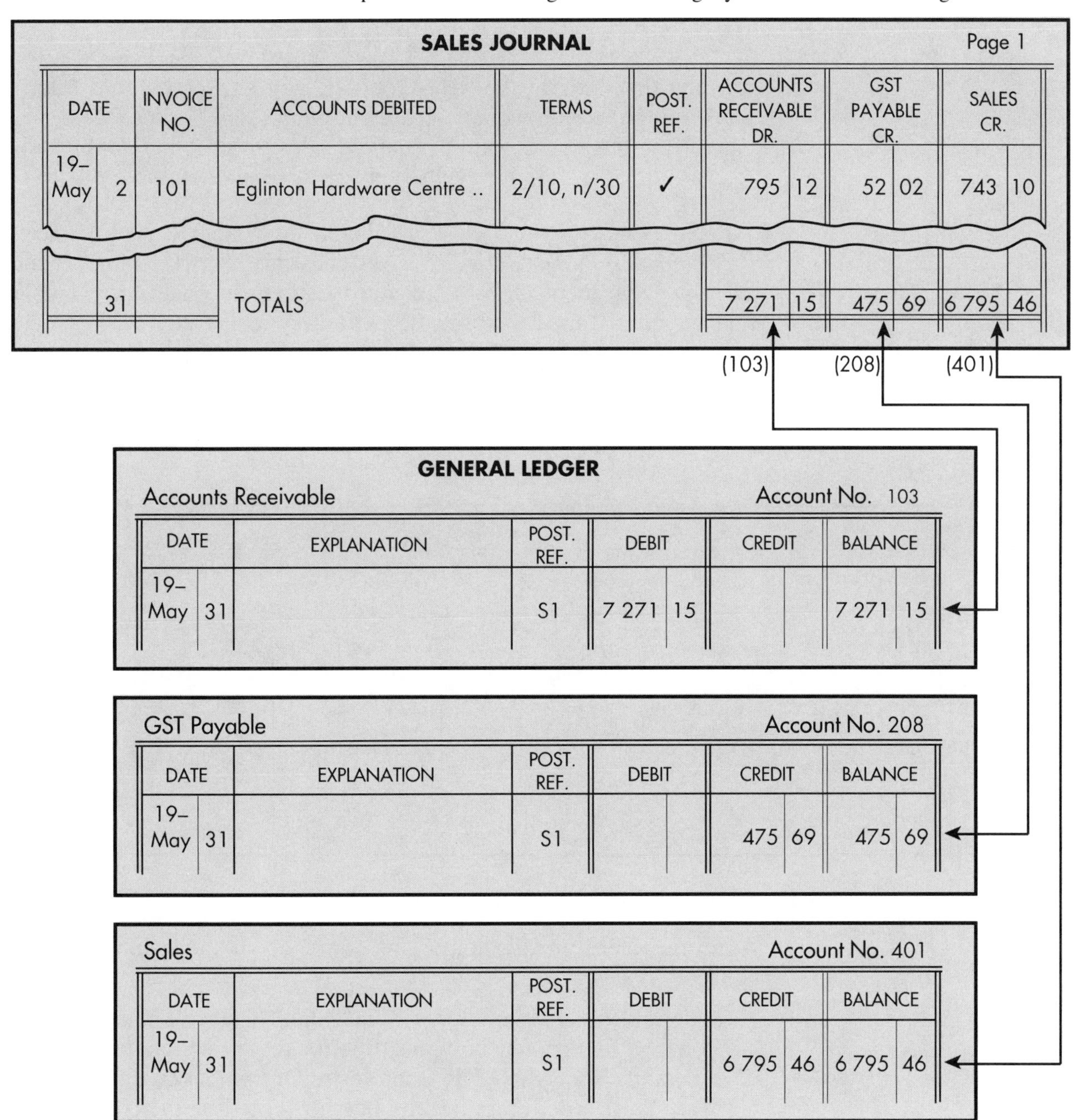

SALES JOURNAL Page 1

DATE		INVOICE NO.	ACCOUNTS DEBITED	TERMS	POST. REF.	ACCOUNTS RECEIVABLE DR.	GST PAYABLE CR.	SALES CR.
19– May	2	101	Eglinton Hardware Centre ..	2/10, n/30	✓	795 12	52 02	743 10
	31		TOTALS			7 271 15	475 69	6 795 46
						(103)	(208)	(401)

GENERAL LEDGER

Accounts Receivable — Account No. 103

DATE		EXPLANATION	POST. REF.	DEBIT	CREDIT	BALANCE
19– May	31		S1	7 271 15		7 271 15

GST Payable — Account No. 208

DATE		EXPLANATION	POST. REF.	DEBIT	CREDIT	BALANCE
19– May	31		S1		475 69	475 69

Sales — Account No. 401

DATE		EXPLANATION	POST. REF.	DEBIT	CREDIT	BALANCE
19– May	31		S1		6 795 46	6 795 46

- The Sales CR. total **only** is posted to the Sales account in the same manner as for Accounts Receivable. Since Sales is a revenue account, the total is posted to the credit column. Again, the account number (401) for Sales is placed in parentheses below the total in the Sales Journal.

EXPANDING THE SALES JOURNAL

In your first look at the Sales Journal, you studied a three-column type. In practice, however, such a simple journal is rare. Most merchandising businesses require detailed sales information, and for this reason, the Sales column is divided into several columns.

Analysis of Sales Most merchandising businesses require some form of sales analysis, that is, a breakdown of their sales by product line, by department, or by some other feature. Suppose, for example, management wanted monthly sales figures in the income statement broken down into two distinct product lines, say Hardware Sales and Electrical Sales. The Sales Journal on page 515 can easily be expanded to include the other money columns as illustrated below.

SALES JOURNAL Page 1

DATE		INVOICE NO.	ACCOUNTS DEBITED	TERMS	POST. REF.	ACCOUNTS RECEIVABLE DR.	GST PAYABLE CR.	HARDWARE SALES CR.	ELECTRICAL SALES CR.
19–									
May	2	101	Eglinton Hardware Centre	2/10, n/30	✓	795 12	52 02	722 10	21 00
	5	102	Plaza Home Hardware	2/10, n/30	✓	687 80	45 00	153 20	489 60
	9	103	Woodbridge Hardware	1/20, n/30	✓	1 043 57	68 27	975 30	
	14	104	Summers Hardware Limited	1/15, n/60	✓	1 540 00	100 75	962 93	476 32
	17	105	Markham Home Hardware	2/10, n/30	✓	890 40	58 25		832 15
	24	106	Eglinton Hardware Centre	2/10, n/30	✓	571 81	37 41	434 30	100 10
	27	107	Hyland Hardware	1/20, n/30	✓	952 48	62 31	250 16	640 01
	30	108	Thornhill Home Hardware	2/10, n/30	✓	789 97	51 68	590 73	147 56
	31		Totals			7 271 15	475 69	4 088 72	2 706 74
						(103)	(208)	(401)	(402)

Analysis: Here are the important points about the columnar Sales Journal:

- Sales are divided into different accounts. This columnar journal contains four money columns: one for recording the debit to Accounts Receivable DR., one for recording the credit to Hardware Sales CR., if applicable, one for recording the credit to Electrical Sales CR., if applicable, and one for GST Payable CR.
- Every sales invoice is recorded as a debit to Accounts Receivable and a credit at least to **one** of the two categories of sales revenue, and a credit to GST Payable.
- During the month, daily postings are made from the Accounts Receivable DR. column of the Sales Journal, or directly from

the source documents to the individual customer accounts filed in the Accounts Receivable Ledger.

- At the end of the month, the column totals of this columnar Sales Journal (sometimes called the multi-column Sales Journal) would be proved (or verified) to show that the total debits of Accounts Receivable agrees with the total credits of the individual sales columns, and the GST Payable CR. column. The proof is illustrated here.

Sales Journal Proof
May 31, 19–

Hardware Sales credit	$4 088.72
Electrical Sales credit	2 706.74
GST Payable credit	475.69
Accounts Receivable debit	$7 271.15

- Once the Sales Journal proof is obtained, the column totals are posted to appropriate General Ledger accounts. The total of the Accounts Receivable column would be posted to the debit side of the Accounts Receivable control account. In the case of the Scarborough Wholesale Hardware example, the totals of the sales columns would be credited to the Hardware Sales and Electrical Sales accounts. The total of the GST Payable CR. column would be credited to the GST Payable account in the GL.

GENERAL LEDGER

Accounts Receivable 103

Debit		Credit	
May 31	7 271.15		

GST Payable 208

Debit		Credit	
		May 31	475.69

Hardware Sales 401

Debit		Credit	
		May 31	4 088.72

Electrical Sales 402

Debit		Credit	
		May 31	2 706.74

- After the column totals are posted to the General Ledger, account numbers of the accounts posted are placed in parentheses directly below each column total. These numbers are important because they indicate that the totals have been posted to the General Ledger.

Since the General Ledger now contains the monthly totals for sales analyzed by product line, a monthly income statement may be prepared as shown in the partial income statement below. (Assume that all sales for the month have been only on a credit basis.)

Scarborough Wholesale Hardware
Partial Income Statement
For the Month Ended May 31, 19—

Revenue from Sales:		
Hardware Sales	$4 088.72	
Electrical Sales	2 706.74	
Total Gross Sales		$6 795.46

The above example illustrates how information in the journal and in the ledger makes for more informative financial statements. In very large businesses with many product lines and departments, the computer is used extensively for the following:

- to produce the columnar Sales Journal
- to update individual customer accounts in the Accounts Receivable ledger and appropriate accounts in the General Ledger
- to prepare month-end trial balances and financial statements

RECORDING SALES RETURNS AND ALLOWANCES

Credit memo: a statement issued by the seller, granting a reduction in the invoice price for damaged or returned goods.

If a customer finds it necessary to return part or all of an order of merchandise, the business uses the contra revenue account called Sales Returns and Allowances (Sales R & A). Under certain conditions, the customer will keep the goods and request an adjustment to the invoice price. If the customer's claim and/or return is justified, the seller will issue a source document called a credit memo. A credit memo granting an allowance to Eglinton Hardware Centre is illustrated.

This document generates a General Journal entry and postings as illustrated opposite.

SCARBOROUGH WHOLESALE HARDWARE
330 PROGRESS AVENUE
SCARBOROUGH, ONTARIO M1P 2Z5

CREDIT MEMO

NO. **CM-01**

TO: Eglinton Hardware Centre
1975 Eglinton Avenue East
Scarborough, Ontario M1L 2N1

DATE: 19– 05 25

Our GST Reg'n No.: #12345	Your Order No. 645890	Our Invoice No. 106

We have credited your account as follows:

Allowance granted for three No. 53Y519 wrench sets received in damaged condition:

3 sets $9.50	$28.50
7% GST	2.00
Total Credits	$30.50

GENERAL JOURNAL Page 3

DATE		ACCOUNT TITLE AND EXPLANATION	POST. REF.	DEBIT	CREDIT
19–					
May	25	Sales Returns and Allowances	402	28 50	
		GST Payable	208	2 00	
		Accounts Receivable/Eglinton Hardware Centre	103/✓		30 50
		Credit memo CM-01, Invoice 106			

Double-posting: posting to the controlling account in the General Ledger and also to the individual account in the subsidiary ledger.

GENERAL LEDGER

Accounts Receivable 103	
	30.50

GST Payable 208	
2.00	

Sales Returns and Allowances 402	
28.50	

SUBSIDIARY LEDGER

Eglinton Hardware Centre	
	30.50

Analysis:

- The original copy of the credit invoice would normally be sent to the customer as a notification to the buyer that the claim has been allowed.

- Another copy is used by the accounting department to record the General Journal entry.
- The General Journal has been used because such entries are usually infrequent. Therefore, a special journal is not required.
- The General Journal entry reduces the amount in the customer's account by the amount authorized on the credit memo. Since a portion of the GST will also be refunded, the GL account GST Payable is debited (reduced). It is important to note that the allowance for GST can **only** be made if a credit memo is issued.
- The credit entry must be **posted twice**: once to the Accounts Receivable control account in the General Ledger, and once to the customer's account in the subsidiary ledger. This keeps the balance in the control account the same as the total of all customers' accounts. (In practice, the customer's account in the Accounts Receivable Ledger is posted directly from the source document regularly.)
- Note the entries beside the credit entry in the Post. Ref. column of the General Journal. The number 103 indicates posting to the Accounts Receivable control account (103). The check mark indicates that the amount has also been posted to the individual customer's account in the General Ledger. Daily posting is required, because the General Journal, if totalled, produces no meaningful number.

Although the General Journal accounts are not normally updated until the end of the month, some accounting systems do update the GL accounts affected by the General Journal on a daily basis. This is especially true when a computer and appropriate General Ledger software are used.

In summary, General Ledger accounts must be updated at the end of each month to produce balances for the preparation of monthly financial statements. All subsidiary ledger accounts must be posted daily to provide current information on these accounts, for example, if a customer wants to know the outstanding balance immediately. When a General Journal is used, posting from this journal may occur daily to make sure **all** accounting information is transferred from this journal to the accounts affected.

PREPARING MONTHLY TRIAL BALANCES

The trial balance is an important accounting check, which is made before financial statements are prepared. This check compares the sum of debits to the sum of credits to ensure that they are equal. Only

General Ledger accounts are checked. Before the GL accounts debits and credits can be checked, it must be confirmed that the total shown in the Accounts Receivable control account is correct. To do this, a Schedule of Accounts Receivable is prepared from the monthly balances of all customer accounts in the subsidiary ledger, as illustrated below.

Schedule of Accounts Receivable: a list of all customers' account balances, the total of which must agree with the control account balance.

The total shown on the Schedule of Accounts Receivable should agree with the figure in the Accounts Receivable control account in the GL. Because these figures were arrived at in different ways, the proof is a good test of accuracy.

Scarborough Wholesale Hardware
Schedule of Accounts Receivable
May 31, 19–

Eglinton Hardware Centre	$1 336.43
Hyland Hardware	952.48
Markham Home Hardware	890.40
Plaza Home Hardware	687.80
Summers Hardware Limited	1 540.00
Thornhill Home Hardware	789.97
Woodbridge Hardware	1 043.57
Total of Accounts Receivable	$7 240.65

GENERAL LEDGER

Accounts Receivable 103

Debit	Credit
7 271.15	30.50
Balance 7 240.65	

ACCOUNTS RECEIVABLE LEDGER

Eglinton Hardware Centre

Debit	Credit
795.12	30.50
571.81	
Balance 1 336.43	

Hyland Hardware

Debit	Credit
952.48	

Markham Home Hardware

Debit	Credit
890.40	

Plaza Home Hardware

Debit	Credit
687.80	

Summers Hardware Limited

Debit	Credit
1 540.00	

Thornhill Home Hardware

Debit	Credit
789.97	

Woodbridge Hardware

Debit	Credit
1043.57	

Here is a useful summary of preparing trial balances under the multiple-journal system:

General Ledger Trial Balance All accounts with balances are listed in the order in which they are found in the GL. Note that the individual accounts payable and accounts receivable are replaced by the control accounts.

Subsidiary Ledger Trial Balances (Schedules of Accounts) A separate alphabetical listing of all subsidiary ledger accounts with **outstanding** balances is called a Schedule of Accounts Receivable. There is a schedule for every separate subsidiary ledger. Two common subsidiary ledgers are the Accounts Receivable Ledger and the Accounts Payable Ledger. The totals of these two schedules must agree with the corresponding control account balances in the GL. Only if they agree can the next step in the cycle—preparation of the worksheet—be done.

In large businesses, different people prepare the trial balances. For example, the accounts receivable clerk may prepare the Schedule of Accounts Receivable, and a General Ledger clerk (or junior accountant) the General Ledger trial balance. In this way, the need for internal control, namely the division of duties or responsibilities, is met.

PROBLEMS

Journalizing common merchandising transactions in a three-column Sales Journal.

P 13-1 The following are transactions for the month of October in the current year for the Red Bay Woodsman Company. Account for GST, where indicated.

Oct. 3 Sold cordwood to J. LaPierre on account. Invoice No. 101. Terms 2/10, n/30. $165.00 plus $11.55 GST.

10 Sold timber logs to Chien Lumber Mills on account. Invoice No. 102. Terms 1/15, n/60. $1500.00 plus $105.00 GST.

20 Sold on account to Singh Wood Products Ltd., 350 bags of cedar chips. Invoice No. 103. These chips cost $3.00 per bag, and were sold n/30. *Hint*: Do not forget to add $73.50 GST.

29 Sold cordwood to Peter Smith on account. Invoice No. 104. Terms 2/10, n/30. $120.00 plus $8.40 GST.

a. In a three-column Sales Journal, page 67, record each of the transactions.

b. Total the journal correctly, checking to ensure that the debit and credit totals are equal. (In other words, do a journal proof or **cross-footing**.)

c. Indicate which entries would be posted **daily** by writing DP in the Post. Ref. column. Indicate which accounts would be posted **monthly** by placing MP under those accounts.

Posting from a multi-column Sales Journal. Preparing a journal proof and a trial balance.

P 13-2 T. Ossington owns and operates a small printing business called Top-Notch Printing in Prince Rupert, British Columbia. The transactions affecting credit sales for the month of June are illustrated below.

SALES JOURNAL Page 15

DATE 19–5		INVOICE NO.	ACCOUNT DEBITED	TERMS	POST. REF.	ACCOUNTS RECEIVABLE DR.	GST PAYABLE CR.	SALES FLIERS CR.	SALES DOCUMENTS CR.	SALES OTHER CR.
June	1	9876	Michael's Ltd.	n/15		197 95	12 95		185 00	
	4	9877	ACME Ads Ltd.	n/15		481 50	31 50	450 00		
	7	9878	A. Deler	n/15		69 55	4 55			65 00
	12	9879	Richmond Chev. Car Sales	n/15		909 50	59 50		600 00	250 00
	19	9880	Michael's Ltd.	n/15		224 70	14 70	210 00		
	25	9881	ACME Ads Ltd.	n/15		352 03	23 03	329 00		
	28	9882	ACME Ads Ltd.	n/15		781 10	51 10	730 00		
	30		Totals			3016 33	197 33	1 719 00	785 00	315 00

GENERAL JOURNAL Page 10

DATE 19–5	ACCOUNT TITLE AND EXPLANATION	POST. REF.	DEBIT	CREDIT
June 21	Sales Returns and Allowances		20 00	
	GST Payable		1 40	
	Accounts Receivable/Michael's Ltd.			21 40
	Invoice No. 9880.			

a. Open a partial General Ledger with the following accounts: Accounts Receivable control (120), GST Payable (208), Sales Fliers (401), Invoice Sales (402), Other Sales (403), and Sales Returns and Allowances Fliers (405).

b. Open an Accounts Receivable Ledger with the following customer accounts: Acme Ads Ltd., 860 Redcliff Dr., Medicine Hat, Alberta, T1A 3E3; A. Deler, 444 13th Ave., Medicine Hat, Alberta, T1A 4F2; Michael's Ltd., 900 West 7th Street, Medicine Hat, Alberta, T1A 3B4; Richmond Chevrolet Car Sales, 3300 13th Ave., Medicine Hat, Alberta, T1A 4F9.

c. Prepare a journal proof of the Sales Journal.

d. Post to the General Ledger and the subsidiary Accounts Receivable Ledger using the information above.

e. Prepare an appropriate schedule at the end of the month to check the accuracy of the control account.

Journalizing to a three-column Sales Journal and posting to ledgers.

Preparing a trial balance.

P 13-3 Pittana's Wholesale Plumbing Supply uses a three-column Sales Journal similar to the one illustrated on page 519. Sales and returns transactions for April are summarized below. Note: GST must be accounted for where indicated.

19-1

April 3 Sold on account to The Water Doctors, Invoice No. 224, goods totalling $410.00 plus $28.70 GST. Terms 2/10, n/30.

6 Sold on account to First Rate Plumbing, Invoice No. 225, $800.00 plus $56.00 GST. Terms 2/10, n/30.

10 Sold on account to AAA Plumbing Contractors, Invoice No. 226, goods for $937.00 plus $65.59 GST. Terms 2/10, n/30.

11 Issued a credit memo on Invoice No. 225 for defective goods, $50.00 plus $3.50 GST.

18 Sold on account to Baker Street Hardware, merchandise totalling $8600.00 plus $602.00 GST. Invoice No. 227; terms 3/10, n/60.

19 Sold on account to Wai Lai Contracting Ltd., $6200 of merchandise plus $434.00 GST. Invoice No. 228; terms 3/10, n/60.

20 Issued a credit memo No. 26 to Wai Lai Contracting Ltd., for incorrect goods, $300.00 plus $21.00 GST.

27 Sold to The Water Doctors, Invoice No. 229, goods for $750.00 plus $52.50 GST. Same terms as previous entry for this business.

a. Open Accounts Receivable Control, GST Payable, Sales, and Sales Returns and Allowances accounts in the General Ledger. Assign appropriate account numbers.

b. Open the following accounts in the Accounts Receivable Ledger: AAA Plumbing Contractors, Baker Street Hardware, First Rate Plumbing, Wai Lai Contracting Ltd. and The Water Doctors.

c. Journalize the transactions in the appropriate journal. *Note*: You may require a General Journal.

d. Make all necessary daily postings as you complete the journal entries. Proof your Sales Journal and make the necessary monthly postings.

e. Verify the control account by preparing a schedule for the Accounts Receivable Ledger, in good form.

MINI-CASES

Designing an accounting system.

MC 13-1 Raymond Wong owns and operates a part-time mail-order computer business. He started the business four years ago in his basement, and it has now grown to the point where Raymond thinks he could expand to a retail location and work full-time. To date, Raymond has done his own bookkeeping, using a General Journal. He anticipates rapid growth in all the areas of his business, which includes hardware sales, software sales, repairs, and installations. ''The problem,'' Raymond says, ''is that I want to make sure each area of the business is profitable. Right now, I haven't got the time or patience to check all the records to find this out.'' Raymond believes so strongly in his products and service that he offers a fifteen-day money-back guarantee, no questions asked. Raymond thinks it works satisfactorily now, but he is not really sure, since he keeps no records of returns, but merely makes a journal entry of a debit to Sales and a credit to Cash.

a. Describe in detail to Raymond a method of recording his transactions that would provide him with the information he needs.

b. Design the forms he would need for **a**.

Using journals in an accounting system.

MC 13-2 Mary Cole, a student in an introductory accounting class, works part-time in the accounting office of a local specialty shop selling only women's fashions. When the topic ''Posting Credit Sales'' was presented, Mary reported that journals are not used in her office. She explained that sales slips are posted directly to the customers' accounts and no entries are made in journals. Furthermore, she stated that management has not yet considered the use of a computer to process accounting data.

a. Name and briefly explain one benefit of the direct posting method identified by Mary.

b. Is there a disadvantage in the elimination of journals in Mary's office? Explain.

c. Can all journals be eliminated from an accounting system? Explain.

JOURNALIZING AND POSTING COST OF GOODS SOLD TRANSACTIONS

At this point, a review of the concepts introduced in Chapter 12 for Cost of Goods Sold is a good idea. Focus your review on the periodic inventory method, which uses the Purchases account, **not** the Inventory account, and related General Ledger accounts to record the purchase of merchandise. This topic will deal only with purchases of merchandise on account in a credit purchases system. Topic 3 will deal with the purchase of merchandise for cash and also the Cash Payments Journal.

ANALYZING THE CREDIT PURCHASES SYSTEM

Purchase invoice: a bill received by the buyer for merchandise purchased on credit.

When a business buys something on account, it expects to receive a document, the invoice, from the seller. The seller of the goods treats this document as a sales invoice. To the business buying the goods, this document is the purchase invoice. The system flowchart opposite traces a purchase on account from beginning to end.

In a large business, a separate person would be assigned to each of these different duties: (1) ordering the merchandise, (2) receiving the merchandise, (3) storing the merchandise, and (4) accounting for the merchandise. Note that no one person is allowed to control all four of the operations involved. The management of the business is exercising the internal control measure of division of responsibility.

Analysis: Study these points as you trace the credit purchase in the flowchart.

STOCKROOM INVENTORY CARD

No. 534 5197
Item Wrench Set
Location: Aisle 12 Bin 5
Maximum 100 Minimum 10

Date	Quant. Rec'd	Unit Cost	Quant. Sold	Balance
Jan. 10	100	2.59		100
20			10	90
Feb. 3			30	60
12			15	45
Mar. 8			35	10
10	90			100
Apr. 10			20	80
25			25	55
30			15	40
May 2			30	10

Preparing the Purchase Requisition

A **purchase requisition** is required from the department requesting the merchandise. In larger businesses, a stockroom **inventory card** would be maintained on each product to keep track of the number currently available for sale. As computerization advances into these businesses, this paper-based task will be replaced with a computer-based inventory, which may be instantly updated by information sent from computerized cash registers. Whether done on paper or with a computer, the basic process is similar. The marginal illustration shows an inventory card used to keep track of wrench sets.

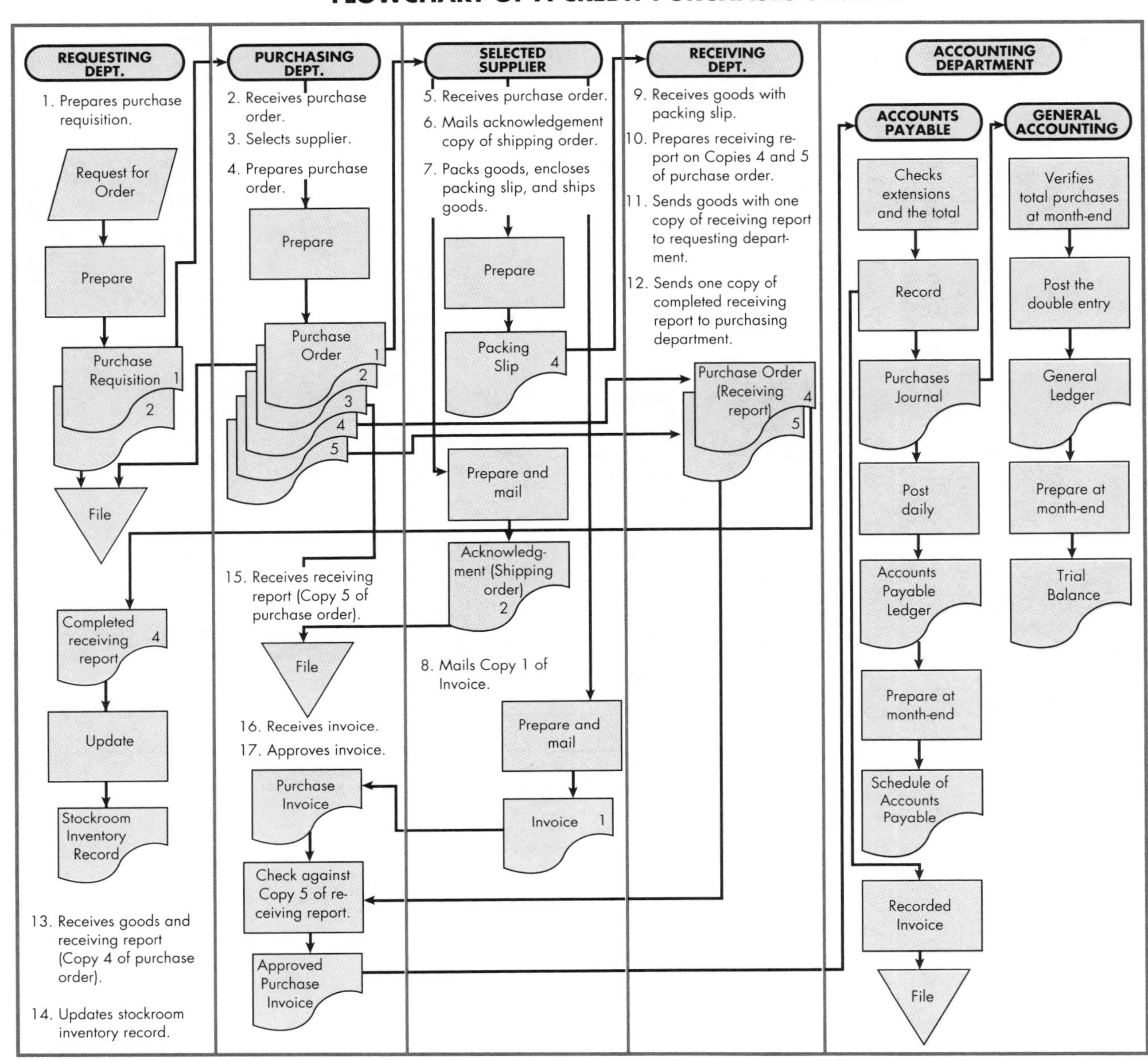
FLOWCHART OF A CREDIT PURCHASES SYSTEM
REQUESTING DEPT.
1. Prepares purchase requisition.
Request for Order
Prepare
Purchase Requisition 1
2
File
Completed receiving report 4
Update
Stockroom Inventory Record
13. Receives goods and receiving report (Copy 4 of purchase order).
14. Updates stockroom inventory record.
PURCHASING DEPT.
2. Receives purchase order.
3. Selects supplier.
4. Prepares purchase order.
Prepare
Purchase Order 1
2
3
4
5
15. Receives receiving report (Copy 5 of purchase order).
File
16. Receives invoice.
17. Approves invoice.
Purchase Invoice
Check against Copy 5 of receiving report.
Approved Purchase Invoice
SELECTED SUPPLIER
5. Receives purchase order.
6. Mails acknowledgement copy of shipping order.
7. Packs goods, encloses packing slip, and ships goods.
Prepare
Packing Slip 4
Prepare and mail
Acknowledgment (Shipping order) 2
8. Mails Copy 1 of Invoice.
Prepare and mail
Invoice 1
RECEIVING DEPT.
9. Receives goods with packing slip.
10. Prepares receiving report on Copies 4 and 5 of purchase order.
11. Sends goods with one copy of receiving report to requesting department.
12. Sends one copy of completed receiving report to purchasing department.
Purchase Order (Receiving report) 4
5
ACCOUNTING DEPARTMENT
ACCOUNTS PAYABLE
Checks extensions and the total
Record
Purchases Journal
Post daily
Accounts Payable Ledger
Prepare at month-end
Schedule of Accounts Payable
Recorded Invoice
File
GENERAL ACCOUNTING
Verifies total purchases at month-end
Post the double entry
General Ledger
Prepare at month-end
Trial Balance

When the number of units declines to a minimum level, a purchase requisition is completed, requesting the number of units necessary to bring the inventory back to the acceptable level.

Preparing the Purchase Order In a large business, the requisition would be sent to the **purchasing department**, which is responsible for finding the best supplier of the requested goods. The purchase conditions — price, delivery, credit terms, and reliability — are carefully considered before a particular supplier is chosen. The purchase order is a multi-part form as shown below. Copy 1 goes to the supplier, who will consider this order as an authorization to ship the goods. In a small business, the owner/manager usually prepares the purchase order, commonly known as the ''P.O.'' This arrangement

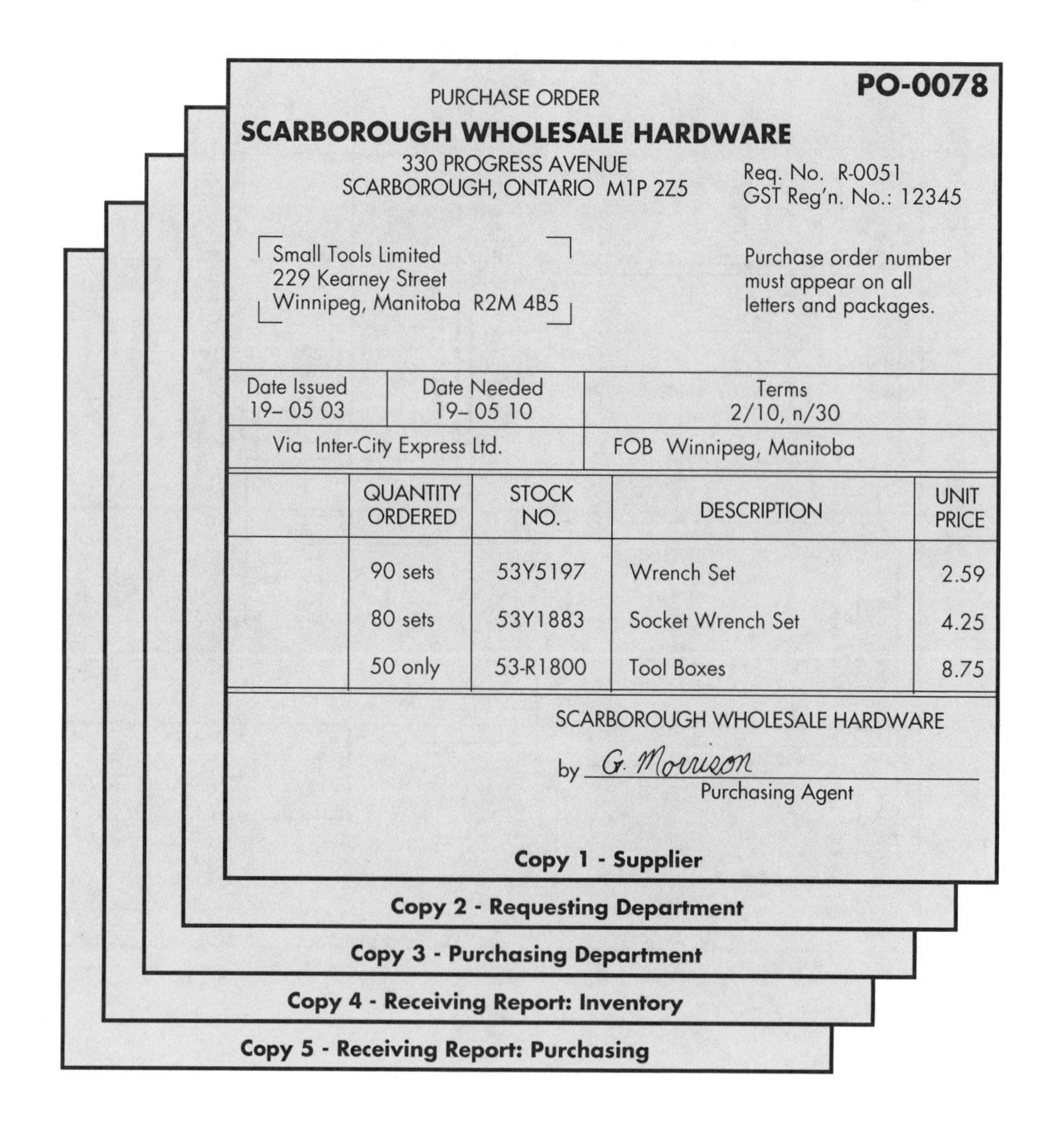

PURCHASE ORDER **PO-0078**

SCARBOROUGH WHOLESALE HARDWARE

330 PROGRESS AVENUE
SCARBOROUGH, ONTARIO M1P 2Z5

Req. No. R-0051
GST Reg'n. No.: 12345

Small Tools Limited
229 Kearney Street
Winnipeg, Manitoba R2M 4B5

Purchase order number must appear on all letters and packages.

Date Issued	Date Needed	Terms
19– 05 03	19– 05 10	2/10, n/30
Via Inter-City Express Ltd.		FOB Winnipeg, Manitoba

	QUANTITY ORDERED	STOCK NO.	DESCRIPTION	UNIT PRICE
	90 sets	53Y5197	Wrench Set	2.59
	80 sets	53Y1883	Socket Wrench Set	4.25
	50 only	53-R1800	Tool Boxes	8.75

SCARBOROUGH WHOLESALE HARDWARE

by G. Morrison
Purchasing Agent

Copy 1 - Supplier

Copy 2 - Requesting Department

Copy 3 - Purchasing Department

Copy 4 - Receiving Report: Inventory

Copy 5 - Receiving Report: Purchasing

replaces the internal control measure—that is, division of duties—in a large business, since the owner has control over the entire process.

In the illustration, there are five copies of the purchase order. Any special instructions, such as shipping instructions, are entered on the form. The illustration contains the shipping instructions "Via Inter-City Express Ltd., FOB Winnipeg, Manitoba," which means several things: (1) a specific trucking business has been chosen (Inter-City Express Ltd.), and (2) the buyer is willing to pay the shipping charges from Winnipeg (the origin of the goods) to its own place of business in Scarborough, Ontario (the destination). This is referred to as the FOB shipping point, meaning that the buyer pays the freight charges from the shipping point. The supplier can therefore quote its lowest price, without having to include a shipping charge. The buyer would then debit this expense to the Freight-in or Transportation-in account, which is used under the periodic inventory system, that in turn becomes part of the Cost of Goods Sold.

FOB Shipping Point: buyer agrees to pay the shipping charges from the shipping point to their place of business.

Sometimes the purchase order may state FOB destination, which means the supplier must pay the shipping costs to the destination. The buyer has no freight charges. For example, FOB Halifax would mean "Free on Board to the destination Halifax," that is, the supplier must make allowance in the price for its expense of shipping the goods. Whoever pays the shipping charges generally selects the method of shipping (truck, train, or air).

FOB Destination: seller agrees to pay the carrier for all transport costs from the shipping point to the buyer's place of business.

Receiving the Merchandise The supplier will ship the goods with a packing slip that lists only quantities, not prices. The actual sales invoice is usually sent separately, and when received by the buyer, it becomes the buyer's purchase invoice.

The **receiving department** uses two copies of the purchase order, as illustrated on page 533, to verify the order when it is received. One copy becomes the **receiving report**, used to update the inventory card or system, and the second copy is sent to the Purchasing department. This copy is used to cross-check the purchase order with the actual invoice when it arrives, to ensure goods were received as ordered.

Receiving the Purchase Invoice When the purchase invoice is received, it is sent to the purchasing department. It is purchasing's responsibility to check the purchase order against the purchase invoice for any changes, before passing it along to the accounting department (or accounts payable division) for payment. Any differences among the purchase order, the shipping order (packing slip), and the purchase invoice must be cleared up before the invoice can be approved for payment. Once the invoice is approved, it is usually stamped and then forwarded to the **accounting department** for

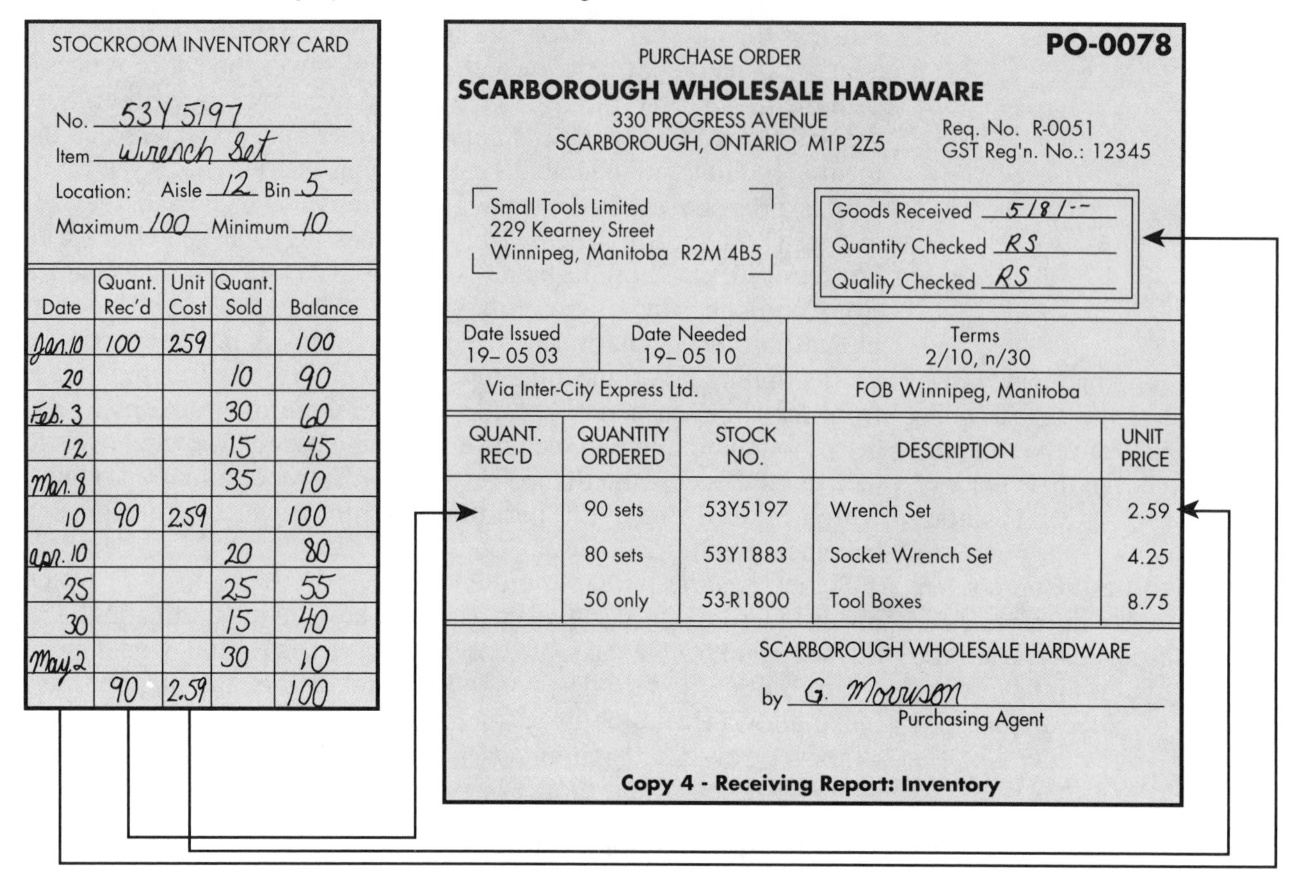

STOCKROOM INVENTORY CARD

No. 53Y5197

Item Wrench Set

Location: Aisle 12 Bin 5

Maximum 100 Minimum 10

Date	Quant. Rec'd	Unit Cost	Quant. Sold	Balance
Jan. 10	100	2.59		100
20			10	90
Feb. 3			30	60
12			15	45
Mar. 8			35	10
10	90	2.59		100
Apr. 10			20	80
25			25	55
30			15	40
May 2			30	10
	90	2.59		100

PURCHASE ORDER **PO-0078**

SCARBOROUGH WHOLESALE HARDWARE

330 PROGRESS AVENUE
SCARBOROUGH, ONTARIO M1P 2Z5

Req. No. R-0051
GST Reg'n. No.: 12345

Small Tools Limited
229 Kearney Street
Winnipeg, Manitoba R2M 4B5

Goods Received 5/8/--
Quantity Checked RS
Quality Checked RS

Date Issued	Date Needed	Terms
19– 05 03	19– 05 10	2/10, n/30
Via Inter-City Express Ltd.		FOB Winnipeg, Manitoba

QUANT. REC'D	QUANTITY ORDERED	STOCK NO.	DESCRIPTION	UNIT PRICE
	90 sets	53Y5197	Wrench Set	2.59
	80 sets	53Y1883	Socket Wrench Set	4.25
	50 only	53-R1800	Tool Boxes	8.75

SCARBOROUGH WHOLESALE HARDWARE

by G. Morrison
Purchasing Agent

Copy 4 - Receiving Report: Inventory

recording and payment. An approved purchase invoice is illustrated on page 537.

Analysis:

- The accounting department now has a source document, which provides objective evidence that a purchase of merchandise had occurred. This evidence is an application of the **objectivity principle**.
- The Goods and Services Tax (GST) is calculated on the amount before taxes at a rate of 7%. Generally, a business will recover any GST paid on merchandise purchased for resale, or for use in the business.
- The total amount owing is recorded in the buyer's books as an account payable. The cost principle indicates that the **laid-down** cost—the total cost of getting the merchandise to the point of sale, including taxes and freight—is to be recorded by the buyer

SMALL TOOLS LIMITED
229 KEARNEY STREET
WINNIPEG, MANITOBA R2M 4B5

INV. NO. **0387**

SOLD TO: Scarborough Wholesale Hardware
330 Progress Avenue
Scarborough, Ontario M1P 2Z5

SHIP TO: Same as above

INVOICE DATE: 19– 05 09
GST REG'N. NO.: 42799
TERMS: 2/10, n/30

Customer Order No.	Date	Shipped Via	FOB	No. of Cartons
PO-0078	19– 05 03	Inter-City Express Ltd.	Winnipeg	3

QUANTITY SHIPPED	STOCK NO.	DESCRIPTION	GST RATE	UNIT PRICE	AMOUNT
90 Sets	53Y5197	Wrench Set	7.0	2.59	233.10
80 Sets	53Y1883	Socket Wrench Set	7.0	4.25	340.00
50 Only	53 [illegible]	Tool Boxes	7.0	8.75	437.50
				AMOUNT BEFORE TAX	1 010.60
				GST 7%	70.74
				TOTAL AMOUNT OWING	1 081.34

APPROVED	DATE 5/10/--
QUANTITIES RECEIVED	G. Morrison
PRICES CHARGED	G. Morrison
EXTENSIONS & TOTALS	S. Davies
DATE PAID	
CHEQUE NO.	

Input tax credit: relates to any GST paid on purchases for resale or use in the business.

as the cost of the merchandise (to be debited to Purchases). The Goods and Services Tax is an **exception** to this principle, since any GST paid on purchases becomes an input tax credit and will reduce the overall GST payable by the business. Therefore, the GST must be subtracted from the **total amount payable**, and the resulting figure is debited to Purchases. In a small business, the GST may be debited to GST Payable. If the transaction was recorded in the General Journal, the entry would look like this:

Purchases	1 010.60	
GST Payable	70.74	
Accounts Payable/Small Tools Limited ...		1 081.34

- Refer to the illustration on page 540 to see how this entry is recorded in a Purchases Journal. *Note*: Alternative methods of accounting for the GST input tax credit are examined in the next chapter.

- In Chapter 9, you learned that the cost principle defined the cost to use when an invoice offered discount terms. The utility bill, illustrated on page 349, shows that if the bill is paid within 15 days a discount is offered. Otherwise, the gross amount is due after this time. In strict accounting theory, the invoice should be recorded at the **cash equivalent price** on the invoice, as of the day it is received and approved. In other words, cost should be recorded as the gross amount less the early payment discount. This is called the net amount method of accounting for invoices, and it strictly follows the cost principle.

Net amount method: a method of accounting for invoices wherein all cash discounts are removed to account for the net cash equivalent price of invoices.

Gross amount method: a method of accounting for invoices wherein the total amount owing shown on the invoice is recorded, and all cash discounts are accounted for only when the cash is transacted.

In practice, however, many merchandising businesses use the gross amount method to account for invoices. Under this method, the gross amount of the invoice is recorded, and no discount is recorded until the invoice is paid within the discount period allowed. At this time, the discount is recorded in a contra account to the invoice. Since the discount is shown as a contra entry (deduction) to the gross invoice amount, the result is that the net cash equivalent price is reported on the financial statements.

We will use the gross amount method to account for all invoices, so that the cost recorded is the total amount payable on the invoice. Discounts will be recorded only as the invoice is paid, and the discount taken. Accounting for discounts will be examined in Topic 3. The net amount method of accounting for invoices is best learned in more advanced courses of financial accounting.

- Scarborough Wholesale Hardware uses the periodic inventory method. Therefore, the cost principle requires that the amount to be recorded is the total of purchases on the invoice, $1010.60. The GST paid ($70.74) may be debited to GST Payable. This amount is an input tax credit, which will reduce the tax payable to the government (GST collected on Sales), and is **not** part of the cost of purchases. *Note:* Alternative methods of accounting for the GST paid are treated in the next chapter.
- Under the periodic system, Purchases is an expense (part of the total expense called Cost of Goods Sold). The expense principle dictates that expenses must be recognized when incurred, which is not necessarily when payment is made. This invoice was stamped and approved on 05 10 —, which is the date Accounting will recognize the debt by making a debit to the Purchases account.

Accounting for the Purchase Invoice The purchasing department sends approved invoices to the division of accounting called Accounts Payable. It is the responsibility of accounts payable:

(1) to record the dollar amount in accordance with the cost principle. For our example, accounts payable will recognize the expense Purchases, since the periodic inventory method is used. It will also recognize the GST calculated on the invoice as a debit to GST Payable

(2) to record the expense Purchases in a special journal designed to record credit purchases

(3) to post purchases transactions to a subsidiary ledger (or Accounts Payable Ledger) to maintain accurate information in individual creditor accounts

(4) to maintain a file on each of the suppliers to ensure that payment is made by the stated due dates and that all available purchase discounts are taken

(5) to update the General Ledger at the end of the month by posting amounts to Purchases, GST Payable, and Accounts Payable control accounts

A/P CLERK

Duties include matching invoices with purchase orders and other documents, and coding invoices and entering them into a computer. Interaction with suppliers also.

2-3 years A/P experience is preferred. Computer knowledge a must.

Excellent working conditions and a comprehensive benefits package.

Please submit your resume and salary requirements to:

In tracing the systems flowchart, you will have noted that several individuals are involved at different stages. This not only improves internal control by dividing responsibility, but also the efficiency of the purchasing system, by allowing each individual to specialize. In a large merchandising business, there might be several clerks working in the Accounts Payable department.

In summary, all credit purchases result in a source document called the **purchase invoice**. It is recorded in a Purchases Journal, followed by the ledger.

ILLUSTRATING THE PURCHASES JOURNAL

Purchases Journal: a chronological record of merchandise purchases on credit.

A special journal called the Purchases Journal is often used to record merchandise purchases on credit. A simple three-column Purchases Journal is illustrated on the next page.

In practice, each business will design the layout of the journal to best meet its needs.

Analysis: Notice the similarity of this journal to the three-column Sales Journal described in Topic 1 (page 515). Both journals are similar. Here are some special points to consider:

- Only credit merchandise purchases are recorded in the three-column Purchases Journal. The Purchases DR. column is used to record the debit to the Purchases account. The GST Payable DR. column is used to record the GST calculated on the purchase invoice. The total of the two amounts, representing the total amount owing, is recorded in the individual accounts payable identified in the Account Credited column.

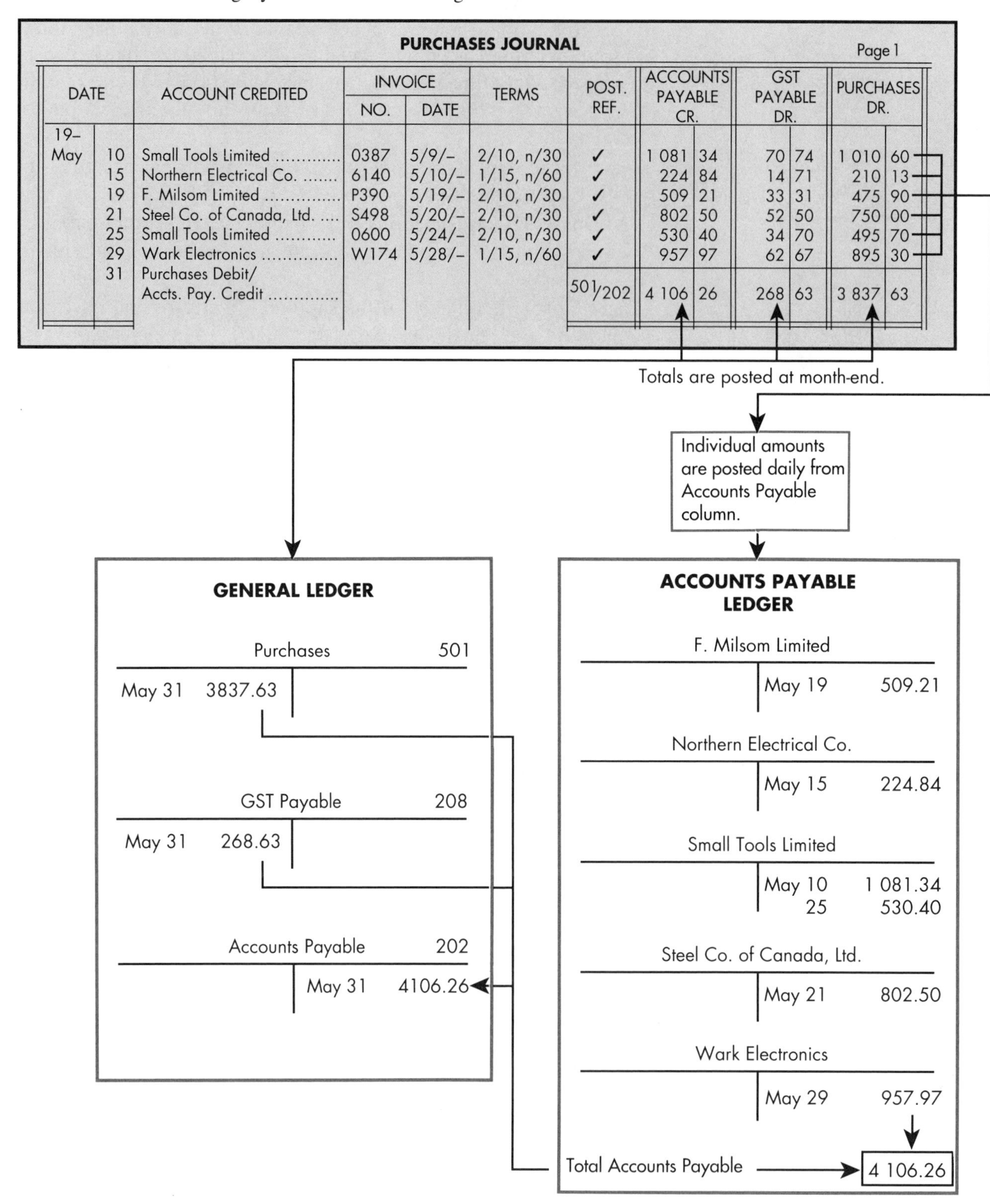

PURCHASES JOURNAL Page 1

DATE		ACCOUNT CREDITED	INVOICE NO.	INVOICE DATE	TERMS	POST. REF.	ACCOUNTS PAYABLE CR.	GST PAYABLE DR.	PURCHASES DR.
19– May	10	Small Tools Limited	0387	5/9/–	2/10, n/30	✓	1 081 34	70 74	1 010 60
	15	Northern Electrical Co.	6140	5/10/–	1/15, n/60	✓	224 84	14 71	210 13
	19	F. Milsom Limited	P390	5/19/–	2/10, n/30	✓	509 21	33 31	475 90
	21	Steel Co. of Canada, Ltd.	S498	5/20/–	2/10, n/30	✓	802 50	52 50	750 00
	25	Small Tools Limited	0600	5/24/–	2/10, n/30	✓	530 40	34 70	495 70
	29	Wark Electronics	W174	5/28/–	1/15, n/60	✓	957 97	62 67	895 30
	31	Purchases Debit/ Accts. Pay. Credit				501/202	4 106 26	268 63	3 837 63

- On the basis of the expense principle, the invoice must be recognized on the date the invoice is approved for payment. The first column, the Date column, is used to record this date, which is usually stamped on the invoice by the purchasing department. Note that this date will usually be several days after the supplier's billing (invoice) date.
- The next column, Account Credited, records the supplier's name.
- Each of the individual creditor's accounts is part of the subsidiary Accounts Payable Ledger, which must be posted daily to ensure up-to-date information is maintained in each creditor's account. Note that the amount to be posted is taken from the Accounts Payable CR. column, which represents the total amount owing.

Accounts Payable Ledger: the file of all individual creditor accounts.

- The next two columns record the invoice number and the invoice date (Invoice No. and Invoice Date). The invoice date is the billing date of the supplier, and should not be confused with the date when the expense is recognized by the buyer.
- The next column (Terms) contains the payment terms, indicating if any discount is available for early payment.
- The next column is the Post. Ref. column. When the entry is posted from the Purchases Journal to the subsidiary Accounts Payable Ledger, a check mark (✓) is placed in this column. *Note:* In the illustration below of the subsidiary ledger account for Small Tools Limited, the invoice numbers are often copied into the Explanation column of the ledger account.

Name Small Tools Limited
Address 229 Kearney Street, Winnipeg, Manitoba R2M 4B5

DATE		EXPLANATION	POST. REF.	DEBIT	CREDIT	BALANCE
19–						
May	10	Inv. 0387	P1		1 081 34	1 081 34
	25	Inv. 0600	P1		530 40	1 611 74

- Finally, the three money columns in the Purchases Journal are used to record a compound entry: a debit to the Purchases account, a debit to the GST Payable account, and a credit to the

Schedule of Accounts Payable: a list of all creditor account balances, the total of which must agree with the controlling account balance in the GL.

Accounts Payable control. This posting is performed at the end of the month. At this time, a Schedule of Accounts Payable is prepared, as shown below. The total of this schedule must agree with the balance in the Accounts Payable control account. Since the posting to the Accounts Payable control and also the posting to the subsidiary Accounts Payable Ledger are usually done by different persons, this provides an important cross-check for internal control purposes. Only if these two balances agree may the accounting process proceed.

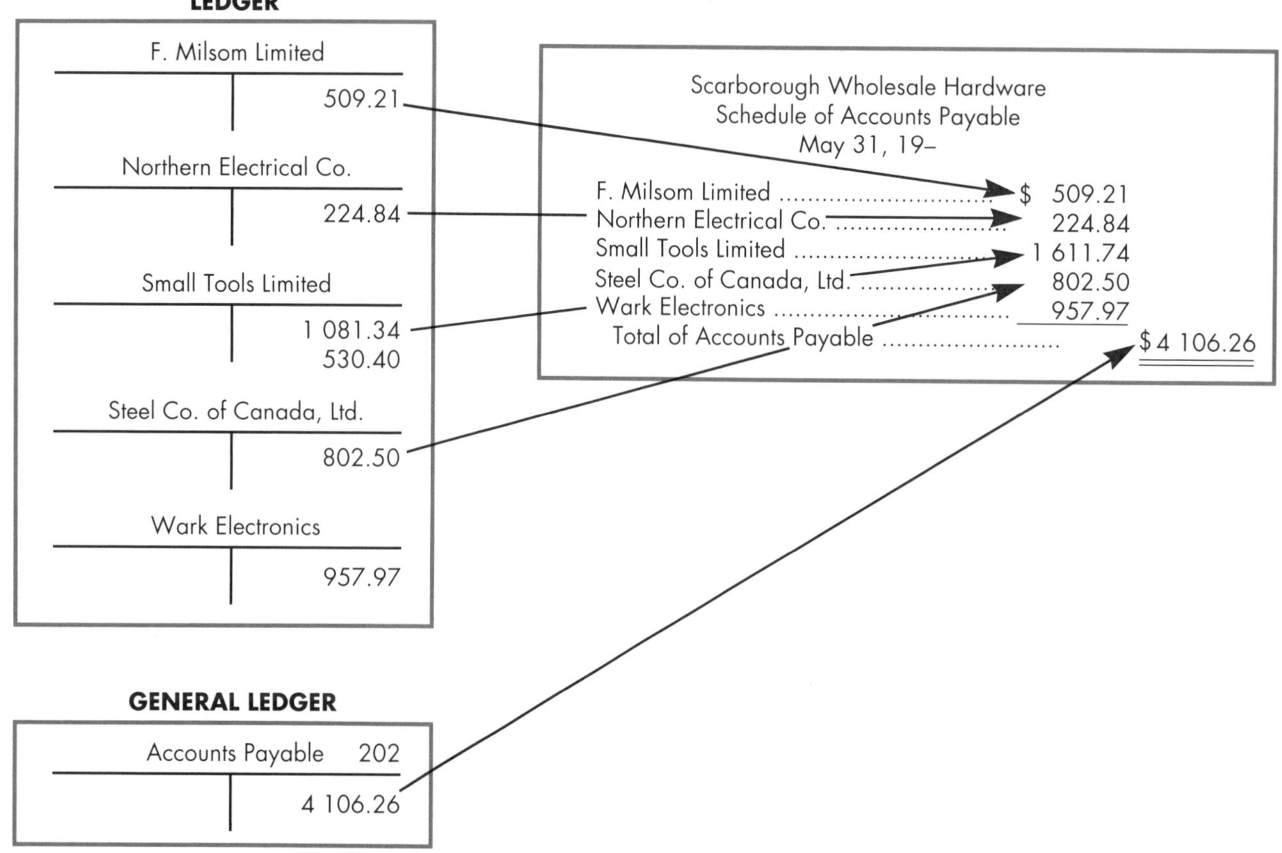

POSTING ACCOUNTS PAYABLE DIRECTLY

In Topic 1, you learned that some businesses prefer to post directly from the source documents to the subsidiary ledger accounts. If this process is followed, two copies of the invoice are usually requested from the seller. One copy is used to update the customer's account in the subsidiary ledger, and the second copy goes to the general accounting division to update the General Ledger accounts and the Purchases and Accounts Payable control accounts.

Some businesses will eliminate the journal completely. Instead, they make an adding machine tape of the totals of all purchase invoices, which is compared at month-end to the Schedule of Payables prepared by the subsidiary ledger clerk. This shortcut illustrates yet another measure of internal control, even if it is somewhat informal.

EXTENDING THE PURCHASES JOURNAL

In modern accounting, there is little need for the simple three-column Purchases Journal. Instead, a **columnar Purchases Journal** is used. It is similar to the columnar Sales Journal, except that purchases are recorded, not sales. The columnar Purchases Journal permits identification of different merchandise purchases, as well as expenses and assets other than merchandise purchases on account and recording of any purchase where there is a credit to Accounts Payable. The columnar Purchases Journal (page 544) illustrates these various entries.

Analysis: The first five columns are similar to those used in the three-column Purchases Journal.

- The first money column is headed Accounts Payable CR. This journal records all transactions that result in an increase in accounts payable. The total amount owing is recorded in this column.
- The offsetting debit will be placed in either the **Purchases** column or the **Sundries** column, and the **GST Payable DR.** column. The total entries to Purchases added to the GST Payable DR. entry must equal the amount in the Accounts Payable CR. column.
- The GST Payable DR. column serves to record the tax inputs, that is, the GST we will pay on Purchases. This will eventually be offset against GST Payable CR. which is collected on sales.
- The Purchases column records the debit entry (for the purchases only, not including GST) for the type of merchandise purchased. Here, two types of merchandise are recorded: hardware and electrical.
- The Sundries column will receive debits to any account except Purchases, such as an expense account or an asset account.

Before any posting to the General Ledger occurs, a Purchases Journal Proof or **cross-footing** must be done to ensure accuracy of debits and

COLUMNAR PURCHASES JOURNAL

DATE		ACCOUNT CREDITED	INVOICE NO.	INVOICE DATE	TERMS	POST. REF.	ACCOUNTS PAYABLE CR.	
19– May	2	Bell Canada	81390	5/1/–	net 30 days	✓	17	05
	10	Small Tools Limited	0387	5/9/–	2/10, n/30	✓	1 081	34
	10	Inter-City Express Ltd.	4187	5/10/–	net 30 days	✓	24	15
	15	Northern Electrical Co.	6140	5/10/–	1/15, n/60	✓	224	84
	16	Public Utilities Co.	4X20	5/16/–	net 10 days	✓	45	80
	19	F. Milsom Limited..............	P390	5/19/–	2/10, n/30	✓	509	21
	21	Steel Co. of Canada, Ltd. ...	S498	5/20/–	2/10, n/30	✓	802	50
	25	Small Tools Limited	0600	5/24/–	2/10, n/30	✓	530	40
	29	Wark Electronics	W174	5/28/–	1/15, n/60	✓	957	97
	30	Craig Motors, Ltd.	X200	5/28/–	net 60 days	✓	5 000	00
	31	Totals					9 193	26
							(202)	

credits. This proof compares the total of all debit columns to the total of the Accounts Payable column, and these totals should be the same.

Posting to individual creditor accounts must be done daily, to ensure accurate, up-to-date information. The amount posted must be the total amount owing: Purchases plus GST. Proof of posting is a check mark in the Post. Ref. column.

Purchases Journal Proof

Hardware Purchases DR.	$2 456.30
Electrical Purchases DR.	1 381.33
GST Payable DR.	601.43
Sundries DR.	4 754.20
Accounts Payable CR.	$9 193.26

Posting to the General Ledger is done at month-end. For each money column headed by a GL account (Accounts Payable CR., Purchases Hardware DR., GST Payable DR., etc.), the account number to which it is posted is placed in brackets, just below the total. The existence of this number in brackets is proof that the total has been posted to the General Ledger.

Each entry in the Sundries column requires a separate posting to the GL. Note that the Sundries column has its own Post. Ref. column in which to indicate the account that has been posted. Since each entry has been posted individually, the total of the column is not posted.

Page 1

GST PAYABLE DR.	PURCHASES HARDWARE DR.	PURCHASES ELECTRICAL DR.	SUNDRIES ACCOUNT DEBITED	SUNDRIES POST. REF.	SUNDRIES AMOUNT DR.
1 12			Telephone Expense	515	15 93
70 74	1 010 60				
1 58			Hardware Transport-in	503	22 57
14 71		210 13			
3 00			Utilities Expense	516	42 80
33 31	200 00	275 90			
52 50	750 00				
34 70	495 70				
62 67		895 30			
327 10			Delivery Equipment	112	4 672 90
601 43	2456 30	1 381 33			4 754 20
(208)	(501)	(502)			(✓)

When all entries in the Sundries column have been posted, a check mark is placed below the total.

RECORDING TRANSPORTATION-IN

You have learned that an FOB shipping point quoted on a purchase order means that the buyer is prepared to pay the shipping cost from the seller's place of business to the buyer's location. If the carrier's bill is paid in cash at the time of delivery, the entry will be recorded in the Cash Payments Journal, by debiting Transportation-in (or Freight-in), debiting GST Payable, and crediting Cash for the total of the freight bill and the GST.

If, however, the carrier allows credit terms, which is frequently done if the carrier is used regularly, an account payable must be credited. In the columnar journal, this is easily done in the Sundries column. In a one-column journal system, the entry must be recorded in the General Journal, as illustrated on page 546.

Analysis:

- The first debit entry is to GST Payable.
- The second debit is to an expense account called Transportation-in, which will become part of the larger expense called Cost of Goods Sold.
- The credit entry is to Accounts Payable/(customer name).

GENERAL JOURNAL Page 2

DATE		ACCOUNT TITLE AND EXPLANATION	POST. REF.	DEBIT		CREDIT	
19–							
May	10	GST Payable	208	1	58		
		Transportation-in	502	22	57		
		Accts. Pay./Inter-City Express Ltd.	202/✓			24	15
		Freight charges payable in 30 days.					

- The credit entry must be posted twice: once to the Accounts Payable control account, and once to the individual creditor's account in the Accounts Payable Ledger.
- A check mark is placed in the Post. Ref. column of the General Journal, next to the account number of the Accounts Payable control, to indicate that it has also been posted to the individual creditor's account in the subsidiary ledger.

RECORDING PURCHASES RETURNS AND ALLOWANCES

Sometimes a business returns purchased goods because they are unsuitable or damaged. In other cases, the goods may be still usable, although not perfect, so the buyer may request an allowance on the price. Other reasons for adjustments include a mathematical error on the invoice, or a shortage in shipped goods. When such an occurrence arises, many of the larger merchandising businesses will prepare a debit memo. The debit memo is a source document sent to the seller to indicate that the seller's Accounts Payable account will be debited as a result of the return or requested allowance.

Debit memo: a source document created by the buyer to notify the seller that the account payable has been decreased by the amount of the purchase return or allowance requested.

Analysis:

- A minimum of two copies is usually made.
- The original copy is sent to the seller, while the buyer retains the second copy, which is sent to the accounting department.
- The debit memo contains a complete explanation of the reason for the debit.
- Note that the GST charged on the goods is also accounted for. *Note:* The return of part of the GST is **only** possible if a debit memo is issued.
- It is signed by the authorized purchasing agent.

SCARBOROUGH WHOLESALE HARDWARE DEBIT MEMO

330 PROGRESS AVENUE
SCARBOROUGH, ONTARIO M1P 2Z5

DM-14

TO: Small Tools Limited
ADDRESS: 229 Kearney Street
Winnipeg, Manitoba R2M 4B5

DATE: 19– 05 26
GST REG'N. NO.: 12345

WE DEBIT YOUR ACCOUNT AS FOLLOWS:

Return of merchandise. 10 only Tool Boxes No. 53-R1800 arrived badly damaged and are being returned via Inter-City Express Ltd.

10 @$8.75	$87.50
7% GST Payable	6.13
Total Debit	$93.63

References: Your Invoice No. 0600, dated 19– 05 24
Our Order No. PO-0091, dated 19– 05 20

G. Morrison
Purchasing Agent

Because transactions involving returns and allowances occur infrequently, the entries are usually made to the General Journal, not a special journal. Refer to the illustration below.

GENERAL JOURNAL Page 2

DATE		ACCOUNT TITLE AND EXPLANATION	POST. REF.	DEBIT		CREDIT	
19–							
May	26	Accts. Pay./Small Tools Limited	202/✓	93	63		
		Purchases Returns and Allowances	503			87	50
		GST Payable	208			6	13
		Issued DM-14 for return of damaged goods.					

Analysis:

- The debit entry must be double-posted: once to the Accounts Payable control account in the GL, and once to the individual creditor's account in the Accounts Payable Ledger. Once posted, the Post. Ref. column will show the account number of the GL account, and a check mark for the subsidiary ledger posting.
- The credit to Purchases Returns and Allowances is posted to the GL. The net effect of this entry is to decrease the cost of Purchases. Therefore, Purchases Returns and Allowances is contra to the Purchases account.

- The credit to GST Payable is posted to the GL account.

When the seller receives the purchaser's debit memo, the seller will prepare a credit memo similar to that discussed in Topic 1. When the purchaser receives a copy of this credit memo, he or she will attach it to the debit memo and file both. No accounting entry is necessary.

Some businesses do not prepare a debit memo, but instead send the goods back to the seller. The seller then prepares a credit memo, which, when received by the purchaser, will serve as the source document for the entry. The actual practice depends on the arrangements between buyer and seller. In any event, the result is to reduce the cost of Purchases from the original amount.

You have now examined all but one account necessary to prepare the Cost of Goods Sold figure: Inventory (beginning balance), Purchases, Purchases Returns and Allowances, and Transportation-in. The remaining account, Purchases Discounts, affects the payment of cash and is dealt with in Topic 3.

PROBLEMS

Journalizing and posting to the Purchases Journal.

P 13-4 R.M. Benham Company is a wholesale business that uses the three-column Purchases Journal. The following journal illustrates some typical business transactions.

PURCHASES JOURNAL — Page 34

DATE		ACCOUNT CREDITED	INVOICE NO.	INVOICE DATE	TERMS	POST. REF.	ACCOUNTS PAYABLE CR.	GST PAYABLE DR.	PURCHASES DR.
19–									
Apr.	2	Kelly Supplier	1214	Apr. 1	2/10, n/30		8 560 00	560 00	8 000 00
	5	C. & O. Wholesaler.......	6334	Apr. 3	1/15, n/60		12 840 00	840 00	12 000 00
	10	Mini-Works Ltd.	A-663	Apr. 10	n/30		5 885 00	385 00	5 500 00
	13	Kelly Supplier	1383	Apr. 12	2/10, n/30		8 025 00	525 00	7 500 00
							35 310 00	2 310 00	33 000 00

a. Open General Ledger accounts for Accounts Payable (207), GST Payable (208), and Purchases (501).

b. Open a subsidiary ledger for accounts payable accounts for C. & O. Wholesaler, Kelly Supplier, and Mini-Works Ltd.

c. Complete the appropriate daily postings, and then the mid-month postings for R.M. Benham Ltd.

Journalizing and posting using the Purchases Journal, GL, and Accounts Payable Ledger.

P 13-5 Dripless Plumbing Supply Company uses a three-column Purchases Journal. The following are approved purchasing transactions for the month of March. You must account for GST where indicated.

Mar. 4 Purchased merchandise from DJS Enterprises, dated Mar. 1, Invoice No. 47392; terms 2/10, n/30, for $9200 plus $644 GST.

7 Bought small parts from Sutherland Distributors, dated Mar. 6, Invoice No. 287 for $6500 plus $455 GST; terms n/30.

12 Bought 10 000 metres of copper pipe at $2.50 per metre from El Cupric Inc. Invoice No. 45829 dated Mar. 9. Terms: 2/10, 1/15, n/30. Add $1750 GST.

22 Purchased glues and adhesives from The Very Tacky Company for $11 000 plus $770 GST. Invoice No. 1600 dated Mar. 12 with terms 2/10, n/60.

27 Bought general purpose plumbing supplies from Marikosan Plumbing Wholesalers. Invoice No. 348 dated Mar. 25 for $7300 plus $511 GST, with terms 2/10, n/30.

a. In the General Ledger, open accounts for Purchases, GST Payable, and Accounts Payable (control). Assign appropriate account numbers.

b. In a subsidiary ledger, open the necessary creditor accounts.

c. Complete the journalizing in a journal similar to the one used in Problem 13-5. *Note*: You must account for any GST Payable.

d. Post the daily entries to the appropriate accounts.

e. Post the month-end totals.

f. Prepare a Schedule of Accounts Payable in proper form, to prove the accuracy of the Accounts Payable control account.

Journalizing and posting using multi-column Purchases Journal, GL, and Accounts Payable Ledger.

Preparing a journal proof and supporting schedule.

P 13-6 Challenge Problem Krawchuk Greenhouses Ltd. uses a General Journal, a multi-column Purchases Journal, a General Ledger, and a subsidiary Accounts Payable Ledger. They sell the following product lines: evergreen trees, bulbs and seeds, box plants, and fertilizers and chemicals. The business purchases all items for resale, except box plants, which they grow in their greenhouses. The terms offered by their suppliers are as follows:
B.C. Tree Farms: orders over $1000 are 2/10, n/30 with free shipping; otherwise, terms are n/60, FOB shipping point.
CIL Canada Ltd.: 1/15, n/60; FOB shipping point.

Dow Chemical of Canada Ltd.: n/45, FOB destination.
Holland Bulb and Seed Suppliers: n/30 for orders under $450, and 2/10, n/30 for orders of $450 or more. FOB shipping point.

a. Open the following GL accounts and assign appropriate account numbers: Accounts Payable Control, Purchases/ Evergreens; Purchases/Bulbs & Seeds, Purchases/Fertilizers and Chemicals, Purchases Returns and Allowances, Transportation-in, Utilities Expense, Gas Expense, and GST Payable.

b. Open a subsidiary ledger for Accounts Payable for: B.C. Tree Farms, 175 Broadway E., Vancouver, British Columbia, V5T 1W2; CIL Inc., Courtright, Ontario; CP Express, P.O. Box 1674, Don Mills, Ontario, M3C 2H8; Dow Chemical of Canada Ltd., Modeland Road, Sarnia, Ontario, N7S 4X4; Holland Bulbs & Seed Suppliers, 921 Erie E., Windsor, Ontario; Varna PUC, Varna, Ontario; Union Gas Limited, Chatham, Ontario.

c. Record the following transactions for the month of April in the appropriate journal. *Note:* You must calculate GST Payable on all purchases. For the purposes of this exercise, assume all items incur GST (which may not, in fact, be true when the new legislation is implemented in practice). Use the following columns in the columnar Purchases Journal.

COLUMNAR PURCHASES JOURNAL

DATE	ACCOUNT CREDITED	INVOICE		TERMS	POST. REF.	ACCOUNTS PAYABLE CR.	GST PAYABLE DR.	PURCHASES DR.		SUNDRIES		
		NO.	DATE							ACCOUNT DR.	PR	AMOUNT

Apr. 1 Bought 1200 1.5-m spruce trees @ $1.80 each from B.C. Tree Farms, Invoice No. 0093, dated April 1.

1 Purchased from Holland Bulbs & Seeds, 5000 tulip bulbs @ $0.75 each, 15 000 dozen daffodil bulbs @ $0.59 per dozen, and 17 000 seed packets at $0.20 per packet. Invoice No. M-1666 dated Mar. 26.

4 Purchased from CIL, Invoice No. 89-775, dated Apr. 2, 3200 22-kg bags of lawn fertilizer @ $20 per bag.

7 Invoice received from Union Gas for natural gas used to heat greenhouses during February. Due date May 2. Invoice No. 3377 dated April 2 for $10 500.

11 CP Express delivered order (Invoice No. M-1666). Offered terms of n/30 for charges of $73.

15 Purchased from Dow Chemical, 200 10-kg bags of broadleaf weed killer @ $22 per bag; 14 dozen cans of all-purpose insecticide @ $43.50 per dozen. Invoice No. DZ-3245 dated April 15.

20 CP Express delivered the CIL order. $142. Terms n/30.

24 Received an Invoice No. ON-3362, dated April 15, from Varna PUC for $433. Terms n/25 from billing date.

30 Received an order from B.C. Tree Farms by CN Express. When the shipment was examined, it was found that 19 trees were 1 m or less in height, which would cost a total of $67 less than the invoice price. The company intends to keep the trees but is requesting an adjustment as indicated. Debit memo DM-156 was prepared.

d. Post all daily items as they occur to the appropriate ledger.

e. Total the Purchases Journal, prepare a journal proof, and post the month-end totals.

f. Prepare a Schedule of Accounts Payable to verify the GL control account.

MINI-CASES

Determining posting date from a columnar journal.

MC 13-3 In posting purchases invoices recorded in a columnar Purchases Journal, a confused accounting clerk raised this question: ''What date do I use when I post amounts from the journal to the individual creditor accounts? Should I use the date of the invoice, the date when the invoice is approved for payment, or the current date when I actually post the accounts?''

a. How would you answer this clerk's question? Explain your answer.

Discussing laid-down cost principle and the GST.

MC 13-4 Two students with differing views were heard discussing interpretations of the cost (laid-down) principle when it was applied to Purchases invoices containing the new federal GST. Student A stated that the strict theoretical interpretation of the cost principle requires that the amount of the GST paid must be part of the total to be debited to the asset acquired, or the expense incurred. On the other hand, student B disagrees by saying that any GST on a purchase invoice, paid by a business, is regarded as a GST input credit, and as such, the amount is not part of the laid-down cost of acquiring the asset, or incurring an expense.

a. Whose view do you support? Explain your answer.

JOURNALIZING AND POSTING CASH TRANSACTIONS

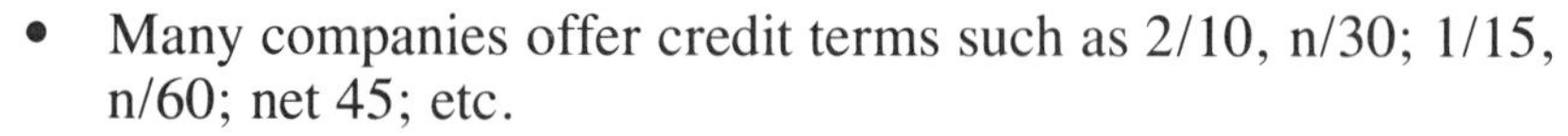

Much of this topic will be review, since accounting for Cash was discussed in Part 2. The focus of this chapter is the cash discount offered to a credit customer.

RECEIVING CASH FROM CREDIT CUSTOMERS

Earlier you learned two important points:

- Many companies offer credit terms such as 2/10, n/30; 1/15, n/60; net 45; etc.
- Many companies require that a source document be prepared for every cheque that is received. This **Remittance Slip** provides internal control. A typical remittance slip is illustrated in the margin.

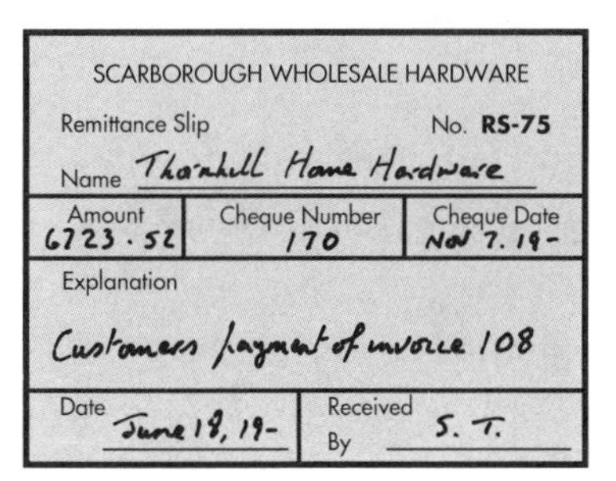

SCARBOROUGH WHOLESALE HARDWARE

Remittance Slip No. **RS-75**

Name Thornhill Home Hardware

Amount	Cheque Number	Cheque Date
6723.52	170	Nov 7. 19-

Explanation

Customers payment of invoice 108

Date June 18, 19- Received By S. T.

Analysis:

- As with most source documents, the remittance slips are pre-numbered. This allows accounting to control all incoming cheques, since each slip must be accounted for.
- The person opening the mail would complete the slip with the following information: the name of the drawer (the party who signed the cheque), the amount, the cheque number, the cheque date, a simple explanation for the cheque, the date the cheque was received, and the person's initials.
- The cheque will be endorsed ''For Deposit Only,'' to prevent unauthorized cashing of the cheque, and it is included in the daily bank deposit.
- The remittance slip is sent to accounting for recording.

In the Accounting department, the remittance slip is treated as the source document. All cheques received are debited to Cash, for the full amount of the cheque. In this example, the cheque is a customer's payment for an invoice, and therefore Accounts Receivable is credited for the invoice amount. Because we are using the **gross amount method**, and the customer has paid within the discount period, the account Sales Discount must be debited with the amount of the discount. Examine the entry as recorded in the Cash Receipts Journal illustrated opposite.

Journal Entry For Cash Discount

CASH RECEIPTS JOURNAL Page 3

DATE		ACCOUNT CREDITED	EXPLANATION	POST. REF.	GENERAL LEDGER CR.		ACCOUNTS RECEIVABLE CR.		GST PAYABLE CR.		SALES DISCOUNT DR.		NET CASH DR.	
19– June	8	Thornhill Home Hardware	For Invoice 108	✓			789	97			14	77	775	20

Discount Calculation

$789.97	Total amount owing
– 51.68	GST
$738.29	Sale Only

$738.29
x 0.02
14.7658
Rounded to $14.77

Analysis:

- Special money columns are used, as in the other special journals, in order that the double entry may be recorded on a single line.
- The Net Cash DR. column records the actual amount of the cheque.
- The Sales Discount DR. column records the amount of the cash discount, if any, as calculated. See the calculation in the margin. *Note:* Any discount must be calculated only on the total before taxes, **not** the total amount owing, which includes the total plus GST. For the reason of administrative simplicity, it is not possible to refund part of the GST when a cash discount is given to a customer. The discount is calculated on only the total before taxes and no accounting for GST takes place. However, the seller does record the full amount of the GST invoiced and collected, and the purchaser records the GST paid as an input tax credit. Since the purchaser recovers any GST paid as an input tax credit, this treatment of the GST does not result in additional costs to the business.

Note: If the net amount method of invoicing is used, GST is calculated only on the net amount; any subsequent charge for late payment will *not* be GST taxable.

- The total amount owing is recorded in the Accounts Receivable CR. column.
- A check of the debits and credits on this line indicates that the entry balances.

Net Cash DR.	+	Sales Discount DR.	=	Accounts Receivable CR.
$775.20	+	$14.77	=	$789.97

- The first money column, General Ledger CR., would be used to credit any GL account other than Accounts Receivable. Examine the illustration opposite.

POSTING FROM THE CASH RECEIPTS JOURNAL DURING THE MONTH

A complete set of entries recorded in a Cash Receipts Journal is illustrated opposite.

Analysis:

- The four money columns, Accounts Receivable CR., Sales Discount DR., GST Payable CR, and Net Cash DR. list month-end totals. The posting of these totals will be discussed later. The GST Payable CR. column appears in this journal, since it is needed to record the GST charged on cash sales. As you will see in the illustration, the total cash sales for the week is also recorded in this journal.
- The General Ledger CR. column contains entries to many unrelated accounts so that each entry must be posted individually, on the day it was recorded. The total will be useful for cross-footing, but cannot be posted itself.
- Once each General Ledger CR. entry is posted to an account, the account number is written in the Post. Ref. column beside the first money column, as proof of posting.
- Each entry in the Accounts Receivable CR. column is also posted daily, for the same reasons. These postings will be made to the individual customer accounts in the subsidiary Accounts Receivable Ledger. The proof that posting has taken place is a check mark in the Post. Ref. column. The corresponding posting reference in the ledger account is the journal name and page number, for example, "CRJ3" represents "Cash Receipts Journal, page 3."

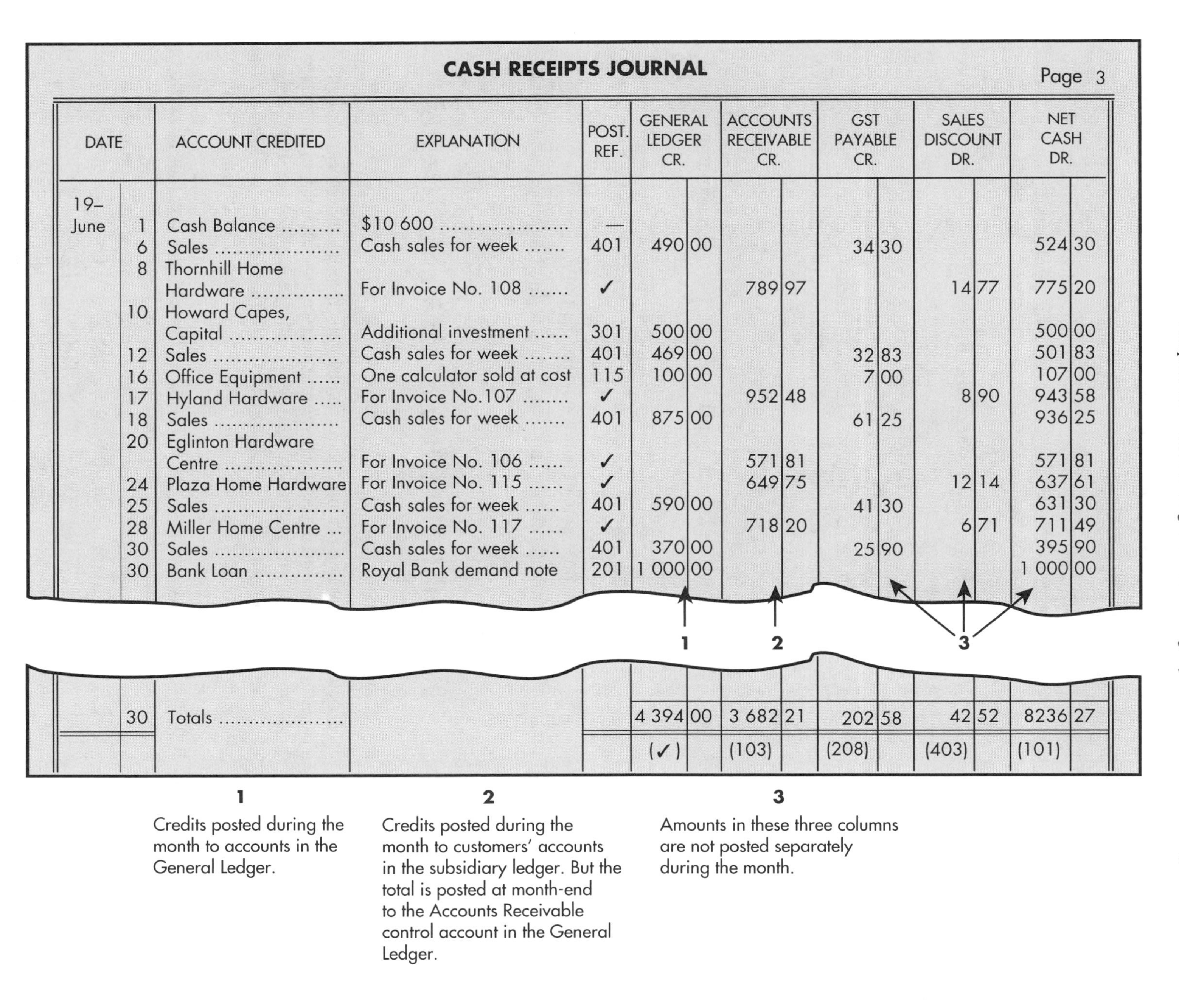

CASH RECEIPTS JOURNAL Page 3

DATE		ACCOUNT CREDITED	EXPLANATION	POST. REF.	GENERAL LEDGER CR.	ACCOUNTS RECEIVABLE CR.	GST PAYABLE CR.	SALES DISCOUNT DR.	NET CASH DR.
19–									
June	1	Cash Balance	$10 600	—					
	6	Sales	Cash sales for week	401	490 00		34 30		524 30
	8	Thornhill Home Hardware	For Invoice No. 108	✓		789 97		14 77	775 20
	10	Howard Capes, Capital	Additional investment	301	500 00				500 00
	12	Sales	Cash sales for week	401	469 00		32 83		501 83
	16	Office Equipment	One calculator sold at cost	115	100 00		7 00		107 00
	17	Hyland Hardware	For Invoice No.107	✓		952 48		8 90	943 58
	18	Sales	Cash sales for week	401	875 00		61 25		936 25
	20	Eglinton Hardware Centre	For Invoice No. 106	✓		571 81			571 81
	24	Plaza Home Hardware	For Invoice No. 115	✓		649 75		12 14	637 61
	25	Sales	Cash sales for week	401	590 00		41 30		631 30
	28	Miller Home Centre ...	For Invoice No. 117	✓		718 20		6 71	711 49
	30	Sales	Cash sales for week	401	370 00		25 90		395 90
	30	Bank Loan	Royal Bank demand note	201	1 000 00				1 000 00
	30	Totals			4 394 00	3 682 21	202 58	42 52	8236 27
					(✓)	(103)	(208)	(403)	(101)

1
Credits posted during the month to accounts in the General Ledger.

2
Credits posted during the month to customers' accounts in the subsidiary ledger. But the total is posted at month-end to the Accounts Receivable control account in the General Ledger.

3
Amounts in these three columns are not posted separately during the month.

POSTING FROM THE CASH RECEIPTS JOURNAL AT MONTH-END

42.52	+1
8 236.27	+1
4 394.00	−1
3 682.21	−1
202.58	−1
0.00	T1

Prior to the posting at month-end, the money columns must be checked for mathematical accuracy and debits must equal credits. You can do this by simply adding the debits and then subtracting credits to obtain a zero balance, as you did with the trial balance zero-proof. Refer to the marginal illustration.

Analysis:

- Once the equality of debits and credits has been proved, the journal may be ruled off for the month, as illustrated.
- The totals of the money columns representing one account (Accounts Receivable CR., Sales Discount DR., and GST Payable CR.) are posted to the appropriate General Ledger accounts.
- Since each of the individual entries in the General Ledger CR. column have been posted daily, the total is not posted. For this reason, a check mark is placed in the Post. Ref. column instead of an account number.
- Although individual entries are posted daily from the Accounts Receivable column to the subsidiary ledger, the total must also be posted to the General Ledger control account. This total will therefore have an account number below it.
- Note that all other totals are posted to their appropriate General Ledger accounts, and the account numbers are written below the totals.

PREPARING MONTHLY STATEMENTS TO CREDIT CUSTOMERS

Many companies mail a monthly account statement to their credit customers. The statement indicates this important information: this month's opening balance (last month's closing balance), all purchases made during the month in chronological order, all payments received on account during the month, any finance charges added to the account due to late payment, and the outstanding balance as of the date of preparation.

There are two common forms of statement: the non-descriptive form and the descriptive form.

In the non-descriptive form, illustrated on page 557, only the date, reference number, and amount for individual entries are shown. The statement usually has a tear-off portion identifying the customer account and balance, which is returned with the payment. This ensures that payments are recorded in the correct account.

SCARBOROUGH WHOLESALE HARDWARE
330 PROGRESS AVENUE
SCARBOROUGH, ONTARIO M1P 2Z5

STATEMENT OF ACCOUNT

TO: Thornhill Home Hardware
67 Grandview Avenue
Thornhill, Ontario L3T 1H3

Date 19– 06 30

Amount Enclosed $ ____________

Please return this stub with your cheque.

DATE		REFERENCE	CHARGES	CREDITS	BALANCE
Balance Forwarded: 19– 05 30					775.20
June	8	RS-75		775.20	0.00
	25	120	1 000.00		1 000.00
	27	CM-08		100.00	900.00

In the descriptive statement on page 558, details of each entry are given, allowing the customer to perform a detailed check against his or her own records. This type of statement usually also has a tear-off portion.

With either type of statement, the customer should check the statement against personal records, in case of error. Any discrepancies should be resolved as soon as possible with the seller's Accounts Receivable department.

Cycle billing: billing according to alphabetical sequence of last names at designated dates during the month.

In a large business with many customers, such as utility companies and department stores, it is not practical to send a statement to all customers on the same day. These firms practise cycle billing, where the list of customers is broken down into alphabetical groups. For example, customers in the group A to F may be billed on the 10th of the month, those in G to N will be billed on the 15th, those in O to S, on the 20th, and so on. This system reduces a massive work volume at the end of the month.

Tickler File

MAKING PAYMENTS TO CREDITORS

Credit terms outline the terms and dates for payment. In a large business, the accounts payable department is responsible for payment of all invoices within a certain time period. If sellers offer discounts such as 2/10, n/30, this department has even a greater responsibility, since these discounts can be substantial.

As discussed in Chapter 9, a tickler filing system enables the department to file invoices according to discount due date. The tickler system will have one file, or slot, for each day of the month. Every

MAY'S DEPARTMENT STORE

AMOUNT ENCLOSED $

PLEASE ENTER AMOUNT OF PAYMENT ABOVE.

MRS H J KELLER
843 DRIFTWOOD RD
LONDON ONT N6H 4H9

BRANCH AND ACCOUNT NUMBER	
457	740-351-40
TORONTO	

PLEASE DETACH THIS PORTION OF STATEMENT AND RETURN WITH YOUR PAYMENT

YOUR ACCOUNT NUMBER: 740-351-40 YOUR BRANCH NUMBER: 457

STATEMENT DATE	PREVIOUS BALANCE	TOTAL CHARGES	TOTAL CREDITS	NEW BALANCE	PAYMENT REQUIRED
SEP 1/–	40.03	34.51	40.03	34.51	34.51

DATE	REFERENCE	GENERAL DESCRIPTION	AMOUNT
		CREDITS	
Aug 14	1870073		
	BOX 4000	PAYMENT - THANK YOU	40.03 CR
		CHARGES	
Aug 22	5271645		
	LONDON	MISSES CO ORDINATES	16.67
Aug 22	5271645		
	LONDON	MISSES CO ORDINATES	13.34
Aug 22	5271645	GST	2.10
Aug 22	5271645	PROV. SALES TAX	2.40

day, the clerk will pull the invoices from that day's file. The authorized person will decide whether or not to take the discount. If approval is given for payment, the invoice can be paid by cheque in the full amount less the discount. If, for some reason, payment is delayed, the invoice is refiled in the tickler system on the last day for payment.

Good internal control requires that all payments be made by serially numbered cheques. This provides a ''paper trail'' for an audit, and helps prevent unauthorized payments. The cheque record or cheque voucher should be checked for accuracy before a transaction is journalized. The journal entry should include the following:

- a debit entry to Accounts Payable for the total amount owing
- a credit entry to Purchases Discounts for the amount of the cash discount, if any, calculated on the price of the goods only, exclusive of GST

- a credit entry to Cash for the exact amount of the cheque

A well-designed Cash Payments Journal would allow the above compound entry to be entered on one line. The journal should also be designed to accommodate a variety of debit transactions that might result from a cheque being issued. Examine the illustration below.

CASH PAYMENTS JOURNAL Page 3

DATE		ACCOUNT DEBIT	EXPLANATION	CHEQUE NO.	POST. REF.	GENERAL LEDGER DR.	ACCOUNTS PAYABLE DR.	GST PAYABLE DR.	PURCHASES DISCOUNT CR.	NET CASH CR.
19–										
June	1	Mortgage Payable	June mortgage	612	220	250.00				250.00
	4	Small Tools Limited	Invoice No. 0600 ..	613	✓		408.20		7.63	400.57
	5	Office Equip.	Typewriter	614	115	600.00		42.00		642.00
	7	Transportation-in	Reimer Transport	615	402	40.00		2.80		42.80
	12	Wark Electronics	Invoice No. W174 .	616	✓		895.30		8.37	886.93
	16	Telephone Expense	June bill	617	518	18.95		1.33		20.28
	18	R. Stone Limited	On account	618	✓		100.00			100.00
	20	Advertising Expense ..	City Press	619	519	175.00		12.25		187.25
	23	Northern Electrical Co.	Invoice No. 6270 ..	620	✓		750.90		7.02	743.88
	26	Utilities Expense	Gas & electricity	621	520	38.50		2.70		41.20
	28	J. Thompson Ltd.	Invoice A25K30	622	✓		800.00		14.95	785.05
	30	Howard Capes, Drawing	Personal withdrawal	623	302	100.00				100.00
	30	Totals				1 222.45	2 954.40	61.08	37.97	4 199.96
						(✓)	(202)	(208)	(504)	(101)

Analysis:

- Five money columns allow the clerk to record any cash payment transaction on a single line.
- As with all columnar journals, each line must have equal debits and credits.
- Since each line represents a cash payment, there will be a cheque number for each line.
- Entries in the Accounts Payable DR. column will be posted daily to the individual creditor accounts in the subsidiary ledger. A check mark in the Post. Ref. column indicates the item has been posted.
- Entries in the General Ledger DR. column will also be posted daily to the appropriate accounts in the GL. The account number to which it is posted will appear in the Post. Ref. column. Since

each entry is posted daily, the total is not posted. This fact is indicated by a check mark in brackets below the total.

- Prior to month-end posting, the journal must be checked to ensure that debits equal credits. This check is essential before the totals are posted to the General Ledger. Once this proof is completed, the journal may be ruled off for the month.
- Column totals, except for General Ledger DR., are posted at the end of the month to the General Ledger. The account number to which the total is posted is placed in brackets below the total.

SUMMARIZING TRANSACTIONS AFFECTING SALES AND COST OF GOODS SOLD

Because a periodic inventory system is being followed, the Inventory account has not been affected. Also bear in mind that the Gross Amount method of recording invoices has been used. Therefore, entries for cash discounts for sales and purchases occurs at the time the cash is actually received or paid out.

Study the chart that follows. In particular, try to relate each transaction to the correct journal.

TRANSACTION	SOURCE DOCUMENT	RECORDED IN	POSTING PRINCIPLES
Sales for cash.	Cash proof	Columnar Cash Receipts Journal	Cash debit is posted as part of the total at month-end. Individual Sales credits are posted during the month unless a special column is provided for Sales Credit. GST is posted at month-end.
Sales returns or allowances for cash.	Cash proof	Columnar Cash Payments Journal	Individual Sales Returns and Allowances are posted from General Ledger Debit column during the month. Cash credit is posted as part of the total Net Cash Credit at month-end.
Sales on credit.	Sales invoice	Three–column Sales Journal	Individual customer accounts are posted daily to Accounts Receivable Ledger. Column total is posted at month-end to debit Accounts Receivable and to credit Sales in the General Ledger, and to credit GST Payable.
		Columnar Sales Journal	Daily posting from Accounts Receivable Debit column to subsidiary ledger. Column totals are posted at month-end to appropriate accounts of the General Ledger.

(Continued on next page.)

(Continued from opposite page.)

Sales returns or allowances for credit.	Credit memo	General Journal	Daily posting as transaction occurs. Debits are posted to Sales Returns and Allowances in General Ledger; and GST Payable in GL; credit is double-posted: once to the customer's account in the subsidiary ledger, and once to Accounts Receivable control account in the General Ledger.
Customer's cheque received.	Remittance slip	Columnar Cash Receipts Journal	Daily posting from Accounts Receivable Credit column to customer accounts filed in subsidiary ledger. At month-end the column totals are posted to the General Ledger for Accounts Receivable CR., Sales Discount DR., and Cash DR.
Merchandise purchases for cash.	Cheque record (stub or voucher)	Columnar Cash Payments Journal	Individual Purchases debit is posted during month unless a special column is provided for Purchases Debit. Cash credit is posted as part of the total Cash Credit column at month-end. GST is posted at month-end.
Purchases returns or allowances for cash.	Remittance slip	Columnar Cash Receipts Journal	Cash debited is posted as part of the total at month-end from the special money column for Cash Debit. Purchases Returns and Allowances are posted during the month from the General Ledger Credit column. GST is posted at month-end.
Merchandise purchases for cash.	Purchase invoice	Two-column Purchases Journal	Daily posting to credit of individual creditors' accounts filed in the subsidiary Ledger. Entry to General Ledger for total posted at month-end to debit of Purchases. Total of purchases + GST to credit of Account Payable control account.
		Columnar Purchases Journal	Daily posting from Accounts Payable Credit column to individual accounts in subsidiary Ledger. All column totals are posted at month-end to appropriate accounts in the General Ledger.
Purchases returns or allowances for credit.	Debit memo (Some firms wait for seller's credit memo.)	General Journal	Daily posting as transaction occurs. Posting of debit entry: once to individual creditor's account in subsidiary ledger, and once to Accounts Payable control account in GL. The credit entry is posted to Purchases Returns and Allowances in the General Ledger, for amount of purchases; GST to GST payable.
Cheque issued in payment of purchase invoice.	Cheque record (stub or voucher)	Columnar Cash Payments Journal	Daily posting of amounts recorded in Accounts Payable Debit column to individual accounts in subsidiary ledger. Column totals are posted at month-end to debit of Accounts Payable, to credit of Purchases Discount, and to credit of Cash.

PROBLEMS

Journalizing in a Cash Receipts Journal.

Totalling and proving columns.

Analyzing postings.

P 13-7 Paulo's Fishing Shack is in the business of selling fishing equipment, and also does repairs.

a. In a journal similar to the one illustrated below, record the cash inflow transactions that follow. *Note:* Paulo extends credit terms of 2/10, n/30 on all credit sales. GST must be accounted for where indicated.

EXAMPLE:

CASH RECEIPTS JOURNAL Page 21

DATE	ACCOUNT CREDIT	EXPLANATION	POST. REF.	GENERAL LEDGER CR.	ACCOUNTS RECEIVABLE CR.	SALES DISCOUNT DR.	GST PAYABLE CR.	CASH DR.
July 1	Cash Balance	$550						

July 5 ABCO Fishing Repairs Ltd. paid their account in full after the discount period. $220.00 plus $15.40 GST.
7 Cash sales for the week totalled $2113.00 plus GST.
10 Sold equipment for $840.00 plus $58.80 GST.
14 Cash sales for the week totalled $1987.00 plus GST.
16 The Fishing Hole Inc. sent a cheque for $619.19 to pay Invoice No. 459 in full. The invoice was billed at $630.99. The Fishing Hole Inc. has taken a 2% cash discount of $11.80
30 Borrowed $2000.00 in the form of a demand loan from the Bank of Montreal. (No GST implications.)

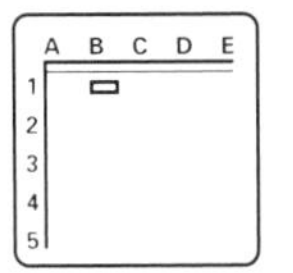

b. Total the journal at month-end. Prove the journal and indicate in the Post. Ref. column (with a DP) those items which should be posted on a daily basis, assuming a subsidiary ledger is used. Place an MP in the correct locations to indicate where any monthly posting takes place.

Journalizing in a Cash Payments Journal.

Totalling and proving columns.

Analyzing postings.

P 13-8 The Handyman Hardware Store uses a Cash Payments Journal similar to the one on page 559.

a. Using a similar Cash Payments Journal, record the following cash outflow transactions. You must account for GST as indicated.

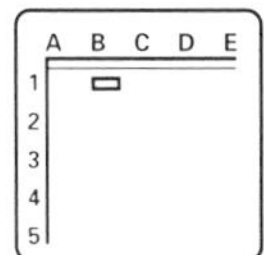

Aug. 3 Paid Burton Hardware Suppliers in full. Invoice No. 247 for $3210.00 offered terms of 2/10, n/30. Cheque No. 234 for $3145.80 was dated on the last day of the discount period and mailed.

8 Paid the monthly mortgage payment of $1053 with Cheque No. 235. (Ignore GST in this transaction.) *Note:* All further payments will be by consecutively numbered cheques.

15 Paid Mascarin Suppliers in full. Invoice No. 4398 totalled $1749.00, including $114.42 GST on terms n/30.

21 Paid Northern Electric for Invoice No. 23345, $145.00 plus $10.15 GST.

28 The owner, Cheryl Sigfrid, withdrew funds for personal use, $500.00.

31 Paid $2010 to the newspaper, *The Enquiring Mind*, for advertising. Invoice No. 00239 offered no terms of discount. This amount included $140.70 GST.

Journalizing to the Cash Receipts and Cash Payments Journal.

Preparing a journal proof.

P 13-9 Challenge Problem DePietro Toys Ltd., located in Saint John, New Brunswick, uses a Cash Receipts Journal and a Cash Payments Journal similar to those illustrated in this chapter. The following transactions took place during the month of February. Credit terms are 2/10, n/60 for all customers. All cash payments **include GST**, unless otherwise noted; cash sales figures do not—you must calculate and add.

Feb. 1 Cash balance $9200.00.

2 Received from C. Leung $389.00 as payment in full on her account. No discount was taken. (There is no GST accounting here. Why?)

3 Paid the electricity bill from the PUC for the month of January. Issued Cheque No. 807 for $639.00 including $41.80 GST.

6 Cash sales for the week totalled $6245.00. Calculate and add GST.

8 The owner, G. DePietro, invested an additional $7600.00 into the business.

10 The company purchased new office equipment from Grand & Toy Ltd. for $1600.00 plus $112.00 GST, issuing Cheque No. 808.

12 Issued Cheque No. 809 for $1050.00 to pay Mattel Toys in full. The firm took full advantage of the 2% discount offered. Total amount owing was $1070.00.
13 Cash sales for the week totalled $8733.00.
15 Issued Cheque No. 810 for $4372.00 to pay the firm's employees. GST does not apply to payroll transactions.
18 Received on account from Tellawoman Company $3434.58 as payment in full of their account of $3500.00, which included GST of $228.97. This business took the discount allowed.
20 Cash sales for the week totalled $6482.00.
24 The owner issued Cheque No. 811 for $750.00 to pay her personal rent. (There is no GST on residential rent.)
27 Cash sales for the week totalled $6862.00.
28 Issued Cheque No. 812 to Carlin Real Estate Co. The cheque for $1926.00 represents the rent on the company building for the month of March. GST of $126.00 is included.
28 Issued Cheque No. 813 for $4124.00 which represents payroll for the employees.

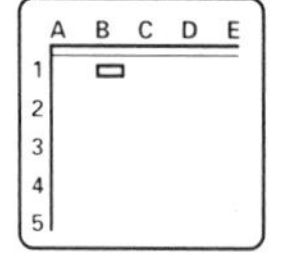

a. Journalize the above transactions in the Cash Receipts and Cash Payments Journals.

b. Indicate in both journals the items which must be posted daily, by placing DP in the Post. Ref. columns.

c. Total the journals and prepare journal proofs to ensure equality of the debits and credits.

MINI-CASES

Analyzing posting requirements of a columnar journal.

MC 13-5 Cara Hughes is a high-school student who is part of a co-op program. Her placement is with a small advertising firm that has always used a single journal system. Cara has mentioned the multi-purpose columnar journal to her employer, Sam A. Nachronistic. Sam dislikes the paperwork that goes with a single journal, and has asked Cara to explain the columnar journal. After her explanation, he has one question, "I see how this saves me a great deal of time. But I see a further shortcut. I don't have to post the total of the Accounts Receivable column, since I have already posted each individual entry to the customers' accounts; I know exactly what they owe me. I can save even more time!''

a. Do you agree with Sam? Explain any shortcomings in Sam's idea.

Analyzing internal controls.

MC 13-6 Dan Davis has no accounting background, but through persistence has landed an entry-level job in the Accounts Payable section of a major department store. Dan's job is to fill out cheques for payment to suppliers. Once filled out, the cheques are signed by the comptroller and mailed. During his first day on the job, Dan is anxious to perform well and to make no mistakes. All went well until about 15:00, when he made an error filling out a cheque. Not thinking, he tore up the cheque, discarded it, and filled out a new one from the cheque register. When Dan took the stack of cheques to the comptroller for signature at the end of the day, the comptroller immediately noticed a cheque was missing, and inquired of Dan.

a. How did the comptroller know a cheque was missing?

b. As the comptroller, explain briefly to Dan the importance of keeping all cheques, even those that are unusable.

USING THE COMBINATION JOURNAL

You have now been introduced to an accounting five journal system comprising of four specialized journals, the General Journal, the General Ledger, and the subsidiary ledger system. This system is very valuable to a large company that processes a sufficient number of transactions to require separate people working in each of these areas. In such a business, the division of responsibilities is very important to maintain good internal control.

In many small businesses, however, the number of transactions is usually small enough that one employee does all the bookkeeping without the aid of a computer. In fact, it is often the owner who maintains the books. This does not mean that the business is limited to using the General Journal. Accountants have designed a journal which combines all the journals into one. It is referred to as the Combination Journal, sometimes known as the synoptic or multi-columned journal. Synoptic means to present a general view of the whole. The Combination Journal is used to record all types of transactions, because it includes many columns: individual columns for accounts used frequently, such as Cash, Accounts Payable, GST Payable, and Accounts Receivable, and a Sundry or GL account column

Combination Journal: a multi-columned journal that takes the place of the entire five-journal system.

for all other entries. The opposite illustration demonstrates how these columns can be arranged to allow all the transactions to be recorded in the one journal.

Analysis: Let's now examine a series of transactions in the General Journal and compare them to similar entries in the Combination Journal. The General Journal format is illustrated below.

General Journal Format

19–				
Sept. 25	Cash	101	5 000	
	P. Bet, Capital	301		5 000
	Owner invested cash in the business.*			

	Land	130	20 000	
	Building	132	60 000	
	GST Payable	208	5 600	
	Cash	101		10 000
	Mtg. Payable	250		75 600
	Bought land and building with cash and mortgage.*			

*Normally an explanation requires only one line in the General Journal.

- The owner invests $5000 cash in the business.
  The General Journal entry would appear as shown above. Note that the entry requires three lines: one for the debit entry to Cash, one for the credit entry to Capital, and one for the explanation. Now refer to the illustration of the Combination Journal opposite. Note that the entire transaction is recorded on one line, and requires only one posting. The General Journal entry required two postings.
- The company buys land for $20 000 and a building for $60 000. It agrees to pay $10 000 in cash, and the rest in the form of a mortgage.
  The General Journal entry requires six lines and five postings, whereas the Combination Journal requires only three lines and three postings, as shown.
- The company sells goods on account to the XYZ Company for $7000. Remember 7% GST is added to all sales.

COMBINATION JOURNAL Page 3

	DATE 19–	ACCOUNT TITLE AND EXPLANATION	POST. REF.	GENERAL LEDGER DEBIT	GENERAL LEDGER CREDIT	ACCOUNTS RECEIVABLE DEBIT	ACCOUNTS RECEIVABLE CREDIT	ACCOUNTS PAYABLE DEBIT	ACCOUNTS PAYABLE CREDIT	PURCHASES DEBIT	PURCHASES DISCOUNTS CREDIT	SALES CREDIT	GST PAYABLE DEBIT	GST PAYABLE CREDIT	CASH DEBIT	CASH CREDIT	CHQ. NO.	
1	Sept. 1	Cash Balance $5 600	–															1
2	3	J. Ball Invoice No. 106	✓			107 00						100 00		7 00				2
3	5	Postage Expense } Replenish Petty Cash	512	32 00									2 24					3
4		Transportation-in }	508	55 00									3 85					4
5		P. Bet, Drawing }	303	100 00														5
6		Supplies Expense	520	23 00									1 61			217 70	736	6
7	7	Cash Sales for Week	–									400 00		28 00	428 00			7
8	10	J. Ball Payment Rec'd	✓				100 00								100 00			8
9	12	M.&C. Ltd. 2/10, n/30	✓						620 60	580 00			40 60					9
10	14	Parkview Motors–Truck	140	10 000 00					10 700 00				700 00					10
11	14	Bank Loan Payable	202		10 000 00										10 000 00			11
32	19	Carried Forward		10 210 00 10 210 00	10 000 00 10 000 00	107 00 107 00	100 00 100 00		11 320 60 11 320 60	580 00 580 00		500 00 500 00	748 30 748 30	35 00 35 00	10 528 00 10 528 00	217 70 217 70		32
		↑ Page End	↑ Daily Posting															

COMBINATION JOURNAL Page 4

	DATE 19–	ACCOUNT TITLE AND EXPLANATION	POST. REF.	GENERAL LEDGER DEBIT	GENERAL LEDGER CREDIT	ACCOUNTS RECEIVABLE DEBIT	ACCOUNTS RECEIVABLE CREDIT	ACCOUNTS PAYABLE DEBIT	ACCOUNTS PAYABLE CREDIT	PURCHASES DEBIT	PURCHASES DISCOUNT CREDIT	SALES CREDIT	GST PAYABLE DEBIT	GST PAYABLE CREDIT	CASH DEBIT	CASH CREDIT	CHQ. NO.	
1	Sept. 19	Balance Brought Forward ..	–	10 210 00	10 000 00	107 00	100 00		11 320 60	580 00		500 00	748 30	35 00	10 528 00	217 70		1
2	19	Cash Sales for Week	–									200 00		14 00	214 00			2
3	20	Telephone Expense	530	85 00									5 95			90 95	737	3
4	25	P. Bet, Capital (Investment)	301		5 000 00										5 000 00			4
5	25	Land	130	20 000 00														5
6	25	Building	132	60 000 00														6
7	25	Mortgage Payable	250		75 600 00								5 600 00			10 000 00	738	7
8	25	XYZ Company	✓			7 490 00						7 000 00		490 00				8
9	30	Wages Expense	528	500 00												500 00	739	9
10	30	Totals		90 795 00	90 600 00	7 597 00	100 00		11 320 60	580 00		7 700 00	6 354 25	539 00	15 742 00	10 808 65		10
11				(✓)	(✓)	(110)	(110)		(205)	(501)		(401)	(208)	(208)	(101)	(101)		11

Accts. Rec./XYZ Co.	210/✓	7 490	
Sales	401		7 000
GST Payable			490
Sold goods on account to XYZ Company.*			

*Normally an explanation requires only one line in the General Journal.

The General Journal requires four lines of journal space and four postings. Remember that the accounts receivable must be posted twice; once to the subsidiary ledger account and once to the control account. The greatest advantage of the Combination Journal in this transaction is this: it requires only one line of journal space and only one posting to the subsidiary ledger. The sales entry is under its own column heading, and it, as well as the GST and the Accounts Receivable control account, can be posted once at the end of the month, as totals.

Advantages of the Combination Journal

- Time is saved because fewer daily postings are required. Many items are recorded in specialized columns and are posted only as totals at month-end. Thus, there is less chance of error.
- It requires less space for the same information.
- Since all journal entries are combined, a business can be easily reviewed from this type of journal. No other sources need to be consulted.
- One person can easily handle all the journalizing for a small business on one page.
- In the developmental stages of a new business, the Combination Journal may be ideal because it can be readily expanded into a five-journal system.

Disadvantages of the Combination Journal

- The frequency of error increases with the number of columns used.
- The journal must be large, making it awkward and cumbersome.
- Some entries may require several lines of journal space, whereas a compound entry involves several accounts for which there are no special money columns.

- The internal control measure of division of duties is violated, because one person handles all the journal entries.
- This system is best suited to manual accounting, as it does not lend itself easily to computerized accounting.

MORE ABOUT THE COMBINATION JOURNAL

Refer to the illustration of the Combination Journal on page 567 as you examine the following points.

- The name, month(s) of operation, and page number of the journal are at the top.
- The column headings highlight the key accounts used in the business. These will vary from business to business. Columns are provided for explanations, posting references, and cheque numbers.
- Daily posting is required from the General Ledger column to the GL accounts, and from the Accounts Receivable and Accounts Payable columns to the subsidiary ledgers, if used. The other accounts with their own columns can be posted to the GL as totals at the end of the month.
- At the end of each page of work, the columns are totalled and "pinhead totals"—very tiny pencilled numbers—appear at the bottom of the columns. These totals are used to proof the accuracy of debits and credits on that page, before the totals are entered as "Brought forward" on the top of the next page. *Note:* Pinhead totals are illustrated here only; they are omitted in future illustrations.
- When the Combination Journal is being closed, a procedure similar to the one described above is used. The columns are totalled showing pinhead totals. The total of debits is compared to the total of credits. If accurate, the totals are copied in ink, and the date and money columns are double-underlined.

Note: As each column total is posted, the GL account number is recorded beneath the total in brackets. Also, you will see that the GL column totals are not posted, because each of the individual items was posted daily. Check marks in brackets below the double-underlined totals verify this fact.

TOPIC 4 PROBLEMS

Analyzing the Combination Journal.

P 13-10 Refer to the Combination Journal on page 567, and then answer the following questions.

a. Why is the cash balance of $5600.00 not recorded in the Cash account debit column?

b. Why are four lines used to record the transaction of September 5?

c. What is the purpose of the debit and credit columns in the General Ledger?

d. Under what circumstances would a transaction be recorded in the General Journal, rather than the Combination Journal?

e. Are there any numbers that should be posted under the circumstances in **d**?

f. Outline briefly the steps required to complete the journal at month-end.

g. Locate a transaction that was completed on one line in the Combination Journal that would take multiple lines in the General Journal.

Journalizing common transactions in a Combination Journal.

P 13-11 Crystal George practices law under her own name. She employs a receptionist who also maintains her accounting records. The records consist of a Combination Journal and a General Ledger. (The GL will not be used in this problem.)

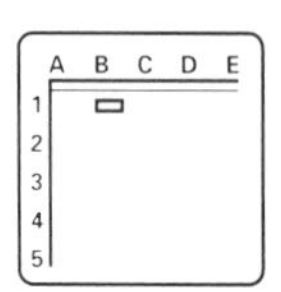

a. Complete the necessary journal entries in the Combination Journal for the month of July, 19—. Read all transactions first and decide which accounts will receive special money columns in your Combination Journal.

July 1 Opening cash balance is $2450.00.
3 Received on account from Connelly Computer Ltd. $1600.00 plus $112.00 GST.
6 C. George invested an additional $5000.00 into the practice.
6 Paid CCH Canadian Ltd. $2086.50 for taxation books, added to the firm's law library. GST of $136.50 is included in the cheque. Cheque No. 251. (Cheque numbers from here on are sequential.)
7 Paid receptionist weekly pay, $325.00. (No GST.)
10 Performed legal services for L. Benham on account. $2200.00. Calculate and add GST Payable.

12 Purchased office supplies on account from Wilson's Office Supplies Ltd. for $300.00, terms n/30. (Calculate and add GST Payable.)
15 Paid receptionist weekly pay, $325.00.
16 Paid the monthly telephone bill of $190.00. (Calculate and add GST Payable.)
20 Performed legal services for Tex Brackett for cash. $1676.00. (Calculate and add GST Payable.)
21 Paid receptionist weekly pay, $325.00.
23 C. George wrote a cheque in the amount of $500.00 for personal use.
24 Arranged a loan for $12 000.00 with the Royal Bank of Canada. Cash was deposited in the chequing account. (There is no GST.)
27 Bought additional office furniture from Steelcase Office Furniture Company on account for $3246.00, terms 2/10, n/60. Calculate and add GST Payable.
28 Paid receptionist weekly pay of $325.00.
30 Paid PUC Invoice No. 666 in full in the amount of $478.00 for electricity. This amount includes GST Payable of $31.27.
30 Paid Globetrotters Realty $1765.50 for August rent. This includes GST Payable of $115.50.

b. Total the journal, check the totals to prove that debits equal credits, and then rule off the journal for month-end.

Journalizing and posting using Combination Journal, GL, and subsidiary ledgers.

Preparing a supporting schedule and trial balance.

P 13-12 Cosentino Photo Studios provides portrait sittings and all types of photographic equipment and supplies. The firm uses a Combination Journal, a General Ledger, subsidiary Accounts Receivable Ledger, and subsidiary Accounts Payable Ledger. The owner's husband, Ross Cosentino, does all the bookkeeping. This allows June to concentrate on the photographic end of the business. An employee handles the daily counter sales and reservations. All cash outflow is paid by cheque. The firm offers credit terms of n/30 to all customers.

a. Open GL accounts as follows: Cash, $8700; Accounts Receivable control; Inventory; Processing Supplies; Equipment; Accounts Payable control; GST Payable; June Cosentino, Capital, $20 000; June Cosentino, Drawing; Photo Services; Photographic Sales; Photographic Sales Returns & Allowances; Purchases; Purchases Returns & Allowances; Purchases Discounts; Rent Expense, $1800; Telephone Expense; Wages Expense.

b. Open the following Accounts Receivable Ledger accounts: M. Davis, H. Morrison, and G. Yee.

c. Open the following Accounts Payable Ledger accounts: Adams Photo Services, Fuji Films Ltd., and Kodak Ltd.

d. Journalize the following transactions for the month of October, starting on page 23. Account for GST where indicated.

Oct. 2 Bought photo supplies from Kodak Ltd. on account for resale, $1250 plus GST.
4 Took family portrait for M. Davis. Invoice No. 2845, $249 plus GST.
5 Sold camera equipment to G. Yee on account for $875 plus GST on Invoice No. 2846.
8 Paid the monthly rent to Aziz Realty Ltd., for $1800 plus GST, using Cheque No. 835.
10 Paid Bell Canada for the monthly phone bill of $42 plus GST, using the next consecutively numbered cheque.
13 Received an Invoice No. T-324 dated Oct. 12 from Adams Photo Services. It was for services performed for the company (use Purchases) for $750 plus GST.
15 Purchased from Kodak, on account, processing supplies needed for the business for $1621 plus GST.
19 Paid Adams Photo Services in full. Terms offered on Invoice No. T-324 stated 1/10, n/30.
20 Took wedding pictures for H. Morrison. Invoice No. 2847 for $2315 plus GST.
21 Sent to G. Yee finished prints left for processing. Included Invoice No. 2848 for $27 plus GST.
25 Purchased store supplies on account from Fuji Ltd., for resale, $387 plus GST.
27 J. Cosentino withdrew $400 for personal use.

e. Complete all necessary daily postings. Total and prove the accuracy of the Combination Journal.

f. Post the necessary totals.

g. Prepare schedules of the subsidiary ledgers to verify the accuracy of the control accounts.

h. Prepare a trial balance for the end of October.

TOPIC 4 MINI-CASES

Explaining the advantages and disadvantages of a Combination Journal.

MC 13-7 Students in an introductory accounting class are discussing the advantages and disadvantages of the Combination

Journal. One student defended the Combination Journal on the grounds that it is designed to meet the needs of the individual businesses. Other students wanted an explanation of the student's statement.

a. If you were the student in question, how would you explain the statement that "the Combination Journal is designed to meet the needs of individual businesses"?

Using a Combination Journal in manual vs. computerized systems.

MC 13-8 Student A defended the use of the Combination Journal for small businesses which plan to use a microcomputer to process their GL, Accounts Receivable Ledger, and Accounts Payable Ledgers. Student B disagreed, indicating that the Combination Journal is related only to a manual accounting system.

a. Which view do you support? Explain your answer.

Locating errors in a trial balance using multiple journals.

MC 13-9 The TMW Company uses the five-journal system (page 574) to record all transactions. Upon completion of all journalizing and posting at the end of March 199–, the company accountant cannot obtain a successful trial balance. She begins checking to determine where the error might be. She has asked for your assistance and has provided you with the following information:

Sales Journal totals: Accts. Rec. $10 000, Sales $9500.

Purchases Journal totals: General Ledger $400, Accts. Pay. $8200, Purchases $7800.

Cash Receipts Journals totals: General Ledger $150, Sales $500, GST Payable $50, Accts. Rec. $8000, Cash $8700.

Cash Payments Journal totals: General Ledger $650, Accts. Pay, $6500, Purchase Discounts $100, Cash $7050.

a. List the checks you believe should have occurred before the trial balance was attempted.

b. What check has the accountant forgotten?

c. Why is there an error?

d. Indicate what must be done to produce the correct balance.

GENERAL JOURNAL

Date	Account	PR	Debit	Credit
March10	Sales Return and Allowances	403	100	
	Accts. Rec./Woodwell Ltd.	✓/		100
20	Accounts Payable/ Petertown Comp.	/✓	50	
	Purchases Return and Allowances	505		50

ACCOUNTS RECEIVABLE LEDGER

ABC Comp.		Woodwell Ltd.	
8 000	8 000	2 000	100
0		1 900	

ACCOUNTS PAYABLE LEDGER

B-1 Ltd.		Petertown Comp.	
3 500	4 000	50	4 200
		3 000	
	500		1 150

GENERAL LEDGER

Accts. Rec. Control		Accts. Pay. Control	
10 000	8 000	6 500	8 200
2 000			1 700

COMPREHENSIVE CASE STUDY 10

Journalizing and posting using multiple journals and subsidiary ledgers; preparing schedules for subsidiary ledgers; and preparing a trial balance.

J.J. Carbuncle Wholesale Jewellers uses the five-journal system, a General Ledger, and subsidiary Accounts Receivable and Accounts Payable Ledgers in maintaining its accounting records. It is company policy to accept all discounts offered to the firm. Sales data is broken down under four headings: Diamond Jewellery, Other Jewellery, Watches, and Other.

Other information:

(i) Credit terms: 2/10, n/30 to all credit customers.
(ii) Next cheque number: 432 (all outflows paid by cheque).
(iii) Next sales invoice: No. S2001.

a. Open a Sales Journal with the following headings: Date, Invoice Number, Account Debited, Terms, Post. Ref., Accounts Receivable, Diamond Jewellery, Other Jewellery, Watches, Other, GST Payable. The page number is 66.

b. Open a Purchases Journal with the following headings: Date; Account Credited; Invoice Number and Date; Terms; Post. Ref.; Accounts Payable; Purchases Accounts: Diamond Jewellery; Other Jewellery; Watches; Other; GST Payable; Sundry Items: Account DR; Post. Ref., Amount. Page number 54.

c. Open a Cash Receipts Journal with the following headings: Date; Account Credited; Explanation; Post. Ref., General Ledger; Accounts Receivable; Sales Discounts; Sales Accounts: Diamond Jewellery; Other Jewellery; Watches; Other; GST Payable; Cash. The page number is 98.

d. Open a Cash Payments Journal with the following headings: Date; Account Debited; Explanation; Cheque Number; Post. Ref.; General Ledger; Accounts Payable; Purchases Discounts; GST Payable; one blank column; Cash. The page number is 78.

e. Open a General Journal, page number 12.

f. Open the General Ledger accounts from the trial balance provided.

g. Open the subsidiary Accounts Receivable Ledger from the information provided below.

h. Open the subsidiary Accounts Payable Ledger accounts as at June 30, 199-, from the information provided below.

J. J. Carbuncle Wholesale Jewellers
Trial Balance
June 30, 199–

Account	No.	Debit	Credit
Cash	101	10 200	
Accounts Receivable	110	8 025	
Inventory	112	8 000	
Office Supplies	125	800	
Land	140	25 000	
Building	145	85 000	
Vault and Storage Equipment	150	30 000	
Delivery Equipment	155	8 500	
Bank Loan Payable	201		15 000
G.S.T. Payable	208		525
Accounts Payable Control	210		6 500
Mortgage Payable (due 1995)	240		45 400
J. J. Carbuncle, Capital	301		100 010
J. J. Carbuncle, Drawing	302	2 600	
Sales:			
Diamond Jewellery	401		18 000
Other Jewellery	402		6 000
Watches	403		3 000
Other	404		2500
Sales Returns and Allowances	406	1 200	
Sales Discounts	407	3 200	
Purchases:			
Diamond Jewellery	501	6 000	
Other Jewellery	502	2 000	
Watches	503	600	
Other	504	1 000	
Purchases Returns and Allowances	506		350
Purchase Discounts	507		170
Transportation-in	510	420	
Property Tax Expense	520	980	
Telephone Expense	525	650	
Delivery Expense	530	900	
Utitlities Expense	535	2 010	
Office Supplies Expense	540	370	
		197 455	197 455

Accounts Receivable Information:	
Miller Jewels	$1605.00
Northland Gems Ltd.	2140.00
Sabrina's Precious Stones	3210.00
Taylor's Treasures	1070.00
	$8025.00

Accounts Payable Information:	
Diamond Discount Dealers	$4000.00
Precious Gems Wholesale	2400.00
Wholesale Watches Inc.	100.00
	$6500.00

i. Journalize the following information in the appropriate journals. Post daily as required. All Accounts Receivable accounts include GST. Sales figures are exclusive of GST, which must be calculated. Wages do not incur GST; neither do mortgage charges. Property taxes are expensed as paid.

CASH INFLOW TRANSACTIONS

July 3 Received payment in full from Northland Gems Ltd. within the discount period.
9 Sold a watch for $185 cash.
14 Received payment in full from Taylor's Treasures, with discount taken.
20 Sold an opal bracelet for $673.
25 Received payment in full from Miller Jewels, no discount taken.

CASH OUTFLOW TRANSACTIONS

July 2 Paid the second instalment of property taxes. $1345.
5 Paid Diamond Discount Dealers in full, taking the allowed discount of 3%.
10 Paid employee wages of $3400.
14 Paid CN Express $45 plus GST for delivery to a customer.
18 Paid $350 towards the loan at the bank.
20 Paid the telephone bill of $124 plus GST.
25 Bought five crystal vases from a local manufacturer after obtaining an approved purchase order, P-1025. $362 plus GST.
30 Paid employee wages of $3400.
30 Paid the monthly mortgage instalment of $1650. $450 to Mortgage Payable, and $1200 to Mortgage Interest Expense.

SALES TRANSACTIONS

July 5 Sabrina's Precious Stones: 3 diamond pins @ $200 each, 8 digital watches @ $22 each.

9 Miller Jewels: 6 crystal vases @ $65 each; 15 pairs of pearl earrings @ $21 per pair; 4 self-winding watches @ $97 each.

22 Taylor's Treasures: 3 diamond brooches @ $325 each; 4 men's diamond rings @ $212 each; 7 women's diamond rings @ $ 286 each.

PURCHASE TRANSACTIONS

July 3 Purchase Order No. P-1023: Precious Gems Wholesale; 12 digital watches @ $16 ea.; 3 diamond pendants @ $164 ea.; 10 school rings @ $7.50 each. Invoice No. 123 dated July 2, 199–. Terms 1/10, n/30.

18 Purchase order no. P-1024: Wholesale Watches Inc.; 5 self-winding watches @ $65 ea., 18 digital watches @ $18 ea. Invoice no. W-222 dated July 15. Terms 2/10, n/30.

GENERAL INFORMATION

July 12 Miller Jewels returned one self-winding watch, and received full credit.

22 The firm returned all five watches ordered from Wholesale Watches Inc. P-1024. The goods were damaged and would not operate.

j. Total and prepare the necessary journal proofs.

k. Post all the journals.

l. Prepare schedules for both of the subsidiary ledgers to ensure accuracy of the control accounts.

m. Prepare a trial balance at the end of July.

CHAPTER 14

ACCOUNTING FOR SPECIAL ITEMS

Topic 1

Accounting for the Goods and Services Tax

Topic 2

Accounting for the Provincial Retail Sales Tax

Topic 3

Accounting for Credit Card and Debit Card Transactions

Chapters 12 and 13 covered common transactions of merchandising businesses. This chapter deals with transactions for what are known as **special items**. Three special items are the federal Goods and Services Tax, the provincial sales tax, and credit and debit cards.

In Canada there will be two levels of sales taxation as of January 1991. The federal Goods and Services Tax (GST) applies to the majority of goods and services sold at all business levels, manufacturing, wholesaling, and retailing. In most provinces, with the exception of Alberta, a retail sales tax is added to the purchase price of most items at the time of purchase. Therefore, a sale of goods and/or services may require both GST and provincial sales tax (PST) in most provinces.

ACCOUNTING FOR THE GOODS AND SERVICES TAX

At the time of writing, the federal government plans to replace the federal sales tax with a 7% tax on the consumption of goods and services—the Goods and Services Tax (GST). The Goods and Services Tax Act has been passed by the House of Commons, but must also be approved by the Senate in order to become law. Once the Act is approved, the Government intends that the GST will take effect on January 1, 1991. **This chapter will deal with the basic accounting concepts of the GST, and the reader must bear in mind that changes to the Act may have occurred after this textbook has gone to press.**

VAT: a value-added tax which places a tax at each level in the chain of distributing the goods or services from the manufacturer to the end user.

To explain the concept of the GST, let's look at the value-added tax, which is used by forty-eight countries around the world. This tax is applied to all business levels—manufacturing, wholesaling, and retailing. The GST works in the same way. If, for example, a retailer purchases goods from a wholesaler, the retailer will pay GST on the amount purchased. The retailer sells the goods and collects the GST from the consumer. Each business that collects the GST is entitled to subtract the GST paid on the purchase from the GST collected on the sale. If the tax paid on the purchase is greater than that collected on the sale, the government will refund the difference. The illustration below traces the GST charged and collected at various stages of the marketing cycle.

Type of Business	Transaction		Tax at Each Stage
Miner	Iron Ore		
	No Taxable Purchases		
	Sells Ore	10.00	0.70
	Collects GST	0.70	
	Remits to Gov't (0.70 – 0) = 0.70		
Steel Manufacturer	Buys Iron Ore	10.00	
	Pays GST	0.70	
	Sells Steel	50.00	2.80
	Collects GST	3.50	
	Remits to Gov't (3.50 – 0.70) = 2.80		
Boat Builder	Buys Steel	50.00	
	Pays GST	3.50	
	Sells Boat	200.00	10.50
	Collects GST	14.00	
	Remits to Gov't (14.00 – 3.50) = 10.50		

(Continued on next page.)

(Continued from previous page.)

Wholesaler	Buys Boat Pays GST Sells Boat Collects GST Remits to Gov't (21.00 − 14.00) = 7.00	200.00 14.00 300.00 21.00	7.00
Retailer	Buys Boat Pays GST Sells Boat Collects GST Remits to Gov't (28.00 − 21.00) = 7.00	300.00 21.00 400.00 28.00	7.00 28.00 Total Tax Collected

In recognition that the GST will strain the administrative resources of small businesses, the government has proposed several measures to minimize the paperwork. Some of these measures are as follows:

Simplified accounting methods: methods available to some businesses to help calculate GST; includes both the quick method and the streamlined accounting method.

- **a small trader's exemption for those businesses with annual sales under $30 000**. A small trader may be exempted from the GST system. This exemption has implications which will be addressed later in this chapter.
- **simplified accounting methods**
  Quick method: This method applies a reduced rate to total sales, with no provision for input tax credits. This method is explained in more detail later.
  Streamlined accounting: A business with annual sales below $2 million and that sells a combination of taxable and zero-rated grocery goods at the retail level will be able to determine GST payable based on the tax status of its inventory, rather than having to track GST at the cash register. This will be explained in detail later in this topic.
- reduced filing of GST returns
- a one-time small business administration fee of up to $1000, which will partially offset the costs to business of administering the GST
- assistance to businesses wishing to modernize their cash registers

IDENTIFYING THE TAX BASE

The GST will affect the vast majority of goods and services consumed in Canada. There will be three basic categories of goods and services:

(1) taxable

(2) zero-rated

(3) tax-exempt

Although items (2) and (3) seem similar, there is a substantial difference between them. On **zero-rated** goods and services, the business will not charge GST on sales, but may still claim input tax credits for any tax paid on purchases. On **tax-exempt** sales, the business will not charge GST on sales, but it will **not** be able to claim any input tax credits on purchases.

It is beyond the scope of this book to explain the GST system in detail. Instead, the basic concepts will be covered, with the reader left the task of determining what details have been finalized by the federal government at the time of proclamation.

Zero-Rated Items

Basic Groceries The vast majority of sales of food for preparation and consumption at home will **not** be subject to GST. Sales of agricultural and fish products will be zero-rated; however, restaurant meals and prepared take-out foods will be GST taxable. Soft drinks, snack foods, and candies and confections will be GST taxable. There has been substantial discussion between government and business and special-interest groups to determine where the lines should be drawn between taxable and zero-rated groups. As the implementation date approaches, these differences between the two groups will be clarified by the federal government.

Prescription Drugs Any drugs prescribed by a physician will be zero-rated.

Medical Devices As was the case under the old federal sales tax system, a wide range of medical devices will be zero-rated. This would include such items as prescription eyeglasses, contact lenses, artificial limbs, wheelchairs and crutches, diabetic equipment and supplies, hearing aids, and hospital beds.

Tax-Exempt Items

Health and Dental Care Almost all health and dental care will be tax-exempt. This will include optometry, chiropractic services, and physiotherapy, as well as the usual health and dental services.

Educational Services This is a very broad category, and reference should be made to the GST provisions for specific details. Educational services includes educational instruction provided by elementary, secondary, and post-secondary institutions, and private secretarial and business schools.

Day-Care Services This category includes all day-care, nursery school services, after-school programs provided by schools and community centres, and day camps.

Legal Aid Services Legal services provided by a provincially authorized legal aid plan will be exempt.

Residential Rents Any long-term, meaning longer than one month, rental accommodation will be exempt from tax.

Financial Services Because of the enormous complexity of the financial services sector, the government made a policy decision in the 1989 budget that certain financial services would be exempt from tax. Generally speaking, loans and deposits, mortgages, and life, property, and casualty insurance will not be taxable, while most of the other services offered by financial institutions, such as safety deposit boxes, will be taxable. At this time, the government is consulting with tax professionals and the industry to clarify the rules for taxation.

Municipal Transit and Passenger Ferries Passenger transportation provided by a municipality on a non-profit basis will be exempt.

ENSURING TAX FAIRNESS

One of the aims of the GST is to make the tax system more equitable. One way the government hopes to achieve this aim is through the Refundable Goods and Services Tax Credit. The credit is paid quarterly and in advance of expenditures by households on taxable goods and services. The amount depends on annual income and family size. In 1991, only families with an annual income of less than $35 000 will qualify for the credit. As family size decreases and income increases, the amount of the credit decreases.

Refundable GST Credit: an amount of money paid by the government to families to offset the impact of GST, based on family size and income.

The government has also decreased the marginal tax rate from 26% to 25% to provide a tax reduction to the middle-income group, since the GST credit will be phased out for this group. As a result of these measures, the government claims that families earning under $30 000 will be actually better off under the new system.

Transitional and Special Rules

There is a multitude of special rules and exemptions that are in the drafting stage. These rules, which will deal with issues such as new and resale housing, small businesses, charities, inventory valuation, and zero-rated versus taxable items, will be finalized when the Act is passed.

WHO PAYS TAX?

Consumers Consumers will pay a 7% GST when they purchase taxable items. At this time, the government offers businesses the option of including the GST in the shelf price, which must be clearly indicated, or calculating the GST at the point of purchase, that is, at the cash register at time of sale. The retail purchaser is assumed to be the ultimate consumer of the product; therefore, there is no provision for recovering any of this GST, other than what is provided through the Refundable GST Credit, as described above.

Businesses with Annual Sales Less Than $30 000 These businesses may choose to operate outside the GST system. If they do so, they cannot charge GST on sales, **nor** can they claim any of the GST paid on purchases (no input tax credits). If they choose to participate, they will charge GST on sales and then deduct input tax credits.

Businesses with Annual Sales Over $30 000 These businesses must collect GST on sales and are required to file and calculate GST collected and paid, depending on their annual sales volumes. For example, if annual sales are less than $500 000, a business may calculate the GST yearly and make quarterly instalments. Those businesses with sales between $500 000 and $6 million will calculate and also remit taxes on a quarterly basis. Finally, businesses with annual sales greater than $6 million must calculate and remit taxes monthly.

Charities, Non-Profit Organizations, Farmers and Fishers, Government, and Educational Institutions All of these groups will receive special treatment. Some groups — agriculture and fishery businesses — will be zero-rated, and some — charities and non-profit organizations — will receive a rebate of up to 50% of GST paid on purchases. Again, reference should be made to the Goods and Services Tax Act for specific rules.

ACCOUNTING FOR GST

Although no specific accounting guidelines have been given for the GST at this point in time, there are some basic principles that can be explained.

To simplify matters in the sections that follow, only one account — GST Payable — will be used to track both the GST paid and GST collected. Alternative methods of tracking the GST will be examined at the end of the topic.

GST Payable as a Current Liability Account Since businesses will be, in effect, collecting tax on behalf of the federal government, any tax collected represents a liability owed to the government. A current liability account, GST Payable, may be set up to record both tax collected on sales and tax paid on purchases. For example, purchase of taxable goods for $200 cash is analyzed in General Journal form as follows:

Purchases	200	
GST Payable	14	
Cash		214

Note that the account GST Payable is debited for the GST paid on the purchase. This debit is an exception to the **laid-down cost principle**, which requires that all costs of the purchase, including taxes and freight charges, be included as the cost of the purchase. Instead, the GST paid on the purchase becomes an input tax credit—a debit to GST Payable. The effect of the debit is to reduce the tax owing to the government.

Input Tax Credit (ITC): a deduction from GST Payable; the amount of GST paid on purchases of goods and services for resale or use in the business.

Now let's assume that the business sells this same item that was purchased for $200 at the marked-up price of $400. The sale would be analyzed in General Journal form as follows:

Cash	428	
Sales		400
GST Payable		28

GST Payable	
14	28
	14

Examine the T-account for GST Payable illustrated in the margin, which shows the two postings as explained above.

Let's also assume that these two transactions were the only ones during the accounting period. The business would then remit to the government the credit balance in the GST Payable account, recording the transaction in the GL as follows:

GST Payable	14	
Cash		14

If for some reason the GST Payable account has a debit balance (tax paid is greater than tax collected on sales), the business would still report to the government, but in this case, the government would refund the amount owing. At this time, the government has indicated that refunds owing would be paid within 21 days. After this period any outstanding refunds would collect interest, and both the refund and interest would be paid to the business.

SALES RETURNS AND ALLOWANCES

When a business sells goods to a customer, and the customer subsequently returns part of the goods or is granted an allowance on the price, the business may make an adjustment for the difference in the GST collected **if a credit memo is issued**. For example, assume $50 of the $400 worth of goods sold to the customer, as shown on the previous page, was returned. The business would refund the $50 plus the applicable GST, and record the transactions as follows:

Sales Returns	50.00	
GST Payable	3.50	
Cash		53.50

GST Payable	
14.00	28.00
3.50	
	10.50

Note that the GST refunded is debited to the GST Payable account, which will have the effect of reducing the tax owing to the government.

The T-account would now appear as in the margin, if the return of goods occurred before the end of the remittance period (when tax must be sent to the government).

Note: **It is important to remember here that this adjustment for GST on returned goods or sales allowances can only be made if a credit memo is issued.**

Cash Discounts

Cash discounts are regularly offered to customers who pay their bills early. An example is a 2% discount for payment within 10 days of the invoice date (2/10, n/30).

If the invoice states an amount with the discount already deducted —**net** amount—the supplier will charge GST only on that net amount. No other adjustments will be required by either party. However, if the invoice shows a **gross** amount, and indicates a discount may be taken for early payment, the supplier will charge GST on the full gross amount. There will be no adjustments or credit notes with respect to cash discounts. The supplier will collect GST on the gross amount, and the buyer will claim an input credit for the full amount of the GST indicated on the invoice, **even when the discount is taken**. This simplifies the paperwork and accounting necessary for cash discounts.

For example, assume that ABC Company has sold GST taxable goods for $500 to the XYZ Company, on terms of 2/10, n/30, under the gross amount method. The XYZ Company's policy is to take trade discounts. ABC Company would record the sale and the subsequent payment by XYZ as follows:

May 1	Accounts Receivable/XYZ Co.	535.00	
	Sales		500.00
	GST Payable		35.00
11	Cash	525.00	
	Sales Discounts	10.00	
	Accounts Receivable/XYZ Co.		535.00

Note that the discount of 2% is taken **only** on the amount of the sale, exclusive of GST.

From the viewpoint of XYZ Company, the same transactions would be recorded as follows:

May 1	Purchases	500.00	
	GST Payable	35.00	
	Accounts Payable/ABC Co.		535.00
11	Accounts Payable/ABC Co.	535.00	
	Purchases Discounts		10.00
	Cash		525.00

Special Journals and the GST As you have seen, the GST will affect the accounting for a great many transactions, since the GST must now be tracked by most businesses on the sale of many goods and services. How will this affect special journals, such as the Sales Journal, the Purchases Journal, and so on? Let's look at an example using the Sales Journal. The traditional Sales Journal has one money column, used to record the amount of the sale. How many columns will be needed in order to account for GST? If you answered "at least two," you are correct; one column records the amount of the sale, and the other records the GST Payable. Since one purpose of a special Sales Journal is to reduce errors, a third column is included to record the total Accounts Receivable amount. This is the sales amount plus the GST payable. In this way each line of the Sales Journal can be balanced, since debits must equal credits. Examine the illustration below:

SALES JOURNAL Page 3

DATE		INVOICE NO.	ACCOUNTS DEBITED	TERMS	POST. REF.	ACCOUNTS RECEIVABLE DR.	SALES CR.	GST PAYABLE CR.
19–								
June	2	4166	Jones Fishing Supply ...	2/10, n/30	✓	214 00	200 00	14 00
	4	4167	Smith Photo Inc.	2/10, n/30	✓	695 50	650 00	45 50
	12	4168	Pittana Charters	2/10, n/30	✓	155 15	145 00	10 15
	18	4169	Martin Distributors	2/10, n/30	✓	98 44	92 00	6 44
	30		Total			1163 09	1087 00	76 09
						(103)	(401)	(208)

POSTING THE THREE-COLUMN SALES JOURNAL

Each day, the figure from the Accounts Receivable DR. column must be posted to the individual customer's account in the Accounts Receivable Ledger. A check mark is placed in the Post. Ref. column opposite the entry to indicate the posting is complete.

At the end of the month, the Sales Journal is ruled, and the money columns totalled. The total of the Accounts Receivable DR. column is posted to the Accounts Receivable control in the GL. The account number (103) is placed in brackets below the total to indicate posting is complete. The totals of Sales CR. and GST Payable CR. are posted to their respective accounts, and the account numbers are placed in brackets below the columns.

UPDATING THE PURCHASES JOURNAL

The reasons for updating the Purchases Journal are the same as those for revising the Sales Journal: there is now a need to track GST paid. A new column, GST Payable DR., is added to record any GST paid on purchases. The amount of the purchases is recorded in the Purchases column, the GST paid is recorded in the GST Payable column, and the total amount owing (Purchases + GST) is recorded in the Accounts Payable column. As with the Sales Journal, each line balances (debits = credits). Similar to the Sales Journal, daily posting of each purchase is required to the Accounts Payable Ledger. The totals of the Accounts Payable column, the GST Payable column, and the Purchases column can be posted at the end of the month. Posting of the Purchases Journal would remain essentially the same as explained in Chapter 13.

REVISING THE COMBINATION JOURNAL

The combination journal is updated in a similar manner. A new column is added for GST Payable. This column has both a DR. and a CR. side, since both debits and credits are recorded in this journal. See the illustration in Chapter 13, page 567 for an example of an updated Combination Journal. Posting of the Combination Journal would essentially remain the same as explained in Chapter 13.

INVOICING REQUIREMENTS

Under the Goods and Services Tax Act, invoicing requirements vary, depending on the level of sale involved. The three levels are (1) total sale under $30, (2) total sale between $30 and $150, and (3) total sale over $150.

All invoices must carry the following information: the business or trading name, the date the GST was paid or payable, and the total amount paid or payable.

If the total sale is over $30, the invoice must also carry the following: an indication of which items are subject to the GST, either the total amount of GST charged **or** a statement indicating that prices include GST, and the business's GST Registration Number.

If the total sale is over $150, the invoice must also carry the terms of sale (cash or credit) and a brief description of the goods or service. An invoice is illustrated on page 590 and shows two types of goods, taxable and zero-rated. Keep in mind that there is no single acceptable format for documents, as long as the document contains the required information.

INTRODUCING SIMPLIFIED ACCOUNTING METHODS

To help businesses calculate the Goods and Services Tax, three simplified accounting methods can be followed—the Quick Method and two streamlined accounting methods.

Quick method: a simple calculation available to some businesses to allow quick calculation of GST Payable.

Quick Method

The quick method is limited to: (a) businesses with annual revenues up to $200 000, and (b) grocery and conven-

MARIKOSAN FOOD AND DRUG WHOLESALE LTD.
256 Brunswick Cr.
London, Ontario
N6G 3LZ

INVOICE NO.: **M—43815**

SOLD TO: Pittana's Convenience Store
96 Empress Avenue
London, Ontario N6G 4T2

Date	GST Reg'n	Terms:
July 7, 1991	No.: 34729	2/10, n/30

ITEM NO.	DESCRIPTION	GST RATE	QUANTITY	PRICE	EXTENSION
G0042	400 g White Bread	0%	100	1.02	102.00
S4177	750 mL Soft Drink	7%	20	0.99	19.80
C6413	28 g Chocolate Bar	7%	50	0.62	31.00
D7236	125 g Toothpaste	0%	12	1.10	13.20
F8412	200 g Potato Chips	7%	12	0.72	8.64
				Total Before Tax	174.64
				GST 7%	4.16
				PST 8%	N/A
				Total Amount Owing	178.80

C. Pittana
Received by:

ience stores with annual sales up to $500 000 **if** basic (zero-rated) groceries make up at least 25% of sales. Using this method, the business would still charge 7% on taxable goods, when calculating

QUICK METHOD PERCENTAGES

Business Group	Maximum Annual Sales	%
Manufacturers and services (Examples: sawmills, bodyshops, electricians, barbers/hairstylists, construction contractors, repair shops)	$200 000	5%
Retailers and wholesalers (Examples: clothing and shoe stores, hardware stores, stores selling less than 25% basic groceries)	$200 000	3%
Grocery and convenience stores, specialty food outlets, etc., selling 25 to 50% basic groceries.	$500 000	1.75%
Grocery and convenience stores, greengrocers, butchers, bakeries, etc., selling over 50% basic groceries	$500 000	1%
Legal, accounting, and financial consulting business	Not eligible	

GST owing. Instead of tracking GST charged on sales, and then subtracting input tax credits, the business multiplies total sales by a specified percentage, which is set by the government according to the type of business. The business **does not** receive specific input tax credits; it is presumed that the specified lower percentage applied to total sales takes into account the approximate amount of tax paid on purchases. There are special provisions for claiming input tax credits for major capital purchases, to ensure that the business is not at a disadvantage because of using this method.

Quick Method
Wholesale Co.

Total Sales for the Period (A)	$25 000
Pre-determined Percentage (B)	3%
GST Payable (A x B)	$ 750

The **Quick Method** does not apply to some types of businesses, such as law, accounting, or financial consulting practices.

Streamlined accounting: a simple calculation available to some businesses to allow easy determination of GST collectable on sales.

Streamlined Accounting

Businesses with annual revenues of up to $2 million that sell a combination of taxable and zero-rated basic groceries at the retail level may elect to use one of two streamlined accounting methods.

Method 1 Retailers will calculate GST owing based on the retail selling price of purchases of taxable goods for resale. The input tax credits as recorded would be deducted from the calculated tax owing. For example, assume a wholesaler pays $8000 for goods for resale, 25% of which are taxable goods, the rest being zero-rated. Assume that after a 50% mark-up, the retail selling price of those taxable

Streamlined Accounting for GST

Method 1	Amount	Tax
Purchase of Taxable Goods for Resale	$2 000	$(140)
Regular Mark-up of 50%	1 000	
Estimated Sales Value	$3 000	210
Net Tax to be Remitted		$ 70

goods is (8000 × 25%) × 150% or $3000. The GST owing on those goods would be $3000 × 7% or $210. From this figure is subtracted any GST paid on purchases. This would be at least $140 ($2000 × 7%) or possibly more, if other taxable items were purchased for use in the business or for resale.

Method 2 This method is similar to Method 1, but instead of the retail selling price, it relies on a prescribed standard mark-up for basic groceries. First, the retailer estimates sales of zero-rated basic groceries by multiplying grocery purchases by a prescribed mark-up. The retailer then subtracts the estimated zero-rated sales from total sales for the period. The difference is the estimated total taxable sales, which is then multiplied by 7/107 to determine the tax on sales for the period. The illustration below is an example.

Streamlined GST Accounting for Retailers:

Method 2

1.	Purchases of Zero-Rated Basic Groceries (GST Inclusive)	$75	
	× Prescribed Mark-up (Illustrative for Groceries)	1.2	
	= Estimated Sales of Groceries	$90	
2.	Total Sales for Period	$310	(including GST)
	− Estimated Sales of Groceries	$90	
	= Estimated Taxable Sales	$ 220	(including GST)
3.	Tax on Sales = 220 × 7/107 =	$14.39	
4.	Subtract Input Tax Credits to determine Tax Owing.		

Finally, the value of any input tax credits are subtracted from the tax on sales to determine tax owing.

Realizing that further refinements will be necessary to the GST system as it is put into practice, the government is consulting with representatives of business and tax professionals. There is also a large body of transitional rules that covers many aspects of the tax conversion, which will not be covered here.

WITHDRAWING BUSINESS ASSETS FOR PERSONAL USE

If the owner of a sole proprietorship business withdraws cash for personal use, accounting principles specify a debit to Drawing, and a credit to Cash. This transaction will remain the same under GST rules. However, a difference arises when the owner takes an asset, for example, a computer or inventory, home for personal use. Under the Goods and Services Tax Act, the owner is said to have acquired the asset at fair market value (FMV), and must collect GST on that item. The owner is viewed as a person who had purchased the asset in the regular manner. Let's look at the example of an owner, Sheila Carty, who operates Sheila's TV and Radio. Sheila takes home a colour TV that has a fair market value of $800, for which the business paid $500. The General Journal entry would be:

S. Carty, Drawing	556	
Purchases (or Inventory)		500
GST Payable		56

Note that the GST is calculated on the basis of fair market value, yet only the **cost** of the item is removed from the inventory.

TRACKING AND REMITTING THE GOODS AND SERVICES TAX

Under the GST system, it is highly advantageous for a business to keep special records of sales and purchases, identifying GST, especially if the business does not intend to use one of the simplified accounting methods. The Sales Journal and the Purchases Journal, in their new format, provide the information necessary for calculating the amount of tax owing at the end of an accounting period.

Alternatively, if special journals are not used, detailed information, such as invoice number and date, is kept in the GST Payable Ledger, and the GST Payable account can be used to calculate tax owing.

COMPLETING THE GST RETURN FOR REGISTRANTS AND REMITTING TAX

All businesses or vendors, called **registrants**, will complete the form Goods and Services Tax Return for Registrants, regardless of the size of the business or the frequency of filing. The illustration on the next page is an example of this form.

The form consists of two parts. The top part is for calculating GST, and is kept by the registrant for the business records. The bottom part is for filling in the amounts as calculated in the top part, and is then filed with the government.

Revenue Canada Customs and Excise — GOODS AND SERVICES TAX RETURN FOR REGISTRANTS — Keep this portion for your records

GST ACCOUNT NUMBER	PERIOD	DUE DATE
105776108	FROM: 91-01-01 TO: 91-01-31	91 02 28

PROTECTED WHEN COMPLETED
Personal information provided on this form is protected under the provisions of the Privacy Act and is maintained in Personal Bank RCC/P-PU-???.
DISPONIBLE EN FRANCAIS

GST Contact Name: JOE SMITH Telephone: (123) 456-7890

123 INC.
M & D'S TIRES
8 MAIN STREET
ANY CITY, PROVINCE
Z1Z 2Z3

INSTRUCTIONS

1. Check the information above for completeness and accuracy. You may change your mailing address, and the name and telephone number of the Goods and Services Tax (GST) contact person in your organization using the change stub on the reply envelope. For other changes contact the number below.
2. Complete SECTION ONE - PERIOD SUMMARY. Refer to the guide to the Goods and Services Tax Return for Registrants. Remember to include taxable supplies at 7% and 0%. Exclude supplies of financial services, and real capital property.
3. Complete SECTION TWO - TAX CALCULATION. Refer to the Guide to the Goods and Services Tax Return for Registrants. A Tax Calculation checklist is provided for your use.
4. Copy the amounts from the shaded boxes in Sections One and Two to the corresponding boxes in the bottom portion. Ensure that your numbers are printed in the boxes as illustrated. Indentify a negative number with a minus sign in the separate box.

   e.g. - 1234567890
5. KEEP THE TOP PORTION. It and any other information used in preparing your return are subject to audit and must be retained for verification purposes.
6. IF YOU NEED ASSISTANCE CONTACT

   1-800-999-9999.

SECTION ONE - PERIOD SUMMARY

Item	Line	Amount
Total Taxable Supplies (Sales and Other Revenue)	101	.00
Total Purchases	102	00

SECTION TWO - TAX CALCULATION

REFER TO THE GUIDE FOR LINE-BY-LINE EXPLANATIONS

Item	Line	Amount	Line	Total
GST Collectible	103	20 790 00		
GST Adjustments	104	0 00		
Total GST and adjustments for period (Add lines 103 and 104)			105	20 790 00
Input Tax Credit (ITC)	106	8421 00		
ITC Adjustments	107	0 00		
Total ITCs and adjustments (Add lines 106 and 107)			108	8 421 00
Net Tax (Subtract line 108 from line 105)			109	12 369 00

OTHER CREDITS IF APPLICABLE...

Item	Line	Amount	Line	Total
Paid by Instalments	110			
Rebates (See Guide)	111			
Total Other Credits (Add lines 110 and 111)			112	
Balance (Subtract line 112 from line 109)			113	12 369 00
Refund Claimed			114	
OR Payment Enclosed			115	12 369 00

If the balance is negative, claim a refund; otherwise remit the amount owing.
A balance of less than $1.00 will neither be charged nor refunded.
All registrants must file a return, regardless of the balance.

Revenue Canada Customs and Excise — GOODS AND SERVICES TAX RETURN FOR REGISTRANTS — Detach and return this portion

GST ACCOUNT NUMBER	PERIOD	DUE DATE
105776108	FROM: 91-01-01 TO: 91-01-31	91 02 28

Name: 123 INC.

Item	Line	Amount
Total Taxable Supplies (Sales and Other Revenue)	101	, , .0 0
Total Purchases	102	, , .0 0
Paid by Instalments	110	, , .
Rebates	111	, , .
Total GST and adjustments for Period	105	, , .
Total ITCs and adjustments	108	, , .
NET TAX	109	, , .
Total Other Credits	112	, , .
BALANCE	113	, , .
Refund Claimed	114	, , .
Payment Enclosed	115	, , .

The information in this return is true and complete to the best of my knowledge.

NAME: ____________ TITLE: ____________

SIGNATURE: ____________ DATE: ____________

It is a serious offence to make a false return.

PRESCRIBED BY THE MINISTER OF NATIONAL REVENUE UNDER THE EXCISE TAX ACT
PLEASE DO NOT WRITE BELOW THIS LINE.

Step 1. Fill in lines 101 and 102, with the total revenues and purchases for the period.

Step 2. Calculate the GST collectible on sales, using an accounting method as outlined previously. To this figure, any adjustments to GST, such as inventory allowances, are added to determine the total GST collectible for the period.

Step 3. Calculate the Input Tax Credits (ITC) (line 106), which is the GST paid on purchases. There is also a line for adjustments in this stage. For our purposes, adjustments will be ignored. The **net tax** (line 109) is calculated by subtracting the Input Tax Credit from the GST collectible.

Step 4. Determine whether the registrant is entitled to any rebates of GST under the special provisions, which will be subtracted, as will any tax paid by instalments. The resulting figure is the Balance, entered on line 113.

Step 5. Copy the figures from the top of the form to the bottom part of the form, sign the form at the bottom, date it, and remit to the government any GST owing.

USING THE GST PAYABLE ACCOUNT TO COMPLETE THE RETURN

If a business is not using special journals for sales and purchases, where GST is tracked separately, the return can still be completed easily using information from the GST Payable liability account. If

GST PAYABLE Account No. 208

DATE		EXPLANATION	POST. REF.	DEBIT	CREDIT	BALANCE	DR./CR.
19–							
Jan.	2	Smith's Supply Invoice No. 2167	J21	840 00		840 00	DR.
	8	Sales for week	J22		599 00	241 00	DR.
	11	ABC Wholesale Invoice No. A-112	J23	257 00		498 00	DR.
	15	Sales for week	J24		762 00	264 00	CR.
	22	Sales for week	J25		619 00	883 00	CR.
	24	Smith's Supply Invoice No. 2649	J25	179 00		704 00	CR.
	25	Ev's Moving Parts Invoice No. B.31	J25	12 90		691 10	CR.
	26	XYC Trading Co. Invoice No. 824	J25	119 00		572 10	CR.
	29	Sales for week	J26		827 00	1399 10	CR.
		Totals		1407 90	2807 00	1399 10	CR.
Jan.	29	Remitted		1399 10 (J26)		0 00	—

this method is used, it is strongly recommended that detailed information be kept in the ledger as to suppliers' names, invoice numbers, and other information so that any particular transaction giving rise to GST implications can be readily identified. The illustration on page 595 is an example of a GST Payable Ledger page, which will be used to complete our sample return.

Analysis:

- Notice that the Explanation column contains the supplier's name and invoice number for each **debit** entry and also the type of transactions giving rise to each **credit** entry. In this example, total sales for the week gives rise to the GST credit entries. If each invoice were posted, the buyer's name and the invoice number would be recorded.
- At the end of the reporting period, the ledger page is ruled off, and totals for the Debit column and the Credit column are calculated. First, the total revenues and total purchases are calculated from the appropriate ledger pages. Second, the figures for GST Collectable and Input Tax Credit are taken from the credit and debit columns of the GST Payable Ledger, respectively. In our example, the GST Collectable is $2807.00, and the Input Tax Credit is $1407.90. If there are no adjustments, the **net tax** is $1399.10, which is also the balance in the GST Payable account. When a cheque is written to the Receiver General for Canada, the journal entry would be as follows:

GST Payable	1399.10	
Cash		1399.10

- Once this entry, when posted, brings the balance of the GST Payable account to zero, recording for the next period may be done.

As an alternative to ruling off the GST Payable account, a monthly statement summarizing the GST transactions for a given month may be prepared as on the opposite page.

If a business is using the multiple-journal system, the information for the calculation can be obtained from the Sales Journal and the Purchases Journal, without ruling off the GST Payable Ledger page or preparing a separate summary of the GST debits and credits posted during the period.

Name of Firm
GST Summary Statement
For the Month Ended January 31, 19—

Total Credits posted to the GST Payable Account	$2 807.00
Total Debits Posted to the GST Payable Account	1 407.90
Balance Owing, if Credit Balance	$1 399.10
Balance Due, if Debit Balance	0

EXAMINING ALTERNATIVE METHODS OF TRACKING THE GST

In the previous sections, only one account—GST Payable—was used to record all aspects of the GST. In practice, however, several accounts may be required when the volume of monthly transactions is large and especially when computer software is used to track the GST.

In general, separate accounts may be created for the key parts required to complete Section Two — Tax Calculation of the GST Return for Registrants. As previously illustrated on page 594, the key parts of this remittance form are boxes for GST Collectable (103), GST Adjustments (104), Input Tax Credit (ITC) (106), ITC Adjustments (107), Paid by Instalments (110), and Rebates (111). With separate account data for these six boxes, the registrant can complete Section Two to account for any Refund Claimed (114) or Payment Enclosed (115).

In the cases that follow, separate accounts will be shown to complete only the GST Collectable and the Input Tax Credit boxes of the remittance form. The accounting of GST Adjustments, ITC Adjustments, Instalments, and Rebates are beyond the scope of this textbook.

Case 1: Manual Method with a Balance Owing Assume a wholesale business called Mississauga Wholesale Hardware exists. Assume also that the summary data below are supported by source documents for the month ended June 30, current year, and that the registrant has elected to report the GST on a monthly basis.

Summary Data:

(i) Total purchases of merchandise for June, $100 000. GST charged on all purchase invoices totalled $7000. Assume terms of net 30 days on all invoices.

(ii) Total purchases of equipment for June, $20 000. GST charged on all invoices totalled $1400. Assume terms of n/30 days on all invoices.

(iii) Total freight-in charges for June, $1000. GST charged on all freight bills totalled $70. Assume terms of n/30 days on all freight bills.

(iv) Operating expense bills paid by cheque for which GST was charged totalled $1800 plus $126 for the GST.

(v) Total credit invoices received from creditors in June for goods returned, $2500. Applicable GST on these credit invoices totalled $175.

(vi) Total sales for June, $300 000. Applicable GST on these invoices totalled $21 000. Assume terms of n/30 on all sales invoices.

(vii) Credit invoices issued to customers for June totalled $3000. Applicable GST on these credit invoices totalled $210.

Mississauga Wholesale Hardware
Partial Chart of Accounts

Current Assets
- 101 Petty Cash
- 102 Cash in Bank
- 103 Accounts Receivable
- 105 GST Refund Receivable

Current Liabilities
- 201 Bank Loan Payable
- 202 Accounts Payable
- 203 GST Payable
- 204 Input Tax Credit (ITC)

To track the GST in the above transactions, assume that Mississauga Wholesale Hardware includes GL accounts as illustrated in the margin. Note the following points when analyzing this partial Chart of Accounts:

- Three GL accounts have been created to track the GST: GST Refund Receivable (105); GST Payable (203), and Input Tax Credit (204).
- GST Refund Receivable is listed under Current Assets. This account will be used whenever the registrant completes the GST Return for Registrants remittance form and concludes that a refund is claimed.
- GST Payable is listed under Current Liabilities. This account will be credited each time a sale is made on which the GST must be collected. The account will be debited for the GST portion of credit invoices issued to customers. Also, the account will be debited each time a cheque is issued to pay any balance owing for GST. As you will learn, the posting of this cheque entry will result in a zero balance to this account.
- Input Tax Credit is listed under Current Liabilities. Since it is shown immediately after GST Payable, the ITC may be analyzed as being contra to the current liability. As a current liability **contra** account, it will be debited for all GST amounts charged on all types of invoices: purchase invoices of merchandise, invoices showing the purchase of equipment; freight-in bills, and bills for which an expense account will be debited. Conversely,

the Input Tax Credit (ITC) account will be credited for all GST amounts quoted on credit invoices received for returned goods and similar adjustments on "purchase" invoices. And as you will learn, the Input Tax Credit (ITC) account will be closed at the end of each month to support the preparation of the GST Return for Registrants remittance form.

Important Note: In practice, some accountants may choose to classify the Input Tax Credit (ITC) account as a current asset. In doing so, they are supporting the theory that a debit amount on a purchase invoice for the GST represents an unexpired cost. However, other accountants may argue that no current asset is possible under GST until the balance of the Input Tax Credit account is matched with the current liability GST Payable at the time the GST Return for Registrants remittance form is completed. In other words, no current asset for GST Refund Receivable can be identified until the Input Tax Credit account balance is subtracted from the balance in the GST Payable account. In this text, we will classify Input Tax Credit (ITC) as a contra account to the current liability GST Payable.

To analyze the tracking of the GST, examine carefully the partial GL, illustrated in T-account form below, showing the summary of debits and credits posted for transactions (i) through (vii).

T-Account GL Summary of Transactions (i) through (vii)

Cash in Bank 102

Debit		Credit	
		(iv)	1 926

Accounts Receivable 103

Debit		Credit	
(vi)	321 000	(vii)	3 210

Equipment 120

Debit		Credit	
(ii)	20 000		

Accounts Payable 202

Debit		Credit	
(v)	2 675	(i)	107 000
		(ii)	21 400
		(iii)	1 070

GST Payable 203

Debit		Credit	
(vii)	210	(vi)	21 000

Input Tax Credit (ITC) 204

Debit		Credit	
(i)	7 000	(v)	175
(ii)	1 400		
(iii)	70		
(iv)	126		

(Continued on next page.)

(Continued from previous page.)

Purchases 501	
(i) 100 000	

Freight-in 502	
(iii) 1 000	

Purchases Returns and Allowances 503	
	(v) 2 500

Sales 401	
	(vi) 300 000

Sales Returns and Allowances 402	
(vii) 3 000	

Operating Expenses 515	
(iv) 1 800	

Analysis: You can easily recreate the double entry for any transaction by identifying the transaction number in each T-account. For example, the first transaction would be analyzed in General Journal form as follows:

		Debit	Credit
(i)	Purchases	100 000	
	Input Tax Credit (ITC)	7 000	
	Accounts Payable		107 000
	To record the total purchases of merchandise for June on account, plus the GST charged on all purchase invoices.		

As you check each numbered transaction, note that each individual double entry must balance because the total debit or debits must equal the total credit or credits.

At month-end, the balances of the two GST accounts — Input Tax Credit (ITC) and GST Payable—can be used to complete Section Two of the GST Return for Registrants as illustrated on the opposite page.

To account for the balance owing, assume that a cheque is made out to the Receiver General of Canada for $12 369.00. Under a manual system, the cheque would be recorded in the Cash Payments Journal and may be analyzed in General Journal form as Transaction (viii) at the top of page 602.

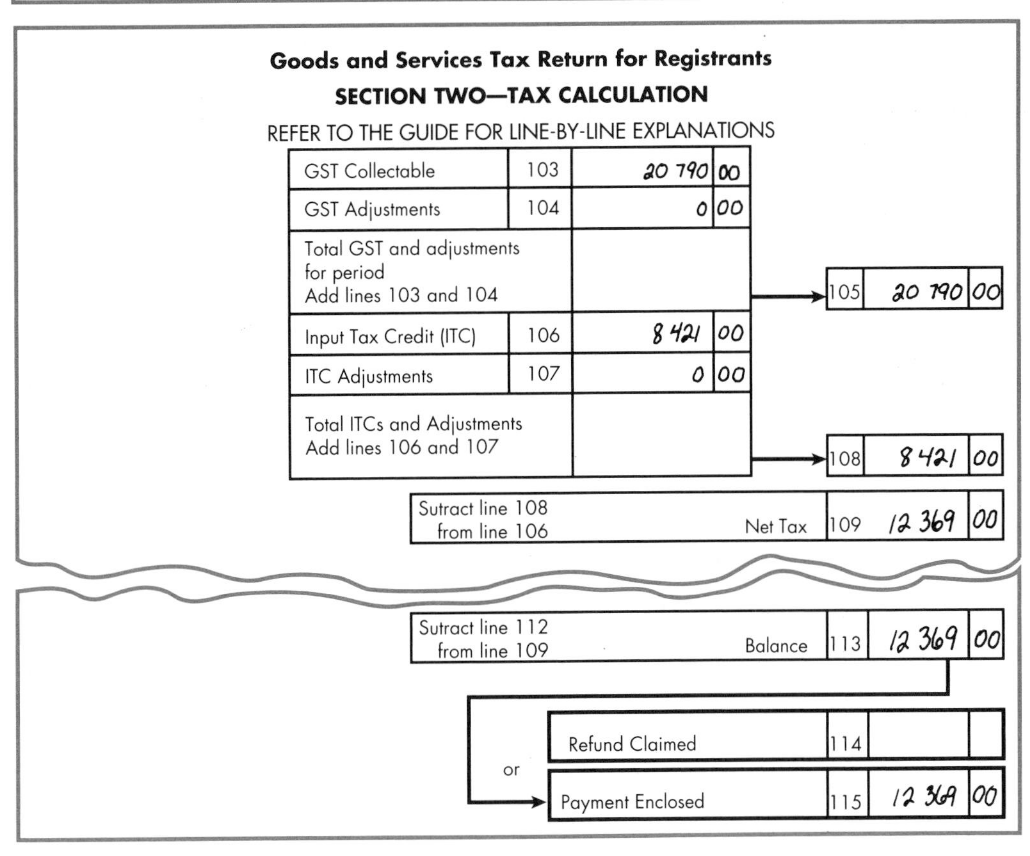

GST Payable 203

(vii)	210	(vi)	21 000
		Balance	20 790

Input Tax Credit (ITC) 204

(i)	7 000	(v)	175
(ii)	1 400		
(iii)	70		
(iv)	126		
Balance	8 421		

Goods and Services Tax Return for Registrants

SECTION TWO—TAX CALCULATION

REFER TO THE GUIDE FOR LINE-BY-LINE EXPLANATIONS

Item	Line	Amount	Line	Total
GST Collectable	103	20 790 00		
GST Adjustments	104	0 00		
Total GST and adjustments for period Add lines 103 and 104			105	20 790 00
Input Tax Credit (ITC)	106	8 421 00		
ITC Adjustments	107	0 00		
Total ITCs and Adjustments Add lines 106 and 107			108	8 421 00
Sutract line 108 from line 106 — Net Tax			109	12 369 00
Sutract line 112 from line 109 — Balance			113	12 369 00
Refund Claimed			114	
or Payment Enclosed			115	12 369 00

		Debit	Credit
(viii)	GST Payable	20 790	
	Input Tax Credit (ITC)		8 421
	Cash in Bank		12 369
	To record Cheque No. 319 in payment of the GST payable at month-end.		

Obviously, the result of posting the above entry will show that both the GST Payable and Input Tax Credit (ITC) accounts will have zero balances as shown below.

GST Payable — 203

	Debit		Credit
(vii)	210	(vi)	21 000
(viii)	20 790		
	Ø		

Input Tax Credit (ITC) — 204

	Debit		Credit
(i)	7 000	(v)	175
(ii)	1 400	(viii)	8 421
(iii)	70		
(iv)	126		
	Ø		

Case 2: Manual Method with a Refund Claimed In this case, we will use the same summary data as outlined under Case 1, except that in Transaction (vi) we will assume that the total sales for June totalled only $100 000, and that the applicable GST on these sales totalled only $7000. With this change, the two GST accounts may be viewed at month-end as illustrated at the top of page 603.

Obviously, the difference between the balances in the two GST accounts shows that a refund of $1631 ($8421 – $6790) will be claimed on the GST Remittance Form. To account for this claimed refund, a General Journal entry would be made as follows:

		Debit	Credit
(viii)	GST Payable	6 790	
	GST Refund Receivable	1 631	
	Input Tax Credit (ITC)		8 421
	To record the refund claimed on the GST Tax Return for Registrants remittance form for June.		

GST Payable 203

Debit		Credit	
(vii)	210	(vi)	7 000
		Balance	6 790

Input Tax Credit (ITC) 204

Debit		Credit	
(i)	7 000	(v)	175
(ii)	1 400		
(iii)	70		
(iv)	126		
Balance	8 421		

The results of posting the double entry on page 602 may be analyzed in T-account form as follows:

GST Refund Receivable 105

Debit		Credit	
(viii)	1 631		

GST Payable 203

Debit		Credit	
(vii)	210	(vi)	7 000
(viii)	6 790		

Balance: Ø

Input Tax Credit (ITC) 204

Debit		Credit	
(i)	7 000	(v)	175
(ii)	1 400	(viii)	8 421
(iii)	70		
(iv)	126		

Balance: Ø

Analysis: Both the GST Payable and Input Tax Credit (ITC) accounts show zero balances. However, the current asset GST Refund Receivable reports that a cheque for $1671 is expected from the Receiver General of Canada's office. When the refund is received, a journal entry would be made by debiting Cash in Bank and crediting GST Refund Receivable. However, if a balance sheet were prepared before the cheque is received, the Current Asset section would report GST Refund Receivable for $1631.

Case 3: Using Microcomputer Software Accounting software developers will modify their existing programs to permit the tracking of all data required to complete the GST Tax Return for Registrants. Although each developer will offer its own unique approach, the following general points may be applied to all microcomputer software programmed to track the GST:

- The GL Chart of Accounts will be expanded to include additional accounts to track the data required to complete the boxes on the Goods and Services Tax Return for Registrants. Therefore, accounts may be created to track the GST Collectable, the GST Adjustments, the Input Tax Credit (ITC), ITC Adjustments, GST Instalments, GST Rebates, and, if applicable, the GST Refund Claimed.
- Exact account titles to track all boxes on the remittance form will vary from one software package to another. However, these titles will usually be related to the function identified in the boxes of the GST Return for Registrants.
- The account title related to "GST Collectable" will probably be a current liability like GST Payable. However, one can expect different titles to support the data required for Input Tax Credit (ITC). As stated earlier, some accountants favour the use of a current asset account while others will recommend the use of a contra current liability account.
- With sufficient accounts to track and complete all required boxes on the GST Return for Registrants, one could expect to see the availability of a special printed report or schedule summarizing the account data for any accounting period. Obviously, such a report will facilitate the easy completion of the GST remittance form.
- The usual short-cuts over a manual system will be available. For example, in printing a sales invoice, the software may allow for the automatic accounting of the sale with GST and PST to the GL and subsidiary ledgers. In other words, the invoicing program will be interfaced with the General Ledger, Accounts Receivable Ledger, and Inventory Ledger so that the resulting journal entry is posted automatically and correctly to all accounts.
- Above all else, the theory of using more than one account to track the GST will be based on what was presented in the two cases under the manual method. Therefore, on completion of the GST Return for Registrants, and if a refund is claimed, an entry would be made through the General Ledger system to close out all GST accounts and debiting a current asset like GST Refund Receivable. On the other hand, if a payment is required to pay a balance owing, an entry would be made to close out all GST accounts and credit a current asset like Cash in Bank.

PROBLEMS

Determining GST status of common goods and services.

P 14-1 Beside each of the following items, write a 7% if the good or service is GST taxable, a 0% if a good or service is zero-rated, or an E if it is tax-exempt.

whole-wheat bread	________	toothpaste	________
digital stereo	________	chair	________
wheelchair	________	candy	________
movie ticket	________	taxi fare	________
haircut	________	coat	________
white milk	________	penicillin	________
contact lenses	________	fresh fish	________
dental fees	________	child care	________
college tuition	________	mortgage	________

Calculating GST paid and GST collectable; calculating net tax.

P 14-2 Megaparts Inc. is a manufacturer of electronic parts for stereos and televisions. The following is a list of purchases (not including GST) it has made over the last three months:

ABC Co.	$4389.00
XYZ Co.	3875.25
NTT Co.	2256.00

Over this period, it has made the following sales (not including GST):

RNE Co.	$7843.00
BWP Co.	8294.45
ORC Co.	3355.55

a. Calculate the total purchases for the three months and the GST paid on those purchases.

b. Calculate total sales for the three months and the GST collected on those sales.

c. Calculate the **net tax** owing for the three months, assuming there are no adjustments necessary.

Journalizing transactions to Sales and Purchases Journals; calculating GST; completing the GST return.

P 14-3 The following is a summary of transactions for ABC Wholesale Company.

Jan. 1 Purchased goods for resale from Martins' Supply costing $4000.00 plus GST. *Hint*: You must calculate and add GST to the cost.

3 Purchased goods for resale from The Wright Place costing $5211.55 plus GST.

6 Sales for the week totalled $6893.33 plus GST.
8 Owner took home a typewriter costing $325.00 for personal use. The typewriter sells for $500.00 retail.
13 Weekly sales, $9712.38 plus GST.
15 Purchased goods for resale from Carters Inc. costing $2288.11 plus GST.
20 Weekly sales, $7703.85 plus GST.
26 Purchased goods for resale from Edwards Ltd. costing $879.99 plus GST.
27 Weekly sales, $9458.55 plus GST.
30 Sales for last two days of the month totalled $437.88 plus GST.

a. Using a Purchases Journal and a Sales Journal, record the transactions.

b. Using the GST Return provided, calculate the amount of tax owing at the end of the period. Assume there are no adjustments.

Journalizing transactions with GST to the GL; posting to T-accounts; calculating GST payable.

P 14-4 Return to Problem 14-3 but in this problem assume that ABC Wholesale Company uses the following GL accounts to track GST transactions: GST Refund Receivable (105); GST Payable (203); and Input Tax Credit (ITC) (204).

a. Record all transactions given in Problem 14-3 in a General Journal. Use both GST Payable and Input Tax Credit to account for the GST charged or collected on sales and charged or paid on purchases respectively.

b. Set up T-accounts for GST Payable (203) and Input Tax Credit (204). Post the data affecting these accounts only from the General Journal in **a** above.

c. Calculate and show balances in the T-accounts posted in **b** above.

d. Calculate the amount of the tax owing at month-end. Assume that ABC Wholesale Company elects to remit the GST on a monthly basis. Therefore, record the double entry in the General Journal assuming a cheque is made out as at February 15 to the Receiver General of Canada for the balance owing on the GST.

e. Make the following changes in the transactions outlined for ABC Wholesale Company in Problem 14-3.

June 6 Sales for the week totalled only $3000. The GST must be added to this amount.
13 Weekly sales totalled only $5000. The GST must be added to this amount.
20 Weekly sales totalled only $4000 plus GST.
27 Weekly sales totalled only $4500 plus GST.

Repeat the General Journal entries for all transactions, including those with the changes given above.

f. Post the results of the entries in **e** to T-accounts for GST Payable and Input Tax Credit.

g. Compute the balances in each T-account in **f** above. Is there a GST balance owing or a claimed refund? Explain your answer.

h. Show an appropriate double entry to reflect the balance of GST in **g** above. Include a short explanation for this entry.

MINI-CASES

Analyzing the net effect of the GST.

MC 14-1 Two accounting students were discussing the Goods and Services Tax. One student complained, "The GST is only 7%, but in reality it is much more than that, since tax is collected at all stages of business, from manufacturing right through to retail. In fact, the real level of taxation is closer to 14%, once you account for all levels. This is why the government has used the value-added type of tax, rather than a straight 7% retail (sales) tax."

a. Using an example with numbers, show the students how the net effect of GST, collected at all levels, is exactly the same as a 7% retail sales tax, applied at one level.

b. If the GST has the same effect as a 7% retail sales tax, why would the government use the complex value-added type of tax instead?

Applying the GST to laid-down cost.

MC 14-2 After completing their study of Chapters 13 and 14 featuring the accounting of the GST, several students discussed the Goods and Services Tax and its effects on applying GAAPs. One student, Mary, admitted total confusion with the GST and the theory of applying it to the cost principle. For discussion purposes, she used the example of a manufacturer purchasing a machine for its plant showing the following costs:

Original invoice cost	$10 000
Less: 2% cash discount	200
Cash equivalent price	9 800
GST at 7%	686
Freight-in	200
GST on freight-in	14
Fee to install in plant	300
Total costs	$11 000

Mary claimed that under the cost principle, the Machinery account should be debited for its laid-down cost, that is, $11 000.

a. Is Mary correct? Explain why or why not.

ACCOUNTING FOR PROVINCIAL RETAIL SALES TAX

This textbook will use Ontario forms and procedures to illustrate the retail sales tax system. The procedures in other provinces will be very similar, although there may be minor differences.

Taxable sales: the sale or rental of all goods except those exempt under the Retail Sales Tax Act.

Collection of Retail Sales Tax

Persons who regularly make taxable sales — all sales or the rental of goods except those exempt under the Retail Sales Tax Act — are required to collect retail sales tax. For the purposes of retail sales tax, you are a "person" if a business is:

- a sole proprietorship (one owner)
- a partnership (more than one owner)
- a corporation (an incorporated business with shareholders)
- an association (a group, such as the Lion's Club or the YWCA)

Retail Sales Tax Vendor's Permit: an identification document issued by the provincial government to all businesses required to collect retail sales tax.

A business must register with the provincial government, and receive a retail sales tax vendor's permit. This document is required before provincial sales tax (PST) can be collected. There is no charge for registering with the government or for the vendor's permit. Any business that sells taxable goods or services must register. Businesses that do not sell taxable items, but consume or use taxable goods, also must register and receive a vendor's permit — for example, a person who sells goods or services at a flea market.

At the time of writing, the sales tax in Ontario is 8%. Therefore, for every dollar of sales, the vendor must collect eight cents on behalf of the Ontario government. To assist retailers to calculate and collect

Ontario Ministry of Revenue / Ministère du Revenu
Retail Sales Tax Branch / Direction de la taxe de vente au détail

Sales Tax Schedule at 8%
Barème de la taxe de vente à 8%

$ Amount *Montant $*			$ Tax *Taxe $*	$ Amount *Montant $*			$ Tax *Taxe $*
.21	to/à	.31	.02	5.82	to/à	5.93	.47
.32	to/à	.43	.03	5.94	to/à	6.06	.48
.44	to/à	.56	.04	6.07	to/à	6.18	.49
.57	to/à	.68	.05	6.19	to/à	6.31	.50
.69	to/à	.81	.06	6.32	to/à	6.43	.51
.82	to/à	.93	.07	6.44	to/à	6.56	.52
.94	to/à	1.06	.08	6.57	to/à	6.68	.53
1.07	to/à	1.18	.09	6.69	to/à	6.81	.54
1.19	to/à	1.31	.10	6.82	to/à	6.93	.55
1.32	to/à	1.43	.11	6.94	to/à	7.06	.56
1.44	to/à	1.56	.12	7.07	to/à	7.18	.57
1.57	to/à	1.68	.13	7.19	to/à	7.31	.58
1.69	to/à	1.81	.14	7.32	to/à	7.43	.59
1.82	to/à	1.93	.15	7.44	to/à	7.56	.60
1.94	to/à	2.06	.16	7.57	to/à	7.68	.61
2.07	to/à	2.18	.17	7.69	to/à	7.81	.62
2.19	to/à	2.31	.18	7.82	to/à	7.93	.63
2.32	to/à	2.43	.19	7.94	to/à	8.06	.64
2.44	to/à	2.56	.20	8.07	to/à	8.18	.65
2.57	to/à	2.68	.21	8.19	to/à	8.31	.66
2.69	to/à	2.81	.22	8.32	to/à	8.43	.67
2.82	to/à	2.93	.23	8.44	to/à	8.56	.68
2.94	to/à	3.06	.24	8.57	to/à	8.68	.69
3.07	to/à	3.18	.25	8.69	to/à	8.81	.70
3.19	to/à	3.31	.26	8.82	to/à	8.93	.71
3.32	to/à	3.43	.27	8.94	to/à	9.06	.72
3.44	to/à	3.56	.28	9.07	to/à	9.18	.73
3.57	to/à	3.68	.29	9.19	to/à	9.31	.74
3.69	to/à	3.81	.30	9.32	to/à	9.43	.75
3.82	to/à	3.93	.31	9.44	to/à	9.56	.76
3.94	to/à	4.06	.32	9.57	to/à	9.68	.77
4.07	to/à	4.18	.33	9.69	to/à	9.81	.78
4.19	to/à	4.31	.34	9.82	to/à	9.93	.79
4.32	to/à	4.43	.35	9.94	to/à	10.06	.80
4.44	to/à	4.56	.36				
4.57	to/à	4.68	.37	20.00			1.60
4.69	to/à	4.81	.38	30.00			2.40
4.82	to/à	4.93	.39	40.00			3.20
4.94	to/à	5.06	.40	50.00			4.00
5.07	to/à	5.18	.41	100.00			8.00
5.19	to/à	5.31	.42	200.00			16.00
5.32	to/à	5.43	.43	300.00			24.00
5.44	to/à	5.56	.44	400.00			32.00
5.57	to/à	5.68	.45	500.00			40.00
5.69	to/à	5.81	.46	GV-13			0418V (89-11)

these amounts, the government supplies businesses with a chart showing the amount of tax to be charged. See the marginal illustration.

Computerized cash register systems can be programmed to automatically differentiate between taxable and non-taxable items, and calculate tax and determine the final total. Let's use the tax schedule in the margin to determine the amount of tax on an item costing $10.51. For ten dollars, the tax indicated on the chart is $0.80. On $0.51 the tax is $0.04. The total tax is $0.80 + $0.04 or $0.84. You can double-check this by multiplying: $10.51 × 8% or $0.84.

Since sales tax is collected by the vendor on behalf of the provincial government, the amount collected represents a current liability owed to the government, since it must be paid within the current operating cycle. The account usually used is called **Provincial Sales Tax Payable**, or simply PST Payble.

For the purposes of the next few examples of accounting entries, the effects of the GST will be ignored, since accounting practice will vary among provinces for reasons explained later in this chapter.

Assume that on April 2, 19—, Walter Frampton sells taxable goods for cash, $800. The accounts affected would be Sales, Cash, and the new account, Sales Tax Payable. The entry in the General Journal would appear as follows:

GENERAL JOURNAL Page 6

DATE 19—	ACCOUNT TITLE AND EXPLANATION	POST. REF.	DEBIT	CREDIT
Apr. 2	Cash		864 00	
	Sales			800 00
	PST Payable	205		64 00
	To record the sale of goods plus the collection of sales tax at 8%.			

Analysis:

- The transaction results in a credit entry to Sales of $800.
- Sales tax is calculated at 8%; therefore the tax to be collected is $800 × 8% = $64.
- The asset Cash increases (debit) by $800 + $64 or $864.

On April 4, goods totalling $100 are sold to J. Arledge on account. The journal entry is illustrated on page 610.

Walter Frampton's business now owes the Ontario government $72, as shown in the T-account in the margin. Each time the business makes a sale of taxable goods, the sales tax owing to the government increases.

PST Payable

	19—	
	Apr. 2	64
	4	8
		72

GENERAL JOURNAL Page 6

DATE	ACCOUNT TITLE AND EXPLANATION	POST. REF.	DEBIT	CREDIT
19—				
Apr. 4	Accounts Receivable/J. Arledge ..		108 00	
	Sales			100 00
	PST Payable	205		8 00
	To record the sale of goods on account plus sales tax at 8%. Terms n/30.			

Analysis: Examine the cash sale and the credit sale illustrated in the General Journal and the related entries in the PST Payable ledger account, and then examine the Combination Journal (opposite) and the example of a five-journal system (page 612).

General Journal Example

PST Payable Account No. 205

DATE	ACCOUNT TITLE AND EXPLANATION	POST. REF.	DEBIT	CREDIT	BALANCE
19—					
Apr. 2	Cash Sale	GJ6		64 00	64 00
4	J. Arledge	GJ6		8 00	72 00
10	P. Frampton			16 00	88 00
20	Cash Sale			80 00	168 00
25	P. Marvel			36 00	204 00

- Notice, in the Combination Journal opposite, the cash sale for $800 on April 2. Because the business must collect sales tax on most sales, a special column, PST Payable CR., has been added to record tax. Keep in mind we are omitting GST in this example.
- Since a separate column is used, no posting is required until month-end. The entry is easier than the General Journal entry on the previous pages; it requires only one line and each item has its own column.
- The credit sale to J. Arledge is shown next. Compare the Combination Journal to the General Journal entry. Examine the receipt of funds from J. Arledge on April 30 in the Combination Journal. *Note:* Posting references are shown only for entries under discussion.

Now examine the same set of entries in the Cash Receipts Journal of the five-journal system shown on page 612.

COMBINATION JOURNAL Page 11

	DATE	ACCOUNT TITLE AND EXPLANATION	POST. REF.	GENERAL LEDGER		ACCOUNTS RECEIVABLE		ACCOUNTS PAYABLE		PURCHASES	PURCHASES DISCOUNT	SALES	PST PAYABLE	CASH		CHQ. NO.	
				DEBIT	CREDIT	DEBIT	CREDIT	DEBIT	CREDIT	DEBIT	CREDIT	CREDIT	CREDIT	DEBIT	CREDIT		
1	19— Apr. 1	Cash Balance $5 400	—														1
2	2	Cash Sale	—									800.00	64.00	864.00			2
3	4	J. Arledge Terms n/30	—			108.00						100.00	8.00				3
4	6	Bought Merchandise	—							650.00					650.00	73	4
5	10	P. Frampton Terms n/30	—			216.00						200.00	16.00				5
6	13	PUC Expense Inv. T-1173	—	85.00											85.00	74	6
7	18	Paid M. & D. Ltd. in Full	—					312.00							312.00	75	7
8	20	Cash Sale	—									1 000.00	80.00	1080.00			8
9	25	P.Marvel Terms n/30	—			486.00						450.00	36.00				9
10	29	Bought Equipment on Acct.															10
11		J. Rosand Ltd.	—	2 000.00					2000.00								11
12	30	Paid Rent Expense	—	480.00											480.00	76	12
13	30	Rec'd from J. Arledge	—				108.00							108.00			13
14	Apr. 30	Totals		2 565.00		810.00	108.00	312.00	2000.00	650.00		2 550.00	204.00	2 052.00	1 527.00		14
15													(205)				15

SALES JOURNAL Page 3

DATE 19—	INVOICE NUMBER	ACCOUNT DEBITED	TERMS	POST. REF.	ACCOUNTS RECEIVABLE DEBIT	SALES CREDIT	PST PAYABLE CREDIT
Apr. 4	V-111	J. Arledge	n/30		108.00	100.00	8.00
10	V-112	P. Frampton	n/30		216.00	200.00	16.00
25	V-113	P. Marvel	n/30		486.00	450.00	36.00
Apr. 30					810.00	750.00	60.00
							(205)

CASH RECEIPTS JOURNAL Page 10

DATE 19—	ACCOUNT CREDITED	EXPLANATION	POST. REF.	ACCOUNTS RECEIVABLE DEBIT	SALES CREDIT	PST PAYABLE CREDIT	SALES DISCOUNTS DEBIT	CASH DEBIT
Apr. 1	Cash Balance	$5 400						
2		Cash sale.			800.00	64.00		864.00
20		Cash sale.			1 000.00	80.00		1080.00
30		On account.		108.00				108.00
Apr. 30	J. Arledge			108.00	1 800.00	144.00		2052.00
						(205)		

Combination Journal Example

PST Payable Account No. 205

DATE		POST. REF.	DEBIT	CREDIT	BALANCE
19—					
Apr. 30	Total	CJ11		204 .00	204 .00

Five-Journal System Example

PST Payable Account No. 205

DATE		POST. REF.	DEBIT	CREDIT	BALANCE
19—					
Apr. 30	Sales Journal Total ...	SJ3		60.00	60.00
Apr. 30	Cash Receipts Journal Total	CRJ10		144.00	204.00

Analysis:

- In the Cash Receipts Journal entry of April 2, the entry takes only one line.

By expanding the journal and including one more column, PST Payable Credit, each account has its own column, reducing the amount of posting.

Examine the Sales Journal for the sale on account. At month-end, the PST Payable account would appear as in the next illustrations of each of the three systems.

No matter which system is used, the business has collected sales tax totalling $204 for the provincial government. The method of remitting this tax will be examined later.

ACCOUNTING FOR SALES TAX ON SALES RETURNS AND ALLOWANCES

Whenever a sale is made, there is a chance that the item sold will be returned for some reason. You have studied the accounting for this transaction, but what happens when sales tax is involved?

Assume that on April 3, goods sold for $25 on April 2 are returned because the goods were damaged. The business agrees to refund the $25 plus provincial sales tax. *Note*: For simplicity, the effects of GST will be omitted. Refer to Chapter 13 for effects under GST. The total to be refunded is $25 × 108% or $27. Compare the General Journal entry on page 615 with the entries in the five-journal and Combination Journal systems illustrated on page 614.

The issuing of a cheque for the cash refund has been analyzed in General Journal form for the five-journal system. Normally it would be recorded in the Cash Payments Journal.

Assume that on April 26, P. Marvel returns $10 of her goods. After negotiating, she agrees to keep the good, if an allowance of $5 is given. Examine the treatment of the transaction under the three systems, as illustrated on pages 616 and 617.

Analysis:

- Because the price was reduced, a portion of the provincial sales tax is refunded.
- Note the increased number of entries in the General Ledger accounts. It is necessary to make these entries since the Combination Journal and the five-journal system do not have a debit column for PST Payable, only **Credit** columns. In the five-journal system, the entry must go into the General Journal, while in the Combination Journal, it can be placed in the General Ledger column.

Sales Discounts and Sales Tax Payable Discounts are taken **only** on the sale, **not** the total amount owing. Refer to the transaction involving J. Arledge. If terms of 2/10, n/30 had been offered and J. Arledge had paid within the discount period, the discount would have been $2 ($100 × 2%). The discount must be taken only on the amount of the sale, which is $100 in this case. Do you remember how purchases discounts were taken when transportation-in was involved? The sales discount procedure is exactly the same.

Finally, note that the Combination Journal illustrated does not have a column for sales discounts. Sales discounts are recorded in the General Ledger Debit column. Because the Cash Receipts Journal has a Sales Discounts Debit column, it should be used as applicable.

REMITTING SALES TAX TO THE PROVINCIAL GOVERNMENT

Normally, at the end of each month, businesses remit to the provincial government any tax collected during that month. *Note*: Some busi-

Five-Journal System

GENERAL JOURNAL Page 6

DATE 19—	ACCOUNT TITLE AND EXPLANATION	POST. REF.	DEBIT	CREDIT
Apr. 3	Sales Returns and Allowances ..		25 00	
	PST Payable	205	2 00	
	Cash			27 00
	Cash refund for goods returned.			
26	Sales Returns and Allowances		5 00	
	PST Payable	205	40	
	Accts. Rec/P. Marvel			5 40
	To record an allowance.			

COMBINATION JOURNAL Page 11

	DATE 19—	ACCOUNT TITLE AND EXPLANATION	POST. REF.	GENERAL LEDGER		ACCOUNTS RECEIVABLE		ACCOUNTS PAYABLE		PURCHASES	PST PAYABLE	SALES	PST PAYABLE	CASH		CHQ. NO.	
				DEBIT	CREDIT	DEBIT	CREDIT	DEBIT	CREDIT	DEBIT	CREDIT	CREDIT	CREDIT	DEBIT	CREDIT		
1	Apr. 1	Cash Balance $5 400	—														1
2	2	Cash Sale	—									800 00	64 00	864 00			2
3	3	Sales Returns and															3
4		Allowances	—	25 00													4
5		Sales Tax Payable	205	2 00											27 00	72	5
6	4	J. Arland (n/30)	—			108 00						100 00	8 00				6
7	6	Bought Merchandise	—							650 00					650 00	73	7
8	10	P. Frampton (n/30)	—			216 00						200 00	16 00				8
9	13	PUC Expense Inv. T-1173	—	85 00											85 00	74	9
10	18	Paid M. & D. Ltd. in Full	—					312 00							312 00	75	10
11	20	Cash Sale	—									1000 00	80 00	1080 00			11
12	25	P. Marvel (n/30)	—			486 00						450 00	36 00				12
13	26	Sales R & A/P. Marvel	—	5 00													13
14		Sales Tax Payable	205	40			5 40									76	14
15	29	Bought Equip. (J. Rosand Ltd.)	—	2 000 00					2000 00								15
16	30	Paid Rent Expense		480 00											480 00		16
17	30	Rec'd from J. Arland					108 00							108 00			17
18	Apr. 30	Totals		2 597 40		810 00	113 40	312 00	2000 00	650 00		2 550 00	204 00	2052 00	1554 00		18
													(205)				

GENERAL JOURNAL Page 6

DATE	ACCOUNT TITLE AND EXPLANATION	POST. REF.	DEBIT	CREDIT
19—				
Apr. 3	Sales R & A		25.00	
	PST Payable	205	2.00	
	Cash			27.00
	To record the refund on the April 2 sale. Cheque No. 72.			
26	Sales R & A		5.00	
	PST Payable	205	0.40	
	Accounts Receivable/ P. Marvel			5.40
	To record an allowance of $5 on merchandise.			

General Journal Example

PST Payable Account No. 205

DATE		POST. REF.	DEBIT	CREDIT	BALANCE
19—					
Apr. 2	Cash Sale			64.00	64.00
3	Sales Return	GJ6	2.00		62.00
4	J. Arledge			8.00	70.00
10	P. Frampton			16.00	86.00
20	Cash Sale			80.00	166.00
25	P.Marvel			36.00	202.00
26	Sales Allowance—Marvel	GJ6	0.40		201.60

Combination Journal Example

PST Payable Account No. 205

DATE		POST. REF.	DEBIT	CREDIT	BALANCE
19—					
Apr. 3	Sales Return	CJ11	2.00		2.00 DR.
26	Sales Allowance—Marvel	CJ11	0.40		2.40 DR.
30	Total	CJ11		204.00	201.60 CR.

(Continued from page 615.)

Five-Journal System Example

PST Payable — Account No. 205

DATE		POST. REF.	DEBIT	CREDIT	BALANCE
19—					
Apr. 3	Sales Return	GJ6	2.00		2.00 DR.
26	Sales Allowance—Marvel	GJ6	0.40		2.40 DR.
30	Sales Journal Total ...			60.00	57.60
30	Cash Receipts Total ..			144.00	201.60

nesses can remit less frequently if their tax collections are low enough.

You should now understand why PST Payable is a current liability account: businesses must remit tax at least every six months.

Registered Vendor Retail Sales Tax Return: the form used for submission of retail sales tax to the provincial government.

To remit the tax, the business must complete a Registered Vendor Retail Sales Tax Return, which is mailed to the business every month by the provincial government. Examine the opposite illustration.

Analysis:

For this business:

- Total of sales in Ontario was $2550.00.
- Tax collected on sales was $196.60.
- Tax on purchases for personal use were nil.
- Payment is being made on time.
- Compensation (payment to the business for collecting the tax) is based on the tax collected. See the marginal illustration. Here, tax collected falls between $16.01 and $400.00, therefore compensation is $16.00.
- There are no adjustments.

Let us follow through the return to determine the final amount.

Line 1:	$2550	Total sales
Line 2:	196.60	Sales tax collected
Line 3:	0	(No purchases)
Line 4:	196.60	Lines 2 + 3
Line 5:	0	No penalty
Line 6:	196.60	Subtotal
Line 7:	16.00	Compensation
Line 8:	180.60	Subtotal
Line 9:	0	No adjustments
Line 10:	180.60	Tax to be paid

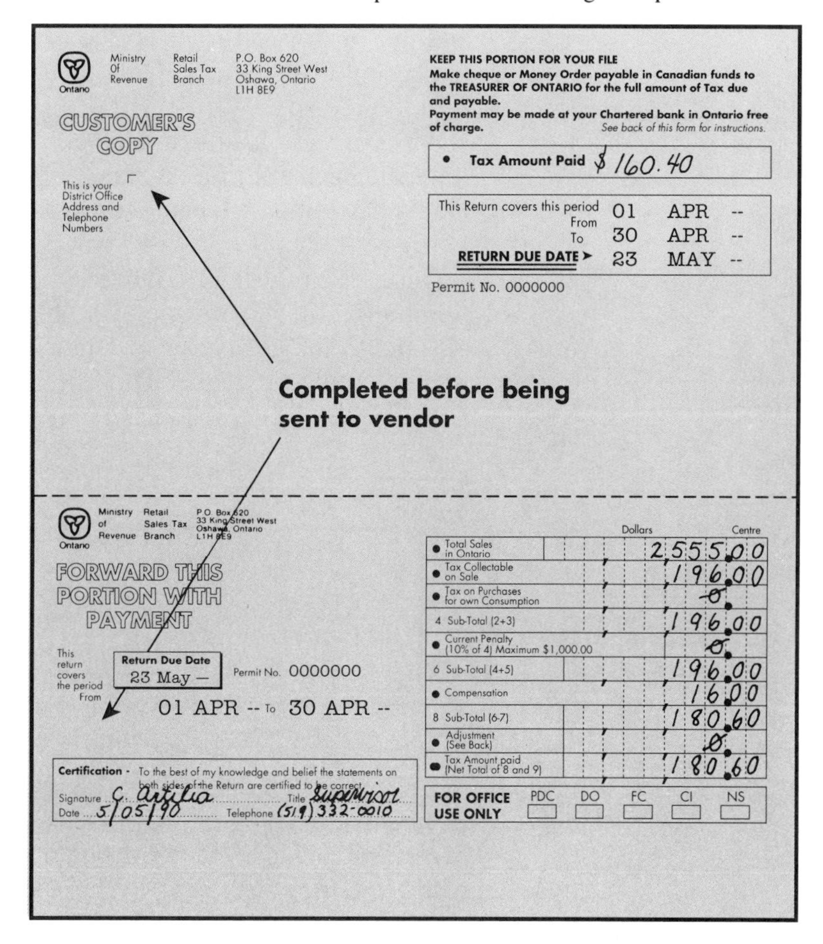

Ontario Ministry Of Revenue | Retail Sales Tax Branch | P.O. Box 620, 33 King Street West, Oshawa, Ontario L1H 8E9

CUSTOMER'S COPY

This is your District Office Address and Telephone Numbers

KEEP THIS PORTION FOR YOUR FILE
Make cheque or Money Order payable in Canadian funds to the TREASURER OF ONTARIO for the full amount of Tax due and payable.
Payment may be made at your Chartered bank in Ontario free of charge. *See back of this form for instructions.*

• **Tax Amount Paid** $160.40

This Return covers this period From 01 APR -- To 30 APR --
RETURN DUE DATE ➤ 23 MAY --

Permit No. 0000000

Ontario Ministry of Revenue | Retail Sales Tax Branch | P.O. Box 620, 33 King Street West, Oshawa, Ontario L1H 8E9

FORWARD THIS PORTION WITH PAYMENT

This return covers the period From 01 APR -- To 30 APR --

Return Due Date 23 May —

Permit No. 0000000

	Dollars	Centre
• Total Sales in Ontario	2,555	00
• Tax Collectable on Sale	196	00
• Tax on Purchases for own Consumption	-0-	
4 Sub-Total (2+3)	196	00
• Current Penalty (10% of 4) Maximum $1,000.00	-0-	
6 Sub-Total (4+5)	196	00
• Compensation	16	00
8 Sub-Total (6-7)	180	60
• Adjustment (See Back)	-0-	
• Tax Amount paid (Net Total of 8 and 9)	180	60

Certification - To the best of my knowledge and belief the statements on both sides of the Return are certified to be correct.
Signature C. Artilia Title Supervisor
Date 5/05/90 Telephone (519) 332-0010

FOR OFFICE USE ONLY PDC DO FC CI NS

Due dates: the date by which the vendor must submit the retail sales tax collected to the provincial government.

Each return mailed by the government to the retailer will carry a due date on the front of the return. Failure to meet this deadline results in a financial penalty (see line 5 above) and the loss of any compensation for that period. Returns are mailed to businesses about three weeks before the due date.

Payments can be made in three ways:

- mail by cheque or money order to the Ministry of Revenue, in the envelope provided. You must allow for delivery time to ensure timely arrival before due date.
- at any chartered bank before the due date. There is no charge for this bank service. Late payments must be mailed to the Ministry.
- in person at a local Retail Sales Tax Office or Ministry of Revenue Information Office.

The return **must** be filed, even if no tax was collected during the period. If this is the case, NIL is written in the appropriate spaces, and the form is returned to the Ministry by the due date. Banks will not accept NIL returns. Only the owner or an authorized person may sign the return.

Any corrections due to changes in operation, ownership, business, trade, legal name, or business mailing address must be reported on the Notification of Change form that is attached to the envelope provided with the return. The form is returned to the Ministry.

Once the return is complete, the business must account for the remittance. In our example, a cheque or money order for $180.60, payable to the Treasurer of Ontario, must be sent. The PST Payable account must be reduced to zero, and the compensation recorded. Examine the General Journal entry below:

May 10	PST Payable	196.60	
	Cash		180.60
	Compensation Revenue		16.00
	To record payment of sales tax less compensation for April. Cheque No. 84.		

Depending on the amount of revenue earned as compensation, the business may open a ''Compensation Revenue'' account, or use a Miscellaneous or Other Revenue account. The same entry would be made in either of the two systems discussed in this chapter.

Maintenance of Records The provincial government requires that every business keep complete and current records of all business transactions. Records may not be destroyed until a set of strict conditions are met in accordance with regulations in each province. These records may be audited at any time.

Sales Tax on Net Sales Sales tax need only be charged on the net sales total. For example, ABC Company sells taxable items at $2 per unit, with a 5% discount for orders greater than 1000 units. If XYZ Ltd. orders 3000 units, the taxable selling price is calculated as shown in the margin.

Likewise, if ABC Company offers a 6% discount for immediate payment in cash, and XYZ Ltd. pays cash for the 3000 units they ordered, the calculation would be as shown opposite.

Retail store coupons: printed forms offering a specified reduction (discount) at a specific store on a particular product.

Discount Coupons Retail stores and restaurants often issue coupons, called retail store coupons and restaurant coupons, that offer a discount on specific products. Since the coupon can be

Dinner Bill	$25.00
Less: Coupon	5.00
Taxable Amount	$20.00
Tax at 8%	1.60
Total Bill	$21.60

Orange Soda	$0.79
Tax	0.06
Pre-Coupon Price	$0.85
Coupon Value	0.25
Net Price	$0.60

Restaurant coupons: printed forms offering some sort of reduction in the price of a meal or a combination of meals.

Manufacturers' coupons: printed forms offering a reduction on the price of a certain product at any store that sells the product.

Money coupons: printed forms representing money, given to customers at the time of a purchase to lower the cost of a future purchase at that store.

Purchase Exemption Certificate: document filed with the seller by the buyer, enabling the seller to buy taxable goods for resale without paying Retail Sales Tax.

redeemed for a discount, the retail sales tax is charged on the net price, which is the total price minus the coupon. For example, if a customer redeems a $5 coupon when paying for a $25 meal, the tax would be calculated as shown above.

Do not confuse retail store and restaurant coupons with manufacturers' coupons and money coupons. Manufacturers' coupons reduce the price of a specific product at any store, and money coupons give the customer the chance to reduce the price of a future purchase at a specific store (for example, Canadian Tire cash discount coupons). They give the customer a reduction in price, but tax must be paid on the price before the discount. For example, if a customer redeems a manufacturers' coupon for orange soda for $0.25, the tax is calculated on the full price, then the coupon value is subtracted from the amount owing. Refer again to the illustration above.

There are many rules and regulations which affect retail sales tax in specific circumstances. Some areas of special rules affect Status Indians, Purchase Exemption Certificates (which allow a business to buy goods free of PST if the goods are for resale), tax-included pricing, and rentals.

Since tax laws are dynamic and vary among provinces, you are advised to contact your local Retail Sales Tax branch for current details.

Retail Sales Tax and the GST The introduction of the GST has complicated the calculation of the provincial retail sales tax. Previously, the federal sales tax was hidden in the retail price upon which the retail sales tax is calculated. Now, if the retailer so chooses, the GST must be calculated at the cash register on the selling price of the goods or services. Then the retail sales tax must be calculated. But on what figure is the retail sales tax calculated? Does the retailer use the price of the goods, or the price of the goods plus GST? The answer to this question will depend on the province where the retailer operates. At this time, Manitoba, Ontario, and British Columbia have indicated that they will not "tax the tax," meaning that they will apply their provincial rate on the price of the goods or services only,

Provincial Retail Sales Tax Rates

Alberta	no tax
British Columbia	6%
Saskatchewan	7%
Manitoba	7%
Ontario	8%
[1]Quebec	9%
Nova Scotia	10%
Prince Edward Island	10%
New Brunswick	11%
Newfoundland	12%

[1]To be integrated with the GST in two years at a combined rate of 7% + 7%.

before the GST is applied. Quebec has announced that it will integrate the GST with its PST over a two-year period once the GST becomes law. At that time, a combined GST and PST (7% + 7%) will be collected by the Quebec government, which will remit the GST portion to the federal government. However, Prince Edward Island, Newfoundland, and New Brunswick have indicated that they will compound the taxes; that is, they will apply the provincial retail tax rate to the total of goods and services **plus GST**. This is, in effect, what was happening before, since the Federal Sales Tax was "hidden" in the price of the goods. Nova Scotia and Saskatchewan have not made a decision either way, but have indicated preference for the compounding method. Examine the illustrations opposite for the differences between the two methods.

Note that the two invoices are not directly comparable, since the provincial tax rate in British Columbia is lower than the rate in Prince Edward Island. The two invoices are identical, except for the last two lines. In British Columbia, the provincial tax is calculated by applying the 6% rate to the price of the goods, whereas in Prince Edward Island, the GST must be calculated and added to the price of the goods **before** the provincial tax is calculated on the invoice amount plus GST.

TOPIC 2 PROBLEMS

Calculating retail sales tax using different rates.

P 14-5 Calculate the retail sales tax that must be charged on each of the items numbered (1) to (10). Find the amount charged in Ontario (8% rate); then find the amount charged in your own province. If you live in Ontario, use British Columbia as the other province. Do the calculations in a table like the one shown below.

Item	Amount	Retail Sales Tax	
		Ontario	Your Province
(1) New car	$9 500.00		
(2) Soft drink	0.79		
(3) Chocolate bar	0.40		

(4) Refrigerator, $959.00; (5) Living room suite, $4 850.00; (6) Television set, $675.00; (7) Roast of beef, $12.80; (8) Repairs to your car, $125.00; (9) Bird feeder, $10.95; (10) Lawn fertilizer, $23.70.

ANYTIME HARDWARE
6427 Burrard St.
Vancouver, B.C.
V6M 4N2

Invoice No.
78642
GST Reg'n. No.
67443

SOLD TO: B. Meilleur
34- West 2nd Avenue
Vancouver, British Columbia V6M 4K2

TERMS: Cash

Item No.	Description	GST Rate	Quan.	Price	Extension
47621	Ladder	7%	1	39.95	39.95
84377	Spray gun	7%	1	612.99	612.99
57334	4 L . Paint	7%	10	24.75	247.50
			A. TOTAL BEFORE TAX		900.44
			B. GST 7% (AxB)		63.03
			C. PST 6% (AxC)		54.03
			D. TOTAL OWING (A+B+C)		1017.50

Tax Not Compounded

ANYWHERE HARDWARE
123 MAIN STREET
Summerside, Prince Edward Island
C1N 1R7

Invoice No.
A-1137
GST Reg'n. No.
45662

SOLD TO: S. Gibson
49 Goodale Drive
Summerside, Prince Edward Island C1N 1R7

TERMS: Cash

Item No.	Description	GST Rate	Quan.	Price	Extension
47621	Ladder	7%	1	39.95	39.95
84377	Spray gun	7%	1	612.99	612.99
57334	4 L. Paint	7%	10	24.75	247.50
			A. TOTAL BEFORE TAX		900.44
			B. GST 7% (AxB)		63.03
			C. PST 10% (A+B)xC		96.35
			D. TOTAL OWING (A+B+C)		1059.82

Tax Compounded

Calculating Retail Sales Tax.

Journalizing remittance of tax.

P 14-6 Refer to the illustration of a sales tax return form shown on page 617.

a. Given the following information, calculate the amount of the cheque to be remitted to the Treasurer of Ontario by completing the return.

b. Complete the necessary General Journal entry to record the results of this source document.

Total Sales for the Month	$18 585.00
PST Collected	1 384.97
Tax on Own Purchases	33.83

Journalizing transactions with Retail Sales Tax to a Combination Journal.

Posting to GL and subsidiary ledgers.

Proving journal and subsidiary ledgers.

P 14-7 Andrea's Flower Shop sells cut flowers and household plants. Andrea uses a multi-columned Sales Journal which includes British Columbia retail sales tax (6%) in a separate column. The following are the transactions affecting credit sales for November. Calculate retail sales tax on all sales. Terms for all sales are n/60.

a. Open General Ledger accounts as necessary.

b. Open accounts receivable ledger accounts for L. Star, B. Dart, D. Ball, and Ingrid Berg. *Hint*: Don't forget the subsidiary ledger order.

c. Journalize the transactions and post daily as necessary.

d. Total the journal and cross-foot as of November 30.

e Post month-end totals and verify the control account in the appropriate manner.

19—

Nov. 1 Invoice No. A-710 for cut flowers was issued to L. Star. Amount, $30 on account.

3 Invoice No. A-711 for a household plant was issued to B. Dart. Amount, $47 on account.

4 Invoice No. A-712 for cut flowers was issued to D. Ball. Amount $24 on account.
Note: Invoices will now proceed in numerical order.

8 Sold one dozen carnations to L. Star on account, $32.

9 Credit memo to L. Star, No. CM-010, re Invoice No. A-713, $17.

11 Sold on account to L. Star, one dozen yellow roses, $48.

12 Sold to Ingrid Berg on account, a cut flower arrangement totalling $78.

14 D. Ball bought a potted plant on account for $33.

15 Credit memo No. CM-011 to Ingrid Berg re Invoice No. A-715, $21.

TOPIC 2 MINI-CASES

Analyzing total tax collected versus total sales.

MC 14-3 Sam deClerk, a high school student, has offered to help his employer complete the monthly Retail Sales Tax Return. Sam had just learned about accounting for taxes in his accounting course. "I'm puzzled," said Sam. "The tax rate here in this province is 8%. Our total sales for the month were $32 468, yet we only collected retail sales tax of $2234.87. By my calculation, we should have collected $2597.44. What happened to the rest?"

a. Explain to Sam the probable reason for the discrepancy, using at least three specific examples.

Journalizing sales and sales returns involving GST and PST in different provinces.

MC 14-4 Ellen Dodman purchased a blouse for $75 at a local retail women's wear shop in Smallville, New Brunswick, on July 16. This sale is both GST and PST taxable. When she got home, she found it was not the same colour as her suit, and decided to return the blouse for a cash refund.

a. Prepare the journal entry that the store would have made on the original purchase.

b. Prepare the journal entry that the store would make to account for the refund.

c. Repeat both **a** and **b** assuming that the store is located in British Columbia.

TOPIC 3 ACCOUNTING FOR CREDIT CARD AND DEBIT CARD TRANSACTIONS

"Plastic money" — everyone has heard that description of **credit cards**. There are bank credit cards (for example, VISA, MasterCard), gasoline cards (Esso, Shell, Petro-Canada), department store cards (Sears, Woolco, Eaton's, K-Mart, The Bay), credit service cards (Carte Blanche, American Express, Diners Club), and finally very specialized service cards, such as the Bell Canada calling card. A calling card allows the holder to make long-distance calls on credit.

This book will discuss only VISA credit cards with illustrations from the Royal Bank of Canada. In most cases, the ideas will be similar no matter which card is considered.

To apply for a VISA card, pick up an application form at your local bank or from any store merchant who accepts the card. An application is illustrated on page 624.

DETACH HERE

ROYAL BANK VISA

APPLICATION FORM

FOR OFFICE USE ONLY

CARDHOLDER NUMBER 4 5 1 0 — 2 0 0

DATE SENT
DATE RETURNED
DATE PLASTIC MAILED

PLEASE PRINT IN BLOCK LETTERS

MR / MRS / MISS / MS — YOUR NAME: FIRST NAME, MIDDLE INITIAL, LAST NAME

MR / MRS / MISS / MS — CO-APPLICANT'S NAME: FIRST NAME, MIDDLE INITIAL, LAST NAME

MAILING ADDRESS: APT./SUITE/P.O. BOX NUMBER OR C/O

STREET NUMBER, NAME, POSTAL STATION OR R.R.

CITY/TOWN — PROVINCE/STATE/COUNTRY — POSTAL CODE OR ZIP CODE

YOUR ROYAL BANK CLIENT CARD NUMBER 4 5 1 9

CO-APPLICANT'S ROYAL BANK CLIENT CARD NUMBER 4 5 1 9

AREA CODE — HOME TELEPHONE — AREA CODE — BUSINESS TELEPHONE — EXTENSION

SOCIAL INSURANCE NO. (OPTIONAL) — BIRTH DATE: MO DAY YR

1 2 3 4 5

HOME ADDRESS, IF DIFFERENT FROM MAILING ADDRESS — HOW LONG? — ☐ OWN ☐ RENT $ ______ PER MONTH — NO. OF DEPENDENTS (EXCLUDE SPOUSE)

PREVIOUS ADDRESS (IF AT PRESENT ADDRESS LESS THAN 2 YEARS) — HOW LONG? — ☐ SINGLE ☐ MARRIED ☐ OTHER — SPOUSE'S NAME

EMPLOYER'S NAME AND ADDRESS — TELEPHONE — OCCUPATION — HOW LONG? — MONTHLY INCOME $

PREVIOUS EMPLOYER (IF WITH ABOVE LESS THAN 2 YEARS) — TELEPHONE — OCCUPATION — HOW LONG? — MONTHLY INCOME $

CO-APPLICANT NOW EMPLOYED BY: NAME AND ADDRESS — TELEPHONE — OCCUPATION — HOW LONG? — MONTHLY INCOME $

NAME AND ADDRESS OF NEAREST RELATIVE NOT LIVING WITH YOU — TELEPHONE — RELATIONSHIP — MOTHER'S MAIDEN NAME (FOR YOUR SECURITY)

REFERENCES

BANK — BRANCH ADDRESS — LOANS $ — SIGNATURE ACCT. NO. — SAVINGS ACCT. NO. — CHEQUING ACCT. NO. — PREVIOUS BANK AND/OR BRANCH IF AT PRESENT LESS THAN 1 YEAR — DID YOU PREVIOUSLY HAVE A VISA CARD ☐ YES ☐ NO

HOME FINANCED BY — ESTIMATED VALUE $ — AMOUNT OWING $ — MONTHLY PAYMENT $

AUTO MAKE & YEAR — FINANCED BY — ESTIMATED VALUE $ — AMOUNT OWING $ — MONTHLY PAYMENT $

OTHER LOANS (CREDIT CARDS/ FINANCE COMPANIES/ DEPARTMENT STORES ETC.) (Indicate acct. nos. if applicable)

NAME — ADDRESS — ACCOUNT NUMBER — AMOUNT OWING $ — MONTHLY PAYMENT $

NAME — ADDRESS — ACCOUNT NUMBER — AMOUNT OWING $ — MONTHLY PAYMENT $

TOTAL $ — TOTAL $

I (the Applicant) certify that the above information is true. If this Application is accepted by The Royal Bank of Canada ("Bank"), I request the Bank to open an account in my name ("Account") and to issue a Visa Card (including renewals and replacements thereof) to each of me and the Co-Applicant (if any). The Co-Applicant and I will be bound by the Bank's Cardholder Agreement (see over for current Cardholder Agreement), as amended or replaced from time to time, which the Bank will send to me. Use of any Visa Card applied for will show that I received such Agreement. I will be responsible for all use of and charges to the Account and the Co-Applicant and I will be jointly and severally liable for all charges incurred by the use of Visa Cards issued in my name and in the Co-Applicant's name and for any other use of the Account by either or both the Co-Applicant and me. I and the Co-Applicant authorize and consent to the receipt and exchange of credit and related information about either or both of us by the Bank, including the sharing and exchanging of such information about either or both of us by the Bank with any credit reporting agency and credit bureau, and any person or corporation with whom either or both of us has or may have financial relations.

CREDIT *LIMIT REQUESTED
$ ______
*Minimum of $1000 and multiples of $500 thereafter.

CHOIX DE LA LANGUE FRANÇAISE
Je préfère recevoir toute communication en français seulement. Je crois comprendre que ce service est offert par l'entremise de votre bureau de Montréal.
Signature du réclamant ______

SERVICE FEE
Tick (✔) One Only
☐ Transaction Fee
☐ Annual Fee
See reverse for explanation

APPLICANT'S SIGNATURE — DATE — CO-APPLICANT'S SIGNATURE — DATE

See over for Cardholder Agreement

The completed form should be mailed to the Royal Bank VISA Centre. If you meet the minimum criteria, and there are no errors or omissions or further questions, you will then receive your credit card, usually by registered mail.

The card displays the following information in raised lettering: your account number, an expiry date (in most cases), and your name. The raised lettering allows transfer of the information to the transaction slips through use of a credit card imprinter. Also printed on the card is the name VISA and the name of the bank that issued the card. Most cards now have a holographic image that changes in colour and shape when tilted slightly. This hologram makes card counterfeiting, which is a serious problem, much more difficult. On the back of the card there will be a small space for your signature, and a magnetic strip. Data is encoded on the magnetic strip that allows a cardholder to access a bank account, or VISA account, through an automatic teller

Point of Sale (POS) terminal: a terminal at a retail store allowing a customer to electronically transfer money from the customer's account to the store's account.

Cardholder agreement: contract between the bank and the cardholder which outlines the responsibilities of the parties.

machine. The Royal Bank also uses this strip on a bank debit card to give a customer access to a bank account through a Point of Sale terminal at selected merchants. The debit card concept is explained later in this chapter.

With the card the bank sends the cardholder a copy of the cardholder agreement outlining the respective privileges and duties of the bank and also the customer, with regard to the use of the card. Some of the information provided explains the cardholder's assigned credit limit —usually from $700 to $1500 to start—where to sign the card, what to do if the card is lost or stolen, how and when payment is required, minimum payments, and how interest is calculated.

If the card is lost or stolen, the cardholder is responsible for up to $50 of charges to the card, even after notification of loss or theft. When payment falls due, the cardholder must pay a minimum of $10 or 10% of the balance, whichever is greater.

When credit cards first came into existence, there was no charge for obtaining or using the card. If the cardholder paid the total outstanding balance within 25 days of the date of the statement, there was no interest charge. This is still true for some types of cards.

Most banks now charge a user fee for the use of the card, although competitive pressures have encouraged some institutions to offer cards with no user fee. User fees range from a flat yearly or monthly rate to an individual transaction fee.

Some banks and trust companies have, in combination with other institutions, offered a specialty card. For example, Canada Trust and MasterCard, in combination with the University of Western Ontario, have issued a special UWO SuperCard. This bright purple (one of the school colours) card bears the university name and official seal, as well as the names Canada Trust and MasterCard. The $45 yearly user fee is divided up, with $25 going to the university alumni fund and $20 going to MasterCard. Every time the card is used, MasterCard sends $0.15 to the university alumni fund.

At present, the method of calculating interest charges on the outstanding balance have remained the same, except that some banks have reduced the number of days before payment is due. There are some exceptions to this: if a cardholder borrows money (a "cash advance") using the card, then interest is charged immediately and daily. Some credit card companies allow cardholders to write special cheques which are drawn against the credit account. These cheques are charged interest just as if it were a cash advance.

Interest rates change according to economic conditions. The law requires that interest rates be stated as an **effective**[1] annual percentage, as well as a monthly rate.

Two basic reasons for paying bills with a credit card are:

(1) the consumer need not carry large sums of cash.

(2) the merchant and the customer both use the card as a method of introduction. The merchant knows that the customer has an established credit rating, and can accept the card for payment, knowing that payment is guaranteed, with no risk of bad debts.

Hot sheet: a list of credit card numbers which should not be accepted by merchants; supplied by the card issuer.

Before accepting the VISA card, the merchant must check that the card is valid. This can be done in two ways. Regularly updated lists, frequently called hot sheets, are sent to merchants, listing the card numbers that are not to be accepted because the card is stolen or credit privileges have been withdrawn for another reason. The card is the property of the bank, not the customer. If the card is stolen, or the bank has requested the card be returned, the merchant can legally withhold the card from the customer, for return to the bank or for destruction.

The second method involves a card scanner (or authorization machine) that is electronically connected to the VISA centre by telephone line. The merchant merely slides the card through a slot at the top of the machine and keys in the dollar amount. The VISA centre computers will indicate very quickly — within 20 seconds — whether the card should be accepted or not. This service costs the merchant about $15 per month in addition to the regular VISA fees. For an extra $10 per month, the merchant can have the authorization machine electronically send the day's transaction data to the VISA centre, without having to complete the usual paperwork at the end of the day.

Each merchant has a "floor limit," usually $50 to $150. Sales over this limit must be approved by the VISA centre before payment can be guaranteed. The merchant telephones the VISA centre on a toll-

[1]The effective annual percentage or interest rate is the interest rate paid over a year, with the increase due to monthly compounding taken into account. For example, an interest rate of 1% per month is not truly 12% per year. Instead, the effective interest rate (r) is:

$$\begin{aligned} r &= (1.01)^{12} - 1 \\ &= 1.12683 - 1 \\ &= 0.12683 \end{aligned}$$

Thus, the effective interest rate is about 12.68%.

free line, gives the merchant number, the card number and expiry, and the dollar amount. A five-digit authorization code will be given to the merchant if the sale is approved, and the merchant writes this number on the credit card slip. Payment is guaranteed on all sales under the floor limit, as long as the card is not stolen. If the merchant uses the **authorization machine**, the floor limit is zero, and all transactions are run through the machine.

If the merchant does not use the authorization machine, a summary document—batch header or sales recap—must be prepared listing the individual transactions, and this document is deposited with the merchant's bank, which treats it like a cash deposit.

ACCOUNTING FOR CREDIT CARD TRANSACTIONS

On June 10, 19—, Martha Roberts, of 1812 Elm Street, Somewhere, Ontario takes her Royal Bank VISA card to Rockstone Clothing Ltd., a local clothing store. Mrs. Roberts makes a few purchases. The total bill is:

Blouse	$ 85.00
Shirt	65.00
Tie	20.00
Total	$170.00

Mrs. Roberts presents her VISA card for payment. The owner, Ms. Rockstone prepares a sales slip similar to the illustration on page 628. Some banks have eliminated the carbon paper, by using carbon-less paper, because of the potential fraud problems caused by people taking the credit card information from discarded carbons. Others have gone to a type of carbon that splits in half, with the result that information is incomplete. The sales slip here is carbonless.

Each item is listed and the list totalled. As of January 1991, GST must be added to taxable items, and in most provinces, provincial retail sales tax must also be added. To simplify our example, both GST and PST will be ignored.

Once the transaction has been authorized, Mrs. Roberts will receive the copy marked "customer copy," and the transaction is complete.

The accounting entry for the merchant appears in the Cash Receipts Journal (if used), since the transaction is treated the same as a cash sale. The entry would debit Cash and credit Sales. Often a special money column is used to identify credit card transactions.

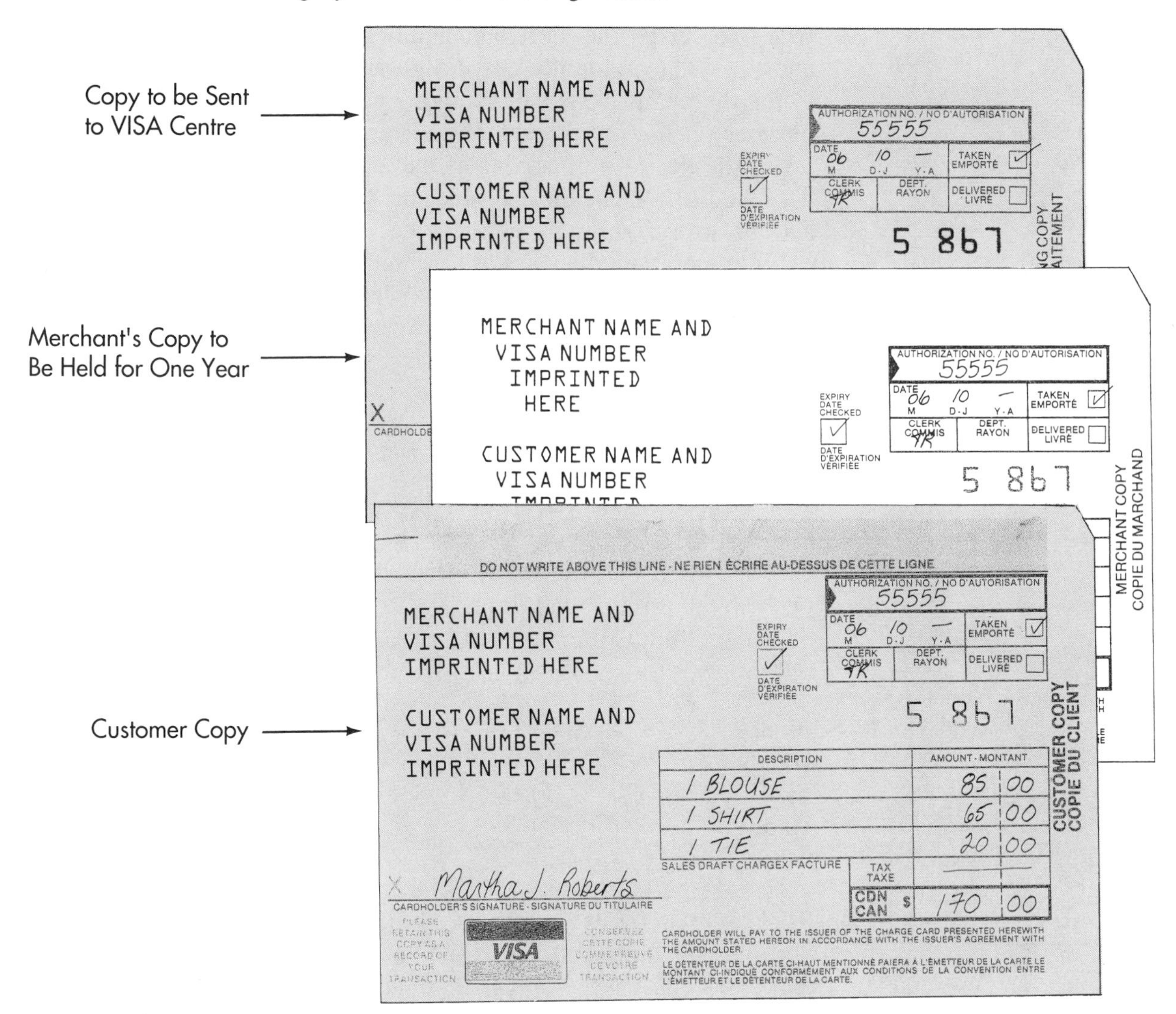

In a General Journal, the transaction would appear as illustrated on the opposite page.

At the end of the day, the merchant usually deposits the day's receipts. The VISA transactions must be summarized for inclusion in the day's deposit, since it is deposited just like cash.

Left Side

CASH RECEIPTS JOURNAL

DATE	ACCOUNT CREDITED	EXPLANATION	POST. REF.	GENERAL LEDGER CR.
19— June 10	Sales	VISA— Mrs. Roberts		

Right Side

Rockstone Clothing Ltd. Page 6

ACCOUNTS RECEIVABLE CR.	SALES CR.	SALES TAX PAYABLE CR.	CASH DR.	DISTRIBUTION TO BANK CREDIT CARDS	
				VISA	MASTERCARD
	170 00		170 00	170 00	

GENERAL JOURNAL Page 10

DATE	ACCOUNT TITLE AND EXPLANATION	POST. REF.	DEBIT	CREDIT
19— June 10	Cash (VISA)		170 00	
	Sales			170 00
	To record the sale of a blouse, a tie and a shirt. Paid by VISA.			

In addition to the sale to Mrs. Roberts, Ms. Rockstone also made two other VISA sales of $65 and $49. A customer also returned unsatisfactory merchandise totalling $15. Since the customer paid with a VISA card, a VISA **credit slip** is completed for the refund. An example of a VISA credit voucher is shown in the illustration.

CREDIT SLIP

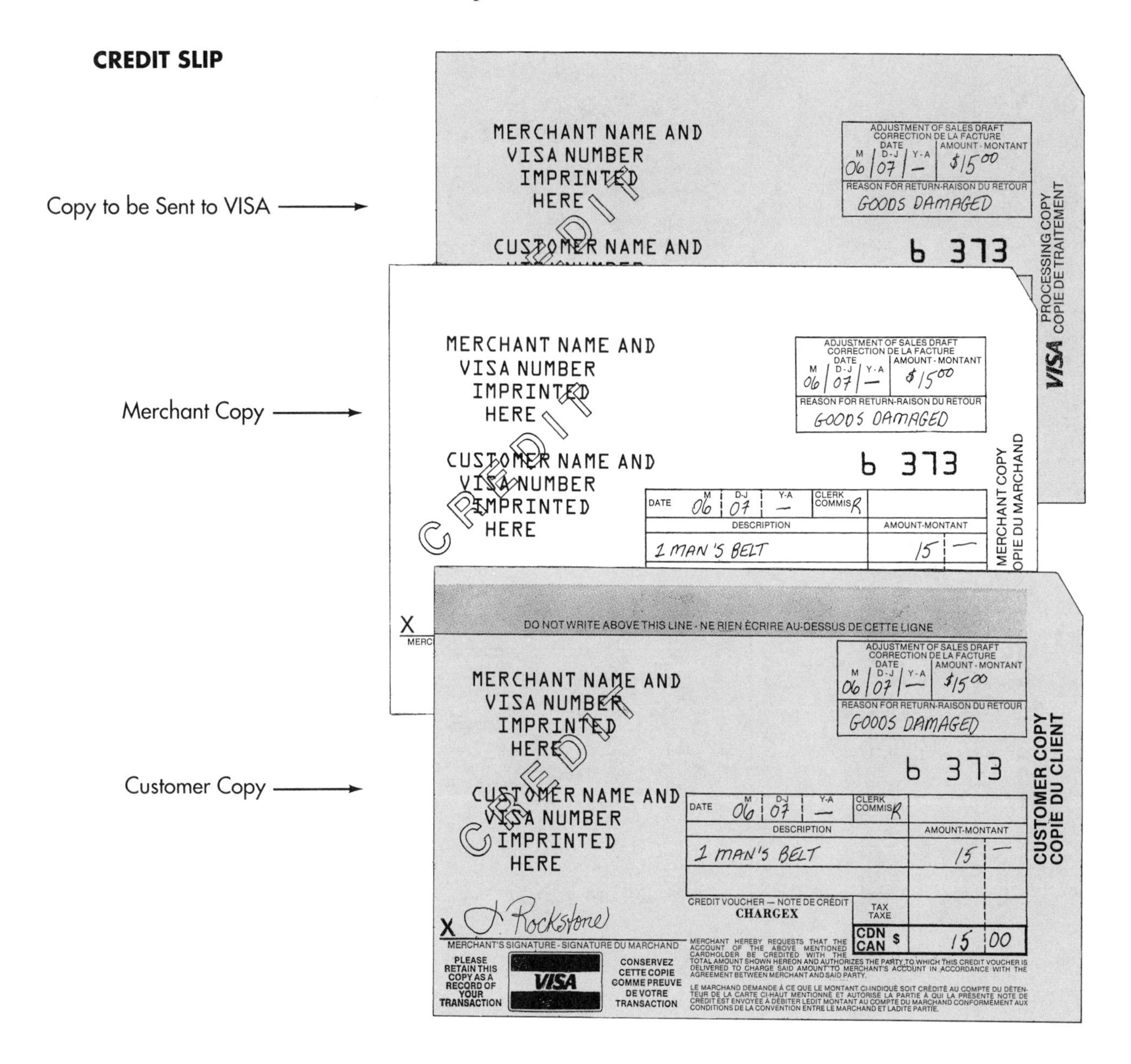

DO NOT WRITE ABOVE THIS LINE - NE RIEN ÉCRIRE AU-DESSUS DE CETTE LIGNE

MERCHANT NAME AND VISA NUMBER IMPRINTED HERE

CUSTOMER NAME AND VISA NUMBER IMPRINTED HERE

ADJUSTMENT OF SALES DRAFT / CORRECTION DE LA FACTURE

DATE M	D-J	Y-A	AMOUNT - MONTANT
06	07	—	$15.00

REASON FOR RETURN-RAISON DU RETOUR: GOODS DAMAGED

b 373

DATE M	D-J	Y-A	CLERK COMMIS
06	07	—	R

DESCRIPTION	AMOUNT-MONTANT
1 MAN'S BELT	15 —
CREDIT VOUCHER — NOTE DE CRÉDIT CHARGEX — TAX TAXE	
CDN CAN $	15 00

X J. Rockstone
MERCHANT'S SIGNATURE - SIGNATURE DU MARCHAND

PLEASE RETAIN THIS COPY AS A RECORD OF YOUR TRANSACTION — VISA — CONSERVEZ CETTE COPIE COMME PREUVE DE VOTRE TRANSACTION

MERCHANT HEREBY REQUESTS THAT THE ACCOUNT OF THE ABOVE MENTIONED CARDHOLDER BE CREDITED WITH THE TOTAL AMOUNT SHOWN HEREON AND AUTHORIZES THE PARTY TO WHICH THIS CREDIT VOUCHER IS DELIVERED TO CHARGE SAID AMOUNT TO MERCHANT'S ACCOUNT IN ACCORDANCE WITH THE AGREEMENT BETWEEN MERCHANT AND SAID PARTY.

LE MARCHAND DEMANDE À CE QUE LE MONTANT CI-INDIQUÉ SOIT CRÉDITÉ AU COMPTE DU DÉTENTEUR DE LA CARTE CI-HAUT MENTIONNÉ ET AUTORISE LA PARTIE À QUI LA PRÉSENTE NOTE DE CRÉDIT EST ENVOYÉE À DÉBITER LEDIT MONTANT AU COMPTE DU MARCHAND CONFORMÉMENT AUX CONDITIONS DE LA CONVENTION ENTRE LE MARCHAND ET LADITE PARTIE.

Before preparing the VISA summary slip (sales recap slip), the merchant will check each transaction slip to ensure that all information was recorded and imprinted correctly. The merchant then completes the VISA summary slip, by listing the amount of each transaction in the spaces provided. Examine the illustration of a sales recap below.

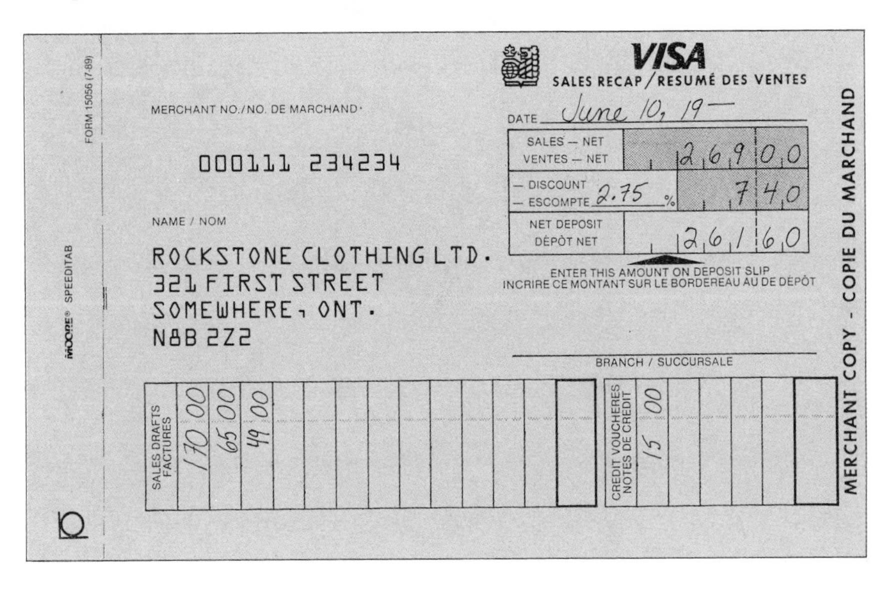

FORM 15056 (7-89)

MOORE® SPEEDITAB

VISA

SALES RECAP / RESUMÉ DES VENTES

MERCHANT NO./NO. DE MARCHAND

000111 234234

DATE June 10, 19—

SALES — NET / VENTES — NET		269.00
— DISCOUNT / — ESCOMPTE	2.75 %	7.40
NET DEPOSIT / DÉPÔT NET		261.60

ENTER THIS AMOUNT ON DEPOSIT SLIP
INCRIRE CE MONTANT SUR LE BORDEREAU AU DE DÉPÔT

NAME / NOM

ROCKSTONE CLOTHING LTD.
321 FIRST STREET
SOMEWHERE, ONT.
N8B 2Z2

BRANCH / SUCCURSALE

SALES DRAFTS / FACTURES
170.00
65.00
49.00

CREDIT VOUCHERES / NOTES DE CREDIT
15.00

MERCHANT COPY - COPIE DU MARCHAND

Note that any credit slips are recorded in a separate column. This slip is then run through the imprinting machine to record the merchant information on it. The date and the net sales information is recorded.

Merchants who offer credit cards to customers must pay the bank for this service by paying a percentage of credit sales. The percentage varies, depending on the size of the average credit sale and the average monthly credit volume. The higher the average sale and the volume, the lower the percentage fee. In our example for Rockstone Clothing Ltd., assume the average credit volume is between $5000.00 and $12 499.00, and that the average draft size (purchase amount) is between $50.00 and $99.99. By referring to the illustration on page 632, you will see that the business discount rate is 2.75%.

Business discount rate: the dollar amount paid to the bank by the merchant in order that the merchant may accept payment with a VISA card. This is usually a percentage (4% – 10%) of the sale price of an item.

Ms. Rockstone will put this discount rate on the VISA summary slip in the spot provided, and calculate the discount by multiplying the net sales by the discount rate, $269.00 × 2.75% is $7.40. This discount, which represents the merchant's cost of the credit services for these transactions, is subtracted from the net sales to determine the net deposit, which is entered on the summary slip.

Ms. Rockstone places the deposit copy of the sales slips, the credit slip, and the summary slip into the special envelope provided, with the summary slip showing through the transparent window. See the illustration on page 633.

Front

ROYAL BANK

VISA
MERCHANT DISCOUNT SCHEDULE

* Average Monthly Volume		Average Draft Size			
		Under $30.00	$30.00 to $49.99	$50.00 to $99.99	$100.00 and Over
		%	%	%	%
$ 1-	$ 999	5.50	4.50	3.50	3.25
1,000-	2,499	4.75	4.00	3.25	2.75
2,500-	4,999	4.50	3.75	3.00	2.75
5,000-	12,499	4.25	3.50	2.75	2.50
12,500-	19,999	4.00	3.25	2.50	2.25
20,000-	29,999	3.75	3.00	2.25	2.25
30,000-	49,999	3.50	2.75	2.25	2.00
50,000-	74,999	3.25	2.75	2.00	2.00
75,000-	149,999	3.00	2.50	2.00	2.00
150,000-	299,999	2.50	2.25	2.00	2.00
300,000-	and over	2.00	2.00	2.00	2.00

*Average Monthly Volume is calculated March 31 and September 30 of each year based on preceding 12 months' sales. Rate change if warranted to be implemented May 1 and November 1 and will apply to the future six month period (See over for further particulars).

FORM 3202 (8-84)

Back

VISA
MERCHANT DISCOUNT SCHEDULE

Discount rates will be reviewed and revised semi-annually during the months of April and October using monthly VISA volume statistics for the previous twelve months. When a change in rate is warranted a letter will be sent advising the new rate and the date it is effective. No advice is forwarded if a change in rate is not in order.

For further information regarding discount policy ask your Service Representative or contact your VISA Centre.

Next, Ms. Rockstone will complete the bank deposit slip — illustrated opposite — by listing all cheques received, and the amount of cash to be deposited, at the bottom of the opposite page. Then the total of the VISA deposit is entered on the deposit slip (Visa, Voucher Total). The deposit slip is then totalled (Net Deposit), and Ms. Rockstone goes to the bank to make the deposit. At the bank, the teller will check the various items against the deposit slip and update the current account of Rockstone Clothing Ltd. by the amount of the deposit.

The bank collects all the VISA deposit envelopes and forwards them to a VISA centre by courier at the end of each banking day.

ROYAL BANK
BANQUE ROYALE

DEPOSIT ENVELOPE **VISA** ENVELOPPE DE DÉPÔT

SALES RECAP / RÉSUMÉ DES VENTES

MERCHANT NO./NO. DE MARCHAND·

000111 234234

NAME / NOM

ROCKSTONE CLOTHING LTD.
321 FIRST STREET
SOMEWHERE, ONT.
N8B 2Z2

DATE June 10, 19—

SALES — NET / VENTES — NET	269.00
— DISCOUNT / — ESCOMPTE 2.75 %	7.40
NET DEPOSIT / DÉPÔT NET	261.60

ENTER THIS AMOUNT ON DEPOSIT SLIP
INCRIRE CE MONTANT SUR LE BORDEREAU AU DE DEPÔT

BRANCH / SUCCURSALE

IMPORTANT

DO NOT INCLUDE **MASTERCARD** ITEMS.
DO NOT **STAPLE** OR **CLIP** CONTENTS.
DO NOT INCLUDE **CHEQUES, CASH** OR **CORRESPONDENCE.**

NE PAS INCLURE DES FACTURES **MASTERCARD.**
NE PAS **BROCHER** OU **ATTACHER** LE CONTENU.
NE PAS INCLURE DE **CHÈQUES, D'ARGENT COMPTANT** OU DE **CORRESPONDANCE.**

Authorization machine: electronic device in a retail store, connected to credit card company computers; automatically checks for invalid cards and acceptable credit balance.

If the merchant is using the authorization machine, all the VISA paperwork is eliminated because all the transaction data can be sent to the VISA centre electronically.

CURRENT ACCOUNT DEPOSIT SLIP

ROYAL BANK

June 10, 19—
DATE

DEPOSITOR'S INITIALS: R
TELLER'S INITIALS:

CREDIT ACCOUNT OF

ROCKSTONE CLOTHING LTD.
321 FIRST STREET
SOMEWHERE, ONT.
N8B 2Z2

00002003

PLEASE LIST FOREIGN CHEQUES ON A SEPARATE DEPOSIT SLIP

VISA AND CHEQUES		DETAILS	CASH (INCL. COUPONS)
261.60	VISA VOUCHER TOTAL	X 1	—
54.00		10 X 2	20.—
61.20		30 X 5	150.—
102.00		10 X 10	100.—
		15 X 20	300.—
		X	
		X	
		COIN	3.25
		CANADIAN CASH TOTAL	573.25
	478.80	VISA & CHQS. FORWARDED	478.80
U.S. CASH		RATE	∅
U.S. CHQS.		RATE	∅
NET DEPOSIT			1052.05

⑆05242⑈003⑆ 154⑈414⑈7⑈ 51

After Ms. Rockstone returns to the store, she will use the sales recap as a source document in order to record the amount of the VISA discount. In General Journal form, it would appear as follows:

VISA Discount Expense	7.40	
Cash		7.40
To record VISA discount expense of June 10.		

PROCESSING A VISA TRANSACTION

VISA Centre The Royal Bank of Canada has VISA centres in Vancouver, Toronto, and Montreal. Each office handles designated areas of the country. Once a deposit envelope arrives at a centre, the data on the recap slip is verified against the sales and credit slips, and the information is entered into a computer. Since the first five digits of the customer account number identify the bank that issued the card, the computer can rapidly sort the information for each of the various banks and record that information on magnetic tape. The appropriate tapes are physically exchanged among the various VISA centres, allowing easy and accurate updating of customer accounts.

Merchant account numbers are also recorded from the slips and internal banking memoranda are issued among the VISA centre and the local bank branches that service the merchant's accounts.

Now that sorting and exchanging of data is complete, the VISA centre updates each customer's account. The account is identified by its number, and all charges are listed, including the transaction date, the store, and the dollar amount. It must be remembered that payments on account received directly at the VISA centre or through bank branches must be recorded in the customer's account as well. On set dates throughout the month, the computer is instructed to produce totals of the charges and payments received and the difference between these two amounts. If a balance has been outstanding for more than 25 days, interest is calculated and added to the total owing. The computer then generates a printed statement that is mailed to the customer. This statement will be examined shortly.

Computer technology makes possible the processing of massive volumes of information in a practical manner.

Customer Statements Throughout the month, cyclical billing takes place. The computer will generate a customer statement similar to the one illustrated below.

Therefore, within a month of the purchase Mrs. Roberts made at

Rockstone Clothing, it will appear on her VISA statement. Let's examine the statement below.

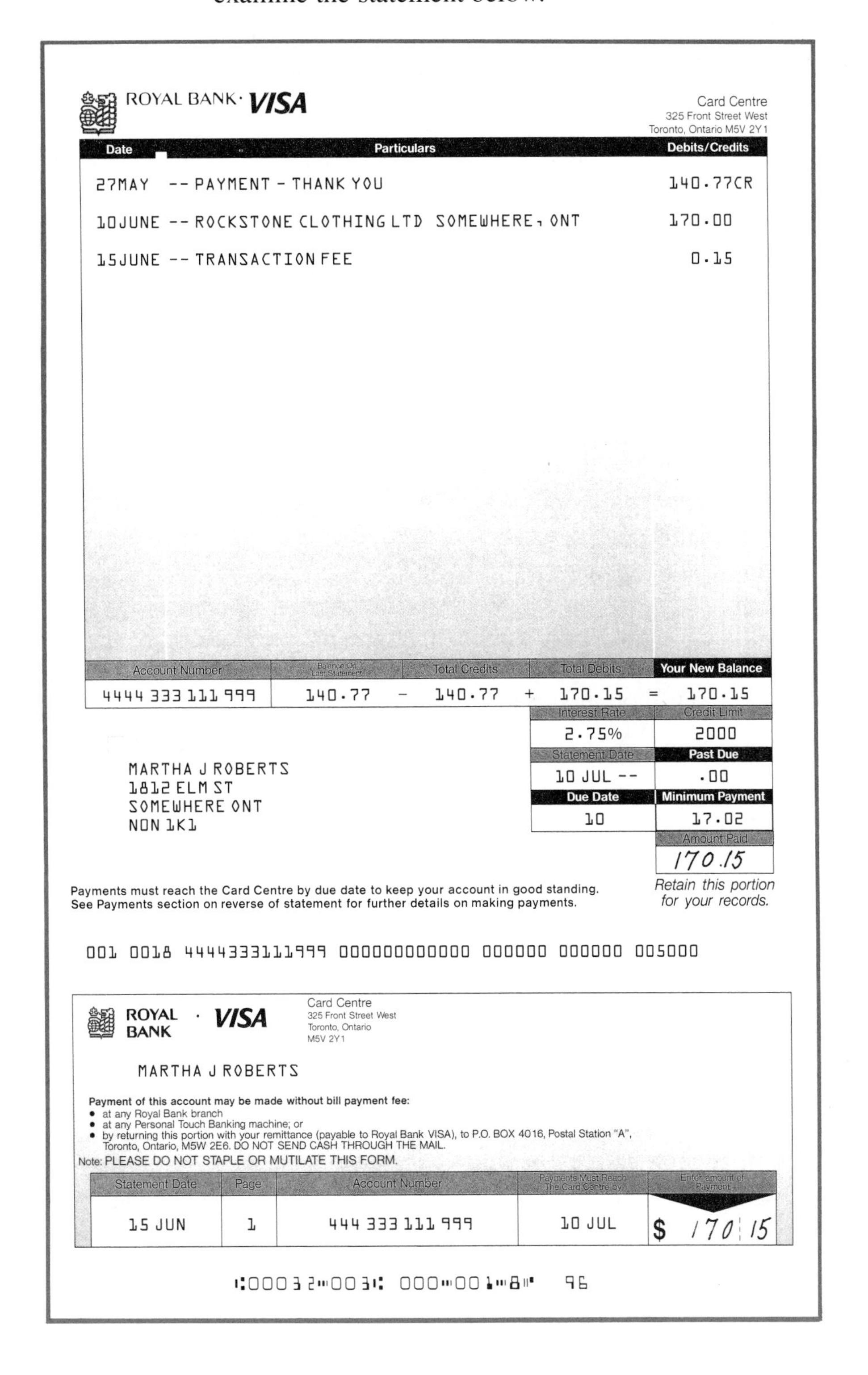

ROYAL BANK · VISA

Card Centre
325 Front Street West
Toronto, Ontario M5V 2Y1

Date	Particulars	Debits/Credits
27MAY	-- PAYMENT - THANK YOU	140.77CR
10JUNE	-- ROCKSTONE CLOTHING LTD SOMEWHERE, ONT	170.00
15JUNE	-- TRANSACTION FEE	0.15

Account Number	Balance On Last Statement		Total Credits		Total Debits		Your New Balance
4444 333 111 999	140.77	−	140.77	+	170.15	=	170.15

Interest Rate	Credit Limit
2.75%	2000
Statement Date	**Past Due**
10 JUL --	.00
Due Date	**Minimum Payment**
10	17.02
	Amount Paid
	170.15

MARTHA J ROBERTS
1812 ELM ST
SOMEWHERE ONT
N0N 1K1

Payments must reach the Card Centre by due date to keep your account in good standing.
See Payments section on reverse of statement for further details on making payments.

Retain this portion for your records.

001 0018 4444333111999 000000000000 000000 000000 005000

ROYAL BANK · VISA

Card Centre
325 Front Street West
Toronto, Ontario
M5V 2Y1

MARTHA J ROBERTS

Payment of this account may be made without bill payment fee:
- at any Royal Bank branch
- at any Personal Touch Banking machine; or
- by returning this portion with your remittance (payable to Royal Bank VISA), to P.O. BOX 4016, Postal Station "A", Toronto, Ontario, M5W 2E6. DO NOT SEND CASH THROUGH THE MAIL.

Note: PLEASE DO NOT STAPLE OR MUTILATE THIS FORM.

Statement Date	Page	Account Number	Payments Must Reach The Card Centre by	Enter amount of Payment
15 JUN	1	444 333 111 999	10 JUL	$ 170.15

⑆00032⑈003⑆ 000⑈001⑈8⑈ 96

Analysis:

- The statement has two parts: the top part, which is retained by the customer, lists all transactions giving the name of the store, the date of the purchase, and the dollar amount. Any payments on account by the customer will be shown here, as well as any interest charged on past due items. This is followed by the account number, the balance on the last statement, any credits and debits on this statement, and the new balance. Next is the statement date, the remaining credit limit, the total of any amount past due, and the due date. Finally, there is a place to record the amount the customer will pay VISA, beside the box where minimum payment is indicated.
- The bottom part is returned to VISA with the payment. This section contains the customer information, the statement date, the page number, the account number, the date by which payment must be made to avoid interest, and the amount of the payment being made.

If Mrs. Roberts sends a cheque to a VISA centre or pays her account at the local bank before the due date, there will be no interest charged. If the card carries a transaction fee instead of an annual fee, this amount will be included on the statement and in the balance owing. A common transaction fee is $0.15 per transaction. Mrs. Roberts will record the amount of her payment on both the top and bottom portions, and return the bottom portion with her cheque to the VISA centre.

We have now covered the basics of credit card transactions. However, it is important to understand that the credit card industry is very competitive, and features, procedures, forms, and rules will vary among card companies. You are encouraged to obtain sample current forms from your local bank.

DEBIT CARDS (POINT OF SALE CARDS)

The Royal Bank has been a pioneer in test-marketing a new type of "plastic money" called the **client card**. This card is part of a system that electronically links the bank and selected merchants. Special equipment, including a card scanner and a small printer, is installed in the merchant's store, and linked by phone line to the bank's computer. At this time, the only merchants participating in the pilot project are Big V Drug Stores, Miracle Mart, and 35 Becker's stores, all of which are in London, Ontario.

When customers open an account, either chequing or savings, they are given a client card, which has a magnetic strip on the back. If the customer requests, the bank will encode data on that strip that will allow the customer to access his or her bank account through an automated teller machine (ATM). In the pilot project, the bank also encodes data that provide for point of sale (POS) transactions on that strip.

If customers want to make a purchase at a store that is part of the project, they present their client card to the cashier. The cashier slides the card through the card scanner (as with an authorization machine), enters the dollar amount, and then hands the customer a small hand-held device resembling a calculator. Clients, in relative secrecy, enter their Personal Security Code, which is the same code they would use to access their bank account through an ATM. The amount is transferred directly from the customer's bank account to the merchant's bank account.

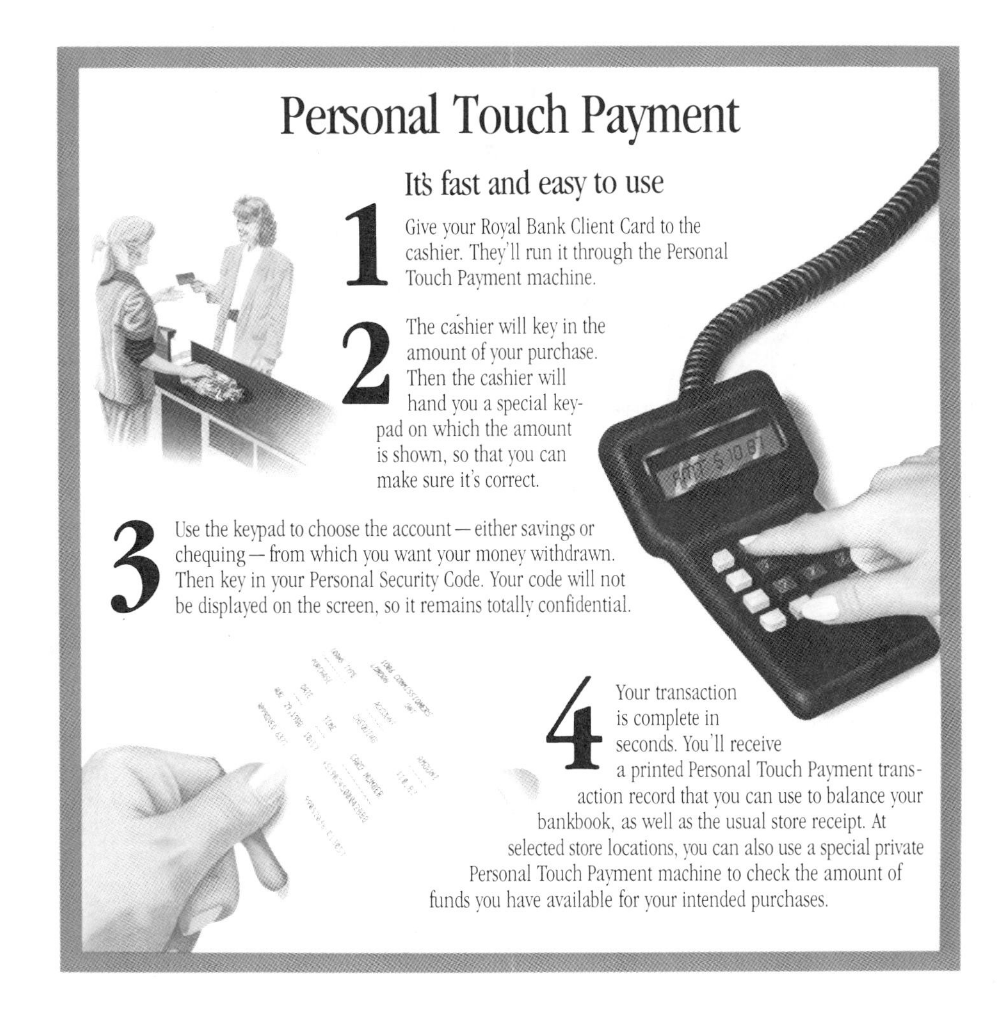

In accounting theory, the transfer from the customer's bank account is debited to that customer's deposit account. As you may recall from the study of bank reconciliation in Part 2 of the text, the customer's deposit account is a current liability account on the banker's books. Therefore, the debit simply decreases the banker's liability to that deposit account. At the same time, when the amount is transferred to the merchant's bank deposit account, the amount is actually credited. By crediting the merchant's deposit account, the bank is increasing its liability to that account.

Then a receipt is printed showing the merchant's name, the amount, and the date of the purchase. All receipts should be kept by the customer to reconcile the bank statement with the VISA statement. **There are no credit privileges on this type of card**. If there are insufficient funds in the account, the transaction is refused by the computer. The customer must keep track of the account balance, since it is not available at all locations. Any transactions made on the client card appear on the regular monthly statement, marked with "POS" for "point of sale," since they are really electronic withdrawals from the bank account, the same as if an ATM was used. The regular transaction fee of $0.45 (the same as a cheque) applies to any POS transaction.

TOPIC 3 PROBLEMS

Analyzing a VISA customer statement.

P 14-8 Refer to the customer statement on page 635 and answer the following questions:

a. When was the last payment received at VISA?

b. How much was sent?

c. How many transactions took place this month?

d. What was the total dollar value of these transactions?

e. Mrs. Roberts owes $87.15. Account for the discrepancy regarding $87.15 and the answer of **d**.

f. When was this statement prepared?

g. What is the due date?

h. What is Mrs. Roberts's credit limit?

i. What is her account number?

j. Was Mrs. Roberts charged any interest on her previous balance? Where would this show up on her statement?

Completing a VISA sales draft.

P 14-9 Given the following information, complete the VISA sales draft.

On August 30, 19—, Mr. Red Fischer bought two pairs of men's shoes at $82.50 each, and shoe polish for $2.79. All this merchandise was purchased at R. & B. Shoes Inc. The store's floor limit is $100, so the clerk, Jim Benham, had to phone for an authorization number (no. 73462). The store is located in Regina, Saskatchewan, and sales tax (7%) was charged on the total amount (ignore any GST effects). Mr. Fischer's VISA number is 1111 222 333 444. The clerk works in department 6 and Mr. Benham takes the goods with him.

Completing a VISA sales recap and bank deposit slip.

P 14-10 Complete the sales recap form and then a deposit slip for Ealing Hardware Supplies, using the following information:

a. Use today's date and your initials as the depositor.

(i) Sales slips: $94.34; $334.72; $134.23; $73.45.

(ii) Credit slips: $12.34; $19.95.

(iii) The firm's monthly VISA volume has been about $23 000.00 per month and the average draft size was $73.45.

(iv) Cash for the day: 18 twos, 2 fives, 6 tens, 21 twenties, and $18.84 in change.

(v) Two cheques were accepted: $372.23 and $29.45.

Journalizing transactions with credit cards to an expanded Cash Receipts Journal.

Proving the journal.

Calculating business discount.

P 14-11 Use an expanded Cash Receipts Journal which includes additional columns to record the VISA and MasterCard sales.

a. Record the transactions in the Cash Receipts Journal, on page 120, in the year 199–.

Apr. 2 Cash balance = $10 200
5 Cash sales for the week totalled $5800; sales tax $348.
9 Sold goods to B. Pilot for $400 plus 10% sales tax. Mr. Pilot used his VISA card to pay the bill.
11 Sold goods to Mary Waters for $290 plus 10% sales tax. She used her VISA card as payment.
15 Borrowed $6000 from the bank on a demand loan.
19 Cash sales for the past two weeks totalled $9200 plus sales tax of $900.
22 Sold goods to Helen Powers for $350 plus 10% sales tax. She paid for her goods with MasterCard.
27 Sold goods to M. Narthwood for $670 plus 10% sales tax. He used his VISA card to make payment.
30 Weekly sales totalled $7000. Sales tax totalled $685.

b. Total the journal and cross-foot to ensure accuracy.

c. Total the columns used for credit cards, and determine what percentage of sales was paid for by credit cards.

d. If average monthly volume is $1700 with an average draft of $102, calculate the VISA discount expense for all transactions, and prepare the General Journal entry to record the expense.

TOPIC 3 MINI-CASES

Analyzing vendor responsibilities under GST and PST rules.

MC 14-5 Geo. Logist owns a tract of land in northern Manitoba. During the summer months he explores this land and collects rocks, unusually shaped driftwood, and rare, highly-coloured fungi. This used to be a hobby for him, but over the last two years, he found that people were willing to pay well for these articles. As a result, Mr. Logist has been selling them from his home for the past six months. He never bothers to keep any records, but simply pockets the cash. Recently when he was talking to a close friend, he realized that he may have some problems with both federal and provincial authorities.

a. What considerations has Geo. Logist totally ignored, and what must be done to fulfil these obligations?

Determining business discount rules.

MC 14-6 Philip Entrepreneur has just established a chain of pet stores, with 6 locations in the province. Philip wants each of his stores to run independently, and has structured all control systems and bookkeeping so that each store can do its own record-keeping. When a representative of a credit card company approached Philip about accepting the company's cards, Philip told her that he thought it was a good idea to accept credit cards, but that he wanted each store to apply separately and keep all credit card transactions in each store. The representative replied that it could be arranged that way, but it would be much to Philip's financial advantage to have each store forward credit card slips to head office, where they could be deposited together.

a. Why would this be to Philip's financial advantage?

Describing advantages and disadvantages of debit cards.

MC 14-7 The newest method of payment, a debit card—like the Royal Bank Client card—is seen by some to be a replacement for credit cards.

a. Why are these cards called debit cards? Explain your answer by using an example and accounting entries.

b. What advantages do debit cards have over traditional credit cards?

c. What disadvantages do you see to debit cards?

d. Do you think that debit cards will become as popular as credit cards? Explain your answer.

COMPREHENSIVE CASE STUDY 11

Spence's Athletic Footwear specializes in athletic shoes (running, football, basketball, etc.). The business has two employees in addition to the owner. It uses a Combination Journal similar to the illustration given earlier. It includes specialized columns for GST and PST (Retail Sales Tax). The business operates a General Ledger, an Accounts Receivable Ledger, and an subsidiary Accounts Payable Ledger. The owner does all the ordering and bookkeeping.

Note: This comprehensive problem involves accounting for GST and Ontario provincial retail sales taxes. All sales involve PST, but since Spence's Athletic Footwear uses purchase exemptions, purchases are PST-free. All sales will involve GST, as will all purchases, except where specifically noted.

Journalizing and posting transactions involving GST and PST, returns and discounts, using Combination Journal, General Ledger, and subsidiary ledgers.

Calculating and remitting GST and PST.

Preparing supporting schedule.

Making a zero-proof trial balance of General Ledger.

a. Open General Ledger accounts for: Cash, $19 500; Accounts Receivable control; Truck; Office Equipment; Bank Loan Payable; Accounts Payable control; PST Payable; GST Payable; Mortgage Payable, $10 000; P. Spence, Capital, $9500; P. Spence, Drawing; Shoe Sales; Sales R&A; Sales Discounts; Purchases/Shoes; Purchases R&A; Purchases Discounts; Transportation-in; Salaries Expense; Interest Expense; Mortgage Interest Expense. Add the appropriate account numbers.

b. Open the following Accounts Receivable Ledger accounts: R.D. Atlas, A.X. Chopping, R.P. Minute, V.F. Runner.

c. Open the following Accounts Payable Ledger accounts: Adidas Outlets, Converse Suppliers.

d. Complete in the Combination Journal the following transactions for the month of March 19-1. (One invoice number and one cheque number will be given. All others follow in numerical order. Sales terms are identical for all companies.)

Mar. 1 Record the cash balance.

1 Sold to V.F. Runner, four pairs of football boots at $72 per pair plus GST (7%) plus PST (8%). (Don't forget, in Ontario, taxes are not compounded.) Terms are 2/10, n/30. Invoice No. T1123.

2 Purchased from Adidas Outlets, 85 pairs of various shoes. Total of Invoice No. P-7082 was $1215 plus GST. Terms 1/15, n/60. FOB Destination.
2 Arranged a bank loan with the Royal Bank of Canada. Principal was $20 000 with interest at 14% annually, due date was March 2, 19-3. Total interest payable in advance. *Hint:* Do not use a cheque. Use a direct deduction from the amount borrowed.
5 Bought office equipment from National Equipment Producers for cash, $2500 plus GST, with Cheque No. 414.
6 The owner invested his personal van for the use of the business. It was appraised at FMV of $3600 by a local auto dealership.
10 Received payment in full from Invoice No. T1123.
11 Sold three pairs of jogging shoes at $62 each, two pairs of soccer shoes at $57 each, and one pair of boxing boots for $92. Issued invoice to R.D. Atlas for the full amount. *Hint:* Don't forget GST and PST.
12 Sold twelve pairs of basketball runners at $37 each to R.P. Minute. *Hint:* Don't forget taxes and invoice number.
15 Paid two employees $800 each to meet semimonthly salary obligations. (No GST or PST is involved.)
17 Issued a cheque to Adidas Outlets for Invoice No. P-7082, taking the full discount.
18 Purchased from Converse Suppliers 55 pairs of shoes at $32 each. Invoice No. T-6717, terms 2/10, n/30, FOB shipping point.
19 Paid to Fidelity Trust Company the monthly mortgage payment, $1300. The interest portion was $800.
21 Received from R.D. Atlas payment in full. *Hint:* Do not forget the discount.
21 Received the order from Converse Suppliers. Delivery was made by CN Express. Their Invoice No. D-1123 was for $57. Prepared and gave driver a cheque for this amount plus GST.
22 After examining the Converse order, a clerk discovered two faulty pairs of shoes. Prepared a debit memo, No. DM-021, totalling $64, and returned the goods with the memo.
23 The owner took home a pair of Converse basketball shoes, which cost the store $42. The shoes sell for $73.
24 Sold 28 pairs of golf shoes, $1458 to A.X. Chopping.

26 Prepared and sent a credit memo, CM-0111, to A.X. Chopping for 3 pairs of golf shoes. Unit cost can be determined from entry of 24th.
26 Received a credit memo, CM-671, from Converse Suppliers for $64. Attach this to the debit memo.
28 Paid Converse Suppliers in full, less discount, less return.
29 Paid semimonthly salaries to employees, $800 each.
30 Calculated and remitted Provincial Retail Sales Tax. Assume there is no data beyond what is given in this problem.
30 Calculated and remitted GST for the month.

e. Total the journal, verify totals, and post.

f. Prepare the appropriate schedules to verify the General Ledger control accounts.

g. If a calculator with a paper tape is available, prepare a zero-proof trial balance of the General Ledger.

CHAPTER 15

REVIEWING AND EXPANDING THE ACCOUNTING OF ADJUSTING ENTRIES

Topic 1

Reviewing and Expanding Adjustments for Prepaid Expenses and Depreciation Expense

Topic 2

Adjusting for Bad Debts Expense

Topic 3

Adjusting for Accrued Revenues, Accrued Expenses, and Unearned Revenues

This chapter will review and expand the accounting of adjustments introduced in Chapter 7. If you have not already done so, complete Chapter 7 before you study the review of accounting principles that support the adjustments treated in Topic 1 of this chapter.

As their name suggests, adjusting entries adjust, update, or correct accounts that change as a result of the ongoing activities of a business. The idea of **change** is the key. If the analysis of an account shows that a change has occurred, an adjusting entry must be made to reflect the change. No matter what type of an adjustment you study, it is this idea of **change** which is the key to understanding and correctly accounting for the change.

Generally, there are four classes of adjustments: for prepaid expenses, for depreciation expense, for bad debts expense, and for a group that includes accrued revenues and accrued expenses, and for unearned revenues.

REVIEWING AND EXPANDING THE ACCOUNTING FOR PREPAID EXPENSES AND DEPRECIATION EXPENSE

Important Note: Chapter 7 in Part 1 of the textbook covers an introduction to the adjustments for prepaid expenses and depreciation expense. Since this material will not be repeated here, it is important that you complete Chapter 7 before you examine the review and expansion of these important adjustments in the material that follows.

ACCOUNTING FOR PREPAID EXPENSES

The accounting of prepaid expenses has been introduced in Chapter 7. Here we review nine points to emphasize the theory of accounting for common prepaid expenses.

Prepaid expenses: short-term pre-payment of expenses whose future benefits will be used up in a later accounting period.

- Prepaid expenses may be regarded as short-term prepayments of common expenses such as insurance expense, supplies expense, rent expense, and advertising expense.
- When initially acquired, prepaid expenses represent a bundle of unexpired costs. The benefits from these costs are expected to be used up within one year of the balance sheet date.
- As unexpired costs are expected to be used up within one year, all prepaid expenses can be thought of as current assets until used.
- When prepaid expenses have been used up in support of revenue-making activities, their costs are said to be expired. Once

this happens, the matching principle requires that they become expenses.

- Many accounting systems debit a current asset account at the time of acquiring all prepaid expenses. For example, Office Supplies on Hand may be debited for $1200 when these supplies are acquired for cash or on account. At the end of an accounting period and if an actual count shows that supplies costing $400 are still on hand, an adjusting entry is required to account for the supplies used (expired).
- The adjusting entry is a debit to Office Supplies Expense and a credit to Office Supplies on Hand for $800. Obviously, the office supplies expense for $800 would be included in the income statement to satisfy the matching principle. The balance in the Office Supplies on Hand account, $400, represents the unexpired cost of supplies and would be reported in the balance sheet as the last group of current assets.
- In acquiring prepaid expenses, some accounting systems prefer to debit the appropriate expense account instead of the current asset account. For example, in paying $1200 for a year's office supplies, the accountant may instruct the clerk to debit Office Supplies Expense and credit Cash for $1200. At the end of the accounting period, if a physical count shows $400 of unused supplies, the matching principle requires that the used-up portion ($1200 – $400) or $800 be included with other operating expenses in the current year's income statement. Therefore, an adjusting entry is required to debit Office Supplies on Hand and to credit Office Supplies Expense for $400. Notice that the end result is exactly the same as achieved under systems that begin by debiting a current asset account and then adjusting to record the expired cost of that current asset. The income statement would report $800 of office supplies expense while the balance sheet would report a current asset for office supplies on hand for $400.
- The decision on whether to begin with a prepaid expense (current asset) account or an expense account is left to management and then becomes part of the overall accounting policy to be followed consistently from one accounting period to the next.
- On a balance sheet, prepaid expenses are reported as the final listing under Current Assets. They may be reported individually without a subheading; or they may be listed under a subheading called Prepaid Expenses and then reported as one subtotal; or their individual account balances may be totalled and reported as Prepaid Expenses.

REVIEWING FIXED ASSET AND DEPRECIATION CONCEPTS

The simple aspects of accounting for the acquisition of fixed assets and of related depreciation expense have been introduced in Chapter 7. Here, we review twelve points to emphasize the theory of acquiring fixed assets and of accounting for depreciation. Then, under separate headings, we examine applications of depreciation that were not covered in Chapter 7.

- In general, fixed assets (also known as Property, Plant, and Equipment or simply Plant Assets) are acquired by business to generate revenue or assist in revenue-making activities for periods longer than one year from the current balance sheet date.
- Common examples of fixed assets are land for business use, buildings, machinery, and equipment. In addition, fixed assets include additions to buildings, improvements to property and plant buildings, and natural resources such as coal mines, timber fields, and oil fields. In this textbook, we are concerned with the accounting of only common fixed assets.
- In the acquiring of any fixed asset, the cost principle requires that all costs related to the acquisition of that asset and any additional costs required to ready the fixed asset for business use be debited to an appropriate fixed asset account. Suppose, for example, a business acquired a new microcomputer system for its office from a dealer under the following contract: price of computer, $10 000; provincial sales tax, $800; shipping charges, $250; and installation labour, $250 on terms of n/30. Under the cost principle, the business would debit Office Equipment and credit Accounts Payable for the total laid-down cost of $11 300 as shown in the margin.

Costing the Office Equipment

Price of computer	$10 000
PST	800
Shipping charges	250
Installation labour	250
Total laid-down cost	$11 300

- The cost principle also requires that no change be made to the laid-down cost during the useful life of any fixed asset. For example, if land is acquired for business use at a cost of $100 000, that cost is maintained in a Land account even though the so-called market value of that land has doubled.
- Since the benefits of all fixed asset acquisitions will last beyond one year, the matching principle requires that the total cost less any estimated disposal value be spread over the useful life of that fixed asset. Suppose, for example, management estimates that after five years' use, the computer above will be no longer useful and has no disposal value. Therefore, the total cost of $11 300 must be spread over its useful life, that is, over five years.

Depreciation: the process of spreading (or allocating) the laid-down cost of fixed assets over their estimated useful lives.

- In accounting theory, the process of spreading the cost of any fixed asset over its useful life is called depreciation. Since the cost of any fixed asset at acquisition represents an unexpired cost, adjusting entries are required to transfer a portion of the unexpired cost to a depreciation expense account.
- In the example of the microcomputer system, a yearly adjusting entry would be a debit to Depreciation Expense/Office Equipment and a credit to Accumulated Depreciation/Office Equipment for $2260 ($11 300 ÷ 5 years).
- The Depreciation Expense/Office Equipment for $2260 would be reported as one of the operating expenses in the income statement of each year's use of the microcomputer system.
- The Accumulated Depreciation/Office Equipment for $2260 would be reported as contra to the cost of Office Equipment reported in the year-end balance sheet. In the second year, the balance of this contra fixed asset account represents the accumulation of the first and second year's depreciation expenses. Therefore, $4520 would be deducted from the laid-down cost of office equipment to report the unexpired cost or book value of the office equipment.
- Following the final year's depreciation entry and assuming that the fixed asset has no further useful life, an adjusting entry would eliminate the fixed asset from the accounting records. For example, after five years' use, the microcomputer would be eliminated by debiting the Accumulated Depreciation account for the balance shown in this contra account, that is, $2260 × 5 or $11 300, and crediting Office Equipment for the same amount.
- One common fixed asset, land, is not subject to depreciation. In accounting theory, land has unlimited useful life. In other words, no estimate may be made on the length of useful life related to the cost of land. Furthermore, the entire cost of land is usually recovered (and often more) when the business ceases to function. Therefore, the cost of land is never depreciated under accounting theory. To ensure that no depreciation is made for land, a separate account for this item is kept in the General Ledger.

Straight-line depreciation: a common method under GAAPs whereby equal amounts of a depreciation expense are spread over the useful life of a fixed asset.

- Under GAAPs, several methods may be used to spread the cost of depreciable assets over their useful lives. In practice, the most common method is called straight-line depreciation. Under this method, the original cost of the asset, less any amount estimated as disposal (salvage) value, is divided by the estimated number of useful years. Thus, equal amounts of depreciation are spread over the useful life of the fixed asset. A second depreciation method will be examined at the end of this topic.

INTRODUCING THE SUBSIDIARY FIXED ASSET LEDGER

In Chapter 7, all fixed asset acquisitions of a similar nature were accounted for in one General Ledger account. For example, the costs of acquiring typewriters, calculators, and other similar equipment for the business were debited to Office Equipment. At year-end, the adjusting entry to record depreciation amounts on each piece of office equipment was debited and credited to one GL expense and one GL contra fixed asset account called Depreciation Expense/Office Equipment and Accumulated Depreciation/Office Equipment, respectively.

Using only one account for each of Office Equipment, Depreciation Expense/Office Equipment, and Accumulated Depreciation/Office Equipment may be adequate for businesses with few pieces of equipment. However, most businesses of reasonable size own many pieces of office equipment, such as typewriters, microcomputers, copiers, calculators, filing cabinets, desks, chairs, etc. It would be most time-consuming and inefficient to compute the total depreciation expense for office equipment especially when individual pieces of equipment are acquired in different accounting periods. Similarly, it would be impractical to open separate GL accounts for each item. Despite these problems, it is necessary to account for all office equipment collectively and individually.

To resolve this issue, many businesses maintain a separate subsidiary ledger system similar to the accounts receivable and accounts payable systems. Therefore, appropriately titled controlling accounts would be kept in the General Ledger, while accounts for individual pieces of office equipment would be filed in a subsidiary ledger called the Fixed Asset Ledger.

Fixed Asset Ledger: a subsidiary ledger containing a separate account for each fixed asset.

To illustrate the relationship between related controlling accounts in the GL and the Fixed Asset Ledger, study the following transactions affecting one piece of office equipment, a typewriter. The transactions occur from the time the typewriter is bought until it is disposed of. To simplify matters, only T-accounts and General Journal entries will be used to analyze all transactions.

January 2, 19-1 Issued a cheque for $700 to purchase an electronic typewriter for the office.

Analysis:

- Record the entry with a debit to the fixed asset Office Equipment and a credit to Cash. In practice this entry would normally be recorded in the Cash Payments Journal under a manual system.

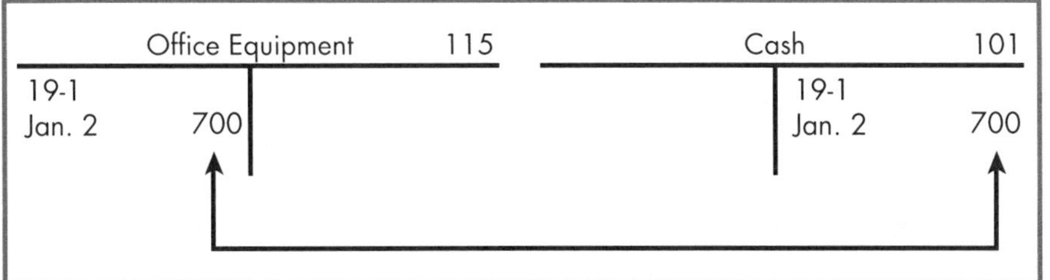

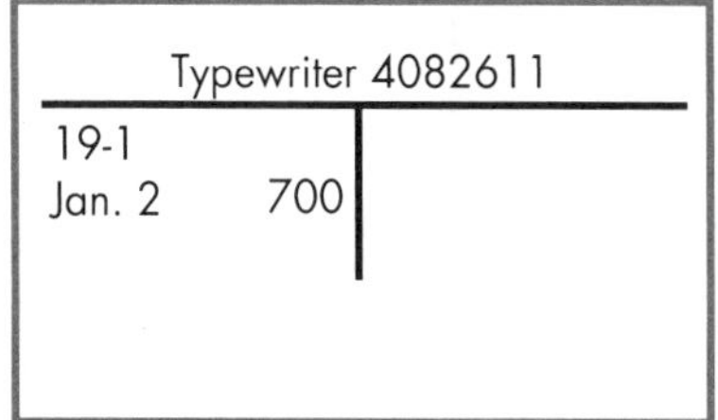

- The Fixed Asset Ledger, in which is maintained an account for each individual fixed asset, must be debited for the same amount as the Office Equipment account.
- In the Fixed Asset Ledger and under a manual system, each asset has its own record, which is usually in the form of a card.
- Each card contains all the information needed for calculating and recording depreciation of the asset over its useful life. Refer to page 652 and examine the ledger card.
- The total of all the individual items is identified in the General Ledger in the Office Equipment account. This General Ledger account acts as a control account similar to the controls for accounts receivable or accounts payable.

December 31, 19-1 An adjusting entry is made to record the dollar result of using the typewriter for one year. Management has estimated a useful life of five years and a disposal value of $100 for this type of office equipment.

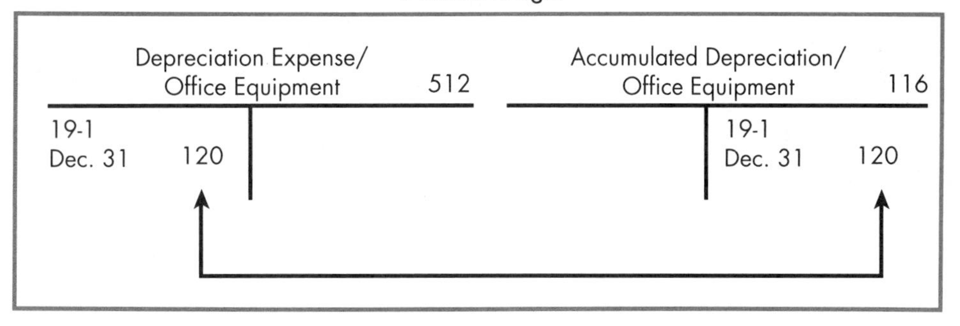

Original Cost	$700
Less: Disposal Value	100
Total Amount Subject to Depreciation	600
Divided by: Estimated Years of Useful Life	÷5
Yearly Depreciation	$120

Analysis:

- The straight-line method of depreciation has been used to calculate the yearly depreciation, as the margin shows. If you wished to know the monthly depreciation, you would divide one year's depreciation by 12.
- The adjusting entry as shown in T-account form would be posted to the General Ledger as well as to the subsidiary fixed asset record card for Typewriter (Serial No. 4082611).

  Note: Although only one piece of office equipment is illustrated here, it is important to realize that the depreciation of each piece would be first calculated from individual ledger cards. Then, the total depreciation would be recorded as the adjusting entry in the General Journal. This total would then be posted to the control accounts in the General Ledger.

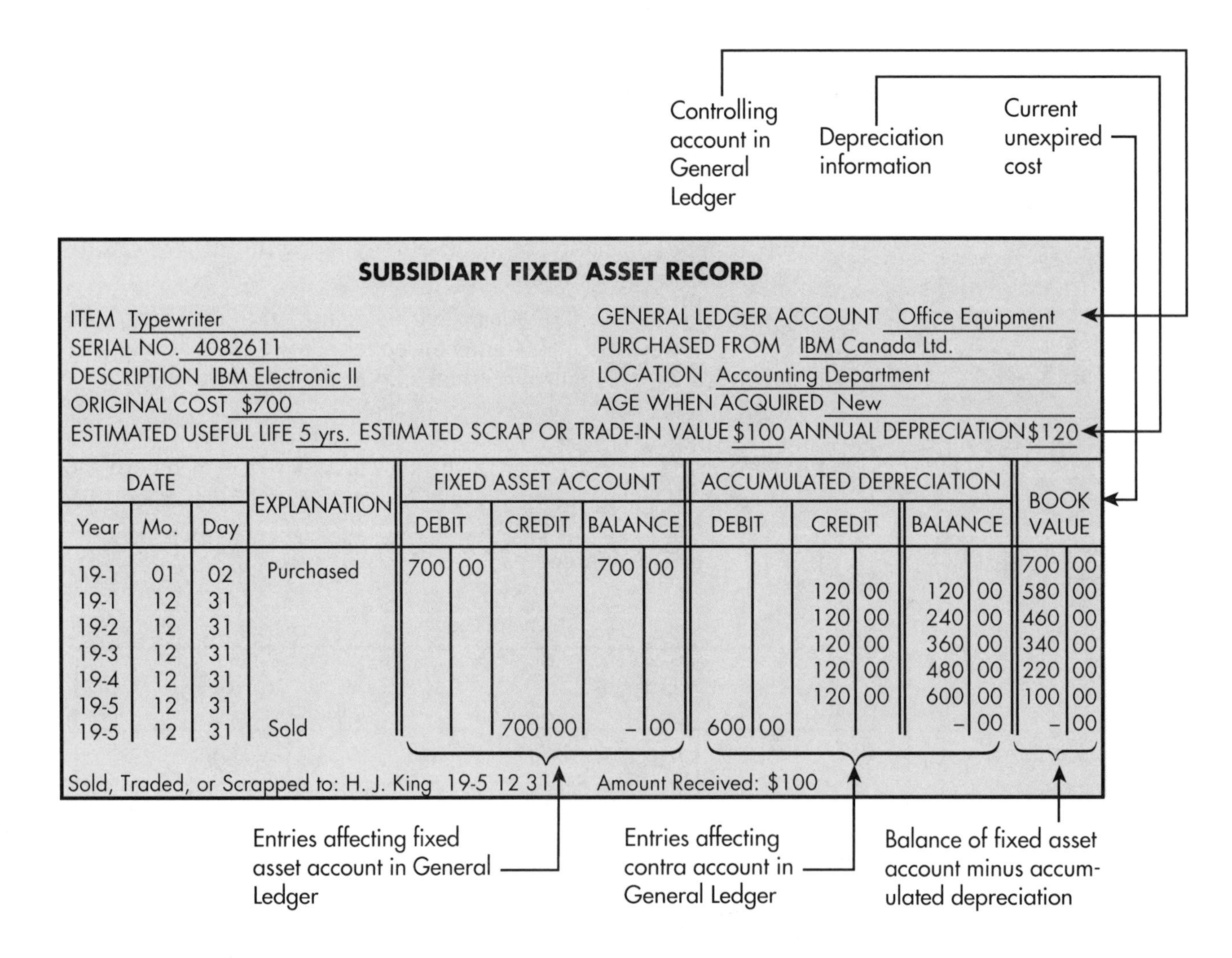

SUBSIDIARY FIXED ASSET RECORD

ITEM Typewriter
SERIAL NO. 4082611
DESCRIPTION IBM Electronic II
ORIGINAL COST $700
GENERAL LEDGER ACCOUNT Office Equipment
PURCHASED FROM IBM Canada Ltd.
LOCATION Accounting Department
AGE WHEN ACQUIRED New
ESTIMATED USEFUL LIFE 5 yrs. ESTIMATED SCRAP OR TRADE-IN VALUE $100 ANNUAL DEPRECIATION $120

DATE			EXPLANATION	FIXED ASSET ACCOUNT			ACCUMULATED DEPRECIATION			BOOK VALUE
Year	Mo.	Day		DEBIT	CREDIT	BALANCE	DEBIT	CREDIT	BALANCE	
19-1	01	02	Purchased	700 00		700 00				700 00
19-1	12	31						120 00	120 00	580 00
19-2	12	31						120 00	240 00	460 00
19-3	12	31						120 00	360 00	340 00
19-4	12	31						120 00	480 00	220 00
19-5	12	31						120 00	600 00	100 00
19-5	12	31	Sold		700 00	– 00	600 00		– 00	– 00

Sold, Traded, or Scrapped to: H. J. King 19-5 12 31 Amount Received: $100

- There is no change at all to the fixed asset Office Equipment; instead, the amount is recorded as a credit to the contra account Accumulated Depreciation/Office Equipment.

Book value: original asset cost less accumulated depreciation.

- The current, unexpired cost of office equipment or the book value is the difference between the two accounts. Remember that the Depreciation Expense account will be closed to the R & E Summary during the closing of the books at year-end.
- In each subsequent year, the Accumulated Depreciation/Office Equipment account will increase by $120 until the end of year 5 when the business disposes of the asset.

ACCOUNTING FOR THE DISPOSAL OF FIXED ASSETS

Two important points must be considered before a fixed asset is removed from the accounting records after that asset reaches the end of its useful life.

- Depreciation expense must first be recorded from the last accounting period right up to the date the fixed asset is disposed of.
- Any loss or gain must be calculated and accounted for in the entry to eliminate the fixed asset from the accounting records.

To illustrate these points, let's follow the entries required to dispose of the office typewriter in three examples. First we will examine how to record the depreciation when the asset is sold.

December 31, 19-5 Assume that this typewriter is sold at year-end. The final year's depreciation is recorded as shown in the T-account analysis below.

General Ledger

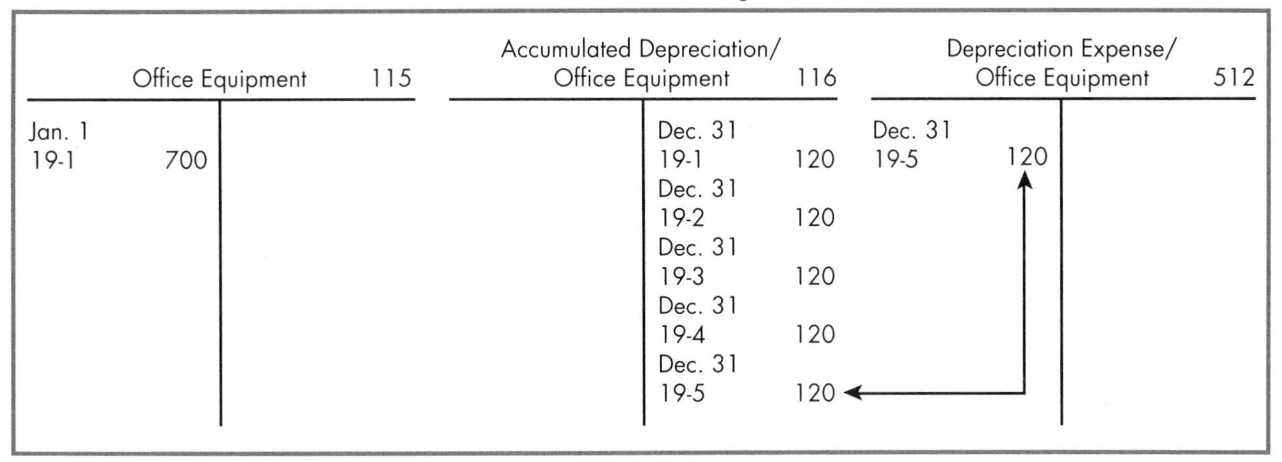

Analysis:

- The Depreciation Expense account shows the posting of the current year's entry, that is, year 5. Why? The matching principle requires that only the fifth year's depreciation expense be matched with revenues earned in year 5.
- The accumulated depreciation account clearly identifies the total of five years of accumulated expired costs for the typewriter.
- The fixed asset account still shows the original cost because no disposal entry has been made.
- The difference between the unexpired cost listed in Office Equipment and the total of the expired costs listed in the accumulated depreciation account is the estimated disposal value of the asset.

Now examine the transaction that actually disposes of or sells the asset. There are three possible outcomes. Study each example separately as they are illustrated below.

Example 1. Sale for Disposal Value, $100 Cash

Analysis:

- The illustration is recorded for you in General Journal form, but it should be properly recorded in the Cash Receipts Journal. The results of posting this entry to the GL are shown in the T-accounts below the double entry.
- The unexpired cost, equal to the disposal value in this case, is also the amount of cash received. Cash is debited for $100.
- Because the fixed asset is no longer owned by the business, it must be removed from the books. Office Equipment/Typewriter 4082611 is credited for $700.
- The fixed asset account, as you know, always has a partner, Accumulated Depreciation/Office Equipment. Its account balance must also be removed. This account is debited for $600.
- Finally, the subsidiary ledger account, Typewriter 4082611, illustrated earlier on page 651, must also be updated in order to close the account.

Notice the useful information that can be obtained from the completed subsidiary ledger card. Keeping a subsidiary ledger for individual fixed asset items offers these advantages:

(1) The individual account is identified by a complete description, which includes the serial number. Consequently, a physical inventory of all fixed assets can be taken to ensure that all units of

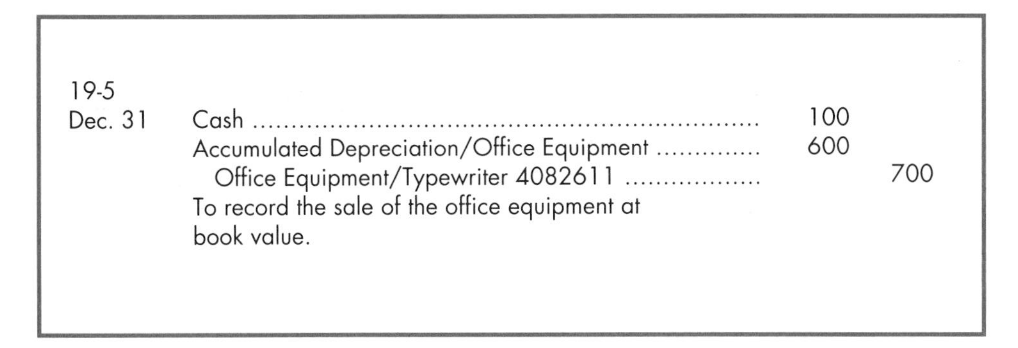

19-5			
Dec. 31	Cash	100	
	Accumulated Depreciation/Office Equipment	600	
	Office Equipment/Typewriter 4082611		700
	To record the sale of the office equipment at book value.		

General Ledger

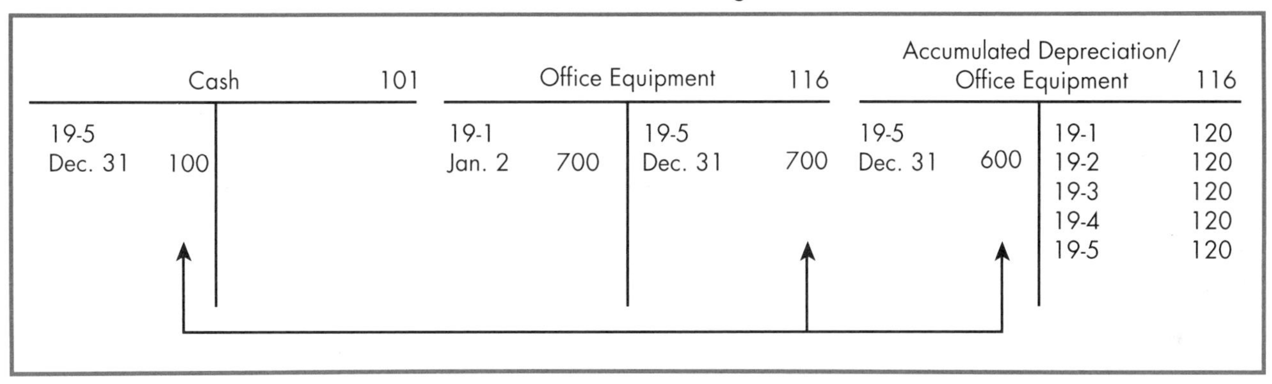

Cash		101	
19-5			
Dec. 31	100		

Office Equipment			116
19-1		19-5	
Jan. 2	700	Dec. 31	700

Accumulated Depreciation/ Office Equipment			116
19-5		19-1	120
Dec. 31	600	19-2	120
		19-3	120
		19-4	120
		19-5	120

office equipment shown by the records are actually on hand. In other words, proper identification of the equipment in the subsidiary ledger ensures a degree of internal control over the fixed assets.

(2) The original cost of the typewriter, the estimated useful life, and the estimated disposal value are clearly indicated so that the periodic calculation of depreciation can be made.

(3) A complete record of both the fixed asset account and its related contra account are maintained on one card. At any time, therefore, the book value—or the current unexpired cost—of the asset can easily be determined.

(4) The individual record also supports information that will be required for filling out tax returns, for obtaining proper insurance coverage, and for supporting claims for losses that may be made against the insurance coverage.

(5) Management is able to follow the useful life of the asset in order to budget for its replacement at least one year ahead of disposing of the asset.

Example 2. Sale for More Than Disposal Value, $150 Cash Assume now that the business received $150 cash for the typewriter. Follow closely the double entry on the next page and its effect on the condensed income statement.

Date	Account	Debit	Credit
19-5			
Dec. 31	Cash	150	
	Accumulated Depreciation/Office Equipment	600	
	Office Equipment/Typewriter 4082611		700
	Gain on Disposal of Fixed Asset		50
	To record the sale of the office equipment in excess of book value.		

Condensed Income Statement
For the Year Ended December 31, 19-5

Sales Revenue	$150 000
Less: Operating Expenses	110 000
Operating Income	40 000
Other Revenue:	
Gain on Disposal of Fixed Asset	50
Net Income	$40 050

Analysis:

- Often, if equipment has been well maintained, it will sell for more than its estimated disposal value, in our example, $150. This is $50 more than the estimated disposal value. What would be the journal entry?
- Since cash was received, the account Cash is debited by $150.
- The asset was sold, and the asset account must be made equal to zero with an equal and opposite entry. Office Equipment is credited by $700.
- The accumulated depreciation account is no longer required; therefore, it is debited by $600. However, at this point, debits do

not equal credits. *Remember:* More was received for the asset than was expected from the original estimated disposal value. For this reason, we say there is a gain on the disposal of a fixed asset. Such a gain is a secondary source of revenue, so you would expect a $50 credit to the account Gain on Disposal of Fixed Asset. Now debits equal credits.

Gain on disposal of a fixed asset: a secondary source of revenue which normally is reported under Other Revenue in the income statement.

Example 3. Sale for Less than Disposal Value, $75 Cash What if the unit could not be sold for its estimated disposal value, but only $75 cash was received instead? Verify your thoughts by examining the double entry below.

19-5			
Dec. 31	Cash	75	
	Accumulated Depreciation/ Office Equipment	600	
	Loss on Disposal of Fixed Asset	25	
	Office Equipment/Typewriter 4082611		700
	To record the sale of the office equipment at a loss.		

Analysis:

Loss on disposal of a fixed asset: a non-operating expense usually reported under Other Expenses in the income statement.

- In this example, a special non-operating expense—a loss on disposal of a fixed asset—of $25 occurs. You would report this loss as one of the Other Expenses in the income statement and subtract it from the Operating Income as illustrated below.

Condensed Income Statement
For the Year Ended December 31, 19-5

Sales Revenue	$150 000
Less: Operating Expenses	110 000
Operating Income	40 000
Other Expenses:	
Loss on Disposal of Fixed Asset	25
Net Income	$39 975

USING THE CAPITAL COST ALLOWANCE (CCA) METHOD

Although the straight-line method is used widely, businesses may select other methods to depreciate different kinds of fixed assets. These alternative methods, which must comply with the GAAPs, will not be examined here since they are studied in more advanced courses.

However, there is another method that does not comply with the GAAPs, but which must be used under the Income Tax Act. Under this act, businesses may deduct amounts for depreciation expense on most of their fixed assets in calculating their net income for income tax purposes. Although most businesses use straight-line depreciation, all businesses must use the Capital Cost Allowance (CCA) method for income tax purposes.

Capital cost allowance (CCA) method: the depreciation method approved by Revenue Canada—Taxation.

Briefly, Revenue Canada — Taxation divides fixed assets into classes. Each class is given a maximum rate of depreciation. CCA may be claimed on depreciable property which is acquired and used to earn income. Several classes and their accompanying rates are shown in the following table.

CAPITAL COST ALLOWANCE (CCA) CLASSES

Class	Description of the Fixed Asset	Rate Allowed
1	Most buildings acquired after 1987 and made of brick, cement, or stone.	4%
2	Most buildings in Class 1 but acquired after 1978 and before 1988.	5%
6	Most buildings acquired after 1978 belonging in Class 1 or Class 3 but buildings made of frame, log, stucco on frame, or galvanized or corrugated iron.	10%
8	Furniture, equipment for the office, fixtures, electrical and radiocommunication equipment.	20%
10	Automotive equipment (vans, trucks, tractors, and passenger vehicles costing under $20 000 and which were acquired before September 1, 1989), electronic data processing equipment and systems software.	30%
10.1	Passenger vehicles used in business and acquired before September 1, 1989 that cost more than $20 000 and passenger vehicles acquired after August 31, 1989 that cost more than $24 000.	30%
12	Computer software (but not including systems software which must be in Class 10), and videotape cassettes acquired for the purpose of renting to persons not exceeding more than seven days in any 30-day period.	100%

The mathematics involved in calculating a CCA can become quite complex depending on the class of asset involved. Here, we will use the simple example of the typewriter owned by a sole proprietor. According to Revenue Canada — Taxation, office equipment is in Class 8. Therefore, the business may use a rate of 20% to calculate as follows:

- In Year 1, only one-half of the fixed asset's original cost can be used to calculate a depreciation expense for income tax purposes, regardless of when the equipment was purchased. Therefore, one-half of $700 is $350. The taxpayer now multiples this amount by 20% to obtain the capital cost allowance (depreciation expense): 20% × $350 or $70. Notice that any estimated disposal (salvage) value is **ignored** in the calculation of CCA.
- At the beginning of year 2, the unexpired cost of the typewriter must be calculated by subtracting the CCA in year 1 from the original cost: $700 – $70 or $630.
- At the end of year 2, the unexpired cost above is again multiplied by 20%: $630 × 20% or $126. Therefore, the CCA is $126.
- In subsequent years, the CCA is calculated only on the resulting balance, or the unexpired cost of the asset. Revenue Canada—Taxation calls this the **undepreciated capital cost**. For this reason, the CCA method is also known as the fixed percentage on declining balance method.

In the table below, note that a larger amount of CCA is allowed in the earlier years of useful life of the typewriter. In other words, a progressively smaller amount is shown as time passes.

Year	Unexpired Cost (Beginning of Year)	Amount of CCA (20%)	Unexpired Cost (Resulting Balance at End of Year)
1	$700 × ½ = $350	$ 70.00	$630.00
2	630.00	126.00	504.00
3	504.00	100.80	403.20
4	403.20	80.64	322.56
5	322.56	64.51	258.05

Capital cost allowances are legal deductions offered to taxpayers as a matter of government policy. The allowance rates are not a true depreciation according to the matching principle. Therefore, most businesses prepare their income statements according to the GAAPs and immediately below the reported net income show a **reconciliation** of that net income for income tax purposes.

As a simple example, assume in the condensed income statement below that all items reported are acceptable for income tax reporting except for the $25 000 of straight-line depreciation expense included in the total expenses. For income tax purposes, assume that Revenue Canada — Taxation allows **twice** the amount for CCA as computed under GAAPs.

Any Single Proprietorship Service Company
Condensed Income Statement
For the Year Ended December 31, 19-2

Total Fees Earned	$150 000
Less Expenses (includes $25 000 of depreciation computed under straight-line depreciation)	100 000
Net Income (under GAAPs)	$ 50 000
Reconciliation for Income Tax Reporting:	
• Re-add Depreciation Expense Not Permitted under Income Tax Rules	25 000
• Subtotal	75 000
• Less CCA Permitted by Revenue Canada — Taxation	50 000
• Net Income for Income Tax Reporting	$ 25 000

Analysis:

- The income statement is first prepared according to the GAAPs. Therefore, the depreciation expense would be calculated using a method that complies with the GAAPs. In this case, we assume the use of straight-line depreciation.
- Since revenues have been matched with related expenses according to the GAAPs, the net income is acceptable for accounting purposes but not for income tax filing.
- A reconciliation below the income statement converts the net income calculated on the basis of the GAAPs to the net income for income tax purposes.

- The first step in reconciliation is to re-add any expense items not approved by Revenue Canada—Taxation. In this case, the straight-line depreciation expense is added to the net income as calculated under GAAPs.
- The subtotal reports the net income before the CCA is deducted.
- The next step is to subtract the deduction permitted by Revenue Canada—Taxation for the CCA. Here, we assume twice the amount as calculated under the straight-line method. Remember that in subsequent years, the amount for CCA will be less than the amount calculated under GAAPs.
- The final step is to report the net income for income tax purposes. This net income would appear on the taxpayer's individual tax return. Of course, the reconciled income statement would also be included.

PROBLEMS

Accounting for prepaid advertising first as a current asset and then as an operating expense.

Making appropriate adjusting entries to support the matching principle.

P 15-1 Nuts and Bolts Hardware Company bought and paid for three months of advertising space at a total cost of $450 on October 1. It is the business's policy to prepare updated financial statements each month.

a. Make the entry to show the purchase of the advertising space in General Journal form. Assume a cash outlay and an accounting policy which uses a Prepaid Advertising account to record this outlay of funds. Post to the appropriate T-accounts.

b. Make the entry to show the adjusting entries on October 31. Post it and indicate the balance in the Prepaid Advertising and Advertising Expense accounts as at October 31.

c. Suppose the accounting policy requires that Advertising Expense is debited at the time of purchasing the three months of advertising on October 1. In General Journal form, prepare the entries to purchase the advertising. Then show an adjusting entry on October 31 to support the matching principle.

Accounting for common prepaid expenses.

Preparing quarterly financial statements from an adjusted trial balance.

P 15-2 Temp Office Services rents office space by paying six months in advance. The business also rents all office equipment by paying three months in advance. Insurance for a company-owned car is prepaid by the year. The trial balance illustrated at the top of the next page outlines the accounts of the business as at June 30, 19-1. Assume that management prepares financial statements at the end of each quarter. The last set of quarterly statements were prepared on March 31 at which time appropriate accounts were closed and carried forward.

Temp Office Services
Trial Balance
June 30, 19—

Cash	101	$ 100	
Accounts Receivable	110	90	
Prepaid Office Rent	115	2 400	
Prepaid Equipment Rent	117	1 500	
Prepaid Car Insurance	119	1 650	
Bank Loan Payable	201		$ 500
S. Flood, Capital	301		3 640
S. Flood, Drawing	305	250	
Stenographic Service Revenue	401		5 000
Telephone Expense	510	150	
Wages Expense	520	3 000	
		$9 140	$9 140

Additional Information:

(i) The office rent was paid in advance on June 1 for six months, totalling $2400.

(ii) The office equipment rent of $500 per month was paid on April 1 for three months in advance.

(iii) The yearly car insurance of $1800 was last paid February 28.

(iv) Last adjustments were done at the end of the first quarter, March 31.

a. Adjust any accounts that require updating so that quarterly statements can be prepared on June 30.

b. Make the necessary General Journal entries to complete the needed adjustments as of June 30. You may wish to use T-accounts to organize your figures. Prepare an adjusted trial balance to assist with the preparation of quarterly financial statements.

c. Prepare an income statement for the three months ended June 30.

d. From the adjusted trial balance, prepare a classified balance sheet as at June 30.

Journalizing the purchase of land and building.

Calculating and journalizing depreciation expense in accordance with the matching principle.

P 15-3 The Rex Wholesale Company purchased a piece of land for $20 000 and the building for $80 000 on January 2, 19-5. The building has an estimated useful life of 20 years and there will be no disposal value expected at that time. The land and building were purchased with a $20 000 down payment and a mortgage was negotiated for the remainder.

a. Record the General Journal entry for the purchase on January 2, 19-5.

b. Record the year-end adjusting entry required for using the straight-line method of depreciation.

c. Compute and indicate the yearly and monthly depreciation expense required under the matching principle.

d. Prepare a partial balance sheet to report the fixed assets at the end of the second year. Assume a year-end of December 31.

Accounting for the purchase of a new drill press for cash.

Calculating the yearly and monthly depreciation expenses using the straight-line method.

Recording the journal entry to dispose of the press at three given cash amounts.

Preparing the subsidiary Fixed Asset Ledger card to report the history of the drill press.

P 15-4 The Saskatchewan Manufacturing Company bought a new drill press on January 2, 19-1 with cost outlays as follows:

Invoice price of new drill press	$8 000
Shipping charges	500
Installation charges	1 800

The company estimates the useful life of the new drill press to be five years, with a disposal value of $300. The company uses straight-line depreciation.

a. In General Journal form, record the double entry to acquire the fixed asset on January 2. Assume a cash outlay for all costs.

b. What is the depreciation expense for 19-2?

c. What is the depreciation expense per month?

d. What is the balance in the Accumulated Depreciation/Factory Equipment account at the end of 19-1? 19-3? 19-5?

e. What is the unexpired cost in the Factory Equipment account on January 2, 19-1? December 31, 19-1? December 31, 19-4?

f. Prepare the General Journal entry to record the depreciation expense on December 31, 19-5.

g. Assume that the drill press was sold on December 31, 19-5 for $300 cash. Record the necessary journal entry in General Journal form. What is the entry if the drill press was sold for $500? $150?

h. Complete a subsidiary fixed asset ledger card similar to the one illustrated on page 652. Make up any information that is required to complete the top portion. Assume that the drill press was sold to K. Hardy for $300 cash.

Calculating and journalizing depreciation expense under the straight-line and CCA methods.

P 15-5 The Niagara Trucking Company, a sole proprietorship, bought a brick building sometime after 1987 for $102 000 to serve as its office. The business estimates the building's useful life to be 25 years with an expected salvage value (disposal value) of $12 000.

Preparing a reconciliation of net income under GAAPs to the net income for income tax purposes.

Preparing partial balance sheets to report the fixed asset under GAAPs and income tax rules.

The business uses the straight-line method of depreciation but is obliged to use the CCA method for income tax purposes. These two calculations are kept in separate records.

a. Record in the General Journal the depreciation entry that is required each year for the straight-line method.

b. Set up a CCA table similar to the one illustrated on page 659 to calculate the CCA for the first five years of useful life of the new brick building. Refer to the Capital Cost Allowance (CCA) Classes table on page 658 for the allowable rate.

c. Assume that a condensed income statement prepared for the year ended December 31, 19-2—the second year of using the new building—reported the following information under GAAPs: Fees Earned, $500 000; Total Expenses (including the amount of depreciation expense using the straight-line method), $400 000; Net Income, $100 000. Prepare an income statement showing the reconciliation of net income for income tax reporting.

d. Show a partial balance sheet at the end of the second year to report the fixed asset under GAAPs. Show a second partial balance sheet to report the fixed asset under income tax rules.

MINI-CASES

Analyzing the need for adjustments.

MC 15-1 Joe Dence has just reviewed the topic on adjusting for prepaid expenses in his introductory accounting class and was still quite confused. "I don't understand," said Joe, "why we have to go through this process of adjusting these accounts. For example, we could just buy enough supplies for this year, and expense them immediately. Then we would not have to make any adjusting entries. For insurance, we will pay it on January 2, expense the entire amount, and then the cost will be completely used up by December 31. Again no adjusting is needed; the process is easier!"

a. Assume you are Joe's accounting teacher and explain to Joe the practical problems with his ideas.

b. If a business were to adopt Joe's ideas, what GAAPs would be violated? Explain your answer.

Analyzing effects of adjustments on financial statements.

MC 15-2 Anna Frank owns and operates Anna's Bananas, a local fruit shop. Her insurance agent has just offered her a reduced price on her insurance, if she pays one year in advance. Anna is tempted by the offer, but is afraid of what a large expense ($4800 for the year) will do to her income statement. ''The bank looks at my income statement every month, and if they see this large expense this month, I may be in trouble.''

a. Explain to Anna how this expense should be handled, and how it would appear to her bank manager on the income statement.

b. What would be the journal entry for one month's insurance expense, if Anna accepted the agent's offer and if Anna debited the initial amount of $4800 to a current asset account?

c. What would be the journal entry for one month's insurance expense, if Anna debited the initial amount of $4800 to an operating expense account?

d. Explain the GAAPs involved in this case.

Analyzing effects of depreciation on financial statements prepared under GAAPs and under income tax rules.

MC 15-3 ''This seems like a lot of unnecessary work to me,'' said Liz Burton, after listening to her teacher's explanation of the adjusting entries related to depreciation. ''Why bother to track these transactions every reporting period? I think accountants are just inventing work for themselves. When I buy a delivery truck for my business, what matters is whether I have enough money in the bank to be able to pay for it. I pay the $20 000, get the truck, and I don't have to worry about 10 years of accounting records if I just make one entry to expense the truck. Nothing could be simpler.''

a. Explain to Liz any problems that her method might create for her business, especially if she ever has to borrow money from the bank.

b. Explain what will happen when Liz files her income tax return based on her method of accounting. What must she do to prepare a proper income tax return?

Analyzing a gain on the disposal of a fixed asset.

MC 15-4 ''I don't see how a person could possibly have a gain on disposal when they sell a fixed asset, especially if the asset is a company car,'' reasoned Kelly Brogham, a junior accounting student. ''Everyone knows that almost all cars decrease in value by almost 30% per year. If I keep my company car for five years, there is absolutely no way I could get gain on disposal when I sell it. It will always be a loss on disposal.''

a. Is Kelly right? Explain your answer, using proper accounting language.

ADJUSTING FOR BAD DEBTS EXPENSE

Bad debts expense: the cost of granting credit to an uncollectable account receivable.

Many businesses sell their goods and/or services to their customers on credit, making their business more attractive to customers. Some credit customers, however, will not or cannot pay their bill when it becomes due. Such an uncollectable account is called a Bad Debts Expense or Doubtful Accounts Expense. Since this is an expense account and the bad debts situation is constantly changing, this account is a good example of one that may be adjusted. The following illustration shows how a bad debt occurs, and also how Wawdel Company deals with it.

December 3, 19-1 Sold merchandise on credit for $200 to Company X; terms 2/10, n/30.

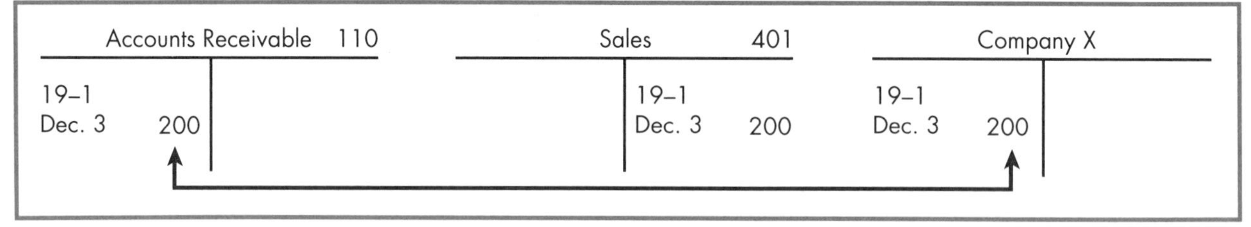

Company X did not take the discount offered, with the result that the $200 amount remained in the 19-1 year-end Accounts Receivable and Sales accounts. Despite all attempts to collect the amount in the early months of 19-2, Wawdel was not able to do so.

ANALYZING THE DIRECT WRITE-OFF METHOD

April 2, 19-2 Three months after the amount was first due, management decides to write off the $200 that Company X owes as a bad debt.

Analysis:

- The expense is called Bad Debts Expense, and like all expenses, it is a debit entry.
- The credit entry directly reduces both the Account Receivable/ Company X, and the Accounts Receivable control account.

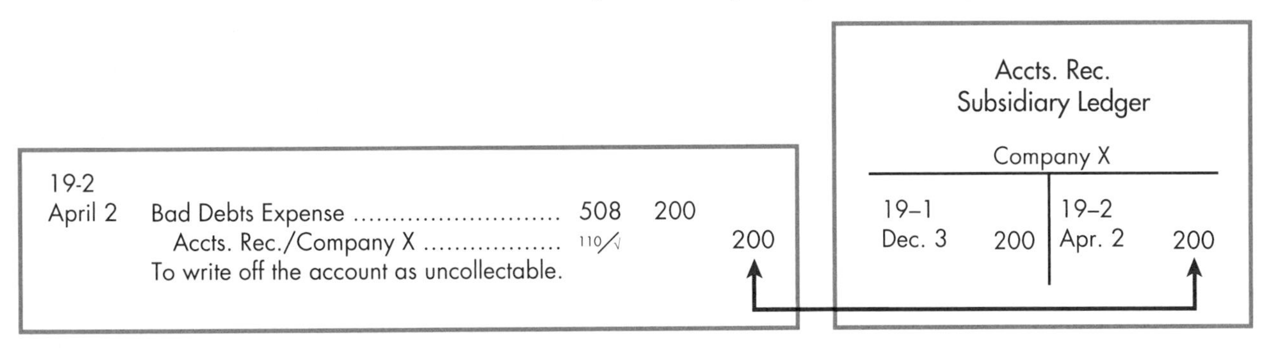

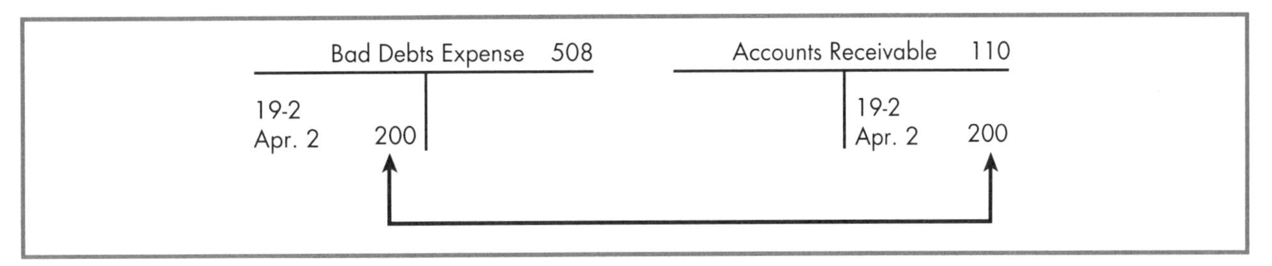

Company X is removed from the books, and the Accounts Receivable control account is reduced.

What is the problem with this method? The bad debts expense is recorded in year 19-2, but the revenue from the sale was recorded in year 19-1. Clearly, this is a violation of the matching principle, because the expense is not matched with the revenue for the same period. As a result, both years' financial statements will be incorrect. Year 19-1 will understate expenses, and therefore overstate net income. Year 19-2 will overstate expenses, and therefore understate net income.

Examine the comparative income statement illustrated below.

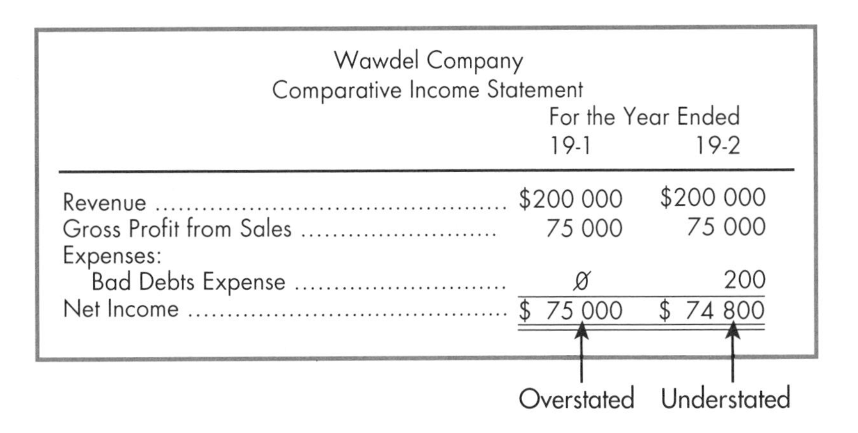
Wawdel Company
Comparative Income Statement

	For the Year Ended 19-1	19-2
Revenue	$200 000	$200 000
Gross Profit from Sales	75 000	75 000
Expenses:		
Bad Debts Expense	Ø	200
Net Income	$ 75 000	$ 74 800
	Overstated	Understated

The owner's equity (capital) in the balance sheet is overstated in year 19-1, because net income was overstated. Although the net income in year 19-2 is understated, and the income statement is incorrect, the figure in the Capital account at the end of the year will be correct (even though the process was incorrect), since the error in year 19-1 will be cancelled out by the opposite error in year 19-2.

Some accountants will argue that the direct write-off method is acceptable if the amounts processed are insignificant. This argument does not alter the fact that the direct write-off method is in clear violation of the matching principle. The proper method of dealing with bad debts will now be examined in detail.

ANALYZING THE MATCHING ENTRY

To solve the problems created by the direct write-off method, an adjusting entry is required at year-end to record the bad debts expense. This immediately creates two problems:

- How much should be debited to the Bad Debts Expense account? The bad debts expense must be estimated. The management will examine past default records and develop a workable policy for estimating. The mechanics of this will be discussed later in this topic. Bad debts are not realized for several months after the actual sale, as illustrated by the Company X example.

- Which accounts receivable should be reduced? None of these accounts can be reduced, since no one has defaulted! Instead, the entire receivable amount is reduced by using an ''allowance'' account called **Allowance for Bad Debts**. This account is a contra account to Accounts Receivable, and will appear immediately after Accounts Receivable on the balance sheet. See the illustration at the top of page 669. Allowance for Bad Debts is the total estimated bad debts for the next accounting period. It is a contra account, since it reduces the amount of the accounts receivable by the estimated bad debts, and has a normal balance opposite to that of Accounts Receivable. In the analysis of the journal entry opposite, notice that Allowance for Bad Debts is assigned the next account number.

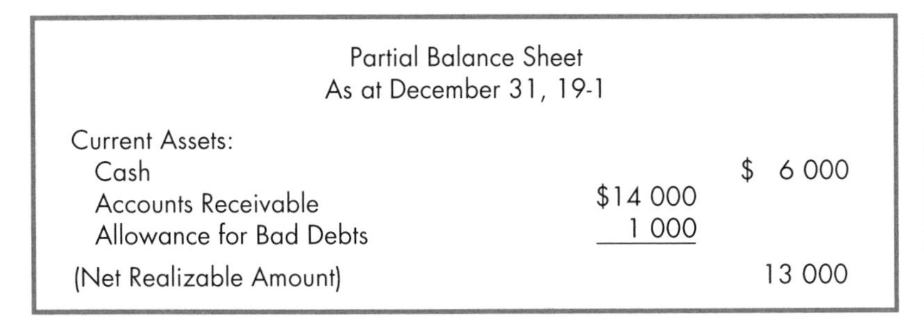

Partial Balance Sheet
As at December 31, 19-1

Current Assets:		
Cash		$ 6 000
Accounts Receivable	$14 000	
Allowance for Bad Debts	1 000	
(Net Realizable Amount)		13 000

Wawdel Company
Chart of Accounts

CURRENT ASSETS
110 Accounts Receivable
111 Allowance for Bad Debts

Let's observe what happens once the business sets up the Allowance for Bad Debts account and makes the Bad Debts Expense entry (adjusting entry) in the General Journal on December 31.

What Happens	Accounting Rule	Entry
The estimated expense for bad debts decreases owner's equity by $1000.	To decrease owner's equity, debit the account that caused the decrease.	Debit: Bad Debts Expense $1000.
The amount realizable from Accounts Receivable decreases by $1000.	To decrease an asset, credit the account.	Credit: Allowance for Bad Debts $1000.

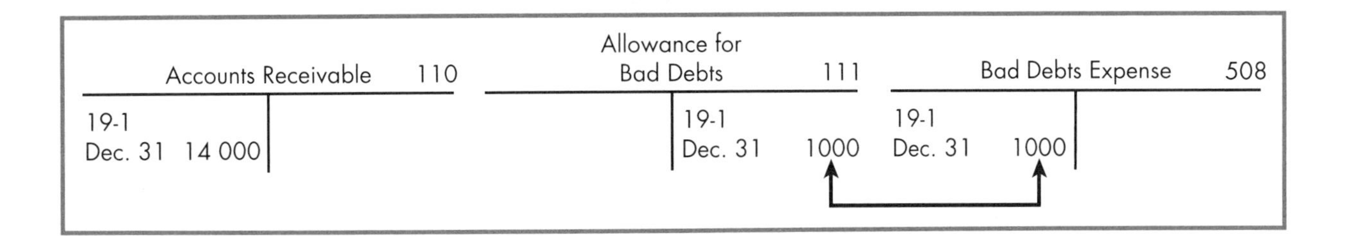

December 31 Wawdel Company estimates that losses due to bad debts will be $1000 in 19-1.

Analysis:

- After the estimate of Bad Debts Expense has been determined, the bad debts expense can be included in the income statement at year-end. See the illustration on the next page.

- Since bad debts expense is only an estimate, the net income is only an approximate, not an exact, calculation.

Wawdel Company
Income Statement
For the Year Ended December 31, 19-1

Revenue	
Revenue from Sales	$200 000
Less: Cost of Goods Sold	125 000
Gross Profit from Sales	75 000
Less Operating Expenses (includes $1000 for Bad Debts Expense)	50 000
Net Income	$ 25 000

These are estimates.

- The allowance for bad debts is now included in the Current Assets section of the balance sheet (see the illustration of Wawdel's partial balance sheet on the previous page), creating a **net realizable** accounts receivable figure. No specific account receivable is affected, but accounts receivable have been reduced overall, in recognition that at least one of these accounts is likely to default at some time during the year.

ANALYZING THE WRITE-OFF

What happens on April 2, 19-2 when management decides to write off Company X's account?

April 2, 19-2 Three months after the account first became due, management decides to write off as a bad debt the $200 charged to Company X's account.

GENERAL JOURNAL Page 10

DATE	ACCOUNT TITLE AND EXPLANATION	POST REF.	DEBIT	CREDIT
19-2				
Apr. 2	Allowance for Bad Debts	111	200 00	
	Accounts Receivable/Company X	110/√		200 00
	To write off the Company X account as a bad debt.			

Analysis:

- After the General Journal entry has been made, the amounts are posted to the appropriate accounts. The debit entry to Allowance for Bad Debts reduces that account by $200 to $800. This means that the business estimates that another $800 of accounts receivable will be uncollectable during this period.
- Nothing happens to Bad Debts Expense. This account was used to match bad debts expense to revenues in 19-1. Its job is done. The Allowance for Bad Debts will now absorb any actual write-offs during the year. Nothing else need be done with Bad Debts Expense until next year, when the estimate of bad debts will have to be made for the next year.
- The credit entry causes the Accounts Receivable/Company X account in the subsidiary ledger to be closed, since the balance in the account is now zero. This is the intent of the write-off. The Accounts Receivable control has also been reduced by $200, since the credit entry was double-posted (refer back to the posting reference in the General Journal entry).
- Accounts Receivable has been reduced by $200, but so has the Allowance for Bad Debts account. Therefore, net Accounts Receivable has not changed. It still reflects the amount of the receivables that the company believes it can collect. Do you remember the estimate we made of uncollectable accounts, and how the Allowance account was created? Now we know which account to reduce; the transactions merely allow us to reduce the Allowance account, and also reduce the specific account receivable.

Net Accounts Receivable: Accounts Receivable less Allowance for Bad Debts.

	Before the Write-off	After the Write-off
Accounts Receivable	$12 000	$11 800
Allowance for Bad Debts	1 000	800
Net Amount of Receivable	$11 000	$11 000

At the end of the year, the Allowance for Bad Debts account might have a balance remaining. If the balance is a credit, the estimate of bad debts was too high. If the balance is a debit, the allowance was too low, and the business lost more to bad debts than was estimated. In either case, the adjusting entry made at the next year-end will take this into account. This entry will be explained in the last part of this topic.

COLLECTING A DEBT PREVIOUSLY WRITTEN OFF

What happens when a customer pays an account that the company had previously written off as a bad debt?

May 5, 19-2 Company X sends a cheque for $200 to settle its overdue account, with a letter of apology for the late remittance. The journal entry would appear as follows:

GENERAL JOURNAL Page 12

DATE	ACCOUNT TITLE AND EXPLANATION	POST. REF.	DEBIT	CREDIT
19-2				
May 5	Accounts Receivable/Company X	✓/110	200.00	
	Allowance for Bad Debts	111		200.00
	To reverse the write-off of Company X.			

Analysis:

- Because the amount Company X owes is no longer on the books, the write-off must be reversed. This will re-establish Company X as a customer on the books.
- Record the receipt of cash in the Cash Receipts Journal, and reduce the Accounts Receivable/Company X account to zero. If a partial payment was received, the account would show a balance still owing. After such an entry is made, a credit report is prepared to determine the new credit standing of this customer.

ESTIMATING BAD DEBTS EXPENSE: TWO METHODS

Several methods may be used to estimate the bad debts expense for an accounting period. Two of these methods will be examined: (1) aging the accounts receivable, and (2) taking a percentage of net sales.

Aging the Accounts Receivable Method In Chapter 8 you learned that many businesses prepare and mail a monthly statement of account in the form of an aged statement. Similarly, many busi-

Aging of accounts receivable: classifying the balance of each account according to the age of the claim.

nesses, particularly large ones with many accounts receivable, use a method called aging of accounts receivable. In the past, this method was long and difficult, but computers with appropriate software can do the job quickly and relatively inexpensively.

Aging requires a classification of every receivable on the business's books into one of the aging categories: current; past due, from 1 to 30 days, or 31 to 60 days, or 61 to 90 days, or over 90 days. The categories are determined by management. The process of aging can be described in four steps:

Step 1. Preparing a Schedule of Accounts by Age Each receivable is listed by name and balance. It is then categorized, as in the schedule illustrated below.

Wawdel Company
Schedule of Accounts Receivable by Age
December 31, 19-2

ACCOUNT WITH	BALANCE	NOT PAST DUE	DAYS PAST DUE			
			1-30	31-60	61-90	Over 90
Anderson Hardware	600	600				
Eglinton Hardware Centre	900	400	500			
Hyland Hardware	700			700		
Reid Home Hardware	300				100	200
Summers Hardware Limited	1 000	900	100			
Thornhill Home Hardware	200	200				
Young Hardware Centre	200					200
Totals	11 500	8 000	1 500	1 100	500	400

A customer may fall under more than one heading, if more than one invoice for that customer is outstanding. Invoices still within credit terms are placed in the **Not Past Due** (or Current) column; all others are broken down according to the given headings. The schedule can be checked for accuracy by comparing the total of all the columns with the total of the Balance column.

Step 2. Estimating the Percentage of Probable Losses Once the columns are totalled, the estimated losses are determined by multiplying each total by a specified percentage. Even the Not Past Due column will generate some bad debts. Generally, the longer money is owed to you, the less chance you have of collecting that money. The percentages are based on management's past experience of actual losses. See the illustration on page 674.

Step 3. Applying the Percentages Prepare a table similar to the one shown. Each total is multiplied by a percentage to obtain an estimate. The estimates are then totalled. This total estimate will be the basis for the year-end adjusting entry.

Percentage of Probable Losses	
Over 90 days	50%
61-90 days	25%
31-60 days	10%
1-30 days	2%
Not past due	1%

Age Group (in days)	Total	Estimated Percentage	Estimated Loss
Over 90	$ 400	50%	$200
61-90	500	25%	125
31-60	1 100	10%	110
1-30	1 500	2%	30
0	8 000	1%	80
	$11 500		$545

Step 4. Recording the Adjusting Entry The estimated loss due to bad debts is now journalized in the General Journal as an adjusting entry at year-end by debiting Bad Debts Expense and crediting Allowance for Bad Debts. One of three situations will exist:

(1) If the Allowance for Bad Debts has a zero balance, the estimated loss is then entered. For Wawdel Company the estimated loss is $545.

(2) If the Allowance for Bad Debts has a credit balance, say $100, then **deduct** the credit balance from the dollar amount calculated, and record only $445 in the journal. When posted, the Allowance for Bad Debts will show $545, which is the amount the business expects to lose. In this way, any errors in last year's estimate are included in this year's estimate. If this was not done, and every year the business overestimated bad debts expense, the Allowance for Bad Debts account would become larger and larger.

(3) If the Allowance for Bad Debts has a debit balance — that is, expense was underestimated last year — say by $155, then **add** $155 to the dollar amount calculated. For Wawdel Company, the journal entry would be $700 ($155 + $545). Since the Allowance for Bad Debts in the journal entry is a credit, when the $700 credit is added to the $155 debit balance, the balance again returns to $545, the amount the business expects to lose. If care is taken, this is a reliable and easy calculation and entry.

Percentage of Net Sales Method Under this method, the percentage is based on past experience within your own business and related businesses. For example, if over the last ten years, your business has lost 0.5% of all net sales to bad debts, this trend will likely continue this year. Four points must be considered:

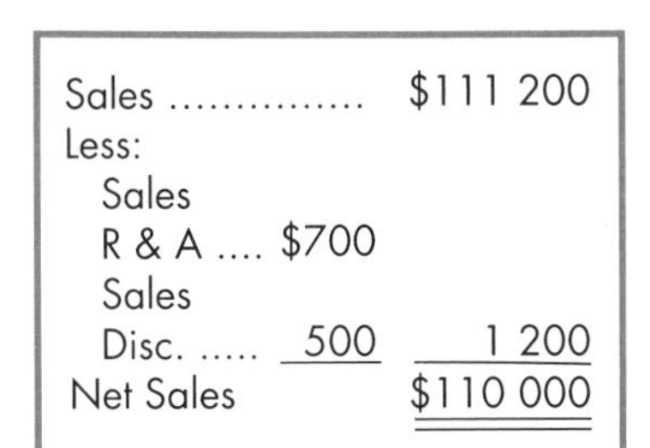

Sales		$111 200
Less:		
Sales R & A	$700	
Sales Disc.	500	1 200
Net Sales		$110 000

- The base is net sales, therefore, Sales Returns and Allowances and Sales Discounts must be deducted first.
- Only credit sales should be examined. You cannot suffer a bad debt if the sale was paid with cash.
- Now that the base or net sales is established (see the calculation in the margin), multiply that number by the percentage calculated for Wawdel Company. Thus, $110 000 × 0.5% = $550.
- The amount of the adjustment will be the computed amount regardless of any previous balance in Allowance for Bad Debts. The estimate is based solely on the relationship between bad debts and net sales, regardless of any entry made in previous periods. This can cause a problem over time if the estimated percentage does not exactly equal the actual losses, as the amount in the Allowance account may continue to grow.

ACCOUNTING FOR GST AND BAD DEBTS

Sale + GST = Total
100% + 7% = 107%

$$\text{GST} = \frac{7}{107} \times \text{Total}$$

If a business has sold taxable goods or services on credit, remitted the GST, and subsequently written off a debt as a bad debt, the business can recover the GST that was remitted. As the GST is included in the amount of the bad debt, the tax adjustment would be 7/107 of the amount written off. For example, if you sold a $300 item, the debt owing would be $321. When this debt is written off, the business would claim an adjustment equal to $321.00 × 7/107 or $21. This value would be entered on the GST Return for Registrants on the line for Adjustments. The journal entry would appear as follows:

Allowance for Bad Debts	300	
GST Payable	21	
Accounts Receivable/Customer		321

If subsequently the customer pays part of the debt that was previously written off, say $100, the business must calculate and remit the GST that was included in that payment. The GST to be remitted would be $100.00 × 7/107 or $6.54. Thus, the journal entry would appear as follows, given that the write-off has already been reversed:

Cash	100.00	
Accounts Receivable/Customer		93.46
GST Payable		6.54

COMPARING THE TWO ASSET ACCOUNTS

Although Accumulated Depreciation and Allowance for Bad Debts are both contra accounts and are similar, it is important to note the differences between them. First, let's look at the similarities:

- Both appear on the balance sheet as deductions from their respective asset accounts.
- Both are created by adjusting entries.
- Both are based on estimates rather than on precisely determined amounts.
- Both show that the debit side of the adjusting entry affects an expense account (Depreciation Expense or Bad Debts Expense).

On the other hand, you should note the important differences between them, as outlined in this table:

DIFFERENCES

Accumulated Depreciation	Allowance for Bad Debts
1. This account does not reduce the related fixed asset to a realizable value. It merely shows what portion of the original cost has expired and has been recorded as expenses.	1. This account serves to reduce the accounts receivable to the amount of cash expected to be obtained through the collection of accounts receivable.
2. This account is debited only at the time the related fixed asset is disposed of.	2. This account is debited each time an individual customer account is written off.
3. This account will have only a credit balance during the lifetime of the related fixed asset.	3. This account may have either a debit or a credit balance at the end of each accounting year. The specific type of balance will depend on the extent of bad debts written off during the accounting period.
4. This account is ''contra'' to a fixed asset account.	4. This account is ''contra'' to a current asset account.

Journalizing adjustments for bad debts.

P 15-6 Make the necessary General Journal entries to record the following adjustments related to bad debts expense. Assume that management prefers to use the method of aging accounts receivable to estimate bad debt expense for each of these cases.

a. The Aged Accounts Receivable Schedule at the end of December shows that $950 is uncollectable. The Allowance for Bad Debts account has no balance.

b. The Aged Accounts Receivable Schedule at the end of October shows $674 is estimated to be uncollectable. The Allowance for Bad Debts account has a credit balance of $95.

c. The Aged Accounts Receivable Schedule at the end of March shows that $1379 is estimated to be uncollectable. The Allowance for Bad Debts account shows a debit balance of $130.

Journalizing common transactions concerning bad debts.

P 15-7 Record in the General Journal the necessary entries for the following unrelated transactions. Use the Allowance for Bad Debts account.

a. Management decides to write off the account of T. Ogden, who has a delinquent balance of $438.

b. The business receives a cheque for $527 in the mail from D. Leenders to cover his account in full. D. Leenders's account had been previously written off as a bad debt. *Remember:* This takes two entries.

c. The business determines that it has net credit sales of $65 000. In the past, this business has lost one-half of 1% (0.5%) of all net credit sales to bad debts. There is no balance in the Allowance for Bad Debts account.

d. The business receives a cheque in the mail from Ralph Highhopes for $100. He wishes to re-establish his business with our firm. His account, totalling $350, had been written off as a bad debt some three months ago.

Journalizing common transactions concerning bad debts.

P 15-8 On December 1, 19-1, the Allowance for Bad Debts account shows a credit balance of $500. In the General Journal, make the necessary adjusting and closing entries for the following transactions. It is recommended that T-accounts be used to organize your work.

Dec. 5 The company decides to write off the account of Mark Fatherson. Fatherson currently owes the company $210.

9 The company also decides to write off the account of G. Howe. G. Howe owes $410.

14 The company receives payment in full from P. Henderson. The Henderson account had been written off as uncollectable. Amount $125.

31 The company uses the aging of receivables method to estimate uncollectable accounts. This year's estimate is $675.

31 The company closes the books.

19-2

Jan. 10 Mark Fatherson sends a cheque to the company for $210. Accompanying the cheque is a letter of apology and an explanation for the late payment.

31 The company receives a letter stating that Betty Upbridge, a customer, has gone bankrupt. A cheque for $51 is enclosed. This is all the company can expect to receive against her outstanding balance of $510.

Using the percentage method to calculate bad debt expense.

Journalizing transactions involving bad debts.

P 15-9 Suppose that, in Problem 15-7, management decided to use the percentage of sales method to estimate the accounting period's bad debts expense. On December 31, 19-1, the trial balance was reported as follows: Sales, $78 354; Sales Returns and Allowances, $569; Sales Discounts, $595. The percentage of net sales believed to be uncollectable is 1%.

a. Prepare General Journal entries for each of the transactions in Problem 15-7 under the above circumstances.

Preparing an Aged Schedule of Receivables.

Calculating and journalizing an adjusting entry.

Closing the Bad Debt Expense account.

P 15-10 Minto Manufacturing Ltd. has prepared the following list of accounts receivable. The balance in the Allowance for Bad Debts account on December 31, 19-1 is $290 CR. The business offers all customers terms of n/30.

Customer	Invoice Date	Amount
Bakers Manufacturing	June 10, 19-1	$ 500.00
Carter Truck Bodies	July 31, 19-1	300.00
Grady Supplies	November 30, 19-1	1 500.00
Markham Production Co.	December 4, 19-1	8 000.00
Regal Products Ltd.	November 1, 19-1	900.00
Regal Products Ltd.	December 1, 19-1	2 300.00

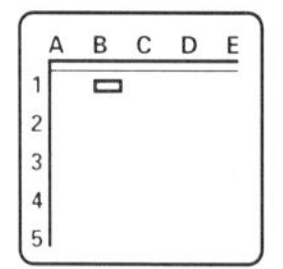

a. Prepare from the list of customers a Schedule of Accounts Receivable by Age, as illustrated on page 673.

b. Prepare a table showing the percentage of probable losses similar to the one shown on page 674. Use the percentages shown on this same page to make your calculations.

c. Prepare the necessary adjusting entry to record the Bad Debts Expense for year-end, and also prepare the closing entry for Bad Debts Expense.

d. In table form, make a comparison of the contra asset accounts called Allowance for Bad Debts and Accumulated Depreciation.

TOPIC 2 MINI-CASES

Analyzing the need for accuracy in estimating bad debts.

MC 15-5 Frank Eager runs his own dry-cleaning business, and does all of his own bookkeeping. Most of his business comes from the people who run other businesses in the mall, and he is in the habit of extending credit to most of them. Frank uses the percentage of sales method to estimate bad debt expense. ''Every year I look at which accounts were uncollectable last year, and calculate the total as a percentage of net sales. Then I double it, to be on the safe side, and that is the number I use for bad debt expense. This method must work well, since the actual bad debts are not even close to the estimate. I guess I'm just a good business person.''

a. Are there any problems with Frank's system? Explain your answer.

b. Explain to Frank the effect on his income statement and also his Capital account if he were to continue overestimating indefinitely.

Analyzing the balance sheet effects of writing off bad debts.

MC 15-6 Leslie Picard runs her own printing business, which she has just purchased from a relative. She has been reviewing the books, since she plans to do all the bookkeeping herself. Leslie found that some bad debts were written off in the General Journal, and is confused. ''I've found this one bad debt written off. The entry looks like this:

Allowance for Bad Debts	75	
Accounts Receivable/S. Jones		75

I don't think this can be right, since the net accounts receivable figure is exactly the same after the transaction. Before, it looked like this:

Accounts Receivable	$4500
Less: Allowance for Bad Debts	500
Net Realizable Accounts Receivable	$4000

After the transaction, it looked like this:

Accounts Receivable	$4425
Less: Allowance for Bad Debts	425
Net Realizable Accounts Receivable	$4000

I don't think these entries have achieved the purpose of writing off the uncollectable debt.''

a. Is Leslie correct? Explain your answer.

b. As Leslie's accountant, explain to her, in your own words, what the entry achieves.

ADJUSTING FOR ACCRUED REVENUES, ACCRUED EXPENSES, AND UNEARNED REVENUE

The reverse side of prepaid expenses is accrued expenses. The term ''prepaid'' means an amount has been paid in advance; thus, you record it as an unexpired cost and list it as an asset. As you will see, ''accrued'' means something built up over time.

To be able to complete adjusting entries for accrued revenue and expenses, a good understanding of both the cash and accrual bases of accounting is necessary. Review carefully the brief discussions that follow.

ACCOUNTING ON A CASH BASIS

Cash basis of accounting: revenue is recorded when cash is received; expenses are recorded when cash is paid.

This is by far the simpler of the two systems, since the cash basis of accounting records an event only when cash is received or spent. For example, cash sales are recorded immediately, since cash is received. A sale on account is ignored, since no cash is received. When the customer pays the account, **then** the sale is recorded. Likewise with purchases, no entry is made unless cash is paid out.

This system makes calculating business profits somewhat difficult. The cash basis is not approved under present GAAPs except in a few special cases, but these are best studied in other accounting courses.

ACCOUNTING ON AN ACCRUAL BASIS

This method, the one you have been studying, allows a business to account for revenue that has been earned, but not yet received (sale on credit), and for expenses incurred but not yet paid (purchases on account). It requires maintenance of inventory records so that the cost of goods sold can be calculated, unlike the cash basis system, which ignores inventory. Under the accrual system, an attempt to match revenues and expenses can be planned and undertaken. It allows the recording of revenue and expenses when they are earned or incurred regardless of the cash consequences.

Accrued expense: an expense that has occurred but has not been recorded or paid.

Accrued: grown or increased, as interest on a debt (receivable or payable) increases day by day. The term applies mostly to a continuing flow of services rather than to physical assets.

An accrued expense is an expense which has been incurred during an accounting period, but has not been paid or recorded. When you see the word "accrued," think of the word "accumulated" or "increased." A good example is employee wages. Every day the employee works, wages accrue, or in other words, accumulate until payday. From the business's point of view, the wages are an accrued expense, one that has been incurred (since the employee worked for the money) but not yet paid or recorded. From the employee's point of view, the wages are accrued, since they have been earned, but not yet received.

These accrued wages must be accounted for at the end of any accounting period. For example, Wawdel Company pays its hourly rated personnel every Friday. Jane Dawson earns $50 per day, or $250 every Friday. Last Friday, June 25, the company recorded in its Cash Payments Journal a debit to Wages Expense and a credit to Cash, both in the amount of $250. The next payday is Friday, July 2, when Jane will receive $250, as usual. But the month-end, June 30, occurs in the middle of the week, and the company wants to prepare financial statements as of June 30. Unless the company prepares an adjusting entry, the wage expense will be incorrect, since part of the week's wages that will be paid on Friday, July 2 are actually an expense from June. Examine the illustration below:

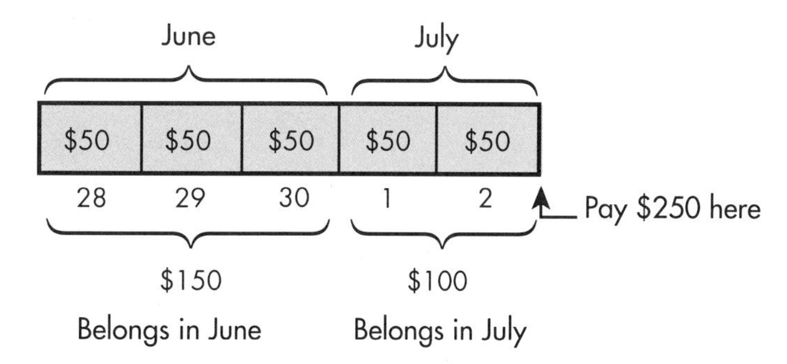

Unless an adjustment is made, the matching principle will be violated, and the financial statements will be incorrect. As the illustration shows, \$150 of the week's wages are properly an expense of June; the balance is an expense of July. What should the business do? Pay the employees twice that week? This is not necessary, since a simple adjusting entry will suffice. The adjustment will record the \$150 wages expense from June in an liability account called Wages Payable, since it is owed, but will not be paid until Friday. On Friday, July 2, the payment of wages will be recorded by crediting Cash and debiting two accounts, Wages Payable for \$150, and Wages Expense for \$100. Refer to the illustrations below.

Week of June 21–25

19–1			
June 25	Wages Expense	250	
	Cash		250
	To record one week's wages for J. Dawson.		

Note: The entry would appear in the Cash Payments Journal.

Week of June 28–July 2

19–1			
June 30	Wages Expense	150	
	Wages Payable		150
	To record the adjustment for wages expense for June 28, 29, 30.		

Note: This is an adjustment and would appear in the General Journal.

19–1			
July 2	Wages Expense	100	
	Wages Payable	150	
	Cash		250
	To record payment of five days' wages owing to J. Dawson.		

Note: July 2 is in a new accounting period. This entry belongs in the Cash Payments Journal.

The June 30 entry is an adjusting entry, which records the wage expenses for June 28, 29, and 30 as an expense for June. If this entry were omitted, three days' wages would be incorrectly recorded as an expense for July. A mismatch would occur. Instead, J. Dawson receives the full week's pay of \$250 on Friday, July 2. Two days' wage expense has been properly recorded as an expense of July, and the account Wages Payable has been reduced to zero. Any time an expense has the potential to be recorded in the wrong period, especially where expenses cover more than one period, an adjusting entry is necessary.

Read carefully the following situation and decide what is the problem. On May 1, 19-1, Wawdel Company borrowed $10 000 from the local bank. The interest rate was 12% per annum, or 1% per month. Interest payments are due November 1 and May 1. Wawdel Company's year-end is December 31. What would be the interest expense on November 1, 19-1? What journal entry would be required, and what journal would it be recorded in? Now the important question is: what journal entry would be required on December 31, 19-1? Check your answer against the following entries.

19–1			
Nov. 1	Bank Loan Interest Expense	600	
	Cash		600
	To record payment of 6 months' interest on the bank loan.		

Note: Record in the Cash Payments Journal.

19–1			
Dec. 31	Bank Loan Interest Expense	200	
	Bank Loan Interest Payable		200
	To record the year-end adjustment for the bank loan interest for two months.		

Note: Record in the General Journal.

An adjustment was necessary on December 31, 19-1, for the accrued interest expense. If no entry was made until the next interest payment day on May 1, a mismatch would occur. The interest expense for the last two months of 19-1 must be recognized as an expense of that period, even though the interest will not be actually paid until May 1. This expense was recognized with the adjusting entry.

Now what would the entry of May 1 look like? Remember that you now have a Bank Loan Interest Payable account created by the adjustment on December 31, which must be eliminated.

19–2			
May 1	Bank Loan Interest Expense	400	
	Bank Loan Interest Payable	200	
	Cash		600
	To record the payment of six months' interest expense on the bank loan.		

Accrued revenue: a revenue that has been earned but not recorded or received.

If an accrued expense is an expense that has been incurred, but not paid or recorded, what then is accrued revenue? An accrued revenue is a revenue that has been earned, but not yet received or recorded. Study the following situation.

Wawdel Company holds an outstanding note receivable for $12 000 that earns interest for the company at 8% per annum. It was purchased October 31, 19-1 and pays interest annually. As of December 31, 19-1, the note has earned interest equal to $160 ($12 000 × 8% × 2/12), which must be recorded as revenue of 19-1, but no interest will be actually received until October 31, 19-2. What type of entry is required?

Date	Account	Debit	Credit
19–1			
Dec. 31	Interest Receivable	160	
	Interest Revenue		160
	To record 2 months' interest earned on our note receivable.		

This is an adjusting entry and belongs in the General Journal. Without this adjusting entry, the 19-1 revenue would be recorded in 19-2. This would be a mismatch of revenue and expenses, and violation of the matching principle. The $200 of interest revenue is recorded on December 31, 19-1 and a receivable is introduced to hold the amount on the business's books until the actual receipt of cash occurs on October 31, 19-2. What entry would be made on October 31, 19-2?

Date	Account	Debit	Credit
19–2			
Oct. 31	Cash	960	
	Interest Receivable		160
	Interest Revenue		800
	To record 10 months' interest earned and 12 months' interest paid on our note receivable.		

Both accrued revenues and accrued expenses will result in year-end adjusting entries to ensure that there are no violations of the matching principle. Without such adjustments, there would surely be mismatches of revenue and expenses in both years. The same is true if one examines the effect such an adjusting entry would have on the year-end financial statements.

When it comes to receiving payment, there are two situations that can arise. The first exists when the company performs the work **before** any payment is received. You have just examined this accrued revenue situation. The second exists when the company is paid in advance for work it will do in the future. For example, Wawdel Company receives $900 in advance to do work for another company, to be performed at the rate of $100 per month for the next nine months. When the cash is received in advance, Wawdel would make this entry:

19–1			
Aug. 1	Cash	900	
	Unearned Revenue		900
	To record receipt of $900. Payment in advance for revenue yet to be earned.		

Unearned Revenue	208
	19–1 Aug. 1 900

Unearned revenue: amounts received as revenue in one period, but not earned until future periods.

Examine the above transaction very carefully. Note that an asset, Cash, has been increased by a debit entry. The new concept is the account called Unearned Revenue. The key word here is **unearned**. This account is a current liability account. Why? Consider the situation on the day the money is received by Wawdel. The business owes the customer either the work promised, or the money that was received for the work to be done. Since the business plans to keep the cash, and do the work, it assumes that it owes the customer the value of the work, which is recorded in the Unearned Revenue account. This record will remain a liability until the work is performed, then the value will be recorded as Revenue.

Examine the circumstances on December 31, 19-1. The business's year-end has arrived, and it is time to ensure that proper matching of revenues and expenses takes place. How many months of work has Wawdel performed as of December 31? Five — from August 1 to December 31. Therefore, five months' revenue must be recorded for 19-1. Entries to Revenue are credit entries; but what entry is the debit? You will recall that when cash was received, an account called Unearned Revenue was created; a current liability with a credit balance. This account will now be debited for the five months' work. The following entry is recorded:

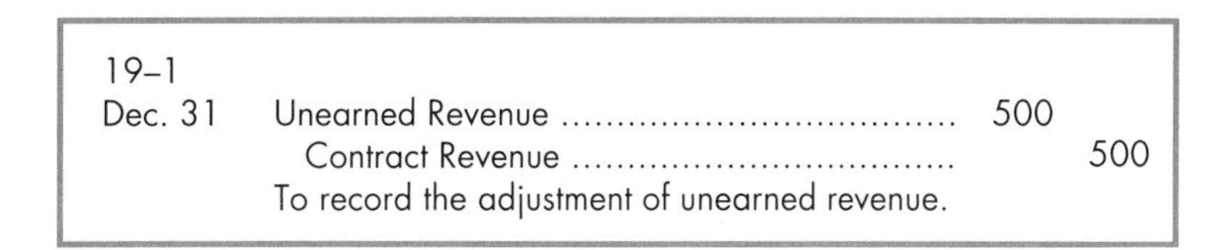

19–1			
Dec. 31	Unearned Revenue	500	
	Contract Revenue		500
	To record the adjustment of unearned revenue.		

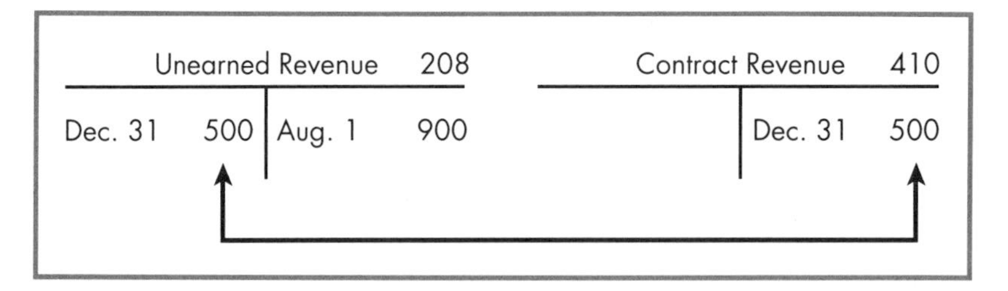

Note that the adjustment matches the revenue that was earned in 19-1 with the expenses of the same period. The liability has been reduced by the amount of revenue earned. The liability account now reflects the correct amount of revenue still unearned (4 months' worth).

This type of adjustment is the last of the four. You have examined prepaid expenses, accrued revenues, accrued expenses, and unearned revenue. Each type of adjustment dealt with a specific situation — a change — that might occur as a business carries on its business activities. It should be noted that entries of another kind called **reversing entries** are sometimes used in combination with adjustments, but these will be left for a more advanced course.

PROBLEMS

Calculating and journalizing accrued interest payable.

P 15-11 The Backside Chair Mfg. Company has an outstanding bank loan for $50 000 at 12% interest per annum. Interest is calculated on March 1 and September 1. The loan was obtained on March 1, 19-1.

a. Record the General Journal entry required for March 1, 19-1; September 1, 19-1; December 31, 19-1; and March 1, 19-2. Assume the business's year-end is December 31.

Calculating and journalizing accrued revenue and unearned revenue.

P 15-12 Mostly Green Lawn Care Company has been hired by Mr. Swank to care for his estate from April 1, 19-1 to October 31, 19-1 at a cost of $250 per month. Mr. Swank agreed to pay the entire amount at the end of the service contract. The business year-end is September 30.

a. Record the adjusting entry required at the business year-end, and then record the entry to receive payment.

b. Assume that Mr. Swank agreed to pay the entire amount in advance on April 1, 19-1. Record the journal entries necessary for April 1, 19-1, September 30, 19-1, and October 31, 19-1.

Calculating and journalizing depreciation, accrued revenue, interest payable, interest receivable, and allowance for bad debts.

P 15-13 The Triple C Company gives you the following information and asks you to prepare all the needed General Journal adjusting entries as of December 31, 19-1.

a. The business owns a building costing $150 000, with a $13 000 salvage value and an estimated life of 25 years. Record one year's depreciation under the straight-line method.

b. The business has agreed to a contract dated October 31, 19-1. The contract calls for Triple C to perform services for three years at a rate of $9000 per year. The business received nothing in advance, but will be paid quarterly.

c. The business has an outstanding loan of $20 000 with the bank. Interest payments are required every six months on April 30 and October 30. The rate of interest is 18%.

d. At the end of the year, December 31, 19-1, the Allowance for Bad Debts has a debit balance of $450. The business ages receivables and determines that $2759 will be uncollectable in 19-2.

e. The business owns Canada Savings Bonds worth $5000. The interest rate is 10% and interest is paid on November 1. The business has owned the bonds for three years.

Calculating, journalizing, and posting to T-accounts for unearned revenue.

P 15-14 The Acme Widget Company hires the ABC Company to perform cleaning services for seven months. The contract is signed on September 1, 19-1 and Acme Widget Co. pays $1400 in advance ($200 per month). Each business has a year-end of December 31.

a. Record the entry required on September 1, 19-1 for the ABC Company.

b. Prepare the necessary adjustments on December 31, 19-1 for the ABC Company.

c. Prepare the T-accounts for all parts of **a** and **b**.

d. Repeat **a** to **c** for the Acme Widget Company.

MINI-CASES

Analyzing cash basis accounting.

MC 15-7 "All this accrual stuff has me confused," complained Al Mummar in accounting class. "The time and money spent in small businesses on accounting paperwork is very high. The cash basis of accounting is a recognized method of accounting. I suggest that everyone start using the cash basis. We only record cash coming and going; we don't have to bother with tracking all these accruals. After all, accounting is accounting, isn't it?"

a. Explain to Al any shortcomings with his suggestion.

Calculating adjustment dates.

MC 15-8 The Excellent Corporation has just signed a long-term contract with a customer to provide services to the customer's business. The three-year contract was signed February 1, 19-1. Excellent Corporation received payment in advance for the first year only of the contract. The following years will be paid in advance, one year at a time, on the anniversary date of the contract. Excellent Corp. has a year-end of April 30, and does financial statements every six months.

a. Over the next three years, Excellent Corp. will require several journal entries. Describe **when** each entry will be made, and what type of an entry it will be (that is, the purpose of each entry).

COMPREHENSIVE CASE STUDY 12

The Peter Pauling Company provides furniture cleaning and repair services for three major hotels. The firm has the following contracts with each hotel:

Hotel Deluxe: The company is required to complete all cleaning and repairs for a flat rate of $250 per month. This has worked well for the company, because there is usually very little repair work to complete. The hotel pays in advance, quarterly (February 15, May 15, August 15, November 15).

12th Street Hotel: The company is called in as required. Furniture cleaning is a flat $25 per piece and repairs are $20 per hour which includes any needed materials. Each quarter (January 1, April 1, July 1, October 1), the hotel makes an advance payment of $550 ($300 for cleaning, $250 for repairs). Any charges over and above must be billed.

Hotel Terrace: This is the firm's largest customer. The contract requires that the firm clean the contents of two floors every month. The firm is paid $750 per month for this service on the 15th of the following month. Repairs are paid on a flat rate, one year in advance on May 1. Amount: $3600.

a. Prepare all necessary General Journal adjustment entries for the company year-end, December 31, 19-4.

Additional Information

(i) All items are paid up to date for all three hotels as you begin work.

(ii) Since October 1, the firm has cleaned 20 items and repaired 7 items at 12th Street Hotel. Each item repaired took one hour.

(iii) All accounts have the exact balances that they should have assuming everything works out perfectly.

(iv) Accounts used by the company are: Cleaning and Repairs Revenue/Hotel Deluxe, Cleaning Revenue/12th Street Hotel, Repairs Revenue/12th Street Hotel, Cleaning Revenue/Hotel Terrace, Repairs Revenue/Hotel Terrace.

CHAPTER 16

COMPLETING THE ACCOUNTING CYCLE

Topic 1
Preparing the Ten-Column Worksheet

Topic 2
Preparing Financial Statements

Topic 3
Completing the Accounting Cycle

Topic 4
Analyzing Financial Statement Relationships

Topic 5
Applying the Electronic Spreadsheet and General Ledger Accounting Package

This chapter will cover the remaining steps of the accounting cycle for a merchandising business. Up to this point in Part 3, you have looked at the following:

(1) originating information from source documents
(2) analyzing those documents and the subsequent recording of transactions in appropriate journals
(3) posting of journal entries to subsidiary and general ledgers
(4) preparing schedules for subsidiary ledgers and preparing a trial balance from the General Ledger

In an earlier chapter, you learned how to complete the six-column worksheet, following the preparation of the trial balance. This working paper was introduced as a rough draft of the financial statements — the income statement and the balance sheet. From the worksheet, the business would then prepare formal financial statements suitable for presentation to the general public. The accounting cycle was completed by the closing entries and the preparation of a postclosing trial balance.

Recall that the adjustments explained in earlier chapters were not included in the first discussion of the accounting cycle, for reasons of simplicity. Adjustments are a major addition to the cycle and result in an expanded worksheet. The first topic of this chapter carefully outlines the changes that occur in the worksheet for a merchandising business. Once the worksheet is completed, financial statements can be prepared, adjusting entries may be recorded, and accounts of the merchandising business can be closed.

PREPARING THE TEN-COLUMN WORKSHEET

Worksheet: an expanded trial balance for computing, classifying, and sorting account balances before preparing financial statements.

The worksheet is the accountant's tool for expanding the trial balance. It allows computing, classifying, and sorting of account balances for preparation of the period-end financial statements. It is not a permanent document of the business and is usually prepared in pencil. This is the only document where erasing is permissible. Now let's have a look at the actual process of preparing the worksheet.

STEP 1 COMPLETING THE TRIAL BALANCE SECTION

The first step is to copy the period-end trial balance onto the worksheet by listing the account name in the Account Title column, and placing the balance in either the debit or credit column. Be careful that the balance is entered in the correct column. Refer to the work-

Wawdel Company
Worksheet
For the Month Ended August 31, 19–

	ACCOUNT TITLE	ACCT. NO.	TRIAL BALANCE		ADJUSTMENTS		ADJ. TRIAL BALANCE		INCOME STATEMENT		BALANCE SHEET		
			DEBIT	CREDIT	DEBIT	CREDIT	DEBIT	CREDIT	DEBIT	CREDIT	DEBIT	CREDIT	
1	Cash	101	10 700										1
2	Petty Cash	102	50										2
3	Notes Receivable	103	60 000										3
4	Accounts Receivable	104	6 400										4
5	Allowance for Bad Debts	105		20									5
6	Interest Receivable	106	500										6
7	Merchandise Inventory, Aug. 1	110	4 200										7
8	Supplies on Hand	112	400										8
9	Prepaid Insurance	114	550										9
10	Land	150	24 000										10
11	Building	155	96 000										11
12	Accum. Deprec./Building	156		700									12
13	Warehouse Equipment	160	4 000										13
14	Accum. Deprec./Whs. Equip.	161		210									14
15	Office Equipment	165	7 200										15
16	Accum. Deprec./Off. Equip.	166		550									16
17	Delivery Trucks	170	40 000										17
18	Bank Loan	201		5 500									18
19	Unearned Revenue	202		500									19
20	Accounts Payable	203		6 800									20
21	Bank Loan Interest Payable	204		75									21
22	Unemployment Insurance Payable	210		60									22
23	CPP Payable	211		120									23
24	Income Tax Payable	212		800									24
25	GST Payable	213		42									25
26	Group Insurance Payable	214		124									26
27	Mortgage Payable	250		100 000									27
28	R. Wawdel, Capital	301		115 530									28
29	R. Wawdel, Drawing	302	705										29
30	Sales	401		32 536									30
31	Sales Returns & Allowances	402	220										31
32	Sales Discounts	403	145										32
33	Purchases	501	5 800										33
34	Transportation-in	502	150										34
35	Purchases Returns & Allowances	503		210									35
36	Purchases Discounts	504		160									36
37	Advertising Expense	510	185										37
38	Utilities Expense	512	60										38
39	Delivery Expense	514	180										39
40	Wages & Salaries Expense	516	1 600										40
41	Payroll Tax Expense	518	864										41
42	Interest Expense	520	28										42
43			263 937	263 937									43
44													44
45													45

sheet above. Note that the account numbers have been included in a separate column between the Account Title column and the money columns. As in the trial balance, account numbers are sequential.

Let's stop here for a moment to review the worksheet heading.

- The heading answers the questions **who** (the name of the company), **what** (the name of the document: worksheet), and **when** (the accounting period for the month, quarter, or year ended). The date may not be abbreviated, and because you will be listing income statement accounts as well as balance sheet accounts, the date identifies the **period** being measured (in this case, for the month ended August 31, 19—).

- The six-column worksheet which you worked with earlier in Chapter 5, Topic 1 is now expanded to include the adjustments you studied in Chapter 15. Examine once again the illustration on page 693. You will see that two more sets of columns have been added. These include the Adjustments and the Adjusted Trial Balance columns. The worksheet now has ten columns. In practice, worksheets may contain six, eight, ten, or more columns. In this book, you will deal only with the six- and ten-column worksheets.

- The worksheet Trial Balance section is identical to the formal General Ledger trial balance. In fact, often the business will dispense with the formal trial balance and prepare the Trial Balance section of the worksheet directly from the ledger accounts. After the trial balance is prepared, it must be checked to ensure that debits equal credits. If they are not equal, the worksheet preparation must stop until the error is corrected.

- In a merchandising business, you must remember that there is a Merchandise Inventory account. When you examine it closely, you will find that the amount listed in the trial balance is the **beginning** inventory. Since the ending inventory amount is not disclosed here, the business must use the periodic inventory method to calculate the cost of goods sold. Be prepared to find where the ending inventory figure is recorded on the worksheet.

- Finally, you should be able to identify a number of accounts in the trial balance that may require adjusting entries (prepaid assets, accumulated depreciation, etc.). Because there are no related expired cost (expense) accounts for any of these accounts, you know that the trial balance amounts are unadjusted, beginning-of-the-year figures. As we complete each section of the worksheet, you will examine these accounts as well.

STEP 2 COMPLETING THE ADJUSTMENTS SECTION

In Chapter 15, you learned how to resolve mismatches between revenues and expenses through the use of adjusting entries. In practice, adjusting entries are calculated and recorded on the worksheet before they are journalized and posted. Since the worksheet contains only beginning-of-the-year figures, the information required to do adjusting entries will not be found there. We would require additional information such as:

- a year-end count of office and/or store supplies
- the unused portion of prepaid rent or prepaid insurance
- the amount of an accrued revenue or expense
- the total of aged receivables or a percentage of net sales taken to estimate the amount of bad debts expense for the accounting period
- the depreciation calculations for the business's fixed assets
- the change in an unearned revenue account

Each of these various adjustments will now be examined. Remember, you will be looking for a **change**. *Note:* The letters A to J in the following headings can be traced to the corresponding entry on the worksheet (see page 697).

A. Adjusting for Supplies Used Look at the Supplies on Hand listing. You will find a debit entry for $400 which represents the amount of supplies on August 1, 19— . Assume that the unused supplies have been counted on August 31, 19—, and that the total is $300. The change is $100 ($400 − $300). Supplies costing $100 have been used up (expired) resulting in an expense, Supplies Expense. To record this change, debit $100 to Supplies Expense, and credit $100 to Supplies on Hand, which reduces the account to $300, representing the cost of supplies on hand. Since there is no Supplies Expense account listed, it must be recorded on a new line (44), in the Account Title column, beneath the trial balance items. The debit entry for Supplies Expense can then be recorded in the debit column of the Adjustment section. Each adjustment, as it is recorded, is identified with a letter of the alphabet. This letter is a reference tool to permit easy identification of related entries and to assist in the preparation of General Journal entries in the future.

Supplies Expense 521	
(A) 100	

Supplies on Hand 112	
	(A) 100

Summary:

(1) Analyze the complete double entry. T-accounts are often useful, as illustrated.

(2) Record the entries opposite the listed accounts in the appropriate debit or credit column, or open any account not previously listed in the trial balance.

(3) Letter-code all adjustments for reference and ease of journalizing in the future.

B. Adjusting for Expired Insurance Assume that your insurance policy was bought on July 1, 19— for $600. The cost per month is $50 ($600 ÷ 12). The adjustment necessary for August is $50, which is one month's expense. The entry required is to debit Insurance Expense and to credit Prepaid Insurance. Note the letter B.

C. Adjusting for Bad Debts Assume that management has estimated uncollectable accounts for August to be $120, using the aged accounts receivable method. As you will remember, the Allowance for Bad Debts account balance must be considered in calculating the adjustment. Since the Allowance for Bad Debts account shows a credit balance for $20, the adjustment will be for $100 ($120 − $20). Notice the letter C, and that once again the Bad Debts expense account is listed below the trial balance.

D. Adjusting for Interest Receivable The business's note receivable pays $500 per month or $6000 per year. Payment is received June 30 and December 31. Examine the entry on the worksheet. Coded D, the debit is to the Interest Receivable account, and the credit is to Interest Revenue, in the amount of $500. *Note:* One month's adjustment for July has already been recorded, as reflected in the preliminary trial balance by the debit to Interest Receivable for $500.

E. Adjusting for the Accrued Interest Expense The business's bank loan of $5500 requires interest payments on March 31, June 30, September 30, and December 31. The interest rate of 16.36% creates an interest expense of $900 per year or $75 per month. The adjustment is coded E, with a debit to the Bank Loan Interest Expense account and a credit to Bank Loan Interest Payable ($75). *Note:* One month's adjustment for July has already been recorded, as reflected in the preliminary trial balance by the credit to Bank Loan Interest Payable for $75.

F. Adjusting for Depreciation of the Building Assume management has estimated a useful life of twenty years with no dis-

Wawdel Company
Worksheet
For the Month Ended August 31, 19–

	ACCOUNT TITLE	ACCT. NO.	TRIAL BALANCE		ADJUSTMENTS		ADJ. TRIAL BALANCE		INCOME STATEMENT		BALANCE SHEET		
			DEBIT	CREDIT	DEBIT	CREDIT	DEBIT	CREDIT	DEBIT	CREDIT	DEBIT	CREDIT	
1	Cash	101	10 700										1
2	Petty Cash	102	50										2
3	Notes Receivable	103	60 000										3
4	Accounts Receivable	104	6 400										4
5	Allowance for Bad Debts	105		20		(C) 100							5
6	Interest Receivable	106	500		(D) 500								6
7	Merchandise Inventory, Aug. 1	110	4 200										7
8	Supplies on Hand	112	400			(A) 100							8
9	Prepaid Insurance	114	550			(B) 50							9
10	Land	150	24 000										10
11	Building	155	96 000										11
12	Accum. Deprec./Building	156		700		(F) 400							12
13	Warehouse Equipment	160	4 000										13
14	Accum. Deprec./Whs. Equip.	161		210		(G) 30							14
15	Office Equipment	165	7 200										15
16	Accum. Deprec./Off. Equip.	166		550		(H) 70							16
17	Delivery Trucks	170	40 000										17
18	Bank Loan	201		5 500									18
19	Unearned Revenue	202		500	(J) 250								19
20	Accounts Payable	203		6 800									20
21	Bank Loan Interest Payable	204		75		(E) 75							21
22	Unemployment Insurance Payable	210		60									22
23	CPP Payable	211		120									23
24	Income Tax Payable	212		800									24
25	GST Payable	213		42									25
26	Group Insurance Payable	214		124									26
27	Mortgage Payable	250		100 000									27
28	R. Wawdel, Capital	301		115 530									28
29	R. Wawdel, Drawing	302	705										29
30	Sales	401		32 536									30
31	Sales Returns & Allowances	402	220										31
32	Sales Discounts	403	145										32
33	Purchases	501	5 800										33
34	Transportation-in	502	150										34
35	Purchases Returns & Allowances	503		210									35
36	Purchases Discounts	504		160									36
37	Advertising Expense	510	185										37
38	Utilities Expense	512	60										38
39	Delivery Expense	514	180										39
40	Wages & Salaries Expense	516	1 600										40
41	Payroll Tax Expense	518	864										41
42	Interest Expense	520	28										42
43			263 937	263 937									43
44	Supplies Expense	521			(A) 100								44
45	Insurance Expense	523			(B) 50								45
46	Bad Debts Expense	525			(C) 100								46
47	Interest Revenue	405				(D) 500							47
48	Bank Loan Interest Expense	530			(E) 75								48
49	Deprec. Expense/Bldg.	550			(F) 400								49
50	Deprec. Expense/Whs. Equip.	552			(G) 30								50
51	Deprec. Expense/Off. Equip.	554			(H) 70								51
52	Deprec. Expense/Trucks	556			(I) 500								52
53	Accum. Deprec./Trucks	171				(I) 500							53
54	Fees Earned	407				(J) 250							54
55					2 075	2 075							55

posal value, and uses the straight-line method. Annual depreciation is $4800 annually ($96 000 ÷ 20) and monthly depreciation is $400 ($4800 ÷ 12). The entry is coded F, and the debit is to Depreciation Expense/Building and the credit is to Accumulated Depreciation/ Building in the amount of $400.

G. Adjusting for Depreciation on Warehouse Equipment Most businesses have equipment that (1) was purchased at various times, and (2) has various disposal values. To calculate depreciation, you must examine the subsidiary **Fixed Asset Ledger** and add together the yearly amounts of depreciation estimated for each piece of equipment. Assume that this has been done, and that the total shows that the depreciation expense for the current year is $360. The depreciation expense for August must be $30.

H. Adjusting for Depreciation on Office Equipment The Fixed Asset Ledger cards were examined, and they revealed total depreciation for office equipment of $840 for the year. The adjustment for August is $70.

I. Adjusting for Depreciation on Delivery Trucks Assume that two delivery trucks were purchased on July 31, 19—. Each truck cost $20 000, and each has a useful life of five years and a disposal value of $5000. Straight-line depreciation will be used. Since this is a new purchase, the contra account Accumulated Depreciation/Trucks does not yet exist. To record this adjustment, the account must be added to the appropriate part of the trial balance. The base cost of the trucks is $40 000 less disposal of $10 000. The annual depreciation is $6000 ($30 000 ÷ 5) and the monthly depreciation is $500.

J. Adjusting for Unearned Revenue Assume that the business contracted one month earlier, on July 2, to perform services for the R. & R. Company for three months at $250 per month. The full $750 was paid in advance and recorded in the liability account Unearned Revenue. The adjustment recorded at the end of July reduced Unearned Revenue by $250—one month's revenue—and a similar adjustment is required now. The entry is a debit to Unearned Revenue and a credit to Fees Earned, for $250.

An examination of the remainder of the accounts reveals no further adjustments are necessary. A single line is drawn across the bottom of both the debit and credit columns, and the columns are totalled. The totals must agree before you may proceed. If they do not agree, you must recheck your work and correct any errors. Use the transaction codes to trace through each entry to ensure debits equal credits.

Once the two columns agree, the traditional double line is drawn across both the debit and credit columns.

STEP 3 COMPLETING THE ADJUSTED TRIAL BALANCE SECTION

After the adjustments are recorded, and the totals are balanced, the next step is to calculate the adjusted trial balance figures. Some figures, the ones that were not adjusted, can be transferred directly to the Adjusted Trial Balance columns. For example, the Cash account shows a $10 700 debit balance. Since Cash is not adjusted, record that amount in the debit column of the adjusted trial balance. Refer to the illustration on page 700. The same procedure will apply to the Petty Cash, the Notes Receivable, and the Accounts Receivable accounts.

The next account, Allowance for Bad Debts, has a credit balance of $20 and a credit adjustment of $100. To extend this account, add the two credit amounts, and write the total, $120, in the credit column of the Adjusted Trial Balance section.

Interest Receivable has a $500 debit balance and a debit adjustment of $500. Add the two figures, and place the total in the debit column of the adjusted trial balance.

Merchandise Inventory requires no adjustment. Transfer the debit balance to the debit column.

Next, examine the account Supplies on Hand, which has an opening balance of $400. Subtract the credit adjustment from the balance ($400 – $100) and extend the $300 difference into the debit column of the Adjusted Trial Balance section.

Finally, if you had to create additional accounts because of the adjustments, transfer the amounts in those accounts to the Adjusted Trial Balance section. Draw a single line across both columns of the adjusted trial balance and total the debit and credit columns. If they balance, you may proceed. If they do not, locate the error before you proceed. Once they balance, double-underline the two columns.

STEP 4 MOVING THE ADJUSTED TRIAL BALANCE AMOUNTS INTO THE STATEMENT COLUMNS

After the Adjusted Trial Balance columns have been proven correct, the individual amounts must be sorted between the Income Statement columns and the Balance Sheet columns. Here are three rules that will help you to decide which columns to use:

Wawdel Company
Worksheet
For the Month Ended August 31, 19–

	ACCOUNT TITLE	ACCT. NO.	TRIAL BALANCE DEBIT	TRIAL BALANCE CREDIT	ADJUSTMENTS DEBIT	ADJUSTMENTS CREDIT	ADJ. TRIAL BALANCE DEBIT	ADJ. TRIAL BALANCE CREDIT	INCOME STATEMENT DEBIT	INCOME STATEMENT CREDIT	BALANCE SHEET DEBIT	BALANCE SHEET CREDIT	
1	Cash	101	10 700				10 700						1
2	Petty Cash	102	50				50						2
3	Notes Receivable	103	60 000				60 000						3
4	Accounts Receivable	104	6 400				6 400						4
5	Allowance for Bad Debts	105		20		(C) 100		120					5
6	Interest Receivable	106	500		(D) 500		1 000						6
7	Merchandise Inventory, Aug. 1	110	4 200				4 200						7
8	Supplies on Hand	112	400			(A) 100	300						8
9	Prepaid Insurance	114	550			(B) 50	500						9
10	Land	150	24 000				24 000						10
11	Building	155	96 000				96 000						11
12	Accum. Deprec./Building	156		700		(B) 400		1 100					12
13	Warehouse Equipment	160	4 000				4 000						13
14	Accum. Deprec./Whs. Equip.	161		210		(G) 30		240					14
15	Office Equipment	165	7 200				7 200						15
16	Accum. Deprec./Off. Equip.	166		550		(H) 70		620					16
17	Delivery Trucks	170	40 000				40 000						17
18	Bank Loan	201		5 500				5 500					18
19	Unearned Revenue	202		500	(J) 250			250					19
20	Accounts Payable	203		6 800				6 800					20
21	Bank Loan Interest Payable	204		75		(E) 75		150					21
22	Unemployment Insurance Payable	210		60				60					22
23	CPP Payable	211		120				120					23
24	Income Tax Payable	212		800				800					24
25	GST Payable	213		42				42					25
26	Group Insurance Payable	214		124				124					26
27	Mortgage Payable	250		100 000				100 000					27
28	R. Wawdel, Capital	301		115 530				115 530					28
29	R. Wawdel, Drawing	302	705				705						29
30	Sales	401		32 536				32 536					30
31	Sales Returns & Allowances	402	220				220						31
32	Sales Discounts	403	145				145						32
33	Purchases	501	5 800				5 800						33
34	Transportation-in	502	150				150						34
35	Purchases Returns & Allowances	503		210				210					35
36	Purchases Discounts	504		160				160					36
37	Advertising Expense	510	185				185						37
38	Utilities Expense	512	60				60						38
39	Delivery Expense	514	180				180						39
40	Wages & Salaries Expense	516	1 600				1 600						40
41	Payroll Tax Expense	518	864				864						41
42	Interest Expense	520	28				28						42
43			263 937	263 937									43
44	Supplies Expense	521			(A) 100		100						44
45	Insurance Expense	523			(B) 50		50						45
46	Bad Debts Expense	525			(C) 100		100						46
47	Interest Revenue	405				(D) 500		500					47
48	Bank Loan Interest Expense	530			(E) 75		75						48
49	Deprec. Expense/Bldg.	550			(F) 400		400						49
50	Deprec. Expense/Whs. Equip.	552			(G) 30		30						50
51	Deprec. Expense/Off. Equip.	554			(H) 70		70						51
52	Deprec. Expense/Trucks	556			(I) 500		500						52
53	Accum. Deprec./Trucks	171				(I) 500		500					53
54	Fees Earned	407				(J) 250		250					54
55					2 075	2 075	265 612	265 612					55

(1) If the amount is a debit in the Adjusted Trial Balance section, move it to the debit column of the appropriate statement.

(2) If the amount is a credit in the Adjusted Trial Balance section, move it to the credit column of the appropriate statement.

(3) There are two statement columns, the Income Statement or Balance Sheet. Generally, asset, liability, and owner's equity accounts will appear on the balance sheet; revenue and expense accounts appear on the income statement. There are some notable exceptions, such as Merchandise Inventory, which will be discussed shortly.

Study the illustration that follows on pages 702 and 703, as you read the analysis.

Analysis: Each account balance in the Adjusted Trial Balance section must be copied to either the debit or credit column of its related statement section. Assets, liabilities, and owner's equity accounts (Capital, Drawing) must be moved to the Balance Sheet columns. Similarly, revenue, contra revenue, costs (Cost of Goods Sold), expense, and contra expense accounts must be copied to the correct Income Statement columns.

One group of accounts requires careful analysis. A merchandising business using a periodic inventory method does not calculate the cost of each good sold as each sale is made. This is why no account for Cost of Goods Sold will be found in either the trial balance or the adjusted trial balance. Instead, a group of costs is used to make an indirect calculation of the Cost of Goods Sold. The accounts required are (1) Merchandise Inventory, which you will remember shows the beginning amount only, (2) Purchases, (3) Transportation-in, (4) Purchases Returns and Allowances, and (5) Purchases Discounts. In addition, one more figure is required: the ending inventory. Analyze how each of these accounts is identified on the worksheet.

Inventory, Aug. 1			$4 200	
Purchases		$5 800		
Transportation-in		150		
Cost of Delivered Goods		5 950		
Purchases R & A	$210			
Purchases Discount	160	370		
Net Purchases			5 580	
Cost of Goods Available for Sale			9 780	
Less: Inventory, Aug. 31			4 000	
Cost of Goods Sold				$5 780

Wawdel Company
Worksheet
For the Month Ended August 31, 19–

	ACCOUNT TITLE	ACCT. NO.	TRIAL BALANCE		ADJUSTMENTS		ADJ. TRIAL BALANCE		INCOME STATEMENT		BALANCE SHEET		
			DEBIT	CREDIT	DEBIT	CREDIT	DEBIT	CREDIT	DEBIT	CREDIT	DEBIT	CREDIT	
1	Cash	101	10 700				10 700				10 700		1
2	Petty Cash	102	50				50				50		2
3	Notes Receivable	103	60 000				60 000				60 000		3
4	Accounts Receivable	104	6 400				6 400				6 400		4
5	Allowance for Bad Debts	105		20		(C) 100		120				120	5
6	Interest Receivable	106	500		(D) 500		1 000				1 000		6
7	Merchandise Inventory, Aug. 1	110	4 200				4 200		4 200	4 000	4 000		7
8	Supplies on Hand	112	400			(A) 100	300				300		8
9	Prepaid Insurance	114	550			(B) 50	500				500		9
10	Land	150	24 000				24 000				24 000		10
11	Building	155	96 000				96 000				96 000		11
12	Accum. Deprec./Building	156		700		(F) 400		1 100				1 100	12
13	Warehouse Equipment	160	4 000				4 000				4 000		13
14	Accum. Deprec./Whs. Equip.	161		210		(G) 30		240				240	14
15	Office Equipment	165	7 200				7 200				7 200		15
16	Accum. Deprec./Off. Equip.	166		550		(H) 70		620				620	16
17	Delivery Trucks	170	40 000				40 000				40 000		17
18	Bank Loan	201		5 500				5 500				5 500	18
19	Unearned Revenue	202		500	(J) 250			250				250	19
20	Accounts Payable	203		6 800				6 800				6 800	20
21	Bank Loan Interest Payable	204		75		(E) 75		150				150	21
22	Unemployment Insurance Payable	210		60				60				60	22
23	CPP Payable	211		120				120				120	23
24	Income Tax Payable	212		800				800				800	24
25	GST Payable	213		42				42				42	25
26	Group Insurance Payable	214		124				124				124	26
27	Mortgage Payable	250		100 000				100 000				100 000	27
28	R. Wawdel, Capital	301		115 530				115 530				115 530	28
29	R. Wawdel, Drawing	302	705				705				705		29
30	Sales	401		32 536				32 536		32 536			30

31	Sales Returns & Allowances	402	220				220		220				31
32	Sales Discounts	403	145				145		145				32
33	Purchases	501	5 800				5 800		5 800				33
34	Transportation-in	502	150				150		150				34
35	Purchases Returns & Allowances	503		210				210		210			35
36	Purchases Discounts	504		160				160		160			36
37	Advertising Expense	510	185				185		185				37
38	Utilities Expense	512	60				60		60				38
39	Delivery Expense	514	180				180		180				39
40	Wages & Salaries Expense	516	1 600				1 600		1 600				40
41	Payroll Tax Expense	518	864				864		864				41
42	Interest Expense	520	28				28		28				42
43			263 937	263 937									43
44	Supplies Expense	521			(A) 100		100		100				44
45	Insurance Expense	523			(B) 50		50		50				45
46	Bad Debts Expense	525			(C) 100		100		100				46
47	Interest Revenue	405				(D) 500		500		500			47
48	Bank Loan Interest Expense	530			(E) 75		75		75				48
49	Deprec. Expense/Bldg.	550			(F) 400		400		400				49
50	Deprec. Expense/Whs. Equip.	552			(G) 30		30		30				50
51	Deprec. Expense/Off. Equip.	554			(H) 70		70		70				51
52	Deprec. Expense/Trucks	556			(I) 500		500		500				52
53	Accum. Deprec./Trucks	171				(I) 500		500				500	53
54	Fees Earned	407				(J) 250		250		250			54
55					2 075	2 075	265 612	265 612	14 757	37 656	254 855	231 956	55
56										14 757			56
57	Net Income									22 899	⟶	22 899	57
58											254 855	254 855	58
59													59

- The beginning inventory is shown in the Adjusted Trial Balance section. It is shown as a debit balance, so it must be copied to the debit column of the Income Statement section. Why this section? As a debit here, the balance is treated as part of the cost of goods sold, which is also part of the income statement. In other words, the effect of the debit is to decrease owner's equity in the accounting equation since the beginning inventory *is assumed to have been completely sold*.
- The amount of Purchases is a debit balance in the Adjusted Trial Balance section. As a debit, it must be copied to the debit side of the Income Statement section, where it is part of the Cost of Goods Sold. In theory, under a periodic system, these purchases are assumed to have been completely sold; consequently, the debit indicates the effect of decreasing owner's equity in the accounting equation.
- Transportation-in is directly related to Purchases in order to calculate the cost of delivered goods. The account balance is a debit; therefore, it must be copied to the debit side of the income statement. Since transportation-in adds to the cost of goods sold, and since the cost of goods sold decreases the owner's equity in the accounting equation, the figure is correctly analyzed as a debit to the income statement.
- Purchases Returns and Allowances and Purchases Discounts are both contra accounts to Purchases. Both have credit balances. Since both accounts have the effect of decreasing the cost of purchases, they must decrease the cost of goods sold. Another way to express this idea is to say that both must increase owner's equity in any accounting equation; consequently, both must be credits in any income statement analysis. At this stage of the analysis, you will probably realize that the Income Statement columns on the worksheet are simply a tool for calculating the net income (or loss) through a series of debits and credits.
- The placement of the ending inventory figure must be considered the critical part of this analysis. Under the periodic method, the final inventory balance is not shown in the Trial Balance section, or the Adjusted Trial Balance section. At the end of the accounting period, a physical count will provide input for the calculation of the cost of remaining inventory. Assume that at the end of August the final inventory figure is $4000. There are three important points to be considered here:

(1) The final inventory is acknowledged on the Merchandise Inventory line. Notice that the account code remains the same. You

will learn how to update this account through a series of closing entries later in this chapter.

(2) The final inventory must appear in **two** places. First, it is an asset of the business. Therefore, it must appear on the balance sheet. Enter this amount on the debit side of the Balance Sheet section, on the Merchandise Inventory line. Secondly, the final inventory figure is needed to calculate cost of goods sold for the income statement, and therefore must appear in the Income Statement columns. Will the entry be a debit or a credit? The final figure has the effect of decreasing the cost of goods sold; therefore, the figure must be entered as a credit in the Income Statement section. As a credit here, the figure is correctly analyzed as contra to the ''costs'' entered in the debit column. To review this point, refer back to the illustration on page 701 which shows the method of calculating indirectly the cost of goods sold for a business using a periodic inventory method. It may help you to remember that the final inventory is entered on the worksheet as a double entry: a debit to the Balance Sheet section to indicate the correct cost of the remaining asset, and a credit to the Income Statement section to indicate the contra effect of the cost of goods available for sale.

As an alternative, the final inventory, properly dated, may be shown on the worksheet on a separate line **below** the trial balance figures as a double entry: debit to the balance sheet and credit to the income statement. This entry is illustrated below.

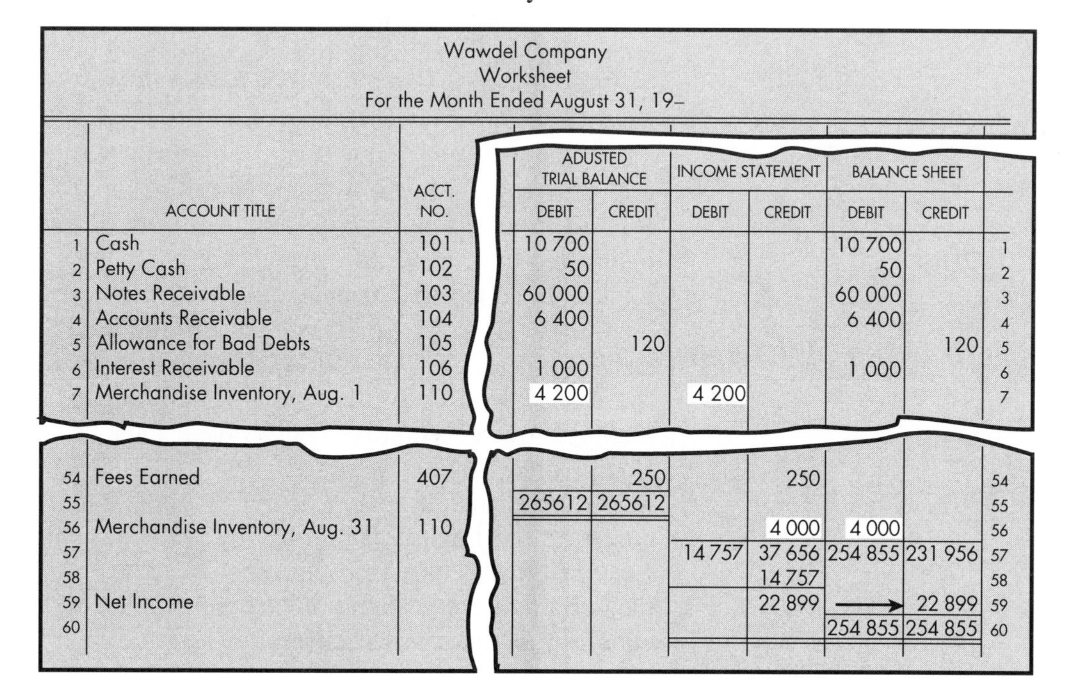

Wawdel Company
Worksheet
For the Month Ended August 31, 19–

	ACCOUNT TITLE	ACCT. NO.	ADJUSTED TRIAL BALANCE		INCOME STATEMENT		BALANCE SHEET		
			DEBIT	CREDIT	DEBIT	CREDIT	DEBIT	CREDIT	
1	Cash	101	10 700				10 700		1
2	Petty Cash	102	50				50		2
3	Notes Receivable	103	60 000				60 000		3
4	Accounts Receivable	104	6 400				6 400		4
5	Allowance for Bad Debts	105		120				120	5
6	Interest Receivable	106	1 000				1 000		6
7	Merchandise Inventory, Aug. 1	110	4 200		4 200				7
54	Fees Earned	407		250		250			54
55			265612	265612					55
56	Merchandise Inventory, Aug. 31	110				4 000	4 000		56
57					14 757	37 656	254 855	231 956	57
58						14 757			58
59	Net Income					22 899 →		22 899	59
60							254 855	254 855	60

STEP 5 CALCULATING THE NET INCOME (OR LOSS) AND COMPLETING THE WORKSHEET

After all amounts have been transferred or recorded into the two statement columns, the totals of the statements must be recorded. First, rule a single line across both columns below the last number recorded. Second, total the debit column of the income statement (expenses, contra revenue, and ending inventory), and then total the credit column (revenues, contra expenses, and ending inventory). Refer to the simplified illustration. Do the columns balance? They

Calculation of
Net Loss

	INCOME STATEMENT		BALANCE SHEET		
	DEBIT	CREDIT	DEBIT	CREDIT	
51	12 000	9 000	20 000	23 000	51
52	9 000				52
53	3 000 →		→ 3 000		53
54			23 000	23 000	54
55					55
56					56

will balance only if revenues equal expenses (no profit or loss). If the credit total is larger than the debit total, a net income exists. If the opposite situation exists, a net loss occurs. In either case, the smaller number is subtracted from the larger to obtain the net loss or net income. Refer now to the opposite illustration. You will notice that the smaller number was placed below the larger number, and subtracted to obtain the net income in this case.

Now total the balance sheet columns. Again, if there is a net income or loss, the columns will not balance. As you will recall, net income is added to owner's equity through closing entries. The net income (or loss) figure is necessary in the Balance Sheet columns, in order for them to balance. In which column should this figure be recorded? You know that net income belongs to the owner, and increases owner's equity. Therefore, it must be recorded on the credit side. Conversely, net loss decreases owner's equity, and must be recorded on the debit side. Refer again to the opposite illustration to confirm this. Label this number by placing either Net Income or Net Loss in the Account Title column opposite the number. Now, total the debit and credit columns of the balance sheet. The totals must be equal, or an error has occurred.

Wawdel Company
Worksheet
For the Month Ended August 31, 19–

	ACCOUNT TITLE	ACCT. NO.	TRIAL BALANCE		ADJUSTMENTS		ADJ. TRIAL BALANCE		INCOME STATEMENT		BALANCE SHEET		
			DEBIT	CREDIT	DEBIT	CREDIT	DEBIT	CREDIT	DEBIT	CREDIT	DEBIT	CREDIT	
1	Cash	101	10 700				10 700				10 700		1
2	Petty Cash	102	50				50				50		2
3	Notes Receivable	103	60 000				60 000				60 000		3
4	Accounts Receivable	104	6 400				6 400				6 400		4
5	Allowance for Bad Debts	105		20		(C) 100		120				120	5
18	Bank Loan	201		5 500				5 500				5 500	18
19	Unearned Revenue	202		500	(J) 250			250				250	19
20	Accounts Payable	203		6 800				6 800				6 800	20
21	Bank Loan Interest Payable	204		75		(E) 75		150				150	21
22	Unemployment Insurance Payable	210		60				60				60	22
23	CPP Payable	211		120				120				120	23
53	Accum. Deprec./Trucks	171				(I) 500		500				500	53
54	Fees Earned	407				(J) 250		250		250			54
55					2 075	2 075	265 612	265 612	14 757	37 656	254 855	231 956	55
56										14 757			56
57	Net Income									22 899	→	22 899	57
58											254 855	254 855	58
59													59

When the totals are in agreement, double-underline both statement columns.

Now the worksheet is finished, and the accountant has mathematical proof of its accuracy. We can move on to the next phase of the accounting cycle—preparing financial statements.

TOPIC 1 PROBLEMS

Preparing adjustments on a ten-column worksheet.

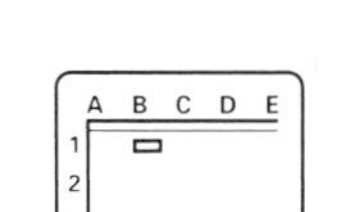

P 16-1 The trial balance for the Snooze Motel for the month ended October 31, 19— is illustrated on page 708.

Given the following additional information, prepare a ten-column worksheet.

(i) An examination of the insurance policy reveals $350 of insurance still in force.

(ii) A count of the office supplies in the back room reveals that $100 of the supplies have been used up.

(iii) The custodial department counted the household supplies and determined that $80 of supplies remains unused.

Snooze Motel
Trial Balance
October 31, 19–

Account	No.	Debit	Credit
Cash	101	$ 100	
Prepaid Insurance	110	500	
Office Supplies on Hand	112	250	
Housekeeping Supplies on Hand	114	150	
Land	150	775	
Building	155	200	
Accumulated Depreciation/Building	156		$ 10
Equipment	170	175	
Accumulated Depreciation/Equipment	171		25
Accounts Payable	203		15
Unearned Revenue	205		150
Mortgage Payable*	250		260
M. Albert, Capital	301		1 455
M. Albert, Drawing	302	165	
Concession Revenue	401		150
Accommodation Revenue	405		600
Telephone Expense	510	50	
Cleaning Expense	513	70	
Wages Expense	514	210	
Miscellaneous Expense	516	20	
		$2 665	$2 665

*The mortgage payable is secured by the land and the portion falling due within this current year is $12.

(iv) The building depreciation for the period totalled $15. The Accumulated Depreciation/Equipment account increased by $55.

(v) The motel has earned, but not received, concession revenue of $22.

(vi) The motel owes to its employees $31 for wages earned, and as of October 31, 19—, this amount has not been paid.

(vii) G. Peabody, on vacation with his family, paid fees for the hospitality suite on October 15, 19— for the next three months. The suite rents for $50 per month.

Preparing adjustments on a ten-column worksheet.

P 16-2 Illustrated on the opposite page is the trial balance for Regina Rugs as at December 31, 19-4.

Given the following information, prepare a ten-column year-end worksheet.

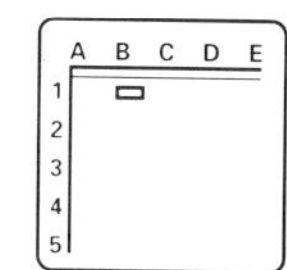

Use your school's spreadsheet software or the traditional manual method to solve this problem.

Regina Rugs
Trial Balance
December 31, 19–4

Account	No.	Debit	Credit
Cash	101	$ 5 500	
Accounts Receivable	105	8 000	
Allowance for Bad Debts	106		$ 40
Inventory January 1, 19-4	110	12 500	
Office Supplies on Hand	115	1 200	
Prepaid Insurance	120	2 700	
Land	150	12 000	
Building	160	53 000	
Accumulated Depreciation/Building	161		2 800
Trucks	165	25 000	
Accumulated Depreciation/Truck	166		1 500
Office Equipment	171	6 000	
Accumulated Depreciation/Equipment	172		2 800
Bank Loan Payable	210		11 000
Accounts Payable	212		2 900
Unearned Revenue	215		1 800
Property Taxes Payable	220		1 400
P. Matthews, Capital	301		88 160
P. Matthews, Drawing	302	1 100	
Carpet Sales	410		76 000
Sales Returns and Allowances	411	500	
Sales Discounts	412	2 300	
Installation Fees Earned	420		25 500
Purchases	501	62 000	
Transportation-in	502	5 800	
Purchases Returns and Allowances	503		300
Purchases Discounts	504		4 100
Wages Expense	508	18 900	
Supplies Expense	520	400	
Telephone Expense	525	1 400	
		$218 300	$218 300

(i) The physical inventory count revealed $11 950 of material in the warehouse.

(ii) All but $150 of the unearned revenue had been earned by year-end. (One-third is installation; two-thirds are carpet sales.)

(iii) The staff determined that there is still $250 of unexpired insurance at year-end.

(iv) There are no office supplies left at year-end.

(v) The business uses the straight-line method of depreciation. Building: salvage value of $3000, useful life of 25 years.

Trucks, each with zero salvage value and a useful life of 5 years. Equipment: salvage value of $500, useful life of 11 years.

(vi) The company decides to write off A. Mitchell's debt of $50 as uncollectable. Ignore GST effects.

(vii) The aging of the receivables produces an estimate for bad debts for the year of $90.

(viii) Interest on the bank loan is 12% per annum. Payments are required on January 31 and July 31. The last instalment was paid on July 31. Nothing has been paid or recorded since that date.

(ix) Two rugs were installed by the PDQ Company. The material was paid for and recorded immediately, but the charges for installation are still unrecorded and unpaid, totalling $80.

(x) Two days' wages totalling $260 are outstanding and unrecorded.

Preparing adjustments on a ten-column worksheet.

P 16-3 Given the trial balance illustrated opposite and the following additional information for H & P Fisheries Enterprise, prepare a ten-column worksheet for the month ended July 31, 19-3.

(i) Insurance was purchased January 2, 19-3 for one full year. Adjustments have been recorded every month to date.

(ii) A review of the supplies reveals the following amounts still available: Warehouse, $2000, Marine Supplies, $5900.

(iii) Building: salvage value of $6000, useful life of 40 years. Straight-line method.

(iv) Depreciation for the month: Boat, $884; Equipment, $611.

(v) On July 31, 19-3 the company negotiated a bank loan for $10 000. It has not yet been recorded.

(vi) Mortgage interest for the month is not yet recorded. The payment was mailed out by cheque, but the amount has not yet been recorded. The rate of interest is 12% per annum.

(vii) Fuel received during July but not yet recorded or paid for totals $1100.

(viii) The mortgage payable is secured by the boat and the current portion owing is equal to $5000.

TOPIC 1 MINI-CASES

Analyzing the need for a trial balance on a worksheet.

MC 16-1 Sam Shortcut has just listened to his teacher's explanation of how to prepare a ten-column worksheet. "There is really no need

H & P Fisheries Enterprise
Trial Balance
July 31, 19–3

Account	No.	Debit	Credit
Cash	101	$ 11 600	
Accounts Receivable	105	7 500	
Allowances for Bad Debts	106		$ 50
Warehouse Supplies	110	2 200	
Marine Supplies	111	6 150	
Prepaid Insurance	114	990	
Land	150	12 000	
Building	155	48 000	
Accumulated Depreciation/Building	156		10 500
Boat	160	152 000	
Accumulated Depreciation/Boat	161		47 870
Equipment	170	22 000	
Accumulated Depreciation/Equipment	171		10 110
Accounts Payable	201		1 250
Mortgage Payable	260		88 000
H. Williamson, Capital	301		49 888
H. Williamson, Drawing	302	18 000	
Fish Sales	401		96 580
Fuel Expense	505	6 700	
Maintenance Expense	510	1 580	
Depreciation Expense/Building	515	525	
Depreciation Expense/Boat	516	5 066	
Depreciation Expense/Equipment	517	3 667	
Insurance Expense	520	990	
Mortgage Interest Expense	525	5 280	
		$304 248	$304 248

to total the trial balance columns on the worksheet,'' said Sam. ''We'll just copy the numbers from the trial balance. The trial balance was already balanced when it was done previously, so we don't have to do it again. It's just a waste of time!''

a. Explain to Sam any flaws you see in his reasoning.

Analyzing the relationships among worksheet columns.

MC 16-2 Paula McLaren is in the process of attempting her first worksheet for a merchandising business. She has done everything correctly so far, but when she gets to the Income Statement column totals, she stops with a worried look on her face. ''I must have made an error somewhere here,'' she mused. ''I know these columns are supposed to balance: the Trial Balance columns do, the Adjustments columns do, the Adjusted Trial Balance columns do, yet the Income Statement columns do not.''

a. Has Paula made an error? Explain to Paula what the Income Statement columns should look like, and why.

Analyzing alternatives to a ten-column worksheet.

MC 16-3 After completing their study of the ten-column worksheet for a merchandising business, two students offered interesting alternatives to the preparation of this working paper.

Paul Abrams proposed that completing the Adjusted Trial Balance section was a waste of time. Instead, he eliminated this section stating that it was just as easy to calculate mentally any adjustment and then move the resulting balance to the appropriate financial statement section. In his concluding remarks, the student emphasized that an eight-column worksheet is faster and accomplishes what the ten-column one does.

Sheri Reis demonstrated the use of a plain sheet of paper divided into four sections as a simple worksheet as follows:

ASSETS	REVENUE
LIABILITIES AND OWNER'S EQUITY	EXPENSES

She explained that accounts and their balances would be taken from the preliminary trial balance and placed in the appropriate section of this sheet. She concluded by saying that the four-box method simplifies the preparation of financial statements.

a. How would you evaluate the alternatives presented by the two students? Explain what you see as the strengths and weaknesses of their respective presentations.

PREPARING FINANCIAL STATEMENTS

This topic will deal with preparing financial statements from the related worksheet, which is Step 6 in the accounting cycle.

PREPARING THE INCOME STATEMENT

The first statement to be prepared must be the income statement, since it will provide the net income or net loss figure necessary to complete the balance sheet. The completed worksheet contains all the information necessary to complete both statements. All you have to do is arrange the information into the correct sequence and format of a formal financial statement. A popular method is to divide the statement into sections: Revenue from Sales, Cost of Goods Sold, and Operating Expenses. If other revenues or expenses exist, they are appended to the end of the statement under those titles. The appropriate calculations using these figures will result in either net income or net loss. The next illustration will help you prepare the formal statement from the worksheet.

COMPARING MULTIPLE-STEP TO SINGLE-STEP INCOME STATEMENTS

The illustration on pages 714 and 715 shows a multiple-step statement. Revenues and expenses are grouped into multiples, in order to report partial incomes, such as Gross Margin from Sales, and Operating Income. This method allows management to report in detail. The advantage of this type of statement is the amount of disclosure it provides. The purpose of accounting is to provide information for decision making, and better decisions may often be made with more complete information. The main disadvantage of this multiple-step statement is its complexity. Only revenue related to sales can be listed under the initial Revenue heading. Since this statement reports a partial income — **Gross Margin from Sales** — no other type of revenue can be included if a meaningful comparison of numbers is to take place. To take care of other, non-operating revenues, the income statement is expanded to include the categories Other Revenues and Other Expenses, which appear after Operating Income. Refer again to this illustration.

The illustration on page 716 shows a single-step statement. The main advantage is its simplicity. The main disadvantage of this statement is its lack of reporting detail, because this method reports all sources of revenue under one heading. Similarly, only one heading — Expenses — is used, since multiples are not reported. Because all expenses are reported under this heading, cost of goods sold is also included as a single number supported by a separate schedule.

Another important point is illustrated by the single-step statement. Some accountants prefer to avoid the use of account titles on financial statements by using account names similar to those illustrated in the single-step statement Expense section. Such account names are common in both single- and multiple-step statements.

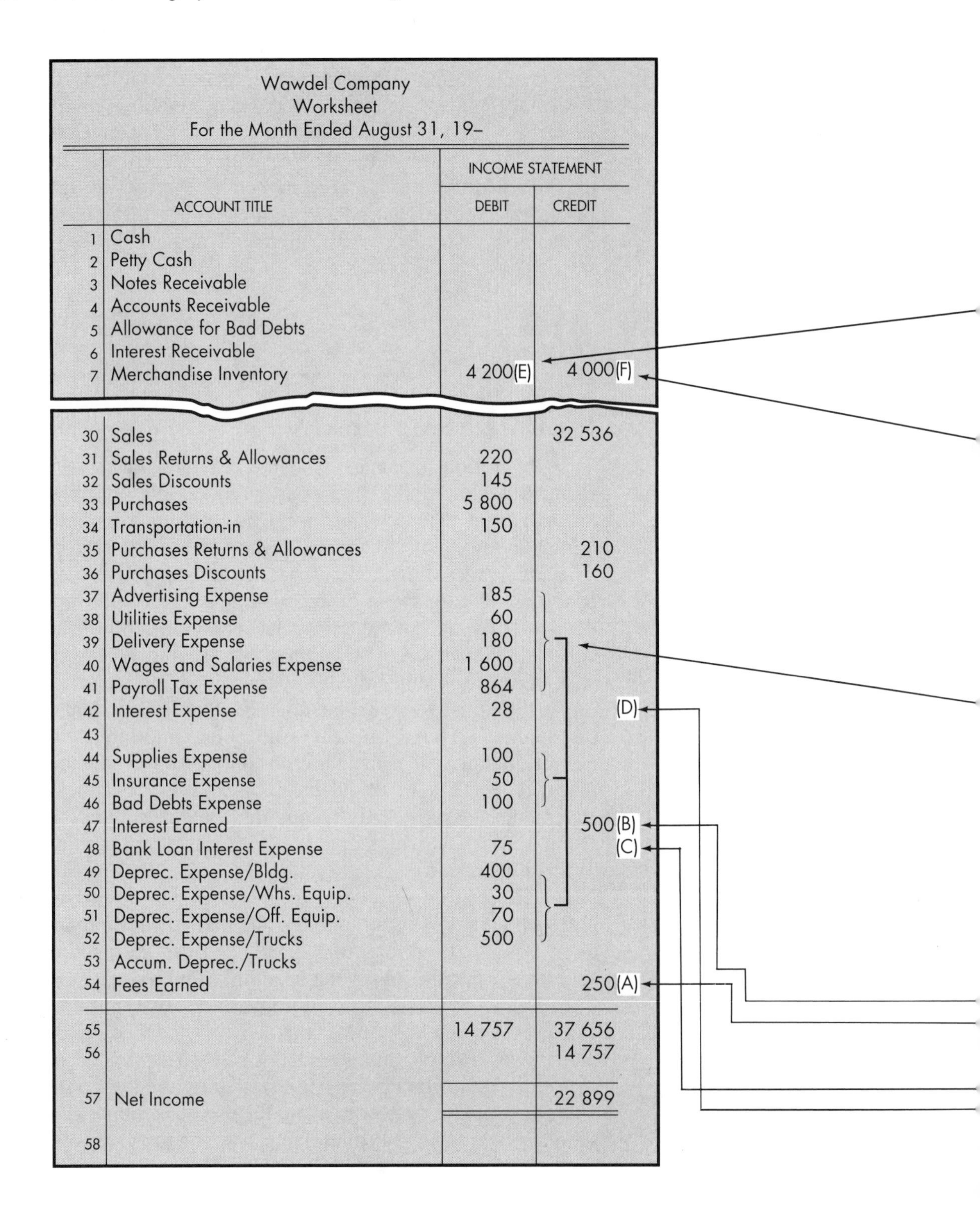

Wawdel Company
Worksheet
For the Month Ended August 31, 19–

	ACCOUNT TITLE	INCOME STATEMENT DEBIT	INCOME STATEMENT CREDIT
1	Cash		
2	Petty Cash		
3	Notes Receivable		
4	Accounts Receivable		
5	Allowance for Bad Debts		
6	Interest Receivable		
7	Merchandise Inventory	4 200(E)	4 000(F)
30	Sales		32 536
31	Sales Returns & Allowances	220	
32	Sales Discounts	145	
33	Purchases	5 800	
34	Transportation-in	150	
35	Purchases Returns & Allowances		210
36	Purchases Discounts		160
37	Advertising Expense	185	
38	Utilities Expense	60	
39	Delivery Expense	180	
40	Wages and Salaries Expense	1 600	
41	Payroll Tax Expense	864	
42	Interest Expense	28	(D)
43			
44	Supplies Expense	100	
45	Insurance Expense	50	
46	Bad Debts Expense	100	
47	Interest Earned		500(B)
48	Bank Loan Interest Expense	75	(C)
49	Deprec. Expense/Bldg.	400	
50	Deprec. Expense/Whs. Equip.	30	
51	Deprec. Expense/Off. Equip.	70	
52	Deprec. Expense/Trucks	500	
53	Accum. Deprec./Trucks		
54	Fees Earned		250(A)
55		14 757	37 656
56			14 757
57	Net Income		22 899
58			

Wawdel Company
Income Statement
For the Month Ended August 31, 19–

Sales Revenue:				
Gross Sales				$32 536
Less: Sales Returns and Allowances			$ 220	
Sales Discounts			145	365
Net Sales				32 171
Cost of Goods Sold:				
(E) Inventory, August 1			4 200	
Purchases		$5 800		
Add Transportation-in		150		
Cost of Delivered Goods		5 950		
Less: Purchases Returns and Allowances	$ 210			
Purchases Discounts	160	370		
Net Purchases			5 580	
Cost of Goods Available for Sale			9 780	
(F) Less: Inventory, August 31			4 000	
Cost of Goods Sold				5 780
Gross Margin from Sales				26 391
Operating Expenses:				
Advertising Expense			185	
Utilities Expense			60	
Delivery Expense			180	
Wages and Salaries Expense			1 600	
Payroll Taxes Expense			864	
Supplies Expense			100	
Insurance Expense			50	
Bad Debts Expense			100	
Deprec. Expense/Building			400	
Deprec. Expense/Warehouse Equipment			30	
Deprec. Expense/Office Equipment			70	
Deprec. Expense/Trucks			500	
Total Operating Expenses				4 139
Operating Income				22 252
Other Revenues:				
(B) Interest Earned		500		
(A) Fees Earned		250	750	
Other Expenses:				
(C) Interest on Bank Loan		75		
(D) Other Interest Expense		28	103	647
Net Income				$22 899

Single-Step Income Statement

Wawdel Company
Income Statement
For the Month Ended August 31, 19–

Revenues:		
Gross Sales		$32 536
Less: Sales Returns and Allowances	$220	
Sales Discounts	145	365
Net Sales		32 171
Interest Earned		500
Fees Earned		250
Total Revenue		$32 921
Expenses:		
Cost of Goods Sold (see separate schedule)	$ 5 780	
Advertising	185	
Utilities	60	
Delivery	180	
Wages and Salaries	1 600	
Payroll Taxes	864	
Supplies Used	100	
Insurance Used	50	
Bad Debts	100	
Depreciation/Building	400	
Depreciation/Warehouse Equipment	30	
Depreciation/Office Equipment	70	
Depreciation/Trucks	500	
Interest on Bank Loan	75	
Other Interest Expense	28	
Total Expenses		10 022
Net Income		$22 899

ILLUSTRATING A SEPARATE COST OF GOODS SOLD STATEMENT

Some businesses prepare a single-step income statement that shows only a total figure for Cost of Goods Sold. To calculate this figure, the business produces a Schedule of Cost of Goods Sold. Refer to the illustration opposite.

Gross margin: the difference between net sales and cost of goods sold.

The income statement provides a key figure, Net Sales less Cost of Goods Sold, which is called Gross Margin from Sales, or gross profit. Note that while some businesses prefer the former term, both are used in practice.

Wawdel Company
Schedule of Cost of Goods Sold
For the Month Ended August 31, 19–

Merchandise Inventory, August 1			$4 200	
Purchases		$5 800		
Transportation-in		150		
Cost of Delivered Goods		5 950		
Purchases Returns and Allowances	$210			
Purchases Discounts	160	370		
Net Purchases			5 580	
Cost of Goods Available for Sale			9 780	
Less: Merchandise Inventory, August 31			4 000	
Cost of Goods Sold				$5 780

Condensed Income Statement

Wawdel Company
Condensed Income Statement
For the Month Ended August 31, 19–

Revenue from Sales:		
Net Sales		$32 171
Cost of Goods Sold (see separate schedule)		5 780
Gross Margin from Sales		26 391
Operating Expenses:		
Selling Expenses	$3 354	
General and Administrative	785	4 139
Operating Income		22 252
*Other Revenues and Expenses:		
Other Revenues	$ 750	
Other Expenses	103	647
Net Income		$22 899

*This is another presentation of the other revenues and other expenses. Compare this to the method used in the multiple-step presentation shown earlier. **Note:** Only totals were used in the above illustration, to save space. Ordinarily all items would be listed. This type of presentation is frequently referred to as a condensed statement.

Multiple-Step Classified Income Statement

Wawdel Company
Income Statement
For the Month Ended August 31, 19–

Revenue from Sales:			
Sales		$ 32 536	
Sales Returns and Allowances	$ 220		
Sales Discounts	145	365	
Net Sales			$32 171
Cost of Goods Sold (see schedule)			5 780
Gross Margin From Sales			26 391
Operating Expenses:			
Selling Expenses:			
Advertising	$ 185		
Utilities	48		
Delivery	180		
Wages and Salaries	1 280		
Payroll Taxes	691		
Supplies	80		
Insurance	40		
Depreciation/Building	320		
Depreciation/Warehouse Equipment	30		
Depreciation/Delivery Truck	500		
Total Selling Expenses		$ 3 354	
General and Administrative Expenses			
Utilities	$ 12		
Wages and Salaries	320		
Payroll Taxes	173		
Supplies	20		
Insurance	10		
Bad Debts	100		
Depreciation/Building	80		
Depreciation/Office Equipment	70		
Total General and Administrative		785	
Total Operating Expenses			4 139
Income From Operations			22 252
Other Revenues:			
Fees Earned	$ 250		
Interest Revenue	500	$ 750	
Other Expenses:			
Other Interest Expense	28		
Bank Loan Interest Expense	75	103	647
Net Income			$22 899

ILLUSTRATING THE CLASSIFIED INCOME STATEMENT

As you will remember in the single-step statement, all expenses of the merchandising business were recorded under the heading Expenses. Many larger businesses require a more detailed breakdown of the business operating expenses, in order to make better business decisions. Typically, the operating expenses are broken down into two sections: Selling Expenses and General and Administrative. Note as well that the non-operating expenses—Other Interest Expense, and Bank Loan Interest Expense—are reported after Income from Operations. In the illustration on page 718 these two expenses are grouped together as Other Expenses. The following are the important points of analysis for this new area of study.

Selling expenses: one class of operating expenses related directly or indirectly to the selling function of the business.

Selling Expenses In general, selling expenses include all expenses of storing and preparing merchandise for sale, advertising and promotion, and actually making sales, such as salaries for the sales personnel. In addition, the expense of delivering the goods from your business to the customer is usually regarded as a selling expense. Many of the selling expenses—advertising, delivery, depreciation on warehouse equipment, and depreciation on delivery truck expenses—do not require a separate division in the General Ledger.

There are other expenses that require special identification and some equitable division between the two classes. For example, all the salaries and wages expense cannot be listed together in one account. Why? There are salaries paid to sales personnel and to administrative personnel, and if we want to keep track of selling expenses, the sales staff's salaries will have to be recorded separately. There are many methods to do this. If a business's premises house both the selling and administrative departments, some division of the salary expense and other expenses — perhaps by a percentage of floor area occupied — must be applied. For example, if sales occupies 80% of the area, it might be fair to assign 80% of the cost for utilities, taxes, depreciation, etc., to Selling Expenses and 20% to General and Administrative Expenses.

This type of discussion is introductory cost accounting, the study of which is best left to a more advanced course.

General and Administrative Expenses In general, this classification includes expenses involving the general office, the accounting office, and the personnel of those offices. In addition, costs involving the credit and collection departments fall under this expense classification. Examples of general and administrative expenses might include bad debts expense and depreciation expense for office equipment. Other expenses might fall into a grey area, as was the case with selling expenses. Office supplies, payroll taxes expense, and insurance expense will require an equitable division between selling and general and administrative expenses.

General and administrative expenses: a large class of operating expenses related to the non-selling aspects of the business.

Finally, the division of expenses means that there must be an allocation of responsibility regarding the budgeting of these expenses. A budget is a co-ordinated plan estimating the future transactions covering a planned time period. It is another major subdivision of accounting best left for advanced courses.

Budgeting: a co-ordinated plan to estimate the future transactions covering a planned period of time.

Income from Operations Another feature of the classified income statement is income from operations or operating income. The statement attempts to match revenues from operations with the expenses from operations. Any other source of revenue and expense (such as Gain on Disposal of Fixed Assets) is to be reported in its own section after Income from Operations. When these final items are added to or subtracted from the income from operations, the net income or net loss results. Examine the statement in the illustration on pages 717 and 718.

Income from operations: the excess of matching revenues and expenses that are related to the main operations of the business.

ILLUSTRATING A CONDENSED INCOME STATEMENT

For some purposes, a business will not wish to present a classified income statement, with all of its complex details. Instead, they will prepare a condensed or shortened version, similar to the one presented earlier at the bottom of page 717. Since the business will still prepare a Schedule of Cost of Goods Sold, the final figure is available for use in the condensed income statement. Totals for Sales and for General and Administrative Expenses can be generated relatively easily from the General Ledger accounts.

Note that the details within each section have been omitted. The figures included will be net sales, cost of goods sold, gross margin from sales, the selling and general and administrative expenses, operating income, any other (non-operating) revenues and/or expenses, and net income or loss. These condensed statements are prepared for ease of understanding by the general public. However, accountants support the principle for more disclosure, and detailed statements are required by Revenue Canada—Taxation, and also by management.

PREPARING THE BALANCE SHEET

The classified balance sheet is prepared after the income statement. You will recall that you have studied two formats of the balance sheet: the account form and the report form. The report form is most popular for an annual report presentation. This format is better suited for typing and also programming via a computer system. The report form is illustrated on page 722.

The treatment of mortgage payable is new and of particular importance on the balance sheet.

Analysis:

- It is important to tell the reader of the balance sheet as much information about the mortgage as space permits. This usually means adding this information: the type of mortgage, the due date, and the assets pledged as security.
- There should be a notation made beside each asset used to secure a mortgage payable, to the effect that the assets have been pledged.
- The portion of the mortgage that falls due during this accounting year must be identified in the Current Liabilities section.
- The current portion must be subtracted from the total amount of the mortgage owing as presented in the Long-Term Liabilities section. Examine the illustration on the next page.

PREPARING THE STATEMENT OF OWNER'S EQUITY

To reduce the size and complexity of the classified balance sheet, some businesses prepare a separate Statement of Owner's Equity, like the one illustrated below.

Wawdel Company
Statement of Owner's Equity
For the Month Ended August 31, 19–

R. Wawdel, Capital, August 1		$115 530
Net Income	$22 899	
Less: R. Wawdel, Drawing	705	
Increase in Capital		22 194
R. Wawdel, Capital, August 31		$137 724

Wawdel Company
Balance Sheet
As at August 31, 19–

ASSETS

Current Assets:			
Cash		$ 10 750	
Notes Receivable		60 000	
Interest Receivable		1 000	
Accounts Receivable	$ 6 400		
Less: Allowance for Bad Debts	120	6 280	
Merchandise Inventory (at cost)		4 000	
Supplies on Hand		300	
Prepaid Insurance		500	
Total Current Assets			$ 82 830
Fixed Assets (at cost):			
Land (Security for Mortgage Payable)		24 000	
Building (Security for Mortgage Payable)	96 000		
Less: Accumulated Depreciation/Building	1 100	94 900	
Warehouse Equipment	4 000		
Less: Accumulated Depreciation/Office Equipment	240	3 760	
Office Equipment	7 200		
Less: Accumulated Depreciation/Office Equipment	620	6 580	
Delivery Trucks	40 000		
Less: Accumulated Depreciation/Trucks	500	39 500	
Total Fixed Assets			168 740
Total Assets			$251 570

LIABILITIES AND OWNER'S EQUITY

Current Liabilities:		
Bank Loan Payable	$ 5 500	
Accounts Payable	6 800	
Unearned Revenue	250	
Interest Payable on Bank Loan	150	
Unemployment Insurance Payable	60	
CPP Payable	120	
Income Tax Collected from Employees Payable	800	
GST Payable	42	
Group Insurance Payable	124	
Current Portion of Mortgage Payable	4 000	
Total Current Liabilities		17 846
Long-Term Liabilities:		
10% Mortgage Payable, due 20–(secured by Land and Building)	100 000	
Less: Current Portion	4 000	96 000
Total Liabilities		113 846
Owner's Equity:		
R. Wawdel, Capital	115 530	
Add: Net Income	22 899	
	138 429	
Less: R. Wawdel, Drawing	705	
Total Owner's Equity		137 724
Total Liabilities and Owner's Equity		$251 570

Specific information regarding capital is illustrated in this document that is separate from the classified balance sheet. The final Capital amount is then placed in the balance sheet. The size and complexity of the balance sheet is reduced, while the reader who requires more detailed information about capital can refer to this statement. The details might include:

- the beginning capital balance
- any additional investments
- the net income or loss for the period
- the personal withdrawals of the owner

Not all the above information is available from the worksheet. Beginning capital plus additional investments would be found in the Capital account. The Statement of Owner's Equity reports changes in the equity of the owner of a single proprietorship. As you will recall, the equity is the owner's claim against the assets of the business. Equity is made up of the owner's investment and any net income. Partnership equity is presented in a Statement of Partnership Equity. Corporations present equity to the shareholders in the Statement of Retained Earnings.

LIABILITIES	
Total Liabilities	$113 846
OWNER'S EQUITY	
R. Wawdel, Capital	137 724
Total Liabilities and OE	$251 570

STATEMENT OF OWNER'S EQUITY		
R. Wawdel, Capital, January 1 ...		$10 000
Additional Investment		1 200
Total Investment		$11 200
Net Loss for the Year	$550	
R. Wawdel, Drawing	950	
Decrease in Capital		1 500
Capital, December 31		$9 700

Additional Investment and Net Loss Illustrated

PROBLEMS

Preparing formal statements from a ten-column worksheet.

P 16-4 Refer back to Problem 16-1 (the Snooze Motel) and prepare the following from the completed worksheet.

a. a formal income statement (classification is not necessary)

b. a formal balance sheet in report form

Preparing an income statement Cost of Goods Sold Schedule, and balance sheet from a ten-column worksheet.

P 16-5 Refer back to Problem 16-2 (Regina Rugs) and prepare the following from the completed worksheet.

a. Cost of Goods Sold Schedule

b. a formal income statement (classification is not necessary)

c. a formal balance sheet in report form

Preparing a formal income statement and balance sheet from a ten-column worksheet.

P 16-6 Refer back to the worksheet of Problem 16-3 (H & P Fisheries Enterprise) and prepare the following.

a. a classified income statement for the month-end

b. a classified balance sheet in report form

MINI-CASES

Analyzing column relationships on a worksheet.

MC 16-4 "You know, I'm not sure my dad understands accounting," said Colleen Kirton. "In my accounting class, we were discussing the purpose of various financial statements, and so I asked Dad to give me one of his business's statements to show me how the business is doing. I expected him to give me an income statement and a balance sheet, but all he gave me was a Statement of Owner's Equity. This doesn't tell me what I need to know, namely how much profit he made last year."

a. Is Colleen correct? Explain why or why not.

b. List all the valuable pieces of information that are revealed by a Statement of Owner's Equity.

Choosing an appropriate format for financial statements.

MC 16-5 Jim Edwards has been asked by his boss to prepare a balance sheet for inclusion in the annual report. "Choose the type of balance sheet you think is appropriate, and use the most practical format," instructed Mr. Cratchit. "And be neat," he said, "since someone will have to type it out."

a. What type of report do you think would be most appropriate here? Why?

b. From a **practical** standpoint, which format do you think is best? Why?

Analyzing the need for additional information on financial statements.

MC 16-6 ''Accountants sure do like to write a lot,'' complained Wendy Whiner. ''These classified income statements, with 'multiples,' are time-consuming to construct, and I don't really see their purpose. For example, what good is the calculation for Gross Margin from Sales?''

a. Explain to Wendy what information the Gross Margin from Sales reveals that might be otherwise hidden in a single-step income statement.

b. Explain to Wendy why certain items, such as Bank Loan Interest Expense, are not classified as Operating Expenses.

COMPLETING THE ACCOUNTING CYCLE

Six steps of the accounting cycle have been discussed:

- originating the accounting data
- journalizing
- posting
- preparing trial balances
- preparing a worksheet
- preparing financial statements

The last three steps of the cycle will now be dealt with:

- making adjusting entries
- making closing entries
- preparing a postclosing trial balance

MAKING ADJUSTING ENTRIES

Revenues and expenses in the worksheet reflect current balances, since adjustments were completed within the worksheet. And because the financial statements were prepared from the worksheet, they, too, are current. However, adjustments were not entered in the GL and therefore the GL accounts are not current. To update the GL

General Journal Adjusting Entries

19–				
Aug. 31	Supplies Expense	521	100	
	Supplies on Hand	112		100
	A count of supplies revealed $300 of supplies on hand. ($400 – $300 = $100)			
31	Insurance Expense	523	50	
	Prepaid Insurance	114		50
	Examination of the insurance policy reveals $50 of insurance has been used up.			
31	Bad Debts Expense	525	100	
	Allowance for Bad Debts	105		100
	The aged accounts receivable reveals $120 of uncollectable accounts for the period. The Allowance for Bad Debts accounts requires an additional $100 ($120 – $20).			
31	Interest Receivable	106	500	
	Interest Revenue	405		500
	Interest earned on the note equals $500 per month.			
31	Bank Loan Interest Expense	530	75	
	Bank Loan Interest Payable	204		75
	The monthly interest accrued equals $75. ($900 ÷ 12)			
31	Depreciation Expense/Building	550	400	
	Accum. Deprec./Building	156		400
	($96 000 ÷ 20 = $4 800 ÷ 12 = $400)			
31	Deprec. Exp./Warehouse Equip.	552	30	
	Accum. Deprec./Warehouse Equip.	161		30
	*($360 ÷ 12 = $30)			
31	Deprec. Exp./Off. Equip.	554	70	
	Accum. Deprec./Off. Equip.	166		70
	*($840 ÷ 12 = $70)			
31	Deprec. Exp./Trucks	556	500	
	Accum. Deprec./Trucks	171		500
	*($30 000 ÷ 5 = $6 000 ÷ 12 = $500) (Base cost $40 000 less $10 000 disposal cost = $30 000.)			
31	Unearned Revenue	202	250	
	Fees Earned	407		250
	Each month $250 is earned by partial completion of the contract.			

*Calculation usually performed in detail on supporting schedules maintained on each separate assets.

accounts, we must journalize and post the adjusting entries. Compare the illustration of General Journal adjusting entries opposite to the worksheet adjustment column (page 697). Notice that the posting reference account numbers have been shown, indicating that posting has taken place as soon as the journal entries were completed.

MAKING THE CLOSING ENTRIES

You studied closing procedures in Topic 1 of Chapter 6. Take a few minutes to go back and review these procedures. The closing entries bring all revenue, expense, and drawing accounts to zero in order that those accounts will be ready to receive entries for the next accounting period. Additionally, in a merchandising business, the beginning inventory account must be balanced, and then updated with the most recently calculated inventory figure, called **ending inventory**. This account is updated via a clearing account called the Revenue and Expense Summary. The process for updating is summarized as follows:

(1) All revenue accounts are debited with equal and opposite amounts to those in the ledger account. The R & E Summary records the single credit entry to offset the debit entries.

(2) All expense accounts are credited with equal and opposite amounts. The R & E Summary records the single debit entry to offset the credit entries.

(3) The old merchandise inventory figure is eliminated with an equal and opposite credit entry. The R & E Summary account supplies the equal and opposite debit entry.

(4) The new inventory figure is brought into the Inventory account with a debit entry. The Summary supplies the equal and opposite credit entry.

(5) The R & E Summary is totalled and then closed to the Capital account.

(6) Finally, the Drawing account is closed to Capital with an equal and opposite credit entry.

When the worksheet is available, all closing information can be found in the Income Statement columns, with the exception of the drawing amount.

A short-cut, using only two compound journal entries, will close the revenue and expense accounts and deal with the merchandise inventory amounts. Simply, each item in the credit column of the income statement must be debited, with the R & E Summary providing the offsetting credit. Similarly, anything in the debit column must be credited, with the R & E Summary providing the offsetting debit.

Of course, the entries will still have to be posted to individual accounts. Next, the R & E Summary must be closed to Capital, as must Drawing. Although many businesses use this short-cut, it does not lend itself to an easy explanation regarding the handling of beginning and ending inventory. However, it does save time if properly handled.

The following is a step-by-step breakdown of the closing procedure. Follow the General Journal entries and related T-accounts for these closing entries. All the accounts are located in the worksheet, the income statement, and the balance sheet of the Wawdel Company.

Closing the Revenue Accounts Close the revenue accounts, namely, Sales, Interest Earned, and Fees Earned to the R & E Summary. Revenue accounts are temporary because they are closed at the end of the period. The R & E Summary account will now have a credit balance.

GENERAL JOURNAL Page 10

DATE 19–	ACCOUNT TITLE AND EXPLANATION	POST. REF.	DEBIT	CREDIT
Aug. 31	Sales	401	32 536	
	Fees Earned	407	250	
	Interest Earned	405	500	
	R & E Summary	399		33 286
	To close the revenue accounts.			

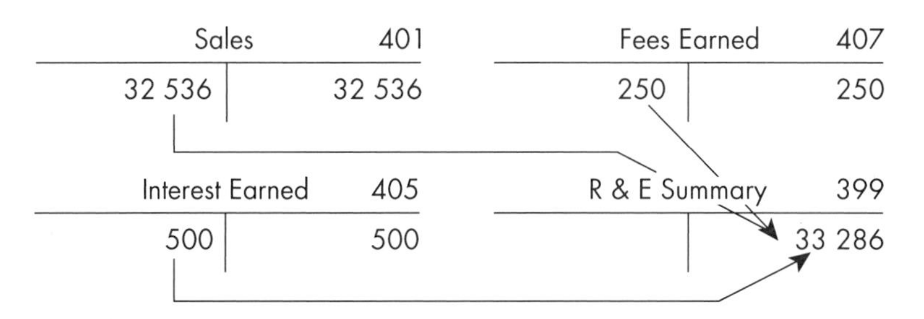

Transferring Contra Revenue Accounts Transfer the two contra revenue accounts, Sales Discounts and Sales Returns and Allowances, to the R & E Summary. After this entry is posted, the balance in the Summary account will equal the net sales figure plus the total of other revenue as reported on the income statement.

GENERAL JOURNAL Page 10

DATE 19–	ACCOUNT TITLE AND EXPLANATION	POST. REF.	DEBIT	CREDIT
Aug. 31	R & E Summary	399	365	
	Sales Returns and Allowances	402		220
	Sales Discounts	403		145
	To close the contra sales accounts.			

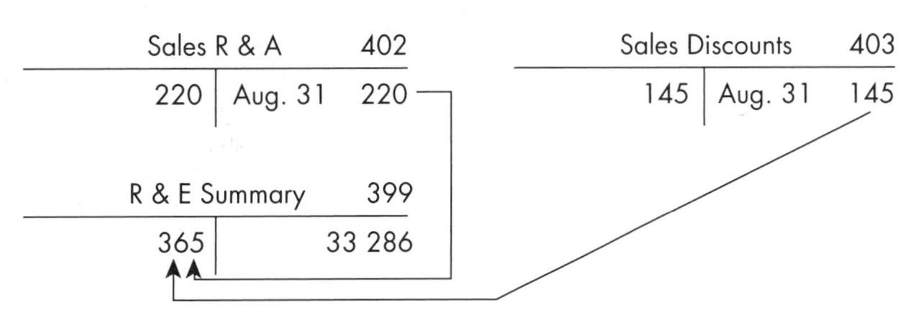

Transferring the Beginning Inventory Transfer the beginning inventory by debiting the R & E Summary and crediting the Merchandise Inventory account. This entry, when posted, causes the inventory account to equal zero, thus closing the account. The R & E Summary balance would be reported on the side on which it is found in the worksheet of the income statement.

GENERAL JOURNAL Page 10

DATE 19–	ACCOUNT TITLE AND EXPLANATION	POST. REF.	DEBIT	CREDIT
Aug. 31	R & E Summary	399	4 200	
	Merchandise Inventory	110		4 200
	To close the beginning inventory figure.			

Merchandise Inventory 110

Debit	Credit
4 200	Aug. 31 4 200

R & E Summary 399

Debit	Credit
365	33 286
4 200	

Recording the Ending Inventory Record the ending inventory on the debit side of the inventory account and the credit side of the R & E Summary. When posted, this transaction will record the current inventory balance in the inventory account. Note how the balance of the Summary account reflects the same position, the credit side, as it is found on the worksheet. The debit to inventory reflects the debit balance found in the balance sheet.

GENERAL JOURNAL Page 10

DATE 19–	ACCOUNT TITLE AND EXPLANATION	POST. REF.	DEBIT	CREDIT
Aug. 31	Merchandise Inventory	110	4 000	
	R & E Summary	399		4 000
	To re-open the merchandise inventory.			

Merchandise Inventory 110

Debit	Credit
4 200	4 200
Aug. 31 4 000	

R & E Summary 399

Debit	Credit
365	33 286
4 200	4 000

Transferring the Purchases Costs Next transfer the two purchases costs, Purchases and Transportation-in. To bring these accounts to zero, credit them with amounts equal to their balances, with a single offsetting debit entry to the R & E Summary.

GENERAL JOURNAL Page 10

DATE 19–	ACCOUNT TITLE AND EXPLANATION	POST. REF.	DEBIT	CREDIT
Aug. 31	R & E Summary	399	5 950	
	Purchases	501		5 800
	Transportation-in	502		150
	To close Purchases and Transportation-in.			

(Continued on next page.)

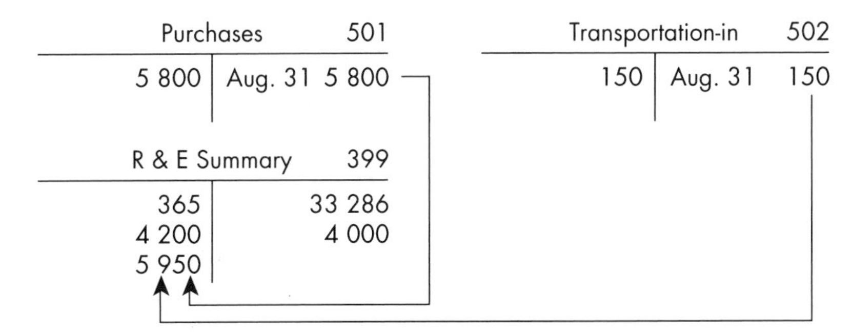

Transferring Reductions to Purchase Price Transfer the entries that cause the purchase price to be reduced. These include Purchases Returns and Allowances and Purchases Discounts. Debiting these two accounts brings their balance to zero. The total credit is recorded in the R & E Summary.

GENERAL JOURNAL Page 10

DATE 19–	ACCOUNT TITLE AND EXPLANATION	POST. REF.	DEBIT	CREDIT
Aug. 31	Purchases Returns and Allowances	503	210	
	Purchases Discounts	504	160	
	R & E Summary	399		370
	To close the contra Purchases accounts.			

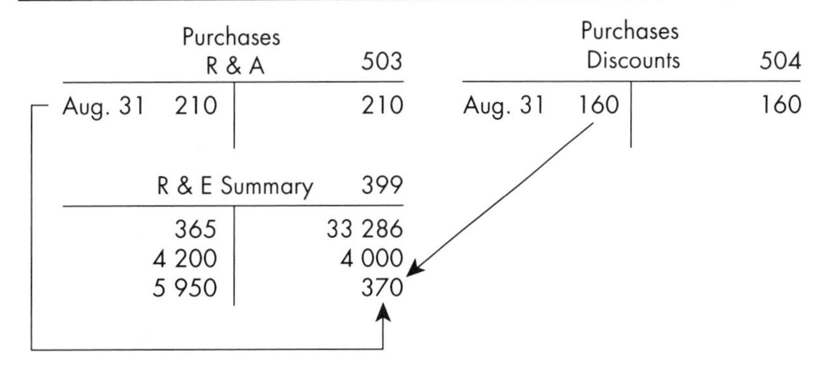

Closing Expense Accounts Through a compound entry, all the expenses (operating plus other expenses) shown on the income statement can now be closed. Each individual account requires a credit entry which, when posted, will produce a zero balance in that account. The R & E Summary will be used to record the single debit entry.

GENERAL JOURNAL Page 11

DATE 19–	ACCOUNT TITLE AND EXPLANATION	POST. REF.	DEBIT	CREDIT
Aug. 31	R & E Summary	399	4242	
	Advertising Expense	510		185
	Utilities Expense	512		60
	Delivery Expense	514		180
	Wages and Salaries Expense	516		1 600
	Payroll Tax Expense	518		864
	Interest Expense	520		28
	Supplies Expense	521		100
	Insurance Expense	523		50
	Bad Debts Expense	525		100
	Bank Loan Interest Expense	530		75
	Deprec. Expense/Building	550		400
	Deprec. Expense/ Warehouse Equip.	552		30
	Deprec. Expense/ Office Equip.	554		70
	Deprec. Expense/Truck	556		500
	To close the expense accounts.			

Closing the R & E Summary The balance in the R & E Summary account must now be transferred to the Capital account. Whether the entry is a debit or a credit will depend on what type of balance is in the account. You know that the purpose is to reduce each expense account to zero, so you will have to debit or credit an equal and opposite amount to the balance in the account. The offsetting entry will be to Capital, since the net income or net loss increases or decreases owner's equity through the Capital account. Examine first the illustration of the R & E Summary below and then the General Journal entry used to close the account.

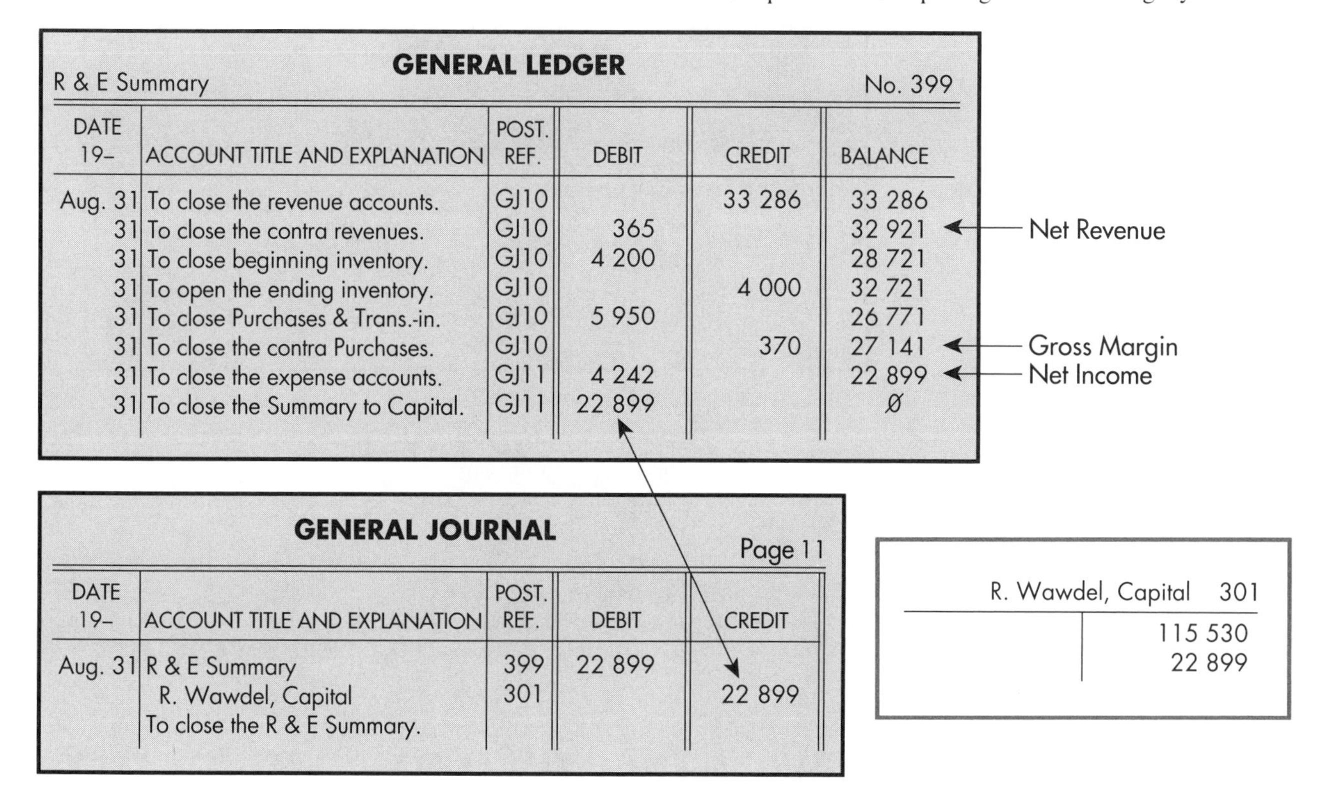

GENERAL LEDGER

R & E Summary — No. 399

DATE 19–	ACCOUNT TITLE AND EXPLANATION	POST. REF.	DEBIT	CREDIT	BALANCE
Aug. 31	To close the revenue accounts.	GJ10		33 286	33 286
31	To close the contra revenues.	GJ10	365		32 921
31	To close beginning inventory.	GJ10	4 200		28 721
31	To open the ending inventory.	GJ10		4 000	32 721
31	To close Purchases & Trans.-in.	GJ10	5 950		26 771
31	To close the contra Purchases.	GJ10		370	27 141
31	To close the expense accounts.	GJ11	4 242		22 899
31	To close the Summary to Capital.	GJ11	22 899		Ø

GENERAL JOURNAL

Page 11

DATE 19–	ACCOUNT TITLE AND EXPLANATION	POST. REF.	DEBIT	CREDIT
Aug. 31	R & E Summary	399	22 899	
	R. Wawdel, Capital	301		22 899
	To close the R & E Summary.			

R. Wawdel, Capital 301

Debit	Credit
	115 530
	22 899

Closing the Drawing Account Finally, the owner's Drawing account must be closed to the Capital account, in order that the Capital account reflect the true owner's claim on the assets at the end of the period. This also brings the balance of the Drawing account to zero. You will recall that a sole proprietor does not draw a salary, but withdraws funds as an advance against future profits of the business. Since net income increases the Capital account, Drawing, which is an ''early withdrawal'' of net income, should be subtracted from the income in the Capital account. If a net loss is reported, this loss plus the drawing should be totalled to show a net decrease in Capital for the period. This last closing entry on page 733 meets that requirement.

GENERAL JOURNAL Page 12

DATE 19–	ACCOUNT TITLE AND EXPLANATION	POST. REF.	DEBIT	CREDIT
Aug. 31	R. Wawdel, Capital	301	705	
	R. Wawdel, Drawing	302		705
	To close the Drawing account.			

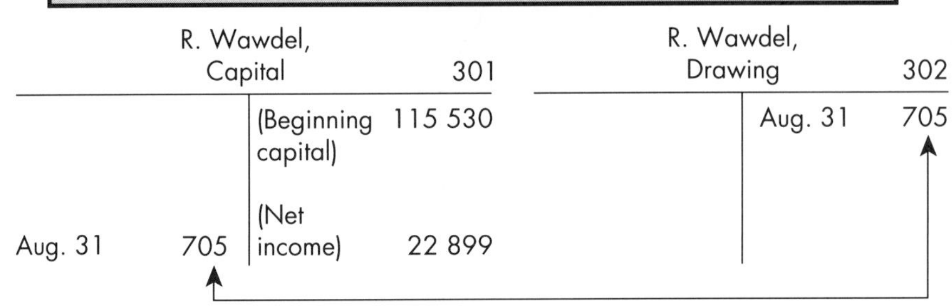

PREPARING THE POSTCLOSING TRIAL BALANCE

The final step in the accounting cycle is to prepare the postclosing trial balance. This balance is a final check to ensure that all the permanent accounts are in balance at the end of a cycle. Three checks occur when the postclosing trial balance is prepared:

- The debit and credit totals must be equal.
- There must be only permanent accounts listed.
- The balance in the Capital account of the postclosing trial balance must be equal to the total owner's equity in the Owner's Equity section of the balance sheet.

If you examine the accounts in the postclosing trial balance, you will find them identical to the accounts in the balance sheet, with one exception, Drawing. This is because both statements list permanent accounts, yet the temporary account Drawing is needed on the balance sheet for reporting purposes. When the postclosing trial balance is complete, the accounting cycle is also complete, and the books are ready for the next accounting cycle.

Wawdel Company
Postclosing Trial Balance
August 31, 19–

Cash	$ 10 700	
Petty Cash	50	
Notes Receivable	60 000	
Accounts Receivable	6 400	
Allowance for Bad Debts		$ 120
Accrued Revenue Receivable	1 000	
Merchandise Inventory	4 000	
Supplies on Hand	300	
Prepaid Insurance	500	
Land	24 000	
Building	96 000	
Accumulated Depreciation/Building		1 100
Warehouse Equipment	4 000	
Accumulated Depreciation/Warehouse Equipment		240
Office Equipment	7 200	
Accumulated Depreciation/Office Equipment		620
Delivery Trucks	40 000	
Accumulated Depreciation/Trucks		500
Bank Loan Payable		5 500
Unearned Revenue		250
Accounts Payable		6 800
Bank Loan Interest Payable		150
Unemployment Insurance Payable		60
CPP Payable		120
Income Tax Payable		800
GST Payable		42
Group Insurance Payable		124
Mortgage Payable		100 000
R. Wawdel, Capital		137 724
	$254 150	$254 150

PROBLEMS

Journalizing adjustments and posting to T-accounts.

Journalizing closing entries.

Preparing a postclosing trial balance.

P 16-7 Refer to the worksheet of Problems 16-1 and 16-4 (the Snooze Motel).

a. Journalize the adjustments in the General Journal, and include a brief explanation for each adjustment.

b. Open T-accounts for Capital, Drawing, R & E Summary, and Insurance Expense accounts. Record the balance of each, taking the figures from the adjusted trial balance.

c. Journalize, in the General Journal, all necessary closing entries, and include a brief explanation for each entry.

d. Indicate how each of the accounts would appear after closing information has been posted into each account.

e. Prepare a postclosing trial balance.

Journalizing adjustments and posting to T-accounts.

Journalizing closing entries.

Preparing a postclosing trial balance.

P 16-8 Refer to the worksheet of Problems 16-2 and 16-5 (Regina Rugs).

a. Journalize the adjustments in the General Journal, and include a brief explanation.

b. Open T-accounts for Capital, Drawing, R & E Summary, and Bank Loan Interest Expense. Record the balance of each from the adjusted trial balance.

c. Journalize, in the General Journal, all necessary closing entries, and include a brief explanation for each entry.

d. Indicate how each of the T-accounts would appear after closing information had been posted into each account.

e. Prepare a postclosing trial balance.

Journalizing adjustments and posting to T-accounts.

Journalizing closing entries.

Preparing a postclosing trial balance.

P 16-9 Refer to the worksheet of Problems 16-3 and 16-6 (H & P Fisheries Enterprise).

a. Journalize the adjustments in the General Journal, and include a brief explanation for each adjustment.

b. Open T-accounts for Capital, Drawing, R & E Summary, and Marine Supplies Expense. Record the balance of each from the adjusted trial balance.

c. Journalize, in the General Journal, all necessary closing entries, and include a brief explanation for each entry.

d. Indicate how each of the T-accounts would appear after closing information has been posted.

e. Prepare a postclosing trial balance.

MINI-CASES

Analyzing the need to journalize worksheet adjusting entries.

MC 16-7 ''Why are we doing this?'' asked Cynthia Lavelle, as she journalized and posted the adjusting entries that had been prepared on a worksheet. ''We already have the adjustments figured out, and we have accurate financial statements, which is the goal of the whole process. Why do we have to now journalize the adjustments?''

a. Explain to Cynthia why the journalizing is necessary, and what would happen if it were not done.

Analyzing the need for a postclosing trial balance.

MC 16-8 David Packham, a junior accounting student, has just completed studying the accounting cycle, and has a question. "Why," he asked, "is it necessary to complete a postclosing trial balance? We know everything balances, because the worksheet balances and the formal balance sheet balances. There is no way that the ledger could be out of balance."

a. Is David correct? Explain why or why not, using concrete examples of what might be incorrect, if anything.

Rebuilding a partial worksheet.

MC 16-9 Rossanni Wholesalers had just finished preparing the worksheet so they could prepare financial statements, when the fire sprinkler system went off, partially destroying the worksheet. Rather than starting from scratch, the accountant has suggested you try rebuilding the old one from the information that is left.

Rossanni Wholesalers
Worksheet
For the Month Ended May 31, 19–

	ACCOUNT TITLE	ACCT. NO.	TRIAL BALANCE		ADJUSTMENTS		ADJ. TRIAL BALANCE		INCOME STATEMENT		BALANCE SHEET		
			DEBIT	CREDIT	DEBIT	CREDIT	DEBIT	CREDIT	DEBIT	CREDIT	DEBIT	CREDIT	
1	Cash		10								10		
2	Accounts Receivable		25		(E) 10								
3	Allowance for Bad Debts			3		(A) 2							
4	Inventory		15								17		
5	Supplies on Hand		4										
6	Prepaid Insurance		7			(B) 4							
7	Land		20										
8	Building		35										
9	Accumulated Depreciation			15		(C)						19	
10	Delivery Truck		8										
11	Accumulated Depreciation			2		(D)						3	
12	Bank Loan Payable			7									
13	Accounts Payable			5									
14	Mortgage Payable			31									
15	M. Rossanni, Capital			69								69	
16	M. Rossanni, Drawings		6										
17	Sales			55		(E)				65			
18	Sales Discounts		2										
19	Purchases		41										
20	Purchases R & A			1									
21	Purchases Discounts			2									
22	Transportation-in		3										
23	Heat Expense		10										
24	Delivery Expense		4										
25			190										
26	Wages Payable												10

ANALYZING FINANCIAL STATEMENT RELATIONSHIPS

The financial statements of any business are a detailed summary of the financial position of that business. In Chapter 5, Topic 3, you learned what financial statements do and do not say. This topic will introduce several ideas and techniques used to analyze financial statements.

COMPARING CONSECUTIVE FINANCIAL STATEMENTS

One of the most effective methods of examining the success of a business is to study its performance over a number of years. A **comparative balance sheet** is one method. Study the illustration below. It is not related to any of the Wawdel Company examples given pre-

Wawdel Company
Comparative Balance Sheet
as at December 31
(in thousands of dollars)

ASSETS

	19-5	19-4	19-3	19-2	19-1
Current Assets	870	880	700	750	740
Fixed Assets	1 500	1 400	1 400	1 000	900
Total Assets	2 370	2 280	2 100	1 750	1640

LIABILITIES AND OWNER'S EQUITY

	19-5	19-4	19-3	19-2	19-1
*Current Liabilities	780	730	590	550	600
Long-Term Liabilities	1 000	1 000	1 000	960	800
Capital	590	550	510	240	240
Total Liabilities and Owner's Equity	2 370	2 280	2 100	1 750	1 640

*Assume that the current portion of the mortgage payable is included in this total. Mortgage Payable, under Long-Term Liabilities, has the current portion subtracted from it.

viously. As well, all illustrations that follow in this topic show the current portion of the mortgage payable in the current liability figures, and the total of mortgage payable less the current portion in the long-term liability figures.

Analysis: This type of presentation makes it easy to focus on **trends** in the data. If a particular item changes radically from year to year, or constantly increases or decreases, more research into the cause is indicated.

Often, an examination of the dollar amounts reveals little information. If, however, the dollar amounts are converted to percentage changes, the results are often more revealing. Study the trend percentages below.

Wawdel Company
Trend Percentages* From Base Year 19-1

	19-5	19-4	19-3	19-2	19-1 (Base Year)
Current Assets	118%	119%	95%	101%	100%
Current Liabilities	130%	122%	98%	92%	100%

* All numbers are rounded.

$$\text{Trend Percentage} = \frac{\text{Comparison Year}}{\text{Basic Year}} \times 100\%$$

Therefore, for 19–2, $\frac{19\text{-}2}{19\text{-}1} \times 100\% = \frac{750}{740} \times 100\% = 101.35\% = 101\%.$

These analyses permit the reader to judge the performance of the business. For example, one may be concerned regarding the percent increase of current liabilities in comparison to current assets. An examination of dollar amounts only—Current Assets, $870; Current Liabilities, $780—does not illustrate the problem as clearly.

One way of simplifying the comparison is to use a **common-size method**. This means, for example, that the total asset and the total liability figures are set at 100% (the base amount) and all other figures are calculated as a percentage of these totals. See top of page 740.

The same type of comparison can be made for an income statement. Study the next two illustrations on page 740 (bottom). *Note:* Other Revenues and Other Expenses have not been included to ensure simplicity.

Examination of the dollar values will give a hint of the problem, but the percentages clearly show the problem.

Wawdel Company
Common-Size Balance Sheet
as at December 31

ASSETS

	19-5	19-4	19-3	19-2	19-1
Current Assets	37%	39%	33%	43%	45%
Fixed Assets	63%	61%	67%	57%	55%
Total Assets	100%	100%	100%	100%	100%

LIABILITIES AND OWNER'S EQUITY

	19-5	19-4	19-3	19-2	19-1
Current Liabilities	33%	32%	28%	31%	36%
Long-Term Liabilities	42%	44%	48%	55%	49%
Capital	25%	24%	24%	14%	15%
Total Liabilities and Owner's Equity	100%	100%	100%	100%	100%

A final method for presenting statement information is illustrated opposite and on page 742. These comparisons show a breakdown by month for both the income statement and the balance sheet. With both dollar and percentage changes presented, the reader can collect needed information easily and quickly. All these statements can be accurately and quickly prepared by the computer using appropriate software, once the required data is entered.

Wawdel Company
Comparative Income Statement
Years Ended December 31

	19-3	19-2	19-1
Net Sales	1 200	900	800
Cost of Goods Sold	1 000	700	600
Gross Margin on Sales	200	200	200
Operating Expenses	50	40	30
Net Income	150	160	170

Wawdel Company
Comparative Common-Size Income Statement
Years Ended December 31

	19-3	19-2	19-1
Net Sales	100.0%	100.0%	100.0%
Cost of Goods Sold	83.3%	77.8%	75.0%
Gross Margin on Sales	16.7%	22.2%	25.0%
Operating Expenses	4.2%	4.4%	3.75%
Net Income	12.5%	17.8%	21.25%

Scotts Company
Comparative Income Statement
For the Months Ended May 31, 19– and April 30, 19–

	Month Ended May 31, 19–	Month Ended April 30, 19–	Increase(*) or Decrease	
			Am't	%
Revenue	2 000	1 800	200*	11.1%
Cost of Goods Sold	1 800	1 620	180*	11.1%
Gross Margin from Sales	200	180	20*	11.1%
Expenses:				
Taxes	25	25	0	—
Telephone	10	12	2	16.7%
Hydro	18	16	2*	12.5%
Wages	100	100	0	—
Advertising	39	21	18*	85.7%
Total Expenses	192	174	18*	10.3%
Net Income	8	6	2*	33.3%

CALCULATING RATIOS FOR SHORT- AND LONG-TERM ANALYSIS

A person may want to know more about a particular business and its probability of future success. Two major groups spend time analyzing financial statements: **insiders** and **outsiders**.

Insiders are the owners and managers of the business. They are the primary users of the comparative and common-size statements. They use the information gained through these statements, and information gained through ratios, to aid in making business decisions. They watch for danger signs that the business has financial difficulties. Positive trends are noted and used to further the success of the business.

Outsiders include creditors (trade creditors, banks), potential investors, and government agencies (Revenue Canada — Taxation, Statistics Canada). Outsiders use the comparative statements far less than insiders; on the other hand, they are more interested in the information that follows.

Scotts Company
Comparative Balance Sheet
May 31, 19–

Description	April	May	Dollar Increase(*) or Decrease	Percentage Increase(*) or Decrease
ASSETS				
Current Assets:				
Cash	50	55	5*	10%*
Accounts Receivable	60	67	7*	11.7%*
Inventory (at cost)	100	110	10*	10%*
Total Current Assets	210	232	22*	10.5%*
Fixed Assets (at cost):				
Land	400	400	0	—
Building	900	1 000	100*	11.1%*
Total Fixed Assets	1 300	1 400	100*	7.7%*
Total Assets	1 510	1 632	122*	8.1%*
LIABILITIES				
Current Liabilities:				
Bank Loan	70	55	15	21.4%
Accounts Payable	25	30	5*	20.0%*
Property Taxes Payable	15	0	15	100.0%
Current Portion of Mortgage Payable	10	10	0	—
Total Current Liabilities	120	95	25	20.8%
Long-Term Liabilities:				
Mortgage Payable less Current Portion	340	330	10	2.9%
Total Liabilities	460	425	35	7.6%
OWNER'S EQUITY				
R. Tram, Capital	1 047	1 202	155*	14.8%*
Net Income	6	8	2*	33.3%*
	1 053	1 210	157*	14.9%*
Less: Drawing	3	3	0	—
Total Equity	1 050	1 207	157*	15.0%*
Total Liabilities and Owner's Equity	1 510	1 632	122*	8.1%*

A series of calculations, called **ratios**, reveals something about various aspects of the business. This book will only touch upon the more elementary calculations. If you wish to learn more, consult a more advanced accounting text.

First, we will discuss ratios that can be used for short-term calculations.

Working Capital Working capital is the difference between the current assets and current liabilities of a business. It measures the amount of current assets available to pay current liabilities. In year 19-2, Wawdel Company has working capital of $140 ($740 − $600). Here, a comparison of the working capital for different years could prove interesting: in 19-2, $200; in 19-3, $110; in 19-4, $150; in 19-5, $90.

Working Capital
= Current Assets
− Current Liabilities

Adequate working capital allows a business to pay its bills on time, take advantage of valuable purchase discounts, and expand its business without the need to borrow. Lack of adequate working capital is a major cause of business failure.

Current Ratio or Working Capital Ratio This ratio is calculated by dividing Current Assets by Current Liabilities. For Wawdel Company in 19-1, the ratio is $740 ÷ $600 = 1.23 : 1. This means that the business has $1.23 of current assets to pay every $1.00 of current liabilities. The rule of thumb is that an adequate current ratio is 2 : 1. This will depend, however, on the type of business. A high ratio is a good indicator for one business but not for another business. For example, a grocery store with a steady inflow of cash needs a much lower current ratio (1.5 : 1) than a business that builds road graders (5 : 1). Representative ratios for various industries and businesses can be obtained from statistical sources, such as Statistics Canada or Dun & Bradstreet Canada. Finally, a strong current ratio might be misleading if a large portion of current assets is not easily converted to cash. For example, inventory, a current asset, often inflates the current ratio, but usually generates cash rather slowly.

Current Ratio
= Current Assets
÷ Current Liabilities

Quick Ratio (Acid-Test Ratio) The last point leads us to the necessity of another test. The quick ratio, like the current ratio, indicates how quickly a business can pay its current debts. But it is a more stringent test than the current ratio, because all items that can-

$$\text{Quick Ratio} = \frac{\text{Current Assets} - \text{Inventory} - \text{Prepaid Items}}{\text{Current Liabilities}}$$

not be quickly converted to cash, such as inventory and prepaid expenses, are not included in the calculation. This leaves cash, marketable securities, and accounts receivable as the only current assets in the calculation. Wawdel Company's current assets and quick ratio appear in the next illustration.

Current Assets, 19–1:		
Cash	$100	Quick Assets
Accounts Receivable	240	Quick Assets
Inventory	300	
Prepaids	100	

$$\text{Quick Ratio} = \frac{\text{Quick Assets}}{\text{Current Liabilities}} = \frac{\$340}{\$600} = 0.57{:}1$$

The illustration indicates that if Wawdel Company had to pay all its current liabilities immediately, it would have only $0.57 in quick assets to cover each $1.00 of debt. Some creditor(s) would not receive payment.

Other indicators of the short-term strengths and weaknesses of a business are inventory turnover and accounts receivable collection period.

$$\text{Inventory Turnover} = \frac{\text{Cost of Goods Sold}}{\text{Average Inventory}}$$

Inventory Turnover This is how often the entire inventory is sold and replaced during a stated period of time, usually a year. It is calculated by dividing Cost of Goods Sold by the Average Inventory.

$$\text{Average Collection Period} = \frac{\text{Average Accts. Rec.}}{\text{Net Credit Sales}} \times 365$$

Accounts Receivable Collection Period This is how many days it takes to collect the average receivable. It can be compared to the terms offered by the business. For example, if the business offers terms of 2/10, n/30 and the collection period is 40 days, it would indicate that the business is not being paid on time. Management would try to determine why, and correct the problem. It is calculated using the formula in the margin. In order to do this calculation, one must have a figure for Net Credit Sales.

The following indicators can be used for long-term ratio analysis.

Wawdel Company 19–1

$$\frac{\text{Total Liabilities}}{\text{Total Assets}} \times 100\%$$

$$= \frac{\$1400}{\$1640} \times 100\% = 85\%$$

Debt Ratio This ratio, usually calculated as a percentage, divides total liabilities by total assets. It tells the analyst what percentage of the total assets have been financed by debt to outsiders, and what percentage of the total assets belong to the owners.

> Rate of Mark-up on Cost
> $$= \frac{\text{Mark-up}}{\text{Cost}} \times 100\%$$

Rate of Mark-up on Cost This last calculation provides both short-term and long-term information. You have learned to calculate gross margin from sales by subtracting cost of goods sold from net sales. These numbers can readily be converted to common-size percentages, as illustrated previously. Gross margin is always expressed as a percentage of net sales. For example, Wawdel Company's gross margin in 19-1 was 25% of net sales; in 19-3, it was 16.7%.

Mark-up generally refers to the increase over cost that the business adds to an item before selling the item, in order to generate profits. The following illustration demonstrates how mark-up is calculated.

> Common-Size Comparison
>
> | | | |
> |---|---|---|
> | If Selling Price | = | 100% |
> | then Cost Price | = | 75% |
> | and Gross Margin from Sales | = | 25% |
>
> The ratio of mark-up to cost price is 25/75 * 100% = 33.33%. (* is a symbol for multiplication.) If the cost price is $200, the dollar mark-up must be $200 * 33.33%, producing a selling price of $266.67 ($200 + $66.67).

However, accountants usually prefer the following calculation.

> Selling Price = 100/75 * Cost Price
> = 100/75 * $200 = $266.67
>
> A second approach: If (Cost Price) $200 = $75%, then (Selling Price) x = 100%. Solving for x: x = $200 * 100/75 = $266.67.

Businesses may find it necessary to adjust their mark-ups, and therefore their gross margin, for several reasons. It may be necessary to match the competition. The business's suppliers may have gradually increased their prices over the years, while the business itself has not increased its prices, in spite of increasing costs. This would gradually erode the business's gross margin. In the Wawdel Company example on page 740, the percentage mark-up on cost in 19-1 is (25/75 × 100%) or 33.33%; in year 19-2, (22.2/77.8 × 100%) or 28.5%; and in year 19-3, (16.7/83.3 × 100%) or 20.0%.

Competitive companies in the same type of business will have similar mark-ups. If one business tries to underprice the competition by reducing its mark-up, the others will probably be forced to follow suit. This is most likely the situation that Wawdel Company is facing; hence, the constant drop in percentage mark-up is explained. *Note:* Because the mark-up and the gross margin from sales are the same, sometimes the rate of gross margin is referred to as the **rate of mark-up on sales**. To prevent confusion, the rate of mark-up will always be based on cost and the rate of gross margin on sales on the selling price.

Many other ratios and tests are commonly used in practice, but these are best left for more advanced courses. It should also be noted that analyzing financial statements requires a great deal of practice and skill to make informed judgements.

PROBLEMS

Calculating differences between years in dollars and as percentage changes.

P 16-10 When using comparative statements, you must calculate differences between years in dollars, and often as percentages.

a. Calculate the dollar differences for each of the following examples. Indicate positive changes with an asterisk.

b. Calculate the percentage for each. Indicate a positive change with an asterisk. *Remember:* The least recent date is the base figure.

Company A

	19-2	19-1
Assets	$6 000	$5 000

Company B

	19-4	19-3	19-2	19-1
Net Sales	$12 500	$11 000	$10 000	$9 000

Company C

	19-4	19-3	19-2	19-1
Net Sales	$28 000	$21 000	$22 500	$25 000
Operating Expenses	23 500	24 000	21 000	19 500
Net Income	?	?	?	?

Calculating differences between years in dollars and as percentage changes.

P 16-11 Calculate the dollar difference and then the percentage change for each of the values in the comparative income statement shown here.

XYZ Company
Comparative Income Statement
For the Months Ended March 31, 19– and February 28, 19–

	Month Ended Mar. 31, 19–	Month Ended Feb. 28, 19–	Increase(*) or Decrease	
			Am't	%
Revenue from Sales	8 500	7 000		
Operating Expenses:				
Rent	2 500	2 500		
Wages	3 000	3 000		
Telephone	150	110		
Heat	600	800		
Miscellaneous	95	60		
Total Expenses	6 345	6 470		
Net Income (Loss)	2 155	530		

Preparing a common-size income statement.

P 16-12 Refer again to XYZ Company's comparative income statement on page 747.

a. Prepare a common-size income statement similar to the one on page 741. Since you only have two months to compare, you will need only two columns.

Calculating ratios.

P 16-13 From the information in PQR Company's balance sheet, given opposite, do the following exercises.

a. Calculate **(i)** the working capital, **(ii)** the current ratio, **(iii)** the quick ratio, and **(iv)** the debt ratio.

b. Could each of the following be calculated for PQR Company? **(i)** accounts receivable collection period, **(ii)** inventory turnover. If it is **not** possible, state the reason.

Calculating percentage relationships on an income statement.

Calculating values using percentages.

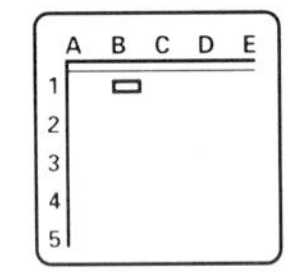

P 16-14 Answer the questions about Computing Company given below. Use a form similar to the following.

	Month											
	A	B	C	D	E	F	G	H	I	J	K	L
Net Sales	$100											
Cost of Goods Sold												
Gross Margin												

a. Using the figure given for month A, determine the net sales for the other eleven months, assuming a sales increase each month of 10%.

b. Determine all the cost of goods sold figures, assuming they are always 40% of net sales.

c. Determine gross margin for each month.

d. Determine the rate of gross margin from sales for each month.

e. Determine the rate of mark-up for each month.

PQR Company
Balance Sheet
as at December 31, 19–

ASSETS		
Current Assets:		
Cash	$ 1 000	
Accounts Receivable	2 500	
Inventory (at cost)	2 400	
Prepaid Rent	900	
Total Current Assets		$ 6 800
Fixed Assets (at cost):		
Land	$10 000	
Building (security for mortgage)	$25 500	
Less: Accumulated Depreciation	5 300	20 200
Total Fixed Assets		$30 200
Total Assets		$37 000
LIABILITIES		
Current Liabilities:		
Bank Loan Payable	$ 2 700	
Accounts Payable	450	
Wages Payable	150	
Current Portion of Mortgage Payable	500	
Total Current Liabilities		$ 3 800
Long-Term Liabilities:		
Mortgage Payable (due in 30 years and secured by the building)	$15 000	
Less: Current Portion	500	
Total Long-Term Liabilities		14 500
Total Liabilities		18 300
OWNER'S EQUITY		
Tom Terrific, Capital	$16 500	
Net Income	5 400	
	21 900	
Less: T. Terrific, Drawing	3 200	
Total Owner's Equity		18 700
Total Liabilities and Owner's Equity		$37 000

Calculating selling price from cost using percentage mark-up.

Calculating gross margin.

P 16-15 The White Night Sales Company has a 35% mark-up.

a. Calculate the selling price for each item.

b. Indicate what the rate of gross margin from sales would be for each item.

Item	Cost Price	Selling Price
A	$700.00	
B	100.00	
C	61.46	

MINI-CASES

Analyzing the need for financial analysis.

MC 16-10 ''All these ratios are good for number-crunchers, but to a businessperson all that matters is how much cash is in the bank,'' said Toni Lamberta. ''You can calculate all the working capital figures and ratios you like, but if you have the cash, you can pay the bills. If you don't have the cash, then the creditors will have to wait.''

a. Is Toni correct? Why or why not?

b. Explain to Toni the advantages you might see in indicators or ratios.

Analyzing the tools used to compare businesses of different sizes.

MC 16-11 ''These calculations are no good to me at all,'' sighed Anne Finigan. ''I've just completed calculations for working capital, and dollar-increases for these two companies that I want to invest in. But the problem is, the two companies are very different in size: one is very large; the other, very small. I cannot compare these numbers in any meaningful way.''

a. Is Anne correct? Explain why or why not.

b. What could Anne do to improve her analysis?

APPLYING THE ELECTRONIC SPREADSHEET AND GENERAL LEDGER ACCOUNTING PACKAGE

USING TEMPLATES ON AN ELECTRONIC SPREADSHEET

In Chapter 6, you learned how to prepare a six-column worksheet using an electronic spreadsheet and utilizing the sum function, among other functions and commands. You then used the spreadsheet to examine some "what if" situations, which should have emphasized to you how powerful a tool a spreadsheet can be.

Since Chapter 6, you have learned the accounting theory behind adjusting entries, and how to record these entries on a ten-column worksheet. How can you modify the six-column electronic worksheet to accommodate the two new sets of columns (adjustments and adjusted trial balance)? You must insert four new columns between the trial balance credit column and the income statement debit column. Next, use the sum function to total each column. These totals will prove the equality of debits and credits. What other relationships do we know exist among these columns? Let's use the example of Prepaid Rent, which must be adjusted at period-end. In the Trial Balance column, there will be a debit balance, representing the value of Prepaid Rent. For this example, let's assume that the value 6400 is recorded in cell C8. See page 752. You know from theory that this account will be credited with the amount of the adjustment which is assumed to be 800, and the result will be reported in the adjusted trial balance. This means that columns E and F will record the adjustments, and columns G and H will record the adjusted trial balance. Now let's determine the necessary formula. If we write out the relationship for the Prepaid Rent row, it would look like this:

Trial Balance Debit + Adjustment Debits − Adjustment Credits = Adjusted Trial Balance Debit

Now, it is necessary to translate this formula to the worksheet. You know that the formula must be entered in the cell where the answer is to appear. For our purposes, we know that Prepaid Rent will still have a debit balance after the adjustment. Move the cursor to cell

	A	B	C	D	E	F	G	H
1					WORKSHEET			
2								
3		Account	Trial	Balance	Adjustments		Adjusted Trial Balance	
4		No.	DR	CR	DR	CR	DR	CR
5	Cash							
6	Acc. Rec.							
7	Inventory							
8	Ppd. Rent		6400			800	5600	
9	Equipment							
10								
11								
12								
13								
14								
15								
16								
17								
18								
19								
20								
G8								

G8. Now enter the formula: +C8 +E8 −F8. This formula means: take the value in cell C8, add the value in E8, subtract the value in F8, and put the result in G8. Now, enter the value of the adjustment, 800, in cell F8. See page 753. The spreadsheet will automatically calculate the adjusted value and place it in the appropriate cell. This process can be followed for all adjustments.

If you wish to construct a more complex worksheet, try linking together the debits and credits of the adjustments. For example, you know that the credit entry adjustment to Prepaid Rent is offset by a debit to Rent Expense. You also know that the credit entry was in cell F6. Move the cursor to cell C20 (or the cell used for a debit to Rent Expense). Place the formula +F6 in that cell. Now, when you place the Prepaid Rent adjustment in cell F6, the spreadsheet will automatically put the same value in cell C20 as the Rent Expense. The same process can be followed for all adjustments, depending on how complicated you want the worksheet to be.

	A	B	C	D	E	F	G	H
1				WORKSHEET				
2								
3		Account	Trial Balance		Adjustments		Adjusted Trial Balance	
4		No.	DR	CR	DR	CR	DR	CR
5	Cash							
6	Acc. Rec.							
7	Inventory							
8	Ppd. Rent		6400			800	5600	
9	Equipment							
10								
11								
12								
13								
14								
15								
16								
17								
18								
19								
20	Rent Exp.		800					

Template: a pre-defined spreadsheet containing formulas to perform a particular function.

This process may seem like a lot of work, especially if this worksheet has to be constructed from scratch each time you want to use one. A better method is to use templates. A template is a pre-defined spreadsheet that performs a particular function, into which a user inserts the data under scrutiny. For example, a worksheet template that you have constructed can be saved initially, **without any data in it**. It would contain all the necessary columns, the account titles, and the mathematical relationships among the various elements. You might save it under the name WRKSHEET. The next time you wish to use it, you would retrieve it from the disk, enter the trial balance data, and the adjustments, and the computer will perform the rest of the calculations. You would **not** save it under the same name, but another **new** name, such as JULY91. This way, the template is not destroyed, or altered in any way, but is ready to use for the next period.

Let us look at two very useful templates that might be used in an accounting setting. These templates are for calculating depreciation and financial ratios.

Depreciation Template The template illustrated on page 755 provides depreciation calculations for three types of depreciation: straight-line, declining balance—as with capital cost allowance—and usage basis. You may not have studied all of these types. If you want to learn more, ask your teacher for help. There are two main parts to this template: the data section, where the user enters the items of information, and the calculation section, where the calculations are automatically performed.

Where indicated you would enter the original cost, the salvage value if any, and the useful life in years, which will allow calculation of the straight-line depreciation. The spreadsheet calculates automatically the book value, the depreciation expense, and the accumulated depreciation for six years. As you will recall, a fixed asset cannot be depreciated below zero book value. If a ''1'' appears in the indicator column, it means that a full year's depreciation can be taken that year. The first ''0'' from the top indicates the first year that full depreciation cannot be taken, and that a manual calculation is necessary for that year. It may be that no depreciation can be taken that year, or that only part can be taken: inspection will tell.

The next section reports by the declining balance method. To do this, you must enter the rate of depreciation as a decimal in the data section. For example, if an asset is to be depreciated at 30% per year, enter .3 as the declining balance rate. The other columns are read the same as explained above.

Ratio Template The second template, the **ratio calculator**, will calculate various ratios, based on the financial statement data you enter. See page 756. Some of the ratios and indicators present in this template are also beyond the scope of this book, but are presented for your interest. To perform all calculations, you would need a balance sheet, an income statement, dividend rates, and share price information.

It is not necessary to do all calculations. You may do as many as you need, by just entering the data required. For example, if all you want is the current and acid test ratios, you only need enter current assets, current liabilities, prepaid items, and inventory. You will note that there are two spots for inventory: beginning inventory and ending inventory. The third figure, average inventory, is calculated by the spreadsheet. If you only have the ending inventory figure, enter it as **both** the beginning and the ending figure.

	A	B	C	D	E	F	
1		DEPRECIATION CALCULATOR					
2							
3	FACTS:		STRAIGHT-LINE:				
4	========================		==========	==========	==========	==========	==========
5	(Round to nearest $)		YEAR	BOOK VALUE	DEPR. EXP.	ACC. DEPR.	INDICATOR
6	Original Cost:	2000	1	2000.00	360.00	360.00	1
7	Useful Life (yrs.):	5	2	1640.00	360.00	720.00	1
8	Salvage Value:	200	3	1280.00	360.00	1080.00	1
9	Productive Life (units):	9000	4	920.00	360.00	1440.00	1
10	Declining Balance rate:	.3	5	560.00	360.00	1800.00	1
11	Units Produced Yr. 1:	1000	6	200.00	360.00	2160.00	0
12	Units Produced Yr. 2:	1000					
13	Units Produced Yr. 3:	2000					
14	Units Produced Yr. 4:	2300	DECLINING BALANCE:				
15	Units Produced Yr. 5:	1800	==========	==========	==========	==========	==========
16	Units Produced Yr. 6:	700	1	2000.00	600.00	600.00	1
			2	1400.00	420.00	1020.00	1
			3	980.00	294.00	1314.00	1
			4	686.00	205.80	1519.80	1
			5	480.20	144.06	1663.86	1
			6	336.14	100.84	1764.70	1
			USAGE:				
			==========	==========	==========	==========	==========
			1	2000.00	200.00	200.00	1
			2	1800.00	200.00	400.00	1
			3	1600.00	400.00	800.00	1
			4	1200.00	460.00	1260.00	1
			5	740.00	360.00	1620.00	1
			6	380.00	140.00	1760.00	1

Both of these templates are good examples of how a spreadsheet might be used in an accounting setting. They would be recalled from disk, the data would be entered and the answers recorded. The template remains available for next time.

```
                              RATIO CALCULATOR
==========================================================================
ENTER COMPANY DATA BELOW:
(Round to nearest $)

          Current Assets:   2000                 Current Ratio:         2
     Current Liabilities:   1000                Acid-Test Ratio:        1
     Beginning Inventory:   1000          A/R Collection Period:  33.45833
        Ending Inventory:   1000             Inventory Turnover:       16
       Average Inventory:   1000             % Return on Assets:  1.454545
      Prepaid Item Total:     10             % Return on Equity:  3.333333
  Beginning Total Assets:   1000           Times Interest Earned:       8
     Ending Total Assets:   1200             Earnings per Share:    19.75
    Average Total Assets:   1100            Price/Earnings Ratio: 1.265823
              Total Debt:    200              Dividend Yield (%):     .04
          Beginning A/R:   1000            Net Income/Sales (%):       10
             Ending A/R:   1200               Gross Profit (%):        20
            Average A/R:   1100              Debt/Equity Ratio:  .1666667
      Cost of Goods Sold:  16000
               Net Sales:  20000
        Net Credit Sales:  12000
            Gross Profit:   4000
              Net Income:   2000
        Interest Expense:    200
      Income Tax Expense:    200
 Beginning Owner's Equity:    500
    Ending Owner's Equity:    700
          Average Equity:    600
Preferred Share Dividends:     25
   # of Common Shares O/S:    100
    Market Price of Share:     25
      Dividends per Share:      1
```

OTHER GENERAL LEDGER PACKAGE APPLICATIONS

Many of the problems presented in this chapter can be solved by using a General Ledger accounting package. Usually, all that is required is that your teacher construct a series of files containing a trial balance. From this, you can perform almost all of the tasks required. For example, look at Problem 16-1. You are given a trial balance, and asked to prepare a worksheet. This problem continues in Problem 16-4, where you are asked to prepare formal financial statements. If the trial balance were set up as GL files, the package would generate a worksheet for you, which you could complete manually. These adjustments could then be journalized, formal statements produced, and a post-closing trial balance prepared, all on the computer. An explanation of how to construct these data files is beyond the scope of this book, since different packages have different requirements. Reference should be made to the appropriate section of the manual for the accounting package that you are using.

Other problems that lend themselves to a GL package are Problem 16-2, which is continued in Problem 16-5, and 16-3, which is continued in Problem 16-6.

PROBLEMS

Using a spreadsheet template to calculate ratios.

Evaluating results of calculations.

P 16-16 Refer to the statements you prepared in Problem 16-4 (the Snooze Motel). Using the template RATIOS on a spreadsheet like Lotus 1-2-3® or Microsoft Works® disk, calculate as many ratios as possible. For each indicate what you would compare the value to, and whether the value is acceptable by that measure.

Using a spreadsheet template to calculate ratios.

Evaluating results of calculations.

P 16-17 Refer to the statements that you prepared for Problem 16-6 (H & P Fisheries Enterprise), and using the template RATIOS on a spreadsheet like Lotus 1-2-3® or Microsoft Works®, calculate as many ratios as possible. For each, indicate what you would compare the value to, and whether the value is acceptable by that measure.

Using a spreadsheet template to calculate depreciation in different situations.

P 16-18 Using the template DEPREC and a spreadsheet like Lotus 1-2-3® or Microsoft Works®, and the provided data, calculate the missing information.

a. Straight-line: cost = $22 000, salvage = $4000, estimated life = 4 years, depreciation expense for year 3 = ?

b. Straight-line: cost = $17 356, salvage value = $3652, estimated life = 5 years, depreciation expense year 4 = ?

c. In **a**, what if salvage is only $100?

d. In **b**, what if salvage is zero?

e. Declining balance: cost = $45 000, salvage value = $4200, rate = 30%. What is the depreciation expense for year 4?

f. In **e**, what if the salvage value is zero?

MINI-CASES

Using spreadsheet templates.

MC 16-12 Fred Wright was puzzled by something he had learned in accounting class. "Today we learned how to construct a ten-column worksheet using an electronic spreadsheet. I really don't see the benefit, though. We spent hours entering formulas into the spreadsheet, and it did the calculations almost instantly when we entered the data. I could have saved a lot of time by doing this on a paper worksheet. I would have been done in less than half the time."

a. What concept has Fred failed to grasp about this use of the spreadsheet?

b. How **should** Fred use this worksheet he has created?

Explaining the declining balance method formula on a spreadsheet template.

MC 16-13 Refer back to Problem 16-18, **e** and **f**. Your answer for both parts should be the same. Explain why. *Hint:* If you are unsure, examine the formulas that are used in the template.

Analyzing the use of different GL packages with different capabilities.

MC 16-14 Four students, each using a different GL accounting package, were asked to present their views on redoing an accounting cycle problem solved previously through the traditional manual method.

Christie Davis had no problems except that her GL software could not print a separate Statement of Owner's Equity.

Kelly Longmore mentioned that his software did not produce a ten-column worksheet and, consequently, he had to prepare one manually.

Shannon Meilleur stated that all of the steps in the traditional accounting cycle were not covered by her software package. Accordingly, she could not produce a postclosing trial balance.

Courtney Gibson did not understand how to handle the beginning and ending inventories even though a six-column worksheet was printed for the preliminary trial balance, the adjustments, and the adjusted trial balance.

a. Do the experiences of these students prove that there are serious limitations with General Ledger accounting packages? Explain your answer based on your experience.

INDEX

Note: The symbol *def.* precedes pages containing a definition in the margin or text; *illus.* precedes pages containing an illustration; *prob.* precedes pages containing a problem; *M.C.* precedes pages containing a Mini-Case; *C.C.* precedes pages containing a Comprehensive Case Study.